HERACLIUS, EMPEROR OF BYZANTIUM

This book evaluates the life and empire of the pivotal yet controversial and poorly understood Byzantine emperor Heraclius (AD 610–641), a contemporary of the Prophet Muḥammad. Heraclius' reign is critical for understanding the background to fundamental changes in the Balkans and the Middle East, including the emergence of Islam, at the end of Antiquity.

Heraclius captured and lost important swathes of territory, including Jerusalem, Syria, and Egypt. Skills in exploiting divisions within the ranks of his opponents, and encouraging the switching of sides and the breakdown of morale, provided Heraclius with the greatest triumphs; yet they proved to be of little value when he finally confronted the early Islamic conquests. The author synthesizes diverse primary sources, including those in Greek and Arabic, in the light of recent historical scholarship. The varied Mediterranean and Middle Eastern context stretches from North Africa to Syria, Armenia, and what is modern Iraq.

WALTER E. KAEGI is Professor of History and Permanent Voting Member, Oriental Institute, University of Chicago. His publications include *Byzantium and the Decline of Rome* (1968), *Byzantine Military Unrest 471–843* (1981), *Army, Society and Religion in Byzantium* (1982), *Some Thoughts on Byzantine Military Strategy* (1983), and *Byzantium and the Early Islamic Conquests* (1992, paperback 1995).

HERACLIUS
EMPEROR OF BYZANTIUM

WALTER E. KAEGI

CAMBRIDGE
UNIVERSITY PRESS

CAMBRIDGE UNIVERSITY PRESS
Cambridge, New York, Melbourne, Madrid, Cape Town, Singapore, São Paulo

Cambridge University Press
The Edinburgh Building, Cambridge CB2 8RU, UK

Published in the United States of America by Cambridge University Press, New York

www.cambridge.org
Information on this title: www.cambridge.org/9780521814591

First published 2003
Reprinted 2004
Hardback version transferred to digital printing 2007
Digitally printed first paperback version 2007

A catalogue record for this publication is available from the British Library

Library of Congress Cataloguing in Publication data
Kaegi, Walter Emil.
Heraclius: emperor of Byzantium / Walter E. Kaegi.
p.   cm.
Includes bibliographical references and index.
ISBN 0 521 81459 6
1. Heraclius, Emperor of the East, ca. 575–641.   2. Byzantine
Empire–History–Heraclius, 610–641.   3. Emperors–Byzantine
Empire–Biography.   I. Title.
DF574 .K34   2002
949.5′013′092 – dc21
[B]   2002023370

ISBN 978-0-521-81459-1 hardback
ISBN 978-0-521-03698-6 paperback

Contents

Maps

Figures

(Photographs courtesy of Cabinet des Médailles, Bibliothèque Nationale,
Paris (Fig. 1), and of Dumbarton Oaks Collection, Washington, DC
(Figs. 2–6))

Acknowledgments

This book began to take form in the middle of the 1990s, after I became convinced of the need for a study that takes account of recent scholarship and editions of sources. I thank the Social Science Research Council for a 1996–1997 grant that permitted me to visit Tunisia in order to understand a region where Heraclius once lived. The National Humanities Center and its Director, W.R. Connor, and Deputy Director, Kent Mullikin, gave me a warm and stimulating environment and resources to begin this book during the course of a Fellowship in academic year 1996–1997. A Fulbright Fellowship to Iraq in the summer of 1988 helped me immeasurably. The University of Chicago Division of Social Sciences and its Dean and my colleague, Richard P. Saller, graciously allowed me the time off to work on this project, as well as divisional funding for my expenses. I thank the libraries of the University of Chicago, Duke University, the University of North Carolina at Chapel Hill, and the Dumbarton Oaks Center for Byzantine Studies for their indispensable help. The Map Collection of Regenstein Library and its head, Christopher Winters, have me in their eternal debt. I am grateful for the aid of Jeanne Mrad, Director, and the use of the facilities of the Centre d'Etudes Maghrébines in Tunis and Dr. Abdelmajid Ennabli, Director of the National Museum at Carthage, and his wife Liliane Ennabli, in support of my work in Tunisia during 1996 and 1997. I owe much to Todd Hickey, David Olster and my Oriental Institute colleagues Fred Donner, John Sanders, and Tony Wilkinson. Special gratitude goes to Wolfram Brandes, Robert Hewsen, Tim Greenwood, Holger Klein, Cécile Morrisson, Stephen Rapp, Irfan Shahid, and Constantin Zuckerman, who generously shared valuable research with me in advance of publication. My wife Louise showed me understanding and patience while I withdrew to write. The Canadian Constantinopolitan Association of Toronto, and the University of Toronto, East Carolina University, Duke University, the students and other participants in the University of Chicago Workshop in Late Antiquity and Byzantium, and the Center for Middle Eastern Studies at the University of Chicago gave me opportunities to speak on and discuss aspects of Heraclius. I owe a deep debt to Dumbarton Oaks and to the Cabinet des Médailles, Bibliothèque Nationale, Paris, for kind permission to consult and to use illustrations from their respective magnificent collections of Byzantine coins. I have produced the maps with the indispensable expertise and aid of the University of Chicago Digital Media Lab, and its Manager, Roberto Marques, and his colleagues Josh Bartos and Dale Mertes. I am heavily indebted to my editor, William Davies, and my copyeditor, Ann Johnston, whose patience and wisdom have assisted me enormously. I try to acknowledge my debt and gratitude to other individual scholars, without whose assistance and vigilant criticism I could not have completed this book, at appropriate places in the footnotes.

Spelling names from so many languages is a challenge. There is no simple solution. I normally use the Greek or Arabic form of names, but I allow very familiar names to retain their most commonly understood form, such as Heraclius, or Caesarea.

Abbreviations

AABSC	*Abstracts, Annual Byzantine Studies Conference*
AB	*Analecta Bollandiana*
ACO	*Acta Conciliorum Oecumenicorum*
Azdī	al-Baṣrī, Muḥammad b. ʿAbdullāh Abū Ismaʿīl al-Azdī
Al-Balādhurī, *Futūḥ*	al-Balādhurī, Aḥmad b. Yaḥyā *Kitāb Futūḥ al-Buldān*, ed. de Goeje
BAR	*British Archaeological Reports*
BCH	*Bulletin de Correspondance Hellénique*
BEIC	Kaegi, *Byzantium and the Early Islamic Conquests*
Beihammer, *Nachrichten*	Beihammer, *Nachrichten zum byzantinischen Urkundenwesen in arabischen Quellen*
BF	*Byzantinische Forschungen*
BGA	*Bibliotheca Geographorum Arabicorum*
BMGS	*Byzantine and Modern Greek Studies*
Byzsl	*Byzantinoslavica*
ByzStratos	Zia Stratos, ed., Βυζάντιον. Ἀφιέρωμα στόν Ἀνδρέα Στράτο. *Byzance. Hommage à Andreas Stratos. Byzantium. Tribute to Andreas Stratos*
BZ	*Byzantinische Zeitschrift*
CC	*Corpus Christianorum*
CFHB	*Corpus Fontium Historiae Byzantinae*
CMH	*Cambridge Medieval History*
CSCO, SS	*Corpus Scriptorum Christianorum Orientalium*, Scriptores Syri
CSHB	*Corpus Scriptorum Historiae Byzantinae*
DO Cat	P. Grierson, *Catalogue of the Byzantine Coins in the Dumbarton Oaks Collection and in the Whittemore Collection*

DOP	*Dumbarton Oaks Papers*
EHR	*English Historical Review*
EI ¹	*Encyclopedia of Islam.* 1st edn., 8 vols. Leiden: Brill, 1913–1936; repr. Leiden, 1987
EI ²	*Encyclopedia of Islam.* 2nd edn. Leiden: Brill, 1960–
EO	*Echos d'Orient*
FHG	*Fragmenta Historicorum Graecorum*
GCS	*Die griechischen christlichen Schriftsteller der ersten Jahrhunderte*
Jaffé, *Regesta*	Philip Jaffé, *Regesta Pontificum Romanorum.* Leipzig: Veit; repr. Graz: Akademische Druck- und Verlagsanstalt, 1956
JAOS	*Journal of the American Oriental Society*
JJP	*Journal of Juristic Papyrology*
JÖB	*Jahrbuch der Österreichischen Byzantinistik*
JRS	*Journal of Roman Studies*
JSAI	*Jerusalem Studies in Arabic and Islam*
Kūfī	Ibn Aʿtham al-Kūfī, Abū Muḥammad Aḥmad
MGH	*Monumenta Germaniae Historica*
NC	*Numismatic Chronicle*
OCP	*Orientalia Christiana Periodica*
ODB	*Oxford Dictionary of Byzantium*, ed. A.P. Kazhdan, New York: Oxford University Press, 1991
PBE	*Prosopography of the Byzantine Empire*
PG	*Patrologia Graeca*
PL	*Patrologia Latina*
PLRE	*Prosopography of the Later Roman Empire*
PMBZ	*Prosopographie der mittelbyzantinischen Zeit*
PO	*Patrologia Orientalis*
REArm	*Revue des Etudes Arméniennes*
REB	*Revue des Etudes Byzantines*
RN	*Revue Numismatique*
Stratos, Βυζάντιον	Stratos, Βυζάντιον στόν Z' αἰῶνα
al-Ṭabarī	al-Ṭabarī, Abū Jaʿfar Muḥammad b. Jarīr, *Taʾrīkh al-rusul waʾl mulūk*, ed. by M.J. de Goeje et al.
al-Ṭabarī, *History*	*The History of al-Ṭabarī* (see respective translated volumes)
Ṭabarī/Nöldeke	Theodor Nöldeke, *Geschichte der Perser und Araber zur Zeit der Sasaniden aus der arabischen Chronik des Tabari*

TM	*Travaux et Mémoires* (Paris)
TMD	Ibn ʿAsākir, *Taʾrīkh madīnat Dimashq*, ed. ʿUmar ibn Gharāma ʿAmrawī
VV	*Vizantiiski Vremennik*
ZDMG	*Zeitschrift der deutschen Morgenländischen Gesellschaft*
ZRVI	*Zbornik, Radova Vizantoloshkog Institut, Srpska Akad. Nauk.* (Belgrade)

Introduction

The life of Flavius Heraclius has never been the subject of a biography in English. The mere existence of a gap does not in itself warrant investigating, writing, or reading about him or any other subject. But there are some reasons for the omission and for the effort to understand him. George Finlay allowed him some pages in his survey of Greek history[1] but nineteenth-century concepts of nationalism and blood stock distorted his interpretation into an almost unrecognizable Heraclius:

It was perhaps a misfortune that Heraclius was by birth a Roman rather than a Greek, as his views were from that accident directed to the maintenance of the imperial dominion, without any reference to the national organization of his people... Heraclius, being by birth and family connections an African noble, regarded himself as of pure Roman blood, superior to all national prejudices, and bound by duty and policy to repress the domineering spirit of the Greek aristocracy in the State, and of the Greek hierarchy in the Church.[2]

Thomas Hodgkin disparagingly remarked,

The young Heraclius, as liberator of the Empire, has something about him which attracts our sympathy and admiration; but when we are reading his story... it is impossible not to feel how thoroughly barbarised were all, even the best men of

---

[1] George Finlay, *History of Greece* (Oxford, 1877) I: 311–350, esp. p. 313,

The reign of Heraclius is one of the most remarkable epochs in the history of the empire and in the annals of mankind. It warded off the almost inevitable destruction of the Roman government; it laid the foundation of that polity which prolonged the existence of the imperial power at Constantinople under a new modification, as the Byzantine monarchy; and it was contemporary with the commencement of the great moral change in the condition of the people which transformed the language and the manners of the ancient world into those of the modern nations. The Eastern Empire was indebted to the talents of Heraclius for its escape from those ages of barbarism which, for many centuries, prevailed in all western Europe.

[2] Finlay, *History of Greece* I: 314–315.

this epoch of the Empire . . . so great is the fall from the tragic beauty of the deeds of the Greek tyrannicides to the coarse brutality of the murderers of Phocas.[3]

J. B. Bury's chapters on him in his 1889 *History of the Later Roman Empire from Arcadius to Irene*,[4] are very out of date. The formerly standard 1905 biography *L'Imperatore Eraclio* by Angelo Pernice acknowledged that the historical understanding of Heraclius in his day was very inadequate: "Heraclius still appears to be one of the strangest and most incoherent figures that history has recorded. His reign is still considered as alternations of wondrous actions and inaction."[5] Even more obsolete are those nineteenth-century biographies by L. Drapeyron[6] and Tryphon Evangelides,[7] which, moreover, are difficult to obtain. The latter two authors were educated generalists who wrote many other books on historical subjects; they were not Byzantine specialists. Heraclius received only a short and unexceptional entry, although its author conceded that he was one of the greatest Byzantine emperors, in the eleventh edition of the *Encylopaedia Britannica*.[8] J. Kulakovskii[9] and A. Stratos[10] included extensive but error-studded chapters on Heraclius in their broader histories. Despite the voluminous quantity of his writings, Stratos did not understand the seventh century or Heraclius in particular. His coverage of the first decade of Heraclius' reign is vague, while his chronology and understanding of the last two decades are deficient.

Periodization has many pitfalls. For some historians and for varying reasons the reign of Heraclius marks the beginning of a different period of Byzantine history,[11] one that some would term "Middle Byzantine History."

[3] Thomas Hodgkin, *Italy and her Invaders* (London, 1880–1889; repr. New York: Russell & Russell, 1967) VI: 7.

[4] John B. Bury, *History of the Later Roman Empire from Arcadius to Irene* (London: Macmillan, 1889; repr. Amsterdam: Hakkert, 1966) II: 207–273.

[5] Angelo Pernice, *Imperatore Eraclio, saggio di storia bizantina* (Florence: Galletti e Cocci, 1905) vii.

[6] Ludovic Drapeyron, *L'Empereur Héraclius et l'empire byzantin au VII siècle* (Paris: E. Thorin, 1869).

[7] Tryphon Evangelides, *Herakleios ho autokrator tou Byzantinou (575–641 m.Chr.) kai he kata ton Z' m. Chr. aion katastasis tou Byzantiakou kratous* (Odessa: P. Zervates-Perakes, 1903).

[8] Maximilian Otto Bismarck Caspari, s.v. "Heraclius," in *Encylopaedia Britannica* (11th edn., Cambridge, New York, 1910) XIII: 310.

[9] Julian Kulakovskii, *Istoriya Vizantii* (Kiev, 1913–1915) III: 18–170.

[10] Andreas Stratos, Τό Βυζάντιον στόν Z' αἰῶνα (Athens, 1965–1969) vols. I–III; English translation: *Byzantium in the Seventh Century*, trans. Marc Ogilvie-Grant, Harry Hionides (Amsterdam: Hakkert, 1968, 1972) vols. I–II. The Greek edition is preferred for precision and detail.

[11] George Ostrogorsky, *History of the Byzantine State*, trans. J.M. Hussey (New Brunswick: Rutgers UP, 1969). Romilly Jenkins, *Byzantium: the Imperial Centuries* (New York: Random House, 1966); M. Whittow, *The Making of Byzantium* (Berkeley: University of California Press, 1996) 38–88; Warren Treadgold, *A History of the Byzantine State and Society* (Stanford: Stanford University Press, 1997) 287–306, 371–379, who describes Heraclius as "an imposing but tragic figure, who had outlived his reputation and his success" on p. 306, but also as "an informed, experienced, and intelligent strategist" on p. 307.

Periods are less alluring today than formerly, the issue still deserves some sifting.

Different generations have possessed their own respective Heraclii. Today historians know much more about the historical context in which Heraclius lived, due to advances in archaeology and to improved interpretation of literary evidence, the asking of questions that earlier historians did not pose, and the edition of many new texts in many languages. Even assumptions about much basic chronology are different. There is still more that we do not know than that we do know about him. The art historical evidence is increasing and interpretations of that material are changing. While far from perfect, a much better understanding, and a different one, has evolved of conditions in many provinces from Africa to Mesopotamia before, during, and after Heraclius' reign than scholars possessed a century ago. New hagiographic material and new methods for examining long edited hagiographic texts enrich and illumine perceptions about Heraclius. Much historical criticism has clarified or raised issues differently concerning Heraclius, the Byzantine Empire, the Eastern Mediterranean and western Asia in his lifetime. New interpretations of the rise of Islam increase the need for another look at his life and reign. A new seventh century is emerging although its interpretation, as well as his place in it, is in flux. Not only the seventh century, but also the broader Late Roman cultural, religious, economic, and political context has undergone reinterpretation and more accurate adjustment of focus. The old Heraclius and the related paradigm of Byzantine history have been deconstructed. No adequate biography exists. This is not a time to be self-satisfied, for many gaps and controversies bedevil the investigator. It is necessary to sift the scattered and fragmentary specialized scholarship, which contains many improvements over the older received picture, to attempt to develop a synthesis.

Heraclius' reputation has undergone many vicissitudes. William of Tyre envisioned him as the originator of the Crusades.[12] The last resident Latin Patriarch of Jerusalem (late twelfth century) was Eraclius or Heraclius, around whose name and its association with the Byzantine Emperor Heraclius a number of prophecies swirled.[13] Some medieval French

---

[12] Late twelfth century, on Heraclius: William, Archbishop of Tyre, *Chronicon* 1.1–2, ed. R.B.C. Huygens (*CC*, Continuatio Medievalis, 63; Brepols: Turnhout, 1986) 105–107, and Eng. trans., *History of Deeds Done Across the Sea*, trans. E.A. Babcock and A.C. Krey (Columbia Records of Civilization; New York: Columbia University Press, 1943) 60–61. For a lovely late twelfth-century miniature of an equestrian Heraclius with the Cross, see Stuttgarter Passionale (Stuttgart: Württembergische Landesbibl., Cod. bibl. fol. 56, fol. 90v.

[13] B.Z. Kedar, "The Patriarch Eraclius," in *Outremer: Studies in the History of the Crusading Kingdom of Jerusalem* (Jerusalem: Yad Izhak Ben-Zvi Institute, 1982) 177–204.

romances have Emperor Heraclius as their focus.[14] In the Italian Renaissance he was the subject of two famous frescoes by Piero della Francesca (ca. 1452–1466) at S. Francesco, in Arezzo: his victory over the Persian King Khusrau II and his restoration of the Cross to Jerusalem. Both themes would have been appropriate in an era of heightened concern about rising Ottoman power. His profile embellished an early fifteenth-century Renaissance bronze medal of unknown provenance, which was fashioned with an intriguing, albeit wholly fanciful, bust of him on the obverse and an equestrian portrait on the reverse.[15] In the seventeenth century his triumph over Khusrau II and the restoration of the Cross to Jerusalem ceased to be the center of attention. Pierre Corneille wrote a very fanciful play *Héraclius* about him and his relationship with his imperial predecessor, Phokas. Corneille concentrated on the instability of the regime of Phokas and a fictitious marital crisis.[16] Heraclius did strike the imagination of posterity. There are other controversies about the meaning and nature of the "Age of Heraclius" and his legacy. But Heraclius after Heraclius is not the principal object of this study.

This is an attempt to investigate Heraclius as a man and an emperor, who confronted crises in both public and private dimensions of his life. It is not an easy task. The investigator must not only penetrate the carapace of panegyrical verse and rhetorical and historical prose but also try to piece together scraps and traces of diverse provenance. His and his dynasty's poets and historians needed to smooth over the origins of his power to create legitimate foundations for his power, however tenuous they might be. That could never be seamless; there were always some traces of the irregular origin of his power. One had to represent him as both full of guile and stratagems yet legitimate and a representative of and guarantor of order. He used guile to seize power. There would always be an uneasy and delicate case for the origins and solidity of his authority. No perfectly smooth interface could cover all of the different layers of cultural and regional influences on him or the layers of sources, tensions, and contradictions in his representation and the transmission of image and tradition about him.

[14] Gautier d'Arras, *Eracle*, ed. Guy Raymond de Lage (Classiques français du moyen-âge; Paris: H. Champion, 1976).

[15] Stephen K. Scher, curator/editor, *The Currency of Fame: Portrait Medals of the Renaissance* (New York: Abrams, 1994). The entry for the medal of Heraclius is found on pp. 34–37 with black and white plates; a color plate with obverse and reverse is on p. 65. The artist is unknown, Heraclius is in profile, the medal is bronze, cast. One is in the Cabinet des Médailles in Paris (Bibliothèque Nationale), and the other in the British Museum. There is also a medal of Constantine that is closely related to the one of Heraclius. These are copies of original gold and jeweled medals bought by the Duke of Berry. I thank M.-L. Dolezal for this reference.

[16] Pierre Corneille, *Héraclius, empereur d'Orient: tragédie* (Rouen, 1647, distrib. at Paris); new edn, Paris: Cicero éditions, 1995.

The historian needs to peel off paradoxical layers of either panegyrical or hostile characterizations in order to achieve at least some appreciation of Heraclius. Favorable representations of him as a new David, new Moses, new Constantine, or new Scipio coexist with others that portray him as self-deceived, arrogant, sinful, and a preeminent example of divine wrath. He and his associates encouraged the dissemination of his reputation as an imitation or equal of earlier great historical and Biblical models, but diverse critical constituencies constructed and transmitted a conflicting memory of him. Historians have to evaluate these overlapping and conflicting images, which bear only limited resemblance to realities.

Heraclius was an important and relatively, for his time, long-lived emperor, who experienced an era of dramatic change, what might be called a turning-point or decisive moment. He was controversial in his own lifetime and he is controversial today: institutions, religious policies, minority policy, especially toward Jews, Copts, and Armenians, his economic and fiscal policies, and his defense policies against the Muslims are all disputed. Heraclius remains an enigmatic and untypical emperor. His was a reign of action on many fronts, a reign filled with war, triumph, and tragedy. His personal life is as puzzling and controversial as his public life. One cannot penetrate his psyche to know with confidence how he felt. Psychohistory as presently constituted cannot furnish the methodology to explain those mysteries. He had serious medical problems. He experienced unidentified phobias and illness. He had marital and succession problems. He suffered anxieties and sorrows concerning his children by two marriages. There was a lot of trauma in his life, but many of his contemporaries endured other severe traumas themselves. Although an indubitable Christian, he apparently had strong astrological interests and tried various devices for peering into the future. One must investigate, however imperfectly, the limits of what he knew and how his range of knowledge and acquaintance with recent events affected and restricted his perceptions about policy options, other decisions, and plans. The recent past weighed heavily on him at the beginning of his reign, especially strife in the Balkans as well as civil war. Other focal points of military problems in his early years were parts of the eastern frontier with Persia: Caucasus, Northern Syria and Northern Mesopotamia. One needs to ask how much he changed his attitudes and practices and his group of associates and counselors over the course of his lifetime.

It is not easy to understand Heraclius the man, and the degree to which he changed or grew during the course of his lifetime. Even in his own lifetime it would have been difficult to understand his family life or even life at his imperial court, for that was available to the public only in limited and very authorized glimpses. His geographical experiences were much more varied than those of his recent predecessors. While every span of years contains unique and discrete experiences, the range and variance of those events and challenges in his lifetime and reign were truly unprecedented. We cannot even understand his relations to his leading ministers, such as his chamberlains (*cubicularii*).[17] We do not know how he consulted and how he made decisions. Few insights exist into how the process of government worked during his reign, let alone how the normally unrecorded yet important encoded processes worked, that is, understandings, unwritten etiquette and assumptions, facial expressions, gestures, signals in corridors, and the deliberate release, suppression, or distortion of information. Only restricted and often overly tantalizing bits can be recovered from that rich past. There can be no doubt that he developed a good relationship with Sergios, Patriarch of Constantinople (610–638), but no extant source provides details of the quality, character, and texture of that relationship. Only the formal dimensions of it appear in the sources.

A common theme in most accounts of Heraclius across literatures, including histories, is his error in religious judgments. He has left an imprint in Arabic, Latin, and Greek sources, as well as some in other languages. The interpretation of those sources is not simple. No Byzantine author expresses any yearnings for a return to the age of his imperial predecessor, Phokas. The historian cannot trust every literary tradition nor use one tradition exclusively. No one tradition provides a complete picture of Heraclius, nor can the historian take something from each tradition, to make a composite compromise interpretation that "splits the difference" in interpretations. His relationship with Zoroastrianism and with the rise and expansion of Islam are among the most important aspects of his reign. Both non-Constantinopolitan perspectives as well as Constantinopolitan ones deserve investigation.

Differing religious frames of reference between the seventh century and our own impede understanding Heraclius. One cannot understand him in a non-religious context, for his was a very religious age. Recent scholarship has contributed to appreciating how differently he and his contemporaries perceived matters and reached decisions in the light of their and their public's religious convictions and expectations. Theirs was a world in which one expected sudden divine intervention for salutary purposes and in the

---

[17] On Byzantine eunuchs, see Mathew Kuefler, *The Manly Eunuch* (Chicago: University of Chicago Press, 2001) and a forthcoming monograph by Kathryn Ringrose.

form of wrathful retribution for individual and collective transgressions. The observant were always watching for signs that suggested, foretold, or proved and reinforced such expectations. They perceived, decided, and acted accordingly. But he in his turn sought to influence contemporary and posterior public impressions and images of himself.

The primary sources have been subject to differing levels of analysis for many years. Here are some broader remarks about them, but for fuller remarks, see the specialized literature.[18] Foremost among seventh-century Greek texts is the contemporary *Chronicon Paschale*, which is useful insofar as its compiler has provided entries for events.[19] The historian Theophylact Simocatta has left correspondence as well as a history with allusions that reflect contemporary political outlooks although they lack much actual subject matter from the reign of Heraclius.[20] The works of George of Pisidia, now being translated and commented upon by Mary Whitby, are difficult but contemporary and essential.[21] Some papyri are valuable contemporary records for one province: Egypt.[22] The speech of Theodore the Synkellos for the siege of Constantinople in 626 is obscure and admittedly an embellished piece of rhetoric, but it does contain valuable material concerning events and their framing and exposition.[23] Two much later histories (early ninth century and late eighth century, respectively) provide essential evidence for the skeletal construction of the reign. Yet they each have problems. The *Chronographia* of Theophanes is often careless in details and owes much to a late eighth-century Syriac prototype of Theophilos of Edessa, but one

[18] For selected sources: *Prosopographie der mittelbyzantinischen Zeit. Erste Abteilung (641–867). Prolegomena*, ed. F. Winkelmann, R.-J. Lilie, C. Ludwig, et al. (Berlin, New York: De Gruyter, 1998).

[19] Michael and Mary Whitby, Introduction to their translation of *Chronicon Paschale* x–xiii.

[20] Michael Whitby, *The Emperor Maurice and His Historian* (Oxford: Clarendon Press, 1988); Whitby, "Theophylact the Historian and the Miracles of Artemius," *Electrum* 1 (1997) 222–234.

[21] The best critical edition and translation into Italian of the panegyrical poems only is [Giorgio di Pisidia], *Poemi, Panegirici epici*, ed., trans. Agostino Pertusi (Ettal: Buch-Kunstverlag-Ettal, 1959). See *Carmi di Giorgio di Pisidia*, ed. Luigi Tartaglia (Turin: UTET, 1998) for a complete collection and translation of the poems, but many in uncritical editions. And see Joseph D.C. Frendo, "The Poetic Achievement of George of Pisidia," in *Maistor: Classical, Byzantine and Renaissance Studies for Robert Browning*, ed. A. Moffat (Byzantina Australiensia, 5; Canberra: Australian Association for Byzantine Studies, 1984) 159–187. Mary Whitby, "Defender of the Cross: George of Pisidia on the Emperor Heraclius and His Deputies," in *The Propaganda of Power: The Role of Panegyric in Late Antiquity*, ed. Mary Whitby (Leiden: Brill, 1998) 247–273.

[22] Kaegi, "Egypt on the Eve of the Muslim Conquest," in *Cambridge History of Egypt*, ed. C. Petry (Cambridge: Cambridge University Press, 1998) I: 39. Apion family holdings: Todd M. Hickey, Ph.D. diss. University of Chicago (2001): "A Public 'House' but Closed: Fiscal Participation and Economic Decision Making on the Oxyrhynchite Estate of the Flavii Apiones."

[23] Critical edition by L. Sternbach is best: *Analecta Avarica*, Rozprawy Akademii Umiejętnosci, Wydzial Filologiczny, Ser. 2, Vol. 15 (Cracow: Polska Akademia Umiejętnosci, 1900); but there is a French translation with notes by Ferenc Makk, *Traduction et commentaire de l'homélie écrite probablement par Théodore le Syncelle sur le siège de Constantinople en 626* (Acta Universitatis de Attila Jozsef Nominatae, Acta Antiqua et Archaeologica, 19; Opuscula Byzantina, 3; Szeged, 1975).

cannot avoid using it.[24] The *Short History* of Nikephoros draws on some of the same sources as Theophanes but is not identical and lacks chronological specificity.[25] Of more complexity are two very different seventh-century provincial non-Greek sources. The virtually contemporary *Chronicle* of John of Nikiu, which was written in Coptic but survives only in an Ethiopic translation, and Sebeos, the former with the perspective of an Egyptian, the latter with that of an Armenian.[26] The *History* attributed to Sebeos is a compilation in Armenian of extracts from various sources, arranged in rough, but not always precise, chronological order. It is of disjointed and uneven coverage and value; most of it was put together no later than 655 with a prophetic and apocalyptic motive to correlate Biblical prophecy and contemporary times. Its authorship remains controversial. Although it supplies some valuable unique material, it is not an objective history, and requires scholars to exercise caution in its utilization.[27] It drew, among other sources, on separate biographical works about Armenian princely families, including one on the Bagratuni family. The tenth-century Armenian *History of the House of Artsrunik'* by Thomas (T'ovma) Artsruni probably derives in part from a common source that the compiler of the *History* attributed to Sebeos also consulted, possibly a Sasanian royal history and a list of Sasanian commanders and officials.[28]

Other non-Greek sources offer difficulties and some rewards. There are some near contemporary as well as later Syriac materials.[29] All of the Arabic materials, except for the Qur'ān, which has its own difficulties for use by an historian, are later, whether Christian or Muslim.[30] The Christian Arab history of Eutychios (Sa'īd ibn Baṭrīq) requires use with caution, because it contains many errors. Yet these Arabic traditions, especially the Muslim

[24] Theophanes, *Chronographia*, ed. C. De Boor (Leipzig: Teubner, 1883); L.I. Conrad, "Theophanes and the Arabic Historical Tradition," *BF* 15 (1990) 1–44. *The Chronicle of Theophanes Confessor*, trans. Cyril Mango and Roger Scott (Oxford: Clarendon Press, 1997), with valuable annotation.

[25] Cyril Mango, "The *Breviarium* of the Patriarch Nikephoros,"in *Byzance: Hommage à A.N. Stratos* (Athens, 1986) II: 539–552; Mango edn. and trans. of Nikephoros, *Short History* 5–19.

[26] R.W. Thomson, with assistance from Tim Greenwood, carefully translated. James Howard-Johnston has produced an historical commentary: *The Armenian History Attributed to Sebeos* (Translated Texts for Historians; Liverpool: University of Liverpool Press, 1999); see also the Italian translation by Claudio Gugerotti, *Storia* (Verona, 1990).

[27] I deeply thank Tim Greenwood for sharing his evaluation of the Sebeos *History* with me in advance of publication of his monograph, *A History of Armenia in the Seventh and Eighth Centuries*.

[28] Thomas (T'ovma) Artsruni, *History of the House of Artsrunik'* (Detroit: Wayne State University Press, 1985). I again thank Tim Greenwood for an analysis of the relationship of this work with that of the *History* attributed to Sebeos.

[29] *The Seventh Century in the West-Syrian Chronicles*, ed., trans. Andrew Palmer (Liverpool: Liverpool University Press; Philadelphia: University of Pennsylvania Press, 1993).

[30] Nadia El Cheikh-Saliba, "Byzantium Viewed by the Arabs" (unpub. Ph.D. diss. in History, Harvard, 1992), for Arab perceptions of Byzantium, including Heraclius.

ones, preserve some important details.[31] One cannot construct the last ten years of the reign of Heraclius without consulting them, although one must be mindful of problems in their use. It is absurd to attempt to reject all of these and to seek to comprehend the Islamic conquests only from Graeco-Syriac sources.[32] Some Arabic accounts are admittedly fabulous and can only be used for understanding later literary imagination and the fluctuating image of Heraclius in an alien culture.[33] I have previously explained my position on using such sources. New research has reaffirmed the existence of an essentially historical core of authentic early Islamic traditions among the larger number of spurious ones.[34] Although a recently identified lead seal of Jabala b. al-Ayham does not corroborate every Muslim tradition, it demonstrates that Muslim traditions can preserve historical details that have disappeared in Christian historiographical traditions.[35] On the other hand, Arabic sources can be of very little help in understanding internal Byzantine developments and conditions.

Other kinds of sources exist. Greek hagiography is helpful for understanding the mentality, flavor, and feel of the era, but was not written with the intent of providing a history of the reign or insight into the thoughts and actions of Heraclius.[36] Saints Theodore of Sykeon and Anastasios

---

[31] Suleiman A. Mourad, "On Early Islamic Historiography: Abu Ismail al-Azdi and His *Futuh al-sham*," *JAOS* 120 (2000) 577–593. Eutychios, *Gli anni*, trans. B, Pirone (Cairo, 1987).

[32] Fred M. Donner, *The Early Islamic Conquests* (Princeton: Princeton University Press, 1981) 142–146; Donner, *Narratives of Islamic Origins* (Princeton: Darwin Press, 1998); R. Stephen Humphreys, *Islamic History: A Framework for Inquiry* (2nd edn. Princeton: Princeton University Press, 1991).

[33] For more critical remarks and bibliography: Robert Hoyland, *Seeing Islam as Others Saw It* (Princeton: Darwin Press, 1997). However interesting and potentially contemporary, there are problems in drawing on the poetry of al-'A'sha: Rudolf Geyer, *Gedichte von Abu Bashir Maimun ibn Qais al-'A'sha* (E.J.W. Gibb Memorial Series, II.5; London: Luzac, 1928).

[34] Kaegi, *BEIC* 2–25. Alexander D. Beihammer, *Nachrichten zum byzantinischen Urkundenwesen in arabischen Quellen* (Bonn: Habelt, 2000), judiciously uses Muslim traditions for the seventh century. A new effort: David Cook, "The Beginnings of Islam in Syria During the Umayyad Period" (Ph.D. diss., University of Chicago, 2002). Irfan Shahid is also developing a sound and important case for some Islamic traditions.

[35] A lead seal that indicates that Jabala held the prestigious Byzantine rank of *patrikios*: Werner Seibt, *Die byzantinischen Bleisiegel in Österreich* (Vienna: Verlag der Akademie, 1978) No. 129, p. 262. Discussion: I. Shahid, "Sigillography in the Service of History: New Light," in *Novum Millennium: Studies on Byzantine History and Culture Dedicated to Paul Speck*, ed. Sarolta Takács, Claudia Sode (Burlington, VT: Ashgate, 2001) 369–377.

[36] Bernard Flusin, *Saint Anastase le Perse* (Paris: CNRS, 1992), is exemplary hagiographical analysis. See *Vie de Jean de Chypre dit l'Aumônier* in *Vie de Syméon le Fou et Vie de Jean de Chypre*, ed. A.J. Festugière (Institut français d'archéologie de Beyrouth, Bibliothèque archéologique et historique, 95; Paris: Geuthner, 1974) 255–637; for the historicity of information in Leontios' *vita* of St. John, see Vincent Déroche, *Etudes sur Léontios de Néapolis* (Acta Universitatis Upsaliensis, Studia Byzantina Upsaliensia, 3; Uppsala: Alqvist & Wiksell, 1995). Another valuable saint's life: *Vie de Théodore de Sykéôn*, ed. trans. A.J. Festugière (Subsidia Hagiographica, 48; Brussels: Société des Bollandistes, 1970).

the Persian are the two richest hagiographical subjects for the study of Heraclius. There are questions concerning whether hagiographic, patristic, and apologetical texts actually reflect seventh-century events and perceptions, or whether they may in fact be corrupt and therefore virtually worthless interpolations from the eighth or ninth centuries.[37]

Epigraphic sources are of limited help but numismatics is a significant tool for this reign, for improving understanding of a number of topics. The sigillographic record is also helpful and a control on chronology, numismatics, and literary vagueness, as the above-mentioned seal of Jabala indicates.[38] Art objects, especially silver and mosaics, also have their utility but present many problems of interpretation. Archaeological excavations help in some instances. Latin sources preserve some traditions of generally limited value. Even some Latin sources as well as Theophanes draw on Syriac and Arabic traditions from the east and so often cannot be treated as completely independent sources.

A history of Heraclius and his times requires coverage of such a disparate group of topics as to be a universal rather than a concentrated history. Among the many issues there is a seemingly simple one: was Heraclius a failure or a success? Was he a great reformer? The older paradigm created by George Ostrogorsky of Heraclius the great reformer has disintegrated. For Ostrogorsky, Heraclius was the linch-pin for a total interpretation of Middle Byzantine History.[39] Ostrogorsky's Heraclius was a creator of institutions and above all was the fundamental Byzantine institutional reformer. That model is no more.[40] The adherents to his model have aged and dwindled with the passing of time and retirements, as has happened with scholarly "schools" in other disciplines.[41] The criticisms of J. Karayannopoulos,[42]

---

[37] Paul Speck, *Beiträge zum Thema Byzantinische Feindseligkeit gegen die Juden im frühen siebten Jahrhundert* (*Varia* VI, Poikila Byzantina, 15; Bonn: Habelt, 1997), but cf. the skeptical and critical review by Andreas Külzer, *BZ* 91 (1998) 583–586.

[38] *Catalogue of Byzantine Seals at Dumbarton Oaks and in the Fogg Museum of Art*, ed. J. Nesbitt and N. Oikonomides (4 vols.; Washington: Dumbarton Oaks, 1991–2001) and its bibliography); G. Zakos, A. Veglery, *Byzantine Lead Seals* (Basel, 1972).

[39] George Ostrogorsky, *History of the Byzantine State* (n. 11) 92–108.

[40] Bibliography: John Haldon, *Byzantium in the Seventh Century* (2nd. edn., Cambridge: Cambridge University Press, 1997) 42–53; Haldon, "Military Service, Military Lands, and the Status of Soldiers: Current Problems and Interpretations," *DOP* 47 (1993) 1–67; W. Brandes, *Finanzverwaltung in Krisenzeiten. Untersuchungen zur byzantinischen Verwaltungsgeschichte zwischen dem ausgehenden 6. und dem beginnenden 9. Jahrhundert* (Frankfurt, 2002).

[41] Broader phenomenon of older cohorts of a paradigm eventually dying out, swept into "the dustbin of historiography," whether or not converted: Peter Novick, *That Noble Dream* (Cambridge: Cambridge University Press, 1988) 348.

[42] J. Karayannopoulos, "Über die vermeintliche Reformtätigkeit des Kaisers Herakleios," *Jahrbuch der Österreichischen Byzantinischen Gesellschaft* 10 (1961) 53–72.

P. Lemerle,[43] A. Pertusi,[44] and others have accomplished their tasks, even though their critiques did not achieve or indeed seek any consensus on any new interpretation of Heraclius. Their achievements were more destructive than constructive. Today there is much less interest in institutional history and institutional interpretations of the causes, nature, and markers of historical change and historical significance, irrespective of what role, if any, Heraclius had with any or all institutions. Byzantinists' obsession with institutions may seem anachronistic and puzzling to other historians. There is no new model. In different eras Heraclius has been interpreted in different ways. Heraclius did innovate, consciously or unconsciously, in creating and augmenting public culture through ceremonies, yet at the same time those who surrounded him stressed that he and his age hearkened back to a former great age, that of Constantine I, rather than to a new one. So Heraclius the innovator remains a real but elusive topic that again deserves review. The nature of the most significant Heraclian innovation has shifted away from the institutional one that fixed many historians' attention in the 1950s.

Leaving aside Byzantinists' interpretations, there is another element in the current context for those attempting any interpretation of Heraclius. This is an era in which the "great man in history" no longer dominates historical interpretation, so some may question the advisability of writing a biography or a history of any reign. The "longue durée" became subject to an acceleration in change in his lifetime and reign, and during that of his son and grandson. The contingent was especially important in those compressed decades. His judgments, made under sharp constraints of time, were important. The picture of Heraclius has changed greatly during the course of the twentieth century, but at this moment it is not in focus. There is no positive scholarly consensus. This study may not solve that problem. The task is a formidable one. It will be impossible to satisfy everyone. However, enough material does exist to begin the process of recovery and reconstruction. The task does involve the study of that now unpopular subject, "histoire événementielle,"[45] but it cannot remain limited to it.

[43] Paul Lemerle, "Quelques remarques sur le règne d'Héraclius," *Studi medievali*, ser. 3a, 1 (1960) 347–361.

[44] Agostino Pertusi, "La formation des thèmes byzantins," in *Berichte zum XI. Internationalen Byzantinisten-Kongress* (Munich, 1958) I: 1–40; Pertusi, edition and commentary on Constantine VII Porphyrogenitus, *De thematibus* (Studi e Testi, 160; Rome: Biblioteca Apostolica Vaticana, 1952) 103–111; also Pertusi, "Nuova ipotesi sull'origine dei 'temi bizantini'," *Aevum* 28 (1954) 126–150.

[45] *La Nouvelle Histoire* (Paris: Retz, 1978); cf. W.E. Kaegi, "The Crisis in Military Historiography," *Armed Forces and Society* 7 (1981) 299–316.

The story of Heraclius, as depicted in several literary historical traditions, is almost Herodotean in his experience of fickle fortune's wheel of triumph and then tragedy, of ignorance or excessive pride, error, and disaster. At one level his name is associated with two categories of classical nomenclature: (1) ancient classical offices such as the consulship, as well as (2) many of the most exciting heroes, places, precedents, and objects of classical, ancient Near Eastern, and Biblical antiquity: Carthage, Nineveh, Jerusalem, the vicinity of Alexander the Great's triumph over the Persians at Gaugamela, Noah's Ark, the Golden Gate in Jerusalem, Arbela, the fragments of the True Cross, Damascus, Antioch, perhaps even ancient Armenia's Tigranocerta, and of course, Constantinople. He and his writers sought to associate his name with famous names from antiquity: Alexander, Scipio, and Constantine I, and with the Biblical Moses and David. Yet he will have to compete with a new name: Muḥammad. No preceding or subsequent Byzantine emperor saw so much: the Araxes, the Khābūr, Tigris, the Euphrates, and the Sea of Galilee (Lake Tiberias). No Byzantine emperor except possibly Constantine I personally traversed so much of the Byzantine Empire, and even Constantine did not see as much of western Asia and the Caucasus as Heraclius. But this is not just a parade or evocation of famous names, places, and objects. It is an action-filled life amid strange and terrible happenings: pestilence, apparitions in the sky, ominous portents on land, reports of astonishing and memorable dreams, and massacres. It was an era of extreme and unprecedented acts. A world began to totter. Uncertain is the extent to which this unique kaleidoscope of experience affected the perception, mentality, and decision-making of Heraclius.

Most historians would probably concede that Heraclius was an important Byzantine emperor but the precise ingredients of that importance are in doubt for them. He did not earn the Byzantine epithet "great," unlike Emperors Constantine I or Theodosios I, in part because of his controversial ecclesiastical policies, specifically his preferences in Christology. Modern historians might well prefer to avoid bestowing an epithet on a sovereign who failed to receive it in antiquity or during the Middle Ages, given that that very category is in disfavor today. Heraclius comes across as a decisive person in his individual as well as in his public sphere of conduct. No source claims or suggests that he was a weak sovereign or person. He had great organizing abilities, and a powerful personality. He was dynamic. He was able to impress his subjects and contemporary intellectuals. He showed leadership. That is the case in a number of different literary traditions and languages. Heraclius had a longer reign than any of his predecessors since Justinian I, and it would be only a century after his death, and almost precisely a century, until another emperor, Constantine V (741–775), would reign for so long. In total, few Byzantine emperors would have such a lengthy reign.

Heraclius was controversial while living and is controversial today. Controversy did not die with him. On the eve of and immediately following his death there were bitter disputes about his intentions concerning his succession among his children. Did he make a difference? The answer is emphatically, yes. Things could have gone other ways, with other outcomes. Some might argue that the empire could have completely disintegrated in the early seventh century, say, between 610 and 630, if he had not imposed his will on it to hold at least some of it together. He did make a difference. Yet he could not overcome everything, in such a large number of challenges. How far can one go with counterfactual reasoning about him (what ifs?)? The best counsel is: be cautious.

Lacunae exist in our knowledge of Heraclius. First of all there are doubts about basic chronology, sometimes due to conflicting reports in the sources, at other times due to omissions of information about certain of his activities. Heraclius and his advisers left no diaries, memoirs, or personal letters. There are no archives of original documents. It is impossible to know biographical details about him that might be standard for nineteenth- and twentieth-century figures. The chronology is inexact for some important events. But it is not the worst-documented period of the Byzantine Empire, for there is more documentation than for some other reigns of the seventh century, or for many of those of the fifth century.

Mysteries abound. The ultimate goals of Heraclius remain obscure. What did Heraclius really want? Heraclius was a fallible mortal, but he did respond to many contemporary challenges and crises. He tried to interpret the future but made some erroneous decisions. The role that Heraclius envisioned himself playing in history is another important topic, yet others may doubt whether this a reasonable question to ask. Was he obsessed with imprinting himself on history? Did he possess any feelings of ethnic or regional identity and if so, what kind? What was his real attitude toward his family? It appears that his family was very important to him. He relied heavily on members of his family to serve in major official positions. What is the reason for so many changes in civic and religious ceremonies during his reign? And why was there so much innovation in the liturgy? Was he the first Byzantine emperor to call himself *Basileus*? His is a reign that looks forward as well as backward. It is part of Late Antiquity but it is also something else. What was happening to culture in his reign and to what extent did those changes owe anything to him?

More than any Byzantine predecessor since the end of the fourth century Heraclius was an emperor on the move. He did not perpetually reside in Constantinople. That mobility in itself probably created a very different style of government and relationship with civilian and ecclesiastical subjects than his predecessors had. It also required a different relationship with Constantinopolitan bureaux than had been the norm. He was much more dependent on efficient communications with Constantinople and with his deputies than were his predecessors. He probably developed a feel for having a traveling court. This surely caused bureaucrats at Constantinople to have to adjust to new ways of governance and communication with the top imperial decision-maker. It also caused military commanders to adapt to the realities of a campaigning soldier–emperor; that change caused adjustments in the functioning and discretion of local commanders.

Emperors who undertook ambitious tasks of learning lived in the century that preceded Heraclius. Justinian I wrote tracts on theology, while Emperor Maurice either wrote or caused the composition of a treatise on military tactics, organization, and strategy. It was not unprecedented for an emperor to ruminate, to be a man of thought as well as of action. Heraclius did not break new ground in doing that. Yet his intellectuality requires more inquiry and assessment.

This study necessarily investigates events. Archaeology is unlikely to resolve some issues concerning this aspect of Heraclius' life. It is important to appreciate contingencies in any attempt to understand him and his reign. Some of Heraclius' greatest successes derive from his ability to take advantage of contingencies and timing. An appreciation of timing and fleeting opportunities is essential in any investigation of Heraclius. There are paradoxical elements in his case as a military commander. How could one who was so militarily successful against the Persians have been such a disastrous failure against the Muslims – or was he a total failure against them? For some the military dimension is uninteresting, because of the present disfavor in which military history is held. The *Strategikon* of Maurice provides some insight into contemporary military thinking and practice.[46] But Heraclius is more than a military commander. A related question concerns Heraclius' religious devotion and how one attempts to investigate and assess it. He is a leader of the faithful, one who marshals the strength of Christendom, who catches the imagination of Christians and non-Christians, whether or not they really understood him.

---

[46] *Das Strategikon des Maurikios*, ed. George T. Dennis, with German translation by E. Gamillscheg (*CFHB* 17; Vienna: Verlag der Akademie, 1981), and English translation by George T. Dennis, University of Pennsylvania Press, 1984.

The life of Heraclius is intrinsically sufficiently interesting to deserve a biographical investigation written in English. Many of the questions that one asks today are somewhat different from what an historian might have asked about Heraclius a century ago, but others are probably similar. In him the historian has a man and emperor who encountered and overcame many successive crises but not all of them. He eventually succumbed. He was a man of action as well as one possessed by the search for religious truth and religious power. He had to fit and fill many roles while he struggled with his personal and familial difficulties in a world that he knew was not always forgiving or benevolent. Lemerle forty years ago asked a basic question as to whether Heraclius dominated an era or was himself dominated by that era:

In summary. Heraclius failed in his national labor for the restoration of the empire and the protection of its integrity, . . . he even failed in his effort for the succession. It would be naive to complain against him, but one may wonder whether this man really dominated his age, whether he had not rather been dominated by it, and by the magnitude of the above-mentioned events.[47]

Scholarly evaluations of Heraclius have varied widely. His nineteenth-century biographer Drapeyron commented with perplexity:

. . . the strange man whom we study has prodigious faculties, which, far from being balanced as in Epaminondas, are unevenly developed. He has more sensibility than intelligence, more intelligence than will. He will be dragged to action by his ardent sympathy, and then he will have, but very falsely, the illusion of unparalleled energy. But he will be enchained, whether by this love of God, of men, and in particular of one in his family, he comes to hover on some cloud. Thus he depends completely on the exterior.[48]

It was Ernst Stein who began the process of positive reevaluation of Heraclius in the early 1930s even though he never wrote a detailed or rigorous biography of Heraclius. Stein, whose life was greatly disrupted and probably shortened by the European turmoil and violence of the 1930s and 1940s, is seldom read today. For Stein, who wrote a contribution on him for a multi-contributor volume entitled *Menschen die Geschichte machten* ("Men Who Made History"), the final evaluation was very favorable.[49] It was Stein who influenced George Ostrogorsky's vision of Heraclius as a great reformer, which Ostrogorsky developed into a broader paradigm later in the 1930s, "der grosste Herrscher der byzantinische Geschichte

---

[47] Lemerle, "Quelques remarques" 361.   [48] Drapeyron, *L'Empereur* (n. 6) 28.
[49] Ernst Stein, "Heraclius," in *Menschen die Geschichte machten*, ed. Peter Rohden, G. Ostrogorsky (Vienna: L.W. Seidel & Sohn, 1931) I: 257–264.

[the greatest ruler of Byzantine history]."[50] For Stein, at the beginning of the 1930s, the foundations of the Byzantine Empire were created by Heraclius:

...die späteren Grundlagen des Byzantinischen Reiches – der während des folgenden halben Jahrtausends noch immer bedeutendsten, ja man kann fast sagen, allein die Merkmale eines wirklichen Staates tragenden christlichen Macht – von ihm geschaffen sind [the later foundations of the Byzantine Empire, which during the following half-millennium were still the most important, one can even say the sole benchmark of a real state wielding Christian power, were shaped by him].

He asserted that Heraclius was "ein kühner Feldherr und vielleicht noch kühnerer Sozialreformer [a bold field commander and perhaps still bolder social reformer]."[51] But some thirty years later for Lemerle the reign of Heraclius had "l'apparente contradiction interne [apparent internal contradiction]." Lemerle's final assessment of Heraclius was a "Bilan tout négatif d'un règne qui eût pu être l'un des plus glorieux de l'histoire de Byzance [totally negative balance of a reign that might have been one of the most glorious of Byzantium]."[52] The majority of contemporary scholars tend to follow the lead of Lemerle by avoiding any identification of the reign of Heraclius as pivotal for Byzantine social and institutional policy, even though conceding that it was pivotal for imperial power and for failed religious policy.

Heraclius was no fool. Despite his mistakes, he showed some foresight and he did attempt to make some major changes. The exact character of some of his fiscal changes remains controversial and very poorly documented. His ultimate intentions remain obscure. Today his greatest achievements in the eyes of historians may be the changes that he made in public culture in his empire, in addition to his military successes on the battlefield and in holding a critical mass of the empire together in an era of epoch-making change that he did not and perhaps could not master or check.

Some of the debate about Heraclius has shifted to issues of interpreting culture, art, and mentalities in that era, as well as to reexamining visual and literary representations of Heraclius. Some scholars may wish to explore the ideological framework of the era of Heraclius. Others will contest whether ideology is or can be a valid term for conceptual analysis prior

---

[50] George Ostrogorsky, *Geschichte des byzantinischen Staates* (Munich: C.H. Beck, 1940) 54–69, esp. 54, and supporting articles, e.g: "Über die vermeintliche Reformtätigkeit der Isaurier," *BZ* 30 (1929–1930) 394–400.

[51] Ernst Stein, in *Menschen die Geschichte machten* (n. 49) I: 257.

[52] Lemerle, "Quelques remarques" 355.

to the nineteenth century and may join those who stoutly reject seeing or reading in any ideological theme whatever, especially any political one, in such indubitably genuine and famous products of the Heraclian era as the David Plates. Differing religious frames of reference between the seventh century and our own impede understanding Heraclius. His was a very religious age, in which one expected sudden divine intervention for salutary purposes and in the form of wrathful retribution for individual and collective transgressions. The observant were always watching for signs that suggested, foretold, or proved and reinforced such expectations. One perceived, decided, and acted accordingly.

Among the most interesting facets of and issues for the historian in interpreting Heraclius' life, reign, and age is evaluating the extent to which, in a time of rapid and major change, one man did or could affect or change history. His is a major case with which to test hypotheses about that problem; indeed most estimates of Heraclius and his historical significance must come to grips with it. This is not primarily an inquiry into institutional history or institutional questions. Instead, it will investigate Heraclius' drift or mastery in the face of historical contingency and varied crises. It, in the end, is an interpretation, not merely a recounting and ordering of chronology and facts.

Heraclius was an emperor in whose lifetime the world no longer remained under control and was rapidly fragmenting without total collapse. His world was one in which old answers and policies no longer sufficed, one in which action became necessary and consumed his life. He did devote much time to crafting his image, to developing a new sacrality that included many more public ceremonies, and he aggressively sought to deflect criticism from himself to an array of scapegoats, which requires that the modern historian remain vigilant and use critical judgment. He was no military or institutional genius or great social or economic reformer.

The picture of Heraclius that emerges in clearer focus is a more limited one of a leader with extraordinary skills at combining political and military policies and tactics, who was able to achieve more through political reversals, political negotiations, intrigue, exploitation of internal divisions within the ranks of his foes, a good sense of timing, and intelligence than through any decisiveness as a commander on the battlefield. He was no Trajan or Gaius Marius or Alexander the Great. Although he was no superman, he achieved much with the materials and opportunities that were at hand. Heraclius was a man with flaws whose life and achievements were flawed, but despite his fallibility and his many crises he never abandoned his struggles. He left his shadow over an age that was full of attention-grabbing shocks. It is necessary to explore these problems and his many ambiguities. In a world of uncertainties his place is more uncertain today than ever. His was a life mixed with victory, anguish, and repeated struggles. He and his reign represent both an end and a beginning. The very uncertainty of his present station encourages and makes this process of reevaluation imperative.

CHAPTER I

Armenia and Africa: the formative years

The seventh century did not begin auspiciously.[1] True, the Empire's borders still stretched from the Pillars of Hercules, that is, the straits of Gibraltar, in the west, to the Gulf of 'Aqaba and the edge of the Caucasus (Map 1). There was, of course, no contemporary consciousness about the start of any new century. St. Theodore of Sykeon foretold calamities that would cover Heraclius' era: speaking of the Emperor Maurice, who he predicted would soon die (as it happened, in 602), he said "after him there will be worse calamities, such that this generation has no idea of." On another occasion, he announced, "Pray, my children, great tribulations, terrible scourges threaten the world."[2] It was a troubled time that was about to worsen, one that would engulf virtually the total sweep of our subject's lifetime. We know very little about Flavius Heraclius' early years. Heraclius the Younger was a virtual contemporary of an illustrious man whom he presumably never met, the prophet Muhammad, who was born about five years earlier, and who died nine years before Heraclius himself did. How much the name evoked the hero Herakles in Heraclius the Younger's mind is unknown, but it was auspicious of his future exertions.[3] It may have been a stimulus to heroic efforts. For others Heraclius commemorated prominent saints, not any ancient mythological hero. But it was his unidentified grandparents who had chosen his father's and therefore implicitly his name.

[1] John Haldon, *Byzantium in the Seventh Century* (2nd. edn., Cambridge: Cambridge University Press, 1997); W.E. Kaegi, "Reconceptualizing Byzantium's Eastern Frontiers," in *Shifting Frontiers in Late Antiquity*, ed. R. Mathisen and H. Sivan (Aldershot: Variorum, 1996) 83–92.

[2] *Vie de Théodore de Sykeôn* c. 119, 127 (I: 96, 103, II: 99, 107 Festugière).

[3] His court poets, such as George of Pisidia, certainly invoked the name of Herakles in praise of Heraclius: *Heraclias* 1.78–79, II 20–23 (243, 252 Pertusi); Mary Whitby, "A New Image for a New Age: George of Pisidia on the Emperor Heraclius," in *The Roman and Byzantine Army in the East*, ed. E. Dabrowa (Krakow: Uniwersytet Jagiellonski Instytut Historii, 1994) 206–208; Th. Nissen, "Historisches Epos und Panegyrikos in der Spätantike," *Hermes* 75 (1940) 302–303.

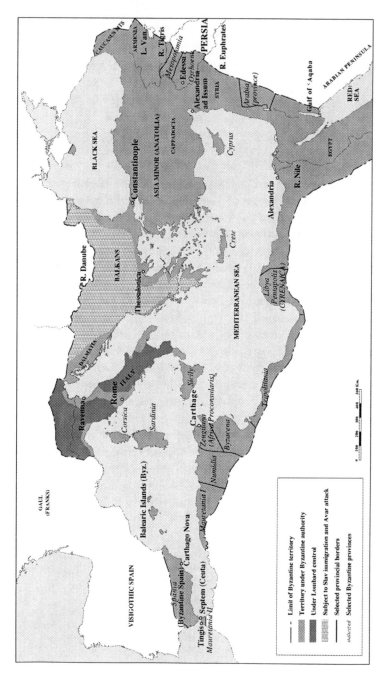

Map 1 The Byzantine Empire in AD 600

Heraclius the Younger was born son of Heraclius the Elder and Epiphania ca. 575, and was probably of Armenian descent[4] (one early and one late source call him Cappadocian, but that is not irreconcilable with being Armenian).[5] The question of the origins of Heraclius the Elder is important. If one assumes that his origin is African or Edessene Syrian or Armenian or Cappadocian non-Armenian, each of these categories creates a different group of possible assumptions about the heritage and context in which both Heraclii grew up and developed. And is the place of birth also the identifier of ethnic identity or not? The preponderance of evidence points to an Armenian origin for Heraclius the Elder, although his wife may well have had Cappadocian origins. Furthermore, the epithet "Cappadocian" leaves many questions unanswered. The term Cappadocia can refer to lands as far as the Euphrates. We have no evidence on what Armenian consciousness, if any, either Heraclius possessed. Greek panegyrists would not have wished to call attention to any Armenian origins of Heraclius. Although the achievements of his father, Heraclius the Elder, were modest, later historians magnified his military achievements as part of their program to exalt and praise his son. His father, also named Heraclius, had been a prominent general in 585, apparently second in command to Philippikos, the supreme regional commander, the Master of the Soldiers

---

[4] *PLRE* III; 586–587, s.v. "Heraclius 4"; A. Pernice, *Imperatore Eraclio* (Florence, 1905). Armenian origin: Theophylact Simocatta, *Hist.* 3.1.1; other information on background: Theophylact Simocatta, *Hist.* 2.3.2, 2.5.10, 2.10.6, 3.6.2; John of Nikiu, *Chronicle* 109.27 (trans. R.H. Charles, Oxford, Oxford University Press, 1916). Theophanes, *Chron.* A.M. 6078, 6100, 6101, 6102. Any genealogy of the family earlier than that of Heraclius the Elder is too speculative to consider here: Cyril Mango, "Deux études sur Byzance et la Perse Sassanide," *TM* 9 (1985) 113–114, in favor of the possible identification of a late fifth-century Heraclius with this family. Other Byzantine commanders in Africa, such as John Troglitas and Solomon, had backgrounds and experience in the east, as of course, did Belisarios, so it is not in principle difficult to find a Byzantine commander in Africa who had experience and origins in the east. The author of the *History* attributed to Sebeos, although written in Armenian, does not specifically identify Heraclius as Armenian, which may be a meaningless ethnic designation for that historical context, or identify his birthplace, but for a very probable Armenian attribution, see Cyril Toumanoff, *Studies in Christian Caucasian History* (Washington: Georgetown University Press, 1963) 192–193; Toumanoff, "Caucasia and Byzantium," *Traditio* 27 (1971) esp. 157–158; D. Kouymijian, "Ethnic Origins and the 'Armenian' Policy of Emperor Heraclius," *REArm,* n.s. 17 (1983) 635–642; Toumanoff, "The Heraclids and the Arsacids," *REArm,* n.s. 19 (1985) 431–434, hypothesizes some genealogical tie with the ancient dynasty of Arsacids. Also: Irfan Shahid, "The Iranian Factor in Byzantium during the Reign of Heraclius," *DOP* 26 (1972) 310. The relevant text is from Sebeos, *History* 144–145 (109 Thomson, n. 673); *Storia* c. 42 (111 trans. Gugerotti = 108 trans. Macler). A.A. Vasiliev, *History of the Byzantine Empire* (Madison: University of Wisconsin Press, 1952) 193, accepted this allusion by Sebeos to the Arsacid antecedents of Heraclius' grandson, Constans II, as likewise referring to Heraclius himself.

[5] John of Nikiu, *Chron.* 106.2, 109.27 (167, 176 Charles) mentions Cappadocia; the twelfth-century poet and historian Constantine Manasses, *Brev. Chron.* 1.3664–5 (ed. Odysseus Lampsides, *CFHB* 36; Athens: Academy, 1997, 197) proclaims in verse that "his fatherland was the thrice-blessed land of the Cappadocians, his race of distinguished men, and with an abundance of hair."

(*magister militum per Orientem*) in the East 586–588, in a capacity in 586 in which he saw action against the Persians at Solachon, and again in the same year he was at personal risk in scouting near the siege of Chlomaron.[6] It is possible that Heraclius the Elder actually exercised authority as *magister militum* twice during the absence of Philippikos from the troops. Philippikos sent Heraclius the Elder to raid Persia late in 586 and again in late 587. Philippikos left him in command of the empire's eastern army for a time in spring 587 while Philippikos was ill and visited Constantinople. Philippikos ordered him to return to Armenia when Emperor Maurice appointed Priskos to replace Philippikos in 588, so Heraclius avoided the difficult situation of having to welcome Priskos,[7] who replaced Philippikos and then encountered a mutiny of the troops who still wanted Philippikos.[8] In 589 he served under the *magister militum per Orientem* Komentiolos[9] in the east, near Nisibis, at the battle of Sisarbanon. He was the lieutenant of General Philippikos.

Precisely where the young Heraclius was during these activities of his father is uncertain – perhaps near him, perhaps in Armenia, perhaps at Constantinople. Ca. 595 Heraclius the Elder was *magister militum per Armeniam*, which reinforced his ties with Armenia. Presumably his son Heraclius would either have accompanied him or visited him while he performed those responsibilities, whether or not he had visited him during his earlier military service.[10] Later Heraclius the Younger enjoyed a reputation for being very learned. There is no information on what kind of education he received as a child or during his teenage years, including when, where, and how he became literate. Armenia did not lack learned scholars, as the contemporary case of the scholar Ananias of Shirak testifies.[11] Presumably Heraclius was bilingual (Armenian and Greek) from an early age, but even this is uncertain, as is whether he learned to speak or read any other languages. Similarly there is no evidence concerning any acquaintances and friendships that Heraclius the Younger made at that time, or the nature or intensity of his relations with the church, or concerning any youthful religious experiences, including mentoring, that he received. His was an era in which impressive ascetics made terrifying predictions and seemed able

---

[6] *PLRE* III: 1022–1026, s.v. "Philippicus 3."   [7] *PLRE* III: 1052–1057, s.v. "Priscus 6."

[8] Theophylact Sim. *Hist.* 3.1.1–2; W.E. Kaegi, *Byzantine Military Unrest* (Amsterdam, Las Palmas: Hakkert, 1981) 68–72; M. Whitby, *The Emperor Maurice and His Historian* (Oxford: Oxford University Press, 1988) 287–290.

[9] *PLRE* III: 321–325, s.v. "Comentiolus 1."   [10] *PLRE* III: 584–585, s.v. "Heraclius 3."

[11] Paul Lemerle, "Note sur les données historiques de l'Autobiographie d'Anania de Shirak," *REArm*, n.s. 1 (1964) 195–201; J.-P. Mahé, "Quadrivium et cursus d'études au VIIe siècle en Arménie et dans le monde byzantin d'après le 'K'nnikon' d'Anania Sirakac'i," *TM* 10 (1987) 159–206.

to make miraculous cures of various medical and mental afflictions, but we do not know whether he or his father consulted or had special contact in that stage of his life with any of them. Presumably he learned how to ride a horse and how to handle some weapons in those years.

Military service in Armenia provided Heraclius the Elder with an up-to-date acquaintance with conditions there, giving his son Heraclius the Younger some memories and ties and opportunities or future opportunities on which to build his network of friends, as well as intelligence about conditions and terrain there – including roads, weather, and communications; the people – their ways and outlooks; and the availability of provisions for man and horse. They learned of the latest developments in warfare between Persians and Byzantines. Heraclius the Elder served in those years of the 580s and 590s in precisely the regions in which his son Heraclius the Younger would be leading imperial armies in the coming decades. So paternal advice about military conditions there would have been invaluable for his son, as well as whatever personal ties and obligations the father made with local inhabitants, especially their leaders. This is a great gap in our knowledge. But the later military successes and routes of Heraclius the Younger on his subsequent campaigns, his ability to recruit troops, his readiness to undertake certain kinds of military risks in such difficult and dangerous terrain, all surely owed much to his father's previous service there, his advice to his son, and whatever goodwill and ties his father had built during his years of service there. Probably the father never wrote all or possibly any of it down, but communicated it orally to his son over a period of years. In upper Mesopotamia both necessarily would have gained at least a little familiarity with Arabs, whether those pasturing their flocks in the vicinity or those who actually were military allies, scouts, or couriers for the Byzantines, and possibly something of those who served the Persians. What opinions they developed about Arabs at that time are matters only for speculation. We cannot determine which towns and routes Heraclius the Younger visited during those years.

Heraclius the Elder had, during his military service in the east, the opportunity to develop impressions about sensitive issues of military unrest and about prominent personalities among the empire's commanders and their impact on military units. He heard a lot about commanders such as Priskos and Philippikos, reached his own conclusions, and probably passed them on to his son. Although he did not serve in the Balkans, in so far as is known, he probably shared the attitudes and possible prejudices of eastern commanders and soldiers about service and about the personalities and character of military units in the Balkans. As a commander who served in the east, he was surely aware of the unpopularity among Armenians of transfer to and military service in the Balkans. All of this wisdom and prejudice was part of the heritage his son Heraclius received from him.

Up to this point in the lives of both Heraclii, as far as is known, Heraclius the Elder's service had been in or near landlocked areas of the interior inhabited by Armenians.[12] None of those areas had ever been heavily Hellenized or Romanized, whether in language, culture, or physical monuments, that is, public buildings, statuary, *fora*, or amphitheaters and arenas. These areas were by no means exclusively Armenian, but were inhabited by diverse ethnic groups. Except for possible visits to Constantinople, there is no evidence of familiarity with maritime regions of the empire, naval warfare or shipping. Their familiarity would have been of warfare and terrain in the Caucasus and the plains and plateaus of extreme upper Mesopotamia, regions of severe winters and summers, with harsh changes of climate, difficulties of travel and regions of limited supplies for an army, if not the need to bring one's own supplies on any substantial military expedition. It was a world of many stone fortifications, and parts of this territory required careful attention to accumulation of supplies of water, due to the parched summer conditions. Waterways, except for the upper Tigris and Euphrates, were not navigable in those regions, and even these waterways were probably of limited value to the Byzantines, because of their routes. Horses were useful in parts of this country, especially upper Mesopotamia and even some parts of the Armenian highlands.

Heraclius learned much from his father about Persian ways of war and diplomacy. His father had some actual combat and scouting experience against the Persians. That action took place in extreme upper Mesopotamia. The *Patria* of Constantinople reports that Heraclius the Younger dreamt of empire while residing in the former residence of Sophiai, built twenty-eight years earlier either for Sophia, wife of Emperor Justin II, or for Anastasia, widow of Tiberius II, and mother-in-law of Emperor Maurice, in Constantinople, presumably after his father was finished with his campaigning or while not campaigning against the Persians.[13] By implication there he gained the ambition for imperial power, presumably having tasted of imperial splendor at that residence. That may be a later invented story,

---

[12] On contemporary Armenian geography: Ananias of Shirak, *The Geography of Ananias of Shirak, Asxarhacouyc, The Long and Short Recensions*, ed., trans., comment. R.H. Hewsen (Beihefte zum Tübinger Atlas des Vorderen Orients, Reihe B, Geisteswissenschaften, 77; Wiesbaden: Reichart, 1992).

[13] Gilbert Dagron, *Constantinople imaginaire* (Paris: Presses Universitaires de France, 1984) 321; *Patria Constantinopoleos*, ed. Th. Preger, K III 125. The reference in the *Patria* is problematic and may conflate Heraclius and his father.

intended to demonstrate the fated and inevitable nature of his rise to the throne, but it may contain a kernel of truth. It is entirely possible that the family of Heraclius the Elder did temporarily reside in that palace as recipients of imperial hospitality to a favored prominent commander, and to reinforce their mutual ties. Heraclius the Elder did enjoy the favor of Emperor Maurice. Probably Heraclius the Younger resided there immediately before his father's assumption of new responsibilities in Africa. Both Heraclii owed a lot to Maurice, respected him, and naturally retained a favorable memory of and loyalty to him. Subsequently Heraclius the Younger wished to associate his cause with the revenge for injustice to Maurice. There may be cold political calculations in the subsequent posthumous praise and lament at the Heraclian court for Maurice, but with it was some genuine admiration and recognition that without his sponsorship, the Heraclii would have had less lustrous careers. No record exists of actual face-to-face audiences of either Heraclius with Maurice.

By approximately the year 600, or in any event by 602, Heraclius the Elder had received appointment as exarch in Africa (a kind of governor-general, who held civilian and military powers, whose seat of power was Carthage[14]) on the authority of Emperor Maurice, who still reigned. Recent scholarship does not ascribe as much significance to the institution of the exarchate as was the case at the end of the nineteenth and early in the twentieth century. A number of important sixth-century Byzantine military commanders in North Africa had held military commands or originated in the east and then came to serve in Africa: Belisarios himself, Solomon, and John Troglitas, Theoktistos, Sergios (nephew of Solomon), Artabanes, and Rufinos.[15] Heraclius' appointment and experience fit into the larger pattern of many Byzantine military commanders in Africa, and like Solomon, he had an Armenian background. His rotation from the east and Dara and Nisibis region to Africa was not unusual.[16] One does not

---

[14] Charles Diehl, *L'Afrique byzantine* (Paris, 1896, repr. New York: Burt Franklin, n.d.), also Diehl, *Études sur l'administration byzantine dans Exarchat de Ravenne (568–751)* (Paris, 1888).

[15] *PLRE* III, s.v. "Belisarius," "Solomon," "John Troglitas," "Theoctistas 2," "Sergius 4," "Artabanes 2," "Rufinus 2." Hence it is unnecessary to seek some remote African ancestor for Heraclius the Elder: D. Pringle, *The Defence of Byzantine Africa* (Oxford, 1979) 1–34. On exarchate: Pringle, *Defence of Byzantine Africa* 41–42, 57. Of course there are *magistri militum, duces,* and exarchs for whom our biographical information is so incomplete that it is impossible to determine their previous military experience and its location.

[16] Transfers between east and west in an earlier century of the Later Roman Empire: Hugh Elton, *Warfare in Roman Europe AD 350–425* (Oxford: Oxford University Press, 1996) 212–214. Even a fifth-century Heraclius came from the Edessa region to lead troops in Africa. He was sent by Emperor Leo I against the Vandal king Geiserich: Theophanes, *Chron.* A.M. 5963 (182–183 Mango) so the cases of sixth-century officers with eastern experience, esp. in vicinity of upper Mesopotamia, are part of a much broader pattern.

know what changes and improvements he made in Africa as a result of his earlier experiences in the east against the Persians. Because the inhabitants of North Africa had previously encountered Byzantine commanders with military experience not unlike that of Heraclius the Elder, both they and he had precedents. There may have been some difficult adjustments for both parties, but this was not the first time such a commander with this kind of background had come to Africa. The name Heraclius probably found a positive reception in Africa, because Tebessa, now in eastern Algeria near the Tunisian frontier, was a site associated with a Christian martyr named Heraclius.[17] It is unknown whether Heraclius the Elder drew on reports of the experiences of some of his predecessors from the eastern front to help him adjust more easily and to avoid any previous mistakes or problems. There was an interchange and rotation of military commanders between the critical eastern commands in the vicinity of Dara and Africa. There was no simple, single pattern for it, but the career of Heraclius the Elder was no unusual case in that respect. How much improvement or change in military arrangements and tactics occurred in both regions as a result of those rotations is uncertain.

Heraclius the Younger probably spent his twenty-fifth through thirty-fifth years in North Africa with his father, a key period of his maturation. Because there is no diary, local history, chronicle, or letters that report the activities of either Heraclius during most of their stays in Africa, one must make inferences. The early Frankish historian Fredegarius (ca. 656, rather close to the reign of Heraclius) reports that Heraclius had "often" fought lions in the arena and even wild boar in unfrequented places, although he is not more specific as to locality.[18] Africa possessed both lions and boar, and

---

[17] Y. Duval, ed., *Loca Sanctorum Africae* I: 126.

[18] Fredegarius 4.65 (= *The Fourth Book of the Chronicle of Fredegar*, ed. trans. J.M. Wallace-Hadrill (London: Thos. Nelson, 1960) 52–53). Although previous emperors had abolished the custom of using panthers and lions and other beasts apparently as punishments, this allegedly resumed in the reign of Phokas, according to John of Nikiu, *Chronicle* 107.10 (168 Charles). But John is not speaking about conditions in Africa. It had become a rarity in the east, if we can trust him. But John may refer to punishments, not to optional combat by free men. It is not likely that there were many arenas in Armenia and in upper Mesopotomia. I am unaware of the excavation of arenas in those regions. Nor would Heraclius probably have engaged in such activity while campaigning against the Persians. He could have engaged in such combat in Constantinople, and despite the opposition of the church, there were at least sporadic instances of animal combat at Constantinople, and those could have included lions. There could be Constantinian associations with such practices, and Heraclius sought to associate his name with Constantine I. The tradition of animal combat is better attested for Africa, where the supply of animals was presumably still plentiful at the beginning of the seventh century and traditions of such past combats were ubiquitous. Steven H. Wander, "The Cyprus Plates and the Chronicle of Fredegar," *DOP* 29 (1975) 345–346, does not discuss Fredegarius' reference to lions. See A.P. Kazhdan, "Animal Combat," in *ODB* 100. Mary Whitby, "A New Image" (n. 3) 218–220, for images of struggle against beasts.

had a long tradition of human combat with wild beasts, as extant mosaics in Sousse and Sfax and the Bardo Museum in Tunis attest. Perhaps Heraclius as a younger man, between the ages of twenty-five and thirty-five, had actually fought lions in controlled situations in Africa, where he had learned of traditions of such combats. Fredegarius' detail that Heraclius fought in the arena makes it conceivable that the locality of such combat was Africa, but fighting lions in the arena is an heroic activity (whether historical or unhistorical) for Armenians as well,[19] so this may be a *topos* and nothing more. He would have engaged in such activity while relatively young, which accords with his stay in Africa. Such prowess probably earned him respect in Africa and among the Byzantine officials and soldiery stationed in Africa, and he was able to draw on those feats to increase his reputation and renown in the future. Renown for such combat also evoked the labors of his mythological namesake, Herakles, who had slain the Nemean lion as one of his distinguished labors.[20] Contemporaries could not have avoided making that association. One can always ask whether this is a mere imperial *topos* and nothing more. That is possible, but it is more likely that he had, in Africa, observed and in some fashion participated in vestigial remnants of the old arena combats of Roman North Africa. He made the most of his stay there, not ignoring local ways and local conditions. He did not isolate himself from Africans and their ways of doing things. He enjoyed his stay in Africa, which contributed to his growth and development as well as providing the resources and springboard for his rise to power. There is no way of knowing how much of Africa he visited outside Carthage.

The elder Heraclius and his son found themselves in a rich land. Byzantine Africa at the beginning of the seventh century was not in economic or demographic decline.[21] Africa contained far more splendid Roman traces

---

[19] Sebeos, *Hist.* ch. 20, 93 (39–40 Thomson), for Smbat Bagratuni's combat with lions in the arena.

[20] George of Pisidia, *Heraclias* 1.78–79, 2.19–23 (243, 252 Pertusi). J. Trilling, "Myth and Metaphor at the Byzantine Court," *Byzantion* 48 (1978) 250–251, for arguments that the "David Plates" date from early in Heraclius' reign, although certainly after his seizure of Constantinople and probably after 613, and on pp. 260–261, more discussion of the Herakles conceit.

[21] M.G. Fulford, "Carthage: Overseas Trade and the Political Economy c. AD 400–700," *Reading Medieval Studies* 6 (1980) 68–80; S. Ellis, "Carthage in the Seventh Century: an Expanding Population?" *Cahiers des Etudes Anciennes* 17 (1985) 30–42; Ellis, "North African Villages in the Byzantine Period," *XXe Congrès des Etudes Byzantines* I:*Séances Plénières, Pré-Actes* (Paris 2001) 78; Stefano Tortorella, "La ceramica fine da mensa africana dal IV al VII secolo d.c.," in *Società romana e impero tardoantico* III: *Le merci gli insediamenti*, ed. Andrea Giardina (Rome: Laterza, 1986) 211–225. An opposing but unpersuasive view: W.H.C. Frend, "The End of Byzantine Africa: Some Evidence of Transitions," in *Histoire et Archéologie de l'Afrique du Nord, IIe Colloque International (Grenoble, 5–9 avril 1983)* = *Bulletin Archéologique du Comité des Travaux Historiques et Scientifiques*, n.s. 19B (1985) 387–397. Geographical limits: Pringle, *Defence of Byzantine Africa* 28–29, 59–63.

than did the Balkan towns from which many Late Roman emperors took their origins. Archaeologists and historians have modified the earlier picture of decline that Charles Diehl had sketched in his *Afrique byzantine*. Byzantine military authorities had devised ways, within their limited financial means and military capacities, to contain the Berber threat. Africa was not without problems, but life there was not on the edge of a precipice.[22] Life was, in fact, far more secure than in the contemporary imperiled Byzantine Balkans or the empire's even more imperiled eastern frontier lands of Mesopotamia and the Caucasus.[23] There is evidence in the western Mediterranean for seventh-century trade between Africa and Gaul.[24] Yet, as in contemporary Italy, there was an understandable impetus for the assertion of local interests and for decentralization.[25]

Churches and agriculture were thriving at and near the coasts. Grain had been important in Mesopotamia: it was also important in Africa, especially in the vicinity of Vaga or modern Beja, in the Mejerda River plain. The Arab memory of the seventh-century Byzantine Africa that they had found and conquered was of a land extremely rich in agriculture based on one principal crop, the olive, even though its grain was also important. Maritime trade was also brisk, probably involving grain, olive oil, and perhaps some wine. Fish and shellfish were plentiful. The landed elite left their principal testimonial in the form of sepulchral mosaics, the overwhelming number of which, insofar as it is possible to ascertain a date, predate the seventh century. This elite was not supine; it could be assertive, but we do not have detailed information about individual families at the beginning of the seventh century, or their familial life. We can only make inferences about their political and economic attitudes. We do not have their account

[22] Averil Cameron, "Gelimer's Laughter," in *Tradition and Innovation in Late Antiquity*, ed. Frank M. Clover and R.S. Humphreys (Madison: University of Wisconsin Press, 1989) 171–190; also Averil Cameron, "Byzantine Reconquest of North Africa," *Graeco-Arabica* 5 (1993) 153–165.

[23] Michael Hendy, *Studies in the Byzantine Monetary Economy* 21–168. Although Hendy emphasizes (172, 620–621) the relatively smaller importance of Africa in contrast to the wealth of Egypt, one historian attributes a significant aspect of the decline of the western Roman Empire in the fifth century to the loss of Africa: Hugh Elton, *Warfare in Roman Europe* (n. 16) 267: loss of control of Africa, "important as a reservoir of manpower and money, and similar to Egypt or Anatolia in the East." If Africa ever held such importance, it would have been somewhat reduced by the seventh century, and never was really equivalent to Egypt. Yet loss of control of it by Phokas was serious, especially when coupled with that of Egypt, and the imperiled situation in northern Syria and upper Mesopotamia and the restive situation in the Balkans. Africa's importance to the empire as a source of revenues rose enormously when Egypt was lost to the Persians and again to the Muslims.

[24] Cécile Morrisson, "Les monnaies byzantines," in Y. Solier and colleagues, "Les épaves de Gruissan," *Archaeonautica* 3 (1981) 35–52.

[25] André Guillou, *Régionalisme et indépendance dans l'empire byzantin au VII siècle: L'exemple de l'exarchat et de la Pentapole d'Italie* (Rome: Istituto Storico Italiano per il Medio Evo, 1969) 231–254.

books.[26] Almost no one remained alive at the beginning of the seventh century who could remember the actual Byzantine reconquest of Africa from the Vandals in the early 530s. Yet some probably could explain and list some of the lessons learned in subsequent military campaigning and preventive defenses constructed against the Berbers.

Later, as emperor, Heraclius, by 630 or 632, took decisive anti-Jewish measures. Yet there is no evidence concerning his (or his father's) acquaintance, experience, or relations with Jews either in the east, until he was twenty-five, or in the following decade, during his stay in Africa, where their prominence in some trade, such as cloth, would likely have caught his attention. There is simply no evidence concerning his opinions about them or theirs about him at that phase of his life, or during his revolt against Phokas between 608 and 610.

Even less certain is what Heraclius learned or knew about Africa's historical heritage and the Roman presence in it. Scipio Africanus receives mention by at least two authors of Heraclius' court, the poet George of Pisidia, and the historian Theophylact Simocatta.[27] But there is no definitive proof that Heraclius took any special interest in Scipio while in Africa, let alone that he attempted to visit any sites connected with Scipio, some of which, like Zama, were distant from Carthage and probably not identified then. He was in the midst of a glorious Roman military past of conquest and victory, but what consciousness of it he had is unclear. The name of Scipio, then, was not unknown but whether it was any kind of inspiration for him, and not merely a literary *topos* for his later panegyrists, is unclear. Equally unclear is whether the general Philippikos, who explicitly is said to have studied Scipio's campaigns against Hannibal, ever later discussed such campaigns with Heraclius after he seized the throne. Heraclius' actual

---

[26] Jean Durliat speculates about the independent attitudes and actions of substantial African landowners in the seventh century: "Les grands propriétaires africains et l'état byzantin (533–709)," *Cahiers de Tunisie* 29 (1981) 517–531, esp. 525–529; also Durliat, *Dédicaces d'ouvrages de défense dans l'Afrique byzantine* (Paris: Ecole française de Rome, Collection 49, 1981) 113.

[27] George of Pisidia, *Heraclias* 1.97, 98 (*Poemi, Panegirici epici* 244 Pertusi). But this comparison of Heraclius with Scipio is a commonplace of Late Roman literature, especially that in Latin. Irfan Shahid has cogently argued for an interpretation that de-emphasizes Scipio Africanus in the line of George of Pisidia: "Heraclius Pistos en Christo Basileus," *DOP* 34–35 (1980–1981) 225–237. Heraclius' (and before him, Maurice's general and son-in-law) *magister militum per Orientem* Philippikos had studied Scipio's campaigns against Hannibal: Theophylact, *Hist.* 1.14.2–4 (40 Whitby, and n. 76 p. 40): "When Hannibal the Carthaginian General was ravaging the European territory of the Romans, the elder Scipio committed the war at home to deferment, attacked the Carthaginian land, and drove the enemy to serious trouble" (Theophylact 1.14.3). This may be an intentional allusion to Heraclius' "Scipionic" campaign against Persia or simply a *topos*. Scipionic associations or memories may have existed in Heraclius' Africa but we have no sure way of probing them and their effects, if any, on him.

experiences in Africa and his later memories of Africa mixed with familial ties and with interpolated conversations and nostalgia, may have created a different view of Africa while he was emperor than when he really lived in Africa with his father as exarch.

Heraclius the Elder's brother Gregory[28] was also in Africa, significantly, with his own son Niketas. So an entire family was ensconced, providing a stronger power base. His was a closely knit family. Yet it was not a narrow Armenian family. Heraclius the Younger himself had the reputation of being accomplished in speech.[29] It is possible that he did learn some Latin and that he could understand something beyond Greek and Armenian. His family members had broad experience and exposure to conditions and people outside Armenia. Their diversity of experience enriched them and helped them to understand complexities and to be flexible in handling different people and problems.

Through his uncle and cousin, the younger Heraclius probably learned more of conditions out in the countryside. The exact location of the seat of the exarch in the city of Carthage has not been identified. With his father being exarch, he surely learned of conditions in the hilly country to the west and southwest in Africa Proconsularis, of the fortifications of the mountain passes or *cleisurae* in the interior to bar the Berbers, and of the stone forts erected at strategic points throughout Africa ever since the Byzantine reconquest in the reign of Justinian I, less than three-quarters of a century earlier. He certainly became familiar with the riches of Africa in terms of agriculture, fertility, and tax revenues, whether from agriculture or from land and maritime trade. He learned to appreciate the sea. He probably learned much about Berbers, their past and potential future threats to Byzantine authority and hegemony, and something of their leaders and the possibilities of using them as allies in warfare, in an era of serious manpower shortages. It is uncertain whether he personally visited the adjacent rich province of Byzacena, to the south of Africa Proconsularis, which also was under the jurisdiction of his father, the exarch. He cannot have avoided gaining an appreciation of the proximity of Africa to Sicily and Italy and the great commercial, fiscal, and strategic value of all of these to the empire, their synergistic significance, and their bustling activity. The dynamics of this region were very different from that of landlocked Armenia and upper Mesopotamia, with their – at least Armenia's – harsh winters and the domination of their economies by the Byzantine military, which was not the case in Africa or Sicily. We do not know whether Heraclius the Younger

---

[28] *PLRE* III: 546, s.v. "Gregoras 3."   [29] Hrabanus Maurus, *PL* 110: 132C.

ever personally set foot in Italy or Sicily while sailing to or from Africa, or under any other circumstances during his residence in Africa. Information about the beleaguered position of the Byzantines in Italy, under pressure from the Lombards, who were still trying to increase the regions under their control, presumably reached Carthage and his father's headquarters, and in turn him, but we do not know his reactions to or opinions about it.

Fredegarius describes Heraclius as "handsome, tall, braver than others and a fighter." He had matured with those characteristics by the time that he reached Africa. Fredegarius adds that being "well-read" Heraclius practiced astrology.[30] Another Latin tradition transmitted by the Carolingian scholar Hrabanus Maurus reports that Heraclius was *"vir armis strenuus, lingua eruditus, corpore decorus, et quamvis saeculari actui deditus, totus tamen erat fide catholicus; et ergo Dei cultoribus supplex, benevolus ac devotus."*[31] It is probable that Heraclius used his public speaking ability in Africa, but how well he had developed it before coming to Africa, or what form it took in Africa, where Latin was the dominant public tongue, is unknown. Hrabanus' list of attributes may simply be stock descriptions of what one expected in a good emperor. It is likely as well that Heraclius already was well read in Africa, but there is no evidence of any contacts by him with astrologers during his years there. For Leo Grammatikos, a tenth-century Byzantine historian, Heraclius was "robust, with a broad chest, beautiful blue eyes, golden hair, fair complexion and wide thick beard."[32] Family was important to him. His relations with his uncle and first cousin were excellent. He probably gained a better appreciation of the Roman Latin heritage, however superficial, while in Africa, for its monuments, statuary, mosaics, and ruins would have surrounded him, and especially so in Carthage and its vicinity. Many Roman constructions had been dismantled in order to reuse their stones for other construction, including new fortifications and churches. But there was still a strong Roman heritage evident everywhere. There were Greek-speaking inhabitants, some of whom have left inscriptions, but they were a minority in a Latin-speaking world. The Roman and Latin imprint would have been much stronger in Africa than anything

---

[30] Fredegarius 4.65 (52–54 Wallace-Hadrill). Cf. Georgios Kedrenos, *Historiarum compendium*, ed. I. Bekker (*CSHB*, Bonn, 1838) 1.714. Barry Baldwin, "Physical Descriptions of Byzantine Emperors," *Byzantion* 51 (1981) 19, does not cite Fredegarius, whose indeterminate source may well be oriental. See M. Mango, "Imperial Art in the Seventh Century," in *New Constantines: The Rhythm of Imperial Renewal*, ed. Paul Magdalino (Aldershot: Variorum, 1994) 124–126.

[31] Hrabanus Maurus, *PL* 110: 132. Hrabanus' source is unknown. Although non-contemporary, this report is of some value.

[32] Leo Grammatikos, *Hist.*, ed. I. Bekker (*CSHB*, Bonn, 1842) 147. Trans. by Constance Head, "Physical Descriptions of the Emperors in Byzantine Historical Writing," *Byzantion* 50 (1980) 230–231; another physical description: Georgios Kedrenos, *Hist.* 1.714 (*CSHB*).

that he or his father would have experienced in Armenia, other parts of the Caucasus, or near the Persian frontier in any part of upper Mesopotamia. This was a very different and broadening experience. His engagement to marry a girl from a very prominent local family reinforced that. He did not restrict himself to Armenian circles or to the circles of those who came from the east. Presumably his family approved and encouraged his action. The Christian church was very active in the vicinity of Carthage and so he would have in some way encountered the devotional commitment among local Latin Africans. Yet no local African chronicler or panegyrist has left any record of Heraclius in Africa or Africa's impressions of Heraclius.

It is unclear precisely what official capacity Heraclius the Younger held in Africa. Certainly he aided his father, the exarch, but his precise title is unknown. Did it remain the same throughout his stay in Africa, until his revolt against Phokas in 608?

Probably Heraclius the Younger learned something of Roman fortification methods in North Africa in the face of raids from Berbers in the past, recently, presently, and prospectively. One does not know anything about the transfer of military techniques from North Africa to Byzantine frontiers in the east and vice versa.[33] In general, it appears that Byzantine defense efforts in Africa did not involve intensive search and destroy efforts, but instead, defensive tactics to hold critical regions, crossroads, with fortified bastions and places of asylum for troops and civilians and limited numbers of livestock, usually at sites chosen for the availability of fresh water or supplies from large cisterns.[34] Whether or not Heraclius the Younger made any inspections of such sites out in the countryside, he surely heard about them from those visiting his father's seat of administrative control in Carthage. Worth attention is the extent to which any of the conditions and methods or failures in Africa impressed themselves on Heraclius. It is worth reflecting on the extent to which he learned anything of value to retain and to exploit or avoid when he later campaigned in western Asia or was involved in making policy decisions about setting defense policies for western Asia. His later order, in the middle or late 630s, to avoid fighting the Arabs in the open, to avoid the dangers of their potential ambushes, may have been the result of his or his father's experiences or the counsel of others who had faced Arabs in western Asia, but his own observations or

[33] D. Pringle, *The Defence of Byzantine Africa*, does not discuss this issue, perhaps because there is insufficient evidence. On the geography of Byzantine control, arguing for a larger region than often has been assumed: Pol Trousset, "Les 'Fines Antiquae' et la reconquête byzantine en Afrique," in *Histoire et Archéologie de l'Afrique du Nord, IIe Colloque International (Grenoble, 5–9 avril 1983)* = *Bulletin Archéologique du Comité des Travaux Historiques et Scientifiques*, n.s. 19B (1985) 361–376.
[34] Pringle, *Defence of Byzantine Africa* 94–112.

perceptions in Africa about the best ways to handle Berber raiders and unsuccessful ways of coping with them may have also influenced or reinforced
his preferences for how to fight Arab raiders. Some of the terrain in Africa
Proconsularis resembled that of western Anatolia, and there was much grain
and pasturage for sheep, but unlike Armenia and upper Mesopotamia, this
was a land of the olive.

Heraclius may have seen or more likely simply heard something of oases
in Africa, and their irrigation systems, and possibly learned of their vulnerability to raids from Berbers, lessons that he may have made use of when
he invaded Persian Mesopotamia several decades later. What he cannot
have learned in Africa is how to handle large armies, because the Byzantine
garrisons and their scattered deployments could not have given him or anyone else any experience with that challenge. That he might have learned
from chatting with his father about experiences in the east. He could have
learned something of the latest experiences in blocking *cleisurae* in North
Africa, but nothing of large-scale mobile warfare or large battle formations
and the latest techniques and practices for large-scale combat. Yet he would
have learned how Byzantines coped with challenges in North Africa, not
a carbon copy of the situation in western Asia or the Caucasus. He would
have observed how one coped with a dearth of soldiery. We do not know
how local recruitment functioned in Africa, or precisely what relations the
authorities had with Berbers and to what degree, by 600, the government
made any use of Berbers as military allies. These experiences may have
been much more important for Heraclius than any theoretical ones about
the combining of civil and military powers in the exarchate that previous
scholars speculated would have been the principal effect on Heraclius the
Younger of having stayed in Africa. Others could not easily have learned
by reading or having others consult military manuals about warfare and
defenses in Africa, because, for example, the contemporary *Strategikon*,
which was written ca. 600, contains no discussion of Berbers or anything
else about warfare in North Africa or fortification in North Africa.[35] One
could have consulted the writings of Prokopios of Caesarea, or Corippus'
Latin verse panegyric *Johannidos,* but there were no known military manuals that explained warfare in Africa ca. 600 or later. So one could not easily
learn about it by reading. It was difficult to find a substitute for the direct
experience, wisdom, and stratagems that Heraclius had gained and learned
there.

[35] Maurikios, *Strategikon,* ed. G.T. Dennis, trans. E. Gamillscheg (*CFHB,* Vienna: Akademie der
Wissenschaften, 1981); Eng. trans. by G.T. Dennis, *Maurice's Strategikon: Handbook of Byzantine
Military Strategy* (Philadelphia: University of Pennsylvania Press, 1984).

Heraclius' African years gave him a perspective that no other Byzantine emperor had, with the possible exception of some members of his own dynasty, because of his, their ancestor's, involvement in Africa. He had some feel for a central Mediterranean perspective.

Although there is no evidence that Heraclius made any travels west of Carthage, for the Byzantine hold on Mauretania was tenuous and only at a few ports, such as Septem (Ceuta) and possibly Tingis (Tangier), as far as we know, he learned something of the western Mediterranean, Gibraltar's straits, Spain, and shipping from Gaul and the islands of Sardinia and Corsica.[36] This was an asset for him. He probably heard something of the mineral riches and maritime potential of Carthago Nova (modern Cartagena) in Spain, the strategic and commercial significance of the straits of Gibraltar and of the special value of the stronghold of Septem as a listening and observation post, and of the vague trading potential of Mauretania's Atlantic coast and its river mouths. There was potential out there in the west, and it was not to be forfeited lightly. Everything did not depend on the environs of the Bosphoros, or on the eastern frontier.

There was another dimension, there was depth, to the empire. While in Africa Heraclius gained an appreciation of the interrelationship of African geography and the potential for shifting troops from Africa to Egypt and possibly even on further east to help to defend the empire from external invaders, be they Persian or Arab. He probably learned something of such ancient Tripolitanian ports and emporia as Gigthis and Tripoli, both of which still functioned in the seventh century. His experiences in the west made it more difficult for his opponents to understand him fully, because they had no basis for sharing or comprehending what he had experienced. He took advantage of his Armenian background and familiarity with circumstances in the Caucasus and on a critical part of the empire's eastern frontier. These assets helped to make him unique.

Heraclius' experiences in Africa brought an introduction, addition, or some might say an injection or intrusion of an African, Latin African or central Mediterranean dimension into an already rather matured Byzantine worldview. It was a different, although not entirely new element in what had become a very stable, traditional, and slowly changing outlook. It was a dash of something new and different. It was potentially stimulating and

---

[36] Broader perspectives: Paul Reynolds, *Trade in the Western Mediterranean, AD 400–700: The Ceramic Evidence* (Oxford: *BAR* International Series 604, 1995), esp. fig. 174, "Shipping Routes." Also: Michael McCormick, "Bateaux de vie, bateaux de mort. Maladie, commerce, transports annonaires et le passage économique du bas-empire au moyen âge," in *Settimane di Studio del centro italiano di studi sull'alto medioevo* 45 (Spoleto, 1998) 35–118; McCormick, *Origins of the European Economy: Communications and Commerce AD 300–900* (Cambridge: Cambridge University Press, 2001).

creative. Its addition did not in itself solve anything, but it gave him new or different ways of looking at things. It was, to be sure, untried. Even his and his father's initial travel to Africa from Constantinople, certainly by ship, probably via Greek ports, islands, including Sicily, to Africa, opened new perspectives and enriched his understanding of his world, conditions, and opportunities. He saw something very different from the highlands of landlocked Armenia and the plains and fortresses of upper Mesopotamia. He came to understand that there was a very rich and abundant world to the west, one that had some similar but also very different conditions from the lands where he had lived and his father had exercised various military commands. His travels to and from Africa and his stay there were stimulating and exerted a life-long effect on him and even more, an effect beyond the term of his own life, on most of the members of his dynasty who succeeded him on the throne.

Heraclius' experiences in Africa taught him that there was another rich land in reserve, one sheltered at that time from the threats of the eastern and Danubian frontiers. It was lush, a kind of paradise, however much of a veneer of coastal strip to which it was limited. It was potentially a source of comfort, that everything did not stand or fall in terms of landbased threats to the empire, that it was a rich land sheltered by the sea from the land threats of the Avars, Slavs, and Persians From the perspective of Carthage it was almost too easy to ignore the dangers of rebellion (reprisal from Constantinople) and risks of Berber raids from the not-too-distant interior. From the port and hill (Byrsa Hill today) of Carthage it was easy to ignore, misunderstand, or underestimate the severity of problems elsewhere in Africa or elsewhere in the empire. Life was splendid, easy, and even lush there, far from other worries. Because descendants of his first marriage to an African, Fabia/Eudokia, continued his dynastic line, some particulars of his African heritage and connections may have survived a little better than others, namely, better than traditions favorable to his niece and second wife Martina and their offspring.

Above all, Heraclius the Younger probably gained some appreciation of the Roman Empire's Latin side, not merely, as he would have seen in Constantinople and other places in the east, the Roman Empire through a Greek filter. There is no evidence as to whether he ever learned to speak or understand, let alone read, Latin, however. Other emperors had often known the Latin perspective from the very different Latin world of the Balkans. But Latin Africa's conditions and perspectives were very different from those of the disappearing Latinity and Latin thought world of the Balkans; Africa was wealthier and enjoyed a much milder climate, more agricultural abundance, and relatively more security. So Heraclius had the opportunity to acquire a unique group of experiences that helped to shape his unique outlook.

Heraclius' mother Epiphania[37] remained, or at least for some part of the time stayed, in the east, reportedly in Cappadocia, with her son's fiancée Fabia/Eudokia, while her husband and son and brother-in-law were serving in Africa. These women probably provided later insights, perhaps very valuable ones, to Heraclius about Cappadocia, but were unlikely to have been able to communicate with him while there. For that and other reasons, Heraclius and his father potentially had various means of receiving communications from the east about the situation there, but only with great difficulty, given that Cappadocia was in the Anatolian interior. Late in his stay in Africa Heraclius the Younger became engaged to marry Fabia, who changed her name to Eudokia,[38] the daughter of an African landowner Rogas,[39] so he sank his roots deep there and had even more family ties. There is no information on how he met her or how the marriage was arranged. It did not take place until immediately after he had seized power, and in fact it occurred the same day as his coronation and her elevation to the rank of Augusta and her imperial coronation, 5 October 610. Presumably that substantial and very prominent landowning family was Latin-speaking. Eudokia was with his own mother somewhere in Cappadocia.

The reason for their residence in Cappadocia is unclear, perhaps an attraction of a more protected life in the east. We do not know the background of Epiphania. Perhaps she inherited property or had family of her own in Cappadocia, or possibly there was even the desire of the imperial government to retain some hold on governors by insisting that key members of their families remain at home as potential hostages for internal security reasons. Epiphania may have had Cappadocian origins. John of Nikiu reports a confused and sensational story that Emperor Phokas summoned Epiphania and Fabia/Eudokia from Cappadocia with sexual desires for Fabia in mind.[40] It is possible that Epiphania had been in Cappadocia when she received the call to go to Constantinople, allegedly to the convent of Nea Metanoia, under the supervision of Theodore. It is quite likely that the women were at great personal risk in Constantinople until the triumph of Heraclius. Reports of Phokas' sexual desires for Eudokia are probably just salacious and malevolent gossip, but she was at risk there. Heraclius

---

[37] *PLRE* III: 445, s.v. "Epiphania 1."   [38] *PLRE* III: 457, s.v. "Eudocia *quae et* Fabia (= Aelia Flavia)."
[39] *PLRE* III: 1089, s.v. "Rogatus 2." Theoph. *Chron.* A.M. 6102 (427–428 Mango-Scott). *PLRE* III: 457, s.v. "Eudocia."
[40] John of Nikiu, *Chronicle* 106.1–6 (167 Charles). John, for example, wrongly identifies Fabia as the daughter of Epiphania.

and Eudokia were part of a well-traveled empire-wide elite whose ties and relationships crisscrossed the entire empire, in an era when the empire's girth still had a very long stretch.

Priskos, the powerful Count of the Excubitors or imperial watch, and probably Prefect of the City of Constantinople, and son-in-law of the usurping Emperor Phokas, who had seized power after violently overthrowing and murdering Emperor Maurice and his family in late 602, reportedly contacted Heraclius the Elder and encouraged him to open revolt against the government.[41] A crisis of legitimacy existed from the beginning, because Phokas' usurpation had broken the precedent of no successful violent usurpation since the reign of Constantine I, a record that the ecclesiastical historian Evagrios Scholastikos had proudly boasted as recently as the year 594.[42] The rebellion of General Narses at Edessa had already failed, with an ensuing brutal repression in 603/604. The new emperor had no constitutional or legitimate basis for his authority; there was only the naked power that he wielded for the moment. The murder of Maurice and his family shocked contemporaries, and caused some to tremble and wonder about and fear for the future of the empire, as the early seventh century (630s) *Doctrina Jacobi nuper Baptizati* indicates.[43] There was no immediate acceptance of Phokas everywhere in the empire. There was some resistance, which Phokas sought to repress.[44]

Motives for rebellion against Phokas were multiple. The regime lacked legitimacy, having seized power violently and, in the eyes of many, profaned its seizure of power by murdering the reigning emperor Maurice and his family. Widespread reports of a tyrannical reign of terror with ruthless purges and displays of cruelty all added justification to any explanation for the very serious decision to rise in rebellion.[45] Yet there is a need for caution, because only the justifications of the rebellious cause remain today, not the explanations on the part of Phokas and his officials for their actions.[46] The

---

[41] Nikephoros, *Short History* 1 (34–37 Mango); *PLRE* III: 1056–1057, s.v. "Priscus 6."

[42] Evagrios, *Hist. eccl.* 3.41, ed. J. Bidez and L. Parmentier (London: Methuen, 1898, repr. Amsterdam: Hakkert, 1964) 143–144. W.E. Kaegi, *Byzantium and the Decline of Rome* (Princeton, 1968) 220–221; David Olster, *The Politics of Usurpation in the Seventh Century* (Amsterdam, Las Palmas: Hakkert, 1993) 23–24, 139–142.

[43] *Doctrina Jacobi nuper Baptizati* 3.10, 3.12, ed. trans. Vincent Déroche, *TM* 11 (1991) 168–169, 170–171.

[44] Sebeos, *History* 106, ch. 31 (57–58 Thomson); *Chronicon Paschale* 142–143 Whitby. Olster, *Politics of Usurpation* 101–115; Olster, *Roman Defeat, Christian Response and the Literary Construction of the Jew* (Philadelphia: University of Pennsylvania Press, 1994).

[45] Contemporary reputation: Olster, *Politics of Usurpation* 165–182, 183–185. George of Pisidia, *Heraclias* 2.8–36 (250–253 Pertusi); *Vie de Théodore de Sykéôn* c. 125, 133 (I: 100–101, 105–106; II: 104–105, 110–111 Festugière).

[46] Olster, *The Politics of Usurpation* 1–21. Purges: *Chronicon Paschale* 143–146 Whitby; Olster, *Politics of Usurpation* 67–80.

court poetry and historiography of the reign of Heraclius cannot provide a sure guide to the truth. It is difficult but necessary to discount the later Heraclian court propaganda about the events of 608–610. Heraclius the Younger probably burned with ambition to become emperor himself. Simple ambition for power was a large part of the explanation for the rebellion.

The author of the *Patria* may well be correct that at Constantinople Heraclius or his father conceived the ambition or dream of becoming emperor, at the palace of Sophiai.[47] Heraclius and his father may have feared that they too might fall victim to the purges of Phokas, and so acted preemptively to forestall that fate, but there is no explicit evidence that the life of either one was in mortal danger before they began to plan their rebellion and to contact others to join them. But there is no doubt that there was an atmosphere of terror abroad that could have contributed to their decision to act. Stories of Phokas' alleged desire to violate Heraclius' fiancée Fabia may be retrospective, but they became another justification for the revolt and may have circulated in some sensational fashion even at that time.[48] Heraclius the Elder had previously served in the east where he had direct experience with military mutiny, most notably that at Monokarton, where troops rejected Priskos in favor of their previous commander Philippikos.[49] He had not been an instigator, but had been closely associated with Philippikos. He was familiar with techniques, practices, and psychological dimensions of military unrest. No doubt he had heard much about the Phokas rebellion on the Danube in 602 by word of mouth from other commanders. So he was no novice, and his son had probably heard much from others as well.

The powerful Egyptian family of Apiones may well have opposed Phokas, and may have helped Niketas' ultimately victorious campaign in Egypt.[50] Indicative of Phokas' stature there is his huge column in the Forum in Rome. Under Justinian, the Apiones seem to have supported the Blues (in Constantinople), but they funded both Blue and Green factions in Egypt (there are many more references to the Blues, however; the last one in 618).

---

[47] *Patria Constantinopoleos* 3.125 (= *Scriptores originum Constantinopolitarum*, ed. Th. Preger, II: 255).

[48] Ps.-Isidore, *Continuationes Isidorianae Byzantia Arabica et Hispana*, ed. Th. Mommsen (*MGH AA* 11) 334.

[49] Kaegi, *Byzantine Military Unrest* 68–72; M. Whitby, *The Emperor Maurice and His Historian* 287–288.

[50] Pope Gregory I the Great advised Apion III's wife Eusebia to stay out of things. If so, they may have helped Niketas in Egypt during the revolt. Gregory I favored Phokas: Gregory I, *Registrum epistolarum* 13.34–35 = ed. Paul Ewald and Ludwig Hartmann (*MGH Epistolae*; Berlin: Weidmann, 1899) 2.397–398. Under Justinian, the Apiones seem to have supported the Blues (in Constantinople), but they funded both Blues and Greens in Egypt. Apion III's marriage to the western Eusebia, as well as the subsequent relationship with Gregory (through mother-in-law Rusticiana) is a good example of "relationships crisscrossing the Empire." I thank Todd Hickey for advice.

Additional assistance for the rebels came from other quarters. The widely respected and revered ascetic St. Theodore of Sykeon, who was a close friend of the Phokas family, when summoned to an audience with Emperor Phokas, spoke his mind. He then spoke privately with Patriarch Thomas, who had inquired about reports of a processional cross wavering and trembling, explaining the significance of this fearsome phenomenon:

> The trembling of the cross forecasts a crowd of misfortunes and perils for us. Yes, it forecasts fluctuations in our faith, and apostasies, invasions of many barbarian peoples, floods of blood scattered, ruin and captivity for everyone, the desolation of the holy churches, the halting of the divine service, the fall and upsetting of the Empire, embarrassments without number and serious times for the state. In short, it announces that the coming of the Enemy [devil] is soon.[51]

Such predictions and anxieties fanned unrest and a readiness to change secular obedience. He had already admonished Phokas to halt his massacres, and conditioned his prayers for the emperor on that change of practice.[52] The spread of such reports can only have damaged the repute of Phokas' regime with the broader public, encouraged the hopes of rebels, and strengthened their conviction that their cause was just.

There were other calculations in favor of rebellion, or at least perceiving that the risk/reward ratio tilted in favor of rewards. Distance from Constantinople, the relative wealth of Africa, the reluctance, probably, to release grain and revenues from Africa to the regime of Phokas all coalesced to impel Heraclius the Elder to proclaim rebellion against Phokas in 608. News of the decision of the Persian King Khusrau II Parviz's decision to go to war to overthrow Phokas, followed by large-scale Persian mobilization and invasion of Byzantium's eastern frontier, tempted Heraclius the Elder: the usurping emperor Phokas' attention necessarily had to be focused on the threatened eastern frontier and on various internal conspiracies in the east.[53] Persian victories began to diminish the prestige of Phokas ever since they captured the important Byzantine fortress of Dara, in upper Mesopotamia, in 605. The Persians in 609 took advantage of the civil war between Heraclius and Phokas to begin some decisive advances: Mardin and Amida may have fallen in 609, and probably it was the turn of Edessa in 610. Whether or not Heraclian rebellion was a stab in the back, Phokas' regime

---

[51] *Vie de Théodore de Sykéôn* c. 134 (I: 106; II: 110–111 Festugière).

[52] *Vie de Théodore de Sykéôn* c. 133 (I: 105; II: 109–110 Festugière). The hagiographer, of course, may wish to defend the reputation of St. Theodore by emphasizing that although he was contemporary with Phokas, he had no complicity in his regime, even though he agreed, for common weal, to pray for him under certain conditions.

[53] Olster, *The Politics of Usurpation* 81–97, on the early years of the Persian war in the reign of Phokas.

was losing its reputation, one that a military regime could ill afford to do; subjects are seldom forgiving of military regimes that are losing wars. Phokas could not spare troops and a fleet to suppress a rebellion in the west. There is no evidence for any direct coordination of actions by the Lombards in Italy with the Persians' military movements, but the Persian invasion created opportunities for the Lombards to have a freer hand in Italy as well. Grain shipments to Constantinople stopped. This was no simple case of east–west rivalry. But the conspiring rebels understood that the army in the Balkans and Asia Minor constituted no monolith. There was no necessary reason to subject oneself to the rude usurper from the Danubian regions, an area to which Armenians did not like to be sent for military duty, and one whose military units were not especially on good terms with units from the east, like those where Heraclius the Elder had formerly commanded. Once someone had seized power for himself, it was possible for others to try to emulate him.

But there was a high cost to rebellion: the penalty for failure was a terrible death and likely mutilation for the rebel and a commensurately grisly end for the members of his family, and, of course, the confiscation of their property. Phokas had already exacted that in several purges. But Africa's success record in rebellions and usurpations had not been very good in the past: long ago Gordian I and Gildo had both failed. Presumably no one looked carefully at those dismal records. North Africa lacked the good timber and iron that were essential materials for war, but they could be imported from elsewhere. In principle, the Lombards in Italy would have welcomed such a rebellion, because it would make it even less likely that the Byzantines could muster any serious military forces for intervention in Italy when the imperial government in Constantinople was facing such serious internal threats and the very real Persian threat. Another risk was assisting the Persian offensive. There is no evidence of any direct diplomatic relations between Heraclian rebels and the Persians, and for different reasons both would have denied it: Heraclians to avoid charges of treason and causing harm to the empire, and the Persians to deny any hint of legitimacy or prospect of formal recognition to the cause of Heraclius, and hence of any possibility of formal diplomatic recognition and cessation of hostilities in the future.

Heraclius the Elder took an unusual direction: he had himself and his son Heraclius proclaimed consul, which may have taken place at the decree of the senate of Carthage, whose members had no legal right to designate a Roman consul. However, no primary sources report any such action by any senate at Carthage during the administration of Heraclius the Elder. The

Fig. 1. Consular solidus from the revolt of Heraclius and his father. Heraclius on the left, with his father (short beard) on the right; inscription: *Dominus Noster Heraclius Consul*; Alexandria, Egypt (obverse, Cécile Morrisson, *Catalogue des monnaies Byzantines*, I: 250, Bibliothèque Nationale, Paris. No. 9/Ar/AV/01. Schl. 2569).

consulate had become an anachronistic institution by the beginning of the seventh century. Since the middle of Justinian I's reign, the emperor was *ex officio* the consul. No private individuals had been proclaimed consul since then. However, the uniqueness of the office, which once had combined civil and military executive powers, and its sole association with reigning emperors since Justinian could indicate, without explicitly saying so, that Heraclius the Elder was claiming to be emperor. It also was a very circumspect statement, underscoring deference to Rome's past and to legitimacy, even though its arrogation by Heraclius the Elder was a brash and illegal act. He struck coins at Carthage and at Alexandria showing himself with his son Heraclius the Younger on his left – significantly, the normal place for an emperor – both wearing consular robes, so the coinage in several senses was an assertion of the claim to imperial power by both, but in particular by Heraclius the Younger, who himself was also represented as consul (Fig. 1).[54]

Previous and later usurpers in Late Antiquity and the Early and Middle Byzantine periods did not resort to consular claims in their striving for

[54] Philip Grierson, "The Consular Coinage of 'Heraclius' and the Revolt against Phocas of 608–10," *NC* 10 (1950) 71–93; A. Cumbo, "La monetazione numismatica di Eraclio," *Numismatica*, ser. 2, 3 (1962) 7–8, Nos. 12–13; David Olster, "The Dynastic Iconography of Heraclius' Early Coinage," *JÖB* 32/2 (1982) 399–405; Gerhard Rösch, "Der Aufstand der Herakleioi gegen Phokas (608–610) im Spiegel numismatischer Quellen," *JÖB* 28 (1979) 51–62. One lead seal with a less distinctive inscription displays Heraclius and his father bareheaded and dressed as consuls: M. Braunlin and J. Nesbitt, "Selections from a Private Collection of Byzantine Bullae," *Byzantion* 68 (1998) 168–169. Braunlin and Nesbitt also publish a copper dodecanummion from Alexandria (No. 1) that shows the two Heraclii bareheaded in consular dress: "Thirteen Seals and an Unpublished Revolt Coin," *Byzantion* 69 (1999) 187–191. Cécile Morrisson publishes the lead seal (No. 11 in the display case of Late Roman coins and other related objects) in the Carthage Museum that reconfirms the numismatic evidence that the two rebellious Heraclii claimed to be consuls: C. Morrisson, "Du consul à l'empereur: Les sceaux d'Héraclius," in *Novum Millennium: Studies on Byzantine History and Culture Dedicated to Paul Speck*, ed. Claudia Sode, Sarolta A. Takács (Burlington, VT: Ashgate, 2001) 257–266. I thank Dr. Morrisson for discussing the Carthage seal, which I had seen at the museum, with me in advance of publication. It differs from the one that that Nesbitt and Braunlin publish. But see Wolfgang Hahn, *Moneta Imperii Byzantini* (Vienna, 1975) II: 84–87.

imperial power; this was a unique case. Hypothesis: Heraclius called himself and his father *consules*, probably by stretching a tenuous line of reasoning that the governor's power in Africa Proconsularis was consular (a *consularius*) and thus he, as a kind of proconsul, held proconsular powers. In no way would that normally entitle one to call oneself consul, but the two Heraclii may have stretched the term, using it as a pretext or claim, however specious or false. A *consularius* was equivalent to a consul.[55] Greek (or "Oriental") sources, especially the poet George of Pisidia, would never refer to this problem or device, which involves Latin matters and concepts. Latin sources are otherwise lacking. But there were Latin inscriptions lying all around in Africa referring to recent *magistri militum* and other prominent officials as ex-consuls. This was an appeal, however tortuous, to an ancient legitimacy after a violent and bloody usurpation.

All of this evidence raises question of who was advising Heraclius Senior or his son concerning old Roman precedents and legalisms and procedures. Presumably it bears some relationship to that of using the senate for diplomacy with the Sasanians shortly after Heraclius' accession. To whom did such procedures appeal within the empire? To nostalgic and well-educated elites and even antiquarian-minded persons in the east and west? To the Constantinopolitan and provincial senatorial class before and after Heraclius' seizure of power? Yet Emperor Phokas may have had some support in the west, from church circles, especially papal. Probably the ubiquitous Latin Roman heritage in Africa influenced the decision of Heraclius the Elder to resort to this claim. It impressed him and his son strongly, probably because they gained exposure and acquaintance with all kinds of insignia and symbols of Roman authority and legitimacy in Old Rome, in forms and specificity much more intensive than would have been the case in the Byzantine east where they had previously lived. The claim to the consulship also underscored Phokas' illegitimacy.

John of Antioch and the later Byzantine (late eighth-century) historian Nikephoros claim that Priskos, the Prefect of the City and son-in-law of Phokas, who bore a grudge against Phokas, wrote to Heraclius the Elder, promising his support for any rebellion. This suspicious tradition is probably a later fabrication. According to John of Antioch, Priskos sent one letter to Heraclius the Younger and one to his father after the revolt started.[56]

---

[55] Th. Mommsen, *Römisches Staatsrecht* (2nd. edn., Leipzig: S. Hirzel, 1887) II: 71–132, Kübler, *RE* IV: 1,138–142 s.v. "consularis"; A.H.M. Jones, *The Later Roman Empire 284–602* (Oxford: Blackwell, 1964) 134–135, 142–144; R. Mathisen, "Emperors, Consuls, and Patricians," *BF* 17 (1991) 173–190.

[56] John of Antioch, *FHG* V: 37–38 (Dindorf). Grierson only briefly mentions, without elaboration, that the African governors were ex-consuls in honor: "The Consular Coinage of 'Heraclius'" 79 n. 22.

That would have been an important encouragement and indication of major dissension at Constantinople, in the very bowels of the government. But a critical issue is when Priskos began his communications: before or after the revolt had begun.[57] Nikephoros states that the two senior brothers, Heraclius the Elder and Gregory, consulted among themselves and then sent out their sons in a race for the throne; then that the first to reach Constantinople would be emperor, a fanciful story to be sure, for the coinage indicates that Heraclius the Younger was from the beginning the real claimant to the throne.[58] Probably others gave advice and counsel, but their names and roles are unknown.

The Heraclian rebellion received support in the central Mediterranean outside Africa Proconsularis, it appears, probably from the smaller numbers of Byzantines and nominal Byzantine subjects in ports along the Mediterranean coast. Their help was valuable, and it also at a minimum allowed the rebels not to worry about their rear. That assistance probably included ships and provisions. But the actual number of assembled rebels is uncertain, as is the amount of funds they amassed for their endeavor. One does not know the number of potentially available Byzantine or locally recruited troops in Africa.[59] There may have been some elements of regional rivalry in the rebellion. Phokas had no ties either with Africa or with Armenia or the eastern frontier. There was no reason to expect special support from him or to expect local civilians or troops in garrisons to favor him. The fact that his seizure of power became the pretext for the Persians to invade could not have endeared him to African subjects of the empire, yet they would have been expected to pay increased taxes and other costs of the consequences of Phokas' seizure of power. How much the power of the personalities of the members of the Heraclius family helped to attract enthusiasm for the cause of rebellion is uncertain. The evidence is that they were popular. Although the rebellion received some ecclesiastical support in Egypt, after the overthrow of the Patriarch, it is noteworthy that there were no reports of prominent African clergy or monastics supporting or blessing the rebellion or the departure of Heraclius' fleet. They may have done so, but if they did, the poets, panegyrists, hagiographers and historians of Heraclian court propaganda have left no record. Perhaps they did not celebrate it because there were no important ecclesiastics or monastics involved, or they had no great reputations in the Greek-speaking world. In any case, that silence is noteworthy.

---

[57] Nikephoros, *Short History* 1 (34–37 Mango). David Olster, *The Politics of Usurpation* 119, 128–131, is rightfully skeptical of reports that Priskos actually instigated the revolt, arguing that this is retrospective Heraclian propaganda.

[58] Nikephoros, *Short History* 1 (34–37, 173 Mango).

[59] Pringle, *Defence of Byzantine Africa* 17, 68–79.

Although the story of a race between the cousins Heraclius the Younger and Niketas is a fable, it is true that Niketas departed by land, from Africa, with the assistance of Mauri, that is, presumably, Berber tribesmen, to reconquer Egypt. The ability of the Heraclian faction to seize Egypt was critical to their ultimate success.[60] It is more than 2,500 kilometers from parts of Africa (more than that from Carthage) to modern Cairo,[61] so that was a considerable logistical challenge for an expeditionary army. It is uncertain whether any precedents from the Vandal defense of Africa against the Byzantines were of use to Niketas. Initially there would have been a theoretical concern to avoid the reverse: a land assault from Egypt and Tripolitania by Phokas' forces.[62] Berbers were raised from Tripolitania and from the Pentapolis (Cyrenaica). Bonakis was sent with 3,000 Byzantine soldiers and a large number of barbarians, presumably Berbers, against Egypt. Niketas was sent with subsidies to persuade Leontios, the Prefect of Mareotis, to switch to the rebels, which he did. Heraclius may have reinforced his relationship with Niketas by becoming his ritual brother.

Secret agreements with Theodore, the former Prefect of Alexandria, and with sons of Menas, the former governor of Alexandria, gave the Heraclian faction additional support in Egypt.[63] Niketas managed to defeat and slay the general who commanded the loyalist forces outside Alexandria. The populace rose and seized the government buildings. Niketas orchestrated a demonstration in Africa and then at Alexandria in favor of accepting Heraclius as emperor.[64] The Patriarch withdrew; John, the Governor, and Theodore, the Treasurer, fled seeking refuge.[65] The rebellion in North Africa was coordinated in some fashion with an uprising at Alexandria.[66] Prophecies by holy men such as the Egyptian stylite holy man Theophilos aided the Heraclian cause.[67] Niketas then sent Bonakis to extend rebel control to the Delta. Only at Semanud and Athrib did local commanders resist the rebels at first. Phokas sent his general Bonosos, who had a reputation for ruthlessness and ferocity, to restore his control. Bonosos sailed from Caesarea Maritima (on the Palestinian coast) to relieve besieged Athrib. He defeated Bonakis, who was captured and executed. He recaptured Nikiu

---

[60] Still useful is N.H. Baynes, "The Military Operations of the Emperor Heraclius," *United Services Magazine*, n.s. 46 (1913) 660–666.

[61] 1,600 miles from the head of Syrtis Minor to the Nile: E.C. Semple, *The Geography of the Mediterranean Region. Its Relation to Ancient History* (London: Constable, 1932) 146, 149.

[62] A.J. Butler, *Arab Conquest of Egypt* (revised edn., Oxford: Clarendon Press, 1978) 1–32. John of Nikiu, *Chronicle* 107.2–4 (167 Charles); also on Berbers: John of Nikiu, *Chronicle* 109.22–24 (176 Charles).

[63] John of Nikiu, *Chronicle* 107.5 (167 Charles).

[64] John of Nikiu, *Chronicle* 110.1–2 (177 Charles).

[65] John of Nikiu, *Chronicle* 107.6–22 (168–169 Charles).

[66] *Chronicon Paschale* 149–150 Whitby.   [67] John of Nikiu, *Chronicle* 108.1–5 (172–173 Charles).

and purged and executed those who supported the rebels.[68] He executed the generals Plato and Theodore and Bishop Theodore of Nikiu. The Green circus faction supported the cause of Heraclius and Niketas between 608 and 610, and battled with the Blue faction in Alexandria, although the exact nature of this brawling is uncertain.[69] The Blues ultimately switched sides, and in order to win favor with the apparent winners, supported the Heraclian forces in their efforts to wrest control of towns in Egypt. The chancellor of Nikiu, Menas, was beaten so severely that he later died. A few rebel soldiers and partisans fled to the security of Alexandria, where Niketas raised new forces. Bonosos then unsuccessfully tried to recover Alexandria for Phokas, but failed in two assaults, fell back on Kariun, and then Dafashir and Manouf. Bonosos had lost his momentum and, discouraged, ultimately fled from the port of Pelusium back to Constantinople, possibly as late as August/September 610 but more likely in early spring 610. The remaining towns and villages of Egypt yielded to the rebels in the spring of 610. Some Egyptians fled east (to Syria) to escape from the fighting in Egypt, others because they were partisans of Phokas and feared reprisals.[70]

Heraclius amassed a fleet, including very many Berbers ("*Mauriton*"), presumably as soldiers, and sailed "from Africa" via islands.[71] The well-informed historian John of Antioch explicitly states that Heraclius came from Africa with many Moors, and he does not say that these ranks also included Egyptians. An inscription at Constantinople indicates participation by members of a tribe from Tripolitania, the Zarakionoi.[72] It is plausible that there was a coordinated pincers operation of Heraclius and his cousin Niketas, who came from Egypt. Heraclius presumably started from Carthage, his father's seat of government, although Hadrumetum (modern Sousse) is not out of the question. His exact route and date of departure are unknown, but he may have passed by Thessalonica.[73] Although he and

---

[68] John of Nikiu, *Chronicle* 107.24–109.13 (169–175 Charles). On Bonosos' terrible reputation: *Vie de Théodore de Sykéôn* c. 142 (II: 111–112 Festugière); Robert Schick, *The Christian Communities of Palestine from Byzantine to Islamic Rule: A Historical and Archaeological Study* (Studies in Late Antiquity and Early Islam, 2; Princeton: Darwin Press, 1995, publ. in 1996) 15–16, 18, 19.

[69] John of Nikiu, *Chronicle* 107.42 (172 Charles). On circus factions: Alan Cameron, *Circus Factions* (Oxford: Oxford University Press, 1976), but for a plea in favor of considering some political role for the factions: Michael Whitby, "The Violence of the Circus Factions," in *Organised Crime in Antiquity*, ed. Keith Hopwood (London: Duckworth, 1999) 229–253.

[70] John of Nikiu, *Chronicle* 109.13–20 (175–176 Charles).   [71] John of Antioch, *FHG* V: 38 (Jacoby).

[72] C. Zuckerman, "Epitaphe d'un soldat africain d'Héraclius servant dans une unité indigène découverte à Constantinople," *L'Antiquité Tardive* 6 (1998) 377–382.

[73] Eutychios, *Hist.* c. 29 (*CSCO* edn., Arabic 122, trans. 102 Breydy = 309 Pirone), for a confused and not entirely convincing reference to Heraclius' presence in Thessalonica. Baynes, "Military Operations," *United Services Magazine* 47 (1913) 30–35. Also, John of Nikiu, *Chron.* 109.25 (176 Charles). Members of the Green faction joined.

his forces may have skirted the shores of Tripolitania and Cyrenaica by
ship, the sea currents along those shores are not good for ships heading
in the direction of Egypt from Africa Proconsularis and Byzacena.[74] He
could have passed by Sicily and mainland Greece to Thessalonica and on
to the Dardanelles, but one may question whether he possessed sufficient
forces to fight Phokas' troops in Egypt as well as mount a naval expedition.[75] There is another reason for his possible departure from Carthage
for Constantinople via a northern route. Evidence for the interrelationship of internal security roles of Sicily, Africa and Italy, from the time
of the 536 revolt in Africa until the late seventh century makes it likely
that Heraclius could not dare to leave Africa unprotected until Sicily and
Byzantine forces in Italy were neutralized or covered in some fashion. It
had been standard Byzantine practice since the fifth century to try to crush
revolts in Africa by dispatching a naval strike force via Italy and Sicily.
There was always the possibility that Phokas might somehow strike with
some punitive naval expedition, via Sicily or Italy, against the matrix of the
rebellion, Africa and Heraclius the Elder. But such a threat from Phokas
seems unlikely. The rebels had to keep some naval forces concentrated
to resist any counterthrust by Phokas. But a rebel defensive force could
quickly transform itself into an offensive one. Although his route is uncertain, Heraclius may have chosen the northern option. The size of his force
is unknown. The account of Sebeos conflated Heraclius' father (Heraclius
Senior), Heraclius himself, and his cousin Niketas all under the name
Heraclius in a corrupt section of his history. There is no independent pa-
pyrological or other documentation for the personal presence of Heraclius
in Egypt.[76]

---

[74] M.G. Fulford, "To East and West: The Mediterranean Trade of Cyrenaica and Tripolitania in
Antiquity," *Libyan Studies* 20 (1989) esp. 171; P. Reynolds, *Trade in the Western Mediterranean* fig. 174,
"Shipping Routes." John H. Pryor, *Geography, Technology and War* (Cambridge: Cambridge
University Press, 1988) 21; Semple, *Geography of the Mediterranean Region* 146–147, 149. Peregrine
Horden and Nicholas Purcell, *The Corrupting Sea* (Oxford: Blackwell, 2000) 137–140.

[75] Heraclius' actual route may not have passed by Cyprus, for that reason. His partisans may well
have seized Cyprus, for it was a rich prize to control and to deny to Phokas, but Heraclius the
Younger himself and his main fleet probably headed more directly from Africa for the Dardanelles,
via traditional routes. They may have passed by Crete although there is no explicit testimonial to
this. Heraclius' seizure of Cyprus in person en route to Constantinople in his rebellion is improbable:
contra, Evangelos Chrysos, Ο Ἡράκλειος στήν Κύπρο, Πρακτικά Συμποσίου Κυπριακῆς Ἱστορίας
(Joannina, 1984) 53–62. Inscriptions in Cyprus that mention Heraclius are not datable to 608–610:
J.-P. Sodini, "Les inscriptions de l'aqueduc de Kythrea à Salamine de Chypre," in *Eupsychia: Mélanges
offerts à Hélène Ahrweiler* (Byzantina Sorbonensia, 16; Paris: Publications de la Sorbonne, 1998) 619–
633. Heraclius' partisans and forces may have seized control of Cyprus as part of an effort to hem
in Phokas, create naval bases for possible future naval strikes against him, and to strangle him
economically while simultaneously increasing the economic resources of the Heraclian faction.

[76] Sebeos, *History* 106, ch. 31; 112, ch. 34 (58, 65 Thomson); T. Hickey gave advice.

Alexandria was the likely place of origin for adequate ships and sea-
men for Heraclius' formidable naval expedition, irrespective of his port
of departure. Could Heraclius have moved from Carthage to Alexandria
by land and then embarked on a ship and led a fleet for Cyprus or along
Mediterranean coast to Alexandretta (modern Turkish Iskenderun)? That
would have exposed Africa and Heraclius' father at Carthage to possible
naval counterthrusts by Phokas and his partisans. Moreover, the presence
of Komentiolos, the brother of Phokas, with a sizeable army intact on
the Anatolian plateau (whether or not Komentiolos at that moment occupied, as he did later, Ankyra) made any land thrust via Asia Minor toward
Constantinople very risky. Theophanes states that Niketas "came from
Alexandria and the Pentapolis, having with him a big host of infantry."[77]
It is unclear whether Niketas came by land or sea, and whether this was a
pincers operation coordinated with Heraclius.

In summary, the present documentation does not permit the identification of the precise route that Heraclius took from Carthage to Constantinople. A number of plausible alternative routes exist: (1) sailing via the
northern route, near Sicily, and Crete and the Aegean Islands, or (2) sailing from Carthage along the southern Mediterranean coast to some
Cyrenaican ports and thence north to Crete, the Aegean Islands and on
to Constantinople, (3) by sailing from Carthage to Alexandria and thence,
with a fleet manned by Egyptians, along the Levantine coast to Cyprus
and then along the Anatolian coast and Dodecanese to Constantinople, or
(4) traveling by land from Carthage to (a) Egypt or (b) Cyrenaica and then
gathering ships, perhaps of primarily Egyptian provenance, and an expeditionary force that either sailed (i) directly north to Crete or (ii) along the
Levantine coast, by way of or near Cyprus, and then along the Anatolian
coasts and Dodecanese, to Constantinople. No primary source provides an
absolutely secure confirmation for any one of these options, each of which
has its own logic and difficulties.

Theodore the Illustrius and a number of senators deserted to Heraclius,
which created a trend of wavering and doubt as to the future of Phokas.[78]
Presumably he had at least passive acquiescence, perhaps direct support,
in Italy and Sicily, for otherwise his move would have gravely endangered
his father and uncle in Africa. Niketas proceeded with military forces by
land. His exact itinerary and its chronology are indeterminate. It appears
that they reached the vicinity of Constantinople after, but not long after,
those of Heraclius. But there are no reliable dates. It was a bold move

---

[77] Theoph. *Chron.* A.M. 6102 (298 De Boor; 427 Mango-Scott).
[78] John of Nikiu, *Chronicle* 109.26 (176 Charles).

that presaged future ones by him, especially in confronting the Persians.[79] It does appear that Cyprus and the Syrian port of Alexandretta, that is, ancient Alexandria ad Issum and vicinity, fell into the hands of partisans of Heraclius, because the two mints struck coins for Heraclius there.[80] Those were serious losses for Phokas, depriving him of important naval bases and tax revenues, cutting off key sea lanes, and sealing off Syria. However, the problems in the vicinity of Alexandretta probably assisted the Persians in decisively breaking through the Byzantines' defenses to the east. The Persian victories and breakthrough were directly attributable to the civil war between Heraclius and Phokas, not to losses by the armies of Phokas; later Heraclian panegyrics and propaganda hid that fact. Phokas found himself and his forces in an untenable position, squeezed between the rebellion in the west and the approaching Persians in the east.[81] It likewise appears that the Danubian or Balkan front was quiet in the reign of Phokas, that major new incursions and inroads by Avars and Slavs took place only after the end of the reign of Phokas.[82] The striking of revolt coins at Alexandria in Egypt and in Cyprus does not prove the personal presence of Heraclius at either place. There is no epigraphic attestation for the presence of Heraclius on Cyprus in 609–610.

For whatever reason, Phokas failed to devise a naval or coastal defense to stop Heraclius the Younger before he passed through the Dardanelles and Sea of Marmara and landed his forces. Heraclius first took the key port of Abydos on the straits.[83] He proceeded on to Herakleia. Stephanos the Metropolitan of Kyzikos took a crown (*stemma*) from the church of the Virgin of Artakes and gave it to Heraclius, so he was crowned emperor before he reached Constantinople. He won a naval clash near the port of Sophia at Constantinople. Phokas had expected him to land near the Land Wall, and accordingly dispatched his brother general (former *curopalates* and former *magister militum per Orientem*, probably now *magister officiorum*)

---

[79] This generalization applies to Heraclius' actions against the Persians in 613, 622, and several subsequent campaigns in the east, including his final triumphant one in 627–628.

[80] Cécile Morrisson, *Catalogue des monnaies byzantines de la Bibliothèque Nationale* (Paris: Bibliothèque Nationale, 1970) 245–251, Philip Grierson, *Catalogue of the Byzantine Coins in the Dumbarton Oaks Collection* (Washington: Dumbarton Oaks, 1968) II: 207–215, 231–232, 330–331. Michael Hendy, "On the Administrative Basis of the Byzantine Coinage c.400–c.900 and the Reforms of Heraclius," in *The Economy, Fiscal Administration and Coinage of Byzantium* (Northampton: Variorum, 1989) VIII: 148, accepts Grierson's thesis on the mints of Alexandretta and Cyprus. Wolfgang Hahn's thesis that the Alexandria in question is the Egyptian one is unconvincing: *Moneta Imperii Byzantini* II: 85–87.

[81] A. Christensen, *Iran sous les Sassanides* (2nd. edn., Copenhagen, 1944) 447–448.

[82] R.-J. Lilie, "Kaiser Herakleios und die Ansiedlung der Serben," *Südost-Forschungen* 44 (1985) 17–43; Paul Lemerle, *Les plus anciens recueils des miracles de St. Démétrius* (Paris, 1979, 1981) II: 85ff., 179–194; F. Curta, *The Making of the Slavs* (Cambridge, 2001) 338.

[83] Theophanes, *Chron.* A.M. 6102 (298–299 De Boor).

Domentiolos or Domnitziolos with troops for that contingency, but had to withdraw them when Heraclius chose to attack from another direction.[84] Heraclius had arrived with his ships at the Sea of Marmara in midsummer, but waited to gain more support. The explanation may involve collaboration and switching sides by certain coastal defense forces and their commanders, similar to what had taken place in parts of Egypt, or simply surprise. Heraclius' fleet had passed by islands where he apparently encountered no significant resistance, if any at all. Perhaps he even continued to gain new supporters for his rebellion, which thereby gathered more momentum. There is a tendency to waver in civil war and to try to join the winning side. Such calculations probably motivated commanders, troops, and civilian subjects whom Heraclius encountered en route from Africa to Constantinople. The full truth remains shrouded.

Heraclius landed near the "circular fort," that is, a fort near the Hebdomon, outside the city walls of Constantinople on 3 October. General Bonosos fled on Sunday 4 October, abandoning seaward defenses, and was later blamed for burning the Caesarius quarter of Constantinople (near the harbor of Theodosius), which in fact resulted from the action of others. Disorder spread quickly. He found a boat, but was killed as he fled into the sea; his body was recovered, and burned at the Forum of the Ox.[85] The Green faction freed Heraclius' mother Epiphania and his fiancée Fabia from the monastery of the Nea Metanoia, and set fire to the Caesarius quarter, goaded by the charioteer Kalliopas, who had a grudge against Phokas. This was sports faction violence, but with political significance. Chaos spread, but organized opposition to Heraclius disintegrated. Priskos, the Prefect of the City, played it very safe. He pretended to be ill, called excubitors (the watch) and *bucellarii* (private guards)[86] to his mansion at the Boraidon, and then made contact with Kalliopas and his allies. The principal support for Phokas had rested among the excubitors and Bonosos, whose death was the cause for the breakdown of organized resistance. Probably the Persian menace in the east had tied down some good troops, whom Phokas dared not attempt to withdraw from the front to assist him at Constantinople.

Phokas was captured by the Patrician Probos (or Photios) at the palace, and led off through the harbor in the direction of the mansion of Sophia.

---

[84] *PLRE* III: 417, s.v. "Domnitziolus 1." Coronation at Cyzicus: Theophanes, *Chron.* A.M. 6102 (299 De Boor).

[85] Forum of the Ox: Janin, *Constantinople byzantine* (Paris: Institut français d'études Byzantines, 1964) 69–71.

[86] Eric McGeer, *ODB* 316, s.v. "Boukellarioi"; O. Schmitt, "Die Buccellarii: Eine Studie zum militärischen Gefolgschaftswesen in der Spätantike," *Tyche* 9 (1994) 147–174; John Haldon, *Byzantine Praetorians* 96–107, 210–227.

He was put on a boat, and taken to Heraclius, who was still, presumably for security reasons, on shipboard in the harbor. Heraclius actually landed on 5 October.[87]

Phokas' own savage fate was symptomatic of the ferocity that his own mutiny and assassination of Maurice and Maurice's family had engendered. On Monday 5 October,

> Photios, the curator of the palace of Placidia, and Probos the Patrician seized Phokas stark naked from the Archangel in the Palace, and led him off through the harbor in the direction of the mansion of Sophia; after throwing him into a skiff, they displayed him to the ships; and then they brought him to Heraclius. And his right arm was removed from the shoulder, as well as his head, his hand was impaled on a sword, and thus it was paraded along the Mese, starting from the Forum. His head was put on a pole, and thus it too was paraded around. The rest of his body was dragged along on the belly, and brought in the direction of the Chalke of the Hippodrome. Behind his corpse Leontios the Syrian, the former *sakellarios* (Treasurer), was also dragged: as he was still breathing, someone gave him a blow with a piece of wood by the Chalke of the Hippodrome, and then he died. His head was removed and then his corpse and that of Phokas were borne off to the Ox, where they were burnt.[88]

According to another vivid tradition, Heraclius interrogated Phokas, asking "Is it thus, O wretch, that you have governed the state?" Phokas answered, "No doubt you will govern it better." Heraclius' angry and rapid response was clear. He ordered Phokas' mutilation and execution while he was still tied up in the boat in the harbor,[89] as well as that of Phokas' brother the General Domentiolos, General Bonosos, and Phokas' *sakellarios* Leontios the Syrian.[90] Phokas' body was cut into pieces, with the pieces displayed, such as his hand impaled on a sword. He was skinned and his other extremities mutilated. Leontios' body and that of Phokas were burned in the furnace of the Ox, as was, given the interests of the Green circus faction with settling sports grudges, the race-starter and sergeant of the city prefect, who handled arrests.[91] John of Nikiu was not as well informed as the author of the *Chronicon Paschale*, and instead claims that senators and officers seized and slew Phokas, after Phokas and his chamberlain Leontios had in a final fit of destructiveness thrown the imperial treasury into the

---

[87] On dating execution of Phokas and coronation of Heraclius to 5 October, persuasive are Michael Whitby, *Chronicon Paschale* 152–153 and Grierson, *DOCat* II.1: 147, 216, but arguments for dating Heraclius' coronation to 6 October: C. Zuckerman, "La petite Augusta et le Turc. Epiphania-Eudocie sur les monnaies d'Héraclius," *RN* 150 (1995) 124; for 7 October: *PLRE* III: 587, 1032.

[88] *Chronicon Paschale* 700–701 (151–152 Whitby).   [89] John of Antioch, *Hist.* (*FGH* V: 38 Dindorf).

[90] Nikephoros, *Short History* 1 (36–37 Mango).

[91] *Chronicon Paschale* 151–152 Whitby.

sea "and so thoroughly impoverished the Roman Empire."[92] The story became, no doubt, another way to put the blame for the lack of public funds on Phokas, not on Heraclius or the civil war that he initiated. The public excoriation and encouragement of popular physical abuse of Phokas already had precedents in the public shaming of Phokas' prominent supporters in urban Egypt. Heraclius encouraged the ventilation of public anger, public humiliation, and condemnation of an opponent. He would utilize this technique on numerous future occasions. Heraclius and his allies continued to draw on and perfect this technique for destroying opponents, whether political or ecclesiastical, by public denunciations, by encouraging public taunts and even mutilations. He would use it until his decease.

The savagery of the overthrow of Phokas, even though rationalized by the brutality and cruelty of the slain emperor, still required smoothing over with appropriate religious ceremonial. The staging of several pageants helped him to accomplish this.

On the same day, 5 October, Patriarch Sergios crowned Heraclius emperor at the chapel of St. Stephen in the palace complex (or, less likely, in Saint Sophia Church). Immediately afterward Sergios performed the marriage ceremony of Fabia/Eudokia and Heraclius in the same chapel, and Sergios then crowned Fabia/Eudokia as empress.[93] The chapel or oratory of St. Stephen contained the supposed relic of St. Stephen and was the standard locale for crowning empresses. The senate had voted him the crown: "Herakleios was proclaimed emperor by the senate and people and was invested by the bishop with the imperial crown." Thus the very ancient Roman principle that legitimate authority of an emperor derived from the act of the senate and people proclaiming the investiture with imperial authority. It took on special significance in light of recent violent usurpation. In an era of crises of legitimacy, the invocation of the role of the senate and people in providing some procedural stability and legitimation was important, as it had often been in earlier crises of that kind in the Roman Empire, given that there never had been a written law of succession.[94] On the following day, 6 October, the flag of the Blue faction was burned in the Hippodrome at Constantinople, together with the head of the *sakellarios* Leontios and an image of Phokas, as the Green faction sought

---

[92] John of Nikiu, *Chronicle* 110.4–7 (177–178 Charles).

[93] Theoph. *Chron.* A.M. 6102 (299 De Boor); Ioli Kalavrezou, "Helping Hands for the Empire: Imperial Ceremonies and the Cult of Relics at the Byzantine Court," in *Byzantine Court Culture*, ed. H. Maguire (Washington: Dumbarton Oaks, 1997) 53–79, esp. 59–66.

[94] Nikephoros, *Short History* 2 (36–37 Mango). Senate: Haldon, *Byzantium in the Seventh Century* 166–171.

its vengeance.[95] So local sports grievances became intertwined with higher political ambitions. The swift execution of Phokas and his most prominent officials eliminated key elements of the regime and prevented any return to the *status quo ante quam*. Heraclius continued to move swiftly. Facts and a new political reality and environment were created expeditiously. Heraclius did not technically assume the consulship that year, which emperors normally held, perhaps because his father was still consul, or, as is conceivable, to save the very considerable expenditures (especially for public sports spectacles) that a consul had to pay in celebration of holding that office.[96]

There were other accounts of the accession and coronation. Reports that Heraclius declined the first offer of the imperial crown should receive a skeptical response, unless one interprets that as a standard gesture, for the *refusatio imperii* had become a rite since the first century: first refusal, then acceptance when the offer was again pressed.[97] Allegedly he informed the senate and people that he was returning to his father and left them to choose the person who would be their emperor, whereupon they elected Heraclius, who accepted only after hearing their entreaties.[98] That may well have been the public procedure, however carefully orchestrated behind the scenes. Order was restored quickly in Constantinople. Nikephoros claimed that Heraclius had the crown first offered to Priskos, who declined, and was subsequently given the command of expeditionary armies in Caesarea, because the Persians had invaded and occupied Caesarea of Cappadocia. Heraclius claimed that he himself had come to punish Phokas, not to take the empire, but after Priskos had declined, Heraclius consented to be crowned by the Patriarch Sergios. The elder Heraclius fades out of sight, perhaps because incapacitated by old age or disinterest, or because the ambitions of his son drove the whole process from the beginning. There is no mention of any claim of Heraclius the Elder to become emperor. Heraclius the Younger notified his father of his election as emperor and his father not surprisingly rejoiced at the news. He appears to have died soon after. Even his date of death is unknown, as well as the date he ceased to be exarch in Africa.[99]

---

[95] *Chronicon Paschale* 152–153 Whitby.

[96] *Chronicon Paschale* 153 n. 428 Whitby. On costliness of the consulship: Michael Hendy, *Studies* 192–195.

[97] John of Nikiu, *Chronicle* 110.9 (178 Charles). The author of the *Chronicon Paschale* also quotes a letter from Heraclius to Khusrau II in which it was explained that Heraclius had really planned to return to Africa after overthrowing Phokas: *Chronicon Paschale* 708 (161 Whitby). That is a *topos* of the regime's propaganda. On the gesture of refusing power in the Early and Late Empire: Jean Béranger, "Le refus du pouvoir," *Principatus* (Geneva: Droz, 1973) 165–190, and Béranger, *Recherches sur l'aspect idéologique du principat* (Basel: Reinhardt, 1953).

[98] *Chronicon Paschale* 708 (161 Whitby).

[99] John of Nikiu, *Chronicle* 110.10–13 (178 Charles); *Chronicon Paschale* 708 (161 Whitby).

Heraclius' cousin Niketas had seized Egypt by 610 and remained there to control it, although he may have engaged in indeterminate military campaigns to mop up the last supporters of Phokas in Syria and Palestine. In any case he returned to Egypt to act as Prefect Augustalis. It was important to insure that Egypt remained in reliable hands, because it was a rich province, possibly contributing 30 percent or more of the revenues of the Prefecture of the East to the imperial treasury.[100] The new government would not have wished some other politically ambitious figure to stir up new unrest there as they had recently done themselves. The office of Augustalis was the perfect position for Niketas to hold when the new government was consolidating its authority. He and Heraclius the Younger enjoyed excellent relations. His control of Alexandria was tight, including, of course, control over revenues.

News of the change of power spread quickly. Already the great ascetic St. Theodore of Sykeon in the vicinity of the border between the provinces of Bithynia and Galatia predicted: "Soon we shall receive news of change of regime." "A few days later, 7 October, there came to the blessed [Saint Theodore], from the mouths of a courier who was passing by, the news of the assassination of Emperor Phokas and the proclamation of the friend of Christ and very pious Emperor Heraclius."[101] Not all of Phokas' family were detested by everyone, for St. Theodore of Sykeon, a friend of the Phokas family, reportedly wrote to Heraclius, asking that he spare the *curopalates* Domnitziolos, nephew of Phokas (?son of Domentiolos). Heraclius granted his petition, asking that St. Theodore "pray for him and his reign."[102] It was indeed desirable for the new regime to gain, in so far as practicable, the support and prayers of ecclesiastics and ascetics, whose attitudes and actions would receive popular notice.[103]

One potentially powerful member of the family of Phokas remained at large: Phokas' brother, the Patrician Komentiolos, who commanded an army in the east, at Ankyra.[104] He apparently led his armies into winter quarters at Ankyra. He may have been *magister militum per Orientem*. He arrested Heraclius' envoy Philippikos, who probably sought to negotiate an end to his armed resistance, but was assassinated in turn, after some delay, by the Armenian commander Justinos, which terminated this brief challenge to the new government. Thus ended the last part of the regime of Phokas.

[100] Michael Hendy, *Studies* 172, 620–621.

[101] *Vie de Théodore de Sykéôn*, c. 152–153 (I: 121–124; II: 127–129 Festugière); W.E. Kaegi, "New Evidence on the Early Reign of Heraclius," *BZ* 66 (1973) 308–330.

[102] *Vie de Théodore de Sykéôn* c. 152 (I: 122; II: 127 Festugière). The saint and Domnitziolos had enjoyed very good relations: *PLRE* III: 417–418, s.v. "Domnitziolus 2."

[103] Not a new phenomenon: Emperor Leo I sought the support and advice of Daniel the Stylite in the fifth century: "Vita S. Danielis Stylitae," ed. H. Delehaye, *AB* 32 (1913) 155, 157, 158–159, 161, 164, 167–168, 169, 173, 179, 182, 184–185.

[104] *PLRE* III: 326, s.v. "Comentiolus 2." *Vie de Théodore de Sykéôn* c. 152, 161 (II: 128–129, 148 Festugière).

But it is uncertain how much time it took to eliminate Komentiolos. It is equally unclear how much territory Komentiolos ever controlled. Did his authority, for example, extend to Antioch or any coast? Did other army units waver and consider allying with Komentiolos? It is unclear who considered supporting him. In a fluid situation, he hesitated and temporized too long. There were first attempts at negotiations, so Heraclius did not immediately gain control of all of Anatolia and of all Byzantine armies in the east on seizing power at Constantinople. Komentiolos was unable to accomplish anything in winter quarters. The best evidence is that Komentiolos was not attempting very actively to rally more troops and officials against Heraclius. He lost whatever opportunity he temporarily possessed. Probably he wished to try to wait and see.

The best solution for the new government of Heraclius was the most possible rapid elimination of Komentiolos. Heraclius had sent Eutychianos as commander of an army, presumably of substantial size, to watch and contain Komentiolos, who occupied a strategic location. He also sent General Philippikos, son-in-law of the late Emperor Maurice, to try to negotiate with Komentiolos. There might have been a major battle to settle his challenge. That would have risked wasting still more valuable lives of soldiers at a moment when the empire could ill afford to lose them. Eutychianos and others were sufficiently concerned about the outcome to seek the spiritual guidance of St. Theodore of Sykeon, to save lives. Presumably Komentiolos feared for his own life, given the fate of his brothers, so he saw little future for himself if he surrendered or came to a negotiated settlement. He also had no hope of fleeing to the Persians, who had announced strong opposition to the Phokas regime. Hence his desperate if senseless effort to prolong resistance to the newly established regime of Heraclius. He probably hoped to see if other opposition arose against it. But even his brief interlude of separate power caused a potential crisis and complicated any Heraclian efforts to make peace with the Persians or to gain control of the Byzantine armies that were in a position to resist the Persians. St. Theodore of Sykeon predicted what occurred: his swift end. There is no evidence that his passing met with any great lament. But his revolt or continued wielding of power gave the Persians an important opportunity to break through on the eastern front during the gap in time before Heraclius could consolidate his control over all armies in the east. They made the most of their opportunity. There was a fleeting period of confused authority and uncertainty and divided allegiance. The armies and the soldiers would have been on their own. Normal communications and pay would have broken down. It was uncertain who was in charge, who would win, and who cared enough for the troops and officers and civilians in exposed and endangered districts who had to face the Persians. Some prominent individuals, such as Strategios *paneuphemos* ("Pseudo-Strategios"), who married into the powerful Egyptian Apion family, managed to navigate a successful passage from the regime of Phokas to that of Heraclius without great difficulty.[105] It would have been imprudent to purge them because Heraclius needed them. The same logic applied to Patriarch Sergios, who had given invaluable service to Heraclius.

The elimination of Komentiolos did not end all internal problems: there remained a crisis of legitimacy that a second violent seizure of power and the wholesale execution and mutilation of members of Phokas' family could not eradicate. The public was still shocked, with trepidation and unease about whether this violence signified divine wrath. There remained the uneasy relationship of Heraclius with the strongman Priskos, who had already shown himself to be treacherous to his father-in-law Phokas, and who now controlled the largest and best field army, now facing the Persians in Anatolia. He was a dangerous dissembler. Given the realities of a Persian invasion, that was a very dangerous situation. Recent urban unrest in Alexandria and Antioch, which included Jewish–Christian clashes at Antioch, added to the internal instability.[106] Heraclius' own chancery, purportedly in the name of the senate and people, described the Persians' military victories as having resulted in the "great diminution" of the empire, and having "humbled" it.[107] Other contemporaries, in the *Doctrina Jacobi nuper Baptizati*, would use similar language two decades later.

The crisis of legitimacy brought in its wake not only shock, but drift, which included the spread of public expressions of hostility and collective violence on a large scale in a number of cities across the east: Constantinople, Antioch, and Alexandria, as well as some clashes in smaller Egyptian towns. The crowd is important in the early seventh century, even though we can only dimly see its faces and hear its voices. It is changeable; it made various alliances with domestic groups, and it is angry. It is impossible to arrive at reasonable estimates of the numbers involved. The crowd never succeeds in mastering events. The sixth century had experienced important popular

---

[105] *PLRE* III: 1203–1204, s.v. "Strategius 10." Palme has argued convincingly that he joined the Apion family via marriage to Praeiecta, the daughter of Apion II (cos. ord.). Apion III would be their son, and he is the one that Pope Gregory I advises (through wife Eusebia) after Phokas' usurpation. Strategios Paneuphemos is still an important player into the seventh century (e.g. Monophysite Union): B. Palme, "Die doma gloriosa des Flavius Strategius Paneuphemos," *Chiron* 27 (1997) 95–125, esp. 98.

[106] David Olster, *Roman Defeat, Christian Response, and the Literary Construction of the Jew* (Philadelphia: University of Pennsylvania Press, 1994) 73, 93.

[107] *Chronicon Paschale* 707, 708 (160, 161 Whitby).

eruptions, such as the Nika Riot of 532, but in the early seventh century, connected to the breakdown of authority with the overthrow of Maurice, there arose singular examples of popular fury: the so-called Levantine riots at Antioch, the rioting at Beirut in 608/9, which Bonosos suppressed, the rioting at Alexandria connected with the overthrow of the Patriarch and partisans of Phokas in 608–610, rioting at Constantinople associated with or contemporary with the overthrow of Phokas. No one person orchestrated these events. The Green and Blue factions had a role. The cases of urban violence followed the sharp outbreak of military unrest in Asia, especially in northern Syria and then in the Balkans, leading to the ultimate rising that brought Phokas to the throne for eight years. There are no surviving memoranda from these crowds. Saints' lives and contemporary, or virtually contemporary, apologetical tracts such as that of the *Doctrina Jacobi nuper Baptizati* indicate the volatility of public moods and the evident wish to vent frustrations collectively. There was sufficient urban life for these riots to spread and be noted and recorded. They were a prominent component of early seventh-century life. For the Emperor Heraclius and his advisers, they constituted another element of instability about which one needed to be wary, and if possible, one wished to try to channel, contain, or control. But it is not always easy to control ugly gushings of frustration about military reverses, humiliations, material shortages, health problems, and ominous signs.

The empire needed a rest but was not to receive one. Pressures and crises escalated. In his first great crisis, the challenge of seizure of power in civil war, Heraclius had triumphed. He had learned how to use naval power. He had learned how to rely less on open battle than secret communication with waverers among leading elements of the ranks of his opponents. He would make use of that technique, with varying results, repeatedly in the future. Yet victory in civil war was very different from winning decisive victory in major battle, let alone campaigns, in the open field against external enemies of the empire, whether those to the north, Avars and Slavs, or to east, the Persians. Except for some clashes in Egypt that Niketas won, there had been no great battles in this civil war. Nor had there been great sieges. Heraclius and his partisans had been, for the most part, on the offensive, not the defensive. How Heraclius and his military team might perform in defense was still an unknown. He had not allowed Phokas to pin him down in positional warfare. That next war would involve very different tests. In this civil crisis he had shown his ability to respond flexibly to rapidly changing events, variables, risks, and contingencies, some of which required immediate decisions on his part. He did not shrink from them and he thrived on risk. Unlike his Persian rival Khusrau II, he had triumphed on his own terms, without foreign assistance, in civil war. He would not forget what he had learned in the civil war with Phokas. In the future he would wage both external and civil war against his Persian foe. During the civil war he had invoked religion and God's help on his behalf. He would repeatedly resort to and polish the technique of encouraging public ventilation of frustration and anger against a prominent leader whom he wished to ruin. He had now set the precedents for his much greater future use of it. He possessed extraordinary military and political qualities that would prove valuable in the future. But he also depended on blessings and association with holy men. At this moment of his triumph he was approximately thirty-five years old, no longer a youth.

CHAPTER 2

Internal and external challenges in the first decade of the reign

The contemporary historian Theophylact Simocatta stated in grandiloquent yet clichéd terms sometime in the 630s that, after overthrowing Phokas, Heraclius revived philosophy and history, and restored their position in the imperial palace. How much new imperial patronage and encouragement of learning took place shortly after 610 under Heraclius may be moot. For Theophylact, "through the reverses of others she [history] makes them more wary, directing them in the light of their predecessors' mistakes. In success she increases their prosperity, raising them up from small beginnings to dizzy heights of achievement."[1] Reversals of fortune and dizzy heights characterize Heraclius' own record, although Theophylact intended his phrasing in a different sense. He implies that Heraclius gave new importance to history after seizing power. Heraclius may have already begun his own consultation of history for discovery of military wisdom, including tactics and possible stratagems of his opponents, presumably, the Persians.[2] There is no firm independent confirmation. It is difficult to imagine how Heraclius could have found free time to read and ponder historical lessons, given the pressing external situation. He was probably too busy coping with diverse emergencies to read much philosophy or history soon after his accession. Theophylact developed a literary conceit here that should not unduly concern the investigator of Heraclius.

Heraclius now confronted challenges of consolidating the power that he had seized. He had demonstrated unusual skills, both military and political, in civil war. One key question internally would be: could he prevent a recrudescence of civil war or not, now that there was, like it or not, a continuing crisis of imperial legitimacy?[3] But external challenges were at least as

---

[1] Joseph D.C. Frendo, "History and Panegyric in the Age of Heraclius: The Literary Background to the Composition of the *Histories* of Theophylact Simocatta," *DOP* 42 (1988) 146–147.

[2] See translation by Frendo, "History and Panegyric in the Age of Heraclius" 146.

[3] Legitimacy and the rationale for the rehabilitation of Emperor Maurice: Frendo, "History and Panegyric in the Age of Heraclius" 153–155.

pressing. The first years of the new emperor were mixed. Primary sources are fragmentary, limited, and diverse with respect to their character and their provenance. There is no detailed history, no archive of documents, no trove of correspondence, nor any diary for the historian to probe. Instead there are glimmerings of information in saints' lives, chronicles, inscriptions on coinage, papyri, and religious tracts, which require filtering, assembly, interpretation, and synthesis. Sasanian sources are not very helpful, despite the prominent role of Sasanian armies and diplomatic decisions in that period. Muslim sources are erroneous or misleading or too sketchy to help very much in understanding these years of Heraclius' reign. Yet this was a critical era in which Heraclius established many basic precedents for his reign, an era in which he reportedly found the external situation so perilous on so many fronts that "he was perplexed about what to do."[4] There are various curious but questionable anecdotes, of unknown origin, about him and his reign, and many gaps and unanswered questions. We hear nothing more about his father Heraclius.

Energy and decisive actions in diverse fields filled the first five years of Heraclius' reign. He moved quickly to place his distinctive stamp on internal and external policies, to master and to conciliate. His successes were initially greater in confronting internal than external crises. The situation demanded more than a strong man. A spiritual dimension was always present in Byzantium, and the exigencies sharpened the need for all to find that indispensable spiritual assistance and legitimation. He demonstrated a strong interest in religious affairs from the beginning. Although some of that public commitment to religion may have represented mere calculation to win popular support and to meet expectations, there almost certainly was a strong impulse in him to find and to immerse himself in genuine religious experiences. He had already displayed icons on his ships, invoking their aid in his struggle against Phokas in 608–610.[5] But in early 610 Heraclius used strong pressure, including the intervention of his cousin Niketas, to secure the election of John the Almsgiver as Patriarch of Alexandria.[6] Niketas and John became ritual brothers through the rite of *adelphopoiesis*. Matters were still unsettled. John of Nikiu reported that although Heraclius the Elder had received news of his son's victory and rejoiced in it, "Now great uncertainty prevailed in the churches because of the long duration of the

---

[4] Theophanes, *Chron.* A.M. 6103 (299–300 De Boor).

[5] George of Pisidia, *Heraclias* 1.218, 2.15 (*Poemi* 250, 252 Pertusi); Theophanes, *Chron.* A.M. 6102 (298 De Boor).

[6] A.J. Festugière, introduction to his edition and translation of Leontios, *Vie de Syméon le Fou et Vie de Jean de Chypre* (Paris: Geuthner, 1974) and anonymous *vita*, *Vie de Jean de Chypre* 4 (322–323 Festugière).

Fig. 2. Heraclius' portrait from a solidus ca. 613–616, with his son Heraclius Constantine, Constantinople (obverse, *DOCat* 8j.4).

war, and every one was full of apprehension over the victory which had been won over Bônâkîs, and the disquietude which had been occasioned in regard to his (Heraclius') son."[7]

Patriarch Sergios of Constantinople, who had become Patriarch on 18 April 610, managed to survive the change of dynasty and to win the confidence of Heraclius. What circumspect role he may possibly have played on behalf of Heraclius during the final months of the civil war is unclear. He had been a deacon of the Great Church, but he came from Syria where his parents had been Jacobite Monophysites.[8] He also had good relations with the then very influential and universally respected St. Theodore of Sykeon. Both Sergios and Heraclius had strong reasons to make their relationship a close one: they needed each other. Their relationship would be long and friendly. Sergios came from a region that was then facing Persian invasion. It is uncertain what counsel, if any, he gave Heraclius concerning the situation in his native countryside and its cities and towns, or what policies he should follow at that time. More immediate were the needs at Constantinople, where the burden of ecclesiastical expenditure was high. In May 612, presumably after discussions with Heraclius, a new regulation restricted numbers of personnel of the Great Church and its bureaucracy: new members of the church staff would not receive pay from the imperial fisc. Heraclius issued an imperial Novel (law) to ratify this. Part of the rationale for this policy may well have been the financial exigencies of the empire. Just as Niketas reportedly had sought to draw on Patriarchal funds in Alexandria, so these new regulations probably had as one of their aims to halt the hemorrhaging of funds because of too many clergy (whose numbers had now reached more than 600) to support on the budget of the Great Church.[9] Sergios and Heraclius developed a close relationship but it is unknown how early this relationship began.

---

[7] John of Nikiu, *Chronicle* 110.12 (178 Charles). On *adelphopoiesis*, Claudia Rapp is preparing groundbreaking research.

[8] Jan Louis Van Dieten, *Geschichte der Patriarchen von Sergios I. bis Johannes VI. (610–715)* (Amsterdam: Hakkert, 1972) 1–56.

[9] Van Dieten, *Geschichte der Patriarchen* 4.

Some events provide insight into the sensitivities of popular emotions. Already holy men had prophesied that Heraclius would become emperor.[10] It was necessary for Heraclius and his advisers to take such emotions into consideration when making policy and thinking of the possible or probable consequences of ceremonies and acts. An earthquake disturbed Constantinople on 20 April 611. Accordingly, on 22 April public prayers were offered on the Campus Martius in the form of a litany and the Trisagion.[11] On 7 July 611 a daughter, Epiphania, named for Heraclius' mother, was born to Eudokia and to Heraclius at the palace of Hiereia, on the Asiatic shore, south of Chalcedon. On 3 May 612 Heraclius II Constantine was born in the suburban palace of Sophianae. But tragedy quickly offset the joy of having an heir for the throne. On 13 August 612 Eudokia herself died of epilepsy at the then suburban palace of Blachernae. Her body was brought by boat to the imperial palace in Constantinople, and she was then buried in the Church of the Holy Apostles, the traditional imperial burial church.[12]

A strange story reports that a maidservant of a resident of the city disrupted Eudokia's funeral by ominously spitting out of a window and soiling the deceased empress' burial dress. The outraged and superstitious public burnt the offending servant alive, and vainly sought to find her mistress, who managed to escape. That was an unsettling event on which various contemporaries put different interpretations. The story emphasizes the sacrality of the empress' body and was probably circulated to discredit the reputation of Heraclius' niece and second wife, Martina, and her sons and their claim to their imperial succession shortly after Heraclius' death. A subsequent cult celebrated Eudokia on 13 August. Some, like the probably contemporary source of the *Short History* of Nikephoros, deplored the motives and actions of the mob, whose vicious reaction denoted the jittery Constantinopolitan mood at the beginning of Heraclius' reign.[13]

Eudokia and Heraclius had been married less than two years. Her death was difficult for him, and for their subjects, leaving him with two infants

---

[10] For example, Theophilos, the pillar-sitting Egyptian holy man: John of Nikiu, *Chron.* 108.1–5 (172–173 Charles).

[11] *Chronicon Paschale* 702 (153 Whitby).

[12] Averil Cameron, "Notes on the Sophiae, the Sophianae and the Harbour of Sophia," *Byzantion* 37 (1967) 11–20.

[13] Nikephoros, *Short History* 3 (40–41 Mango). Zonaras, *Hist.* 14.14, III: 305 Dindorf. Cf. Paul Speck, *Das geteilte Dossier. Beobachtungen zu den Nachrichten über die Regierung des Kaisers Herakleios und die seiner Söhne bei Theophanes und Nikephoros* (Bonn: Habelt, 1988) 241f. Fabia/Eudokia in the *Synaxarium* of Constantinople: Areti Papanastasiou, "Saint Eudokia the Empress," *AABSC* 27 (2001) 24; *Synaxarium ecclesiae Constantinopolitanae*, ed. H. Delehaye (Brussels: Société des Bollandistes, 1902, repr. 1964) 890.

and an empire still in crisis. It did not bode well. Recent mob action in the various cities of the empire, not just at Constantinople, had involved burning, torture, mutilation of individuals, burning and shredding of hated physical symbols or objects, shouting taunts as well as celebratory cheers, mass devotion and contrition, and collective thanks. Heraclius probably remained a mourning widower for some time.[14] This was a lonely period of his life.

The lapse in normal imperial succession due to violent usurpations increased the need for compensating legitimization, which may explain the noticeable increase of imperial participation in elaborate ceremonies and rituals. A purpose would be increasing or restoring public respect for the office of emperor.[15] New rituals appeared with the reign of Heraclius. The need for more legitimation probably stimulated this trend.[16] Another possible reason for this phenomenon was the conscious or unconscious need to offer a different psychological release or outlet in an era of increasingly rigid formal theology, increasingly severe literalism in theology, and what some scholars describe as a harsher tone in the heightened obsession with theological truth, with a closing down of the possibility of dogmatic theology.[17] Heraclius for his part may have encouraged the development of new rituals and ceremonies because he understood the need to communicate with his subjects and to enable them to participate with him in public ceremonies and spectacles. For reasons of security and for the purpose of respecting and honoring his rank, subjects were not to approach him, but they were able to see him. There were many occasions of public spectacles in which he participated, together with members of his family. This was not an innovation but his subjects at Constantinople had many opportunities to see or hear of public ceremonies and processions in which their emperor participated. This was consistent with his personal participation in military campaigns, which was a departure from recent practice. Those occasions allowed numbers of his provincial subjects to see him as well, including at ceremonies of formal departure for and formal return from campaigns and visits to the provinces. He began to change some of the physical aspects of Constantinople, to place his own stamp on the capital and to eradicate that

---

[14] Speck, *Das geteilte Dossier* 33–43, shows that Theophanes' ascription of an early remarriage of Heraclius to his niece Martina is incorrect.

[15] Ceremonial precedents in the reign of Heraclius: Michael McCormick, *Eternal Victory* (Cambridge: Cambridge University Press, 1986) 70–71, 75, 191–196.

[16] New ceremonials: Averil Cameron, "Images of Authority: Elites and Icons in Late Sixth-Century Byzantium," *Past and Present* 84 (1979) 16–26; Averil Cameron, "The Theotokos in Sixth-Century Byzantium," *Journal of Theological Studies*, n.s. 29 (1978) 79–108.

[17] Patrick T.R. Gray, "Theological Discourse in the Seventh Century: The Heritage from the Sixth Century," *BF* 26 (2000) 219–228.

of his predecessor. Phokas erected a composite column to the east of the Church of the Forty Martyrs (on the south side of the main street called Mese, between the Tetrapylon and the Forum of Theodosius). This construction apparently was just being finished when Phokas fell from power. Heraclius retained the column but transformed it by placing a cross on it in 612.[18]

Ceremonies with Heraclius' children were one feature of his emphasis on ceremonial. This helped to assuage the pain of the death of Eudokia, and celebrate the perpetuation and future of the dynasty. On 4 October 612 Heraclius' one-year-old daughter Epiphania was escorted in a chariot by court officials, who included the *cubicularius* (chamberlain) Philaretos and the *castrensis* Synetos, to the oratory of St. Stephen in the palace, where she was crowned, and then proceeded to the Great Church.[19] A number of ceremonies and displays of the imperial children were essential carefully scripted parts of the pageantry of his reign.

Heraclius also needed to assert his authority and win respect from the public, to negate or fill the void of the crisis of legitimacy. Whether or not it was calculated, certain actions of his contributed to impressing the public with his firm commitment to insuring justice within the empire. One involved an unidentified ceremonial, a public procession. A conspicuously wealthy *candidatus* (imperial deputy who wore a white cloak), Boutilinos or Bitilinos, engaged in a rural boundary dispute with a widow, in the course of which Boutilinos' servants clubbed one of the widow's sons to death. This may have taken place in Thrace. The widow managed to reach and touch Heraclius when he was participating in a public procession, showed him her late son's bloody clothing and demanded vengeance, "or if not, so may your children perish." Heraclius ordered a legal inquiry, but ordered her not to approach him again. The woman departed, bewailing the lack of justice. Boutilinos, fearing the outcome, participated in one circus faction's association at the hippodrome, presumably with hostile intentions against the widow. Heraclius took notice, ordered the Prefect to arrest him, and encouraged a legal inquiry. He finally ordered the slaying of Boutilinos and also Boutilinos' servants to slay one of themselves in recompense. The story magnifies Heraclius' reputation as a guarantor of justice, as an avenger of the weak, as one who would not shrink from punishing the powerful and

[18] *Chronicon Paschale* 698–699 (148 Whitby) for original erection of the column by Phokas; p. 703 (155 Whitby) for Heraclius placing a cross on it. The column remained a fixture in Constantinople for many centuries: C. Mango, "Epigrammes honorifiques, statues et portraits à Byzance," in Ἀφιέρωμα στόν Νίκο Σβορῶνο, ed. V. Kremmydas, Chrysa Maltezou, Nikolaos M. Panagiotakis (Rethymno, 1986) I: 30.

[19] *Chronicon Paschale* 703 (154 Whitby).

prominent. On the other hand, there is careful attention to inflicting retribution on those directly and indirectly responsible for the wrongful death, those of higher and lower class. So the story magnifies Heraclius' reputation without encouraging hopes for any stern clash between the imperial government and elites. One does not know the outcome of the actual property dispute, except that presumably it too was the subject of legal inquiry and therefore of formal justice and redress. This story spread and eventually found its way into historical narratives of the reign. Such prominent acts and their publicizing probably increased Heraclius' authority and respect for his rule and helped him to govern.[20] They reduced the possibility of additional rebellions and unrest. This does not mean that Heraclius' decision was made purely for political calculation and effect. The placement of this story very early in the narrative of Nikephoros implies that the event occurred at the beginning of Heraclius' reign. The brashness of the threat to Heraclius' children and even the widow's physical approach to Heraclius are striking in the story, which evidently circulated after Heraclius' death, probably to the benefit of his dynastic successors. This legend contributed to his being held in popular awe. It shows the fear that the potential for imperial investigation could strike into even elite sectors of society. This is a story more of retribution than of actual fairness.

But Heraclius also had a reputation for fairness that may have received assistance from another source: monumental remains in Constantinople. He apparently set up a scale (*hexamon*) in the golden-roofed Basilica colonnade in Constantinople.[21] It is unknown when in his reign this was done, however. The reference is too sketchy to conclude anything more about its nature or historical context. Somehow he set up or authorized to be set up some kind of weight or measuring scale that survived long after him in the city of Constantinople. Probably it sought to establish some fair standard that the emperor guaranteed and publicized. There are no details, but that was an era of irregularities and troubles with measures and weights, for Patriarch John the Almsgiver exerted himself on behalf of fair weights and measures in Alexandria as well.[22] Another possible purpose for erecting this scale was to emphasize his role as a guarantor of equity in order once again to smooth over the irregular circumstances of his own accession to imperial power.

---

[20] Nikephoros, *Short History* 4 (42–43 Mango).

[21] Anonymous, *Parastaseis Syntomoi Chronikai* 37 = *Constantinople in the Eighth Century*, ed. Averil Cameron and J. Herrin (Leiden: Brill, 1984) 96–99.

[22] However, one cannot explicitly connect the concerns of Patriarch John with the physical or actual scale of Heraclius at Constantinople.

External crises impinged. Heraclius unsuccessfully sought to communicate with the Persian King Khusrau II, seeking a termination of hostilities now that Phokas was overthrown. He tried to make peace in the first year of his reign.[23] Khusrau haughtily rejected that overture, as he would continue to do, probably believing that there was no reason to halt while his armies were winning and conquering more Byzantine territory. If anything, his aims probably widened as his victories raised even more hopes for more military opportunities, and the possible disintegration of the Byzantine Empire.[24] Lack of Persian archives makes it impossible to document their goals, but the best explanation appears to be that the constitutional crisis, civil war, and their initial victories whetted the Persians' appetite for booty, power, and territory, and unwisely for them, discouraged any efforts at limited conquests. Instead their striving for maximal gains raised Persian hopes of the destruction of the Byzantine Empire, or at least encouraged probing how far they could conquer.[25] No document conclusively proves that an explicit goal of Khusrau II and his advisers was the restoration, or even the surpassing, of the former limits of the Achaemenid Empire, but that is conceivable.[26]

Some of Khusrau's generals, such as Shahrbaraz, may have developed their own goals and ambitions as they extended their string of victories. The year 609 was the occasion of the great Persian breakthrough. The Persians exploited the Byzantine civil war, which made it impossible for Phokas to concentrate on developing a unified defense. The continuing resistance by Komentiolos, brother of Phokas, for however a brief time in late 610 and possibly early 611 after the fall of Phokas, slowed Heraclius' consolidation of authority in central and eastern Anatolia and provided the Persians with a great military opportunity, which they exploited to the fullest. Dangers multiplied and intensified on the empire's eastern frontiers at several points. By applying pressures and probing at several points, the Persians compelled the Byzantines to maintain at least two major defensive

[23] Agapios, *Kitāb al-Unvān, PO* 8: 450 (Vasiliev).
[24] *Chronica Minora*, ed. Ignatius Guidi (*CSCO*, SS ser. 3, 4; Paris, Leipzig, 1903–1905) trans. 22; *Chron. 1234* (= [Anonymous] *Chronicon ad annum Christi 1234 pertinens*, ed. J.B. Chabot (*CSCO*, SS 14; Louvain, 1937)) 173–177; *Chronicon miscellaneum ad annum Domini 724 pertinens* (in *Chronica Minora*, ed. Guidi) trans. 113; Michael the Syrian, *Chronique* II: 378 (Chabot). Sebeos, *History* 113, ch. 34 (66 Thomson); *Storia* c. 32 (86–87 Gugerotti). Agapios, *Kitāb al-Unvān, PO* 8: 450. This effort to open communications probably is different from the one that the *Chronicon Paschale* reports for 614/615. It is unlikely that Heraclius made no attempts to make peace immediately after seizing power in October 610 – his later attempts at peace naturally passed over this initial rebuke, trying, unsuccessfully, to smooth over matters by avoiding mention of such initial snubs.
[25] Bernard Flusin, *Saint Anastase le Perse* (Paris: CNRS, 1992) II: 67–97.
[26] Michael Whitby, "The Persian King at War," in *The Roman and Byzantine Army in the East*, ed. E. Dabrowa, 227–263.

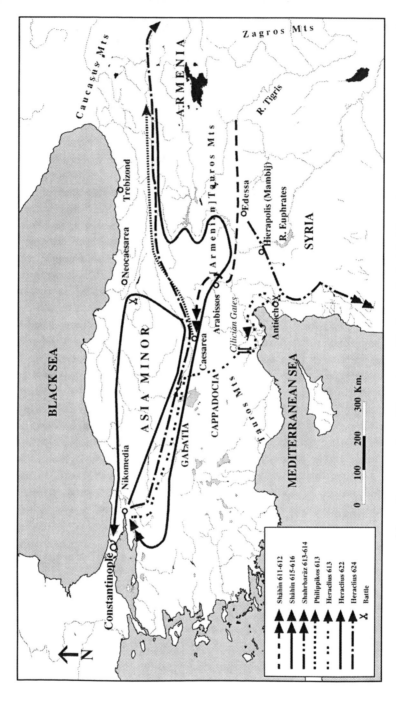

Map 2 Some campaigns of Byzantine and Persian armies in Asia Minor, 610–622

groupings of troops. There were two separate major fronts: in the Caucasus, that is, Armenia, and on the Euphrates frontier (Map 2).

Some of the earliest Byzantine reverses occurred in Armenia. There was no sudden and easy breakthrough on this front. Sasanian armies initially failed near Elevard, but won successes in the plain of Akanich, in the district of Shirak, but the Persians then returned into their territory of Atrpatakan.[27] The Persian commander Senitam Chosrov defeated the Byzantines in the districts of Basean and in the district of Taron.[28] Ashtat Yestayar led another Persian expedition into the district of Basean, between Du and Ordru, then captured and garrisoned Theodosiopolis (Erzurum), followed by Kitris/Dzitharoc.[29] Shāhīn Patgosapan then defeated and expelled Byzantine troops in the Theodosiopolis region, perhaps in 609–610. Inhabitants of Theodosiopolis were deported to Ecbatana (Hamadan). The result was the virtual conquest of Byzantine Armenia by the Sasanians. It had been a slow process. Komentiolos, brother of Phokas, may have been trying to check these Persians up to his own death in late 610 or early 611. Shāhīn had then pushed on into Cappadocia, to Casearea.[30]

The Persians likewise had smashed through the eastern front, took Dara possibly in 605 and other key cities in upper Mesopotamia, including Edessa in 610, Tella, Amida in 609, and Ra's al-'Ayn.[31] In 610 they crossed the Euphrates and soon crossed the Taurus passes into the Anatolian plateau itself and began devastating it.[32] Khusrau II claimed to have Theodosios, the son of the murdered Emperor Maurice, in his possession. Theodosios allegedly had fled to the protection of Khusrau II, who made use of this impostor. The real Theodosios apparently perished in the massacre of Maurice's family at the accession of Phokas.[33] The abortive rebellion of General Narses in 603 allowed the proclamation of the false Theodosios as emperor at Edessa. This impostor helped to persuade some Byzantine-held cities, such

---

[27] Sebeos, *History* 108–110, ch. 32–33 (60–62 Thomson); *Hist.* c. 22 (57–60 Macler), *Storia* c. 30 (83–84 Gugerotti). The chronology of these campaigns and their relations to those in Syria are confused.

[28] Sebeos, *History* 109–111, ch. 32–33 (60–62 Thomson); *Storia* c. 30 (84 Gugerotti).

[29] [Anonymous], *Narratio de rebus Armeniae* 112–113, trans., comment. G. Garitte, 41, 259–263; Sebeos, *History* 111, ch. 33 (64 Thomson); *Hist.*, c. 23 (62 Macler), *Storia* c. 31 (85–86 Gugerotti).

[30] Sebeos, *History* 111, ch. 33 (63–64 Thomson); *Storia* c. 31 (85–86 Gugerotti). Flusin, *Saint Anastase le Perse* I: 81.

[31] Sebeos, *History* ch. 32–33 (62–63 Thomson); *Narratio de rebus Armeniae* 112–113 (41 Garitte).

[32] *Vie de Théodore de Sykéôn* c. 153 (I: 123–124, II: 129 Festugière); Theophanes, *Chron.* A.M. 6103 (299 De Boor); Clive Foss, "The Persians in Asia Minor and the End of Antiquity," *EHR* 90 (1975) 721–743; W.E. Kaegi, "New Evidence on the Early Reign of Heraclius," *BZ* 66 (1973) 308–330; Olster, *Politics of Usurpation* 81–97.

[33] Theodosios had already perished, according to official Heraclian statements: Theophylact, *Hist.* 8.13.3–6, 8.15.8.

as Theodosiopolis (Erzurum) to surrender to the Persians. The Persian invasions were devastating, in the words of an anonymous Armenian commentator, they brought "great afflictions in Romania."[34] Their commander Shāhīn even occupied, in 611, Caesarea Mazaca, the capital of Cappadocia, an especially embarrassing event if indeed Heraclius' mother Epiphania or any member of the Heraclian family, as the historian John of Nikiu claims, did have Cappadocian ties.[35]

Fear spread widely in neighboring Galatia and Bithynia. The contemporary biographer of St. Theodore of Sykeon reported: "We were all, both those in the monastery and all of the inhabitants of our region, in great fear, lest they make a raid against us." St. Theodore reassured them, "Do not fear, my children, barbarian invasion. My God has been called for help, and He will not permit them to attack our territory, and I shall not see with my own eyes an invasion of the barbarians in this place here."[36] He predicted that the Persians – whom Priskos, head of the imperial guard (Count of the Excubitors), and sent by Heraclius, encircled – would escape. He repeated his prediction that there would be no invasion of the area in his lifetime, but that if there were no repentance, "this people will return with a strong army and will ravage the entire land up to the sea . . . [the hagiographer observed gravely] And that is what happened by the grace of God."[37]

Heraclius departed from long-time precedents and left Constantinople to participate in Priskos' one-year siege or blockade of the Persians at Caesarea. Since the reign of Theodosius I emperors had not really campaigned in person. Some had made a gesture of departing to campaign, but they had not really led armies in the field. It was Priskos who allegedly commented that it was inappropriate for the emperor to come to the camp. Heraclius broke with that long-established tradition by going to the front at Caesarea and again in leading troops soon thereafter against the Persians near Antioch.[38] There were long-term rhetorical and iconographic expectations that the emperor was leader of the empire's armies in war, but that had not been a reality for centuries. This was an important symbolic act, one that Heraclius' subsequent actions reinforced. Heraclius was not creating a new theoretical

---

[34] *Narratio de rebus Armeniae* 116 (42 Garitte).
[35] John of Nikiu, *Chron.* 106.2, 109.27 (167, 176 Charles; 551 Zotenberg). Michael the Syrian, *Chronique* II: 400 (Chabot); *Chron. 1234* (n. 24) 177–178; Theoph. *Chron.* 299 (De Boor); Flusin, *Saint Anastase le Perse* I: 82.
[36] *Vie de Théodore de Sykéôn* c. 153 (I: 123–124, II: 129 Festugière).
[37] *Vie de Théodore de Sykéôn* c. 153 (I: 123–124, II: 129 Festugière).
[38] Kaegi, *Byzantine Military Unrest* 37–39, soldiers became angry with Zeno for failing to go on campaign; Maurice's actions were abortive; but cf. Michael Whitby, "The Persian King at War," in *The Roman and Byzantine Army in the East* 256.

precedent; he was in fact the first emperor to act as soldier—emperor, that is to lead a significant campaign, since the reign of Theodosius I.[39]

But Priskos pretended to be sick, as he had already done, one recalls, when Heraclius besieged Phokas at Constantinople, and declined to meet him for an interview at Caesarea.[40] According to Sebeos, who uses very specific terminology, Heraclius left the siege in the hands of a *curator* (not a normal Armenian word, this is a borrowed technical term).[41] There is no other confirmation of this term for a deputy or even a *vicarius* of some kind. It could be a distortion of the term *curopalates*, but there is no independent confirmation that Priskos held that post. The term *curator* is in greater use in the late sixth and seventh centuries, however, and this may well be an example of an additional title or authority held by Priskos. His snub irritated Heraclius, who hid his pique when he returned to Constantinople early in 612. Shāhīn and his troops managed to escape from the encirclement in the summer. That infuriated Heraclius and others who had expected the surrender or annihilation of the Persians. In addition, the Persian breakout and burning of Caesarea embarrassed and humiliated Heraclius. It cast doubt on his own leadership and signified that the war would last a long time, that the Byzantines were not fighting well.[42] It was not surprising that Priskos suffered the consequences, even if he had not snubbed Heraclius. Heraclius summoned Priskos for the baptism of his son Heraclius II Constantine, suggesting that he invited him to become his son's godfather, on 5 December 612. He brought him before the senate and people, accused him of dishonoring the emperor, and had him tonsured:

> After assembling all the members of the senate and the remaining people of the city together with their bishop Sergios, Herakleios is reported to have asked them: "When a man insults an emperor, whom does he offend?" They answered: "He offends God who has appointed the emperor." And he urged Krispos [Priskos] also to express his honest opinion. The latter, not understanding the play that was being acted, said that a man convicted of such a daring deed should not even have

[39] No emperor had campaigned seriously in person, except for showing his presence on limited forays, since Theodosius I died in 395.

[40] Nikephoros, *Short History* 2 (37–41 Mango). Cf. Kaegi, *Byzantine Military Unrest* 145–148; on *curator* and military commands: Michel Kaplan, "Quelques aspects des maisons divines du Ve au IXe siècle," in Ἀφιέρωμα στόν Νίκο Σβορῶνο (n. 18) I: 77, 88–91. There had been a *curator* for the imperial patrimony in Cappadocia, p. 77; perhaps this was assigned to Philippikos to help him to pay substantial military expenses. For Sebeos, *History* 113, ch. 34 (66 Thomson) and commentary by J. Howard-Johnston on p. 203 for possible explanation of the presence of the term *curator*. I thank Peter Cowe for advice on *curator*.

[41] Sebeos, *History* 113, ch. 34 (66 Thomson); *Hist.* c. 24 (65 Macler); *Storia* c. 32 (87 Gugerotti).

[42] Sebeos, *History* 113, ch. 34 (66 Thomson); *Hist.* c. 24 (65 Macler); *Storia* c. 32 (87 Gugerotti); Kaegi, *Byzantine Military Unrest* 145–148.

the benefit of a lenient sentence. Then the emperor reminded him of his feigned illness at Caesarea, and how he thought of degrading the imperial dignity, and how he [Heraclius] had offered him the empire. And picking up a book, he struck him on the head and then he said: "You have not made a [good] son-in-law. How will you make a friend?" And straightaway he directed that his head should be shorn in the manner of a clergyman and that the bishop should recite the customary [prayers] over the act of tonsure.[43]

Patriarch Sergios presided at the tonsure of Priskos in a formal *ex officio* position.[44] Heraclius then convoked Priskos' guards as *bucellarii* and informed them of their new allegiances, now as his own soldiers, and gave them high preferences, but removed any motivation that they might have had to fight for their former commander.[45] It was a shrewd move. The accusation against Priskos probably helped to relieve Heraclius of the responsibility for the Persian breakout at Caesarea. Priskos became the scapegoat. Furthermore, his tonsure removed the last major internal threat to Heraclius from the past. Counts of the Excubitors, because of their extremely sensitive command of the imperial bodyguard, had been extremely powerful and sometimes dangerously ambitious commanders ever since the creation of the office in the late fifth century.[46] Heraclius neutralized that threat by appointing his reliable cousin Niketas, who had just come from Egypt, the successor to Priskos as Count of the Excubitors.[47] Priskos died a year later in the monastery of the Chora.

Heraclius followed his previous precedents in the public chastizing of Phokas (but in this case of Priskos, no mutilation or execution) and his cousin Niketas' procedures in Egypt of requiring public denunciations of Phokas and his partisans and public support for Heraclius. He resorted to similar public denunciations and humiliations of prominent opponents or scapegoats at critical points throughout his reign and life. It was a way of involving the public in imperial affairs, although there were perils in using such a technique.

Heraclius received Niketas with great ceremony on his arrival from Egypt. He appointed his own brother Theodore to the critical post of

---

[43] Nikephoros, *Short History* 2 (38–41 Mango).

[44] Van Dieten, *Geschichte der Patriarchen* 3.

[45] Cf. Haldon, *Byzantine Praetorians* 376.

[46] Kaegi, *Byzantine Military Unrest* 33–34, 123, 145, 157.

[47] Niketas: *Vie de Théodore de Sykéôn* c. 154 (I: 124–125, II: 130–131 Festugière); *Vie de Jean de Chypre* c. 10, 13, 52 in *Vie de Syméon le Fou et Vie de Jean de Chypre*, ed., trans. A.-J. Festugière (Paris, 1974) 356–357, 361–362, 402–403, 456–457, 462–463, 515–516; *PLRE* III: 940–942, s.v. "Nicetas 7"; Cyril Mango, "Deux études sur Byzance et la Perse Sassanide," *TM* 9 (1985) 105. For caution about references to Niketas: Cyril Mango, "A Byzantine Hagiographer at Work: Leontios of Neapolis," *Sitzungsberichte, Österreichische Akademie der Wissenschaften, Philosophisch-Historische Klasse* 432 (1984) 25–41.

curopalates,[48] which consolidated familial control over major official posts. This very high-ranking official controlled order within the palace, among other responsibilities.[49] By this device he tried to discourage opportunities for rebellion, and in any case, placed trustworthy persons in the most sensitive and powerful positions. The risk in such a policy, of course, was passing over persons better qualified for the positions, fanning frustration at blocked ambitions of capable persons, which could turn to violence or passive alienation within the elite. But it is significant that we hear of no more military conspiracies or rivalries with Heraclius in the east after 612 until very late in his reign. There were problems in Italy, but no documented ones in the east. So the suppression of Komentiolos and of Priskos, and the rapid suppression of conspiracies in Italy all contributed to consolidation of power and the suppression of internal dissent, even though the government suffered very embarrassing external military reverses that could have stimulated military unrest.

Until the fall of Priskos, Heraclius had not eliminated all of the old key personalities and rivalries within officers' ranks that prevailed in the reigns of Maurice and Phokas. After 612 he was free from these, but the Persian invasion did not free him to enjoy his victory over his domestic rivals. Others may well have still harbored enmities and a propensity to older alignments. He owed much to his own father, but he may have inherited some of his paternal enemies.

There were other interesting dimensions to Heraclius' handling of the Priskos episode, which had implications for internal military and political strife within his empire. His own father had a long and close relationship with Philippikos, as was evident back in 589 on the eve of the Monokarton mutiny. Perhaps through no fault of his own, but because he was affiliated with Philippikos, serving as his subordinate, he could not develop good relations with Priskos. It was natural for Heraclius the Younger to cultivate relations with Philippikos, bringing him out of his monastic exile, and first using him to try to negotiate with Phokas' brother Komentiolos in late 610. Heraclius probably sought his counsel on dealing with the Persians and with handling other internal military political problems. When Heraclius needed to worry about eliminating Priskos, it was natural again to turn to Philippikos, who probably had many ties with whomever survived of the former officials and officers of Emperor Maurice. He would have been motivated to support action against his old rival Priskos, and he probably knew many of Priskos' vulnerabilities. After purging Priskos it was again

[48] *PLRE* III: 1277–1278, s.v. "Theodorus 163."   [49] A. Kazhdan, "Kouropalates," *ODB* 1157.

natural and astute of Heraclius to appoint Philippikos to a major military post, again to draw on his experience and his prominence for aid in suppressing any more internal military dissidence and to use his help in trying to check the Persians. Philippikos probably was of some limited help to Heraclius for both purposes. But Heraclius had to turn to another generation, a younger one, to solve future problems. Heraclius' exploitation of his family's relations with Philippikos was an astute and intelligent use of networks of friendships and hostilities.

The desperate military situation in the east and southeast as well as the sensitive considerations of tightening internal security made it impossible for Heraclius to contemplate reinforcing beleaguered Byzantine forces in southern Spain.

Imperial commitments to Christianity were a prominent feature of governmental actions at Constantinople in that era: in 612–613 the cross was placed on top of the composite column that Phokas had erected. That was visual proof of the regime's devotional stance and piety. The cross received more celebration as the reign progressed.[50]

Hagiographical tradition reported that Heraclius and his cousin Niketas benefited from the assistance and supernatural assistance of St. Theodore of Sykeon, among others. Heraclius entrusted Constantinople to Niketas while he visited Priskos and his army at Caesarea during the Byzantine siege of the Persians. When Niketas was very ill during his visit to Constantinople, St. Theodore visited him, saying,

"Rise, my son, it is the time to take up your labors, our government needs you." Niketas uncovered his hands and showed them to the saint, saying, "When will these hands here be able to hold a bow?" Theodore answered him, "Do not lose hope, my son. God, who has created us from nothing, is much more capable of healing our illnesses." Placing his hand on him, he prayed over him, then he blessed a vial of oil and a cup of wine and ordered him to drink it and to swallow it. The blessed man remained in the oratory in that house and, as, thanks to his holy prayer, the very illustrious Niketas recovered much of his health, at the hour of the liturgy he had himself carried in a litter near the oratory. Finally he took a meal with Theodore and let him leave, not without having him accompanied by his slaves. The next day the slaves of the said very illustrious count came back to the saint giving thanks to God and announced that due to his prayers the illustrious count had mounted his horse. Eight hours later he went again on horseback to his villa at Cosmidion, he sent a messenger to the servant of Christ and welcomed him in that place. He banqueted with him and then, having recovered his strength, he went out to meet emperor [Heraclius] who was returning from Caesarea.[51]

[50] *Chronicon Paschale* 703 (155 Whitby).
[51] *Vie de Théodore de Sykéôn* c. 154 (I: 124–125, II: 130–131 Festugière).

Already there was, in the earliest years of Heraclius' reign, a ritual reception for greeting an emperor who now did, unlike his predecessors, leave his capital, go to the battlefield and thereby risk his own life and implicitly bring risk on his empire's weal, and then return. The imperial Book of Ceremonies would provide a number of formal descriptions of elaborate ceremonies from the ninth and tenth centuries for such receptions of a returning emperor, but the act had already begun in his reign, and would, in the course of real events of that reign, become a very common one.[52] We do not know whether Heraclius issued bulletins to his subjects while on that campaign, but he would do so in later years. Probably he did issue them even at that time.

Heraclius then, some time before the end of 612, met with St. Theodore of Sykeon and with Patriarch Sergios. He dined with the saint after the saint blessed him several times. But St. Theodore had closely allied himself with the Phokas family, so Heraclius may always have felt some reserve in his relations with him. Heraclius went to the palace of Sophianae, introduced his infant son Heraclius Constantine to him, for the saint's blessing, which was given.[53] For a combination of religious reasons, and for reassurance of the public that he was doing everything possible to place himself and his family on the right side of divine matters, Heraclius at that time of extreme crisis took the time to meet with, consult, and receive prominent blessings and support from an ascetic like St. Theodore, and of course also from Patriarch Sergios of Constantinople. It was essential to associate himself with the prestige and supernatural powers and legitimacy of a St. Theodore and the Patriarch.

On 22 January 613 Heraclius crowned his son Heraclius Constantine in the palace. They went to the hippodrome, where the senators gave him obeisance, and the circus factions hailed him. Young Heraclius Constantine was carried by the *cubicularius* Philaretos and both went with Heraclius to the Great Church. It was henceforth decreed that acts should be recorded in the name of both emperors, "In the reign of our most sacred lords and greatest benefactors . . . the eternal Augusti and emperors."[54]

Matters lurched dangerously in 613–614, both with respect to external and to internal conditions. No precise or even approximate figures exist on the numbers of troops who were available to Heraclius for resisting the

---

[52] Constantine VII, *De cerimoniis*, ed. J.J. Reiske (*CSHB*; Bonn, 1829) I: 495–508. Expanded edn. and commentary: *Three Treatises on Imperial Military Expeditions*, ed., trans. John Haldon (Vienna, 1990).

[53] *Vie de Théodore de Sykéôn* c. 155 (I: 125–126, II: 130–131 Festugière).

[54] *Chronicon Paschale* 704 (155–156 Whitby). G. Dagron, *Empereur et prêtre. Etude sur le césaropapisme byzantin* (Paris: Gallimard, 1996) 95–96.

Persians. The purges of those loyal to Phokas removed some from the ranks while disease and plague removed uncounted others. It was difficult to recruit, train, and pay the new and old soldiers. There was no respite. The *Strategikon* of Maurikios provides general information about the nature of organization and tactics immediately before Heraclius' and Phokas' reign, but many questions remain. Numbers cannot have remained constant in a rapidly changing and deteriorating military situation.[55]

The Persians penetrated Byzantine defenses on the eastern front in Mesopotamia–Syria in the sixth century, most notably in 540. A number of north Syrian cities had come to terms with the Persians instead of resisting to the death. But the embarrassing Persian penetration of 540 had been essentially an expeditionary raid, devastating to a few localities and those citizens who were slain or deported to Persia, but all in all, it had been swift and temporary. Perhaps some citizens initially expected nothing worse than what happened in 540, but it was much worse. The breakthrough in 610–611 was much more serious, for given the political crisis, the recent civil war, the Persians became an occupying, not merely a raiding, force. In 540, there had been no penetration or occupation of the Anatolian plateau until 611, while in 615/616 an expedition reached Chalcedon itself. And now there was no Belisarios. The *Strategikon* of Maurikios contains a section in Book 11 on how to fight the Persians, but most of that advice is tactical. It does not contain information on specific possible routes of invasion and how to block them. It is unclear just what older historical records on warfare with the Persians were available to, and were actually used by, Heraclius and his advisers in attempting to devise a defense against the Persians. Prokopios' account of the wars with the Persians in the reign of Justinian I might have been helpful, and to a lesser degree, although more recent, were the accounts of Agathias and Menander Protector. Once the Persians broke through, Prokopios' account of 540 would have been of some help, but as the Persians expanded their breakthrough, Byzantine strategists found themselves facing unprecedented military and political challenges. There were no standard formulae or measures to apply.

The Persian threat intensified as King Khusrau II, sensing opportunity and weakness in Byzantium, increased the stakes by sending more troops under General Shahrbarāz to invade Syria.[56] In the meantime he rejected

---

[55] Michael Whitby, "Recruitment in Roman Armies from Justinian I to Heraclius," in *States, Resources, Armies*, ed. Averil Cameron (Princeton: Darwin Press, 1995) 61–124, does not concentrate on the reign of Heraclius, see p. 61 n. 1. See John Haldon, *Warfare, State and Society in the Byzantine World* (London: UCL Press, 1999) 70–71, 99–101.

[56] Flusin, *Saint Anastase le Perse* II: 67–97.

diplomatic overtures to end hostilities now that Phokas, the original pretext for his invasion, was overthrown.

Heraclius recalled Philippikos from the monastery where he had lived since Phokas had forced him into monastic retirement and appointed him as *magister militum per Orientem*. After the embarrassing debacle at Caesarea, Philippikos led the Byzantine troops to make a military demonstration against the Persians. Whether more was intended than that is unclear.[57] He penetrated as far as Ayrarat, then camped near Valarshapat, then moved to the region of Nig, passing by Shirak and Vanand near Theodosiopolis (Erzurum), and returned to Byzantine territory, having avoided battle with the Persians.[58] Khusrau II raised troops to halt the Byzantines, after great loss of life, because of their hasty pursuit and lack of provisions, they subjugated the territory that Philippikos had traversed.[59]

Heraclius found no respite after seizing power from Phokas. He faced serious threats in Armenia and in northern Syria and upper Mesopotamia. First it had been necessary to assign troops to deal with the menace of Phokas' brother Komentiolos, who was still at large. Then Priskos and Heraclius struggled for mastery of the army, and Heraclius ultimately was victor, resulting in the tonsure of Priskos, who had never demonstrated any great ability to command. Heraclius did have time to change commanders, to replace Priskos, with the now divided command of the excubitors going to his cousin Niketas, and initially command of the armies in the east (*magister militum per Orientem*?) to Maurice's old general Philippikos, the former rival of Priskos. The Persians had now tested Heraclius and found him to be vulnerable. He now had to find other commanders. He could no longer draw on the old roster of commanders. Those from the era of Maurice were too old, those from the era of Phokas were purged or dead or untrustworthy. These factors encouraged Heraclius to assume direct command. Although he used his brother Theodore, he could not give him full responsibility. Probably unwilling to raise others, which was risky for reasons of internal security, he elected to command himself.

Heraclius sought to check the Persians near Antioch. During Lent 613, he passed the monastery of St. Theodore of Sykeon, whom he hastily visited for his blessing en route to fight the Persians near Antioch. His cousin Niketas aided him there in fighting the Persians. The saint met him at the threshold of the church. After they mutually embraced, the saint took him

[57] Baynes, "Military Operations," *United Services Magazine* 47 (1913) 195–196.
[58] Flusin, *Saint Anastase le Perse* 87–91.
[59] Sebeos, *History* 114, ch. 34 (67 Thomson); *Storia* c. 32 (87–88 Gugerotti).

into the church, prayed to God for him, blessed him with gifts of flour, apples, wine, and invited him to dinner:

> But the emperor, by reason of his great haste refused to dine or even to accept the gifts offered to him, saying, "Keep them for me, father, and pray for me, I shall pass by on my return, and when I shall take them, I shall stay as long as it pleases you, I shall enjoy your blessings and your very holy prayers in great leisure." . . . Having received his recommendation to God from the saint, he left for the city of Antioch, where he engaged in struggle against the Persians, with the aid of the Patrician and Count Niketas. The blessed [saint] was sad that he left the gifts of his benediction there. He said, "If he had taken them, it would have been a proof of victory and he would return with joy. The fact that he left them is a sign of our defeat, and if he had risen and received the blessing of the saints, that misfortune would not have reached him and as far as us."[60]

But reportedly Theodore foretold one good item for Heraclius: "'Know my son George [author of his *vita*], that by a divine command this emperor will live a long time: he will reign thirty years.' Which happened according to his prediction" [proof that the author of the *vita* wrote this after the death of Heraclius in 641].[61] St. Theodore died on 22 April 613. Another explanation is that Heraclius harbored reservations about becoming too close to St. Theodore, who had maintained very close ties with the family of Phokas.

Not long afterwards Heraclius and Patriarch Sergios resolved to bring St. Theodore's remains to Constantinople to protect them from any possible Persian raid and despoiling, and, not a small consideration, to add another supernatural protection to Constantinople.[62] An elaborate ceremony of reception of the saint's remains was accomplished by the Patriarch, who always enjoyed a close association with him. Heraclius himself knelt before the body in the presence of the senate. Heraclius truly wished to associate the prestige and powers of St. Theodore with himself, his family, his capital, and his empire. Heraclius' predecessor Phokas had similarly tried, together with members of his family, to receive the blessings, legitimacy, and prestige of the saint.

We cannot, because of the inadequate sources, trace the details of the fighting near Antioch, but it resulted in a serious Byzantine defeat. In

---

[60] *Vie de Théodore de Sykéôn* c. 166 (I: 153–154, II: 157–158 Festugière).
[61] *Vie de Théodore de Sykéôn* c. 154 (I 154, II 158 Festugière).
[62] *Chron. 1234* (n. 24) 177; Theoph. *Chron.* A.M. 6102 (299 De Boor). See on the translation of the body of St. Theodore to Constantinople: C. Kirch, "Encomium in S. Theodorum Siceotam," c. 44–46, *AB* 20 (1901) 268–269; cf. A. Pertusi, in *La Persia nel Medioevo* (Accademia Nazionale dei Lincei, Problemi Attuali di Scienza e di Cultura, Quaderno 160, Atti del Convegno internazionale sul tema: La Persia nel Medioevo; Rome: Accademia Nazionale dei Lincei, 1971) 618, for dating the event to an order by Heraclius after the Persian armies reached Chalcedon.

the battle Heraclius and his cousin Niketas suffered defeat at the hands of Shāhīn. Antioch and the surrounding countryside fell.[63] Among the Byzantine soldiers there was Tychikos, who was wounded, but later became the teacher of Ananias of Shirak in the 620s.[64] Broader numbers of casualties are unknown. The outcome was not merely the loss of Antioch and vicinity, but also the severing of communications between Constantinople and Byzantine Anatolia on the one hand, and with Byzantine Syria, Palestine, and Egypt on the other. The Persians deported many Antiochenes after systematically looting the city, as they had previously done elsewhere in Byzantine Mesopotamia. Their slaying of the Patriarch increased bitterness.[65] Heraclius and his own brother Theodore commanded troops defending the area immediately north of Antioch. In that battle, after initial Byzantine gains, the Persians routed them, inflicted serious losses, captured Tarsos and, in effect, the Cilician plain.[66]

Now the empire was cut into two sections. Levantine riots between Jews and Christians late in the reign of Phokas were not the cause of the breakdown of Byzantine resistance to the Persians, but probably left divisive scars. There were reports that the Persians had the help of Jews to capture certain Levantine cities; allegedly they had planned to slay Christians in Mesopotamian cities that the Persians had overrun, but were discovered and prevented from doing so. These stories involved great exaggerations and hysteria.[67] Local magnates probably contributed funds and efforts to fortify towns in northern Syria, such as Anasartha, against the Sasanians in the reign of Phokas and probably, although unattested, at the start of Heraclius' reign, but they could not stem the Persian advance.[68] There was no diehard resistance in upper Mesopotamia or northern Syria to the Persians. Even though local elites sought to construct defensive fortifications, they or their spokesmen generally, with the important exception of Jerusalem, sought to spare themselves and their native towns, and accordingly usually agreed to terms with the Persians.

Niketas continued to command Byzantine forces in Syria and Palestine who were attempting to resist the Persians. Cut off, Apamaea, Emesa, and

---

[63] Sebeos, *History* 114–15, ch. 34 (68 Thomson); *Storia* c. 32 (88 Gugerotti).

[64] Paul Lemerle, "Note sur les données historiques de l'Autobiographie d'Anania de Shirak," *REArm*, n.s. 1 (1964) 195–202.

[65] Agapios, *Kitāb al-Unvān*, *PO* 8: 450 Vasiliev.

[66] Sebeos, *History* 115, ch. 34 (68 Thomson); *Storia* c. 32 (88 Gugerotti).

[67] Eutychios, *Hist.* c. 29 (*CSCO* Scriptores Arabici 121–122, 128–129 = 101–102, 108–109 trans. Breydy = 308–309 Pirone). Agapios, *Kitāb al-Unvān*, *PO* 8: 449 Vasiliev.

[68] Landowners erect fortifications in the Chalkis region: Frank Trombley, "War and Society in Rural Syria c. 502–613 A.D.: Observations on the Epigraphy," *BMGS* 21 (1997) 154–209, esp. 190–191. But see J. Liebeschuetz, *Decline and Fall of the Roman City* (Oxford, 2001) 349–350, 403.

then Damascus fell later in 613, opening the way for Persian penetration further south. The Persians under General Shahrbarāz won a victory over the Byzantines near Adhri'āt (modern Deraa); the particulars are unclear, but it left a permanent resonance among the nascent Arabs, and reportedly is the occasion for the Qur'ānic sūrat al-Rūm.[69] At some point, Niketas won some truce or limited victory over the Persians near Emesa (modern Ḥimṣ), probably in 614; in that battle both sides suffered heavy casualties; reportedly 20,000 fell.[70] In commemoration of that victory, or to transform that action into some kind of victory amid so many serious defeats, Heraclius in 614 erected an equestrian statue to Niketas: "The Emperor, the Army, the cities, and the People erected the statue of Niketas, bold in war, for his great exploits in slaying the Persians."[71] But Caesarea Maritima fell to the Persians, submitting on terms, as did Arsūf and Tiberias. Jerusalem refused to submit to Shahrbarāz, who stormed it after a twenty-one day siege, probably in 614, possibly on 17 or 20 May.[72] The loss of life among armed defenders and civilians was heavy, although apologetical motives may have exaggerated casualties. About 57,000 or even 66,500 inhabitants were allegedly slain, many of them being those who had attempted to take refuge in caves and other hiding places. Another 35,000 were taken prisoner and, with Patriarch Zacharias, were taken away to Persia, along with the presumed relic of the True Cross.[73] The event became an object of liturgical commemoration.[74]

---

[69] *Qur'ān* 30. 1–3; Ḥusayn ibn Muḥammad al-Diyārbakrī, *Ta'rīkh al-khāmis fī aḥwāl anfas nafīs* 1.298.

[70] Agapios, *Kitāb al-Unvān, PO* 8: 450; Ps.-Isidore, *Continuationes* (*MGH* AA 11) 335; Conybeare, *EHR* 25 (1910) 503, or this putative victory may have permitted a temporary search for peace terms: Strategios, *La prise de Jérusalem par les Perses en 614* 5.3–34 (8–11 Garitte). Epigrams: Cyril Mango, "Epigrammes honorifiques, statues et portraits à Byzance," in 'Αφιέρωμα στόν Νίκο Σβορῶνο, ed. Kremmydas *et al.* (n. 18) I: 30–31.

[71] *Greek Anthology* 16.46 (trans. W.R. Paton, Loeb Classical Library, V: 184–185); cf. 16.47 (Loeb V: 186–187): "The Green Faction erected, because of his merits, the statue of Nicetas the great in war, the fearless leader." This latter inscription could refer to Niketas' victories in the civil war against Phocas and Bonosos, not necessarily including any reference to his record against the Persians. The continuation of the chronicle of Isidore of Seville probably has an eastern source: "Nicetaque magister militiae per heremi deserta cum nimio labore Aegyptum pervenit ac nimia virtute et strenuitate adgressus Persis acie caesis Aegyptum, Syriam, Arabiam Iudaeam et Mesopotamiam provincias optimae dimicatione imperii restauravit" (Ps.-Isidore, *Continuationes* (*MGH* AA 11) 335).

[72] Sebeos, *Hist.* ch. 34, 115–116 (69, 207 Thomson). Speck, *Das geteilte Dossier* 66–74. Eutychios, *Hist.* c. 27 (Arabic 98–99, trans. 118–119 Breydy = 306–307 Pirone). *Le Calendrier Palestino-Géorgien du Sinaiticus 34 (Xe siècle)* 67, 226–227, 229 Garitte. Robert Schick, *The Christian Communities of Palestine from Byzantine to Islamic Rule* (Princeton: Darwin Press, 1995) 33–39; Flusin, *Saint Anastase le Perse* II: 156.

[73] Cyril Mango, "The Temple Mount, AD 614–638," *Bayt al-Maqdis. 'Abd al-Malik's Jerusalem,* ed. Julian Raby and Jeremy Johns (Oxford: Oxford University Press, 1992) 1–16, esp. 3–4.

[74] *Le Calendrier Palestino-Géorgien* 67, 226–227, 229 Garitte.

The fall of Jerusalem shocked contemporaries.[75] Sophronios wrote a moving threnody, "Children of the blessed Christians, come to groan for Jerusalem on its raised hills! Weep for the generations of holy Christians, for holy Jerusalem destroyed! Blessed Christ, You who are King, show your anger against the Medes, because they have destroyed the city that was sweet to you. The object of the vows of the entire world has perished. The Heavenly city has suffered a deplorable fate." Sophronios again lamented, "The wave of tears that flow from my eyes are insufficient for such a great funeral. The groaning of my heart is a slight thing for such a cruel sadness." "Brandishing the murderous sword, he slew the multitude of mortals: holy citizens, pure, the old with white hair, children, women. Accomplishing his cruel deed, he looted the Holy City, and with a burning flame, he touched the Holy Places of Christ."[76] The contemporary author of the *Chronicon Paschale* records, "we suffered a calamity which deserves unceasing lamentations."[77] Strategios also bewailed the storming and ravages, "I weep and bemoan the holy city and the glorious churches and the sacred altars and the sanctified priests and the faithful people who were slain without mercy . . ."[78] Again, "In that time, my beloved brothers, great sadness and unspeakable grief befell all Christians in the world, because the chosen and renowned royal city was delivered to devastation, because the holy places and the refuge of all the faithful was delivered to fire, and the Christian people were delivered to captivity and death."[79] It also raised the issue of divine wrath. It greatly embarrassed the Heraclian government and probably raised serious doubts among some of its subjects concerning not merely the conduct of the war, but the genuine conduct and piety of imperial leaders and their advisers and official theology: was something wrong? It led to scapegoating of Jews as collaborators with the Persians, and allegedly involved in treachery against the empire and the Christians. The atmosphere became envenomed. There were Jewish eschatological expectations as well.[80] There were repeated accusations that Jews

---

[75] Schick, *Christian Communities of Palestine* 38–39.
[76] Sophronios quoted in A. Couret, "La prise de Jérusalem par les Perses," *Revue de l'Orient Chrétien,* ser. 1, vol. 2 (1897) 136, 139–140, also poetry on 133–135.
[77] *Chronicon Paschale* 704 (156 Whitby).   [78] Strategios, *Prise de Jérusalem* 1.16.
[79] *Prise de Jérusalem* 15.7 (32 Garitte).
[80] Brannon Wheeler, "Imagining the Sasanian Capture of Jerusalem," *OCP* 57 (1991) 69–85; David Olster, *Roman Defeat, Christian Apologetic and the Literary Construction of the Jew* (Philadelphia: University of Pennsylvania Press, 1994). *Travaux et Mémoires* 11 (1991) contains many papers on Byzantine–Jewish relations and polemics, esp. Gilbert Dagron and Vincent Déroche, "Juifs et chrétiens dans l'Orient du VIIe siècle," 17–46; and Déroche, "La polémique anti-Judaïque au VIe et au VIIe siècle. Un mémento inédit, *Les kephalaia*," 275–311.

betrayed localities in Jerusalem to the Persians and themselves participated in the slaughter of Christians.[81] There is no way to check the veracity of these stories.[82] Archaeological excavations have uncovered human remains that may date to the Sasanian storming of Jerusalem.[83] Jews probably were unhappy with imperial policies, especially with increasing restrictions and the loss of former rights, a process that had been intensifying since the early fourth century.

Patriarch Zacharias was probably arrested by Persians outside the city of Jerusalem, brought by the Porta Probaticae, and then marched out with the relic of the True Cross through that same gate.[84] The fall of Syria and Palestine was not only a psychological shock, especially given that fire-worshipping Zoroastrians and their alleged Jewish allies had triumphed, but with them the empire also lost huge tax revenues, both agricultural and commercial, and valuable skilled populations. That increased the empire's internal crisis and made it more difficult to sustain the cost of the war. The sources probably exaggerate the depredations of the Persians.[85]

The flight of many refugees from Palestine and Syria to Egypt and especially to Alexandria strained the church's resources and added to the psychological distress of the broader population in and around Alexandria.[86] In the desperate search for funds, Niketas had planned to manage the local market for the profit of the government, but he met opposition from his ritual brother, Patriarch John the Almsgiver.[87] But the two became reconciled. The Alexandrian church had amassed an unprecedented amount of financial wealth by 610: 576,000 gold solidi, a sum that the contemporary church

[81] *Prise de Jérusalem* 10, 17–18 Garitte; Strategios, *Expugnationis Hierosolymae A.D. 614 Recensiones Arabicae,* ed. Gérard Garitte (*CSCO,* Scriptores Arabici, 26–29; Louvain, 1973–1974) 24. 9–10 (I: 121–124 Garitte); Eutychios, *Hist.* (129 text, 109 trans. Breydy). Olster, *Roman Defeat* 60, 80; A. Sharf, "Byzantine Jewry in the Seventh Century," *BZ* 48 (1955) 103–115; J. Starr, "Byzantine Jewry on the Eve of the Arab Conquest," *Journal of the Palestine Oriental Society* 15 (1935) 280–293; Schick, *Christian Communities of Palestine* 26–31.

[82] P. Speck, "Die Predigt des Strategios," in his *Beiträge zum Thema Byzantinische Feindseligkeit gegen die Juden* (Bonn: Habelt, 1997) 37–129, is skeptical of such accounts.

[83] Possible evidence for slaughter in 614: Rony Reich, "The Ancient Burial Ground in the Mamilla Neighborhood, Jerusalem," in *Ancient Jerusalem Revealed,* ed. Hillel Geva (Jerusalem: Israel Exploration Society, 1994) 111–118; Aren Maier and Matthew Ponting, "An Archaeological and Archaeometallurgical Study of a Late Byzantine/Early Arab Weapons Hoard from Mamilla, Jerusalem," in *New Studies on Jerusalem. Proceedings of the Second Conference, November 28th, 1996,* ed. Avraham Faust (Jerusalem: Bar-Ilan University, 1996) 45–52.

[84] Strategios in *Prise de Jérusalem* 22–23 (trans. Garitte); 16–17 (Arab edn.); X 1–9 (Georgian edn., 17–18 trans. Garitte).

[85] Agostino Pertusi, "La Persia nelle fonti bizantine del secolo VII," in *La Persia nel Medioevo* (n. 62) 605–632.

[86] Leontios, *Vie de Jean de Chypre* 11 (442, 458 Festugière); anonymous 6, 9, 12 (324, 325–326, 327 Festugière).

[87] *Vie de Jean de Chypre* 13 (462 Festugière).

in Rome probably did not possess.[88] This story associates the Heraclian family with the prestige and holiness of the saint, and provides a hagiographic picture of the ideal relationship of saint and secular ruler or surrogate in the age of Heraclius. Several anecdotes exist about Niketas and John. A symptom of the government's frantic search for funds was an action of Patrician Niketas, who had been so important in electing John Patriarch of Alexandria. Niketas, having observed the generosity of John with alms, came to him and stated, "The empire is hard pressed and needs funds. Instead of heedlessly spending your revenues, give them to the empire for the public treasury."[89] John declined to hand over the funds, but indicated the location of the church treasury, and Niketas' *domestikoi* and soldiers took it away. When he realized that the Patriarch was receiving more funds from Africa in pots marked "honey," he asked forgiveness from the Patriarch, who gave it to him. This anecdote is typical of several later incidents in the reign of Heraclius, in which the government, or its officials, acting with or without authorization from central authorities, because of its urgent need for funds, sought to lay its hands on ecclesiastical wealth for the sake of the state. This incident involving John and Niketas cannot be dated exactly, but probably occurred after the beginning of the great Persian victories in Syria, around 613 or 614.[90] John also, distressed by reports of the destruction at Jerusalem, reportedly gave funds to Patriarch Modestos for reconstruction, but this makes no chronological sense; probably what he did in fact was provide funds for philanthropic assistance to the needy in Palestine in the wake of the Persian invasion.[91]

Patriarch John also gave funds to redeem captives of the "Midianites," whose identity is uncertain, but may well indicate chaos in the regions east of the Dead Sea (Biblical Midian), from which Arab tribesmen raided southern Palestine.[92] He sent his bishop Theodore with Anastasios, the superior of the monastery of St. Anthony, and Gregory, Bishop of Rhinokoloura (modern Al-'Arīsh), to redeem "numerous prisoners, men and women," for a large sum of gold. This is anticipatory of the chaos in the

---

[88] Michael Hendy, "Economy and State in Late Rome and Early Byzantium," in *The Economy, Fiscal Administration and Coinage of Byzantium* (Northampton: Variorum, 1989) I: 12.

[89] Leontios, *Vie de Jean de Chypre* 10 (356, 456–457 Festugière).

[90] Leontios of Neapolis probably inserted these stories in his narrative to attempt to persuade Heraclius or, more likely, Constantine III and his wife Gregoria, the daughter of Niketas, to avoid more seizures of ecclesiastical plate and other wealth in the great fiscal and military emergency at the death of Heraclius in 641. Kaegi, "Egypt on the Eve of the Muslim Conquest" 51, 57–58.

[91] Leontios, *Vie de Jean de Chypre* 18 (468–469 Festugière). See Mango, "The Temple Mount" 5.

[92] Anonymous, *Vie de Jean de Chypre* 10 (326 Festugière). Other indications of marauding Arabs in the south of Palestine: "S. Georgii Chozebitae Vita," *AB* 7 (1888) 129, 134. *Antiochi Monachi Epistola ad Eustathium*, PG 89: 1425, 1424. Schick, *Christian Communities of Palestine* 24–26, 31–33.

same region in the early 630s at the time of the Muslim conquests.[93] Already Arabs erupted in more or less the very region, apparently, where the first Muslim conquests would take place in the early 630s.[94] That is why the Bishop of Rhinokoloura was involved in attempting to ransom captives. There had been troubles with Arabs overrunning and plundering parts of Palestine early in the sixth century.[95] It indicates, not surprisingly, that some Arabs took advantage of Byzantine defeats at the hands of Persians, and Byzantine preoccupation with resisting the Persians, to engage in raiding, plundering, and enslavement of civilians in settled areas, apparently especially in southern Palestine. Such experiences anticipated the future, and probably whetted some Arab appetites, and increased apprehension in settled and urbanized areas of Palestine and Syria.

Religious ceremony continued to be important in Heraclius' reign.

A chant was introduced after the "Let it be directed" at the moment when the presanctified gifts are brought to the altar from the sacristy after the priest has said "In accordance with the gift of your Christ," the congregation at once begins, "Now the powers of the heavens are invisibly worshipping with us: for behold, the king of glory enters in. Behold, the mystic and perfect sacrifice is being escorted. In faith and in fear let us approach, so that we may become partakers in eternal life. Alleluia."[96]

In an era of enormous concern about assuring proximity to the divine, for protection against invasion and enemy threats, the introduction of this liturgical change may have been intended to do the maximum to assure the presence of divine protection and support. It is another case of efforts to change public ceremony to do whatever was possible to bring divine aid.

Patriarch John the Almsgiver's anonymous biographer noted, "At the news that the entire empire had been totally devastated by the Persians, he [John] wished to go to the emperor and support the cause of peace. But when he gave a speech of farewell and addressed it to everybody, the

---

[93] Kaegi, *BEIC* 56–57, 91–94.

[94] H. Delehaye, "Une vie inédite de Saint Jean l'Aumônier," *AB* 45 (1927) 23–24; E. Lappa-Zizicas, "Un épitomé inédit de la vie de S. Jean l'Aumônier," *AB* 88 (1970) 276. Dawes and Baynes' commentary on their English translation of the passage (*Three Byzantine Saints* (Oxford: Blackwell, 1948) 265) referred to Midian, but not to Arabs, which may explain why many scholars overlooked this passage. Sinai problems: Andreas Reichert, "Eine Fluchtberg christlicher Sarazenen bei Pharan im Südsinai. Archäologische Anmerkungen zu einer hagiographischen Anekdote des Anastasios Sinaites," in *Themelia: Spätantike und koptologische Studien Peter Grossmann zum 65. Geburtstag*, ed. Martin Krause, S. Schaten (Sprachen und Kulturen des christlichen Orients, 3; Wiesbaden: Reichert Verlag, 1998) 273–282.

[95] Irfan Shahid, *Byzantium and the Arabs in the Sixth Century* (Washington: Dumbarton Oaks, 1995) I: 182–193, offers the soundest interpretation of the evidence from the panegyrics of Chorikios of Gaza.

[96] *Chronicon Paschale* 705 (158 Whitby).

people of the city did not allow him to leave."[97] This report indicates the kinds of pressures that bore on Heraclius while the Persian military threat increased.

It was Shahrbarāz who overran Syria, Palestine, and Egypt.[98] But it was another prominent Persian general, Shāhīn, who, after the fall of Jerusalem, penetrated with a Persian army as far as Chalcedon. Philippikos, by making a diversionary raid into Persia, contributed to Shāhīn's lifting of the siege in unsuccessful pursuit of Philippikos. Anastasios the Persian, later to become sanctified, participated in that expedition and then deserted while the Persian army was in the east.[99] But Philippikos became ill, had to give up his command, and then died, depriving Heraclius of even more of his old pool of experienced military leadership.

In 614, or more probably 615, a serious formal effort was made, in the name of the Roman (i.e. Byzantine) senate and people, to send a letter to Khusrau II seeking a negotiated settlement. Probably it was not written in the name of Heraclius, because Khusrau II refused to recognize him as the avenger of Maurice and as the rightful imperial successor. In a constitutional sense, then, to the extent that there could be any hope for reception of a letter, it had to be presented not by envoys of the emperor, but by two ex-consuls, the Pretorian Prefect Olympios and the Prefect of the City Leontios, as well as by the *synkellos* Anastasios, who served as the envoys. The nominal excuse for the absence of earlier embassies was civil war and war between Persia and Byzantium. Khusrau II arrested and imprisoned them.[100] It was a ploy to avoid the seemingly intractable issues of protocol that had probably blocked previous attempts to negotiate: Persian refusal to accept an envoy sent in the name of an emperor whom the Persians refused to recognize as legitimate. In an antiquarian and vestigial sense, Roman authority even in the seventh century, as previously in the Roman principate, derived formally from the senate and the people. So there probably was a hope that an embassy representing a legitimating political entity might receive a hearing and have the capacity to act to negotiate terms of peace and diplomatic recognition. It is, of course, unlikely that Khusrau II and his advisers possessed specialists on Roman constitutional matters or really cared about them. They were winning on all fronts and probably saw no reason to halt their armies when they were triumphing.

[97] Anonymous, *Vie de Jean de Chypre* 10 (328 Festugière).
[98] Todd M. Hickey, "Observations on the Sasanian Invasion and Occupation of Egypt" (1992 University of Chicago Department of History seminar paper, now under revision for publication); Hickey, "Who Really Led the Sasanian Invasion of Egypt?," *AABSC* 19 (Princeton University, 1993) 3.
[99] Flusin, *Saint Anastase le Perse* 8 (I: 48–49, II: 87–91 Flusin).
[100] *Chronicon Paschale* 707 (160–161 Whitby).

Allegedly this embassy was encouraged by Shāhīn, who had led an expedition as far as Chalcedon, opposite Constantinople.[101] Heraclius and Shāhīn conferred about possible peace terms after Shāhīn requested such a meeting. Before meeting with Shāhīn, Heraclius significantly had consulted with the Patriarch Sergios, and other important officials.[102] Shāhīn purportedly prostrated himself to Heraclius, which is not out of the question, for he very likely would have been expected to show an emperor some appropriate courtesies. Heraclius crossed the straits, accompanied by a retinue. Shāhīn's speech, in which he counseled in favor of a detente between the two powers of Byzantium and Persia, is noteworthy and prophetic:

> This concord should be as profound as our empires are great; for we know that no other state will ever appear to rival these our empires...if...[you] take up mutual hostility and enmity instead, you will become responsible for many wars (a discordant and hateful action), with the natural result that you will undergo much sweat and toil, suffer many casualties, and expend an enormous amount of money: in a word, the effect of the war will be to bring you great distress.[103]

Shāhīn claimed that he lacked the ability to make terms, but encouraged Heraclius to send an embassy to Khusrau II.[104] Similar themes of the desirability of concord between the two powers exist in earlier speeches, such as those of Khusrau II when he sought the protection and assistance of Emperor Maurice, if we can believe Theophylact Simocatta, who may simply be inventing sentiments of the era of Heraclius.[105] Shāhīn retired to Persia, having devastated much of Anatolia. He brought Heraclius' response to Khusrau II, together with Byzantine envoys.

The letter requests that Khusrau II forgive the failure to engage in written communications earlier to resolve differences, explaining:

> But Phokas who plotted against the Roman state dissolved this arrangement: for after secretly corrupting the Roman army in Thrace, he suddenly attacked our

---

[101] Flusin, *Saint Anastase le Perse* II: 90–93, Acta 8 (I: 48–49 Flusin). Theoph. *Chron.* A.M. 6107–6108 (301 De Boor).

[102] *Chronicon Paschale* 707. Van Dieten, *Geschichte der Patriarchen* 7.

[103] Nikephoros, *Short History* 6 (46–47 Mango).

[104] Nikephoros, *Short History* 6–7 (44–47 Mango). It is incorrect to believe that the Persians penetrated as far as Carthage, because there is no archaeological, epigraphic, or other literary evidence to confirm this late historical reference, as D. Pringle, *Defence of Byzantine Africa* 378–379 n. 13, rightly concludes, *contra* Speck, *Das geteilte Dossier* 75–77. Persistent operations of the Carthage mint in the 620s decisively undermine Speck's hypothesis. Vasiliev clearly read Khalkedonia and not Karkhedonia in the text of Agapios, *Kitāb al-Unvān*, *PO* 8: 451; see for similar reading, Michael the Syrian, *Chronique* 11.1 (II: 401 Chabot). Agapios, Michael the Syrian, and Theophanes draw on a common source. Carthage must be rejected.

[105] Theophylact Simocatta, *Hist.* 4.11.2–9, 4.13.6–9, 4.13.13; Michael Whitby, *The Emperor Maurice and His Historian* (Oxford: Clarendon Press, 1988) 300, 327.

imperial city and killed Maurice who piously ruled over us, and his wife, and in addition his children, relatives, and not a few of the officials. And he was not satisfied with his accomplishment of such great evils, but he did not even render the honor that was appropriate to your superabundant clemency, so that thereafter, incited by our faults, you brought the affairs of the Roman state to this great diminution.[106]

The letter explains that Heraclius was unable because of disturbance and internecine strife to "do what ought to have been done, to present by means of an embassy the honor that was owed to the superabundant might of your serenity." As for Shāhīn, he claimed that he did not have the authority to engage in discussions, but he promised that envoys would be received unharmed and would be able to return. So the letter petitions that the envoys be received by Khusrau and return shortly,

securing for us the peace which is pleasing to God and appropriate to your peace-loving Might. We beg too of your clemency to consider Heraclius, our most pious emperor, as a true son, who is eager to perform the service of your serenity in all things. For if you do this, you will procure a two-fold glory for yourselves, respect of your valor in war and in respect of your gift of peace. And hereafter we shall be in enjoyment of tranquillity through your gifts, which will be remembered for ever, receiving an opportunity to offer prayers to God for your long-lasting prosperity and keeping your benefaction free from oblivion for the eternal duration of the Roman state.[107]

This letter was at some point released to the public, perhaps to persuade it that the government had done the maximum to try to secure peace from the Persians, who had rejected it. Its contents probably resembled those that earlier embassies had unsuccessfully attempted to transmit to Khusrau II. Heraclius' diplomatic initiative failed miserably, because Khusrau II assumed that his armies were winning, that Byzantium's were collapsing, so there was no reason to settle. He rejected Heraclius' ambassadors.[108] The source of Theophanes may be correct, that Khusrau II hoped "to seize the Roman Empire completely."[109] Shahrbarāz had "devastated the entire oriental part of the empire."[110] Sebeos provides the text of an arrogant and haughty response from Khusrau II to Heraclius.[111] But Heraclius was, at a terrible price, learning how to use diplomatic and informal contacts to probe his opponents for vulnerabilities. Heraclius did in fact seek a negotiated

[106] *Chronicon Paschale* 707 (160 Whitby).   [107] *Chronicon Paschale* 709 (161–162 Whitby).
[108] Michael the Syrian, *Chronique* 11.1 (II: 400 Chabot); Theoph. *Chron.* A.M. 6105, 6109 (300–301 De Boor; 430, 433 Mango-Scott), although several embassies are suggested, perhaps more than existed.
[109] Theoph. *Chron.* A.M. 6105, 6109 (300, 301 De Boor).
[110] Nikephoros, *Short History* 6 (44–45 Mango).
[111] Sebeos, *History* 123, ch. 38 (79–80 Thomson); *Storia* c. 36 (95 Gugerotti). Probably the same overture as in Theophanes, *Chron.* A.M. 6105 (300 De Boor).

end to hostilities. But the first problem was gaining Persian recognition of his right to be emperor at all, which King Khusrau II did not concede.[112]

614 was a year of serious defeats for Byzantium. The greatest loss was Jerusalem. But the important city of Salona on the Dalmatian coast also fell in 614 or 615.[113] Sources such as John of Nikiu speak of the devastation of Illyricum, and the enslavement of its inhabitants, with only Thessalonica surviving.[114] Devastation is the term most commonly applied to conditions that inhabitants suffered at the hands of the Persians: "they plundered them and left not a soldier surviving at that epoch."[115] Some of that was an exaggeration, for many did survive in Palestine and Syria and did not suffer the fate of the inhabitants of Jerusalem, which was an exceptional case, but there was much destruction. A major earthquake struck Ephesus in 614,[116] which not only inflicted physical damage, but may also have raised apprehensions about divine wrath and possible portents of more terrible events to come.

The ability of Heraclius' cousin Niketas as a general is moot. His skills in capturing Egypt from Bonosos and Phokas appear to have been more political than military. He negotiated with local Egyptian political and military leaders, the people and the ecclesiastical leadership to win their support. Those were valuable skills. He appears to have won and retained popular confidence, even though some of his relations with his ritual brother Patriarch John of Alexandria, involving matters of money, became testy at times. But John and Niketas maintained a close positive relationship until the death of the Patriarch. What is unclear is exactly what he did after he gained control of Egypt, whether he led Heraclian forces in any invasion of Syria, to wrest it from Phokas. Was it he who captured Alexandretta (Alexandria ad Issum), and possibly also Cyprus, and opened mints and struck coins in the name of Heraclius in 610? Except for references in the Life of St. Theodore of Sykeon, we would not know for certain that he was in Constantinople in 612, well before Heraclius summoned and removed Priskos from command of the excubitors. Where did he accomplish any even ephemeral victories over the Persians? Exactly how did he communicate with Heraclius and Heraclius' brother Theodore after the Persians won a major victory near Antioch? (By boat, one would guess, however awkward that was.) Presumably Heraclius maintained his

---

[112] Evident from the continuation of hostilities and Sebeos' account of Khusrau's arrest of the Byzantine envoys. Whether there was ever any genuine possibility of a negotiated settlement is moot.

[113] R.-J. Lilie, "Kaiser Herakleios und die Ansiedlung der Serben," *Süd-Ost Forschungen* 44 (1985) 34, for the date.

[114] John of Nikiu, *Chron.* 109.18 (175–176 Charles).   [115] John of Nikiu, *Chron.* 109.21 (176 Charles).

[116] C. Foss, *Ephesus After Antiquity* (Cambridge: Cambridge University Press, 1979) 103.

trust in his cousin and did not wish to allow anyone else to exercise that command. How many troops did he command after the Persians had triumphed at Antioch? What did he do to stiffen resistance against the Persians in Palestine and on the Lebanese coast?

There are many questions concerning Niketas and Heraclius, and their efforts to defend Egypt against the Persians. How did Niketas try to prepare the defenses of Egypt? Did he draw on his experience with defeating Bonosos and Phokas in trying to devise such a defense? How good was his intelligence about the intentions and the capacities of the Persians? What was his opinion of Egyptians as soldiers? Did he try to encourage and train Egyptians to defend themselves against the Persians? What impressions of Egypt did he pass on to Heraclius, who himself never personally visited Egypt? Did Niketas draw special conclusions about the possible role of Africa and Africa's military units in fighting the Persians from his own campaigning from Africa in accomplishing the overthrow of Bonosos and the Phokas regime in Egypt in 608–610? We cannot be certain. But Heraclius' view of Egypt and military possibilities in Egypt probably depended most on whatever wisdom and observations Niketas communicated to him. Heraclius' outlook on Egypt would also have received some influence from ecclesiastical and other advisers, but Niketas would have been his closest and most trustworthy counselor concerning Egypt. To what extent did his experiences in waging war from Africa to Egypt and beyond affect Niketas' campaigning and strategic plans against the Persians? To what extent did his reports of experiences affect Heraclius' policy-making?

The Persians' conquests immediately deprived the Byzantine Empire and Heraclius of a huge amount of its population, and therefore tax revenues.[117] How precisely the Byzantine government coped is not entirely clear, given the absence of archives. But a likely immediate result was the raising of taxes, or at least an effort to do so, on remaining territories and the subjects within them, in an effort to squeeze out the maximum revenues in that emergency. Under undetermined military exigencies, probably to pay troops stationed in the vicinity who were trying to resist the Persians, a mint was temporarily opened at Seleucia Isauriae (modern Silifke) to strike bronze coinage, folles and half-folles.[118] The loss of the coastline determined the location of the mint in the interior.[119] Niketas' demands from

---

[117] Hendy, *Studies* 172, 620–621, for estimates of the relative proportion of imperial revenues from the Prefecture of the East, and within it, from Egypt.

[118] Philip Grierson, *DOCat* II: 39, 327–329, nos. 179–182. Grierson, "The Isaurian Coins of Heraclius," *NC*, ser. 6, 11 (1951) 56–67; Grierson, "A New Isaurian Coin of Heraclius," *NC*, ser. 6, 13 (1953) 145–146.

[119] Cécile Morrisson, "Numismatique et recherche: vingt cinq ans de recherche et d'études," in Ἀφιέρωμα στόν Νίκο Σβορῶνο (n. 18) I: 175.

the Alexandrian patriarchate of John are only part of that effort, which very probably intensified after the loss of Egypt itself. Among the immediate known consequences was the cancellation of the distribution of the grain dole (*annona*) at Constantinople, in 618 (it was first altered by requiring payment of money for the bread, then simply abolished).[120]

What is certain is that from the beginning the government's priorities favored the eastern front. Problems in the Balkans or Italy had to take second place. That would continue to be the understandable prioritization in the eyes of Heraclius and his advisers.[121]

Heraclius reportedly became so despondent about the beleaguered state of his empire that he considered moving back to Africa, but was dissuaded by the Patriarch Sergios. He allegedly sent ahead a fair amount of his treasures to Africa, but the ship sank (a possible conflation with the report of Phokas throwing treasures into the sea).[122] One later Syrian tradition suspiciously reported that a Byzantine ship with treasure trying to leave Alexandria was blown back to shore by the winds and then captured by the Persians. These treasures all being lost in water have some questionably similar features and their authenticity is therefore doubtful.[123]

One may ask: how feasible would it have been to move the government to Africa? Africa was not the geographic center of the empire, but it was relatively rich and unscathed. He knew that he had favorable support there. But it would not have been practicable to rule the empire from Carthage, because of difficulties with communications. Africa lacked sufficient soldiers. Its language was Latin, not Greek. But the gesture of a threat was sufficient to secure more pledges of loyalty and financial assistance from various quarters at a time of need. There was enough plausibility to his threat that he gained some leverage at a crucial time. He may well have yearned for the security, quiet, and prosperity of Africa, in contrast to the crises that he was confronting. He may have spoken out loud of his wishes, however unrealistic they were. His threat to leave Constantinople

---

[120] *Chronicon Paschale* 711 (164 Whitby). Nikephoros, *Short History*, 12.4–8. The thesis of Kyra Ericsson, "Revising a Date in the Chronicon Paschale," *JÖB* 17 (1968) 17–28, is unsatisfactory, as M. and M. Whitby, "Appendix 3: Ericsson's Postulated Textual Transposition," in their translation of the *Chronicon Paschale* 201–202, have convincingly argued.

[121] I discussed this matter with Paul Lemerle during an invaluable academic year in Paris in 1978–1979. See also, Lemerle, *Les plus anciens recueils des miracles de Saint Démétrius et de la pénétration des Slaves dans les Balkans* (2 vols., Paris, 1979, 1981).

[122] Nikephoros, *Short History* 8 (48–49 Mango); this may have been a device to pressure the Patriarch Sergios into consenting to lend ecclesiastical treasures to the government for the war effort; cf. on Phokas' throwing the imperial treasure into the sea, John of Nikiu, *Hist.* 110.4 (177 Charles). On the alleged destruction of treasure from Alexandria: Butler, *Arab Conquest of Egypt* 78, and references.

[123] I agree with the skepticism of Cyril Mango in his commentary on Nikephoros, *Short History* 8, on p. 177.

also permitted him to cancel the grain distribution. The report of plague at Constantinople is possibly true.[124] The majority of the inhabitants of Africa probably would have welcomed his return. There is no confirmation of this threat in extant Latin sources. Outbreak of plague in Africa may have discouraged him from returning there.

External pressures increased from others who sought to exploit Heraclius' vulnerability, distress, and distraction. The Visigothic King Sisebut took advantage of Heraclius' preoccupation with Sasanian and Avar menaces to occupy such important Byzantine-controlled Hispanic urban centers as Malaca (Malaga) and Assido in 615.[125] The worsening crises in the Balkans and on the eastern fronts compelled Heraclius to consent to peace with Sisebut, giving recognition to the new realities of power in the Hispanic peninsula. Heraclius' Patrician Caesarius participated in those difficult negotiations with Sisebut, which were completed before 617.[126] Such pressures made it even more difficult for Heraclius to contemplate leaving Constantinople to lead any military expeditions against the Persians for the moment. He needed to remain at the Empire's nerve center, in Constantinople, where he best could weigh the news from many directions.

Heraclius' cousin Niketas encouraged and probably also used pressure in favor of the union with the Monophysite churches. Patriarch of Antioch Athanasios visited Alexandria ca. 615–616, and effected union with Anastasios, Monophysite Patriarch of Alexandria.[127] Strategios, an honorary consul, Patrician, and prominent landowner in the Arsinoite nome, who was probably a member of the Apion family, visited Niketas at Alexandria and participated in the discussions on union between the two patriarchs and

---

[124] On plague: Lawrence I. Conrad, "The Plague in the Early Medieval Near East" (Ph.D. diss., Princeton University, 1981). ?Suda [Suidas] II: 583, s.v. "Herakleios," ed. A. Adler; Michael McCormick, "Bateaux de vie, bateaux de mort. Maladie, commerce, transports annonaires et le passage économique du bas-empire au moyen âge," in *Settimane di Studio del centro italiano di studi sull'alto medioevo* 45 (Spoleto, 1998) 52–65. The *Lexikon* dates from the late tenth or early eleventh century, but contains much earlier material: A.P. Kazhdan, s.v. " Souda," in *ODB* 1930–1931.

[125] Isidore of Seville, *Chron.* 129; Isidore, *Historia Gothorum* 61, 62 (ed. Th. Mommsen (*MGH* AA 11) 291–292). Fredegarius, *Chron.* 4.33. Margarita Vallejo Girves, *Bizancio y la Espana Tardoantigua (SS. V-VIII): Un Capitulo de Historia Mediterranea* (Memorias del Seminario de Historia Antigua 4; Alcala de Henares: Universidad de Alcala de Henares, 1993) 287–297.

[126] *Epistolae wisigotae* 5, 6; *Epistolae merowingici et karolini aevi,* I. *Epistolae* 3 (*MGH*; Berlin: Weidmann, 1892) 666–668. Vallejo Girves, *Bizancio y la Espana Tardoantigua* 298–302; Vallejo Girves, "Byzantine Spain and the African Exarchate: an Administrative Perspective," *JÖB* 49 (1999) 13–23, esp. 14–15, 22–23. Also *PLRE* III: 258–259, s.v. "Caesarius 2."

[127] Michael the Syrian, *Chronique* 10.22, 10. 26–27 (II: 364–371, 381–399 Chabot); W.H.C. Frend, *The Rise of the Monophysite Movement* (Cambridge: Cambridge University Press, 1972) 341–342. Louis Bréhier, in *Histoire de l'église,* ed. A. Fliche and V. Martin (Paris: Bloud and Gay, 1938) V: 87.

Fig. 3. Silver hexagram; inscription: *Deus aiuta Romanis*; Constantinople
(reverse, *DOCat* 65.1).

helped to forge the agreement.[128] If the intent of the union was to serve
imperial interests by eliminating any political stumbling block to support
from the civilian population and clergy for the government against the
Persians, it failed. Although the Copts eventually suffered very much from
the Persian invasion of Egypt, the signing of the union did not measurably
stiffen Egyptian resistance or encourage Syrian Monophysites to resist behind Persian lines.[129] Of course such resistance would have been very costly
to those who participated.

The year 615 also marked another innovation: the appearance of an important new Byzantine coin. Symptomatic of the urgency of the situation
was Heraclius' striking of a new silver coin of 6.82 grams weight, the hexagram (Fig. 3). It displayed Heraclius and his son Heraclius Constantine on
the obverse, and a globe cruciger with steps on the reverse, which also carried the inscription *Deus adiuta Romanis* ("May God help the Romans").[130]
Although one cannot ascribe the issuance of this coin to any particular
event, this appeal for divine assistance poignantly reflected and expressed
the stressful and desperate contemporary conditions and anxieties. There
are many unanswered questions concerning the striking of the hexagram.
Simultaneously, the rate of pay for officials, who now received their pay
in *hexagrammata*, was halved.[131] The pay cut in *hexagrammata* also affected soldiers in the army. That was a dramatic and severe slash of salaries.
The copper follis also dropped in weight, from 11 grams to between 8
and 9 grams, and therefore presumably in value, around the year 615/616.
Economically depressive consequences followed wherever there were substantial numbers of men on the imperial payroll. The government had to
reduce its expenses given the loss of so much revenue-producing territory
and the endangering of much of what remained in its hands. It needed its
revenues and resources to attempt to halt the Persians, and there probably

[128] *PLRE* III: 1204, s.v. "Strategius 10."
[129] J. Maspero, *Histoire des patriarches d'Alexandrie* (Paris: Champion, 1923) 330–332.
[130] Grierson, *DOCat* II: 17–18, 115–117. P.A. Yannopoulos, *L'Hexagramme* (Louvain, 1978), dates it to
       614 or 615, but see Cécile Morrisson, *RN*, ser. 4, 20 (1978) 192–197; Hendy, *Studies* 494–495.
[131] Literary recording of the date: *Chronicon Paschale* 706 (158 Whitby).

were additional threats by Avars and Slavs on the northern frontiers, in the Balkans. Its expenditures were primarily military. Adjustments to the new conditions were very difficult. People had to find ways to cope with the straitened circumstances. All of this presumably derived from the effects of the loss of Syria and the Persian invasion of Anatolia, and the endangered status of Egypt, soon to fall to the Persians as well.[132] There is no detailed information on precisely how Heraclius' government reached conclusions about fiscal and commercial policy in that era of crisis.

Shahrbarāz, having conquered Syria, invaded Egypt. The exact details cannot be determined, as the relevant pages of the *Chronicle* of John of Nikiu are missing. We cannot determine how closely Heraclius himself attempted to manage the defense of Egypt.[133] His cousin Niketas was Augustalis, in control of fiscal and military affairs there, using Alexandria as his base. The Life of John the Almsgiver includes details about the Persian invasion, but some have been questioned. The momentum of the Persian victories elsewhere unquestionably helped the Persians to conquer Egypt. There was no incentive for Egyptians to fight to the death when, except for Jerusalem, Syrians and Palestinians and the townspeople of upper Mesopotamia had sought, and many in fact had managed, to negotiate special terms with the Persians.

Shahrbarāz set out from Palestine on the so-called coastal road or *via Maris*, first capturing Pelusium, then Nikiu and Babylon (Old Cairo). After a lengthy siege, Alexandria fell in 619, with the reported assistance of a traitor who guided the Persians to a disused canal, which enabled them to penetrate the city and storm it. The city fell with great loss of life. Niketas, the Augustalis and cousin of Heraclius, had fled, together with the Melkite Patriarch John the Almsgiver.[134] At first John had offered assistance to refugees. It is possible that some of the contacts for religious relics accompanied negotiations for redeeming hostages from marauding Arabs, or simply from other contacts. The Bishop of Tiberias brought a fragment of the Cross to Egypt, for example, and doubtless other relics came in the wake of the flight of so many refugees, some of whom were very distinguished.[135] In a number of cases, the Persians may well have been willing to sell such relics back to Christians for an attractive price. The dynasty's prestige was on the line in Egypt, given that the defense of Egypt

---

[132] Fall in value of follis: Hendy, *Studies* 498–499; Yannopoulos, *L'Hexagramme* 89–90, 95.

[133] Todd M. Hickey, "Observations on the Sassanian Invasion and Occupation of Egypt." Butler, *Arab Conquest of Egypt* 54–92.

[134] *Vie de Jean de Chypre* 52 (515–516 Festugière); anonymous *vita* of John, c. 13 (328, 336–337 Festugière).

[135] Anonymous *vita* of John, c. 11, 14 (327, 328 Festugière).

was in the hands of Heraclius' cousin Niketas. So the fall of Egypt involved a dramatic blow to the imperial budget, to the supply of natural resources, and to the dynasty.

References to betrayal and conspiracies on the part of both Leontios, the biographer of Patriarch John the Almsgiver, and in the life of Samuel, may well reflect the existence of dissidence within the local population – although not split along Melkite–Coptic lines – but may also be a rationalization or effort of the Heraclian dynasty to develop scapegoats for their own failure to defend Egypt successfully. Explanations of betrayal helped to relieve the government of responsibility for the debacle and the losses: the basic plans may have been good, but it was treachery that accounted for the loss and for the Persians' victory. Allegedly the general Isaac[136] handed Alexandria over to the Persians, but this charge is very obscure. Isaac supposedly sought unsuccessfully to kill Patriarch John on the island of Cyprus, although it is unclear whether he was involved in the other conspiracy to kill John at Alexandria shortly before. Isaac himself fell victim to assassins on Cyprus.[137] One might well ask what could have been a better defense by Heraclius and Niketas, given Egypt's isolation and the difficulties of communicating with Constantinople after the Persian occupation of Syria. Niketas fled to Rhodes and then on to Cyprus, according to one account, or possibly on to Constantinople.[138] Niketas allegedly entreated his ritual brother Patriarch John to leave Alexandria to offer prayers for Heraclius: "Do not refuse to take the trouble to go to the queen of cities to accord to the gloriously conquering emperors the favor of your prayers to God." He initially consented, but as they reached Rhodes, he awoke and saw a vision of a eunuch in resplendent clothing, who told him, "Come if it pleases you. The King of Kings calls you." He told Niketas, who then consented to let him go to Cyprus, "You, master, have invited me to the terrestrial emperor, but it is the heavenly emperor who has foreseen this and he has invited My Insignificance instead of you." Niketas' subsequent fortunes are unknown.[139]

Unidentified dissidence on the key island of Cyprus at that time further exacerbated the defense of Egypt: Leontios speaks of the initial reluctance, assuaged by Patriarch John, of the local Cypriot population at the port

---

[136] *PLRE* III: 719, s.v. "Isaacius 7," where the fall of Alexandria is dated to to late 617, but this raises questions about the accuracy of the information in the life of John the Almsgiver and possible chronological discrepancies.

[137] Anonymous *vita* of John, c. 15 (328–329 Festugière).

[138] *Vie de Jean de Chypre* c. 52 (402–403, 515–516 Festugière).

[139] Anonymous *vita* of John, c. 52 (402–403, 515–516 Festugière). Nikephoros, *Short History* 184 Mango commentary.

capital of Constantia to receive Aspagourios, a Byzantine commander with an Armenian name, presumably dispatched by Heraclius to take control of it. The significance and nature of this strife is unclear, but if true, it complicated efforts to hold Egypt.[140] Reports of troubles in Alexandria and on Cyprus may in some way be later projections backward to attempt to justify Egyptian ecclesiastical policies and actions at the time of the Muslim conquest of Egypt between 639 and 642, in an era of much finger-pointing and backbiting.

Patriarch John allegedly stayed at Alexandria as long as possible. But eventually an unidentified conspiracy caused him to fear for his life. In response to the news of that, his biographer explains, he decided to sail from embattled Alexandria[141] to his birthplace, Cyprus.

Italy had its own share of troubles, which the difficult situation in the east exacerbated. The situation at Ravenna, the exarchate's seat of government, festered and grew worse. Heraclius managed, but just barely, to maintain fragile imperial control at Ravenna. Probably both the Lombards and restive locals followed the reports of the military situation on the front against the Persians, and took advantage of the imperial government's preoccupation with that exploding eastern crisis. Persians probably engaged in no direct negotiations with those parties, but Persians, Lombards, and Italians all probably took advantage of the crisis to the discomfort of Heraclius' government. Heraclius appointed and sent (probably spring/summer 616) the exarch Eleutherios to repress and punish the murderer of the preceding exarch, John, who had been slain ca. 615–616, together with other high officials.[142] The Patrician and *cubicularius* and eunuch exarch Eleutherios of Ravenna visited Pope Deusdedit (Pope 615–618) in Rome, then entered Naples and slew (?617?) the rebel John of Conza (Compsa), whose rebellion probably sought to take advantage of imperial difficulties in Egypt and Syria and the impotence of Constantinople.[143] Eleutherios made peace with the Lombard King Agilulf after failing to defeat him.

In 619 Eleutherios attempted to seize power, and had himself crowned, but was slain by soldiers of Ravenna at the Luciolis (Luceoli) castle as he sought to approach Rome from Ravenna.[144] Allegedly Eleutherios had

[140] *Vie de Jean de Chypre*, anonymous *vita* of John, c. 13 (328 Festugière).

[141] *Vie de Jean de Chypre*, anonymous *vita* of John, c. 13 (328 Festugière).

[142] *PLRE* III: 702, s.v. "Ioannes 239."

[143] *Liber Pontificalis*, s.v. "Deusdedit" (I: 319 Duchesne). *Auctorii Havniensis Extrema* 21–23 (*MGH AA* 9: 339); S. Cosentino, *Prosopografia dell' Italia bizantina* (Bologna: Editrice lo scarabeo, 1996) I: 391, s.v. "Eleutherius 4."

[144] *Liber Pontificalis*, s.v. "Bonifatius" (I: 321 Duchesne). Paul Diaconus, *Historia Langobardorum* 4.34 (= *Storia dei Longobardi*, ed. trans. Lidia Capo (Milan: Fondazione Lorenzo Valla, Arnaldo Mondadori, 1998) 208).

attempted to become emperor because of the strained imperial situation in Italy. His rebellion underscored the precariousness of imperial power. Everything was not rosy in the west. There were dangers there too. In its own way, the rebellion of the Heraclii from Africa had tempted other military and political leaders in the west to try to imitate that action and seize power for themselves. In any case, repeated unrest in Italy insured the inability of Italy to provide much in the way of financial assistance to Constantinople, for the Byzantines in Italy found themselves in an extraordinarily difficult military and political predicament and needed aid of every kind to save themselves. It was unrealistic to expect Italy to provide troops to help the imperial government against the Persian menace, nor could the remnants of Byzantine Italy expect any significant dispatch of troops from the east to help with its own local needs and its struggles against the Lombards. Heraclius had to find his soldiers elsewhere to fight the Persians. Centrifugal forces threatened to cause the empire to fly apart, to disintegrate. A positive constant in that era was the government's ability to maintain control of Africa and draw on its considerable revenues and agricultural products, ever more valuable now that Egypt and Syria were lost, together with their crops. Although the abortive rebellions in Italy presumably took advantage of the government's preoccupation with the Persian crisis, it is significant that there was no rebellion against Heraclius in the east. That fact partly derived from the Persians' apparent decision to seek a triumph without any assistance from any internal Byzantine opposition to Heraclius, except for the important exception of some Jews.

The Persians offered the Byzantines nothing, except for selective terms for towns that submitted to Persian authority without violent resistance. But the Persians, after their earlier efforts to claim that Theodosios, son of the late Emperor Maurice, had fled to Persia for protection, seem to have avoided making that case for the Pseudo-Theodosios, or for seeking to encourage the emergence of some other breakaway usurper to split the Byzantines. They were too confident to believe that it was necessary, even though eventually they would suffer their opponent's creation of a very dangerous dissenting usurper within their ranks. Finally, Heraclius' strong exercise of authority, and the penalties for Phokas, his collaborators, and for Priskos, left little doubt as to the eventual fate of would-be usurpers and stooges. He had established tight control over his armies so that others could not lightly repeat what he had recently done: win a military revolt and seize the throne.

The preponderance of evidence indicates that it was during Byzantine preoccupation with Persian advances that the government neglected its interests in the Balkans. Slavs and Avars took advantage of that opportunity to expand.[145] It is impossible to trace the exact location and advance of the Slavs and Avars between the years 610 and 620. It is plausible that Emperor Phokas, given his service on that front, had given some importance to the defense of that region and to grievances of fellow-soldiers from there or who were temporarily stationed there. Heraclius and his father had no such ties and had no known experience or service in the Balkans or along the Danube. Heraclius probably was wary about soldiers from that region who might have sympathies for the cause of Phokas. His territorial priorities were elsewhere. The result was that Avars in some fashion expanded southeastwards, presumably aided or accompanied by Slavs. Between 613 and 615/616 the Avars had captured Naïssus. Refugees from overrun Pannonia, Dacia, and Dardania poured into Thessalonica.[146] Within a decade of the overthrow of Phokas, the Avars had succeeded in penetrating into sections of eastern Thrace that were contiguous with the outer suburbs of Constantinople. That does not mean that the Avars exerted firm rule over that territory in Thrace, but it does mean that they were able to make expeditionary forays into it without serious military impediments, presumably because Heraclius had pulled his best troops out of the Balkans to confront the Persian menace in Anatolia and elsewhere. A shroud remains over the details. But the Avar expansion imperiled commerce and agriculture near Constantinople and the lives and livelihoods of those who lived nearby in Thrace; it imperiled Constantinople itself. The insecure nature of adjacent areas on the land side of Constantinople became another worry. Isidore of Seville claims that in 615 the Slavs took "Greece" away from the Romans or Byzantines.[147] Although there is evidence for Slavic penetration far into mainland Greece (including the Peloponnese) one must be cautious about placing too much trust in the exactitude of this precise year. There very well may have been a migration of the ancestors of the Croatians and Serbs into what had been Illyricum in the reign of Heraclius, as the tenth-century

---

[145] Haldon, *Byzantium in the Seventh Century* 43–45; Lemerle, *Miracles de St. Démétrius* (n. 121) I: 179–194, II: 69–71; John V. Fine, *The Early Medieval Balkans: A Critical Survey from the Sixth to the Late Twelfth Century* (Ann Arbor: University of Michigan Press, 1983) 33–43; Hans Ditten, *Ethnische Verschiebungen zwischen der Balkanhalbinsel und Kleinasien vom Ende des 6. bis zur zweiten Hälfte des 9. Jahrhunderts* (Berlin: Akademie, 1993); F. Barisic, "Car Foka (602–610) i podunavski Avaro-Sloveni," *Zbornik radova Vizantoloshkog Instituta* 4 (1956) 73–86; F. Curta, *The Making of the Slavs* (Cambridge: Cambridge University Press, 2001); John V. Fine, "Croats and Slavs: Theories about the Historical Circumstances of the Croats' Appearance in the Balkans," *BF* 26 (2000) 205–18.

[146] Lemerle, *Miracles de St. Démétrius* c. 197, 200 (= I: 181, 185, 186); see Vl. Popovic, "Les témoins archéologiques . . . ", *Mélanges, Ecole française de Rome et d'Athènes* 87 (1975) 493ff. Also Lemerle, "Invasions et migrations dans les Balkans depuis la fin de l'époque romaine jusqu'au VIIIe siècle," *Revue Historique* 211 (1954) 295–300.

[147] Fine, *Early Medieval Balkans* 62.

Byzantine Emperor Constantine VII Porphyrogenitus reports.[148] This also probably was the era (ca. 614–615) of two Avaro–Slavic attacks against Thessalonica, which, according to later tradition, the intervention of St. Demetrios had thwarted.[149]

The Byzantines failed to defeat the Persians between 610 and 615 for a number of reasons. The seizure of power by Heraclius and the purging of the army of those loyal to Phokas probably were very disruptive. Initially the revolt of Komentiolos made it difficult to assert control of the entire army. The continuation of Priskos as Count of the Excubitors also made it impossible at first to take complete control of his armies and forge them the way that Heraclius wanted. No sources describe actual conditions or the state of morale within the Byzantine army at the end of 610, or in early 611, 612, or 613. There is no detailed record of how Heraclius moved to try to insure the loyalty of his troops, or how he purged the existing military leadership, and whether he found good new commanders. Not until after the purging of Priskos in December 612 was Heraclius able to begin to do that, and by that time the Persians had achieved their decisive breakthroughs in northern Syria and upper Mesopotamia. Insufficient details exist to ascertain what was the problem with the Byzantine army in 613 when Heraclius met defeat near Antioch. After that defeat he and Niketas were fighting separate poorly coordinated campaigns because the Persians had seized the central position between the two. Although it might have seemed easy or tempting for them to make a coordinated pincers attack on the Persians, the bad state of communications did not permit that. Heraclius had no time to reform his armies before decisive battle with the Persians. The military manual, the *Strategikon* of Maurikios, probably from ca. 600, identified some Persian vulnerabilities, but of course provided no sure methodology for crushing them. Heraclius did possess territorial depth, which allowed at great costs to his subjects the trading of space for time to recover and gain his bearings. But the Byzantine defeats probably had a cascade effect.

The Byzantines did not succeed in arousing any fierce defense by local inhabitants, except at Jerusalem, to their regret, against the Persians.[150] Towns and cities and the countryside generally capitulated or negotiated the best terms that they could obtain with the Persians. Nor did the Byzantines succeed in developing any really effective alliance with the local Arab tribes against the Persians. There was no Byzantine Stalingrad in the urban Levant.

---

[148] Fine, *Early Medieval Balkans* 49–59.

[149] Lemerle, *Miracles de St. Démétrius* 1.1, 2.1 (= Lemerle I: 174, 179; II: 185; I: 180–189; II: 87–91, 94–103).

[150] Liebeschuetz, *Decline and Fall of the Roman City* (n. 68) 349–50, 403.

As in the Persians' invasion in 540, towns sought the best deal that they could negotiate. The Persian invasions brought mass flight and mass deportations in their wake, which were disruptive for rural and urban life. Arabs might well have furnished the manpower, mobility, and intelligence know-how that would have been essential to check the Persians. That did not happen. No great new commanders arose from the ranks, perhaps because the newly ensconced imperial family did not want that to happen. Niketas was able to wage a temporarily skillful defense but he ultimately had to abandon that effort and flee from Egypt.

The Persian penetration had its vulnerabilities. The Persians were not popular occupiers. They suffered from logistical difficulties in gaining supplies and communications from Ctesiphon. The occupied lands and peoples were diverse and more numerous than their Persian occupiers. There were religious tensions because of Persian Zoroastrianism, especially in areas such as Palestine with its numerous holy places and very zealous Christians. The Persians themselves lacked cohesiveness. Their ranks were rent with rivalries and suspicions. Some Persians were attracted to Christian beliefs and practices, as in the exceptional case of St. Anastasios the Persian. The Persians had overextended themselves in overrunning and remaining in the Levant and Egypt. They were inexperienced in handling so much territory. Centrifugal forces contributed to the unraveling of their own forces. They did not inaugurate efficient and honest new institutional procedures that might have weaned the local populations' support away from Byzantium. They did not assimilate their conquered peoples. On the other hand, they faced no effective guerrilla warfare in conquered areas, although there probably was some chaos resulting from depredations by nomads who were out of control and who took advantage of the new situation of flux.

The Byzantine army was not in excellent shape on the eve of Heraclius' seizure of power. It had been rent by the trauma of two violent overthrows of emperors, purges, civil war, repression, and serious unrest in the years before Phokas himself had seized power. The failure of the army in 610–615 was the culmination of many older structural problems that no emperor or commander had solved. Rising troubles with the Avars and Slavs in the Balkans created more difficult military dilemmas for Byzantine decision-makers. One should not, of course, view the Persians as completely ineffectual. They had some good commanders and were well motivated in the early stages of the war.

Heraclius had assets as an Armenian. He probably received intelligence about the Persians from Armenians inside and outside Persian military service. He relied on his own political skills to divide and exploit the Persians, not merely on winning in conventional warfare. He had so triumphed against Phokas in 608–610. Informal contacts with some Persian leaders such as Shahrbarāz began quite early, as traditions about the means by which certain relics reached Constantinople indicate. He probably realized that there was no monolithic Persian entity. Yet initial negotiations with General Shāhīn were unproductive, embarrassing, and even fatal to the Byzantine envoys. The struggle became a complex one that cannot be reduced exclusively to military terms.

There was no wholesale exodus of inhabitants of Asia Minor into Constantinople, where there would have been insufficient food and probably insufficient clean water. However serious the ravages at the hands of the Persians, Heraclius resolved to recover that area. There was resilience in Asia Minor – in contrast to the situation in the twelfth and thirteenth centuries. The population somehow endured, even at the cost of great harm to urban life and commerce.

The Byzantine armies suffered from serious financial problems. An empire with an empty treasury could not easily raise or maintain sufficient troops. But Byzantine problems were not limited to financial ones. Territorial losses multiplied and resulted in massive losses of tax revenues. To find new manpower one had to turn to the Kök Turks, but they were valuable for service only in areas that were adjacent to their own. One could not expect them to serve far away from their homes. One could not reliably use barbarians from the Balkans and there is no evidence that there was any consideration of such an option. There was no money to hire Germanic mercenaries from the west, even if a supply had been available. Although the experiences of Niketas in the rebellion against Phokas may have been instructive about the value of Africa as a reservoir or base from which to counterattack against the Persians, it lacked sufficient manpower to contribute significantly to the military effort to expel the Persians from Egypt or the Levant.

The decade ended with the empire and Heraclius in far more perilous and unprecedented straits than at the beginning of hostilities, and with no favorable solutions or coherent plan in sight for the military challenges in Europe, Asia, or Egypt. Heraclius inherited warfare with the Persians. With hindsight some may conceive of alternative strategies that he might have pursued to save Jerusalem and Alexandria, even though their losses were not due to any culpable neglect or misconduct on his part. Under extraordinarily strained conditions, which included much internal strife, much of western Asia and Egypt lay vulnerable to major Persian offensives and occupation. He gave that external military threat his fullest attention.

The sources leave the impression that he assumed the personal responsibility for devising and implementing an energetic military defense against the Persians, even as he pursued every possible option for a diplomatic solution to hostilities. Under difficult circumstances, he developed the best military and diplomatic responses that he judged to be possible. In this first phase of his warfare with the Persians he suffered dramatic losses but began, after yielding up much territory, to learn how to cope, how to conduct simultaneous warfare and diplomacy against Persians, and most of all, how to stabilize the situation to prevent still greater losses. But he and his Byzantine armies found and developed no winning formulae in the years between 610 and 620 to use against the Persians.

CHAPTER 3

Taking the offensive

Heraclius was about forty-five years of age at the beginning of the 620s. By now he had a feel for how to govern. He had taken full measure of the fiscal situation of his empire and understood the fiscal consequences of the loss of Egypt and Syria to the Persians and their savaging of Asia Minor. He understood the problems with his remaining any longer in Constantinople. It was dangerous to allow short-term conditions and positions to harden. The situation demanded an initiative. Either he had to appoint and provide adequate human and material resources to a promising commander, or he had to assume command in the field himself. The latter option required safeguarding central political control in his capital and security for his family. Any lessons that he could have learned from studying Byzantine mistakes in warfare with the Persians between the early 600s and now had become apparent. He himself was still vigorous, and physically and mentally capable of rigorous campaigning. By 622 a second phase of Byzantine–Persian warfare unfolded: in contrast to earlier defensive modes, Heraclius now successfully but gingerly tested techniques of offensive warfare against the Persians in a limited context.

Heraclius' life was filled with alternating periods of great mobility and immobility. The most stationary part of Heraclius' reign, as far as we know from the limited primary sources, were the years from late 614 until the end of 621. Heraclius did not leave Constantinople on major campaigns during that time, except for short trips in the vicinity, just across the straits and in Thrace in attempts through person-to-person diplomacy to solve problems with Persians and with Avars respectively.

The panegyrist George of Pisidia praises Heraclius for having reconciled the quarreling factions of Constantinople.[1] The precise character of the Blue and Green factions is disputed, and scholarly assumptions about their social and economic roles have received justifiable criticism.[2] But the factions

[1] George of Pisidia, *Heraclias* 2.35–61 (*Poemi* 253–254 Pertusi).
[2] Alan Cameron, *Circus Factions* (Oxford, 1976).

had been disorderly at Constantinople at the end of the sixth century and during the reign of Phokas. It was an achievement to have tamed them, and that process of conciliation, the details of which are obscure, appears to have been complete by the beginning of the second decade of Heraclius' reign, that is, by 620, if not well before. The evidence is, in addition to the statement of George of Pisidia, the absence of references to factional rioting or other forms of unruliness that had plagued Constantinople in previous decades. It was a process that complemented his tightening of control over his armies, from the perspective of internal security.

During that time Heraclius consolidated his grip on the armies and purged them of politically doubtful elements. Heraclius could not march out against the Persians until he was certain of internal controls to assure internal security. His cousin Niketas' control of the Byzantine armies in Syria and Egypt between 610 and 619 helped to prevent any recrudescence of provincial or military rebellion. Not only could Niketas, by exercising the most powerful command, remove the possibility of some other rival to the family gaining control of the resources to rebel, he was in a position to move forcefully against any potential rebel civilian or military leader. His presence probably deterred rebellion as the front against the Persians collapsed. The Persians did not succeed, if they tried, to cause any prominent Byzantine civilian and military leaders to switch sides. Disgruntled Byzantine commanders, if there were any, probably saw no incentive to desert. Despite drastic military reversals and heavy economic losses, there were rebellions only in remote regions such as Italy, and significantly not in Anatolia, for example, or at Thessalonica. No internal center of opposition appeared. As it would turn out, the greatest internal security problems and dissension would exist not within the Byzantine, but within the ranks of the Persian forces and their leaders. The Persian King Khusrau II had regained his own throne in 590 only with Byzantine assistance. That event was in the past, but it was a reminder that there might again be many internal fissures within Persian ranks, if one could find the way to exploit them. The trickle and occasional stream of defections from the Persian side, and unofficial contacts with those on the Persian side, indicated that there might be vulnerabilities, that in any case the Persians were not invincible. The need might be for some of the kind of skills that Heraclius had used to overthrow Phokas, not merely the generalship of a Trajanic soldier–emperor on the battlefield. But that would take time and the right opportunities.

Heraclius probably used the two or three years after the fall of Egypt in 619 to observe the Persians, to regroup his forces, and to try to obtain an accurate assessment of the current situation of his empire in many dimensions. No such intelligence reports survive. He probably received assistance in the form of extensive briefing from Niketas, the details of which we do not know, about Persian military capabilities, Byzantine failures and successes, and prospects. Niketas had developed contacts with some person or persons in the entourage of the Persian General Shahrbarāz. This was a second contact with a Persian general, now that the contact through General Shāhīn, on the straits, had failed to halt the war. Heraclius probably engaged in a number of informal probes of Persians, seeking for vulnerabilities to exploit: Persian deserters, generals or other commanders willing to sell information or even to switch sides or to shift their troops to the other side. It was cheaper and less risky than the battlefield to find ways to corrupt and weaken the strength of his opponents. Even his interview with Shāhīn may well have had that objective as a possible, if improbable, option. The Persian forces were not monolithically and homogeneously solid. The presence of Arabs, Armenians and some other Christians within the Persian ranks always created opportunities for defections and leaks of vital information from the other side. Although the military situation looked bleak and the financial situation even graver, there were potential openings to try to exploit or at least to probe. Niketas inexplicably disappears from the extant sources. His date of death is uncertain. He plays no further role in military operations. It is likely that he advised Heraclius about realities and probabilities of defending Byzantine Africa against any Persian thrust from Egypt and likewise, concerning any feasibility of threatening Egypt from Byzantine Africa. His consultations had long-term effects: they probably influenced Heraclian policy towards Egypt long after 619.

Psychological as well as medical, demographic, and economic consequences resulted from the mortality in Constantinople and in the provinces from the plague in roughly the year 619. The incidence of plague reinforced apprehensions about the possibility of divine wrath and the need to change. It likely encouraged the government to reinforce and demonstrate the visibility of its support from the powers of living and dead holy men and other ecclesiastics. Heraclius almost certainly sought additional prayers from holy men and clergy, just as Niketas had unsuccessfully sought to persuade Patriarch John of Alexandria to come to bring his prayers and blessings to him at Constantinople after the fall of Alexandria and Egypt. Much of the empire suffered from plague. Probably there were disruptive medical effects from the Persian invasion, the spread of new disease from Persia, and certainly from the dislocation, uprooting of and massing of civilians in unsanitary conditions. But the plague had spread even to Africa, to Carthage, where there was no Persian invasion.[3] Anastasios the Sinaite, who thrived in the second half of the seventh century, has preserved the memory of one instance of plague in Carthage from the reign of Heraclius:

In the years of the Patrician Nicetas such a wonder occurred in Carthage, in Africa. A certain *taxeotes* [soldier] passed time in the *praetorium* in many sins. A deadly plague having fallen on the city, he became bewildered and went out to his suburb with his own wife, fleeing from the death there. But the devil ever envying the salvation and repentance of men, throwing him into sin, caused him to have sex with the wife of his farmer... After a few days he died, stricken by the plague. There was a monastery a mile distant, in which the wife of the soldier summoned the monks, and coming and taking the remains, they buried them in the church, at the third hour. And chanting at the ninth hour, they heard from the depths a voice saying: "Have mercy on me, have mercy on me." And following the sound of the voice, they came to his tomb, and opening it they found the *taxeotes* crying out. At once they brought him up, and loosening the winding sheets and the bandages, they questioned him, wishing to know what he saw and what had happened to him. He was unable to speak from the number of his lamentations and asked them to take him to the servant of God Thalassios who embellished all of Africa... Thalassios the revered father of Africa comforted him and fixed on him for three days, and after four days he scarcely was able to correct his tongue because of his many wailings and he spoke weeping in this way: "When my soul was about to depart I saw some frightening Ethiopians standing over me. Of which merely the concept of all the punishment was worse, which seeing the soul shuddered and withdrew to itself. And while these things stood by me I saw two beautiful youths come, at the mere sight of whom my soul immediately leaped out to their hands. As though we were in flight we were raised up and found a toll-booth guarding the exit and each toll-booth in the air took account of my sin. They examined every sin of mine, one the lies, another the envy, another the arrogance, in order. When I was taken up by one of them I saw them carry as onto a scale all my deeds and juxtapose the good ones against my bad ones, which they brought to the heavenly toll-booth. Having paid out all of my good deeds, we reached the road leading up to the toll-booth of fornication near the gate to heaven. Seizing me they brought forth every fornication and fleshly sin I committed since the age of twelve. Those

---

[3] Paul Speck, "Epiphania et Martine sur les monnaies d'Héraclius," *RN* 152 (1997) 461, and Speck, *Das geteilte Dossier* 75–77, argues for a Persian occupation of Carthage. But archaeologists find no evidence for any Persian invasion. The continuing production of coins at the Byzantine Carthage mint throughout the relevant years argues against any Persian occupation of Carthage. Speck fails to explain the continuing operation of that mint. Papal correspondence indicates that in June 627 Byzantine civil authorities were in firm control of Africa and had been so in the immediately preceding time: Mansi, *Sacrorum conciliorum nova et amplissima collectio* 10.582; *Regesta Pontificum Romanorum* 2014–2015 (= ed. Philip Jaffé (Leipzig: Veit, 1885–1888; repr. Graz: Akademische Druck- und Verlagsanstalt, 1956) I: 224); André Guillou, "La diffusione della cultura bizantina," in *Storia dei Sardi e della Sardegna*, ed. Massimo Guidetti (Milan: Jaca Book, 1987) 382–384. There is no affirmative evidence for Persian expeditions that far west.

who brought me said, 'God forgave all those bodily sins he committed in the city, for he took refuge from them and left the city.' My denunciators said, 'After he left the city he fell into fornication with the wife of a farmer in the suburbs.' When the angels heard this and found nothing to give up against it, they abandoned me and departed. Then those Ethiopians seized me and struck me and dragged me under the ground. The earth split open and we went through narrow and gloomy places where the souls of sinners were locked up in underground prisons and jails of Hades.... And locked up and in narrow and dark and in the shadow of death I remained there weeping and closed up from the first until the ninth hour. And at about the ninth hour I saw those two saintly angels who led me out of my body appearing there. I began to cry out to them and to lament, to ask them to take me from that place of need that I might turn to God ... Taking heed of me who cried out with need and promised to repent, then one said to the other one: 'Will you reply to him that he may repent willingly to God?' And he said, 'I shall answer.' Then immediately the responder gave me his right hand. Then taking me up they raised me in the earth and brought me into the tomb and said to me, 'Enter what you exited.' I saw my own nature as a jewel crystal radiating forth, but I saw my body as mud and foul-smelling and dark filth, and I was displeased and did not want to enter it. But they said to me: 'It is impossible for you to change in any way except if you do so through your body, through which you sinned. Have faith and enter your body, so that you accomplish what you suffer, or let us turn away whence we took you. In order that you may enter.' At any rate I entered it, and my body took on life, and I began to cry out." ...

The great Thalassios urged him to take food but he would not accept it, only throwing himself on the place in the church on his face and confessing to God. Saying this and living still forty days without food, groaning and weeping and crying, "Woe to sinners and for the punishment that awaits them, especially those who profane their own flesh." So he acted, and departed to the Lord, foreseeing three days in advance his own death again.[4]

Reports in the provinces of extraordinary apparitions involving blacks added unsettling elements to existing uncertainties, and probably increased terror of any news of Persians or others, who probably all became conflated as part of a very terrifying and Godless otherness. The effects intensified

---

[4] Anastasios the Sinaite, c. 40 = ed. F. Nau, "Le texte grec des récits du moine Anastase sur les saints pères du Sinaï," *Oriens Christianus* 2 (1902) 83–87; revised later versions in *Synaxarium ecclesiae Constantinopolitanae*, ed. H. Delehaye, 638–639; and Georgios Monachos, *Chronicon*, ed. C. De Boor (Leipzig, 1904) 678–683. Anastasios was a seventh-century saint who recorded this story within a few decades of its occurrence. Thalassios flourished ca. 630–634: C. Laga and C. Steel in the introduction to their edition of Maximus Confessori, *Quaestiones ad Thalassium* (*CC*, Series Graeca; Leuven, 1980) I: x; cf. Polycarp Sherwood, *Annotated Date-list of the Works of Maximus the Confesssor* (Studia Anselmiana, 30; Rome, 1952) 33–35. Ethiopians as evil devils, in this case, in Alexandria, Egypt: Stephanos Efthymiadis, "Living in a City and Living in a Scetis: The Dream of Eustathios the Banker," *BF* 21 (1995) 21–23, trans. 27–28; and Apostolos Karpozilos, "Η θέση τῶν Μαύρων στό Βυζάντιο," in οι περιθωριακοί στό Βυζάντιο, ed. Chrysa Maltezou (Athens, 1993) 67–81. Plague in reign of Heraclius: Miracle 34, *The Miracles of St. Artemios*, ed. trans. V. S. Chrisafulli and John W. Nesbitt (Leiden: Brill, 1997) 178–179, 48.

challenge and crisis for Heraclius and his advisers. The plague, together with so many other calamities, raised more questions about the possibility of divine wrath and the need to propitiate the Deity.

Religion overhung and suffused most dimensions of life, and those tendencies intensified in emergencies. Possibly in 619 Heraclius received and granted the request of an unidentified chief of the Huns to receive baptism. An earlier precedent existed: Justinian I had welcomed Grod, king of the Huns in the Crimea, into baptism in 529. The exact location and ethnic nomenclature of Heraclius' guest is unknown. Important diplomatic and commercial benefits might also redound to the benefit of the empire from such a move. Heraclius welcomed the initiative. The Hunnic chief and his nobles and their wives were baptized, with distinguished Byzantine men and women, who may well have been members of the senatorial class, acting as respective baptismal sponsors. Heraclius then presented them all with gifts and imperial dignities. So here was a case in which he gladly asserted his role as protector and as a sovereign who sought to expand the faith.[5] This public role probably added to his prestige and offered, in a time of much negative news, something positive to celebrate publicly. This was not a new role, but the reassertion or reminder of very traditional diplomatic and religious roles of the Byzantine emperor. It was a standard diplomatic gambit. Yet it was at least a minor diplomatic triumph which could help to raise morale and could in principle have had positive diplomatic and military consequences. He needed every new ally he could find. The tangible results of this initiative, however, are unknown.

Other events underscored the prominence of religion. Two differing cases involving holy men illuminate the relationship of Heraclius with the holy. He and Patriarch Sergios brought the remains of St. Theodore of Sykeon to Constantinople, where they were welcomed with suitable hymns, in order to save them from possible harm at the hands of the Persians and to reinforce the host of supernatural powers that were mustered to protect Constantinople:

Just as you were charitable to all cities by so moving from city to city, in order that you might transfer your protection to those who beg for it, and so that you might cover with the brightness of your deeds the humility of mind, so now after your death take heed to our supplications, leave your home, make the capital city [Constantinople] your home. Let [the Galatians] accept your presence among us as an aid against the opponents [the Persians]. For many times you have purified their land of demons who dwelled there, contrary to expectations. You who had managed to bring freedom from them now display your assistance to us who

[5] Nikephoros, *Short History* 9 (48–51 Mango).

are wronged, blessing those who love your presence. For the wretch Chosroes [Khusrau II] impelled madly by love of greed sputters great things against us. For the Persian army nursed by many victories will not even briefly consider holding off from approaching you [that is, may approach and threaten you and your remains]. For he having conquered almost all of Asia of the Mysians does not restrain himself from threatening our capital city herself [Constantinople].[6]

After the chanting of people's hymns, Heraclius knelt, bending his knee, before the saint's remains, with the senate of Constantinople in attendance to emphasize the solemnity of the dramatic scene and the solidarity and testimony of prominent constituencies.[7] That initiative also contributed to raising public morale. It showed Heraclius' resolve to try everything to find powers to halt the Persians, deny them control of the valuable remains and potential supernatural powers of St. Theodore, and use them to embellish the capital and to assist in expiating any pollution.

It was probably some time in 622 or 623 that Heraclius took the controversial step of marrying his niece Martina, daughter of his sister Maria by her first marriage, despite the likelihood that the news would cause a scandalous reaction in many ecclesiastical and secular constituencies.[8] The date is controversial.[9] This marriage within the prohibited degrees aroused great controversy, but Patriarch Sergios, after some remonstrances, performed the marriage ceremony and crowned the new bride.[10] However, the controversy continued to trouble Heraclius' reign and his successors'. There is additional evidence for marriage within the prohibited degrees within the family of Heraclius, but however oblivious to religious prohibitions and scandal, elements of the church and public were aware of it. In marrying Martina, Heraclius created another serious and costly element of internal instability and controversy. As it turned out, the incestuous marriage resulted in some severe medical problems for many of their offspring. The first child of the marriage, Constantinus, was baptized by Patriarch Sergios at the Blachernae, and was proclaimed co-emperor with Heraclius

---

[6] C. Kirch, "Nicephori Sceuophylacis Encomium in S. Theodorum Siceotam," *AB* 20 (1901) 268.

[7] Ibid. 269.

[8] C. Zuckerman, "La petite Augusta et le Turc: Epiphania-Eudocie sur les monnaies d'Héraclius," *RN* 150 (1995) 114–115; P. Speck, *Das geteilte Dossier* 33–43; P. Speck, "Epiphania et Martine sur les monnaies d'Héraclius," *RN* 152 (1997) 461, dates the marriage to 622; C. Mango, commentary on Nikephoros, *Short History* 50–53, 179–180. The marriage occurred before March 624, because the *Chronicon Paschale* (713–714) mentions the couple as married at that time.

[9] *PLRE* III: 837–838, s.v. "Martina 1"; also 829, s.v. "Maria 12," and 848–849, s.v. "Martinus 7." There is discussion whether Martina was the daughter of Heraclius' brother Marinus or his sister Maria, which is the most likely explanation. Also see Linda Garland, *Byzantine Empresses* (London, New York: Routledge, 1999) 52–65.

[10] Van Dieten, *Geschichte der Patriarchen* 5–6.

Constantine but then presumably died, as one hears nothing more of him.[11] Many of their other children were born with defects.

The marriage created not only scandal, but also tension and rivalry about the eventual succession to Heraclius. It was a continuing problem or structural flaw. Heraclius' efforts to consolidate power and solidify his dynasty suffered from these problems, which were never really solved. Remarriage theoretically should have helped consolidation, but in this case it created new fissures. Its effects on his armies are uncertain. For some civilians and ecclesiastics it probably was seen as a possible cause of divine wrath, indeed the cause of some of the disasters that were befalling the Empire. Heraclius did not see it that way. But he created a very serious problem for himself. In a sense the crisis of legitimacy that had existed since the overthrow and murder of Maurice and his family was extending itself in a somewhat different form. The marriage may have had a number of objectives. Heraclius tried to create new stability and resolve his dynastic problems by marrying Martina, but this act created new ones.[12] He may also have hoped that the marriage would help give him a structure of a regency while he was absent on campaign, for the situation on the Persian front remained very critical.

Heraclius ascertained that no diplomatic initiative was likely to terminate hostilities with the Persians. Yet the morale of his troops was probably too poor to test them immediately against the Persians. He sought to select tests very carefully, if at all possible. The rebuilding or construction of morale among defeated soldiers was essential. That task probably involved personal encouragement from their emperor, drawing on religious motivations, as well as Heraclius' own and probably also his advisers' reading and studying of ancient Greek and Roman military manuals and precedents for help in creating an effective fighting force.

Heraclius' court poet George of Pisidia reports in an important passage:

It was during the long period of nights that allowed reflection, in which you resolved to cut out at the base the source of the evils, Persia, in so far as it was possible. And wishing to turn your ideas into reality you went to take a vacation in the suburban [palace] not for pleasure – and especially those lonely are accustomed to offer themselves only in the winter season – but in order that you would not be interrupted by decisions of state, nor that your plans would fall into the hands of spies ready to inflict harm by revealing them. For the spy is hidden in the crowd as in a cloud and is difficult to detect. There, at any rate, sovereign, collecting all your thoughts and feeding your mind with learned studies, you read about all of the norms specific to wars and public affairs. . . . Then imitating ancient Elias

[11] *PLRE* III: 348, s.v. "Constantinus 34," with improper and obsolete chronology.
[12] The historical tradition is so hostile to Martina that modern investigators must exercise great caution.

and wandering in the desert, you fed not on food but on ideas. For there were no matters of military formations with which outlines you did not become acquainted: plans, predispositions, shaping, writing out in advance and sketching the diagrams for others, for yourself, for the army, for the [other allied?] peoples, so to speak, anticipating in summary the battles before they took place.[13]

George of Pisidia was probably describing Heraclius' withdrawal across the Bosphoros, to the palace of the Hiereia, to contemplate and retreat some time during the winter of 621–622. At some point in his reign he filled in old cisterns with gardens and parks on that well-loved palace's grounds.[14] The linking of the Hiereia palace with fear of spies for Heraclius is noteworthy. There were security breaches and leaks everywhere. The large numbers of refugees and displaced persons included spies in the ranks. There was no linear front in the Byzantine–Persian war, even in Anatolia. It was risky but not difficult to pass from regions under the control of one side to regions under the control of their enemies. That is why there were so many interceptions of spies and so much intrigue. Few deserved trust. One does not know whether treachery was afoot, but he could not trust allied peoples, such as Arabs, whom his court historian Theophylact Simocatta later characterized as "fickle,"[15] nor all of his Armenians, for example, or the many heterogeneous ethnic groups from parts of the Caucasus. Whether anyone with ecclesiastical grievances would have considered betraying him is unknown, but that was, despite the Persians' Zoroastrianism, another possible source of disloyalty. No doubt many Jews also fell under suspicion. The hordes of refugees from regions now under Persian control could hide spies within their ranks. All of the above groups might have grievances or special interests and would have possible channels by which they could communicate with their fellows inside areas under Persian control. There was no hermetically sealed front. Things were porous. Very probably, of course, Heraclius himself made heavy use of spies against the Persians. Their ubiquitousness is clear. George of Pisidia indicates that Heraclius was correct to take precautions against them and in turn to use them against the Persians. But the poet does reveal some truth: the atmosphere at Constantinople at that time was one of unprecedented suspicion, distrust, tension, uncertainty, and watchfulness.

It is impossible to identify with precision what Heraclius studied while on his retreat, but it is highly probable that among the military manuals

---

[13] George of Pisidia, *Heraclias* 2.102–121, 2.134–142 (256–257 Pertusi).

[14] Theophanes Continuatus, *Chron. Vita Basilii* c. 92, ed. I. Bekker (Bonn, 1838) 338.

[15] Theophylact Simocatta, *Hist.* 3.17.7. Menander Protector, *Hist.* fr. 9.1, trans. R.C. Blockley (Liverpool, 1985) 100–101.

was the *Strategikon* of Maurikios from ca. 600 CE or an abridgment or revised version of it. A substantial corpus of Graeco-Roman and Byzantine military manuals existed at the time of Heraclius' accession. Also extant were earlier tracts and memoranda about military scenarios and plans for invasions of Persia, the heritage of many centuries of Romano-Byzantine warfare with Persia. Many of those contained obsolete details, but may have offered some ideas and cautionary remarks.[16] In addition to diagrams of military formations and evolutions, this type of material probably included gnomic advice about Persians' strengths and vulnerabilities, and preferences and dislikes. It is uncertain who chose the manuals for Heraclius to browse, out of a potentially large clutter of materials, or by what criteria. George of Pisidia may have composed another short poem at this time, one in which he emphasized Heraclius' ability to eliminate the Persian menace, which he describes as a destructive bird: "But if your power so commanded, O sovereign, it would be found with its back split and incinerated, and would learn how justice punishes the disorderly."[17]

The challenges that faced Heraclius at the beginning of the 620s found no real precedents or solutions in recent history. Only the tremors of the third century, which was not well understood in the seventh century, or even now, might have reminded an investigator of anything comparable to the imperial shocks and losses in Egypt, western Asia, and the Balkans. Existing reports of that era would have been sketchy to offer solace or solutions to an emperor who needed urgent expedients. He had to respond, but the options were not easy ones to choose, and older patterns were inadequate. Yet the most likely response was still a cautious and natural one, which sought to act in conformity with a familiar past and familiar patterns, even though it turned out to include ground-breaking innovation. There was a need for new expedients but there was no sure path to find or apply them. Although the Persians were a very old and familiar adversary, and there was a vast treasure of maxims and expedients for use against them, there was no recent or historical parallel for the present challenge.

Because we cannot precisely date Slavic and Avaric invasions, we cannot be certain about the interrelationship of Heraclius' calculations about

---

[16] Kaegi, "Constantine's and Julian's Strategies of Strategic Surprise Against the Persians," *Athenaeum*, n.s. 69 (1981) 209–213; Kaegi, *Some Thoughts on Byzantine Military Strategy* (Brookline, MA: Hellenic College Press, 1983). Contested is the date of a treatise ed. by George T. Dennis, "Anonymous Byzantine Treatise on Strategy," in Dennis, *Three Byzantine Military Treatises* (Washington: Dumbarton Oaks, 1985) 9–135. Salvatore Cosentino dates the text much later than the sixth century: "The Syrianos's Strategikon: a Ninth Century Source?," *Byzantinistica*, n.s. 2 (2000) 243–80.

[17] George of Pisidia, *Epigrammata*, Εἰς ὄρνιν· πρὸς τὸν βασιλέα Ἡράκλειον, *Carmi* 13.109 (502–503 Tartaglia).

the Balkan situation with his decision to campaign personally against the Persians. Military unrest there had recently resulted in the overthrow of Emperor Maurice, which Heraclius could not lightly forget. So the Balkans were not simply a challenge for external frontier defense, but also one of internal security. Of course there would have been a rapid turnover of troops in the span of twenty years that had passed since the rebellion of Phokas.[18] Thessalonica had recently fended off an Avaric assault through its own local resources, both human and material, but also in the eyes of local inhabitants, through the supernatural aid of the city's patron saint, Saint Demetrios.[19]

The empire's problem was not exclusively moral and psychological. There was also the need to find "the sinews of war, wealth,"[20] namely, money to pay for war. There was a need to find the material resources to pay for an effective force and to pay for subsidies to hire foreign soldiers individually or collectively and to purchase some foreign diplomatic support, cooperation, or at least neutrality.

The loss of tax-rich provinces exacerbated the task. Extraordinary measures were required and were taken. It was necessary to seek metal everywhere, even if it meant scrapping very ancient, well-known and possibly well-beloved monuments of the capital. The process took extreme forms: seizure via a forced loan of precious and semi-precious metals in the form of ecclesiastical plate. There was a shortage of precious metals. Relying on his relationship with Patriarch Sergios, Heraclius took precious metal from St. Sophia Church, among others. In the words of Theophanes, "Having taken the money of the holy churches in the form of a loan, pressed by difficulties, he seized the *polykandela* of the Great Church as well as other serviceable equipment and coined large numbers of nomismata and miliaresia."[21] Already, a few years earlier, his cousin Niketas in Egypt had been engaged in similar practices and negotiation with Patriarch John of Alexandria in an effort to tap into the vast wealth of the Alexandrian church. Indeed, John's biographer Leontios appears to have striven to emphasize the deleterious consequences of such wrongful seizures.[22] According to Leontios, Niketas ultimately failed in his efforts and returned the funds to Patriarch

---

[18] Paul Lemerle, *Les plus anciens recueils des miracles de Saint Démétrius et la pénétration des Slaves dans les Balkans* (Paris: CNRS, 1979, 1981) I-II.

[19] Lemerle, *Miracles de Saint Démétrius,* Text II.1, sections 179–192 (text, I: 175–179, commentary, II: 91–94).

[20] George of Pisidia, *Heraclias* 1.163–164 (*Poemi* 247 Pertusi).

[21] Theophanes, *Chronographia* A.M. 6113 (302–303 De Boor). Nikephoros, *Short History,* claims that he seized church plate to help pay tribute to unidentified barbarians, who may or may not have been Avars: c. 11 (54–55 Mango). In any case Nikephoros' reference is one critical of Heraclius' policy.

[22] Vincent Déroche, *Etudes sur Léontios de Néapolis* 150–152, 294–296.

John. Probably commanders throughout the empire attempted to requisition church funds and plate to help to meet the emergency. Part of the impulse for such actions was the lack of other means to float public loans for military or other purposes; that was a deep structural weakness of the Byzantine Empire.[23] It is impossible to calculate the amount of funds raised from such forced loans and seizures. The bronze ox-head from the Forum of the Ox may have been removed for use as a military treasury in the northeast or melted down at that time.[24] These seizures and meltdowns were not unprecedented; they had occurred at various times earlier in antiquity because of desperation and the governmental inability to borrow in any open market of public debt. Resort to this policy had a negative consequence: the supply of plate for forced loans and confiscations was finite. Having seized or commandeered that which was in sight, it was difficult to repeat the exercise successfully.

Heraclius probably used the threat of abandoning Constantinople for Africa to help persuade Patriarch Sergios and the clergy and the Constantinopolitan public to accept, or be resigned to, the forced loan of ecclesiastical plate and to accept other extraordinary governmental measures. The text of Theophanes does not relate the two actions, but the dissemination of the story encouraged acquiescence with this drastic measure of temporary appropriation of the sacred, revered, and highly visible church property. It would have helped to make the seizure more palatable.

It is impossible to determine the exact military situation in Anatolia, but it appears that the Persians did not occupy Anatolia even though General Shāhīn had penetrated as far as Chalcedon itself in 615. There probably had been much devastation and loss of life, but Persian units were not stationed in western and central Anatolia. Probably they were south of the Cilician Gates and in the Caucasus, but again, we cannot fix the precise demarcations between Byzantine- and Persian-controlled territory at the beginning of the 620s, or, to be chronologically more exact, on the eve of Heraclius' departure to campaign in the east on 5 April 622. Persian naval actions against Rhodes in the 620s are difficult to confirm.

George of Pisidia described the mood at Constantinople on the eve of that campaign. Heraclius already was familiar with some problems of

---

[23] Michael Hendy, *Studies in the Byzantine Monetary Economy* 229, 415–417.

[24] Παραστάσεις σύντομοι χρονικαί 42 (Cameron-Herrin 116–117, 229–230), but see criticism of P. Speck, "War bronze ein knappes Metall?," *Hellenika* 39 (1988) 3–17, who offers a complex emendation and reinterpretation of the text, arguing against Kaegi, "Two Studies in the Continuity of Late Roman and Byzantine Military Institutions," *BF* 8 (1982) 87–111. This subject still needs more investigation. Many cases of melting down metal from public monuments occurred in the seventh century.

campaigning in Anatolia, given his experiences there against the Persians in 612 and 613. Heraclius' advisers were split concerning whether he should personally engage in campaigning in 622, according to the poet, but, given that he had already broken the tradition of passivity on the part of emperors, this was no great precedent. Of course Justinian I, who did not go on campaign, had experienced a sharp division of counselors concerning whether he should authorize a naval expedition against the Vandals in Africa in 533.[25] George of Pisidia says of Heraclius' options, "Many who were familiar with the plans and practices of strategy murmured that it was imperative for the emperor to be present with his authority in the dangers of battle, but others, in contrast, countered that option with reasons that it would be dangerous for the empire to risk imperial power in imminent dangers. Others comparing the two reasoned that it was best to wait and yet to participate. But common to these arguments was lack of results."[26] George of Pisidia is probably exaggerating, for panegyrical purposes, the degree of dissent among Heraclius' advisers, and drawing attention to his hero, Heraclius, who ends the suspense by resolving to take up personal command of the armies in the east. Heraclius had not yet conclusively demonstrated his own skills as a military commander who could decisively defeat and expel the Persians. His two earlier personal appearances against them, in 612 and 613, involved Byzantine defeats and humiliations.

The absence of the sovereign compelled the creation of a regency that included the young Emperor Heraclius Constantine or Constantine III, Empress Martina, and the able Patrician Bonos, who was also *magister militum praesentalis*.[27] In effect, Bonos was also a *vicarius*, in Greek *topoteretes*, or substitute for the emperor. His was an extremely sensitive position, which he loyally occupied at Constantinople in the absence of Heraclius.

Heraclius celebrated Easter on Sunday, 4 April 622, at Constantinople, from which he departed on the following day. He had already shifted his principal European armies, that is those whom he normally stationed in troubled Thrace, to Asia in anticipation of the campaign.[28] Heraclius' crossing the straits to assume command of the army against the Persians is the subject of many lines of George of Pisidia's poetry.[29] The figure of Heraclius acting as a bold naval commander even when a tempest blew

[25] Prokopios of Caesarea, *Wars* 3.10.2–18.

[26] George of Pisidia, *Exped. Pers.* 1.111–125 (89–90 Pertusi).

[27] George of Pisidia, *In Bonum patricium* 163–170 Pertusi; see commentary of Pertusi, pp. 170–171. George of Pisidia, *Bell. Avar.* 314 (190 Pertusi). *Script. Orig. Const.* 2.189, 2.245.

[28] Theophanes, *Chron.* A.M. 6112 (302 De Boor).

[29] George of Pisidia, *Exped. Pers.* 1.163–1.238 (92–95 Pertusi).

up is easily expanded by George into a major act of heroism, and it bears comparison with representations of other famous leaders crossing rivers,[30] symbolizing firm leadership and courage in the face of adversity and danger.

After Heraclius overcame the challenge of the waves, his ship sailed to Pylai, in Bithynia (?Gömlek, Gulf of Izmit?), where he arrived the next morning.[31] He took with him a precious icon of the Virgin, an act that embodied the growing significance of veneration of icons and the growing importance of the cult of the Theotokos,[32] to show that he campaigned with the aid of God.[33] He marched into the interior of Anatolia, where he began to collect and form his armies, which had been dispersed during the winter. He organized them and instructed them in drill and maneuver, presumably drawing on conclusions from his studies during his winter's retreat.[34] Contrary to earlier scholarly assumptions, there is no evidence that these activities of Heraclius at that time involved any major comprehensive institutional restructuring of the Byzantine Empire. He probably solidly rebuilt the shattered Byzantine army and whipped it into shape by using traditional procedures: drills, formations, maneuvers, and interfolding new recruits where appropriate to fill gaps in the ranks that had resulted from purges and attrition from battlefield losses, and probably also from deteriorating health and from desertions.[35] The ethnic composition of his army was diverse and polyglot.[36] In addition to drill, Heraclius emphasized inculcation of religion in his soldiers.[37]

Heraclius reportedly addressed his troops:

The possession and the manner of authority has joined me and you. For we exercise the advance of authority not so much by fear as by love. Against the inhuman violence that tyranny arms against the laws, my rule now introduces instead the compulsion of love of mankind and to oppose mine to those others, which always requires well-constructed laws to those raised up in adversity. I so think in this way

---

[30] Louis XIV crossing the Rhine, Washington crossing the Delaware.

[31] George of Pisidia, *Exped. Pers.* 2.8–11 (97 Pertusi). Nicolas Oikonomides, "A Chronological Note on the First Persian Campaign of Heraclius (622)," *BMGS* 1 (1975) 1–9. Thomas S. Brown, Anthony Bryer and David Winfield, "Cities of Heraclius," *BMGS* 4 (1978) 16 n. Paul Speck, "Epiphania et Martine sur les monnaies d'Héraclius," *RN* 152 (1997) 159–160, offers a different but unpersuasive chronology for the campaign.

[32] George of Pisidia, *Exped. Pers.* 1.139–154, 2.86 (91, 101 Pertusi).

[33] George of Pisidia, *Exped. Pers.* 2.24–26, 2.74–79 (97, 100 Pertusi).

[34] George of Pisidia, *Exped. Pers.* 2.38, 54, 56, 76–205; Theophanes, *Chron.* A.M. 6113 (303 De Boor, 435–438 Mango-Scott). Mango, "Deux études" 150–151.

[35] On the meaning of the passage "regions of the themes," Theophanes, *Chron.* A.M. 6113 (303 De Boor; 435, 438 Mango-Scott); see John Haldon, "Military Service, Military Lands, and the Status of Soldiers: Current Problems and Interpretations," *DOP* 47 (1993) 1–67, esp. 4–5; Haldon, *Warfare* 71–74.

[36] George of Pisidia, *Exped. Pers.* 2.165–169 (104–105 Pertusi).

[37] George of Pisidia, *Exped. Pers.* 2.202–203 (106–107 Pertusi).

and form. But the common King and Lord of all and the leader of our armies is He [God] with Whom is the safest course of command in war, through Whom victory follows with deep piety. Believing in Him, I now take up arms with you for the task. It is necessary for us to march out against the enemy who worship idols, who mix blood sacrifices with polluted blood. Those are churches of human misery, contaminated with the worst sensual pleasures. They wish to cut out the grapevine of the sacred word with the barbarian sword. They are the ones about whom David divinely spoke out, saying "blessed is he who strikes down the sons of Persia and smashes them against the rocks."[38]

Heraclius' invocation of Davidic language and imagery here is not the only time that it will occur in his reign.[39] His poet George of Pisidia voiced the hopes of many subjects in wishing "You have put black sandals on your feet. May you color them red with Persians' blood."[40]

General Shahrbarāz had come up from Egypt, which he had conquered,[41] and had assumed command of the Persian army, which was located not far away. The size of his force is unknown. Heraclius feared that the Persians would appear before the Byzantines had concentrated their troops, but that did not occur. His precise itinerary is controversial.[42] The Byzantines may have first reached some unidentified point in Cappadocia, near Caesarea, but it is more likely that he marched straight east, towards Pontos. En route he clashed with a small party of Arabs who were allied with the Persians around. Some, including their leader, were captured and taken to Heraclius, who released them from captivity and they entered Byzantine military service. The Byzantine scouting-party who captured them may itself have been Ghassānid Arabs.[43] This is one of many indications of the Heraclian policy and desire to try to induce defections, on as large a scale as possible, from the Persian side, not necessarily seeking a decision through any victory on the battlefield. It was an understandable tactic, although George of Pisidia calls them "untrustworthy barbarians."[44]

[38] George of Pisidia, *Exped. Pers.* 2.88–115 (101–102 Pertusi). Cf. Psalms 136.9.

[39] Note the David Plates, with their Davidic themes, which probably were created at the end of the decade, perhaps 628–30, after final victory over the Persians. Steven H. Wander, "The Cyprus Plates: The Story of David and Goliath," *Metropolitan Museum Journal* 8 (1973) 89–104.

[40] George of Pisidia, *Epigrammata*, Εἰς βασιλέα Ἡράκλειον, *Carmi* 13.110 (502–503 Tartaglia).

[41] The exact date of the departure of Shahrbarāz from Egypt is unknown.

[42] Thomas S. Brown, Anthony Bryer and David Winfield, "Cities of Heraclius," *BMGS* 4 (1978) 16–17. C. Zuckerman, "The Reign of Constantine V in the Miracles of St. Theodore the Recruit (*BHG* 1764): Appendix. Heraclius' First Campaign in Miracles # 2 and # 3," *REB* 46 (1988) 208–209.

[43] For locating this clash in Bithynia, see James Howard-Johnston, "Heraclius' Persian Campaigns and the Revival of the East Roman Empire, 622–630," *War in History* 6 (1999) 3–4, esp. p. 3 n. 11. On Arabs serving in the Byzantine forces: Irfan Shahid, *Byzantium and the Arabs in the Sixth Century* (Washington: Dumbarton Oaks, 1995) I: 643–644.

[44] George of Pisidia, *Exped. Pers.* 2. 57–59, 2.206–235 (99, 107–108 Pertusi); on untrustworthy barbarians: *Exp. Pers.* 2.238 (108 Pertusi); Theophanes, *Chron.* A.M. 6113(304 De Boor).

The Persian army under Shahrbarāz managed to block the road into the passes that would provide access to the east. He tried to do this after Heraclius reached Hellenopontos, west of Euchaita. But Heraclius outflanked them, and placed his forces in the rear of the Persians, who realized this only about two weeks later. The Persians plundered and burned Euchaita, including the relics and martyrium of St. Theodore the Recruit.[45] George of Pisidia probably is describing in poetic language an actual maneuver of tactical reversal[46] that Heraclius used on that occasion to take the Persians by surprise. The chronology is inexact, but these events took place late in autumn of 622 in eastern Hellenopontos, perhaps about 90 kilometers east of Euchaita, at Ophlimos (Omphalimos).[47] But Shahrbarāz then, moved his troops to outflank the Byzantines, and attempted a night attack that a waning moon frustrated.[48] The Byzantines held a position in the plain to the east of the Persians. Heraclius probably knew that the Persians did not, as the author of the *Strategikon* of Maurikios noted, like to fight on an open field; that is why Heraclius selected it, but they refused to fight.[49] Pisides mentions the defection of a Persian who had fled to the Byzantine ranks, was enrolled in the Byzantine army, and who then, after two weeks, fled back to Persian ranks but was executed for having thrown away his shield. George of Pisidia, in mentioning this, was trying to emphasize Persian perfidy and also the punishment for desertion from the Byzantine army.[50] After some waiting and maneuvering, the Byzantines decisively defeated the Persians, probably in late autumn 622. Heraclius discovered, through personal observation the night before the combat, that the Persians had hidden soldiers in ambush, so in turn he contrived a simulated flight of a small number of his own troops. In conformity with the *Strategikon*, both Heraclius and the Persians had drawn up their forces in three formations. As the author of the *Strategikon* noted, the Persians preferred rough terrain rather than to draw up on open and level ground. The Persians left their cover and rushed to chase the fleeing Byzantines, and in turn were assaulted with losses by Heraclius' Optimates, an elite force.[51] The Persians gave way and then apparently retired from the

[45] Zuckerman, "The Reign of Constantine V" 202–203, 208–210.

[46] Maurikios, *Strategikon* 11.1 (ed. G.T. Dennis, trans. E. Gamillscheg) 356, 358; Eng. trans. by Dennis, 114–115.

[47] Zuckerman, "The Reign of Constantine V" 209–10.

[48] Battle: George of Pisidia, *Exped. Pers.* 3.30–304 (117–129 Pertusi); cf. Oikonomides, "Chronological Note" 4.

[49] Maurikios, *Strategikon* 11.1 (ed. G.T. Dennis, trans. E. Gamillscheg) 356, 358; Eng. trans. Dennis, 114–115.

[50] George of Pisidia, *Exped. Pers.* 3.144–152 (122 Pertusi).

[51] George of Pisidia, *Exped. Pers.* 3.179–304 (123–129 Pertusi). On the Optimates: John Haldon, *Byzantine Praetorians* (Bonn, Berlin, 1984) 95–100, 105–107, 116–118.

entire region. A threat from the west, probably from the Avars' growing menace in the Balkans, compelled Heraclius to return to Constantinople late that summer (622).[52] The Byzantine army went into winter quarters. These victories were in fact limited ones, but they helped to rebuild shattered morale among Heraclius' soldiers, civilians, and elites. They did not change the fundamentals of the strategic situation, but they provided a valuable boost to morale.

George of Pisidia emphasizes that Heraclius' stratagems in these initial tests demonstrated cleverness in war, in conformity with broader Byzantine conceptions of strategy and stratagem.[53] Traditions also circulated about Shahrbarāz's own use of stratagems against the Byzantines.[54] The actual campaigning of 622 did not involve just maneuvers of extremely well-disciplined soldiers. Nor was it a simple contrast of Christian and Zoroastrian beliefs and practices, as George of Pisidia would have it:

You then completed these actions with wisdom, while the supreme head of the infidels did the complete opposite. He entrusted his labor to the indecent sound of drums and cymbals and to the strange dance of women quick to disrobe. You, on the other hand, supreme leader, armed with wisdom, were satisfied with songs drawn from mystic instruments raising the voice of God in your heart. And you had chaste dances of virgins and incorrupt hopes in your mind. They rested their hopes in the moon, but it exalted you through a sudden eclipse. They venerated fire, while you venerated the wood [of the cross] raised on high. It is clear when it was raised, that the fire of the Persians was of no avail.[55]

The reality of warfare in 622 in fact was more complex. At times it was a war of waiting, but also often one of fluidity and instability, with each side encouraging desertions and defections and trying to induce switching or disintegration of the other side. That was preferable because it was cheaper and less risky than fighting. Even the heroic imagery of George of Pisidia's verse allows the reader to discern that fluid and unstable reality. The small-scale desertions that George of Pisidia mentions in the campaign of 622 anticipate the much greater and decisive ones of 627, 628, and 629, which would help bring Heraclius to final victory. Already in 622 Heraclius was finding out that many within the Persian ranks were willing

[52] George of Pisidia, *Exped. Pers.* 3.311–340 (129–131 Pertusi); Theophanes, *Chron.* A.M. 6113 (305–306 De Boor); Oikonomides, "Chronological Note" 6–7. On the Balkans: Fine, *Early Medieval Balkans* 34–59.

[53] Kaegi, *Some Thoughts on Byzantine Military Strategy.* On the earlier Graeco-Roman heritage of stratagems: Everett L. Wheeler, *Stratagem and the Vocabulary of Military Trickery* (Leiden: Brill, 1988).

[54] Al-Mas'ūdī, *Murūj al-dhahab* (= *Prairies d'or*, ed. B. de Meynard, Pavet de Courteille) 2.227.

[55] George of Pisidia, *Exped. Pers.* 2.239–256 (108–109 Pertusi).

to consider defection. The question remained: could the Byzantines trust such defectors? Heraclius needed so many troops that he was willing to enroll some defectors forthwith in his armies, often with mixed results. The porosity of the military forces and flux of loyalties increased risks of espionage and sabotage, which could take place out in the countryside as well as at Constantinople. The recently written *Strategikon* of Maurikios assumes such a world of volatility of loyalties. The realities behind the poetry of George of Pisidia conform to the world of the *Strategikon*. The situation was full of opportunities and challenge by the end of the summer campaign season of 622.

Less apparent is why Heraclius failed to devise better solutions for military problems, whether tactical or operational or strategic, before 622 and 624. Things did start to improve by 622. But it took a long time before the pendulum turned. It was expensive to purchase time through giving up much valuable and populous territory to the Persians. But the passage of additional time enabled him to acquaint himself with their vulnerabilities, including the weaknesses and resentments of their commanders. He came to appreciate ever more the strategic strength of his own position on the Bosphorus and his full range of military options.

A close reading of the texts of George of Pisidia[56] and Theophanes indicates that Heraclius, and possibly also his military advisers, had read the Maurikios *Strategikon* or derivative writings for advice on fighting the Persians. He had studied military writings, which descriptions of his techniques in his campaign of 622 confirm. The author of the *Strategikon* advises using flanking attacks, not frontal ones, when wheeling against pursuing Persians. George of Pisidia indicates that Heraclius simulated a frontal attack after wheeling, but actually used an unspecified stratagem. Persian failure to secure their flanks is noted in the manual. The Persian proclivity to cling to rough terrain also conforms to the descriptive material in the *Strategikon*. One could ask, of course, why he and his commanders could not have gleaned the right lessons, changed tactics, and used all of this earlier to spare his empire and its armies the losses and suffering that they experienced in the first dozen years of his reign. Why could these not have worked for Heraclius and Niketas near Antioch in 613, or earlier? One could ask why had the Persians not learned of this Byzantine knowledge and altered their tactics in the meantime, given that probably at least two decades

[56] George of Pisidia, *Exped. Pers.* 2.260–262, 2.267–273 (109, 110 Pertusi). George of Pisidia, *Exped. Pers.* 3.20:–32 Persians kept to high ground, Heraclius took his position in a plain (Pertusi 116–117). George of Pisidia, *Exped. Pers.* 3.235–241, 251–252 (126–127 Pertusi): Persians flee to steep and rocky locations.

had passed since the compiling of the *Strategikon*. The Persians may well not have known what the Byzantines had concluded about them and, if so, had not communicated this information down the chain of command, and in any case, were unable to change their ways. These clashes were not the decisive ones in the war, and the losses on both sides do not appear to have been high. But more than confidence-building, they may have convinced Heraclius that military manuals could be of some utility, that in them he possessed some valuable insights on how to defeat the Persians. They served as early tests of Persian vulnerabilities and Byzantine cohesiveness and vulnerabilities, and they also enabled him again to have some contact, albeit military and not diplomatic, with General Shahrbarāz. These actions in the summer and in late 622 anticipated the kinds of maneuvers that he later successfully implemented near Nineveh against other Persians and their allies.

Heraclius returned as victor, to the greetings of a joyous citizenry at Constantinople, and was able to enjoy the fame of having triumphed over the Persians.[57] That was an unusual experience for the populace, given so many Byzantine defeats.[58] The entreaties of the inhabitants of his capital for his presence also served as an excuse for him to take temporary leave of his army in Anatolia.

Heraclius and the (unidentified) Khan of the Avars planned to meet outside Constantinople, at Herakleia in Thrace on 5 June 623 to celebrate games, after the Khan had initiated diplomacy for a peace treaty. Heraclius needed a treaty because of his plans for war against the Persians. But the Khan secretly planned an ambush. In the words of the chronicler of the *Chronicon Paschale*: "And about hour 4 of this Lord's Day the Chagan of the Avars signaled with his whip, and all who were with him charged and entered the Long Wall." Heraclius detected it and fled, reportedly carrying his crown under his arm. The Avars, who had entered the Long Walls, plundered that region between the Long Walls and the city walls. Heraclius had sought terms with the Avars to relieve his government of the need to deploy troops on two fronts; during the desperate struggle against the Persians he lacked both the troops and the funds. This Avar surprise was part of a larger pattern of kidnapping participants in peace negotiations. The practice was not unique to the Avars, for indeed the Byzantines and the Romans before them had resorted to such practices when dealing with

---

[57] George of Pisidia, *Exped. Pers.* 3.314–355 (130–131 Pertusi). Theophanes, *Chron.* A.M. 6113 (306 De Boor).

[58] George of Pisidia, *Exped. Pers.* 3.296–304 (129 Pertusi); Theophanes, *Chron.* A.M. 6113 (306 De Boor).

other barbarian peoples. This incident temporarily ruined efforts to reach an accommodation, but the needs of the Empire for a truce in the Balkans remained.[59]

According to Nikephoros, it had been a complicated story. Heraclius had sent the Khan gifts after he was approached about a treaty:

> Greatly pleased at this, he decided to meet the Avar [chief] in the city of Herakleia as has been agreed. He sent in advance some theatrical equipment and made preparation for chariot races to be held at the reception; he also brought along splendid vestments for him [the Chagan] and his companions. He then arrived at Selymbria and lodged there. Three days later the Chagan arrived before Herakleia with a great throng of Avars. After picking among his followers a contingent of the bravest fighting men, he sent them to the overgrown and wooded heights overlooking the so-called Long Walls and scattered them secretly in the bushy hills that are there so that, taking the emperor in the rear, they might encircle him and make an easy prey of him and his retinue. Upon becoming aware of them, Heraclius, greatly astonished at this unexpected event, took off his purple robe and, putting on instead some mean and miserable clothes so as to appear like an ordinary man to anyone he encountered; hiding, furthermore, his imperial crown under his arm, immediately turned to ignominious flight and barely escaped to Byzantium. The Avars set out in hot pursuit and reached the plain in front of the City that is called Hebdomon, where they encamped. Spreading out from there as far as the bridge of the river Barbysses, they grievously devastated the settlements that are there and pitilessly slaughtered the Roman people. They also seized the imperial vestments, the theatrical equipment, and all the men who were transporting [those items]. After taking a great many captives, they carried them off to their own country: the total number amounted to 270,000 men and women, as was mutually confirmed by some of the prisoners who escaped.[60]

Nikephoros has greatly exaggerated the numbers of Byzantine prisoners who fell into the hands of the Avars; perhaps it was 70,000, which would still be a high number, or some more modest amount. The embarrassing and humiliating incident, where the emperor lost his clothes and almost lost his crown, underlined the tenuousness of the situation and the insecurity that prevailed so close to Constantinople. Despite the shock and humiliation, it also shows the adroitness and resourcefulness of Heraclius and the trickery of the Avars. It was a reminder of how dangerous summit conferences, however well-meaning, might be, and how prone all of the parties

[59] *Chronicon Paschale* 712 (165 Whitby). Arguments in favor of 617 or 619: Lemerle, *Miracles de St. Démétrius* 101–103; for 619: Averil Cameron, "The Virgin's Robe: An Episode in the History of Early Seventh-Century Constantinople," *Byzantion* 49 (1979) 43–46; but arguing for 623 are Michael and Mary Whitby, "Appendix 4: The Date of Heraclius' Encounter with the Avars (*CP* s.a. 623)," *Chronicon Paschale* 203–205, and Mango in his edn. of Nikephoros, *Short History* 178. Original argument for 617: N.H. Baynes, "The Date of the Avar Surprise," *BZ* 21 (1912) 110–128.

[60] Nikephoros, *Short History* c. 10 (50–53 Mango).

were to attempting kidnappings and assassinations in such contexts. The looting and the captivity of many Byzantine civilians probably increased popular criticism of Heraclius, some of which may be reflected in the narrative tradition that Nikephoros transmits. It also ratcheted up pressure on Heraclius to ease the situation. He ended by being more vulnerable than before. Favorable preconditions for another offensive against the Persians would be difficult to achieve.

Despite that recent Avar treachery, Heraclius still needed to avoid a two-front war, which he could not afford financially or militarily. He soon swallowed his pride and negotiated a peace treaty with the Avars, who received a hefty monetary payment, 200,000 solidi and valuable hostages, including his illegitimate son John "Atalarichos," his nephew Stephen, son of his sister Maria and Eutropios, and John, the illegitimate son of his powerful aide, the Patrician Bonos, to whom he had entrusted the real power of the regency during his expeditionary campaigning against Persia.[61]

The new treaty with the Avars gave Heraclius the option of removing troops from the Balkans to use in Asia against the Persians. He may have been somewhat wary about using such troops earlier, until he had purged their ranks of those favorable to Phokas, who had started his usurpation from their ranks. Although he seemingly secured his rear through that treaty, the very fact of the earlier Avar treachery was a reminder that the agreement was unstable. The Avars might again violate it for all kinds of reasons: they might calculate that it was in their interest to prevent any overwhelming Byzantine military victory, because Heraclius might then turn victoriously against them. They might try to extort still more money and strive for more plunder and captives in the Balkans. Presumably they received some economic (that is, commercial) advantages from this arrangement, as well as understandings to prevent flight or asylum of their own people in Byzantine territory. Probably there were promises that Heraclius would in turn avoid trying to destabilize the Avars through intrigue among both Avars and other tribes and subjects.

The treaty arrangements with the Avars were uneasy and ephemeral. It is significant that Heraclius found the funds to pay such a large sum to the Avars. It was a major financial sacrifice for the empire at a time when the government and its subjects were already suffering severely and imperial revenues had plummeted. The explanation is that he probably believed that he had no real choice but to complete a treaty even though the other party

---

[61] Nikephoros, *Short History* c. 13 (59, 181 Mango). Avar violation of the earlier negotiations, c. 10 (50–53, 178–179 Mango). Athalarichos' resentment against being treated as an expendable hostage may help to explain his participation in an abortive coup against Heraclius in the mid-630s.

had ruthlessly violated a similar effort a few years before. Heraclius took a characteristically calculated risk in making this treaty and in relying on it as a critical element in his strategy against the Persians. It was a realistic move. This accord was arranged by envoys, not by any face-to-face meeting of the two sovereigns, which had ended so riskily and disastrously a few years before. It probably dates to late 623 or early 624. Theophanes is surely right in claiming that the conscious motive of Heraclius in arranging it was his preparations for the next and very different phase of war with Persia.[62]

[62] Theophanes, *Chron.* A.M. 6111 (302 De Boor). Theodore Synkellos, *Analecta Avarica*, ed. L. Sternbach (Cracow, 1900) 302, lines 28–35.

CHAPTER 4

Peril and hope

The time for testing Heraclius' skills had come with respect to public relations, coalition building, as well as strategy and tactics. Having restored
the morale of his troops and having won at least a psychological victory
in 622 over the Persians, he left Constantinople on 25 March 624 with
"Armenia" his objective.[1] This is the third phase of Byzantino–Persian warfare under Heraclius (Phase I, defeat and stabilization, 610 to 620; Phase II,
testing techniques of offensive warfare, in 622): a shift to large-scale offensive expeditionary warfare, between 624 and 627/628. He had "the appetite
to penetrate into the innermost parts of Persia."[2] He did not return to
Constantinople for four years, until the definitive defeat of Persia and the
overthrow of Khusrau II. Heraclius had his army purify itself for three days.[3]
Khusrau II in turn sent General Shahrbarāz to invade Byzantine territory
in Anatolia. Having reached Armenia, the high ground of which enabled
him to make a credible threat against Persia proper, Heraclius once again
attempted to reopen diplomatic negotiations for a settlement of hostilities
with Khusrau II. Heraclius threatened to invade Persia unless Khusrau II
agreed to peace.[4] But Khusrau apparently saw no advantage in consenting
to a settlement when he was so far ahead. He rejected the overture with an
insulting open letter, which Heraclius may have fabricated or altered and
in any case used to advantage to fan soldiers', popular, and clerical outrage:

Chosroes, honored among the gods, lord and king of all the earth, offspring of the
great Aramazd, to Heraclius, our senseless and insignificant servant. You have not
wished to submit yourself to us, but you call yourself lord and king. My treasure
which is with you, you spend; my servants you defraud; and having collected an

---

[1] Date of departure: *Chronicon Paschale* 713–714 Dindorf.
[2] George of Pisidia, *Heraclias* 1.157–158 (247 Pertusi).
[3] Theophanes, *Chron.* A.M. 6114 (308 De Boor, 440 Mango-Scott). Heraclius orders troops on Persian
campaign to spend three days in purification and prayer. Cf. Haldon, *Warfare, State and Society*,
p. 297 n.22. Heraclius similarly asks his troops to choose a crown of martyrs in return for God's
reward: Theoph. *Chron.* A.M. 6115 (310–311 De Boor, 442–443 Mango-Scott).
[4] Theoph. *Chron.* A.M. 6114 (306 De Boor, 438–439 Mango-Scott).

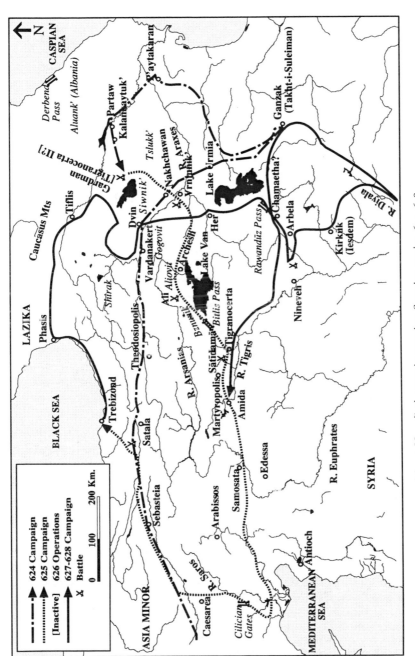

Map 3 Heraclius' campaigns against Sasanian armies, 624–628

army of brigands, you give me no rest. So did I not destroy the Greeks? But you claim to trust in your God. Why did he not save Caesarea and Jerusalem, and the great Alexandria[5] from my hands? Do you not know that I have subjected to myself the sea and the dry land? So is it only Constantinople that I shall not be able to erase? However, I shall forgive you all your trespasses. Arise, take your wife and children and come here. I shall give you estates, vineyards, and olive-trees, whereby you may make a living. And we shall look upon you with friendship. Let not your vain hopes deceive you. For that Christ who was not able to save himself from the Jews – but they killed him by hanging him on a cross – how can the same save you from my hands? 'For if you descend into the depths of the sea,' I shall stretch out my hand and seize you. And then you will see me in a manner you will not desire.[6]

The release or the contrivance of such a letter provided Heraclius with a powerful weapon of propaganda, with patriotic and religious tones. He had it read publicly to Patriarch Sergios and to the elite (magnates), presumably senators and other high officials. He entered St. Sophia Church, placed the letter on the high altar table, and prostrated himself. He underscored the offense to God given by the letter from the Zoroastrian sovereign.

The Muslim historian al-Ṭabarī preserves a later tradition that Heraclius saw a dream in which a person threw down the Sasanian King and stated, "I have delivered him into your hands," which encouraged him to take the offensive against Persia and ultimately to invade it.[7] Heraclius could have floated the story. Other dreams would be attributed to him.

Heraclius, together with his new second wife and niece Martina and two of the children from his first marriage (with Fabia/Eudokia), departed from Constantinople on 25 March 624. He crossed to Chalcedon, then followed the route along the Sea of Marmara. His daughters Epiphania and Eudokia by his first marriage (but apparently not his son Heraclius Constantine) accompanied him as far as the vicinity of Nikomedia where they celebrated Easter on 15 April. He sent his children back to Constantinople while he, Martina, and the Domestikos of the *magister officiorum* Ananianos proceeded to the military expedition. He then named the regency, including his son Heraclius Constantine by his first marriage.[8]

Heraclius' Patriarch Sergios created another liturgical innovation in May 624 at Constantinople. After everyone took the Eucharist, when the clergy were about to replace the flabella, patens, chalices, and other vessels in the sacristy, an antiphon was added to the final verse of Communion: "Let our

[5] To distinguish it from Alexandretta in Syria.   [6] Sebeos, *History* 123, ch. 38 (79–80 Thomson).
[7] *The History of al-Ṭabarī*, V: *The Sāsānids, the Byzantines, the Lakhmids, and Yemen*, trans. C.E. Bosworth (Albany: State University of New York, 1999) 320–321.
[8] Sebeos, *History* 124, ch. 38 (80–81 Thomson); *Storia* c. 36 (95 Gugerotti).

mouth be filled with praise, Lord, so that we may hymn your glory because you have deemed us worthy to share in your Holy Mysteries. Preserve us in your holiness as we rehearse your justice throughout the whole day. Alleluia!"[9] This change was a symptom of the need for spiritual enrichment in a moment of crisis.

Before that liturgical change had taken place, Heraclius had already long departed for the east. His forces allegedly, Sebeos says, numbered 120,000, but this figure is much too high.[10] He went first to Caesarea, in Cappadocia, where he released to his soldiers the text of the supposed letter from Khusrau II, which was contemptuous of Heraclius. This is a reaffirmation of Christian superiority. Caesarea had been the scene of his humiliation in 612, although at that time he did gain an appreciation of its strategic value. He then turned northeast in the direction of Armenia.

It is uncertain how Heraclius devised his long-term strategy and operations for invading the heartland of Persia. Long-standing Roman traditions, which certainly existed a century before Heraclius' operations, advocated very rapid deep strikes as the most effective type of invasion of Persia.[11] Julian had invaded Persia via the Euphrates route in 363 with an estimated 65,000 to 83,000 troops.[12] Warfare between 624 and 628 extended over a vast stretch of Anatolia, the Caucasus, western Iran, and Mesopotamia. This was not fixed positional fighting, but expeditionary warfare of maneuver over vast distances. There was no linear front. Creation, survival, and destruction of armies, not control of towns and territory, were critical. Both opponents heavily depended on adequate provisions for men and beasts as well as accurate knowledge of topography, including routes and the necessary mountain passes and river crossings, for success. Both resorted to stratagems more than massed force, and historical memory records this campaigning in terms of the stratagems of Heraclius and his protagonists, especially Shahrbarāz. Sasanian and Byzantine panegyrists exult and exaggerate feats of their respective sovereigns and commanders while publicizing

---

[9] *Chronicon Paschale* 1.713–714 Dindorf (167–168 Whitby). *PLRE* III: 82, s.v. "Ananianus."

[10] Sebeos, *History* 124, ch. 38 (81 Thomson); *Storia* c. 36 (95 Gugerotti); *Hist.* c. 26 (81 Macler). Probably they numbered a fifth or sixth of that, and in any case not more than a third of that very high figure. See J. Haldon, *Byzantium in the Seventh Century*; Haldon, *Warfare, State and Society* 99–101. James Howard-Johnston, "Heraclius' Persian Campaigns and the Revival of the East Roman Empire, 622–630," *War in History* 6 (1999) 1–44.

[11] Kaegi, "Constantine and Julian's Strategies of Strategic Surprise Against the Persians," *Athenaeum* 69 (1981) 209–213.

[12] On numbers: R. MacMullen, "How Large Was the Roman Imperial Army?," *Klio* 62 (1980) 451–460, esp. 459; MacMullen, *Corruption and the Decline of Rome* (New Haven: Yale University Press, 1988) 173; J.F. Matthews, *The Roman Empire of Ammianus* (1989) 167; J.-M. Carrié, S. Janniard, "L'armée romaine tardive dans quelques travaux récents. 1e partie. L'institution militaire et les modes de combat," *L'Antiquité Tardive* 8 (2000) 321–341.

the embarrassing defeats of their opponents. Traces remain in the written memory.

Heraclius sought allies within the peoples of the Caucasus. This was not a new policy for him, for his initial military actions against Phokas involved recruiting Berbers or Moors, and he had sought to build other alliances while at Constantinople. Now he intelligently sought to expand his forces by drawing on warlike peoples of the Caucasus, whom it was also important to cultivate for information and so they would help with, and not hinder, his logistics and communications.

Heraclius entered Persian territory, according to one chronology, on 20 April 624,[13] allegedly addressing his men by invoking revenge and religious and patriotic sentiments, perhaps with the previous Persian communication in mind:

My brothers, let us keep fear of God in mind and let us struggle to avenge the divine sacrilege. Let us stand courageously against the enemy who have perpetrated so many dreadful acts against the Christians. Let us honor the independent empire of the Romans, and let us stand against the impiously armed enemy. Let us understand that we are inside Persian territory and that flight is very dangerous. Let us avenge the rapes of virgins. Having seen the mutilated members of our soldiers let us labor with our hearts. Danger is not unrequited, but the way to eternal life. Let us stand courageously, and the Lord God will help us and will destroy our enemies.[14]

His soldiers answered: "We have armed our hearts, Emperor, amplifying your mouth's praise. Your words have excited us. Your words have sharpened our swords, made them breathe. We are proud that you are our champion in battle, and we shall obey all of your orders."[15] These are rhetorical evocations of what allegedly was said, not reliable eyewitness transcriptions. They indicate that Heraclius was emphasizing participation and even death in this war as means to heaven. Yet this was no simple religious crusade; it was a multidimensional conflict of which religious zeal was only one component.[16] It is Heraclius and his panegyrists, not the Patriarch or bishops, who are creating any crusade-like features and whipping up religious enthusiasm.

[13] Theophanes, *Chron.* A.M. 6114 (306 De Boor; 439 Mango-Scott).
[14] Theophanes, *Chron.* A.M. 6114 (307 De Boor; 439 Mango-Scott). My translation.
[15] Theophanes, *Chron.* A.M. 6114 (307 De Boor; 439 Mango-Scott).
[16] Crusade is an inappropriate term: G.T. Dennis, "Defenders of the Christian People: Holy War in Byzantium," in *The Crusades from the Perspective of Byzantium and the Muslim World*, ed. Angeliki E. Laiou, Roy Parviz Mottahedeh (Washington: Dumbarton Oaks, 2001) 31–39, and Haldon, *Warfare, State and Society* 27–33, *contra*, Tia Kolbaba, "Fighting for Christianity. Holy War in the Byzantine Empire," *Byzantion* 68 (1998) 194–221; more nuanced: Michael Whitby, "*Deus Nobiscum*: Christianity, Warfare and Morale in Late Antiquity," in *Modus Operandi: Essays in Honour of Geoffrey Rickman* (London: Institute of Classical Studies, 1998) 191–208, esp. 195.

Heraclius encamped near Bathys Rhyax,[17] passed through Satala (Sadak, north of Erzincan), Theodosiopolis (Erzurum), Ayrarat, descended the Araxes River route to Horosan, and destroyed Dvin ("the calamitous destruction of Dwin, among so many deeds, as if one more, one could speak of a calamity by the destruction of a city by a pious emperor, rather than it be preserved in the hands of the impious Khusrau"[18]) and Nakhchawan.[19] It is speculative to argue that he arrived at Nakhchawan around 15–25 June 624.[20]

Learning that Khusrau II was at Ganzak with 40,000 troops, Heraclius set off against him.[21] He sent loyal Arabs ahead, who captured and slew some of Khusrau's guards. Both Byzantines and Persians used Arabs as scouts and advance skirmishers; those of Heraclius may well have been Ghassānids.[22] Khusrau then fled south to Dastagard and his army scattered. Heraclius captured Ganzak, and then pushed on to capture and destroy its renowned fire-temple of Takht-i-Suleiman.[23] He destroyed Thebarmais and its village. He looted and destroyed many towns and much countryside, but Khusrau II had already destroyed much with a traditional scorched-earth policy.[24] Probably Theophanes drew this account from some official or semi-official report issued by Heraclius, or that was very sympathetic to Heraclius and his government and dynasty. The words may well be embellished, but Heraclius did have a reputation for being a good public speaker.[25] Heraclius raided the region of Atrpatakan, as far as the King's residence at Gayshawan.[26]

It is unreasonable to criticize Heraclius for not making a relentless pursuit of Khusrau II into the heart of Mesopotamia at that time. That would have been foolhardy with two major Persian armies and their commanders at his rear. He only dared to do that later when he had defeated more Persian forces and when he had secured the desertion or neutralization of

---

[17] Thomas S. Brown, Anthony Bryer, and David Winfield, "Cities of Heraclius," *BMGS* 4 (1978) 17–22. Location, 28 km west-north-west of Sebasteia. F. Hild, M. Restle, *Tabula Imperii Byzantini* II: *Kappadokien* (Vienna, 1981) 157 -158.

[18] George of Pisidia, *Heraclias* 2.162–166 (258–259 Pertusi). Thomas Artsruni, *History of the House of the Artsrunik'*, ed., trans. R.W. Thomson (Detroit: Wayne State University Press, 1985) 159; Moses Dasxuranci, *History of the Caucasian Albanians* 78–79 Dowsett.

[19] Sebeos, *History* 124, ch. 38 (80–81 Thomson). Theoph. 308 De Boor.

[20] A. Stratos, Βυζάντιον I: 390–391 = *Byzantium in the Seventh Century* I: 154–155.

[21] Sebeos, *History* 124, ch. 38 (81 Thomson).

[22] Shahid, *Byzantium and the Arabs in the Sixth Century* I: 642, 644.

[23] R. and E. Naumann, *Takht-i-Suleiman* (Munich, 1976).

[24] Theophanes, *Chron.* A.M. 6114 (308 De Boor; 439–440 Mango-Scott); Sebeos, *History* 124, ch. 38 (80–81 Thomson).

[25] Hrabanus Maurus, *Homilia* 70, *PL* 110: 132C.

[26] Moses Dasxuranci, *History of the Caucasian Albanians* 2.10 (79 Dowsett).

at least one major Persian commander and his formidable armies. The time was not yet ripe; it was too risky while Heraclius was in Azerbaijan in June 624.[27] That would have been almost the worst possible moment to invade Mesopotamia, for he and his forces would have arrived at the zenith of the summer heat, which is intolerable for military operations, especially for foreigners unfamiliar with coping with those very high temperatures. An impulsive thrust could have been catastrophic; he had made no logistical plans for such an operation.[28] The heat and potential health (that is, disease) problems of central Mesopotamia would at that time of year also have threatened his limited and very valuable experienced manpower, for comparable replacements would not have been easy to find. Already in 624 Heraclius was aware of the heat of central Mesopotamia and its negative effects on unprepared armies from other regions.[29]

Heraclius turned north to winter (624–625) in Caucasian "Albania" after his advisers split concerning whether he should go into winter quarters there or continue to pursue Khusrau II. He made his decision after his soldiers prayed for three days and he consulted the Holy Scriptures.[30] He arrived in Caucasian Albania with 50,000 Persian prisoners of war, whom he released, as winter snows began to fall, in late November. Heraclius endeavored to summon local princes in Albania to meet him and to agree to serve him during the winter and thereafter. Many local chieftains responded favorably, but others refused his invitation or threat, and instead abandoned the city of Partaw at the command of Khusrau II and ensconced themselves in their various mountain fastnesses. The Byzantine army encamped near Partaw at the village of Kalankaytuk', and then crossed the river Trtu (Terter') to the village of Diwtakan.[31] The Byzantine army and its allies threatened many Christians, Jews, and pagans, but a priest Zakaria of Partaw acted to have them spared.

Khusrau II attempted to crush the threat of Heraclius by sending three armies against him. Khusrau ordered Shahrbarāz[32] to follow him and later sent General Shāhīn[33] with another army against him. Persian forces ("The New Army") under Shahraplakan retook many towns and drove the Byzantines back to the region of Siwnik'. Khusrau II in the initial

---

[27] *Contra*: Stratos, Βυζάντιον I: 396–397 = *Byzantium* I: 156–157.

[28] W.E. Kaegi, "Challenges to Late Roman and Byzantine Military Operations in Iraq," *Klio* 73 (1991) 586–594.

[29] Moses Dasxuranci, *History of the Caucasian Albanians* 2.11 (86 Dowsett).

[30] Theophanes, *Chron.* A.M. 6114 (308 De Boor; 440 Mango-Scott).

[31] Moses Dasxuranci, *History of the Caucasian Albanians* 2.10 (80–81 Dowsett). Sebeos, *Hist.* 81–82 Thomson; Thomas Artsruni, *History*, p. 159.

[32] *PLRE* III: 1141–1144, s.v. "Shahrbaraz."   [33] *PLRE* III: 1140–1141, s.v. "Shahin."

months of 625 sent General Sarablangas (Shahraplakan)[34] with elite Persian (Chosroeplekes and Perozitas) units who recovered lost towns and territory and sought to seize passes and *cleisurae* to block Heraclius, who was planning to invade Atropatene and Persia proper. Heraclius reached P'aytakaran, and wished to enter Iberia, crossing the Aluank. Khusrau II also summoned and sent Shahrbarāz with another army from the direction of Armenia to block Heraclius' possible retreat through Iberia (Georgia) and then attack him.[35] Shāhīn led another army of possibly 30,000[36] that sought to catch Heraclius near the Bitlis Pass.

The Lazic and Abasgian and Georgian (Iberian) allies of Heraclius feared encirclement. Heraclius had to extricate himself and his forces from potential annihilation by a rapid series of maneuvers that confused his opponents. Vague sources impede understanding exact topographic details and routes of operations. Shahrbarāz reached Ayrarat, then Gardman. But Heraclius decided to attempt to defeat each in detail: to defeat Sarablangas before Shahrbarāz could unite forces with him. Addressing his soldiers with another injunction, he allegedly remonstrated: "Do not let the number of our enemies disturb us. For, God willing, one will pursue ten thousand. Therefore let us sacrifice to God for the salvation of our brothers. Let us take the crown of martyrdom, so that future time will praise us, and God will return the hostages."[37] Here again there is Heraclian invocation of the promise of eternal life as a reward for death in battle.

Shahrbarāz reached Mrcuin. Heraclius used a stratagem. He sent two false deserters to the Persians, to persuade them that Shāhīn was coming with another army, and that the Byzantines were fleeing. Feigned retreat was an old stratagem. Shahrbarāz and Sarablangas were rivals of Shāhīn, and did not wish him to share in their glory. Heraclius induced them to pursue, he found a grassy plain near "the second" Caucasian Tigranocerta, where he camped and then attacked and defeated in turn Sarablangas and Shāhīn, who fell wounded. Heraclius' forces slew many Persians. His campaign was a text-book execution of the advice of the Maurikios *Strategikon* on how to fight the Persians.[38] He followed the formulae. Theophanes' account of these operations is intelligible in the light of the information in the Maurikios *Strategikon*. Heraclius then went north to the middle Araxes, near

---

[34] *PLRE* III: 1141, s.v. "Shahraplakan."

[35] Moses Dasxuranci, *History of the Caucasian Albanians* 2.10 (79–81 Dowsett).

[36] Sebeos, *History* 124, ch. 38 (81–82 Thomson).

[37] Theoph. *Chron.* A.M. 6115 (310–311 De Boor; 442–443 Mango-Scott). Cf. Theoph. *Chron.* A.M. 6114 (307 De Boor).

[38] John Wiita, "The Ethnika in Byzantine Military Treatises" (Ph.D. diss., University of Minnesota, 1977) 99–108.

Tslukk', and planned to winter in the plain of Nakhchawan. Shahrbarāz followed, as did Shāhīn. Heraclius crossed the Araxes River, at the town of Vrnjunik' and camped there. Shāhīn then appeared but Heraclius defeated him in turn and captured his baggage. Theophanes probably used information from a victory bulletin of Heraclius, not an ideal objective source, but better than some other ones. Shāhīn's remaining forces then joined with Shahrbarāz.[39]

The Abasgians and Lazes deserted after Heraclius withdrew. The Persians planned to assault Heraclius, but there was no combat after he drew up his forces. Heraclius extricated himself, while the Persians found themselves in marshy country.[40] Intending to winter near Lake Van, he went to Baghravand, passed to Apahunik', camped at a village named Hrcmunk. Shahrbarāz marched with 6,000 troops to Aliovit, sent on 6,000 troops to the Arcesh region to try to ambush Heraclius.[41] Heraclius in turn, having learned of this through scouts[42] – espionage was rampant in those campaigns – decided to make a surprise attack with 20,000 troops on Shahrbarāz, who was encamped in the lands of the Salvani. Here again his methods conform to the Maurikios *Strategikon*, whose author emphasized the carelessness with which Persians camped and the vulnerability of their camps to night attacks.[43] Heraclius or his aides took the advice of the author of the *Strategikon* and put it to good effect here. His initial assault wiped out all but one Persian in an advance unit at Ali, who escaped to inform Shahrbarāz, who alone escaped from Arcesh naked and barefoot from the town to reach other troops at Aliovit, while he lost his wives, and all of his men and baggage and his personal effects. This embarrassing defeat[44] probably occurred late in February 625, not at the end of November or early December 625.[45]

The campaign of very early 625 raised Byzantine morale but did not decisively alter the military balance or break Persia's will to continue the war. Heraclius camped somewhere north or northeast of Lake Van, took counsel of his army on 1 March 625 as to how to extricate himself westwards: whether to cross the better pass at Taranta, which was easier but

---

[39] Theophanes, *Chron.* A.M. 6115 (310–311 De Boor; 442 Mango-Scott). Sebeos, *Storia* c. 36 (96 Gugerotti).
[40] Theophanes, *Chron.* A.M. 6115 (310–311 De Boor; 441 Mango-Scott).
[41] Sebeos, *History* 125, ch. 38 (82–83 Thomson).
[42] Sebeos, *History* 125–126, ch. 38 (83 Thomson). Theophanes, *Chron.* A.M. 6115 (311 De Boor; 442–443 Mango-Scott).
[43] Maurikios, *Strategikon* 11.51–53 (358 Dennis-Gamillscheg).
[44] Sebeos, *History* 126, ch. 38 (83 Thomson).
[45] C. Zuckerman, "Heraclius in 625," *REB* 60 (2002) 189–197; *contra*: Stratos, Βυζάντιον I: 429 = *Byzantium* I: 163.

lacked provisions, or the one into Syria and Adana over the Tauros (recall that "Tauros" has a broader meaning in Late Antiquity than it does in the twenty-first century), which offered more difficulties but better supplies.[46] He chose the latter. Heraclius rapidly reached and crossed the Yanarsu (Garzan Su, Nikephorion) River near a point that many identify as the site of the ancient Armenian capital of Tigranocerta (?misidentified by Theophanes as the "Tigris," as it is confused and conflated in the Peutinger Map; perhaps some form of the name "Tigranocerta" or river of Tigran has contributed to the confusion). Seven days after starting out from his encampment north of Lake Van, having managed to cross the Nymphios (Batman Su, Arabic Sātīdamā) River with sharp losses, he reached Martyropolis (Turkish Silvan, or Arabic Mayyafariqīn), and then the Tigris at Amida (modern Diyarbekir). From there he relieved his worried subjects in Constantinople by sending them bulletins,[47] withdrew westwards to the Euphrates, which, despite Shahrbarāz's effort to cut off his retreat, he forded to reach successively Samosata, Germanikeia, and the Saros River (modern Ceyhan River).[48]

Byzantine, Sasanian, and later Muslim stories celebrated the respective stratagems and heroic feats of Shahrbarāz and Heraclius during the latter's rapid retreat, including his posting of guards at the *cleisurae* (fortified passes). Pursuing Perso–Arab forces caught up with retreating Byzantines at the wādī Sātīdamā (Arabic "the bloody" or "bloodthirsty river," modern Turkish Batman Su) River. It is the bloody clash between Heraclius and hotly pursuing Sasanian and allied Arab forces during that campaign of 625 that the pre-Islamic Arab poet al-Aʿshā celebrated and exaggerated as a disaster for Heraclius: "And more than the bold sons of Burjān [?proto-Bulgars?] he [Iyās b. Qabīṣa aṭ-Ṭayy] overcame Heraclius on the day of Sātīdamā (*yawm Sātīdamā*)." The geographer Yāqūt explains, "Khusrau Parwiz sent Iyās b. Qabīṣa al-Ṭayy to slaughter the Romans at Sātīdamā and he slew them and boasted of that." The Arabic glossator to the poetry of al-Aʿshā reports an impossibly garbled but intricate account of events in 625 and 628, jumbling some slaughter of Byzantines at the Nymphios or Sātīdamā with Shahrbarāz's desertion of Khusrau for a coalition with

---

[46] Stratos (Βυζάντιον I: 439–440) could not understand why Theophanes, *Chron.* A.M. 6116 (312–313 De Boor; 444 Mango-Scott) called the route to Amida and Martyropolis Syria, but Theophanes' source thinks in terms of "Asorestan." I accept the chronology of Zuckerman, "Heraclius in 625."

[47] Theophanes, *Chron.* A.M. 6116 (313 De Boor; 444 Mango-Scott). Eutychios, *Hist.* c. 29 (105 Breydy; *Gli anni* 320–321 Pirone). Stratos, Βυζάντιον I: 443–449 = *Byzantium* I: 168, estimates that he reached Amida 15–18 March, left it 20–22 March and reached Samosata three or four days later, on 24–26 March.

[48] Stratos, Βυζάντιον I: 449 = *Byzantium* I: 169, estimates that he reached the Saros on 8–12 April.

Heraclius.[49] Byzantine sources simply refer to Heraclius' crossing the Nymphios, pointedly omitting any humiliating reverse. They even exaggerate the extent of a defeat that Byzantine General Philippikos suffered in 586 at a comparable point on the nearby Yanarsu (Nikephorion, Garzan Su) River where Heraclius' father saw action.[50] Later Arab historical memory of Sātīdamā became confused and separated from the historical context of 625.

The subsequent retreat and maneuvering in 625 near the Saros (Ceyhan) River included another skirmish between Shahrbarāz's and Heraclius' forces in which, according to his official panegyrists, Heraclius distinguished himself by heroically rallying his forces when their Persian foes pursued them.[51] This gave a respite to Byzantine forces, which then managed to pass through the Cilician Gates to the north. A voluntary separation of forces ensued. Heraclius reached the vicinity of Caesarea of Cappadocia, a key base, giving him both defensive and offensive options.[52] After a standoff, Heraclius moved to Sebasteia,[53] crossed the Halys River and wintered (625–626). Khusrau's panegyrists magnified the defeat of Heraclius, while Heraclius' panegyrists in their turn, perhaps in now lost bulletins, sought to cover up embarrassing reverses and exaggerate the emperor's heroic feats in stemming the Persians.

Khusrau II sent his commander Shahrbarāz against Constantinople in 626. Khusrau had not removed Shahrbarāz for failing to destroy Heraclius, but his failure tested Khusrau's patience. At the same time Khusrau entrusted another prominent commander, Shāhīn, with 50,000 troops, including an elite group called the Golden Ones, from Shahrbarāz's forces, and sent them against Heraclius via a northern route. Heraclius deputized his brother Theodore to oppose Shāhīn. Theodore managed to defeat Shāhīn severely at a location that may have been between Koloneia (Shebinkarahisar) and Satala (Sadak, north of Erzincan), probably in July 626. It is probable that Heraclius participated in Theodore's defeat of

---

[49] Rudolf Geyer, *Gedichte von Abu Bashir Maimun ibn Qais al-'A'sha* (London, 1928) poem 36, verse 10, p. 160 and commentary on 159–160. On which see Werner Caskel, "Ein Sonderbarer Anonymus des ersten Jahrhunderts d. H.," *Oriens* 16 (1963) 89–98, esp. 91. I thank Paul Cobb for advice. Sātīdamā: *The Geography of Ananias of Shirak*, trans. and comment Robert H. Hewsen (Wiesbaden, 1992) 59, 160–161, nn. 45–46, 162, nn. 50–51; Yāqūt (= *Jacut's Geographisches Wörterbuch*, ed. Ferdinand Wüstenfeld) 3.6; J. Markwart, *Südarmenien und die Tigrisquellen* (Vienna, 1930) 270–274, explication of al-A'shā poem p. 271.

[50] Theophylact Sim. *Hist.* 2.7.6–2.8.12 (52–54 Whitby trans.); two articles by T. Sinclair, "The Site of Tigranocerta," *REArm* n.s. 25 (1994–5) 183–254; 26 (1996–7) 51–117.

[51] Theoph. *Chron.* A.M. 6116 (313–314 De Boor; 444–445 Mango-Scott).

[52] Sebeos, *History* 126, ch. 38 (83 Thomson).

[53] Stratos, Βυζάντιον I: 454 = *Byzantium* I: 171, estimates that he reached Sebasteia on 20–25 April.

Shāhīn; he may even have led an army himself. The story that the displeased Khusrau II had Shāhīn skinned and salted may be a distorted description of Zoroastrian mortuary practices.[54] Blocked by intervening Sasanian forces, Heraclius could only helplessly observe events in and around Constantinople from a distance.

On 14 and 15 May 626 Constantinople experienced rioting because of popular discontent with John Seismos, whose exact public office is uncertain, because he sought to cancel the bread rations of the *scholae* or imperial guard units and raise its cost from 3 to 8 folles. John allegedly sought to slash the privileges of the *scholae* to conserve resources for the government. Crowds chanted at the Great Church against John, ultimately forcing his removal, and for the Pretorian Prefect Alexander to restore the bread ration.[55] This local riot did not jeopardize the government. Even though the emperor was absent and the situation of the city was perilous, there was, significantly, no effort on the part of anyone to overthrow the regime, the regency, and seize power on behalf of anyone else. That is noteworthy, especially given the recent dismal military situation. The city had only a short respite before more serious problems from outside threatened annihilation. It was a test for both sides as to which had more stamina and cohesion under the strain of protracted war. The public was anxious for Heraclius to return. He in turn attempted to use the rhetoric of George of Pisidia to assuage their fears about his own protracted absences.[56]

Heraclius sent another part of his own army to aid the defense of Constantinople in 626 against threats from Shahrbarāz from the east and from Huns, Slavs, Bulgars, and "Gepids" in the Balkans.[57]

The Persian threat to Constantinople peaked in the summer of 626, because of their successful alliance or entente with Avars. Heraclius authorized the Patrician Athanasios to try a new but unsuccessful diplomatic effort with the Avars, probably in March or April 626. The Persian General Shahrbarāz and his army occupied the area around Chalcedon and laid siege to it, across the straits from Constantinople.[58] They raided and devastated the area and took many captives and generally spread terror. The seventh-century Frankish historian Fredegarius claims that the Persians

---

[54] Theoph. *Chron.* A.M. 6117 (315 De Boor; 447 Mango-Scott).

[55] *Chronicon Paschale* 168–169 Whitby. He may have been prefect of the *annonae*: *PLRE* III: 702, s.v. "Ioannes qui et Seismos 237," where the event is hesitatingly and implausibly misdated to 615.

[56] Mary Whitby, "Defender of the Cross: George of Pisidia on the Emperor Heraclius and His Deputies," in Whitby, *The Propaganda of Power: The Role of Panegyric in Late Antiquity* (Leiden: Brill, 1998) 261–262.

[57] Theoph. *Chron.* A.M. 6117 (315 De Boor, 446 Mango-Scott).

[58] Theodore Synkellos, in L. Sternbach, *Analecta Avarica* 300. Nikephoros, *Short History* 12 (56 Mango).

captured Chalcedon by assault and then burned it.[59] The chronology of
the movements of Shahrbarāz and his forces are inexact, but the usually
trustworthy and contemporary *Chronicon Paschale* reports that he and his
forces had been at Chalcedon for many days before the Avars reached
Constantinople.[60] The movements of Shahrbarāz and the Avars may not
have been precisely and consciously synchronized, but it is likely that they
took account of each other's operations. The issue is whether there was any
advance coordination. The contemporary poetical panegyrist George of
Pisidia states that it existed: "For Slav with Hun, and Scyth with Bulgar
and now Mede making agreement with Scyth, however split by tongue
and geography and however distant from one another, moved all together
against us pretending that their lack of belief was worth more than our
faith."[61] Nikephoros or his source reports, "The barbarians mutually com-
pacted to capture Byzantium."[62]

The Avars did not operate in a vacuum. Their Khan sought to take
advantage of the vulnerable situation of the city during the absence of
the emperor and his army. Given the large number of spies, it was certainly within the capacity of both Avars and Persians to find the means to
communicate with each other, even though communication might have
been irregular. Neither Persians nor Avars left records of their decisions and
actions.

Sources plausibly put the number of defenders of Constantinople at
12,000, under the command of Bonos, the *vicarius* (*topoteretes* or substitute
for Emperor Heraclius), and *magister militum* and Patrician.[63] Heraclius
had entrusted the city to Bonos, and to his children, but reportedly showed
his concern for the city by raising a special prayer to God to save the city:[64]

raising his hands to heaven he cried out to the Lord, "You, Lord, who see and
know everything, know that to you and to the Virgin [the one willingly giving
birth] I have entrusted my children and the city and your people who inhabit it.
I have entrusted to him affairs and the responsibility to deal with the barbarian
animal, the Khagan, as it seems best to him, even if it is necessary to conduct
negotiations with the wretch. Nor can I need to have the decision to triumph over
his wretchedness. But you see how and in what way he intends to act against the
people in your name. You, lord of everything, to whom I have entrusted my soul

[59] Fredegarius, *Chron.* 64 (52–53 Wallace-Hadrill).   [60] *Chronicon Paschale* 170 Whitby.

[61] George of Pisidia, *Bellum Avaricum* 197–203 (185 Pertusi). P. Speck dates this work to the end of
the 620s, presumably between 626 and 629: *Zufälliges zum Bellum Avaricum des Georgios Pisides*
(Munich, 1980) 18–19. His analysis of the contents is thought-provoking, although I do not find
convincing his efforts to impute the poem to the so-called Avar surprise in place of the siege of 626
itself.

[62] Nikephoros, *Short History* 13 (58 Mango, my trans.).   [63] *Chronicon Paschale* 718 (172 Whitby).

[64] Theodore Synkellos, in L. Sternbach, *Analecta Avarica* 302–303.

and life and children and what you have given me, and the city, which you have entrusted to me, guard unharmed what you have trusted to me. For you gave law through Moses, your servant, and you commanded that he remained safe and not be plotted against. Guard for me according to your law the city undamaged and unharmed, which I have committed to the strength of your power and that of the Theotokos, the mother of grace."[65]

Heraclius' children and the Patriarch Sergios prayed for the city.[66]

Theodore Synkellos carefully stressed that Heraclius did not neglect the care and defense of the city.[67] In no sense did Theodore wish nor was it prudent to criticize his emperor. The contemporary George of Pisidia likewise emphasized Heraclius' concern by explaining his instructions to Bonos that prepared Constantinople to withstand the impending siege:[68]

our sovereign, with the sharpest mind, was not absent from our labors even though he was far away, but he was so close in his thoughts even though he was physically distant...but unceasingly being amongst barbarians, like a rose fixed among the thorns and before on our behalf moving in his campaign against the Persians again he did mental battle for us. Constrained by attacks from both directions, he left the nearby labor, and he had the more distant labor. Then he uplifted us by sending letters, like a spent fire is inflamed, in multiplicity ordering the foundations for the walls to be improved as was necessary, to build very high towers, to create bastions, and to make barriers thickly constructed with stakes, and to build a new wall and prepare machines for missiles (arrows) and stones that could be discharged rapidly, and to prepare armed ships which he had not neglected to do before.

George of Pisidia explains further:

And he [Heraclius] sent a mass of soldiery and so neglected his own safety believing that the only secure salvation would be from finding the public safe. He turned almost his entire attention to us lest he would suffer mental harm if he did not suffer every danger for our welfare. In this way ordering and writing everything, he anticipated the recording of the events. He sketched the battle although he was absent, arranging, strategically commanding, and devising the diagrams for constructing the siege machines.

It is inappropriate here to narrate all of the details of the siege, which failed despite Heraclius' absence. According to the *Chronicon Paschale*, the Avar vanguard, which allegedly numbered 30,000, arrived on 29 June 626.[69] The total number of Avar besiegers eventually reached a high number, but

[65] Theodore Synkellos, in L. Sternbach, *Analecta Avarica* 302.31–303.4.
[66] Theodore Synkellos, in L. Sternbach, *Analecta Avarica* 303.5–32, 304.1–16.
[67] Theodore Synkellos, in L. Sternbach, *Analecta Avarica* 303.33–35.
[68] George of Pisidia, *Bellum Avaricum* 246–247, 266–293 (187, 188–189 Pertusi, *Poemi*), and comments of Pertusi, pp. 216–218.
[69] *Chronicon Paschale* 170–171 Whitby.

one that cannot be ascertained with any reliability. Another contemporary, George of Pisidia, spoke of 80,000, which is plausible although probably still too high.[70] The contemporary Theodore Synkellos rightly calls them "myriads," tens of thousands or beyond number.[71] Avars destroyed some buildings, including churches, in the west suburbs. They prevented the inhabitants of the capital from leaving to seek their animals or forage and crops. The Khan constructed a palisade, presumably to protect the besiegers and to channel and trap any sorties or refugees.[72] He had siege machines constructed, including wooden towers and the so-called tortoises (protective constructions for besiegers).[73] After ten days a Byzantine sortie failed because the soldiers had to help rescue threatened civilians and camp followers, whom the Avars sought to capture. The Avars made initial signal fire contact with the Persians across the straits in the middle of July.[74] Athanasios brought the terms of the Khan to Constantinople, which were for its surrender. Athanasios received criticism for listening too much to the Khan. He then reviewed a muster of the defenders, who allegedly numbered 12,000, and reported the strong state of defenses to the Khan. It made no difference. The Khan rejected the final Byzantine overture.[75] On 29 July the actual assault began, with the arrival of the Khan himself and his main army.[76] One cannot trust the exaggerated numbers given for the Avars. It was, however large, probably tens of thousands, including Slavic allies.[77] Theodore Synkellos says,

It was on the land side the most frightening sight to behold, and to see it was to derange the senses. For against each one of our soldiers there were a hundred and more barbarians, all dressed in breastplates and helmeted, bringing every war machine. The sun rising from the east with its rays accentuated the iron, and made them appear frightful, and shook the viewers.[78]

Patriarch Sergios carried the icon of the Virgin around the city walls and through the city as a supernatural defense. On 30 July the Avars set up

---

[70] George of Pisidia, *Bellum Avaricum* 219 (186 Pertusi). On the siege: James Howard-Johnston, "The Siege of Constantinople in 626," in *Constantinople and Its Hinterland*, ed. Cyril Mango and G. Dagron (Aldershot, UK, Brookfield VT: Variorum, 1995) 131–142. Stephan E. J. McCotter, "The Strategy and Tactics of Siege Warfare in the Early Byzantine Period: from Constantine to Heraclius" (Ph.D. diss., Queen's University, Belfast, 1996) 204–214.

[71] Theodore Synkellos, in L. Sternbach, *Analecta Avarica* 300.39.

[72] *Chronicon Paschale* 179 Whitby.   [73] Nikephoros, *Short History* c. 13 (58 Mango).

[74] *Chronicon Paschale* 171 Whitby.

[75] *Chronicon Paschale* 172 Whitby. Theodore Synkellos, in L. Sternbach, *Analecta Avarica* 302.4–8.

[76] *Chronicon Paschale* 173 Whitby.

[77] F. Barisic, "Le siège de Constantinople par les Avares et les Slaves en 626," *Byzantion* 24 (1954) 371–395; P. Speck, *Zufälliges zum Bellum Avaricum des Georgios Pisides*.

[78] Theodore Synkellos, in L. Sternbach, *Analecta Avarica* 305.21–26.

tortoises. On the following day, 31 July, the Avars tried an assault until the eleventh hour, that is, 5 p.m. Towers and trebuchets were put into position. First Slavs attacked, then Avars. An attack in the Pigae area was repulsed.[79] On 1 August, the Avars attempted to bring at least a dozen towers against the walls, between the Gates of Polyandriou and the Romanos Gate, but were defeated after much fighting.[80] The Byzantines took heart that the Virgin was fighting the Avars and protecting them.[81] Bonos offered money for them to leave but they refused. Inside the Golden Horn the Slavs made an attempt to attack with dugout boats.

On 2 August the Khan asked for negotiations and a delegation of five prominent Byzantines (Patrician George, Athanasios, the Patrician and logothete Theodosios, Theodore Synkellos, and Theodore the *kommerkiarios*) was appointed. Three Persian envoys "dressed in pure silk" were present. The Persians offered to send 3,000 troops, or, according to George of Pisidia, 1,000.[82] Again the Khan demanded surrender and for the inhabitants to leave, taking no more than a cloak and shirt with them, to cross over the straits to Shahrbarāz.[83] The Persians allegedly taunted the Byzantine envoys, claiming that, "Your emperor has neither invaded Persia nor has your army arrived."[84] The author of the *Chronicon Paschale* carefully explains that those Persian envoys who had insulted Emperor Heraclius came to a terrible fate for their arrogance. Their interception and beheading is narrated not merely as interception and termination but as an act of benevolence of God, presumably to punish them for their insulting words about the emperor as well as for their hostility to Christianity.[85] On 6–7 August, the Byzantines repelled a major Avaric land assault against the city walls with heavy loss. On 7 August, there was a major naval battle that either resulted in the Byzantine defeat of the Persians, possibly 4,000 horsemen in ships, or Byzantine defeat of an effort to make a connection between Persians and Avars.[86] The Slavs attempted an attack with dugout *monoxyla*, which failed.[87] On 8 August, the Avars began to withdraw their machines and abandoned the siege. Their cavalry burned some suburbs, including the

---

[79] Theodore Synkellos, in L. Sternbach, *Analecta Avarica* 306.   [80] *Chronicon Paschale* 174 Whitby.

[81] Theodore Synkellos, in L. Sternbach, *Analecta Avarica* 306.6–7.

[82] *Chronicon Paschale* 175 Whitby. George of Pisidia, *Bellum Avaricum* 329–331 (191 Pertusi).

[83] *Chronicon Paschale* 175 Whitby. Theodore Synkellos, in L. Sternbach, *Analecta Avarica* 306–307.

[84] *Chronicon Paschale* 721 (Bonn edn., my trans.). This statement is retrospective, for the author knew that by the time of the compilation of this chronicle that Heraclius had successfully invaded Persia and overthrown Khusrau II.

[85] *Chronicon Paschale* 176–178 Whitby. Theodore Synkellos, in L. Sternbach, *Analecta Avarica* 308. Nikephoros, *Short History* c. 13 (58–60 Mango).

[86] Theodore Synkellos, in L. Sternbach, *Analecta Avarica* 308, 310.

[87] Theodore Synkellos, in L. Sternbach, *Analecta Avarica* 311.

churches of Sts. Cosmas and Damian in the Blachernae region.[88] Theodore, brother of Heraclius, reportedly arrived, and there were some negotiations with the Avars, the outcome of which is unknown, except the siege was at an end.[89] Bonos prevented an overzealous Constantinopolitan public, including women and children, from making a premature sortie to try to seize the Avar siege machines. Instead the Khan was allowed to burn them.[90] One wonders whether some payment or gift was given to the Khan to encourage or reward him for withdrawing. The Khan had asked to negotiate with the *kommerkiarios* who probably was Theodore, but Bonos declined and stated that he must now negotiate with Theodore, brother of Heraclius.[91] Theophanes reports that Shahrbarāz remained near Chalcedon and continued during the winter to plunder the countryside and towns there, while the contemporary source Theodore Synkellos says that the Persians withdrew.[92]

The failure of the siege represented a great triumph for Byzantium. To be sure, inhabitants in the Constantinopolitan suburbs had been kidnapped, slain, and wounded, livestock had been driven off or destroyed, and many houses and churches had been plundered and burned. But the walls and the city held. It was a great psychological victory. There was not to be another such coordinated Avaro–Persian action, even though there may have continued to be some cooperation between the two. No one could be sure of that at the time. But communication would not have been easy, even though not impossible. The siege and its defeat were not strictly military actions. They involved espionage and counter-intelligence, diplomatic sparring, and trickery. Such features were typical of other contemporary warfare. There was also the important religious aspect, for the outcome was a religious triumph for the Byzantines.[93] Heraclius had taken a great risk in being absent and his enemies had sought to exploit the situation of his absence; Theodore Synkellos assumes and explicitly argues that the Avar Khan had consciously attacked when he knew Heraclius was absent from Constantinople.[94] But they had wrung no great rewards from their considerable expenditure of efforts, expenses, and manpower. The besiegers had

[88] *Chronicon Paschale* 180–181 Whitby. Also Antoine Wenger, *L'Assomption de la T.S. Vièrge dans la tradition byzantine* 118–23.
[89] Theodore Synkellos, in L. Sternbach, *Analecta Avarica* 312–313.
[90] Theodore Synkellos, in L. Sternbach, *Analecta Avarica* 312–313.
[91] *Chronicon Paschale* 180–181 Whitby. Theoph. *Chron.* A.M. 6117 (316 De Boor). On *kommerkiarios*: Haldon, *Byzantium in the Seventh Century* 232–238.
[92] Theoph. *Chron.* A.M. 6117 (316 De Boor). Theodore Synkellos, in L. Sternbach, *Analecta Avarica* 313.14–27.
[93] Theodore Synkellos, in L. Sternbach, *Analecta Avarica* 314.11–13, 319.18–320.4.
[94] Theodore Synkellos, in L. Sternbach, *Analecta Avarica* 302.17–23.

suffered considerable human losses. But the siege was a terrible warning of the perils of a two-front war. There was no guarantee that a second attempt would also fail, however fervently the Constantinopolitans believed that the Virgin would guard their city. One could not be so sure.

Sources are careful about how their portrayal of Heraclius' absence from the siege. No one could reasonably claim that his absence involved any shirking of responsibilities or fear of danger, because he was on expeditionary campaigning against the Persians, a task that involved much personal risk. The sources tried to prove his solicitude for the inhabitants of his capital, that he took the right decision in not returning for the siege. They wished to show that his mind and concerns were for the capital and its inhabitants.[95] Insofar as any human, in contrast to divine, intervention had any role in the defense of the city, it was Heraclius who was in full charge of those human actions. They cautiously attributed full honor and responsibility to him and to his family, and of course not to any autonomous individual or collective local actions. Even in praising the Patrician Bonos, they try to emphasize the watchfulness and hovering presence of Heraclius.[96] They underscore his indispensability in all of the positive outcomes. Such a representation of Heraclius was even more crucial because of the uneasy and violent origins of his accession to the imperial throne. It would have been normal to emphasize all of these elements for any Byzantine emperor, but in his case it was even more imperative. Theodore Synkellos compared Constantinople with Biblical Jerusalem.[97] He ultimately attributed the defense of the city to the Theotokos.[98] According to the *Chronicon Paschale*, even the Avar Khan claimed to have seen "a woman alone in decorous dress hurrying around on the wall," who presumably was thought to be the Theotokos.[99] Theodore Synkellos' tract is suffused with joy at the relief of the city and praise for the Virgin and her role in defending it. It is also filled with Davidic imagery, a kind of imagery that would be typical in the reign of Heraclius, especially in the next few years. Although the Akathistos Hymn was formerly dated to this period and was thought to be expressing gratitude to God for saving the city from its peril at this time, recent scholarly opinions date it to the fourth or fifth centuries.[100] Byzantine confidence and morale grew, reversing the

[95] Mary Whitby, "Defender of the Cross" (n. 56) 261–262.
[96] George of Pisidia, *In Bonum patricum*, 51–52 (165 Pertusi).
[97] Theodore Synkellos, in L. Sternbach, *Analecta Avarica* 300.
[98] Theodore Synkellos, in L. Sternbach, *Analecta Avarica* 312–313.
[99] *Chronicon Paschale* 725 Dindorf.
[100] The traditional explanation. But it may well date from the fourth, fifth, or sixth century: E.M. Jeffreys, R.S. Nelson, *ODB* 44, s.v. "Akathistos Hymn"; also conversation with Johannes Koder.

recent depths of pessimism and terror. But the empire's adversaries had not yet suffered decisive defeat.

Theodore equated the Persians with the Biblical Assyrians at a moment when Heraclius was on the verge of invading what had once been the core territory of the long-perished and only dimly and very imperfectly remembered Assyrian Empire. Neither Theodore Synkellos nor anyone else recognized that identification and made that association, given their lack of familiarity with facts about ancient Assyria. Nikephoros later continued the tradition of ascribing the victory to divine assistance, especially to the church at Blachernae.[101] Theodore Synkellos also invoked numerology in exalting the defeat of the besiegers, arguing that the Khan had hoped to capture Constantinople on the tenth of the fifth month since the month of April, which, he explains, had Biblical equivalents for other captures of Biblical cities. His explanation may have resonated with Heraclius, who showed a strong personal interest in astrology.[102] The downfall of false astrology was also a theme of writers: George of Pisidia emphasized the confounding and ruin of the false horoscopes of Khusrau II.[103] Such a remark had special significance for Heraclius, even though there was no explicit celebration of the correctness of whatever horoscopes he read.

The Avars and their Slavic allies lacked the technology and the patience to take the city at that time. The Avars were able to construct siege towers and had some kinds of siege engines, but they were no match for the defenses of Constantinople.[104] They and their Slavic and Persian allies lacked the naval resources and training to overcome the sea walls and to master the maritime communications. They also lacked expertise in logistics to calculate, accumulate, and bring up adequate supplies to conduct a long siege. Even the Avar Khan himself allegedly blamed his lack of supplies as the reason for his abandonment of the siege.[105] More important in the eyes of the defenders, if one believes the extant narratives, was divine salvation. The Avars may well have extracted some considerable monetary payment or other material and diplomatic terms from their threat to the city. But to judge from the Byzantine sources, which are not ideal, they either expected to take the city quickly or not at all. When their initial efforts failed, they gave up. It proved impractical for the Persians to give them much

[101] Nikephoros, *Short History* c. 13 (60 Mango). Wenger, *L'Assomption de la T.S. Vièrge* 118–123.
[102] Theodore Synkellos, *Analecta Avarica* 309.12–40, 310.1–25.
[103] George of Pisidia, *Heraclias* 1.61–62 (243 Pertusi).
[104] Byron Tsangadas, *The Fortifications and Defense of Constantinople* (East European Monographs, 71; New York, 1980); McCotter, "The Strategy and Tactics of Siege Warfare in the Early Byzantine Period" 204–214.
[105] *Chronicon Paschale* 180 Whitby.

material assistance. In principle, the combination of the two ought to have accomplished much more.

News of the failure of the siege probably reached Heraclius very quickly.[106] Even if Shahrbarāz's forces blocked couriers from carrying the news by horse across Anatolia to Heraclius, other messengers would have carried it by boat across the Black Sea to some port in Pontos or the coast of Iberia, from where others would have rather quickly made certain it reached Heraclius. Constantinople did receive open or public letters from Heraclius, for they were his medium for maintaining at least some contact and ties with his subjects during his long absence.[107] No one could be certain at the time, but the failure of the siege marked the climax of the Persian War and the most dangerous point in the reign. One can speculate endlessly about counterfactual scenarios that might have happened in 626. But Constantinople did not fall. The Persian-Avar entente did not intensify; if anything, communications became more difficult between the two parties, even though they may have continued to try to coordinate their actions.

The exigencies of the siege and blockade of Constantinople and Heraclius' campaigning in the east made it impractical for him or any of his commanders to offer assistance to the beleaguered Byzantine presence in Spain. The Visigothic King Swintila took advantage of Byzantine weakness in the western Mediterranean and in the Iberian peninsula to complete the conquest of the remnants of Byzantine Spain in 625/6, under circumstances which are obscure. The Byzantines had no viable options.[108]

Heraclius was intent on defeating the Persians at that time. Little did he suspect that he was also gaining an appreciation for logistics and military topography of Anatolia and the Caucasus and northern Syria that would be extremely valuable to him a decade later in attempting to devise defenses against a new enemy, the Muslims. Between 612 and 628 he was criss-crossing parts of Anatolia and the Tauros and the Amanos ranges. He came to learn the value of various nodal points for transportation and the vital role of various mountain passes. He was gaining an appreciation of the relative ease and difficulty in shifting troops, realities of weather conditions, how to calculate timetables for moving troops, possibilities for provisioning troops, and the defensibility of towns. In those campaigns Caesarea of Cappadocia and Theodosiopolis (Erzurum) are both prominent as pivot points. Heraclius surely came to appreciate strategic relationships and the

---

[106] Theodore Synkellos, in L. Sternbach, *Analecta Avarica* 319.27–320.5.

[107] Theodore Synkellos, in L. Sternbach, *Analecta Avarica* 320.5–8.

[108] Margarita Vallejo Girves, *Bizancio y la España Tardoantigua (SS. V-VIII): Un Capitulo de Historia Mediterranea* (Memorias del Seminario de Historia Antigua, 4; Alcala de Henares: Universidad de Alcala de Henares, 1993) 307–310.

dynamics of warfare in different ways than if he had remained at Constantinople. No previous Byzantine emperor had spent that much time or gained such familiarity with the situation in the Caucasus and the southeast. Travel out there also gave Heraclius a different perspective on affairs. He could understand what perspectives might be from different provinces, not just from the point of view of Constantinople. He gained some feel for provincials and their concerns, and how all provincials were not the same, that there was diversity in language, dialect, local customs, climate, and diet. These new perspectives were not exclusively military, but also political: he could better understand how to govern and what was feasible and what was not. His campaigning in 624–625 had demonstrated his cunning, leadership, and resourcefulness. He would soon need to demonstrate them again.

Heraclius departed from the Sebasteia region, made his way to the Pontic coast, embarked his staff and a sturdy but limited number of troops on ships and sailed to Lazica.[109] He himself proceeded in 627 to Lazica, probably part of the way by boat, accompanied by 5,000 soldiers.[110] One thesis maintains that he sailed to Sourmaina (Surmene) in Pontos, and then made his way northeast to Lazic territory,[111] that Heraklonas probably was born there.[112] He passed through the Lazic port of Phasis, at one point, where he met its Bishop Kyros, who impressed him.[113] From there he moved to seek to link up with and recruit Kök Turks,[114] not individual recruits, but units of warriors. As before, Heraclius' skill here was diplomatic as well as military. Heraclius used his diplomatic skills to encourage the Kök Turks to attack Persia, which they did very effectively when it was so vulnerable. He had sent the Patrician Andrew as his ambassador to them early in 625. The return Turkic embassy used the Derbend Pass and then passed through Lazica to reach Heraclius. Negotiations continued in the summer of 625, Heraclius' diplomatic efforts bore fruit in the abortive Turkic invasion of the summer of 626. After devastating much territory but receiving threats

---

[109] Nikephoros, *Short History* 55; Moses Dasxuranci, *History* 83–85. Eutychios, *Hist.* 104 Breydy (320 Pirone). Zuckerman, "The Khazars and Byzantium," in *Proceedings of the International Colloquium on the Khazars* (2002) 10.

[110] Theoph. *Chron.* A.M. 6117 (315 De Boor, 446 Mango-Scott). R.W. Thomson, *Rewriting Caucasian History* (Oxford: Clarendon Press, 1996) 232–235.

[111] Thomas S. Brown, Anthony Bryer, and David Winfield, "Cities of Heraclius," *BMGS* 4 (1978) 22–30, esp. 30.

[112] Brown, Bryer, Winfield, "Cities of Heraclius" 30.   [113] *PLRE* III: 377–378, s.v. "Cyrus 17."

[114] Peter B. Golden, *Khazar Studies* (Bibliotheca Orientalis Hungarica, 25/1; Budapest: Akadémiai Kiadó, 1980) 37–42, 51–59; Golden, *An Introduction to the History of the Turkic Peoples. Ethnogenesis and State Formation in Medieval and Early Modern Eurasia and the Middle East* (Wiesbaden: Harrassowitz, 1992) 127–136, 235–237.

from Khusrau II that he would summon his best generals from the west against them, they abruptly withdrew, having gathered many captives and much booty.[115] But the great booty that they had amassed during their abortive campaign encouraged their cupidity and encouraged their Khan, Yabghu Xak'an, to reassemble his forces and to raid again the next year, 627/628.

Heraclius had to find, create and seal alliances with peoples who could supply him with adequate warriors, especially those who were strategically placed or who possessed urgent specialties in war-making. A prerequisite for success in coalition-building was accurate and timely intelligence, which he appears to have enjoyed. The Kök Turks had been raiding Persian territory successfully, in 626, especially while the Persian armies were campaigning or engaged in occupying Byzantine provinces in the west.

Heraclius himself in early 627 went through Armenia to Bznunik', and from there to Tiflis. Through the chamberlain, Andrew, Heraclius arranged a meeting with Yabghu, the Kök Turk leader.[116] The Kök Turks entered into a ceremony of swearing loyalty to Heraclius in full dress, who shared his crown with Yabghu after the latter dismounted, kissed Heraclius' throat, and swore him loyalty. His commanders all swore loyalty as well. Afterward they celebrated a banquet together, at which occasion Heraclius gave Yabghu jewel-studded earrings and special clothes.[117] Heraclius showed Yabghu a portrait of his sixteen-year old daughter Eudokia, according to Nikephoros, with the intent of starting a process for an eventual marriage tie.[118]

The Kök Turk incursion spread panic in Persia:

Their terror increased at the sight of the ugly, insolent, broad-faced, eyelashless mob in the shape of women with flowing hair who descended upon them, and they trembled before them, especially when they saw their bent and well-aimed bows, the arrows of which rained down upon them like heavy hailstones... and mercilessly slaughtered them in the lanes and streets of the town. Their eyes did not distinguish between the fair, the handsome, or the young among men and women, nor the weak and helpless. They spared neither the lame nor the old,

[115] Moses Dasxuranci, *History of the Caucasian Albanians* 2.11 (82 Dowsett). They probably were Kök Turks, not "Khazars." Peter B. Golden, *Khazar Studies* 37–42, 51–59; Golden, *An Introduction to the History of the Turkic Peoples* 127–136, 235–237; and a communication for which I am very grateful. Only after the fragmentation of these Turks did the Khazars emerge, sometime after 630, as a distinct grouping. See also, A. Bombaci, "Qui était Jebu Xak'an?," *Turcica* 2 (1970) 7–24; Zuckerman, "The Khazars and Byzantium."

[116] Moses Dasxuranci, *History of the Caucasian Albanians* 2.11–12 (85–87 Dowsett).

[117] Theoph. *Chron.* A.M. 6117 (316 De Boor, 447–448 Mango-Scott). Moses Dasxuranci, *History of the Caucasian Albanians* 2.12 (87 Dowsett).

[118] Nikephoros, *Short History* c. 12 (54–57 Mango).

neither did they feel pity, mercy, or compassion for the children who clutched their murdered mothers and sucked blood from their breasts in place of milk. Like fire among straw, they entered in at one gate and emerged through another, and in their wake they left work for the birds and beasts of prey.[119]

Most of the terrified inhabitants of Partaw managed to escape by fleeing to the security of mountain fortresses in the region of Uti, and ultimately on to fortresses in the cantons of Arcax, while their Persian commander Prince Gayshak fled to Persian territory, before the Kök Turks and Byzantines arrived, because they knew that they would be unable to resist.[120] Heraclius and Yabghu besieged Tiflis. Heraclius' forces apparently used the counterweight artillery machine, the trebuchet (*helepolis*), in that siege.[121] Khusrau II sent General Shahraplakan with a relief army of 1,000 cavalry, who emboldened the townspeople to persist in their resistance. Heraclius allowed the Kök Turks to depart because he knew that they were unprepared to engage in a campaign in the hot summer in Mesopotamia, where Heraclius planned to engage in his next operations:

for I can see that you were reared in a cool climate and will be unable to endure the coming of summer in the sweltering land of Asorestan in which the capital of the Persian King lies, on the great river Tigris. When the next year comes and the hot months have passed, return in haste so that we may carry out our plans. I shall not cease to fight the king of Persia and menace and harass his land and people, and I shall arrange things so cunningly that he will be slain by his own subjects.[122]

The Bagratid Stepanos, who ruled K'art'li, maintained loyalty to the Persians, but was slain by the Byzantines while resisting at Tbilisi (Tiflis).

Heraclius here took counsel from the Book of Daniel,[123] which he used to vindicate claims to divine aid, not unlike the consultation that Theophanes had mentioned in his description of Heraclius' decision to choose the route via Syria instead of the other pass. Heraclius apparently made heavy use of Biblical sections to justify himself and his choices. Frequent resort to the Bible reinforced the religious character of this campaign and cause. The townspeople of Tiflis [or those of Kala?] ridiculed Heraclius and the Kök Turk Khan Yabghu Xa'kan. They sketched a picture of the King of the Honk', and jeered him and Yabghu Xa'kan and Heraclius, then stuck a spear through it. The monarchs were irate and swore revenge in the future,

---

[119] Moses Dasxuranci, *History of the Caucasian Albanians* 2.11 (83–84 Dowsett).
[120] Moses Dasxuranci, *History of the Caucasian Albanians* 2.11 (84 Dowsett).
[121] G. Dennis, "Byzantine Heavy Artillery: the Helepolis," *Greek, Roman and Byzantine Studies* 39 (1998) 99–115.
[122] Moses Dasxuranci, *History of the Caucasian Albanians* 2.11 (86 Dowsett).
[123] Thomson, *Rewriting Caucasian History* 234.

when they departed from this siege.[124] In this case Heraclius turned the Bible against a satirical remark of defenders of Kala against him, who had called him a goat. He then had a subordinate besiege the town, capture and fill the mouth of the insolent Jibla with gold, then flay off his skin and send it to Heraclius. This was late August or early September 627.[125] Yabghu returned to his own country having reportedly left 40,000 troops with Heraclius, but this number is probably exaggerated.

Heraclius was not the first nor the last Byzantine emperor to attempt to forge an alliance with Turkic peoples north of Persia: already there had been approaches in the reign of Justin II during the previous century. But he found a powerful lever in the form of the Kök Turks. His alliance with the Kök Turks was more solid and effective than some of his efforts to make alliances with other peoples in the unruly Caucasus, some of whom clearly preferred affiliation with the Sasanian Empire. But the situation was a dynamic one. He did not need to win the compliance and cooperation of every people in the Caucasus. His alliance with the Kök Turks was a powerful one that was mutually beneficial. Probably the Kök Turks also gained plunder and trade privileges, but they also gained rich luxury goods, presents, precious metals, clothes, titles, regalia, and valuable intelligence about the Persians from the Byzantines. As Khusrau II reportedly said, what the Kök Turks seemed to want were "gold and silver and precious stones and muslin and purple robes embroidered with gold and encrusted with pearls."[126] Such objects were not surprising ones to covet. Presumably Heraclius had seen to it that the Byzantines had given some of these to the Kök Turks. The alliance would have more utility in the future. The Persians could not be sure when or where the Kök Turks might again strike. The alliance exposed many areas of Persia's northern frontiers, complicating the deployment of troops and commanders, when they might well be needed to fend off Heraclius as well as to try to hold onto Persian conquests in the west.

Heraclius was winning victories through diplomacy more than through sheer military might. Or as his contemporaries may have put it, he was winning through cunning.[127] These skills he had finely honed. He profited more from them than the Persians, who themselves had sought to use diplomacy with the Avars as a lever and as a diversion. But such skills had their limits. Up to this moment, Heraclius was still playing a winning

---

[124] Moses Dasxuranci, *History of the Caucasian Albanians* 2.11, 13 (86, 94–95 Dowsett).

[125] Thomson, *Rewriting Caucasian History* 234–235. Zuckerman, "The Khazars and Byzantium – The First Encounter." Cf. Moses Dasxuranci, *History of the Caucasian Albanians* 2.16 (104–106 Dowsett).

[126] Moses Dasxuranci, *History of the Caucasian Albanians* 2.11 (82 Dowsett).

[127] Allegedly Heraclius claimed such skills: Moses Dasxuranci, *History of the Caucasian Albanians* 2.11 (86 Dowsett).

game by using diplomacy to win alliances, and to confound and confuse his foe without suffering large human losses on the battlefield. Of course any campaigning involved heavy human losses through medical problems and desertions. But he had not yet demonstrated that he was a great captain. The skills he was demonstrating were a variation on the kind of skills he had used in civil war to overthrow Phokas and his brother Komentiolos. Although it is easy to emphasize that Heraclius was waging a religious crusade through these military operations, as well as against the pagan or shamanistic Avars, he and his fellow Byzantine leaders were always willing, at least ostensibly, to engage in negotiations. They displayed readiness to be flexible, even though such a stance may have masked their real desire to find ways to use trickery to undermine and destroy their opponents without having to risk a test on the field of battle. They shared that predisposition with their opponents. So this was no simple holy war. It involved fight–talk, talk–fight, a type of warfare that characterized violence between Byzantium and Persia in the reigns of Justin II and Tiberius II.

Heraclius had not allowed himself to be diverted from creating the conditions for a decisive blow against Khusrau II. Despite the panegyrists' exaggerations, the decision to risk everything by proceeding to the Caucasus was his. Instead of trying to defend and save every piece of territory and every fortified town in Anatolia, he correctly and boldly struck off to the strategic Caucasus, where he could find recruits, damage Persian prestige, live off the enemy's resources, find alliances, and ultimately post himself to strike against Persia. The Persian decision to strike at Constantinople may well have had as its objective pressuring Heraclius to abandon operations in the Caucasus.

When the siege of Constantinople failed and the Persians and Avars both suffered from failure in their efforts, Heraclius was in a strategic position of inestimable value. Events proved the rectitude of his gamble and judgment in remaining in the east. He was free to pursue his plans to bring the war to the Sasanian heartland, preferably with a minimum of Byzantine human losses, and to the greatest extent possible with the diplomatic, military, and intelligence support of other warlike peoples who were willing to serve against the Persians. His operations in 626 confirm the soundness of his military judgment with respect to tactics and strategy. Throughout he continued to demonstrate his understanding of political realities by his persistent and successful efforts to maintain contact with his subjects during the siege. If the siege had persisted, pressures on him to abandon his operations in the Caucasus would have intensified. He maintained rather good communications with Constantinople, which helped to avoid confusion and despair. Heraclius had a different range of military experience from the Byzantines whom Persians had normally encountered. Whether he had learned unique stratagems or tactics while in Africa is uncertain, and if so, they had not enabled him to beat the Persians in 612 and 613. But they gave him a very different repertory of ways of fighting to other Byzantines whom Persian commanders had met. It was an imponderable, a useful mystery.

Counterfactual speculation about what would have happened if the Avars and Slavs had captured Constantinople can lead to all kinds of curious extrapolations, but would be essentially unhistorical. The Persians themselves never appear to have possessed the means to make a serious effort to capture the city themselves.[128] Their operations in the vicinity of Chalcedon posed a serious threat to Byzantine authority and they did inflict serious physical and monetary damage, as well as escalating psychological terror. Capture of Constantinople would in all likelihood have dealt a decisive blow against the Byzantine Empire at that time, even more serious than in 1204, because there was no reasonably secure heartland elsewhere in Europe or Asia if the capital had fallen.

But Heraclius was not the only one to gain more familiarity with terrain in Anatolia and in the Caucasus. Arabs served prominently as scouts for both Byzantines and Persians. In doing so they were also gaining familiarity with the fundamentals of military campaigning in those regions. Although it was never intended that way, their knowledge might be willingly or involuntarily communicated to or made accessible to other Arabs in the future for objectives that would be harmful to the Byzantines. But no one could imagine or anticipate that in the desperate years of the 620s, when there were more immediate threats.

The narratives of these years continue to highlight hypersensitivity to any insult to the reputation or image of Emperor Heraclius. They stress the terrible fate of those who insult or demean him, while they also point to the equally grim fates of those who insult the Christian name or symbols. The sensitivity to the majesty of the emperor is a standard theme in Byzantine literary and visual representation in any era. One wonders whether during Heraclius' reign, given the irregular nature of his assumption of imperial power, that sensitivity of contemporary authors was an attempt to overcompensate for his irregular accession and any other uneasy associations that might taint it. It may well actually reflect his own hypersensitivity to such deprecations of his majesty and station.

---

[128] McCotter, "Strategy and Tactics of Siege Warfare" 405–429, on Persian capabilities.

The course of events veered sharply. Conventional military strategy and tactics ceased to be the exclusive means for Heraclius to achieve victory. Opportunities arose that permitted him to excel in what he had always done best, namely, seizing on opportunities to create a turning point in a volatile and risky situation that could have gone either way, one in which the outcome was not inevitable. His good sense of timing and his ability to resort to a number of methods that were not exclusively open military combat had served him very well in civil war. Now a situation arose in which he could employ his diverse skills to defeat the Persians and their monarch using battle, diplomacy, deception, and speed to achieve the outcome that he wanted.

Khusrau II became disaffected with his best general, Shahrbarāz. Whether his disaffection resulted from calumny on the part of envious detractors at Khusrau's court is uncertain, although that has been alleged. Khusrau may have feared the accumulation of so much wealth and power in the west by one general, who might be tempted to repeat the actions of the abortive usurper Bahram in the year 590, who came close to depriving Khusrau of his throne. It is said that Khusrau became frustrated with the desultory progress of Shahrbarāz against Byzantium and especially his disappointing performance in the 626 siege or blockade of Constantinople.

The truth has been lost in a panoply of later stories in several languages about the craftiness of Heraclius and Shahrbarāz. The source of Theophanes reports that Khusrau sent a messenger to the Persian officer Kardarigan to kill Shahrbarāz, but Byzantine soldiers in Galatia intercepted the messenger, whose message was taken to Heraclius' son Heraclius Constantine III, who in turn transmitted it to Heraclius. Heraclius informed Shahrbarāz of the letter's contents, and arranged a meeting with him and showed him the letter. Shahrbarāz then made a pact with Heraclius' son and Patriarch Sergios of Constantinople.[129] Presumably that pact relieved Constantinople of the threat of siege and probably established modalities of a relationship between Byzantine authorities and Shahrbarāz, probably including outlines of halting armed hostilities and how to handle any cease-fire problems between the Byzantines and Persians. Shahrbarāz then falsified a letter in the name of Khusrau II to order the slaying of four hundred Persian officers, then reported its contents to them, which naturally enraged them, and thereby persuaded them to join his cause of rebellion against Khusrau II.[130]

[129] Theophanes, *Chron.* A.M. 6118 (323–324 De Boor, 452–453, 458 Mango-Scott).

[130] Walter Kaegi and Paul M. Cobb, "Heraclius, Shahrbarāz, and al-Ṭabarī," in *Al-Ṭabarī: The Historian and His Work*, ed. Hugh Kennedy (Princeton: Darwin, 2002). Cf. critical arguments for plausibility: Beihammer, *Nachrichten* nos. 26, 27, pp. 39–41.

How Shahrbarāz viewed the unfolding of the Avar–Persian siege of Constantinople is unknown. It is unclear what more Shahrbarāz could have done to aid the Avars and Slavs. In principle, the Persians could have brought more naval support from their Levantine or Egyptian ports. But in all likelihood the personnel who would have manned such ships would have had to be Christian. That option would probably have required different Persian policies of conciliating and recruiting among Christians that Shahrbarāz could not have conceived and authorized on his own responsibility alone. Likewise there are no reports of any negotiations at that moment between him and the Byzantines, even though a decade earlier there had been talks between Heraclius and General Shāhīn when Shāhīn had temporarily set himself up in virtually the same location as Shahrbarāz now held.

There is no secure evidence that Shahrbarāz contemplated switching sides during the siege. All evidence is that up to this point he was still loyally following orders from Khusrau II and was doing his best to defeat the Byzantines. Perhaps he or one of his subordinates had been involved in informal contacts, but nothing concrete indicates that he had thus far switched sides or had been derelict in his duties to his king.[131] Yet his actions do appear to have been limited in support of the Avars. His passivity or lack of maximal exertion may well indicate some propensity to weigh options and avoid all-out expenditure of efforts.[132] However, Khusrau II cannot have been pleased with the failure of this siege and assault in August 626, when that news reached him. Even though Shahrbarāz probably was not at fault, his actions displeased Khusrau II. There would be repercussions. The failure of the siege worsened relations between Khusrau II and Shahrbarāz. High officials and subjects of the Sasanian Empire cannot have been happy with the trend of developments. It is even uncertain whether they received accurate reports. The failure of the siege may well have encouraged rivals of Shahrbarāz to lobby and intrigue against him with their sovereign, Khusrau II. In turn the Avar Khan himself experienced rising dissatisfaction with his subject peoples because of the botched siege and his loss of prestige.

Shahrbarāz's forces had been closer to those of Heraclius Constantine and the Patriarch than to Heraclius himself. The omission of the name of Bonos may or may not be significant. He died in May, and was buried at the monastery of St. John the Baptist/Studion, near the Golden Gate, on 11 May 627.[133] His death deprived Heraclius of an important and trusted

---

[131] *Chronicon Paschale* 177 n. Whitby.
[132] Mango, "Deux études sur Byzance et la Perse Sassanide," *TM* 9 (1985) 107.
[133] *Chronicon Paschale* 726–727, cf. 182 Whitby.

ally, but fortunately he died after the end of the siege of Constantinople, when Heraclius was on the offensive. He was no longer indispensable.

Galatia was a crossroads where such an interception of a Persian courier from the King to a prominent officer near Shahrbarāz might well have taken place, where Byzantines might well have stationed patrols and checkpoints. Heraclius and his son Heraclius Constantine III, despite their distance from one another, remained in contact, as we know from reports of Heraclius' conduct during the Avar–Persian siege of 626. Heraclius Constantine III managed to report the capture of the courier to Heraclius, who then took advantage of it to achieve a reversal of alliances, or switching of sides. Heraclius had been expert at that since his rebellion against Phokas in the years 608–610, and during his negotiations with Komentiolos, the brother of Phokas, in late 610. Switched letters do happen, as the history of events in the sixth century already demonstrated (the Ghassānid phylarch al-Mundhīr learned of Justin II's orders to murder him because he mistakenly received a switched letter).[134] There had already been contact between Shahrbarāz's entourage and those close to Heraclius, ever since Shahrbarāz conquered Palestine from the Byzantines in 614. Over the long course of warfare and occupation many opportunities would have arisen for additional contact and probes. The exact date of the interception of the letter and the subsequent negotiations is uncertain. It did not occur before or during the actual Avar–Persian siege of Constantinople, but after it. It required some time for Heraclius and Shahrbarāz to cross-check the information from the interception before embarking on any dramatic policies, probably at least two months or more. The key events probably occurred late in 626 or very early in 627.

The neutralization of Shahrbarāz's army was a turning point. This relieved Heraclius of his fears for the safety of his capital and the imperial family, and of any major threat to his rear. The trustworthiness of the new relationship with Shahrbarāz, whose forces remained intact and strategically well placed, remained problematic. If Heraclius jumped off on a distant expedition into Persian territory, he risked his communications and ultimately himself and his men. If he suffered defeat or encountered great obstacles, Shahrbarāz could always switch again. We cannot trace the exact location and movement of Shahrbarāz and his forces immediately before and after he made this agreement with the Heraclian family.[135] Probably

---

[134] Shahid, *Byzantium and the Arabs in the Sixth Century* I: 354–356. For an early twentieth-century example, in 1907 the Sultan's bureaucracy in Morocco mixed up two letters, engendering rebellion: Douglas Porch, *The Conquest of Morocco* (New York: Knopf, 1983) 120–121.

[135] Important is Cyril Mango, "Deux études sur Byzance et la Perse sassanide," *TM* 9 (1985) 91–118. Paul Speck, *Das geteilte Dossier* 144–152, is learned but unfamiliar with problems in the eastern sources and

Shahrbarāz, to judge from Armenian and Arabic sources,[136] withdrew his men from the vicinity of Constantinople a few days after the lifting of the siege. He then moved from the Anatolian plateau and concentrated his forces strategically in northern Syria, probably in Cilicia and in and around Alexandretta (Alexandria ad Issum) and Antioch. This was an agriculturally rich area where he could find food for his troops and their beasts. From there he could dominate his communications with Persia, could continue to control Palestine. He was sufficiently close to the mountain passes across the Tauros range, if he wished, to resume operations in Anatolia against the Byzantines. Yet he was in a position to intervene relatively expeditiously in affairs in Persia while preserving his communications with Persia. Although the numbers of his forces are uncertain, he commanded Persia's best battle-hardened troops. From his location he could, without loss of life, exert great leverage on both Heraclius and on Khusrau II. His desertion of Khusrau II in turn could have caused some desertions from his ranks, but we have no confirmation of any attrition. Heraclius probably wintered in Constantinople.

The traditions in the Arabic accounts of 'Ikrima,[137] preserved in al-Ṭabarī, and by Ibn 'Abd al-Ḥakam,[138] have some value and differ somewhat from those of Theophanes and Nikephoros, *Short History*.[139] Ibn 'Abd al-Ḥakam claims that Khusrau II became frustrated with the length of time Shahrbarāz spent in the west and ordered that he be executed and that another take his place and bring the armies back. It is a fascinating source on the use of deception by both Byzantine and Persian authorities. It is consistent with other Muslim sources' depiction of Heraclius as a wise ruler who knows more than his subordinates.

Both tradents report Persian anger at Khusrau's treachery, which was discovered through letters, but in neither case through the mediation or forgery of Heraclius. Both depict Khusrau as suspicious, irascible, impatient, and an arrogant ingrate. Neither identifies the specific locality where the meeting between the two commanders took place. Neither mentions the restoration of the Cross or any Christian relics from Jerusalem or

brings forth unconvincing arguments. Important neglected traditions in the gloss accompanying the poetry of al-A'shā: Rudolf Geyer, *Gedichte von Abû Bashîr Maimûn ibn Qais al-'A'sha* (E.J.W. Gibb Memorial Series; London: Luzac, 1928) 158; on him see John Dennis Hyde, "A Study of the Poetry of Maimun ibn Qays al-A'shā:" (Ph.D. diss., Princeton University, 1970).

136 Al-Mas'ūdī, *Livre de l'avertissement et de la revision*, trans. B. Carra de Vaux (Paris, 1897) 216. Al-Mas'ūdī, *Prairies d'or* 2.233 (Berbier de Meynard). Sebeos, *History* 128, ch. 39, 129, ch. 40 (86, 88 Thomson).

137 On 'Ikrima: J. Schacht, "Ikrima," *EI* ² III: 1081–1082.

138 Ibn 'Abd al-Ḥakam, *Futūḥ miṣr*, ed. Charles Torrey (New Haven: Yale University Press, 1922) 35–37. But see more skeptical remarks of Beihammer, *Nachrichten* nos. 26, 27, 39 pp. 39–41, 54–60.

139 Nikephoros, *Short History* 12.51–64 (56–58 Mango, and commentary on p. 181).

elsewhere. Perhaps Muslim traditionists purged the fact that Shahrbarāz was involved in restoring important Christian relics as part of his agreements with Heraclius. Shahrbarāz is depicted as honest and conscientious, in general in a positive light. There is no mention of the erection or dedication of any church of Irene ("Peace") at Arabissos in commemoration of this peace agreement. Muslim traditions do not mention Heraclius' agreeing to support Shahrbarāz to be king or his son to be Shahrbarāz's successor as king. There is a Muslim tradition of the execution of Shahrbarāz's son by 'Umar, so it is possible that the Muslim tradition wishes to suppress any memory of such an agreement. No Muslim account exists of resentment against Shahrbarāz for any alleged slight by Christians, as reported in the *Chronicle of Si'īrt*,[140] or of any possible marriage arrangement between Heraclius' and Shahrbarāz's families, or hostages. However, the stress on Heraclius' suspicions could support the need to supply some kinds of assurances. Zuhrī's tradition, as preserved by Ibn 'Abd al-Ḥakam, is more plausible than that of 'Ikrima. Muslim traditions do not assert, as do the traditions of Theophanes and Nikephoros, that Shahrbarāz himself forged a letter from Khusrau to convince his generals and soldiers to accept his switching of sides in the war. But all traditions associate Shahrbarāz's switching with growing enmity between himself and Khusrau that somehow broke out because Shahrbarāz learned of Khusrau's instructions that he be slain. There is no reference to Niketas, son of Shahrbarāz, in either Muslim text about this meeting. Shahrbarāz, in Ibn 'Abd al-Ḥakam's account, is not the victim of any calumny by other Persians, nor was Khusrau in flight from Heraclius or other Byzantine forces when he summoned Shahrbarāz.

Muslim traditions are vague about specifics, including dates. Their authors may merely seek to report the final moments of irreligion before the coming of Islam and the poor nature and character of the final great Sasanian ruler. They underscore Heraclius' cautiousness and explain the Persian defeat in terms not of any Byzantine revival or competence of Heraclius, but as a result of Persian actions, misgovernment and mismanagement on the part of the Persians, who are the principal responsible actors.

Heraclius, as far as is known, did not receive any units of Persian troops to assist his operations. He may have profited from intelligence that Shahrbarāz supplied, or individual key soldiers or commanders from the ranks of those whom Shahrbarāz commanded, but no entire combat units.

The desertion or studious passivity of Shahrbarāz and his soldiers and commanders is the critical event that permitted Heraclius to invade Persia

---

[140] *Histoire Nestorienne = Chronicle of Si'īrt*, ed. A. Scher, R. Griveau, *PO* 13: 551–552, 556.

and to make the choices that he did. Heraclius was aware of climatic conditions inside Persia and had no desire to attempt any invasion in the peak of the summer heat in central Mesopotamia. He certainly knew of the estrangement of Shahrbarāz from Khusrau II by late summer of 627, which encouraged him to risk military operations in the winter months. He probably decided to strike while the situation was very opportune, and not allow Khusrau II the time to find expedients to adjust to Shahrbarāz's desertion. The situation was very unstable. This was not conventional warfare. He had diplomatic and financial objectives, including internal subversion in Persia. It was imperative for Heraclius to invade the heart of Persia, to strike at Khusrau II, when he did. Ctesiphon, the Sasanian capital, was not necessarily Heraclius' objective. It is unclear whether its capture would have been decisive, except for intensifying the shaking and shattering of Sasanian morale and confidence.

Ancient Roman memoranda advised swift strikes against Persia.[141] But there was no recent precedent for such operations. Heraclius had led troops along the Euphrates, but failed to make any deep penetration. It would have been natural for Persians to expect any new Byzantine operation to take such a direction again. However, any such action on the part of Heraclius would also have threatened Shahrbarāz, who would not have wished Heraclius to place himself between the Persian heartland and Shahrbarāz's possible route of evacuation and escape from Byzantine territory. That might have triggered the overthrow of Shahrbarāz by other commanders within his ranks. The actual route of invasion that Heraclius selected was one that minimized any threat to Shahrbarāz, while Shahrbarāz himself and his troops would not have posed so much of a threat to Heraclius on that route. Heraclius "was troubled by fear of Khoream [Shahrbarāz]."[142]

Heraclius probably profited from excellent intelligence from Armenians and other disgruntled groups from within Persian ranks, in several regions, including but not limited to occupied areas. His Arab scouts may have gained intelligence from contacts with Arabs who served in Sasanian ranks. Possibly there were even other Persian converts to Christianity, not limited to St. Anastasios the Persian and his acquaintances. Some Christians in Persian-occupied Syria served the Sasanian administration and had other ties. Thus a Jacobite named Yunan served as physician to Khusrau II himself but had a relative, Qurra, who was in charge of levying taxes in Edessa,

[141] Kaegi, "Constantine and Julian's Strategies of Strategic Surprise Against the Persians," *Athenaeum* 69 (1981) 209–213.
[142] Sebeos, *Hist.* 127, ch. 39 (84 Thomson).

and was unpopular for that reason.[143] The future St. Anastasios the Persian deserted the Persian army and took residence with and became apprentice to a Christian gold jeweler from Persia who had established himself at Hierapolis, in northern Syria.[144] Another Persian jeweler, who had been Zoroastrian, lived at Jerusalem and also converted to Christianity, and was executed at Edessa.[145] These unidentified Persian immigrants are examples of the mobility of populations, which unwittingly created in itself opportunities for change and disruption. Other apparently Christian Persians resided at Caesarea in Palestine.[146] The temporary removal of the borders probably permitted other Christians from Persia to move into Sasanian-occupied Syria and possibly also into Egypt. New opportunities to make money appeared and attracted some Persians.[147] These new demographic influxes and related upheavals unintentionally created conditions in which networks of espionage could develop, even though there is absolutely no evidence whatever that these above-mentioned gold jewelers ever engaged in or ever contemplated engaging in such activities.

A fifth column may have existed among some Christians. Khusrau II reportedly worried about espionage among Chalcedonian communities in northern Syria. Some Chalcedonians did serve as a supply pool for spies even though other innocent ones suffered from the paranoia that all Chalcedonians were inclined to spy on Persians.[148] Compulsory deportation of Chalcedonians from Edessa and other locales to Persia created even more malcontents who might engage in espionage or sabotage.[149] So Heraclius had many means by which to gain information about conditions within Persia. He needed to reconfirm and assess the quality and accuracy of that information.

Heraclius and his advisers also faced internal troubles. Despite the gravity of the military situation in the east during the troubled years 626–627, discord between secular and ecclesiastical authorities persisted in the far west. Pope Honorius vigorously protested in June 627 the interference of the Byzantine governor (*praeses*) Theodore of Sardinia in matters of ecclesiastical discipline within that island. Honorius invoked precedents from the end of the fourth century in support of his position. The governor of Sardinia attempted to prevent papal jurisdiction from handling a troublesome case of

---

[143] Agapios, *Kitāb al-Unvān*, PO 8: 459.　　[144] *Acta* 8 (ed. B. Flusin) I: 48–49.

[145] *Acta* 10 (I: 50–51 Flusin).　　[146] St. Anastasios the Persian, *Acta* 31 (I: 74–75 Flusin).

[147] Persian communities still existed in parts of Syria at the time of the Muslim conquest, but it is uncertain whether they included earlier migrants or refugees from vanquished factions in the bitter internal Persian struggle for the succession after the murder of Khusrau II. The vanquished may have fled for their lives into Byzantine territory.

[148] Agapios, *Kitāb al-Unvān*, PO 8: 460.　　[149] Agapios, PO 8: 460–461.

clerical discipline by referring it to the judgment of the governor (Pretorian Prefect) of Africa.[150] Honorius protested to Sergius, subdeacon in Africa, hoping that Gregory, Pretorian Prefect of Africa, would discipline the governor of Sardinia for exceeding his authority. The outcome of the dispute is unknown, but it is a reminder that secular and ecclesiastical authorities did not suspend their quarrels for the sake of the struggle against the Zoroastrian Sasanians. The case foreshadows the persistence of disputes in the same region a few decades later even as the Muslim threat grew. Institutional rivalries persisted while the Papacy asserted its prerogatives. Every issue did not find deferral until the end of the desperate military struggle in the east. Old proclivities remained.

Heraclius developed an excellent expeditionary force, perfected tactics, and managed to defeat Sasanian commanders and their forces on several occasions between 624 and 627. He shaped a strategy. In part due to his skills, things were falling into place. With the temporary neutralization of Shahrbarāz, construction of a coalition with the Kök Turks, and superb intelligence on routes and the internal cleavages and strains within the Sasanian Empire, Heraclius was ready to risk a bold thrust into his opponent's interior. But he would adhere to one other persistent practice he had polished in the preceding years: insistence on keeping his subjects informed of military progress from the Byzantine imperial perspective. He had honed his skills at communication and morale-building that would significantly contribute to military effectiveness and ultimate victory in the final phase (Phase 4) of the protracted operations against the Persians.

---

[150] Mansi, *Sacrorum conciliorum nova et amplissima collectio* 10.582; *Regesta Pontificum Romanorum* 2014–2015 (I: 224 Jaffé); André Guillou, "La diffusione della cultura bizantina," in *Storia dei Sardi e della Sardegna*, ed. Massimo Guidetti (Milan: Jaca Book, 1987) 382–384.

CHAPTER 5

The invasion of Mesopotamia

Heraclius' strategy in 627–628 in Phase 4 of his warfare against the Persians was a bold one that allowed him to manage risks rather well. He discerned an opportunity that he exploited to the fullest while understanding his limits. He demonstrated a rare combination of excellent strategic and operational skills. There was no adequate Persian force to interpose between him and the fertile, rich center of the Persian Empire, and the residence and governmental nerve center of Khusrau II. The region of Nineveh was a center of gravity that gave him the initiative and key to the heart of Mesopotamia. It had been critical for Alexander the Great at Gaugamela and again in AD 750 when the battle of the Zāb sealed the fate of the Umayyads. The victory in December 627 created a new dynamic situation, which Heraclius appreciated and exploited. The initiative was his to maintain.

Literary representation depicts Khusrau's surprise at Heraclius' decision to invade in the winter,[1] but he probably already had dispatched the commander Roch Vehan to oppose Heraclius.[2] Victory bulletins of Heraclius, issued to communicate with his subjects, may be the underlying source. Although they are not objective archival documents, they do contain some unique details that indicate what Heraclius and his advisers wanted his subjects to know and to believe.[3] They portray Heraclius, as he no doubt wanted to be, as burning many Persian villages and cities; this was probably conceived to be revenge for Persian ravages in Byzantine territory and to sate the public's desire for such revenge.

[1] Theophanes, *Chron.* A.M. 6118 (317 De Boor).
[2] Sebeos, *History* 126, ch. 38 (83 Thomson); *Storia* c. 36 (97 Gugerotti); *Hist.* c. 26 (83–84 Macler).
[3] Topography of this expedition: Kaegi, "Challenges to Late Roman and Byzantine Military Operations in Iraq (4th–9th Century)," *Klio* 73 (1991) 586–594; and "The Battle of Nineveh," *AABSC* 19 (Princeton University, 1993) 3–4, called attention to the long-overlooked (by Byzantinists) Sarre and Herzfeld, *Archäologische Reise im Euphrat- und Tigris-Gebiet,* in which they identified many placenames cited in the text of the *Chronographia* of Theophanes. Michael McCormick, *Eternal Victory* (Cambridge: Cambridge University Press, 1985) 193–195; J. Howard-Johnston, "The Official History of Heraclius' Persian Campaigns," in *The Roman and Byzantine Army in the East,* ed. E. Dabrowa (Cracow, 1994) 57–87.

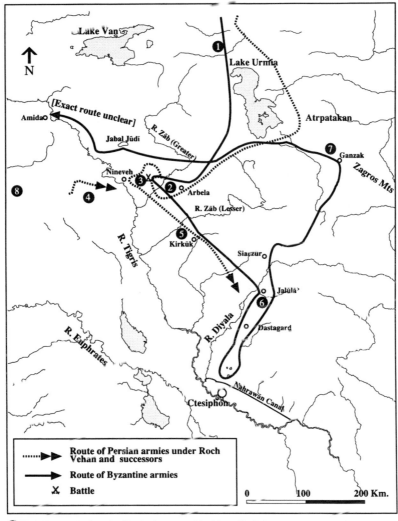

Route of Persian armies under Roch Vehan and successors

Route of Byzantine armies

X Battle

0   100   200 Km.

1. Heraclius invades Sasanian Empire from west side of Lake Urmia in autumn and early winter 627
2. Heraclius reaches and crosses Greater Zāb River.
3. Heraclius draws pursuing Sasanian army of Roch Vehan onto plain in front of Nineveh, where, near village and Karamlays Creek, he suddenly reverses to attack 12 December 627
4. Additional Persian troops seek to join Roch Vehan and block Heraclius
5. Heraclius recrosses Greater Zāb and penetrates to Kirkūk (House of Iesdem)
6. Heraclius crosses R. Diyala at Jalūlā', seizes Sasanian royal residence at Dastagard, threatens Sasanian capital of Ctesiphon before turning back at the Nahrawān Canal, returns north via Siarzūr (Shahrazūr, southeast of Suleimaniya)
7. Heraclius at Ganzak in April 628
8. [Important army of Persian General Shahrbarāz inactive in Syria]

Map 4 Heraclius' campaign in Mesopotamia and southern Azerbaijan, winter 627/628

Heraclius set out from Tiflis, probably in mid-September 627, with his own Byzantine forces and up to 40,000 Kök Turks and their allies, while Yabghu Xak'an continued the siege of the citadel of Tiflis.[4] Sarablangas (Sahraplakan) had a numerically inferior force that was unable to halt his advance.[5] Heraclius passed by Shirak, rejoined the valley of the Araxes, crossed the Araxes near the village of Vardanakert and rested in the region of Gogovit. Khusrau II sent a second Sasanian army under the loyal Armenian Roch Vehan (Greek: Rhazates) to resist Heraclius and his allies. Roch Vehan and his forces believed wrongly that they had routed him. Heraclius surprised them by pushing east and circuited Lake Urmia from the west, using the road via Her and Zarewand. Roch Vehan probably expected that Heraclius would retire west down the Arsanias River in the direction of Anatolia. Instead he entered the region of Atrpatakan and on to Nakhchawan, hurrying by day and night to penetrate the Zagros mountains and descend into the heartland of ancient Assyria. Kök Turks accompanied him, but some deserted him because of the winter conditions.[6] Yabghu Xak'an and his nephew Shat reportedly sent an ultimatum to Khusrau:

If you will not retreat from the king of the Romans and surrender to him all the lands and cities which you have taken by force and return all of the prisoners of his country now in your hands, together with the wood of the Cross which all Christian nations worship and honor; if you will not recall your troops from his territory, the king of the north, the lord of the whole world, your king and the king of kings, says to you: "I shall turn against you, governor of Asorestan, and shall repay you twofold for each deed committed against him. I shall swoop upon your lands with my sword as you descended upon his with yours. I shall not spare you, nor shall I delay to do to you what I said I shall do."

Khusrau rejected the ultimatum: "It was unworthy of you to be paralyzed and to allow yourself to be perverted by the words of the hothead of the Romans, a slave who belongs to me."[7] The Kök Turk assistance was critical to Heraclius' victory in 627/628.

The reliability of the sources of Moses Dasxuranci is doubtful; it is unclear how he would have had access to diplomatic correspondence, except for what might have been released to the public. This is probably an embellished literary rendering of a possibly genuine ultimatum or gesture,

---

[4] Theophanes, *Chron.* A.M. 6118 (317 De Boor) for date and desertions; Stratos, Βυζάντιον II: 566, argues for mid-September, which is plausible.

[5] Theophanes, *Chron.* A.M. 6117 (447 Mango-Scott); Moses Dasxuranci, *History of the Caucasian Albanians* 85, 94–95 Dowsett. Thomson, *Rewriting Caucasian History* 234–235.

[6] Moses Dasxuranci, *History of the Caucasian Albanians* 12 (87 Dowsett).

[7] Moses Dasxuranci, *History of the Caucasian Albanians* 12 (88 Dowsett).

one that emphasizes the overweening arrogance and pride of Khusrau on the eve of his fall.

Theophanes' source asserts that Heraclius addressed his soldiers: "Know brothers, that no one wishes to be our allies, except for God alone and the willing Mother of Him, that he may show his power, since there is no salvation in numbers of men or weapons, but he sends his help to those who place their hope in his mercy."[8]

The exact number of expeditionary troops whom Heraclius commanded is indeterminate; it was conceivably between 25,000 and 50,000 (probably too high). Absurdly exaggerated is one Christian Oriental source's figure of 300,000 Byzantine troops in addition to 40,000 Kök Turks.[9] Heraclius intended to bring the war into the Persian heartland. He possibly used the Rawandūz Pass, but in any case he led this army, and penetrated the Chamaetha region.[10] On 9 October he reached Chamaetha, where he rested one week. Roch Vehan reached Ganzak (alias Takht-i Suleiman)[11] in Azerbaijan and followed behind him, but found the countryside stripped of provisions, which caused great harm to his animals.[12] On 1 December Heraclius reached the Greater Zāb River, having descended out of the mountainous country, crossed the Zāb and camped near Nineveh.

Heraclius simply, after reaching Assyria, descended directly against the heartland of Khusrau's country. The explanation for his move north from the Zāb, when he already had been south, was his desire that the Persian army not place itself, while it was still formidable, in a position to trap and deny him an escape route or withdrawal route, if circumstances should force him to need one. He wanted to draw the Persians to attack him and force them into a battle where he had options for withdrawal. He was planning prudently.

By crossing the Zāb and turning northwest after his descent from Azerbaijan, Heraclius tempted the Persians into thinking that he might withdraw and try to cross the Tigris to return to Byzantine territory via relatively well-known, well-watered and well-provisioned territory in upper Mesopotamia. Khusrau II probably ordered his military commanders to try to prevent Byzantine forces from escaping the Persian heartland unscathed.

What is certain is Heraclius' crossing of the greater Zāb on 1 December at one ford. It is probable that his crossing took more than one day, especially for the animals. In the nineteenth century it took large caravans a whole

---

[8] Theophanes, *Chron.* A.M. 6118 (317 De Boor).
[9] Haldon, *Byzantium in the Seventh Century* 253, for general observations.
[10] Location: Sarre-Herzfeld, *Reise* II: 87.   [11] *Bulletin of the Asia Institute*, n.s. 12 (1998) 249–268.
[12] Theophanes, *Chron.* A.M. 6118 (317 De Boor).

day to ford the Zāb, and an army, even granting variability of estimates for its size from as much as 60,000 to 70,000 to as little as somewhere between 25,000 and 50,000, would have surely taken longer.[13] The Nineveh region supplied Heraclius with adequate water and provisions for his men, mounts, and draft animals.

Roch Vehan found a different ford three miles away from that of Heraclius, probably three miles closer to the Tigris. Heraclius sent out Baanes (Vahan) the *stratelates* (*magister militum per Orientem*)[14] with a few hand-picked soldiers who engaged a unit of Persians, slew their commander (*kometa*) and brought back his head and his gold sword. They also brought back twenty-seven prisoners, among whom was Rhazates/Roch Vehan's *spatharios*, who reported that Roch Vehan sought battle, but was awaiting the arrival of 3,000 more Persian troops that Khusrau was sending to him. That news caused Heraclius to act swiftly by sending his baggage train on ahead and not keeping it near the Zāb. The Persians expected that he would cross the Tigris.

The location of the battle cannot be determined absolutely. Any military force that had descended from the north, as Heraclius had done, following the Zāb and then fording it and pressing west towards Nineveh, had to pass through a plain. From it one could again move easily back south of the Zāb against the Persian King, which is what happened on 12 December 627, after the battle. Heraclius encamped near (πλήσιον) Nineveh and, according to Theophanes' source, which ultimately is probably some official victory communiqué, "discovered a plain suited for battle" (πέδιον ἐπιδέξιον πρὸς πόλεμον) where he arrayed his troops. He was drawing the Persians west from the Zāb, onto the extensive plain east of Nineveh, including that of Karamlays (Karamles, Qeramlis, Kermelis), which early travelers had wrongly identified as the plain of Alexander the Great's battle of Gaugamela or Arbela.[15] Whether the battle of Nineveh was exactly at Karamlays (or less likely nearby Bartallah) is not the point; there is a flat plain in this vicinity, bifurcated by the Karamlays Creek, which drains into the Wādī Shawr.[16]

Consistent with his plan to lure the Persians onto a field of battle, Heraclius probably removed guards from his crossing-point of the Greater Zāb

[13] Potential crossing points of the Zāb near its confluence with the Tigris: Otto Lendle, *Kommentar zu Xenophons Anabasis* (Darmstadt: Wissenschaftliche Buchgesellschaft, 1995) Maps 20 and 21, pp. 165–166, and continuing discussion 165–168.

[14] Theophanes, *Chron.* A.M. 6118 (318 De Boor; 449 Mango-Scott); also *PLRE* III: 161, s.v. "Baanes."

[15] Karl Niebuhr, *Reisebeschreibung* (Copenhagen, 1778) II: 348–349, esp 349n, and Karl Ritter, *Erdkunde* (rev. edn., vol. IX). Correct location of that battle: A.B. Bosworth, *Commentary on Arrian's History of Alexander* (Oxford: Oxford University Press, 1980) I: 293–294.

[16] The poet al-Aʻshā does not refer to this battle.

River. Likewise he probably did not try to keep any communications open in that direction. He wished to give the appearance of making a complete pullback from Persia, that he was going to try either to head north (improbable, given hazards of terrain, climate, hostile ethnic groups) or cross the Tigris and head northwest to Byzantine territory via the traditional route across upper Mesopotamia. Such actions probably allowed the Persians, after they crossed the Greater Zāb below his ford, to bisect Heraclius' former line of march, that is of feigned retreat and flight. The Persians sought to stay closer to the Tigris than Heraclius and to link up with other reinforcements. Heraclius' strategy was a cautious raiding one,[17] although some might consider it to be one of annihilation.[18] He did not attempt to occupy and hold fixed points that would be untenable, nor did he wish to dissipate and waste his limited effectives.

The Byzantines found an open field that they always wanted for use against the Persians, so that they could deploy troops in close order and use their own troops' skills with lances and their foot-soldiers' ability at hand-to-hand, close combat against the Persians' preference for the bow. Book 11 of *Strategikon* of Maurikios extensively discusses this logic for battle-field selection.[19] The fog on the battlefield even more perfectly suited the Byzantines. It hampered Persian archers and apparently prevented Roch Vehan/Rhazates, the Persian commander, from understanding what Heraclius was trying to do. It allowed the Byzantines to approach the Persians without taking serious losses from Persian arrows. Although the Byzantines eventually surrounded the Persians, we do not know the exact formations that succeeded in accomplishing this. The author of the *Strategikon* recommends trying to outflank Persians instead of using frontal attacks.[20] Probably Heraclius suddenly had his troops wheel about to assault the Persians on the plain while the Persians thought that they were successfully pursuing the Byzantines. Both sides made extensive use of cavalry, which was well suited to this plain.

The battle "of Nineveh" took place on the morning of Saturday, 12 December 627. Roch Vehan organized his Persian forces into three masses

[17] On the concept: Archer Jones, *The Art of War in the Western World* (New York: Oxford University Press, 1987) 54–56, 84–85, 675–679.

[18] Haldon, *Warfare* 39–40.

[19] On Persians' methods of fighting: John Wiita, "The Ethnika..." (Ph.D. diss., University of Minnesota, 1977) 61–109, esp. 99–101. Everett Wheeler comments that Greek military texts from many different centuries advocate infantry rushing the Persians, among other reasons in order to neutralize their archers.

[20] On outflanking movements: Maurikios, *Strategikon* 3.14 (184–187 Dennis-Gamillscheg, 49–50 Dennis trans.), but see also 3.10 (176–179 Dennis-Gamillscheg; 46–47 Dennis trans.); Wiita, "Ethnika" 101–102.

and attacked. The seventh-century Armenian source Sebeos states, "They pursued Heraclius. But Heraclius drew them [the Persians] on as far as the plain of Nineveh; then he turned to attack them with great force. There was mist on the plain, and the Persian army did not realize that Heraclius had turned against them until they encountered each other."[21] A volatile and very fluid situation existed. Heraclius was, at Nineveh, in a potentially dangerous situation. He could not return whence he came because his army and the pursuing Persian army under Roch Vehan had consumed all available foodstuffs. The Persians naturally tried to trap him between their armies and cut off his escape over the Tigris.

The accounts in Greek of this campaign neither refer to ruins at Nineveh, nor to Gaugamela, even though (1) there are some more general literary comparisons of Heraclius and Alexander, and (2) some decades earlier the Byzantine historian Agathias had referred to tombs at Nineveh.[22] The place-name of Nineveh was known, but in a Syriac form, as the site of a Christian community. Historians and panegyrists of the late sixth and early seventh century made no effort to associate the location with anything from ancient Assyria in classical or Biblical traditions. Nor can one understand Heraclius' campaigns well from reading extant Muslim historical traditions such as al-Mas'ūdī, who claims that it was Shahrbarāz who caused Heraclius to invade Iraq as far as the Nahrawān canal.[23] Ṭabarī's source confuses events in 627 with Heraclius' campaign in the upper Tigris region in 625, two years earlier.[24]

The battle took place on a plain west of the Greater Zāb that was near (23 or 24 kilometers distant) "Nineveh," which presumably referred to the settlements in the actual ruins of ancient Assyrian Nineveh, with its two mounds of Nebi Yunis and Koyunjuk. The information that identifies the site comes not from descriptions of the actual battle, but its immediate aftermath. Although the Persians suffered heavy losses it was not a rout. Both antagonists remained on the battlefield after the combat. Byzantine cavalrymen watered their horses two arrow-shots' distance from the Persian horsemen who watched over their dead until the seventh hour of the night. When the eighth hour began the Persians suddenly departed, with their baggage.

---

[21] Sebeos, *History* 126, ch. 28 (83–84 Thomson); *Storia* c. 36 (97 Gugerotti).

[22] Agathias, *Hist.* 2.23.10; Averil Cameron, "Agathias on the Sassanians," *DOP* 23–24 (1969–70) 67–183, esp. her trans. on p. 81 and commentary on p. 91.

[23] Al-Mas'ūdī, *Murūj al-dhahab = Prairies d'or* (Berbier de Meynard edn.) 2.227 (= Beirut edn. 1.319).

[24] See Nöldeke's comment: *Ṭabarī* /Nöldeke, *Geschichte der Perser und Araber* 295 n. 2. No comment on Ṭabarī's (or his source's) confusion in *The History of al-Ṭabarī* V: *The Sāsānids, the Byzantines, the Lakhmids, and Yemen*, trans. C.E. Bosworth (Albany: State University of New York, 1999) 322–323.

"They camped at the foothills of a steep mountain."[25] This precious statement of Theophanes helps to eliminate sites within a kilometer or so of
Nineveh, or any of them north of Nineveh. The steep mountain that dominates Nineveh is to the east, above the plain of Karamlays. It is the Jabal
'Ayn al-Ṣafrā' ("Yellow Spring Mountain"), which does have outliers or
foothills, to which the Persians fled from the plain of Karamlays.

The Persians departed for the nearby foothills after the battle. Often
this, according to the *Strategikon*, was Persian practice, to avoid more battle,[26] not a surprising or dishonorable tactic, just a prudent one under the
circumstances. The unidentified foothills of the steep mountain were probably those of the mount of 'Ayn al-Ṣafrā' or, less likely, of Jabal Maqlūb,
to the northwest. As Sir Aurel Stein remarked: "Near the large village of
Bartallah . . . the foot of the Jabal Ain-as-Satrah is approached by a low out-
lier of the southern hill chain stretching to the north-east. Here the level
plain which concerns us may be considered to end."[27] His topographic remarks and a satellite photograph of the region between Nineveh and Jabal
'Ayn al-Ṣafrā' enable one to grasp the essentials of the maneuvering and
battle. They reinforce the trustworthiness of Theophanes and his source
for this section of the *Chronographia*. Occupation of these foothills both
secured the Persians' protection, as the *Strategikon* describes their contemporary preference, and secondly, to the extent that the weather permitted, allowed good visibility for watching the intentions of Heraclius and his army.

At the end of the battle of Nineveh, after the stripping of the dead,
and while the Zoroastrian Persians watched over their dead for a minimal
observance of respect, the Byzantines, at a distance of two arrow-shots
(approximately 266 or 600 meters),[28] watered and fed their horses. There is
a stream, known locally as the Karamlays Creek, which flows into the Wādī
Shawr, at the village of Karamlays, and there are other potential watering
places on this plain, which would be especially true in December. Older
maps show that the Karamlays Creek and its continuation, the Wādī Shawr,
bisect the plain of Karamlays and together constitute the obvious natural
point where a general might choose to stand and fight, supported by an
adequate supply of water. Karamlays Creek is not an insuperable barrier
at the village of Karamlays, but in an otherwise flat plain that is circumscribed by the deeper Wādī Shawr, it provided a certain modest amount
of topographical and psychological support, as well as water. Here was

---

[25] Theophanes, *Chron.* A.M. 6118 (319 De Boor; my translation, see also 450 Mango-Scott).
[26] On Persian preference for rough terrain: Maurikios, *Strategikon* 11 (114 Dennis trans.).
[27] Sir Aurel Stein, "Notes on Alexander's Crossing of the Tigris and the Battle of Arbela," *Geographical Journal* 100 (1942) 161. Correction: Safrah, not Stein's Satrah. I visited the site on 11 August 1988.
[28] Cf. G. Dennis' glossary in his English translation of the *Strategikon* 171.

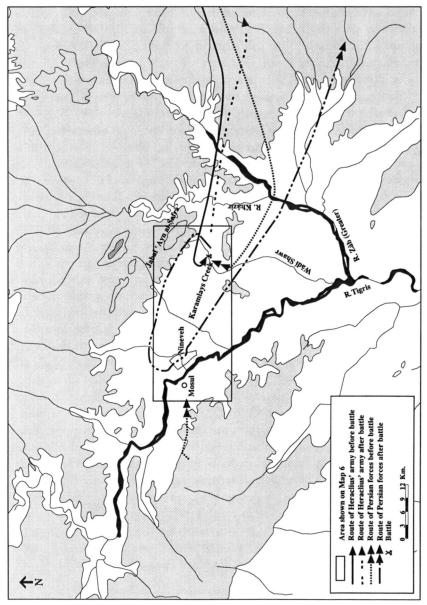

Map 5 Battle of Nineveh, 12 December 627. Reconstruction of the battle in the plain near Nineveh

KEY: 1. Probable site of battle. 2. Karamlays (Kermelis). 3. Karamlays Creek, which splits at village. 4. Bartallah 5. Perimeter of Ancient Nineveh.
6. Mosul. 7. River Tigris. 8. Jabal Maqlūb. 9. Jabal ʿAyn al-Ṣafrāʾ. See Map 5 for location diagram.

Byzantines

Persians

Map 6 Battle of Nineveh, 12 December 627. Reconstruction of the battle in the plain near Nineveh (satellite photograph)

the obvious rallying-point, to which actual fog gave additional assistance and surprise. Presumably Heraclius placed his baggage train, which he had sent on ahead, somewhere west of this creek. According to the historian of the locality, Mr. Habib Hannona, Karamlays Creek "starts at natural springs at a mountain five miles northeast of Karamles near the village of Tarjilla . . . the Wādī Shawr is a seasonal water way about two miles west of Karamles, running north–south, and meets Karamles Creek; together they join the Tigris River near Nimrud. During autumn and winter, the rainy seasons, this wādī with Karamles Creek becomes like a river and is very hard to cross or pass through."[29] This is the most probable spot where Heraclius chose to halt and give battle. Of course one cannot be certain which stream was the one that the Byzantines used, or be sure whether they brought water to their horses from elsewhere, but the existence of streams additionally supports the likelihood that this plain of Karamlays and Bartallah was the approximate one in which the battle of Nineveh was fought. More precision we cannot reasonably expect, given the vagueness of these sources. The terrain around Karamlays is consistent with the few details of the battle of Nineveh that we have.[30] Both sides used cavalry in the battle. Three fords of the Zāb existed in 1873, although their location in the seventh century is uncertain.[31] Heraclius probably channeled the Persians into fighting on terrain of his choice, where at that time of year effectively there was no other easy crossing in any effort to head him off – assuming that his pursuers thought that he was fleeing in order to attempt to cross the Tigris at Nineveh.

Probably Heraclius' advance guard had occupied the ruins of Nineveh itself. The baggage, as per Byzantine advice, may have been in this vicinity, instead of near the actual battlefield, even though the encampment was merely near to Nineveh, not actually in its perimeter. After the battle, when Persian strength was weakened, Heraclius decided to strike south, so guards were pulled in from Nineveh and the Byzantine baggage was sent south of the Greater Zāb with the main army. The leaderless Persians worked their way westwards and occupied Nineveh after Heraclius' forces withdrew from it. They may still have hoped to trap Heraclius at Nineveh, by blocking his anticipated passage across the Tigris to return to Byzantine territory. But they misread his intentions. Heraclius had no reason to string out garrisons that would have been

---

[29] I thank Mr. Waiel Hindo and Mr. Habib Hannona for providing this information.
[30] Josef Cernik, "Technische Studien-Expedition durch die Gebiete des Euphrat und Tigris," *Petermanns Geographische Mitteilungen* No. 45, *Ergänzungsband* (1876) 3–5.
[31] Cernik, "Technische Studien," p. 2.

picked off. By seizing Nineveh itself, he confused the Persians concerning his intentions.

Heraclius allegedly commanded 70,000, while Roch Vehan had only 12,000 before reinforcements came, but all of these numbers are suspect. The Muslim historian al-Ṭabarī reports that at the battle 6,000 Persians were slain out of a total of 12,000, including the Persian commander, Roch Vehan himself. Most of his account is inaccurate.[32] Heraclius probably did take some inventory of his troops at the battle: "When the Emperor Heraclius was making war against Rhazates, he inspected his army in review and discovered that there were two soldiers alone left from the tyrant-loving mob, even though the intervening years had not been numerous."[33] Theophylact saw the disappearance of Phokas' soldiers as proof of divine wrath for their wrongful actions:

For when the Persian war gained free rein, they received their allotted retribution for those wicked enterprises by divinely ordained threats, now being struck down by fire from heaven at the hour of the engagement, at other times being wasted by famine and ravaging, but the majority perished as they surrendered this sinful life in the jaws of cutlass and sword.[34]

One panegyrical official tradition of questionable accuracy depicts a public challenge to combat in which Heraclius distinguished himself by personally cutting down three Persian challengers, first Roch Vehan himself, then two others after Heraclius and his steed suffered wounds.[35] A few fragments of George of Pisidia's *Heraclias* III refer to Heraclius as a kind of magnetic stone in the battle,[36] probably an allusion to the closing of Byzantine ranks around the standard leader, who in this case would be Heraclius, immediately before their charge against the enemy.[37]

3,000 Persian reinforcements for Roch Vehan/Rhazates arrived too late, but it is unclear precisely from which direction (south?) they were coming, although the Persians had already received some reinforcements.[38] They could have simply crossed the Zāb and Khāzir Rivers close to the Persian position in the foothills from where they could watch and shadow the forces of Heraclius. They could even have been coming from west of the

[32] Ṭabari/Nöldeke, *Geschichte der Perser und Araber* 295. *The History of al-Ṭabarī*, V: 322–323 Bosworth.
[33] Theophylact, *Hist.* 8.12.12 (229–230 Whitby).
[34] Theophylact, *Hist.* 8.12.10–11 (229 Whitby).
[35] Theoph. *Chron.* A.M. 6118 (318 De Boor). But Nikephoros, *Short History* 14 (60–61 Mango), for Rhazates/Roch Vehan challenging Heraclius to a duel.
[36] George of Pisidia, *Heraclias* 3 frg. 43–44 (287, 304–305 Pertusi).
[37] Cf. Maurikios, *Strategikon* 3.5, lines 17–25 Dennis-Gamillscheg edition.
[38] Sebeos, *History* 126, ch. 38 (83–84 Thomson); *Patmutiwn Sebeosi*, ed. Abgaryan (Yerevan, 1979) p. 126; *Hist.* c. 26 (84 Macler).

Tigris. The Persians simply moved their camp, presumably out of the plain, after they failed to break up the Byzantines, for its location was now very exposed and made no sense. The Byzantines could neither storm the camp nor prevent them from moving their camp from its probable location not far behind the Persian battle lines. It was therefore on or near the plain, possibly near where the Persians crossed the Greater Zāb downstream from Heraclius' ford. The Byzantine failure to seize the Persian camp and supplies underscores the limited scope of the Byzantine victory at Nineveh in the formal, immediate sense, even though strategically it was a great success.

The battle of Nineveh was one in which Heraclius drew on a standard repertory of Byzantine techniques, as described in the *Strategikon*. This in no way diminishes the appreciation of the very difficult task of successfully commanding and coordinating his troops to achieve the desired result. Heraclius took advantage of the opportunities. He deliberately lured the Persians into battle west as far as the Nineveh plain.[39] He took full advantage of the terrain, either because he received superior intelligence about the terrain and his opponents, or because he possessed the skill to appraise the value of terrain instantly, a quality that early modern commanders called the *coup d'oeil*, the ability to size up terrain with the glance of the eye. The Persian commander Roch Vehan was not very experienced, it appears, in fighting against Heraclius and he, his subordinates, and soldiers paid a very heavy price. The battle of Nineveh involved the use of classic Byzantine techniques of close order attack against the Persians on an open plain. Predictably, immediately following this action, the Persians retreated away from the open plain to rough country where, as the *Strategikon* Book 11 reports, they preferred to stay when they wished to avoid battle with the Byzantines, or at least to cause it to be fought on terms more favorable to themselves and their own military skills.

Victory was not total. There was no Persian rout. But in the volatile world of warfare it was a case of a marginal victory transforming into a decisive one. Nineveh created an accelerating momentum in favor of Heraclius and one of internal disintegration for Khusrau II. The absence of an adequate Persian army to interpose between Heraclius and Khusrau and the agricultural heartland of Mesopotamia, the physical destruction that he unleashed, and the uncertainty of Heraclius' ultimate intentions, created new dynamics. A country tired of protracted war could only ponder how much more destruction Heraclius might wreak. The prestige of Khusrau crumbled; Persians understandably worried and panicked for their lives

---

[39] Sebeos, *History* 126–127, ch. 38 (84–85 Thomson); *Patmutiwn Sebeosi* 126 Abgaryan; *Hist.* c. 26 (84 Macler).

and their property. Heraclius profited from the turn of psychology. This time the Persians folded. Heraclius' contacts with Shahrbarāz and with some key Christians in Persia and with disaffected diverse minorities within Persian ranks were crucial. Heraclius, despite his religious devotion, showed sufficient flexibility to reach accommodations with dissident Christians, even Nestorians, in Persian territory. Flexibility and resourcefulness were valuable.

After defeat, the Persians, in what was a kind of standoff, having lost 6,000 men, kept a watch over the corpses of their dead (σκηνώματα), following Zoroastrian strictures, but for a more limited duration, for one-fifth or so of a day (probably an abbreviated watch for military exigencies).[40] It was a Zoroastrian practice to leave the dead exposed and not touch their clothing or valuables. The Byzantines were free to rob the corpses.

Heraclius' army won much booty: "They carried away many all-golden swords and belts decorated with gold and jewels and the shield of Rhazates [Roch Vehan] having one hundred twenty plates and his breastplate and his caftan with his head and his bracelets and his golden saddle. They also captured alive Barsamouses, the commander of the Iberians serving in the Persian army." Heraclius then encouraged the troops against Khusrau "in order to frighten him," and summoned Shahrbarāz from Byzantium. Yet was he really at Constantinople or merely in its vicinity, after he had made terms with Heraclius Constantine, or are Theophanes and his source merely speaking generally and carelessly of summoning him from Byzantine territory?[41] Heraclius shrewdly waged psychological warfare by terrifying Khusrau into taking precipitous action.

Heraclius all this time probably tried to sow doubts in Shahrbarāz's mind about Khusrau II. Conversely, Persian traditions may well be correct that Khusrau II or his associates attempted to ruin the reputation of Shahrbarāz in the eyes of Heraclius and cause him to distrust Shahrbarāz.

But unlike the poetic panegyrics of George of Pisidia and the victory accounts in Theophanes, reality was not merely conventional military operations or any triumphal religious procession. The new dimension involved the risky and uncertain exploitation of internal Persian divisions for maximal advantage. Heraclius had excelled at handling matters of timing and internal subversion back in 608 and 610, and the opportunity presented itself for him to resort to it again, albeit involving a polity and society that were very different from those of Byzantium.

---

[40] Theoph. *Chron.* A.M. 6118 (319 De Boor; 450 Mango-Scott). Cf. σκηνώματα in *Chronicon Paschale*, where it means simply the dead, pp. 730–731 (185 Whitby).
[41] Theoph. *Chron.* A.M. 6118 (319 De Boor; cf. 450 Mango-Scott).

Persian leaders may have expected Heraclius to return to Byzantine territory in the direction of either Amida (Diyarbekir) or to cross the Tigris and traverse the plain to the Euphrates and from there make his way back to Byzantine territory, as he had done in 625. He surprised them by instead heading into the heartland of Persia, toward the seat of governmental power, where no serious Persian army could stop him. The Persians were too weak to oppose Heraclius' recrossing of the greater Zāb, so they followed. Heraclius seized four bridges over the lesser Zāb, presumably at or near the modern town of Altun Köpru, but the Persians managed to find other crossings that enabled them to bypass Byzantine forces. Uncertain is exactly where the 3,000 Persian reinforcements joined up with remnants of the Persian army of the now dead Rhazates.[42]

It is unclear why Khusrau II persisted at his royal residence of Dastagard and did not flee to Iran to take advantage of the territorial depth of his empire. Dastagard's location astride or near major communications nodal points may have been too embarrassing to concede to Byzantine ravaging. The dynasty's prestige may not have been able to withstand the ravaging of Mesopotamia. Any royal flight of Khusrau endangered the political structure. Yet the Diyala (Torna) River was no place along which to organize any effective defense line.

After crossing the Greater Zāb River unopposed on 21 December, the *tourmarch* George with his horsemen captured bridges over the Lesser Zāb, a distance of 48 Roman miles.[43] Here Theophanes or his source is relying on a victory bulletin of Heraclius. Heraclius followed, crossed the Lesser Zāb on 23 December, and proceeded on to spend Christmas at Kirkūk or Karka de Beth Slokh, at the residences of Yazdin (Iesdem), the influential Christian (Nestorian) financial official (chief administrator of the vital and lucrative land tax) of the Sasanian Empire and its most prominent Christian layman.[44] Heraclius used "Saracen," i.e. Arab, patrols, probably because they knew the language or could communicate with others who might provide information.[45] Heraclius already contacted elite Christian subjects of the Sasanian Empire, who provided him with key contacts and useful information about conditions within Khusrau's empire. The family

---

[42] Thomas Artsruni, *History of the House of the Artsrunik'* 160, says that 4,000 Persians survived the battle of Nineveh. Those 4,000, added to the reinforcements, would make 7,000. Ṭabarī/Nöldeke put the Persian dead at 6,000: *Geschichte der Perser und Araber*, p. 296.

[43] Theoph. *Chron.* A.M. 6118 (320 De Boor, 450 Mango-Scott). A *tourmarch* commanded a *turma* or cavalry unit (very old Roman term). Chronology: B. Flusin, *Saint Anastase le Perse et l'histoire de la Palestine au début du VIIe siècle* II: 271–272, 278–279.

[44] Location: Sarre-Herzfeld, *Reise* II: 88. On Yazdin: *PLRE* III: 612–613, s.v. "Iesdem."

[45] *Chronicon Paschale* 730 (185 Whitby). On these, Shahid, *Byzantium and the Arabs in the Sixth Century* I: 642, 644.

of Yazdin won a prominent place at Heraclius' court in the final years of
the reign. Those ties were already being cemented. Indigenous Christians
also informed him about the location and condition of Christian hostages
and prisoners, and concerning wealth and other resources within Khusrau's
empire, and probably provided intelligence about numbers of troops, given
their familiarity with the Persian military payroll. One will never know the
full truth about those ties, which official bulletins did not divulge.

The halt at Kirkūk is important. There is, significantly, no indication
that Heraclius' army damaged any property at Kirkūk. Kirkūk probably made a psychological impact on the Byzantines, for in the vicinity
eerie flames spurt from petroleum that oozes to the surface (although no
Byzantine source mentions this). Khusrau II reacted by recalling the Persian army, which managed to cross the Lesser Zāb at another ford and
placed itself south of Heraclius. Probably Khusrau himself, on the news
of the approach of Heraclius, departed from Dastagard on 22 January.[46]
Heraclius captured and burned the Persian palace of Dezeridan (Kufri).[47]
The Persian army crossed the Diyala River and encamped there. Heraclius
captured Rousa (Rushanqubadh/Zengabad),[48] which he ravaged. Although
he feared that Persians would block his own crossing of the Diyala River,
they deserted the key bridge at his approach. He crossed the Diyala (Torna)
and then took the palace of Beklal or Jalūlā'[49] on 1 January, and then destroyed it, giving the game in its game preserve to his soldiers. Alexandrians
and Edessenes, whom the Persians had taken prisoner, fled to Heraclius.
Khusrau II, Armenian deserters informed Heraclius, waited for him five
miles in front of Dastagard, at a point called Barasroth. There he learned
from shepherds that Khusrau II had fled to Dastagard with his treasures,
carried by beasts ("loading on elephants and camels and mules in his service household"), when he learned that Heraclius had passed the Diyala
and that he had ordered his army to loot Dastagard. Theophanes' chronology from the departure of Heraclius from Karka de Beth Slokh (Kirkūk)
to Jalūlā' and Dastagard is not out of the question, if one refers not to
the entire Byzantine force, but to mobile units. The countryside between
Kirkūk and Jalūlā' is mostly smooth or only lightly rolling.[50] There is no
obvious fortified line. One could bypass Kufri. Cavalry units could traverse
that distance. Whether the baggage train could is another matter.[51]

---

[46] Here I accept the first of two chronologies proposed by Flusin, *Saint Anastase le Perse* II: 281.
[47] Location: Sarre-Herzfeld, *Reise* II: 88.   [48] Location: Sarre-Herzfeld, *Reise* II: 88.
[49] Location of Beklal and Torna (Diyala): Sarre-Herzfeld, *Reise* II: 88, and 86 n. 8.
[50] As I observed in August 1988.
[51] Flusin, *Saint Anastase le Perse* II: 276, reasonably asks whether such speed was possible. It is a stretch, but it was conceivable.

Heraclius now controlled not only the ancient royal road that stretched from Persepolis into Anatolia, but also that other critical road that is the principal one from central Mesopotamia into Iran. Jalūlā' was a strategic position. He had several options before him. He had cut off central Mesopotamia temporarily from the principal route for communications and reinforcements. The doubtful loyalties of Shahrbarāz and his troops imperiled Khusrau, who could not easily flee into Iran, a flight that would likely have encouraged Mesopotamia to revolt. A move by Heraclius into the interior of Iran would have been very unwise: he lacked adequate numbers of troops, logistics, or intelligence. For a few weeks Heraclius controlled the jugular of the Sasanian Empire.

Heraclius divided his army after crossing the Diyala. One part went to Dastagard and the other one, under his personal command, went to another palace called Bebdarch (Tazaristan/Tachara),[52] ravaged and burned it. At Dastagard Heraclius celebrated Epiphany on 6 January, plundered its game preserve and destroyed the palace. He found three hundred flags that the Persians had captured from the Byzantines over the course of various military actions, vast amounts of spices and other valuable condiments: "... they found much aloe and large woodstocks of aloe, of seventy and eighty pounds, and much silk and pepper and many beyond counting number of shirts of charbasia, sugar and ginger and many other sorts of things, and asimon and shirts made wholly of silk, wool carpets and carpets sewn by needle so many that, because of their weight, he burned them because they were too heavy to carry away."[53] Theophanes' source emphasized the exotic and astounding proportions of the triumph for rhetorical effect. Khusrau had fled Dastagard nine days previously, to Ctesiphon and then to Veh-Ardashir. Heraclius wrote an ultimatum to Khusrau: "I pursue and run after peace. I do not willingly burn Persia, but compelled by you. Let us now throw down our arms and embrace peace. Let us quench the fire before it burns up everything."[54] Heraclius may in fact have released an "open letter," or bulletin, more for propaganda purposes within Byzantium and within his army and to cultivate support, possibly, within Persia. Of course the text can be mere rhetorical exaggeration, again trying to portray the arrogant Khusrau doomed to fall. Heraclius left Dastagard on 7 January.

Heraclius' forces three days later under George the *tourmarch* found the Nahrawān Canal blocked, because the bridge had been broken. He sent a

[52] Location: Sarre-Herzfeld, *Reise* II: 88.
[53] Theoph. *Chron.* A.M. 6118 (322 De Boor; cf. 451 Mango-Scott).
[54] Theoph. *Chron.* A.M. 6118 (324 De Boor; cf. 453 Mango-Scott).

force under Mezezios to probe but it turned back.[55] This was a sign of great prudence on Heraclius' part.[56] Unlike Julian in 363, who became involved in heavily populated central Mesopotamia and its problems of logistics, he turned, utilizing a different route than that by which he had arrived, thus avoiding problems of the exhaustion of supplies along that route. Probably he was unaware of an ancient saying: "many declare that there is a certain decree of Fate that no Roman emperor may advance beyond Ctesiphon."[57]

Grisly scenes filled the last days of Khusrau II. St. Anastasios the Persian, for example, was strangled on 22 January at the village of Bethsaloe.[58] Khusrau ordered the mass execution of prisoners in his prisons.[59] Sons of Yazdin bribed the executioners so Anastasios' remains could be removed by their servants and a few monks. They shrouded his remains in precious clothing and left them at the monastery of St. Sergios the Martyr.[60] Reportedly St. Anastasios foretold the death of Khusrau: "Know brothers, by the grace of God, that tomorrow I shall die. In a few days you will be freed and the impious and bad king will be killed."[61]

The author of the life and acts of St. Anastasios continued, in an almost contemporary narration:

The brother of the monastery . . . having rendered funeral honors to the body of the martyr, having deposited it as was proper in the said monastery of Holy Sergios, stayed there, asked how he could return to the one who sent him. And about ten days later, on the first of February, our very pious and very Christian Emperor Heraclius arrived with the army that followed him. Seeing them, the brother rejoiced and spoke to them in the Roman [Greek] language. They asked him what he was doing there, after he had told them everything in order, they glorified God and told him, "Get up, come with us and save your life." He stayed with them, in great honor, all the time that he spent in Persia, then left with them by way of the land of the Armenians.[62]

Heraclius probably gained valuable information from some of the Christian monks in Persian territory, and their presence reinforced the sacred and moral mission of his expedition, giving additional confidence and momentum to his campaign in the eyes of his soldiers and probably in the eyes

---

[55] Theoph. *Chron.* A.M. 6118 (324–325 De Boor; 453 Mango-Scott).
[56] But note the tradition that the glossator of al-A'shā's poem gives for Heraclius' turning back, a map showing no bridge in Iraq over the water: Geyer, *Gedichte von Abu Bashir Maimun ibn Qais al-'A'sha* (E.J.W. Gibb Memorial Series; London: Luzac, 1928), poem 36, p. 158.
[57] *Scriptores Historiae Augustae*, Carus 9.1. Note the charming story that the author of the gloss to al-A'shā's poem no. 36 cites about the hesitation of Heraclius about proceeding further: Geyer, *Gedichte von Abu Bashir Maimun ibn Qais al-'A'sha*, poem 36, p. 158.
[58] *Acta* 38 (82–85 Flusin); Bethsaloe: Flusin, *Saint Anastase le Perse* II: 243–260.
[59] Ṭabarī 1.1043; Ṭabarī /Nöldeke, *Geschichte* 356; Ṭabarī 378 Bosworth.
[60] *Acta* 39 (84–86 Flusin).   [61] *Acta* 42 (88–89 Flusin).   [62] *Acta* 43 (88–91 Flusin).

of at least some subjects of the Persian Empire. His campaign had thus far greatly embarrassed and troubled Khusrau II, whose authority lost great prestige.

Heraclius turned to establish himself in the north at Siarzūr (Shahrazūr),[63] which he left on 24 February.[64] He marched on to Barza,[65] where he had been staying for seven days when a delegation headed by a Persian general (commander of a thousand, *chiliarch*) Gousdanaspa Razei from Shahrbarāz's army, accompanied by five others–three counts and two officers (*axiomatikoi*)–found him and informed him about the coup that overthrew Khusrau II on 23 February 628.[66]

Khusrau fled Dastagard ill with dysentery. Already he probably was nervous about his succession and reportedly sought to crown his son Merdasan by his wife Seirem. He took Merdasan and another son Saliar with him when he crossed the river Tigris. But his first-born son Siroy and others in the household had previously crossed that river, and summoned Gourdanaspa (Aspad-Gušnasp), who previously commanded Sasanian troops. Siroy promised to raise the pay of the army, give special heed to Gourdanaspa, and make peace with the Byzantines and Kök Turks if Gourdanaspa spoke to the army and persuaded them to support him for the succession. Within this faction were the two sons of Shahrbarāz, the son of Iesdem, the financial official, significantly, and many other sons of leaders. Heraclius offered him weapons. The conspirators arrested Khusrau, reviled him, starved him and mocked him, executed Merdasan and his other sons and after five days ordered Khusrau executed with arrows,[67] on 29 February. The upheaval and flight of Khusrau II created conditions that disrupted his normal security measures and gave a jealous son Kawadh-Siroy and discontented elites the opportunity to overthrow him, which they took.[68] The participation of sons of Shahrbarāz strongly suggests that Shahrbarāz already had some implicit or explicit deal with Heraclius. The

---

[63] V. Minorsky and C.E. Bosworth, in *EI* ² (1996) IX: 218–219 s.v. "Shahrazūr," give a location in the vicinity of modern Suleimaniya, Iraq; Rika Gyselen, *La géographie administrative de l'empire sassanide: les témoignages sigillographiques* (Res Orientales, 1; Paris: Groupe pour l'étude de la civilisation du Moyen-Orient; Leuven: Peeters, 1989) 59–60.

[64] *Chronicon Paschale* 732 Dindorf.   [65] Flusin, *Saint Anastase le Perse* II: 275 n. 65.

[66] Theoph. *Chron.* A.M. 6118 (325 De Boor; 453 Mango-Scott); *Chronicon Paschale* 184 n. 486 Whitby.

[67] Theoph. *Chron.* A.M. 6118 (326–327 De Boor; 454–455 Mango-Scott). Ṭabarī 1.1046–1049, 1059–61 (382–386, 396–399 Bosworth), but Bosworth erroneously emends the text on p. 382 n. 948 to make Aspad-Gušnasp into head secretary; the *Chronicon Paschale* is correct, p. 728, that he was a former army commander. Another version: Thomas Artsruni, *History of the House of the Artsrunik'* 161–162 Thomson.

[68] On some encomiastic and other problems with traditions about Khusrau II and Siroy: Speck, *Das geteilte Dossier* 322–323. Also: D. Frendo, "The Early Exploits and Final Overthrow of Khusrau II (591–628): Panegyric and Vilification in the Last Byzantine-Iranian Conflict," *Bulletin of the Asia Institute*, n.s. 9 (1995) 209–214.

Byzantine invasion and destruction and shredding of his prestige all created conditions in which popular support could quickly fade away. The physical destruction and killing in Persia that Heraclius wrought had a strong psychological effect.[69]

Persian noblemen plotted with Siroes (Siroy), son of Khusrau, and imprisoned Khusrau, according to Nikephoros, "So they imprisoned him in one of the royal palaces and gave him no food, but set before him a heap of gold and silver and precious stones, saying, 'Do enjoy these things which you have loved insanely and massed.'"[70] This is a story that emphasizes Khusrau's arrogance, overweening pride, and fall from such heights. "In this way they starved him to death and proclaimed his son Siroes king of Persia". Siroes wrote to Heraclius seeking to come to terms and added, "that their respective states should be reconciled and embrace peace at God's hands so that each might live in tranquillity." Heraclius responded, calling Siroes his son and declaring that it had never been his wish for a king to lose his glory (once again the theme of not damaging the majesty of the sovereign), "Even though he had inflicted innumerable woes upon Romans and Persians, I would have hastened," he said, "were he to have survived, to restore him to his own kingship, complete though my victory over him might have been. But God, knowing his purpose, has wreaked upon him a just punishment so as to prevent universal destruction, and has now bestowed concord upon us." He appealed for the return of the Cross. Siroy reported that the earlier Byzantine ambassadors had all perished, Leontios by a natural death, and the others by flogging on the orders of Khusrau II when he learned of the invasion of Heraclius.[71]

Executions of prisoners and Zoroastrian apostates, the sight of extensive numbers of cadavers on and beside the roads all heightened an atmosphere of crisis and doom in the final moments of the life of Khusrau II and the initial days after his overthrow. The sight and smell of death seemed to be everywhere and contributed to the macabre mood.[72]

The participation of two sons of Shahrbarāz, together with Gourdanaspa, Shahrbarāz's commander of a thousand troops, in this conspiracy is significant. They helped to make contact with Heraclius, presuming, which we cannot be certain, they had contact with their father Shahrbarāz or his agents. The presence of the two sons in the conspiracy is interesting for another reason. It is surprising that Khusrau would have allowed two sons

---

[69] Eutychios, *Hist.* c. 29 (125–127 Breydy, 105–107 German trans.).

[70] Nikephoros, *Short History* 15 (62–63 Mango, trans. on 63).

[71] Nikephoros, *Short History* 15 (62–63 Mango). See Mango commentary on 182–183.

[72] *Chronicon Paschale* 730–731 (Dindorf); *Saint Anastase le Perse, Acta* 38–43 (I: 82–91 and II: 256–263 Flusin). Ṭabarī /Nöldeke, *Geschichte* 356.

of a rebellious general to remain at large. We do not know what exact role, if any, they had on the eve of Khusrau's execution. They may have been objects of suspicion by Khusrau and his entourage. Their presence could argue for a late date for Shahrbarāz's split from Khusrau, but it is virtually inconceivable that news of Shahrbarāz's defection would not have reached Khusrau very speedily. He may have spared them to use them as hostages. The narrative is too terse to know the full story.

The inclusion of the family of Yazdin (Iesdem) in this delegation to Heraclius is equally significant. Heraclius had already occupied some of their prominent estates at Kirkūk. Members of that Nestorian Christian family were heavily involved in rescuing the corpse of the executed St. Anastasios the Persian from being devoured by beasts.[73] They were powerful, financially well-connected members of the influential Christian community and members of their family would remain prominent, probably due to ties being established, in the court of Heraclius a decade later.[74] This family probably had its own ways to gain intelligence about the situation. Its inclusion in the delegation offered Heraclius an opportunity to contact those in the best position to know Sasanian fiscal revenues (especially revenues from the land tax) and location of movable wealth within the Persian Empire, and also individuals who could provide him with excellent intelligence about Persia outside of pre-existing channels. Given their Christian identity and Heraclius' drive to improve relations with and unify Christians, there was even more incentive for Heraclius to welcome and develop close ties with them.

Constituents of the conspirators' embassy to Heraclius from Persian ranks included two mutually hostile groups. Yazdin's family and Shahrbarāz and his allies were two very different and mutually hostile constituencies. Shahrbarāz reportedly had already been insulted by Shamta, a son of Yazdin, in Edessa, northern Syria, and was angry that Khusrau had not punished that insult. The story may well be false. However, there were rivalries and dislikes between bureaucrats, especially of a fiscal responsibility, and military commanders.[75] Tensions could not be smoothed over and assured more instability in Persia, and more opportunities for Heraclius. The rivalries were such that Heraclius had no monolithic constituency with whom to negotiate arrangements in Persia. Things were spinning out of control there. The two constituencies may have provided Heraclius with conflicting information about Persia's internal dynamics and conditions.

---

[73] *Acta* 39 (I: 84–87 Flusin).   [74] Constantine VII, *De cerimoniis* 2.28 (628–629 Reiske).
[75] *Histoire Nestorienne/Chronicle of Siʿirt*, *PO* 13: 540, 556.

The effects of Heraclius' invasion were devastating for inhabitants of the Persian Empire. Kök Turkish raids in Atrotrapene embarrassed Khusrau II and raised the specter of still worse raids and destruction. The Nestorian Patriarch Ishoyahb III speaks of events that shook the world, causing wild fluctuations in life and making large numbers of people into captives.[76] Heraclius' operations spread terror that contributed to his victory. Heraclius' own victory bulletins emphasized the devastation that he wrought.

The *Acts of St. Anastasios the Persian* date the arrival of Heraclius at Bethsaloe, six miles from Dastagard, on 1 February 628.[77] Heraclius then moved to Ganzak (alias Takht-i-Suleiman) by 11 March,[78] where, on 15 March, he issued a victory bulletin describing his military moves since 17 October. In the meantime he had sent out Arab patrols to Siarzūr (Shahrazūr), Kirkūk, and the Lesser Zāb to check for information about Persian military movements and, it is probable, concerning internal Persian politics. Presumably they also were awaiting more news from Shahrbarāz. By moving in this direction they avoided passing through land devastated and foraged by their armies and also prevented any Persian counter-force from blockading them. The news came from the watch:

...on the 24th of the same month March the men of the watch brought to us in our camp near Canzacon one Persian and one Armenian, who delivered to us a memorandum which came to us from a certain Persian *a secretis*, whose name was Chosdae and rank Rasnan; its contents were that, following Seiroes' proclamation as Persian king, he dismissed them to us, along with other officials and a memorandum which came to us from Seiroes himself; that when Chosdae came to Arman, he resolved to dismiss to us the aforementioned two men, so that some men might be sent in order to escort himself and those with him unharmed.

...on the 25th of the same month March we dismissed to them Elias the most glorious *magister militum*, who is called Barsoka, and Theodotus the most magnificent *drungarius*, together with recruits and 20 saddled pack-horses, in order to meet and escort them to us. With them we resolved to send as well Gusdanaspa the son of Rhazes, the *chiliarch* of the Persian army...[79]

On 30 March Heraclius received word that the snows in the Zagros Mountains made it impossible to cross.[80] Then he moved his own forces to

[76] Ishoyahb III, Patriarch, *Liber epistularum*, ep. 8–9 (ed., trans. R. Duval; *CSCO*, SS, 12; Louvain, 1955) 13–14.

[77] *Acta* 43.4–5. Flusin, *Saint Anastase le Perse* II: 265–276. Stratos, *Byzantium* I: 378–379, note xxxvii.

[78] *Chronicon Paschale* 734.

[79] *Chronicon Paschale* 729–731 (184–185 Whitby). Quotation is from the Whitby translation.

[80] There is no evidence of any conscious study of Julian's campaign by Heraclius or those in his entourage.

Ganzak, where he found ample supplies and quarters for his men and animals. The Persian elite at Ganzak had retired to mountain fastnesses. After messages came from Kawadh/Siroy, Heraclius' staff ordered sixty animals prepared to carry ambassadors to Kawadh/Siroy.[81]

On 3 April Heraclius at Ganzak received Phiak, the *a secretis*, who delivered a memorandum from the Persian King Kawadh/Siroy, "which contained his proclamation and his desire to have peace with us and with every man." Heraclius sent a copy of that missive, with his own, to show the Byzantine public. In the letter Siroy orders the release of all Byzantine prisoners in Persian hands:

we have the intention of releasing each and every man who is confined in prison. And thereafter, if there is anything for the benefit and service of mankind and of this state, and it was possible that it be ordered by us, this we have ordered, and it has been done. And we have this intention that we should live in peace and love with you, the emperor of the Romans and our brother, and the Roman state and the remaining nations and other princes who surround our state.[82]

These clauses therefore included the commitment to free all prisoners, apparently both civilian and military, the extremely broad commitment to perform whatever else would be of service, including restoration of booty, reparations for damages, evacuation of Byzantine territory, and the commitment of his government to make peace not only with the Byzantine Empire, but with other peoples and their leaders, whose numbers included the Kök Turks and other Caucasian as well as Arab allies of Byzantium.[83]

Heraclius resided at Ganzak until 7 April, for a total of twenty-seven days. On 8 April he dismissed Phiak, together with Eustathios, the most magnificent *tabularius*,[84] to direct Byzantine affairs in Persia. On 8 April he also began to move his troops to Armenia. It was probably this Eustathios, together with members of the family of the financial official Yazdin, who sought to recover lost Byzantine spoils, both secular and ecclesiastical, and who may have engaged in making surveys to find such reparations, booty,

[81] *PLRE* III: 276–277, s.v. "Cavades II *qui et* Siroes."

[82] *Chronicon Paschale* 735–736 (188 Whitby). N. Oikonomides, "Correspondence Between Heraclius and Kavadh-Siroe in the Paschal Chronicle," *Byzantion* 41 (1971) 269–281; Beihammer, *Nachrichten* nos. 29, 30, 31, pp. 42–46.

[83] See also [Anonymous] *Chronicon ad annum Christi 1234 pertinens* 184 (trans. Chabot).

[84] *PLRE* III: 472, s.v. "Eustathius 12." Functions of a *tabularius* varied, and might include being recording secretary, military accountant. He was a very important officer of the financial *officia*, for the *tabularii* were the chief clerks of financial *officia* in general, but the *castrensis sacri palatii* had two *tabularii*: one for the emperor, one for the empress (*Not.dig.or.*17.7–8, *occ.*15.8–9). See Sachers, *RE*² IV, s.v. "Tabularius." He could have just been a glorified scribe.

prisoners and hostages, and funds as Hrabanus Maurus suggests:[85] "He made surveys of the kingdom of Persia on his own authority, and he assigned all of the silver in the tower of that man [Khusrau] to his army, but he reserved for the restoration of the churches gold and gems in the form of vessels or utensils." There are later traditions that Heraclius attempted to seize valuable relics in the Caucasus,[86] but such actions, if true, were not necessarily part of any systematic inventory-taking for reparations. There is no doubt that the losses of Christian churches at the hands of the Persians had been considerable, and that there was great desire for reparations, not merely the return of valuable relics and the release of imprisoned ecclesiastics.[87] Members and friends and associates of the family of Yazdin would have known how to calculate and extract maximal amounts of wealth from Persia. They knew where the money was or how to try to find it, for they had the best access to recorded and unrecorded information.[88] An important mutual interest between their religious and communal interests and those of Heraclius quickly emerged. On the other hand, Shahrbarāz and other Persians envied them and their privileged status with Heraclius, in addition to any old grievances from the days of Khusrau II. There were also old religious resentments between Zoroastrians and Christians.[89]

According to Sebeos, Siroy ordered in the presence of Eustathios that a command be sent to Shahrbarāz to regroup his troops, return to Persia, and evacuate Byzantine territories, which he declined to do. Siroy dismissed Eustathios with presents.[90] The argument that Siroy did not agree to restore the frontier as it was in 591 is unpersuasive; he had no choice, given the dire

---

[85] "Descriptiones etiam regni Persarum sub ejus nomine fecit, totumque argentum turris illius in praedam sui exercitus deputavit, aurum vero vel gemmas in vasis vel utensilibus ad restaurandum ecclesiarum, quas tyrannus destruxerat, reservavit," in Hrabanus Maurus, *Homilia* 70, PL 110: 133.

[86] Thomson, *Rewriting Caucasian History* 235–236,

King Heraclius entered Persia and slew King Xuasro. He captured Baghdad and took away the Wood of Life. He returned along the same road to K'art'li in the seventh year since he had set out. The church of the Venerable Cross and the Sion of Tp'ilisi had been completed by Adarnase, *mt'avari* of K'art'li. Then King Heraclius took away from Manglisi and Erusheti the foot-rest and the nails of our Lord Jesus Christ, which had been given by Constantine to Mirian. Adarnase, *mt'avari* of K'art'li, importuned and begged the emperor not to remove these gifts from God. But the emperor did not heed his request and took them away.

Thomson quotes another text on this subject as well. See also, for other fragments distributed by Heraclius in Armenia, on his victorious return from Persia: A. Frolow, *La relique de la Vraie Croix* (Archives de l'Orient Chrétien, 7; Paris: Institut français d'études byzantines, 1961) nos. 56–58, p. 191.

[87] Flusin, *Saint Anastase le Perse* II: 283–284.

[88] Flusin, *Saint Anastase le Perse* II: 246–252, 260–261.

[89] See Joel Walker, "'Your Heroic Deeds Give Us Pleasure!' Culture and Society in the Christian Martyr Legends of Late Antiquity" (unpub. Ph.D. diss., Princeton University, 1998).

[90] Sebeos, *History* 128, ch. 39 (86 Thomson); *Hist.* c. 27 (86 Macler).

military situation for the Sasanian Empire.[91] But enforcement of the terms was not so simple to effect.

A Georgian tradition claimed that on his return from Persia, "Heraclius returned after five years and came to Mc'xet'a. He seized from Monkli and Erushet the Lord's foot-rest and the nails given by Constantine to King Mihram. These he brought with him, not heeding the complaints of Atrnerseh and the tears of the whole land of Georgia."[92] Heraclius had earlier shown an interest in relics. This tradition probably confuses Heraclius' activities before his invasion of Mesopotamia with its aftermath.

Heraclius then sought to have Siroy's decree enforced for the Persian evacuation of Byzantine territory. But Agapios and Michael the Syrian report, credibly, that troops of Shahrbarāz said that they did not recognize Siroy: "We do not recognize Siroes, son of Khusrau and we shall not leave our land."[93] Allegedly Jews encouraged them to refuse to give up territory. Heraclius had sent his brother Theodore to reoccupy such lands. Theodore led a vanguard, followed by Heraclius with the main body of the army. Letters from Shahrbarāz and Siroy were shown to Persian garrisons, who were expected to evacuate. Each city was systematically reoccupied.[94] The greatest difficulty or incident took place at Edessa, where only with difficulty were the Persians persuaded to leave. Then Theodore's troops began to massacre the local Jews, who purportedly had insulted Heraclius and encouraged Persian recalcitrance. Theodore previously had to bring up siege machines and fling more than forty stones before the Persians capitulated. One Jew escaped and appealed to Heraclius, who reportedly sent a letter ordering that any Jewish transgressions be overlooked; and that order was scrupulously followed, "When the letter came, he did not bother them any more."[95] Yet this is an indication of potential tensions with Jews. The Persians were sent back to Persia. Isaiah, the Monophysite archbishop, was dislodged and fled from the cathedral.[96] Heraclius gave the cathedral to the Chalcedonians, while the archbishop of Edessa and some other leading Monophysites waited for him to depart.

Heraclius had not needed to wage battles of annihilation. His marginal victory at Nineveh unhinged and upset the equilibrium of the Persian war effort and deployments. He was able to proceed to reap rewards without any more heavy battle casualties. His principal problem was prevention of

[91] Howard-Johnston, "Heraclius' Persian Campaigns," *War In History* 6 (1999) 27. No reliable sources support his thesis, which is inferential. On the frontier in 591: Whitby, *Emperor Maurice* 197–202.
[92] Thomson, *Rewriting Caucasian History* 235–236.   [93] Agapios, *Kitāb al-Unvān*, PO 8: 466.
[94] Agapios, *PO* 8: 465.   [95] Agapios, *PO* 8: 466.
[96] Michael the Syrian, *Chronique* II: 409–412 Chabot trans. Flusin, *Saint Anastase le Perse* II: 286–287.

desertions or loss for medical reasons, and loss of animals to the rigors of the journey.

Shahrbarāz remained in a strong position. Throughout the expedition into Mesopotamia Heraclius remained wary about Shahrbarāz, who could doublecross him, in the words of Sebeos, "was troubled by fear of Khoream [Shahrbarāz]."[97] He still controlled numerous soldiers, despite the attrition from deserters. Presumably his logistics had been disrupted and his troops were living off the land as best they could in Byzantine territory. Siroy died in September or October 628, having reigned only seven months.[98] Shahrbarāz still controlled Palestine.[99] He was at Antioch, or Alexandretta (Alexandria ad Issum), Syria – one cannot be certain from Sebeos' Armenian text.[100] But almost certainly he departed from Syrian Antioch (that is, Antakya, or the vicinity of modern Turkish Iskenderun), because the source for al-Masʿūdī states that Shahrbarāz eventually departed from Antioch in Syria for Persia after his meeting with Heraclius.[101] Shahrbarāz's principal task was to hold his army together fresh and intact. He did not need to do anything to be able to exert great leverage at that time in the situation.

While engaged in this expedition, Heraclius became familiar with the Christians of northern Iraq, including such influential families as that of Yazdin. He also developed a greater appreciation for their potential, and was tempted to explore improvement in relations with them, including seeking solutions or neutralization for Christological issues. These fleeting moments created great expectations and probably retrospectively colored traditions about hopes for the Christianization of Persia and alleged events back in the reign of the late and murdered Emperor Maurice. This expedition into Persia did not make Heraclius an expert on Christianity in Persia, but it certainly gave him and his entourage a much better acquaintance with the Persian Christians and the opportunities that might exist for improving relations with them, which in turn created other opportunities. The narrative of St. Anastasios the Persian's martyrdom reflects that changing world of expectations. The migration of numbers of Persian Christians into Persian-occupied Byzantine Syria and Palestine accelerated contacts,

---

[97] Sebeos, *Hist.* 127, ch. 39 (84 Thomson).

[98] Moses Dasxuranci, *History of the Caucasian Albanians* 2.13 (92 Dowsett).

[99] Moses Dasxuranci, *History of the Caucasian Albanians* 2.16 (104 Dowsett).

[100] Sebeos, *History* 127, 129, ch. 39, 40 (84–85, 88 Thomson); *Storia* c. 38 (99 Gugerotti); *Hist.* c. 28 (87–88 Macler). Flusin, *Saint Anastase le Perse* II: 295–312.

[101] Masʿūdī, *Prairies d'or* (II: 233 Barbier de Meynard). Ambiguous in referring to Alexandria (whether Syrian or Egyptian) is Sebeos, *History* 129, ch. 40 (88 Thomson); *Hist.* ch. 28 (p. 88 Macler trans.).

and familiarity, and also created still more conditions that were propitious for mutually beneficial relations. Not every Persian Christian saw it that way, however.

Heraclius now had new contacts in Persia, who provided him with many new and better sources of intelligence as well as tools for influencing or attempting to influence affairs inside Persia. He could well think that he had a handle on the dynamics of developments inside Persia. It was to the advantage, in the short term, of Christians in the Persian Empire, especially those in northern Iraq, to give heed to him.

There were Messianic hopes for a new golden age, that Khusrau II had foretold through a horoscope that,

The Babylonian race will hold the Roman state in its power for a threefold cyclic hebdomad of years. Thereafter you Romans will enslave the Persians for a fifth hebdomad of years. When these very things have been accomplished, the day without evening will dwell among mortals and the expected fate will achieve power, when the forces of destruction will be handed over to dissolution and those of a better life hold sway.[102]

That was a retrospective horoscope. Of course references to horoscopes could have a special resonance for Heraclius and some of his contemporaries, because he had a reputation, at least in posterity, for having a strong interest in horoscopes. The explanation for this was vague, "When time had created afresh different forces and the evil had been consumed, success migrated from the Persians, the Babylonian dragon, Chosroes the son of Hormisdas, was slain, and the Persian war was concluded." But from the murder of Maurice "until our present times the Roman realm has had no respite from a variety of extraordinary and intolerably serious misfortunes."[103] George of Pisidia asked, "Where are the inquiries into the mysteries of the stars? Who casts the horoscope of the fallen Khusrau?"[104]

Theophylact Simocatta exulted in the recent Byzantine victory over Khusrau II by composing a speech that he attributed to Domitianus, cousin of the late Emperor Maurice and Bishop of Martyropolis, in 590. He referred to God who granted victory:

For in truth he has acted mightily with his arm, humbling peaks of arrogance, casting down the mighty from their seats, and once more inscribing against Babylon the greatness of the spirit. For lions are enslaved, serpents choked, Bel and Mithras sold into slavery, and the fire mitigated, the fire which could not even conquer the clothing of the martyrs although it was liberally sprinkled with tar and pitch.

---

[102] Theophylact, *History* 5.15.6–7 (153 Whitby).   [103] Theophylact, *History* 8.12.13–14 (230 Whitby).
[104] George of Pisidia, *Heraclias* 1.61–62 (243 Pertusi).

Once again the right hand of the Lord has acted powerfully by condemning the pride of the Chaldaeans, writing his proclamation not on a wall, but in heaven. The scepters of Babylon are rent asunder, the throne of his insolence is cast down, the wine-sodden kingdom abased, the humbled are once more honored, and the conquered hold sway.

... This, martyrs, is your offering from the Babylonian tyrant and foreigner, the fugitive from his own kingdom who is now obedient to the Romans rather than hostile: for such great deeds have you executed against your enemies. The tyrant was confounded at these things, and fear and trembling came upon the earth. For he who was from the beginning has punished the heathens, and this is the transformation of his right hand. From the very peak of heaven is its going forth and its end is as far as the bounds of the earth, and we have beheld its glory full of grace.

... now let the Euphrates in accordance with its name rejoice at the splendors of its Creator and let the Tigris transform its ferocity into benevolence, for it has been liberated from the debauchery of slaughter.[105]

This is less the rhetoric of the year 590 than that of the post-628 mood of victory over Khusrau II. It provides some feel for the retrospective literary representation and constructed memory, but not historical realities, of that era. Hopes and expectations seemed boundless at that brief moment.

George of Pisidia similarly envisions the triumph of Heraclius as a universal birthday, which renews the world, as he addressed Heraclius, "Every region and city is conscious that your achievement constitutes an effective and vital renewal."[106] Beyond the rhetoric and celebratory poetry there were also tough realities to confront.

The years of campaigning had been rough on Heraclius. During his wars with the Persians, in that era of very high infant mortality, he had experienced the death of four children, two boys and two girls.[107] He had in ca. 629 betrothed his daughter Epiphania/Eudokia to the *khan* of the Kök Turks, but after the *khan's* violent death Heraclius ordered her return to Byzantium.[108] Heraclius himself needed to rest. It is impossible today to ascertain whether his lengthy military campaigning caused Heraclius to suffer from Post-Traumatic Stress Disorder, even though the psychological effects of such a mental condition might help to explain some of his subsequent unusual actions and reactions.

---

[105] Theophylact, *Hist.* 4.16.4–15 (128–129 Whitby).
[106] George of Pisidia, *Heraclias* 1.201–203 (248–249 Pertusi).
[107] Nikephoros, *Short History* 18 (66–67 Mango).
[108] Nikephoros, *Short History* 18 (66–67). *PLRE* III: 445–446, s.v. "Epiphania *quae et* Eudocia 2." Peter B. Golden, *Khazar Studies* 51; Golden, *Introduction to the History of the Turkic Peoples* 135–137. But see Paul Speck, "Epiphania et Martine sur les monnaies d'Héraclius," *RN* 152 (1997) 453–465.

Theophanes, possibly having used a lost section of George of Pisidia's poetry, declares that

The emperor [Heraclius] in six years fought and conquered Persia and, in the seventh year, he returned to Constantinople, having achieved all of that in the mystical sense. In effect, God fashioned all of creation in six days and he named the seventh day that of rest. So the emperor also accomplished numerous works during six years, then, in the seventh, having returned to the City in the midst of joy and peace, he rested.[109]

Heraclius' precise itinerary from Jalūlā' to Siarzūr to Ganzak to Armenia (and exceedingly improbably, Georgia) and thence to Edessa and other points in Syria is unknown.[110] Agapios reported that he halted on his return from central Mesopotamia to visit the locally famous traditional site of Noah's ark at Jabal Jūdī. He climbed the mountain near the village of Thamania, where he enjoyed the view in all directions.[111] This may well be merely a story, but given Heraclius' interest in relics, it is conceivable. While traveling back after the end of hostilities he did have the time to take in a few local noteworthy sights. The incident once again reinforces and impresses his figure into the legends of the Christian Orient. Local memory preserved or imputed the incident to reinforce the importance of the site. Here Heraclius is remembered for having shown interest in an important Biblical story. If true, Heraclius and his soldiers traversed extremely rough terrain as they headed west from Ganzak. Routes existed, but they were difficult to traverse unless one skirted Lake Van. Finding adequate provisions might have been a challenge. The exact route is simply unknown. According to Agapios, Heraclius then proceeded "to the vicinity of Amida" to pass "the rest of the winter."[112] It was a strategic city. A *stratelates* Theodore did repair its walls, possibly in 628, and he may have been the brother of Heraclius.[113]

By September or October 628 Siroy had died. The succession crisis increased the leverage of Heraclius in internal Persian affairs. Siroy's son

---

[109] Theoph. *Chron.* A.M. 6119 (327–328 De Boor); George of Pisidia, *Poemi* (292 Pertusi).

[110] Speck, *Das geteilte Dossier* 356–377, unpersuasively argues that Heraclius went to Jerusalem and restored the Cross there in 628. Correct chronology: Flusin, *Saint Anastase le Perse* II: 282–319.

[111] Agapios, *Kitāb al-Unvān*, PO 8: 465. Site: Yāqūt, *Geographisches Wörterbuch* I: 934–935, II: 144 (Wüstenfeld). J. Fiey, *Assyrie chrétienne* (Université de Saint-Joseph, Institut de Lettres Orientales, Recherches, 23; Beirut: Imprimerie catholique, 1965) 749–754, explains that the site is Jabal Jūdī in northern Iraq.

[112] Agapios, *Kitāb al-Unvān*, PO 8: 465. Does this mean winter for the rest of the winter of early 628 or that of 628–629?

[113] Cyril and Marlia Mundell Mango, "Inscriptions de la Mésopotamie du Nord," *TM* 11 (1991) 469–470. It may seem surprising that Heraclius receives no mention if 628 is indeed the date, but there could be explanations for the omission of his name even if he did pass through the city during that period.

Ardashīr III succeeded him, from ca. September 628 to 27 April 630.[114] Ardashīr, too, came to a violent end after a short time, at the hands of the still more ephemeral Shahrbarāz, providing Heraclius with additional leverage.[115] Heraclius' principal but not exclusive lever was Shaharbarāz, with whom he reached an agreement in July 629, at Arabissos. Shahrbarāz had Ardashīr assassinated and succeeded him briefly, from 27 April until 9 June 630. Nikephoros confused the records and exaggerates in claiming that Hormisdas succeeded Siroy and then made a statement about his son to Heraclius, "I am delivering my son who is your slave."[116]

Heraclius' itinerary remains murky. Eutychios reports that Heraclius reached Trebizond and from there took a ship to Constantinople.[117] Other sources do not confirm. However, the majority of sources indicate that his itinerary was westward, possibly via Edessa. But he somehow made his way to Constantinople, although the details remain obscure. Northern Syria, Palestine, and Egypt still remained under the control of Shahrbarāz and his formidable forces. The standoff between Byzantine and Persian troops persisted. Heraclius arranged his troops to form a potentially blocking position in the vicinity of Amida and Edessa in order to prevent any possible reinforcement of Shahrbarāz's forces from the Persian heartland while both leaders attempted to work out the terms for détente, disengagement, and Byzantine evacuation of Persian territories in return for the complete evacuation of Byzantine territories by Shahrbarāz and any other Persian commanders. It was still a risky and delicate situation. Heraclius probably remained very wary of Shahrbaraz. It was out of the question for Heraclius to contemplate any personal visit to Jerusalem while Shahrbarāz retained significant military forces in northern Syria.[118] The kinds of clashes that his brother Theodore encountered at Edessa were difficult enough to face down. It was inconceivable for Heraclius himself to place himself in jeopardy at that time by attempting any visit to Jerusalem until all potentially rowdy Persian troops and sympathizers had evacuated the region.

The people of Constantinople, together with his son Heraclius Constantine and Patriarch Sergios, met Heraclius carrying olive branches and lamps, "praising him with joy and tears. His son approached him and fell at his feet, and they both watered the ground with their tears. On seeing this, the people all raised up hymns of thanksgiving to God. And

---

[114] *PLRE* III: 106, s.v. "Ardashir III."
[115] Agapios, *Kitāb al-Unvān*, PO 8: 467. *Histoire Nestorienne*, ed., trans. A. Scher, R. Griveau, *PO* 13: 553–556.
[116] Nikephoros, *Short History* 16 (62–65 Mango).
[117] Eutychios, *Hist.* 29 (127 text Breydy; 107 German trans.; 322 Pirone).
[118] Sebeos, *Hist.* 127, ch. 39 (84 Thomson).

thus taking the emperor they joyfully entered the city."[119] The exact date of his return to Constantinople is uncertain despite its great importance. Celebrations lasted nine days and nine nights.[120]

Heraclius was in Constantinople in 629, apparently by 21 March 629, when he issued a Novel, his fourth, which took legal force on 1 April 629.[121] It confirmed the privileges of bishops, clergy, and monks in Constantinople and the provinces in their protection against civil and criminal complaints, and protected them against civilian and military officials. In the provinces bishops, clerics and monks could appeal to be heard by the Patriarch of Constantinople, or the Pretorian Prefect of the East, or a deputy of the emperor.[122] The cases of these above clerics were no longer compelled to be heard by a deputy of the emperor or by the office of the Pretorian Prefect of the East. Appeals against decisions of a bishop could be made to a metropolitan, and from those of a metropolitan to the Patriarch. But of equal importance, it for the first time uses the title *basileus* for an emperor, who is also characterized, with his son, as πιστοί ἐν Χριστῷ βασιλεῖς (faithful in Christ).[123] This appears to be a major and lasting innovation in Byzantine imperial titulature.

Other challenges beckoned after the termination of the brilliantly successful military campaign. It was unclear whether he could adjust to the tempo and diverse non-military needs of the postwar empire. Plague spread and killed many in the reign of Heraclius, probably late in the 620s, at any rate while Niketas was still alive. He had died, it appears, by 629. The causes of the plague may be complex, but were possibly related to overcrowding, and massive population shifts of refugees bringing disease from other regions of the Near East and the Mediterranean.[124] As the author of the *Miracles of St. Artemios* stated,

Now it happened in the years of the reign of Heracluis of divine portion that a deadly plague arose and people were suddenly carried off. So it transpired at that

[119] Theoph. *Chron.* A.M. 6119 (328 De Boor).
[120] Eutychios, *Hist.* 29 (127 text Breydy; 107 German trans.).
[121] Johannes Konidaris, "Die Novellen des Kaisers Herakleios," *Fontes Minores* V *(Forschungen zur byzantinischen Rechtsgeschichte* 8) 84–95.
[122] Konidaris, "Die Novellen des Kaisers Herakleios" 103–106.
[123] Konidaris, "Die Novellen des Kaisers Herakleios" 57–60; also Speck, *Das geteilte Dossier* 356–357. For a generally convincing reconstruction of events surrounding the restoration of the Holy Lance and Sponge: Holger A. Klein, "Niketas und das wahre Kreuz. Kritische Anmerkungen zur Überlieferung des Chronicon Paschale ad annum 614," *BZ* 94/2 (2001) 580–587; cf. P. Speck, "Zum Datum der Translation der Kreuzreliquien nach Konstantinopel," in *Beiträge von Paul Speck* (*Varia* VII, Ποικίλα Βυζαντινά, 18; Bonn: Habelt, 2000) 167–175.
[124] *The Miracles of St. Artemios*, ed., trans. Virgil S. Chrisafulli and John Nesbitt (Leiden: Brill, 1997) 48, 178–179.

time that the aforesaid Euphemia succumbed to a deadly affliction since a bubonic tumor was growing in her armpit and she was terminally ill. This Euphemia spent two days mute and speechless, opening neither mouth nor eye nor uttering a word (for over the whole of her body harbingers of death were growing like a pestilence, the so-called black spots; the common people call them "blessings") . . .

Haunting spectres loomed large in popular imagination.

Plague ravaged Byzantine Africa as well, probably late in the 620s. Africa, or at least the Carthage region, did suffer from the plague, probably in the 620s. Some insight into local mentalities comes from a rare text in the works of St. Anastasios the Sinaite,[125] one that is repeated in the Constantinopolitan *Synaxarium*, in which the terrors of the specters of black Ethiopians in a vision are prominent. The localization of the story in Africa probably less than two decades before the beginning of the Muslim conquest (that is, in the 620s) does suggest some of the tensions that probably existed between the Latin and Greek urbanized elites and some parts of the African population. Such terrors might well also have become conflated with those of the imminent Muslim invaders. It may indicate a local propensity to be frightened about the kinds of people who would be among (but not exclusively populate) the invading Muslim armies. The story also indicates, and this appears to be corroborated by recent archaeological work in Carthage,[126] that the population was declining inside Carthage but growing in its suburbs. So great fears accompanied the plague and other disruptions that were contemporary with Heraclius' victorious campaigns.

The contemporary author of the threnody concerning the fall of Jerusalem to the Persians reports that after the death of the Sasanian King Siroy in September 629, and in the brief reign of Ardashīr who reigned for three months, Rasmiozan (that is, Shahrbarāz) was the intermediary whose intervention permitted peace between the Byzantines and Persians.[127] Heraclius had already made a pact with Shahrbarāz at Arabissos. Heraclius also probably heard of the death of Siroy while at Hierapolis.[128] Many events unfolded while Heraclius stayed at the strategic and administratively significant city of Hierapolis.[129] Sebeos claims that when Kawadh/Siroy

---

[125] Anastasios the Sinaite, ed. F. Nau, "Le texte grec des récits du moine Anastase sur les saints pères du Sinaï," c. 40, *Oriens Christianus* 2 (1902) 83–85; revised later versions in *Synaxarium ecclesiae Constantinopolitanae*, ed. H. Delehaye, 638–639; and Georgios Monachos, *Chronicon*, ed. C. De Boor (Leipzig, 1904) 678–683.

[126] Professor Susan Stevens so informs me.

[127] Strategios, *La prise de Jérusalem par les Perses en 614*, 24.3–7 (54 Garitte).

[128] Theophanes, *Chron.* A.M. 6021 (329 De Boor).

[129] Godefroy Goossens, *Hiérapolis de Syrie. Essai de monographie historique* (Leuven: Bibliothèque de l'Université, 1943) 145–174 on its strategic significance; on its significance for Monophysitism: 174–180.

died, Heraclius wrote to Shahrbarāz, offering him a pact and assistance, which he accepted. The essential summit meeting took place at Arabissos, where Shahrbarāz promised to arrange the borders as Heraclius wished, indicating continuing problems with fixing Byzantine–Persian borders.[130] Heraclius and his commanders and soldiers learned to appreciate the value of certain mountain passes in the Tauros Mountains as choke-points during the tense standoff with Shahrbarāz. That experience in 628–629 with sealing passes probably helped Heraclius and his successors to devise defenses against the Muslims in the late 630s and 640s in the same region. Heraclius sent the eunuch Nerses with an unknown but large number of Byzantine troops to assist Shahrbarāz against Persian rivals. Nikephoros or his source probably had access to some court documents or official bulletins. As Nikephoros explained, Shahrbarāz wrote a formal apology for his damages to Byzantine territory, which he claimed that he committed on orders of Khusrau II,

... he begged permission to be received and to present himself like a slave. Upon receiving from the emperor a sworn assurance, he promised to appear before him and bring money from Persia so as to repair whatever he had destroyed in the Roman country. At this juncture the son of Hormisdas fell victim to a plot and was slain; and Shahrbarāz requested from the emperor the Persian crown. The latter gave it to him, and they agreed among themselves that all Roman territory occupied by the Persians should be restored to the Romans. When peace had been concluded, Shahrbarāz immediately returned to the Romans both Egypt and all the eastern lands after withdrawing the Persians that were there; and he sent the emperor the life-giving Cross. Now Heraclius conferred the dignity of Patrician upon Niketas, son of Shahrbarāz, and gave the latter's daughter Nike in marriage to his own son Theodosios, born of Martina.[131]

One may consider Niketas the son of Shahrbarāz (and his brother) a kind of hostage for the observance of Shahrbarāz's agreements with Heraclius.

The marriage plans of Nike and the very young (five or six years old at that time), deaf-mute Theodosios had great implications for Byzantine power in Persia and even for the spread of Christianity in Persia if Shahrbarāz had successfully maintained control of Persia.[132] The marriage of Constantine III looked west, with his marriage to a cousin from Africa, albeit that part of

---

[130] Sebeos, *History* 129–130, ch. 40 (88 Thomson); *Storia* c. 38 (99–100 Gugerotti). Thomas Artsruni, *History of the House of the Artsrunik'* 162, claims that Shahrbarāz (Khoream) handed over Jerusalem, Antioch, Caesarea in Palestine, Tarsus, the greater part of Armenia, "and everything that Heraclius had ever desired." Heraclius gave him a small number of trusted troops to accompany him to Persia.

[131] Nikephoros, *Short History* 17 (65 Mango trans., 64 Greek text).

[132] Mango, "Deux études sur Byzance et la Perse Sassanide" 113–117. But see C. Zuckerman, "La petite Augusta et le Turc," *RN* 150 (1995) 121. Against Zuckerman: Paul Speck: "Epiphania et Martine sur les monnaies d'Héraclius," *RN* 152 (1997) 457–465.

Africa that was adjacent to Egypt. This marriage, however, looked to the east and offered potential bridges to a very different region with different ethnic groups and potential, almost open-ended opportunities for the expansion of Christianity and for securing the eastern borders against any repetition of the horrors of the recent wars.

Tangible fruits appeared immediately. Shahrbarāz's son Patrikios Niketas forwarded the relic of the Holy Sponge to Constantinople, which was fastened to the relic of the Cross on 14 September 629 for exaltation at a special ceremony at Constantinople. Niketas already had met Heraclius in central Mesopotamia, where he and a brother had been serving as virtual hostages. Shortly after transmission and veneration of the Holy Sponge Niketas forwarded the Holy Lance to Constantinople, where it was received on Saturday, 28 October 629. He had brought it from "the holy places," that is, from Jerusalem or its vicinity. Its arrival was heralded, and men and women alternately began its four-day public veneration on 1 November 629: Tuesday and Wednesday by men, Thursday and Friday by women.[133] Niketas' delivery of these two relics was a token of his and his father Shahrbarāz's alliance with Heraclius. It also underscores that up to that point Shahrbarāz still controlled Jerusalem and its environs. It would have been impractical for Heraclius to visit Jerusalem to restore the major relic of the Cross that the Persians had carried away to Mesopotamia while Persians still controlled Palestine and Syria. Treachery could always occur. Otherwise Heraclius could have taken possession of the Holy Sponge and Lance while in the Holy Land and any delivery of those items by any member of the family of Shahrbarāz would have been unnecessary. Niketas had presumably already converted to Christianity and was promised support by Heraclius to inherit the Persian throne from his father.

The transmission of the relics of the Holy Sponge and Lance indicates some significant contacts between those in the Persian ranks and Byzantines. It was an immediate token of Shahrbarāz's alliance with Heraclius, even though he himself did not personally send it to Niketas.[134] The exaltation of the Cross and veneration of the Lance and Sponge all represented a terminus: the process of accumulating relics culminated on the eve of the restoration of the Cross to Jerusalem in early 630 and the association of all of these with Heraclius and his dynasty. These religious ceremonies had a complicated psychological effect at Constantinople: they celebrated the religious dimensions of the war, raised popular consciousness of the issues

---

[133] *Chronicon Paschale* 704–705 (156–157 Whitby). H. Klein is persuasive, see n. 123 above.

[134] The reference in the *Chronicon Paschale* may indicate the author's or contemporary interest at the court of Heraclius in celebrating the role of Shahrbarāz.

at stake, and increased the holiness of Constantinople and the Heraclian dynasty, which had managed to bring them to Constantinople and to associate its name with them. They marked the end of a moment in which the empire and the church were in great jeopardy.

Heraclius and his advisers had been devising ambitious marriage alliances in different directions. It was probably approximately at this time, in 629, that he sent his daughter Eudokia, whom he had previously betrothed, probably in 627, to marry the Khan of the Kök Turks but recalled her on learning of the Khan's death.[135] The failed marriage alliance, which would have involved the dispatch of Heraclius' daughter Eudokia to the Kök Turks, would have given, close to the time of the marriage of Constantine III to Gregoria and of the arrangement of Theodosios to marry Nike, the dynasty and empire solid ties in the east with both Persia and with the powerful, and possibly commercially significant as well, tribe of Kök Turks. The Kök Turks might exercise leverage over Persia, over Armenia, for many Armenians and other peoples of the Caucasus feared the Kök Turks, and constitute a listening post and bridge to peoples in the trans-Caucasus. Both of those marriages would have strongly affected Armenia and the empire's relations with Armenia and Armenians, who were potentially exposed to Kök Turks, Persians, and of course to Byzantines. Yet the hopes for both marriages collided with tragic events: the deaths of both the Kök Turk Khan and Shahrbarāz himself. These were the first serious checks to Heraclius after his triumph over Khusrau II.

The initial triumph of Shahrbarāz in Persia was swift. With the assistance of Nerses, Shahrbarāz seized power and slew Ardashīr on 27 April 630. He undertook an embarrassing and humiliating clash with the Kök Turks, which may have encouraged others to plot his downfall. Shahrbarāz fulfilled his agreement with Heraclius. He made peace with Byzantium and remitted the major relic of the wood of the Cross. The process may have been more complex, not a mere handing over of the Cross to Nerses. Shahrbarāz had the Cross remitted to General David, who probably was David Saharuni, the Persian *marzpan* of Armenia.[136] Yet there are problems with the chronology of Saharuni, who probably put himself at the service of Heraclius in that complex period.

Hopeful scenes also filled some of those days. While at Constantinople, and not later than February 630, Heraclius married his niece Gregoria,

---

[135] Nikephoros, *Short History* c. 18 (66–67 Mango). C. Zuckerman, "La petite Augusta et le Turc," *RN* 150 (1995) 120–122, dates the start of her journey to the Khan to July 629.

[136] Nicole Thierry, "Héraclius et la vraie croix en Arménie," 172–176, for the role of David Saharuni; *PLRE* III: 389–390, s.v. "David Saharuni 6," for alternative chronologies and identifications. Also Beihammer, *Nachrichten* no. 39, pp. 54–60.

daughter of his late first cousin Niketas, to his son Heraclius Constantine.[137] A dynastic motivation was a component of this memorable act. Gregoria came from the Pentapolis to Constantinople. Here again the dynasty re-inforced its ties with Africa. She had already been betrothed to Heraclius Constantine while Niketas had been alive. But this marriage, like Heraclius' to Martina, fell within the prohibited degrees.[138]

On 7 November 630, Heraclius found himself a grandson in the person of Heraclius Constantine's son, also named Heraclius at his baptism on 3 November 631, and then Constantinus at his ultimate coronation.[139] The future of his dynasty appeared to be assured and stable.

---

[137] Nikephoros, *Short History* 17 (64–65 Mango); George of Pisidia, *Bell. Avar.* 537–541 (200–201 Pertusi); *PLRE* III: 349–350, s.v. "Constantinus 38." The exact date of Niketas' death is unknown: Mango, "Deux études," 105; *PLRE* III: 940–943, s.v. "Nicetas 7."

[138] Mango, "Deux études" 105, 113–114, for analysis and a possible explanation.

[139] Theoph. *Chron.* A.M. 6122 (335 De Boor); Georgios Kedrenos 1.750.

CHAPTER 6

Five crucial years: a narrow window of opportunity

Crises did not cease to weigh on Heraclius. His labors were Herculean, even Sisyphean, some might say. His panegyrist George of Pisidia praised him for slaying the Hydra-headed monster,[1] but his challenges between 629 and 633 were indeed Hydra-like. Extraordinary skills in external and civil wars, including the ability to divide his opponents and overcome them in detail, had proved decisive for him in the first two decades since he first rebelled against Phokas. George of Pisidia also called him a new Noah, which is strikingly consistent with his visit, on his return from Persia, to putative remains of Noah's ark in the Armenian highlands. He also hailed him as a new Constantine, an epithet perhaps underscored by his campaign tent, which was reminiscent of the celebrated one that Constantine I had used.[2] But a complex group of new tasks awaited him, ones that required different methods.

A critical span of five years began. Heraclius' activities between returning to Byzantine territory and the outbreak of the first Islamic conquests of Byzantine territory, namely the years from 628 to 633, are pivotal for

---

[1] George of Pisidia, *Heraclias* 1.65–79; *Expeditio Persica* 3.349–359; *In Christi Resurrectionem*, lines 106–111, *Contra Severum*, lines 62–71 = *Carmi di Giorgio di Pisidia*, ed. trans. L.Tartaglia, pp. 132–133, 198–199, 256–257, 266–267. Mary Whitby, "A New Image for a New Age: George of Pisidia on the Emperor Heraclius," in *The Roman and Byzantine Army in the East*, ed. E. Dabrowa (Cracow, 1994) 207–208, and Mary Whitby, "Defender of the Cross: George of Pisidia on the Emperor Heraclius and his Deputies," in Whitby, *The Propaganda of Power* (Leiden: Brill, 1998) 247–273. Herakles analogy: T. Nissen, "Historisches Epos und Panegyrikos in der Spätantike," *Hermes* 75 (1940) 302–303. Claudia Ludwig, "Kaiser Herakleios, Georgios Pisides und die Perserkriege," *Varia* III, Ποικίλα Βυζαντινά, 11, ed. P. Speck (Bonn, 1991) 73–128.

[2] Constantine I's tent, created for an aborted military campaign against the Persians: Sokrates Scholastikos, *Historia ecclesiastica* 1.18.12, ed. G.C. Hansen (GCS; Berlin: Akademie Verlag, 1995) 59; also Gelasios, *Hist. eccl.* 3.10.26–27, *Kirchengeschichte*, ed. G. Loeschcke, M. Heinemann (*GCS*; Leipzig: Hinrich'sche Buchhandlung, 1918) p. 155, for similar phrasing. Cf. Eusebius, *Vit. Const.*, ed. F. Winkelmann (*GCS*; Berlin: Akademie Verlag, 1991) p. 144, note 1/2 lac. Mss. But see Eusebius, *Life of Constantine*, trans., comment., Averil Cameron, S.G. Hall (Oxford: Clarendon Press, 1999) 336. Heraclius used a similar tent of variegated brocade: Ibn 'Abd al-Ḥakam, *Kitāb futūḥ miṣr*, ed. C. Torrey (New Haven, 1922) 37. See C. Rapp, "Comparison, Paradigm and the Case of Moses in Panegyric and Hagiography," in Whitby, *The Propaganda of Power* 292–296.

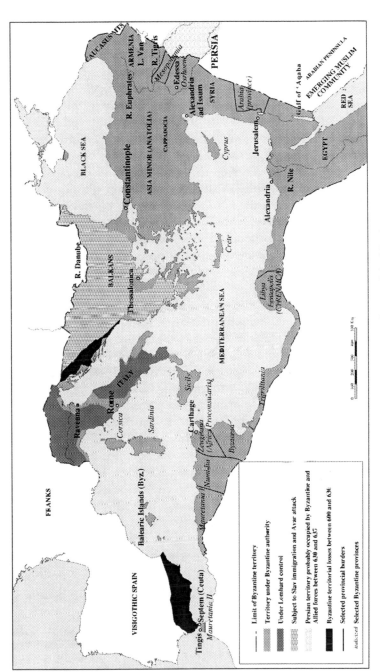

Map 7 The Byzantine Empire in 630, on the eve of the Islamic conquests

FRANKS

VISIGOTHIC SPAIN

Tingis o Septem (Ceuta)
Mauretania II

Balearic Islands (Byz)

Ravenna
Rome o ITALY
Corsica
Sardinia
Sicily
Carthage
Mauretania Numidia
(Caesariensis)
Zeugitana
(AFR Proconsularis)
Byzacena

Tripolitania

MEDITERRANEAN SEA

Crete

Libya
Pentapolis
(CYRENAICA)

R. Danube

BLACK SEA

BALKANS

Thessalonica

Constantinople

ASIA MINOR (ANATOLIA)

CAPPADOCIA

Cyprus

Jerusalem o

R. Nile

Alexandria

EGYPT

CAUCASUS MTS

ARMENIA
L. Van
R. Tigris

Mesopotamia

o Edessa
Osrhoene

R. Euphrates

Alexandria
ad Issum

SYRIA

Arabia
(province)

Gulf of 'Aqaba

PERSIA

ARABIAN PENINSULA

EMERGING MUSLIM
COMMUNITY

RED
SEA

0 100 200 300 4pm 500 Km

- - - Limit of Byzantine territory
Territory under Byzantine authority
Under Lombard control
Subject to Slav immigration and Avar attack
Persian territory probably occupied by Byzantine and
Allied forces between 630 and 637
Byzantine territorial losses between 600 and 630
Selected provincial borders
italicised Selected Byzantine provinces

understanding him and the history of his empire and the entire Mediterranean littoral. The era started with his military and religious triumph. Shahrbarāz and his lieutenants probably handed over the Cross to a reputable Byzantine, who may have been Armenian, to transmit to Heraclius.[3] Heraclius was at the zenith of his influence. He enjoyed the exhilaration and virtual giddiness of the broader public in his military victory, the reaffirmation of the truths and power of Christianity, the end of an era of deprivation, insecurity, and anxiety, and the satisfaction and delight at seeing the discomfort and confounding of the enemies of the empire and the true church. Events started to move fast, even to cascade. Everything seemed to be fluid and malleable. It was an exhilarating time. The rush of events may have made Heraclius and others wonder whether portents indicated that this was indeed some extraordinary time of historical fulfillment. Later stories attribute, without confirmation, astrological inquiries to him in this period, including a prediction of harm to him and his empire from a circumcised people, whom he wrongly concluded to be Jews: "Being well read, he practiced astrology, by which art he discovered, God helping him, that his empire would be laid waste by circumcised races."[4]

Heraclius' titulature changed. Hitherto it had a Justinianic resonance: "Emperor Caesar Flavius Heraclius, faithful in Christ, most serene, supreme, beneficent, peaceful, victor over the Alamanni, the Goths, the Franks, Germans, Antae, Alans, Vandals, Africans, Heruls, Gepids, pious, fortunate, glorious/famous, victor, triumphant, ever venerable Augustus."[5] He changed in 629 to a new formula, which was now written in Greek: to Πιστὸς ἐν Χριστῷ βασιλεύς ("Faithful in Christ, *Basileus* [Emperor]"),[6] which signified a permanent Hellenization of titulature.

Heraclius did not rest long after his victory over the Persians. He demonstrated once more his great energy by turning to handle the numerous challenges that confronted the empire, to which he committed great amounts of personal time, attention, and his prestige. Heraclius' goals included efforts to restore Byzantine control of territory. First this required negotiation with Persian leaders both in Mesopotamia and with Shahrbarāz, who still controlled troops in Palestine and Syria, to secure the orderly evacuation of Byzantine territory by Persian troops. There was a need to watch the

---

[3] Nicole Thierry, "Héraclius et la vraie croix en Arménie" 175–176. But the identification of that official as David Saharuni is doubtful.

[4] Fredegarius, *Chronicle* 65 (53–55 Wallace-Hadrill).

[5] J. Konidaris, "Die Novellen des Kaisers Herakleios," *Fontes Minores* V: 80. On the title: Irfan Shahid, "Heraclius *Pistos Basileus en Christo Basileus*," *DOP* 34–35 (1982) 225–237; Shahid, "On the Titulature of Emperor Heraclius," *Byzantion* 51 (1981) 288–296.

[6] J. Konidaris, "Die Novellen des Kaisers Herakleios," *Fontes Minores* V: 84.

internal situation in Persia, to prevent the reemergence of any leader there who would be dangerous for Byzantium, given Byzantium's recent painful experiences with Persia. There was also the need to secure the return of prisoners, refugees, and stolen property whether public, private, or ecclesiastical. Other goals included holding a triumph in Constantinople to celebrate and to demonstrate to the people that their sufferings had received a just reward, and restoration of the Cross and other holy relics that the Persians had seized to their rightful places. An eighth-century Spanish chronicler commented concerning Heraclius in the twenty-first year of his reign (although his chronology is inaccurate): "who restored many regions that were lost to the Roman state in the east and invaded by the Persians to their former perfect condition and he triumphed victoriously over the Persians" (*qui a re publica Romana multas in Oriente deficientes patrias et a Persis invasas dicioni priscae restaurat ac de Persis victoriose triumphat*).[7] Such was Heraclius' reputation abroad for action in that period. Significantly missing is any reference to activities in or concern for the Balkans.

The empire's mood in 629–630, and probably Heraclius' own, was confident yet conditions were also very fragile. In some localities much physical reconstruction was necessary after wartime ravages. The enormous loss of human life in the Byzantine–Persian War would be difficult to replace in a short time.[8] On another level Byzantine authority needed restoration after a hiatus of more than a decade in Syria and a decade in Egypt. Heraclius' campaigning disrupted life and the economy of the Caucasus, including Georgia.[9] There were troubling issues of disloyalty, misappropriation and restoration of private, public, and ecclesiastical property, both movable and immovable. It was necessary to restore the judicial processes and, above all, the machinery for collecting and distributing tax revenues. Many years had now passed since the violent overthrow and deaths of Emperors Maurice and Phokas. Military victory and restoration of religious relics seemingly erased any conceivable traces of the vulnerability of the Heraclian house and its regime. Internal opposition to the political and military authority of Heraclius was invisible. Yet Heraclius' second marriage, to his niece Martina, remained controversial. No solution existed for theological difficulties of the centuries-long Christological controversy and the legacy of

---

[7] Isidore, *Chron.* 414b, *MGH AA* 11: 479; Hoyland, *Seeing Islam as Others Saw It* (Princeton: Darwin, 1997) 614.

[8] 200,000 men, according to Suda, *Lexikon*, Adler II: 583. Although probably an exaggeration, losses were surely high. Many perished from medical rather than combat reasons.

[9] S. Rapp alerted me to the disruptiveness of Sasanian–Byzantine warfare for the inhabitants of Georgia.

decisions at the Council of Chalcedon in 451. Related to this there were ecclesiological questions about who should control actual local churches and their properties and why.[10] Even the Chalcedonians had grievances concerning forced loans of church wealth to the government during the recent military emergencies of the war against the Persians.

Recent events added new names. Martyrdoms connected with the Persian invasions added St. Anastasios the Persian to the roster of venerated saints; there were enhanced eastern contributions to sacrality at the beginning of the 630s. The process of increasing the veneration of saints continued to spread, deepen, and intensify on different shores of the Mediterranean, from Palestine in western Asia westward to Numidia, in the interior of Byzantine Africa. The cult of the saints was growing and was being enriched. This was not a static society, it was a vibrant and pulsating one, which further complicated any governmental efforts to control or to guide religion and intellectual life. Heraclius did not create or direct that process, but he was contemporary with and had to cope with it. He embraced it. It was an indispensable component of the mental and spiritual environment of the 630s. It was growing.

Developments in Rome reinforced this process. Heraclius now had the time to turn to shoring up his relationships with provincial and ecclesiastical leaders. He reinforced his good ties with Pope Honorius I (625–638), who converted the old Roman senate house, the Curia, into a church in honor of the Nikomedian martyr St. Adriano in approximately the year 630.[11] Honorius probably accomplished this with explicit or tacit imperial permission from Heraclius. The *Liber Pontificalis* states that with the permission of Emperor Heraclius, Pope Honorius also stripped the roof tiles from the Temple of Roma and Venus for the roof of St. Peter's.[12] So paradoxically, Heraclius, although he was an admirer and utilizer of ancient Roman formulas and procedures, was a passive observer and even a participant in

---

[10] For background on Christological controversies, especially after 451, see: J. Meyendorff, *Imperial Unity and Christian Divisions* (Crestwood, NY: St. Vladimir's Seminary Press, 1987); W.H.C. Frend, *The Rise of the Monophysite Movement* (Cambridge, 1972); Patrick T.R. Gray, *The Defense of Chalcedon in the East: 451–553* (Studies in the History of Christian Thought, 20; Leiden: Brill, 1979). For a different perspective: Werner Elert, *Der Ausgang der Altkirchlichen Christologie: Eine Untersuchung über Theodor von Pharan und seine Zeit als Einführung in die alte Dogmensgeschichte* (Berlin: Lutherisches Verlagshaus, 1957).

[11] *Liber Pontificalis*, ed. L. Duchesne (repr. Paris, 1957) 1.324, cf. comment on p. 326; R. Lanciani, "L'aula e gli uffici del senato romano," *Atti della R. Accademia dei Lincei, Memorie, Cl. di Scienze morali, storiche e filologiche*, ser. 3 (1882–1883) XI: 13–14; F. Gregorovius, *History of Rome in the Middle Ages*, trans. Mrs. Gustavus Hamilton (London: G. Bell, 1911; repr. New York: AMS Press, 1967) II: 121–122; Alfonso Bartoli, *Curia senatus. Lo scavo e il restauro* (Rome: Istituto di studi romani, 1963) 72–73.

[12] *Liber Pontificalis* 1.323 (Duchesne).

the transformation of some great relics of Rome's past into Christian ones. Political pressures and trends compelled him to yield sensitive symbols of Rome's heritage to Christian makeover. He probably had no regrets. But years of giving priority to the east had their consequences for Italy. Elsewhere in Italy, as in Rome, there was a drift to implicit or *de facto* assertion of independence from centralized imperial control, as an inscription from the island of Torcello and another from Ravenna testify.[13] But despite the exarch Isaac's apparent claims to some parity with Heraclius, Liguria still remained under Byzantine control at the death of Heraclius.[14]

The drawing power of the Cross and Jerusalem is also evident in those years. Individuals, including ones from rural Egypt as well as from remote Armenia, were attracted to venerate the presumed relics of the Cross that the emperor had restored to Jerusalem.[15] New saintly remains such as those of St. Anastasios the Persian now enriched the land of Palestine. As a political leader, Heraclius had to live in, adjust to, and react to that mental and spiritual ferment, longing, and change. He could not, however, control it and there is no evidence that he ever cynically attempted to do so or even contemplated the prospect. Festivals such as the Exaltation of the Cross enhanced religious ceremonial. The contemporary obsession with obtaining physical relics, whether the Cross, the chair of St. Mark, and other saintly relics, all were part of the same trend.

The overweening concern for relics involved many dimensions. New burials and cult sites for remains took place as far away as Byzantine Numidia, in North Africa.[16] The translation and veneration of relics, such as those of St. Anastasios the Persian from Persia to Caesarea, and the diligent recording and dissemination of accounts of miracles performed by those relics, was one kind of act. Another was the restoration of holy sites in Palestine desecrated by the Persians. But there also were holy sites near Constantinople that the Persians had burnt and desecrated, such as the monastery of St. Olympias, which the superior Sergia restored after

[13] A. Pertusi, "L'iscrizione torcellana dei tempi d'Eraclio," *Bollettino dell'Istituto di storia della società e dello stato veneziano* 4 (1962) 9–38. Salvatore Cosentino, "L'iscrizione ravennate dell'Esarco Isacio e le guerre di Rotari," in *Atti e Memorie della Deputazione di Storia Patria per le Antiche Province Modenesi*, ser. 11 (1993) XV: 23–43.

[14] Cosentino, "L'iscrizione ravennate" 25–27.

[15] Pilgrimages: from Egypt there is Papyrus 55, *Greek Papyri of the Byzantine Period*, ed. G. Fantoni (Griechische Texte, 10; *CPRF*, 14) pp. 107–109; on Armenian pilgrims to the Holy Land in the seventh century, see Kaegi, *BEIC* 30–31, but esp. Michael Stone, "Holy Land Pilgrimage of Armenians before the Arab Conquest," *Revue Biblique* 93 (1986) 93–110; F. Nau, "Le texte grec des récits du moine Anastase," *Oriens Christianus* 2 (1902) 81–82.

[16] Yvette Duval, ed., *Loca Sanctorum Africae*, no. 112 (I: 234–235, 236–239). Elsewhere in Numidia, a chapel was dedicated at Telergma near Timgad as late as 645, in the reign of Heraclius' grandson Constans II: *CIL* VIII: 2389 = 17822; S. Gsell, *Monuments Antiques de l'Algérie* (1901) II: 315.

collecting the bloody relics from the destroyed monastery. Sergia reported the assistance of Sergios the Constantinopolitan Patriarch, although she fails to mention Heraclius in her account ca. 630. So a process of cleanup, rededication, and spiritual invigoration immediately followed the end of hostilities with the Persians. In the case of the monastery of St. Thomas, at Brochthoi, the Patriarch sent John the presbyter, the baker, and other clergy to deposit the relics. That moving and memorable ceremony brought the attendees to fear and trembling. Such acts contributed to the empire-wide atmosphere of spiritual renewal and rededication.[17]

The Patriarchate of Constantinople probably gained even more in importance and influence because of the Persian depredations. Bishoprics and monasteries in Anatolia had suffered grievously during the lengthy war. Many precious relics had been permanently moved to Constantinople, to the greater glory of the Patriarchate, even though that was not the primary motive in transferring them. Likewise the Patriarchate participated in the ceremonies of rededication of relics and monasteries and other holy places, like that of St. Olympias, during the process of reconstruction. Weakened localities became even more dependent on the Patriarchate after the events of almost three decades of civil strife, external warfare and the subsequent local upheavals. This was not the plan of Heraclius, but it affected him and his realm in his final years.

The crafting of the sumptuous silver David Plates is still another part of that process of the Christianization of the secular. It is probable that they were created in this period, immediately following the triumphal return of Heraclius. These important and exquisitely crafted plates may evoke the prevailing triumphal atmosphere, but any ideological message or clear relationship other than chronological with Heraclius remains unproven.[18] Other famous Heraclian silver pieces may date to this period and may also owe their production to the influx of silver as loot and reparations from Persia in 628 and immediately thereafter. The very production and survival of such lavish and beautiful plates are remarkable, given the desperate confiscations of silver plate on several occasions in the seventh century. They testify to the quality of workmanship and the wealth that existed in the age

[17] "Narratio Sergiae de translatione Sanctae Olympiadis," *AB* 16 (1897) 44–51. English translation, with notes: Elizabeth Clark, "Sergia's Narration," in *Jerome, Chrysostom, and Friends. Essays and Translations* (Studies in Women and Religion, 2; New York, Toronto: The Edwin Mellen Press, 1979) 145–157.

[18] The silver stamps on the plates date to the reign of Heraclius. Triumphalism: S.H. Wander, "The Cyprus Plates: the Story of David and Goliath," *Metropolitan Museum Journal* 8 (1973) 89–104; alternative non-imperial reading: Ruth E. Leader, "The David Plates Revisited: Transforming the Secular in Early Byzantium," *Art Bulletin* 82 (2000) 407–427.

of Heraclius. It was the end of an era. Comparable pieces are rare after the middle of the seventh century.[19] The very substantial thesaurized wealth of these objects made them and comparable objects ones that tempted officials and private individuals in times of need. This was a society that still possessed sufficient wealth to devote rich resources to the beautification of churches and private households in the form of silver plate and revetments.

The end of war with Persia allowed a diversion of imperial funds for long-deferred construction. Heraclius probably released funds for rebuilding the Magnaura Palace at Constantinople at that time: "Swiftly the construction of this building was completed by sovereigns who owed the success of their arms to the cross: lord Heraclius and his son Constantine."[20] Contemporary also was the restoration of baths at Constantinople, according to a poem "On a bath renewed by Heraclius": "Time held this bath prisoner like the barbarians previously held cities, but just as he who prevailed over the Scyths and Persians made cities new, and so he displayed this bath new."[21] His immediate successors will repeat this vaunted Heraclian theme of renewal, *ananeōsis*. However, Heraclius' extensive commitments to reconstruction in Constantinople and other cities overextended his tired empire's limited financial resources, while military needs received diminished attention and diminished funding.

The Byzantine and the wider Mediterranean maritime economy began to revive because of the end of hostilities with Persia. Profits and financial opportunities beckoned for the enterprising. Members of the imperial palace staff participated in and encouraged that commercial activity, even though it may have escaped the personal attention of Heraclius himself.[22] Although he may have sought to portray himself as a guarantor of fair weights and measures, there is no evidence that Heraclius took any great personal interest in or possessed any insights about the stimulation or reforming of commerce and finance. Taxation and regulation of this burgeoning maritime and overland commerce was an objective of local bureaucrats as well as

[19] Marlia Mango, *Silver from Early Byzantium. The Kaper Koraon and Related Treasures* (Baltimore: Walters Art Gallery, 1986) pp. 1–15, items E5, E103–E106; M. Mango, "The Monetary Value of Silver Revetments and Objects Belonging to Churches, A.D. 300–700," in S. Boyd and M. Mango, *Ecclesiastical Silver Plate in Sixth-Century Byzantium* (Washington: Dumbarton Oaks, 1992) 123–136.

[20] *Greek Anthology* 9.655; *Anthologie Grecque*, ed., trans. P. Waltz, G. Soury, J. Irigoin, P. Laurens (Paris: Budé, 1974) 8.126; C. Mango in *ODB* 1267–1268, s.v. "Magnaura."

[21] L. Sternbach, "Georgii Pisidae carmina inedita Pars II," *Wiener Studien. Zeitschrift für Classische Philologie* 14 (1892) p. 56, poem No. 47; Εἰς λοετρὸν ἀνανεωθὲν ὑπὸ Ἡρακλείου, *Carmi di Giorgio di Pisidia*, ed. L. Tartaglia, poem 13: 105, pp. 500–501. The wording indicates that the repairs took place after Heraclius' victories in 628.

[22] Trade between Constantinople and Africa: *Doctrina Jacobi nuper Baptizati* 5.20.1.1–50 (215–219) Dagron-Déroche).

those at Constantinople. Yet such initiatives created resentments in many quarters in the far-flung provinces, especially on the part of those who suffered taxation or who even were prevented from engaging in trade.

It was also a time to give thanks to God for divine assistance in crushing the Persians and in restoring the wealth and holy relics to the empire. It was a time for humility as well as exaltation. Heraclius modeled his own public gestures to conform to those expectations, which probably coincided with his own deepest convictions as one who had strong religious feelings and beliefs.

Issues of power and control also needed attention. Heraclius and his advisers took the opportunity to try to secure the family's future hold on imperial power by conceiving and implementing several important marriage alliances, all of which had important consequences for internal and external policies. This was a reasonable and prudent action. The death of four of his children while he campaigned[23] probably upset him. His critics may have regarded those deaths as some kind of divine punishment and warning, but he retained other heirs. Of the greatest permanent significance was the selection of a wife for his presumptive successor, Constantine III. Heraclius summoned Gregoria, daughter of his cousin Niketas, who was deceased by that time, from the African Pentapolis, to marry his son Constantine III, probably no later than February 630.[24] This marriage reinforced the potential influence of Africa within the highest reaches of the court and government. Once again a member of the Heraclian dynasty entered into controversial marriage within prohibited degrees.[25] The date of the death of Niketas is unknown, as are the perspectives that Gregoria brought with her to Constantinople. The Pentapolis itself was not a Latin-speaking region of Africa, but Gregoria brought some of the interests and outlooks from a very different part of the empire into the innermost parts of the imperial family and decision-making matrix. The marriage, which represented an effort to stabilize the dynasty, soon brought forth a son, Heraclius, who was born on 7 November 630. The future of the dynasty seemed to be assured, despite the death of two sons and two daughters while he campaigned away from Constantinople, in and against Persia. Everything seemed to be going well.

Heraclius' date of departure from Constantinople for Jerusalem, his administrative arrangements during his absence from Constantinople, and his itinerary are imprecise. His son Heraclius Constantine, or Constantine III, presumably exercised authority at Constantinople. Heraclius had much

[23] Nikephoros, *Short History* c. 18 (66–67 Mango), commentary on 184.
[24] Nikephoros, *Short History* c. 17 (65 Mango); important comments on chronology, p. 184; *PLRE* III: 547, s.v. "Gregoria 3."
[25] Mango, "Deux études" 105, 113–114.

experience in delegating authority while absent from Constantinople. Peacetime eased communications with his capital and its inhabitants. Probably he continued to issue bulletins, but none is extant. He continued to receive information about conditions at Constantinople. He probably wanted to accustom his subjects to his successor, whom he in turn wanted to gain more experience in ruling.

Local needs may have induced Heraclius to remain in the Levant instead of residing at Constantinople. But there was another possible incentive: expediency. Controversy concerning his marriage to his niece Martina may have led him to prefer to remain far away from his critics in distant provinces, choosing to invoke an impeccable excuse that the imperatives of reconstruction, rehabilitation, and ecclesiastical reconciliation and reunion required his personal presence and attention. We shall never know whether this was a genuine motive or not. Implicitly, his decision to stay away from Constantinople indicates that he had no great fear of a major threat to his control of the empire. Otherwise, even if his marriage was controversial, he would not have dared to remain far away. His earlier provisions for internal security and his external victories had eliminated internal threats for the moment. He felt secure.

Relations with Shahrbarāz were more complex but also included a marital alliance. Fredegarius (that is, his oriental source) may be correct in asserting that for almost three years Heraclius subjugated Persia after invading it.[26] Shahrbarāz evacuated Palestine by way of Antioch in northern Syria,[27] led his Persian troops who engaged unsuccessfully in fighting Khazars (who emerge more distinctly with the breakup of the Kök Turks who had controlled them) near Lake Sevan, then captured Ctesiphon.[28] Shahrbarāz's representative, via a general from Hierapolis who was a relative of Severos, Archbishop of Samosata, who in turn was a brother of the Monophysite Patriarch Athanasios, remitted the relic of the Cross to David Saharuni, who presented it to Heraclius[29] at Hierapolis (Mabbug, Arabic Mambij, northern Syria) in return for Heraclius' support for Shahrbarāz to be King.[30] The itinerary of Heraclius from Constantinople is uncertain

---

[26] Fredegarius, *Chronicle* 64 (53. Wallace-Hadrill).

[27] Specified as Antioch of Syria by al-Mas'ūdī, *Prairies d'or* (II: 233 Barbier de Meynard); cf. A.J. Butler, *Arab Conquest of Egypt* 117n.

[28] B. Flusin, *Saint Anastase le Perse* II: 282–291. C. Mango, "Deux études" 105–117; Walter Kaegi and Paul M. Cobb, "Heraclius, Shahrbarāz, and al-Ṭabarī," in *Al-Ṭabarī: The Historian and His Work*, ed. Hugh Kennedy (Leiden: Brill, 2002).

[29] Flusin, *Saint Anastase le Perse* II: 308–312.

[30] Heraclius and his relations with Armenians and activities in this period: Nicole Thierry, "Héraclius et la vraie croix en Arménie," in *From Byzantium to Iran... In Honour of Nina Garsoian*, ed. J.-P. Mahé and R.W. Thomson (Occasional Papers and Proceedings, 8; Columbia University Program in Armenian Studies, Publication No. 5; Atlanta: Scholars Press, 1997) 165–179.

until he reached Hierapolis, where he received the fragments of the Cross.[31] Already he had chosen Hierapolis as a key city for the consolidation and reassertion of Byzantine authority in northern Syria and as a key point for monitoring the Sasanian military and political evacuation of Byzantine territory. Hierapolis sat astride key communications between northern Syria and Sasanian Mesopotamia, and between Byzantine Anatolia and northern Syria. Heraclius used his brother Theodore there to supervise the Persian withdrawal. It was also an important Monophysite center. At Hierapolis, where he apparently returned after having restoring the relic of the Cross to Jerusalem in spring or summer 630, Heraclius addressed the populace, according to the *Contra Severum* of George of Pisidia.[32] It is a case of Heraclius cultivating the populace by addressing them, as reportedly he soon would when convoking the people and denouncing Kyros, Bishop of Alexandria, and in convoking the populace of Palestine and Syria, according to the source of al-Azdī al-Baṣrī, *Futūḥ al-Shām*, in several towns to warn them of the impending invasion of the Muslims and urge them to armed resistance. It is more evidence for his personal intervention and involvement and assumption of responsibility for ecclesiastical policy, and it is a case of his reaching out to provincial inhabitants, not merely in the capital in formal ceremonies. We need to know more about this.

Shahrbarāz had received assistance from Armenian and Georgian contingents in his own efforts to gain control of Persia. Shahrbarāz himself was quickly slain by troops in Ctesiphon.[33] He probably reached central Mesopotamia well before he seized power briefly (one month). The opaque and fluid internal situation within the Sasanian Empire gave him the opportunity to obtain Christian relics, such as the fragment of the Cross, before his public usurpation of power from Ardashīr III. The precise sequence of events will probably never be clarified. It is unclear when and how Heraclius learned the outcome of these events, perhaps within a couple of weeks of their occurrence. Potentially centrifugal or even disintegrative trends in Persia offered opportunities but also dangers, and there was a question as to how many men and how many of his limited resources Heraclius wished to divert and commit to that destabilizing and rapidly changing situation. No one at that time could predict that Persia would not recover. Heraclius' prolonged stay in northern Syria, at both Edessa and Hierapolis,

---

[31] Theophanes, *Chron.* A.M. 6120 (459 Mango-Scott); Michael the Syrian, *Chron.* II: 427 Chabot. [Anonymous] *Chronicon ad annum Christi 1234 pertinens* 186 (trans. Chabot).
[32] George of Pisidia, *Contra Severum* 8.706–714 (304–305 Tartaglia); *PG* 92: 1673–1674, lines 706–714. Kaegi, "A Misunderstood Place-name in a Poem of George of Pisidia," *BF* 26 (2000) 229–230.
[33] Sebeos, *History* 129–130, ch. 40 (89 Thomson); *Storia* c. 38 (100 Gugerotti).

put him in a position to exercise some leverage in Sasanian affairs. Internal Sasanian rivalries took their own course, but although improbable, there was always the possibility that Heraclius might forcefully intervene again. His support for Shahrbarāz failed, but he was in a position to do more than supervise the reconstitution of borders and older administrative arrangements.

The death of Shahrbarāz raised other problems. Heraclius had to decide how to handle at least a few refugees from among the losing side, whom he had supported, in Persia. There were at least a few more refugees for Byzantium to accommodate. Meanwhile, monetary chaos apparently ensued in the western regions of the Sasanian Empire that abutted Byzantine territory. That did not bode well even for Byzantium.[34]

The Persians did not easily surrender and evacuate Edessa, according to Christian Syriac traditions, in 629–630. There was mistrust on both sides. Some Byzantine troops deliberately remained within Persian boundaries until the Persian soldiers had completely evacuated Byzantine territory. Turbulence in Persia itself did not incline Persian soldiers to obey orders automatically. There was score-settling with Jews in some reoccupied territories, especially in northern Syria and upper Mesopotamia. Heraclius' brother Theodore, who was also *curopalates*, performed the role of visiting Persian-occupied cities in Byzantine upper Mesopotamia in order to inform Persian garrisons of the terms of peace, including their duty to evacuate and return to their own country. At Edessa the garrison refused, stating "we do not know Siroy [Greek, Siroes] and we will not surrender the city to the Romans." Jews joined the Persians and insulted the Byzantines and Theodore, who then bombarded the city with rocks from his siege machines. The Persians yielded and began to evacuate, while Theodore entered the city and commenced the murder and plundering of local Jews. One Jew escaped from Heraclius' brother Theodore's massacre of them at Edessa to find Heraclius at Tella (Constantina), in upper Mesopotamia, and reported those bloody events. Heraclius ordered the sparing of the Jews there.[35] The exact date is uncertain, but it may be as late as summer of 630, and not the hitherto hypothesized 628 or 629.

The same incident appears in the *History* attributed to Sebeos elaborated in a different form. According to that compiler, on the eve of the Byzantine reoccupation of Edessa, the twelve tribes of Israel went up to Edessa, where

34 The confusing economic situation inside Sasanian Iraq: Stuart D. Sears, "A Monetary History of Iraq and Iran, ca. CE 500 to 750" (unpub. Ph.D. diss., Department of Near Eastern Languages and Civilizations, University of Chicago, 1997) 366–376.
35 Agapios, *Kitāb al-Unvān, PO* 8: 466; Michael the Syrian, *Hist.* II: 409–410 Chabot.

they seized control of the city after the Persian troops had evacuated it, shut its gates and fortified it, and refused entry to the Byzantine army of reoccupation. After Heraclius ordered Edessa to be besieged, those Jews realized their inability to resist any longer, so they sued for peace:

Opening the gates of the city, they went and stood before him. Then he ordered them to go and remain in each one's habitation, and they departed. Taking desert roads, they went to Tachkastan [Arabia], to the sons of Ismael, summoned them to their aid and informed them of their blood relationship, . . . yet they were unable to bring about agreement within their great number, because their cults were divided from each other.[36]

The compiler identifies this event as the catalyst for the appearance of Islam (a term that he does not use): a merchant Muḥammad appeared as "a preacher [and] the path of truth," who proclaimed to them: "'With an oath God promised this land to Abraham and his seed after him for ever. . . . love sincerely only the God of Abraham, and go seize your land which God gave to your father Abraham. No one will be able to resist you in battle, because God is with you.'"[37]

The investigator must assess the historicity of this narrative in the *History* attributed to Sebeos, which represents the perspective of some Armenians on events at Edessa, a city of great significance for Armenians because of its influence and ties with respect to culture, commerce, and communications. It is credible that Jews did temporarily seize partial or total control of Edessa in the interim (that is, vacuum) between Persian military evacuation and Byzantine reoccupation. Such activities may well have exacerbated Byzantine–Jewish tensions and led Heraclius and his authorities to expel some or all Jews from that locality. Such actions would have stirred more Jewish resentments. Some Jews may well have taken refuge in regions occupied by Arabs. But an incident or incidents associated with Heraclius' reoccupation of Edessa in 629–630 would not have resulted in the emergence of Islam. This is an early but skewed, conflated, and apparently virulently anti-Jewish account envisioning world history from the narrow scapegoating perspective of Edessa as some Armenians perceived it.[38] However fascinating, it requires examination in a broader and a critical perspective. It reveals some important hate-filled contemporary or near-contemporary perspectives and perceptions, but cannot serve as any definitive and exclusive interpretation of Heraclius' Jewish policies and activities, let alone as the authoritative account of the appearance of Islam.[39] Some Jews may

---

[36] Sebeos, *Hist.* c. 42 [134] (95 Thomson).   [37] Sebeos, *Hist.* c. 42 [135] (96 Thomson).

[38] Robert Hoyland, "Sebeos, the Jews and the Rise of Islam," in *Studies in Muslim–Jewish Relations*, ed. R. Nettler (1996) II: 89–102.

[39] A different interpretation from that of J. Howard-Johnston in his Historical Commentary on Sebeos, *Hist.* 233–240.

have found all kinds of reasons for joining or preferring the new Muslims or proto-Muslims, but one needs to take into account the rhetorical objectives of the compiler. The story does challenge modern historians to investigate the interim and vacuum between the termination of Sasanian occupation and Byzantine recovery or restitution of authority. It is easy to understand how some later narrators erroneously conflated and associated the emergence of Islam with Jewish–Christian clashes at Edessa in 629/630. The role of Theodore and the problematics of the reoccupation of Edessa recurred further south, in the Balqā', where Theodore again acted as point man for Heraclius in an even murkier interim and power vacuum between 629 and 634.

Heraclius may have passed by Damascus on his way to Jerusalem in 630.[40] He certainly visited Tiberias, in Galilee, where he received a delegation of Jews, whom he promised to spare, despite the favorable attitude that some Jews had allegedly displayed to Persians. However, angry Christian clergy and civilians soon reportedly prevailed on him to change his mind.[41] The outcome was a massacre of Jews at Jerusalem and in its environs, reportedly followed by a special fast to expiate the sin of having violated the oath.[42] Heraclius allegedly forbade Jews to live within three miles of Jerusalem.[43] The details are controversial and unclear.[44] His was an era in which anti-Jewish polemic flourished.[45]

The Cross was in a sealed container, which Modestos, soon to be Patriarch, examined and proclaimed to be intact.[46] This was a ceremony proclaiming a non-violation (that is, non-desecration) of the relic, even though it appears that Persians had disturbed and therefore profaned and possibly harmed it. Muslim historiography even recorded a plausible flashback: Heraclius' treading on carpets strewn before him.[47]

[40] Eutychios, *Hist.* 107–109 Breydy (322–325, 332–333 Pirone); Kaegi, *BEIC* 75–78. But see Archbishop Basilios s.v. "Fasting," in *Coptic Encyclopedia* (New York: Macmillan, 1991) 1093–1097, esp. 1093–1094.

[41] Theoph. *Chron.* 328 De Boor.

[42] Flusin, *Saint Anastase le Perse* II: 311; cf. Theophanes, *Chron.* A.M. 6120 (458–459 Mango-Scott); Eutychios. *Hist.* 108–109 Breydy (323–325 Pirone).

[43] Theoph. *Chron.* 328 De Boor (458–459 Mango-Scott); Dagron, "Juifs et Chrétiens dans l'Orient du VIIe siècle," *TM* 11 (1991) 28–29.

[44] Averil Cameron, "The Jews in Seventh-Century Palestine," *Scripta Classica Israelica* 13 (1994) 79–81.

[45] Contemporary with Heraclius, although living also beyond Heraclius' lifetime, was Leontios, Bishop of Neapolis in Cyprus, whose anti-Jewish text survives only in fragments: Vincent Déroche, "Léontios, Apologie contre les Juifs," *TM* 12 (1994) 45–104, probable date between 610 and 640, p. 46.

[46] Suidas, *Lexikon*, ed. A. Adler, II: 582.

[47] Ṭabarī 1.1561–1562.

Heraclius entered Jerusalem by its Golden Gate, after allegedly changing out of imperial dress after portents initially prevented him from entering.[48] Wearing no imperial insignia and dismounted, he carried the relic of the Cross. The symbolism of humility was unmistakable. Martina, Heraclius' wife, accompanied him to Jerusalem.[49] Shahrbarāz's son Niketas had already delivered the Holy Sponge and Holy Lance to Constantinople contemporary with or in the immediate aftermath of Heraclius' meeting with Shahrbarāz at Arabissos in July 629, and those relics had been celebrated at Constantinople on 14 September and 28 October 629 respectively.[50] Heraclius had Modestos named Patriarch of Jerusalem. Heraclius restored the Cross to Jerusalem on 21 March 630.[51] The exact length of his stay at Jerusalem is unknown.

The joyous news swiftly reached Constantinople on St. Lazaros' Day, 31 March 630. "Exult, O Golgotha!" was how Heraclius' panegyrical poet George of Pisidia expressed his emotions to word of the Restoration of the Holy Cross.[52] The anonymous author of the treatise entitled "Return of the Relics of the Holy Martyr Anastasios the Persian from Persia to His Monastery" described the "immense joy and the indescribable happiness seized the entire Universe. It produced what had never been produced. No emperor of the Christians, in human memory, had come to Jerusalem. Only our most serene and very pious emperor came there, with the Life-giving Cross of the Saviour."[53] "He accomplished it in a manner worthy of himself, honoring the one who honored him and reestablishing it in the place that is appropriate for it which assures the security of the world."[54] Sebeos commented,

Great joy manifested itself on the day of entry into Jerusalem: sounds of cries and sighs, tears flowed with immense fervor of emotion in their hearts, inner anguish of the king, the commanders, all the soldiers and the inhabitants of the city. No one could sing the songs of the Lord because of immense and tearing

---

[48] Hrabanus Maurus, *PL* 110: 133–134; Nikephoros, *Hist.* 66 Mango. Cyril Mango, "The Temple Mount, AD 614–638," 1–16, esp. 6.

[49] Strategios, *La prise de Jérusalem par les Perses en 614* 24.8–9 (55 Garitte).

[50] Sebeos, *Hist.* pp. 90–91 Thomson; Flusin, *Saint Anastase le Perse* II: 310. Holger A. Klein, "Niketas und das wahre Kreuz. Kritische Anmerkungen zur Überlieferung des Chronicon Paschale ad annum 614," *BZ* 94/2 (2001) 580–587.

[51] Strategios, *Prise de Jérusalem* 24.9 (55 Garitte). Robert Schick, *The Christian Communities of Palestine* (Princeton: Darwin, 1996). The radical chronology for Heraclius and Jerusalem that P. Speck proposes, *Das geteilte Dossier*, 156–157n, 376–377, is unpersuasive, as are many of Speck's additional arguments in *Beiträge zum Thema Byzantinische Feindseligkeit gegen die Juden* (*Varia* VI; Ποικίλα Βυζαντινά, 15; Bonn: Habelt, 1997) 123, 235–238; cf. Andreas Külzer, *BZ* 91 (1998) 583–6. Correct date: Flusin, *Saint Anastase le Perse* II: 293–309; Beihammer, *Nachrichten* nos. 39, 46, pp. 59–60, 65–66.

[52] George of Pisidia, *In restitutionem S. Crucis* 1.1, 5.108 (225, 229 Pertusi and comment. 230–239).

[53] Flusin, *Saint Anastase le Perse* I: 99.   [54] Flusin, *Saint Anastase le Perse* I: 99.

commotion of the king and the crowd. The Cross was put in its place, and all the objects of the church were put in their place, he distributed alms and money for incense to all of the churches and inhabitants of the city.[55]

The *History* attributed to Sebeos may preserve parts of an Armenian missive to Heraclius expressing joy for his recovery of Jerusalem:

The sound of great evangelical trumpets [blown] by the angels summons us through this letter that has arrived from the divinely-built city, 'which announces great joy to us.' Therefore 'the heavens rejoice, and let the earth exult'; let the church and its children delight in their glory. So let us all with united voice sing the angelic praises, repeating: 'Glory in the highest to God, and peace to earth, goodwill to mankind.'[56]

It expresses the triumphalistic mood of the years 628–33 in Armenia and elsewhere. The foundation of the cathedral of Mren in Armenia 639/640 may also commemorate Heraclius' restitution of the True Cross to Jerusalem.[57]

Jerusalem suffered grave damage when the Persians stormed it in 614. Patriarch Zacharias had died in exile in Persia. Bishop Elias arrived in Jerusalem from Persia, sent by the Catholicos Ishoyahb II of Gadala, with letters for Heraclius and for the Patriarch of Jerusalem. Elias and Anastasios, another monk who diligently cultivated the cult of St. Anastasios the Persian, accompanied Heraclius, after he left Jerusalem, to Mesopotamia, as far as the vicinity of Constantina, where they turned off to Persia.[58]

Many prisoners and hostages from Persia needed to be repatriated and resettled. A number of Christians from Persia, in various capacities, took the opportunity to leave Persia and settle inside the Byzantine Empire, including at Constantinople. That process of migration had started while the Persians occupied Syria and Mesopotamia. Others left Persia when Heraclius' victory temporarily prostrated the Persian government and allowed individuals the opportunity to leave with Byzantine troops. Perhaps some had compromised themselves with Persian authority, feared for their safety and future, and had to flee to Byzantium. Others may simply have opted for better opportunities and left Persia when they had a chance. These migrants would not have been a typical cross-section of Persians. They were overwhelmingly Christian. In any case, there was a considerable movement of populations, some of which would have been disruptive to the migrants and probably also to some communities where they settled. The *vita* and *Miracles* of St. Anastasios the Persian are replete with examples. Displacement of populations brought new cultural ideas and practices

[55] Sebeos, *Storia* c. 39 (100 Gugerotti); cf. *History* 131, ch. 41 (90–91 Thomson).
[56] Sebeos, *Hist.* ch. 36 [118] (73 Thomson).
[57] Nicole Thierry, "Héraclius et la vraie croix en Arménie" 165–176.
[58] Flusin, *Saint Anastase le Perse* I: 103.

as well. The introduction of alien ideas, customs, and languages created a
new mix in some regions, especially urban, of the Byzantine Empire. Newcomers with strange ideas and ways probably aroused some resentments,
which may have found expression in anti-Jewish sentiment, even though
Jews probably were not the most important group of displaced persons.
But the Byzantine-Persian war had brought many changes in its wake, despite imperial efforts to restore the world that had existed before that war's
outbreak.

Ravaged buildings and services needed extensive restoration and rehabilitation. Heraclius probably inspected the damage, to which he could
not have remained oblivious during his visit. Modestos was raised to be
Patriarch of Jerusalem. Heraclius bestowed funds for the embellishment
and restoration of the church at Jerusalem.[59] Modestos soon died, possibly
on 17 December 630.[60] Heraclius may have wished to demonstrate that he
was returning relics to Jerusalem, that he was not concentrating everything
at Constantinople. This would have been a public gesture of humility and
respect for religion.

Heraclius' visit to the Holy Land and his new wealth from his arrangements with the Persians enabled him to show generosity to subjects who
lived elsewhere. Syria and Palestine lie close to the island of Cyprus. Probably during or immediately after his visit to the Holy Land, or possibly while
he stayed at Hierapolis, Heraclius donated some funds for the construction
of an important aqueduct on Cyprus. A Cypriot inscription that probably
dates to 631, at the virtual entrance gates of Salamis/Constantia, celebrates
Heraclius: "These seven arches have been made with the help of God and
also thanks to the generosities of Flavius Heraclius, our master crowned by
God, from the Hippodrome, the sixth month, indiction four."[61] It was natural for Heraclius to contribute to the improvement of local public works
when the financial condition of the empire permitted, and he did so. He also
probably wished to reinforce his ties to the strategically important island,
whose Archbishop Arkadios was a significant participant in contemporary
ecclesiastical politics. The gift of funds for the aqueduct may even have
been an act to help to conciliate Chalcedonians to the policies of Heraclius
and Arkadios.[62] It underlined the close cooperation of the Archbishop and

---

[59] Hrabanus Maurus, *PL* 110: 134. Strategios, *Prise de Jérusalem* 24.10–12 (55 Garitte).
[60] *Prise de Jérusalem* 24.13 (55 Garitte).
[61] Jean-Pierre Sodini, "Les inscriptions de l'Aqueduc de Kythrea à Salamine de Chypre," in *Eupsychia.
Mélanges offerts à Hélène Ahrweiler* (Byzantina Sorbonensia, 16; Paris, 1998) 624–625, no. 1.
[62] Sodini, "Les inscriptions de l'Aqueduc de Kythrea à Salamine de Chypre," 632–633.

Heraclius in matters of local administration on Cyprus. It also fitted into the larger and older pattern of emperors reminding provincial subjects of their ties with and their benefits from imperial munificence.[63]

Heraclius at that time may have encouraged the construction of pentagonal tower fortifications on Cyprus at Kyrenia and the reconstruction of the citadel of Ankara in Anatolia, and possibly also at Dereagzi in Lycia.[64] At Ankara Heraclius' supposed motive was strengthening its citadel against possible repetition of the recent Persian devastation, using models from recently abandoned Balkan fortifications such as Salona.

After a hiatus, including a visit to Constantinople in late 633, and many uncertainties during which Sergios of Joppa was *locum tenens* for the Jerusalem Patriarchate, the monk Sophronios returned to Palestine. Implicitly with the approval or at least passive acquiescence of Heraclius, he became Patriarch of Jerusalem in 633 or, at the latest, in early 634.[65] Sophronios had sworn an oath never to attack Monotheletism, and in fact he never explicitly attacked it. Sergios of Joppa and a number of other ecclesiastics were hostile to this election, which created a prominent seat for opposition to imperial doctrines of Monotheletism (also held by Patriarch Sergios of Constantinople). But Heraclius was unable to stop or reverse this significant election, which was a reminder of the limitations of his own influence even at the zenith of his prestige. Sophronios almost immediately became a difficult controversialist for Heraclius and his chosen bishops to handle. The *Synodicon Vetus* tersely reports that after Heraclius' return to Constantinople Sergios held a synod at Constantinople to affirm Monothelete doctrine, but there is no independent confirmation of this statement.[66]

After his short visit to Jerusalem Heraclius gave gifts to monks and to holy places and then returned to Mesopotamia (the Byzantine province of that name). Strategically located, it was a convenient place from which to scrutinize the Persian situation, the reassertion of Byzantine authority and imposition of controls in areas that Persians had evacuated, and the right

---

[63] Heraclius' apparent contribution to a nymphaeum at Hagioi Deka, near Gortyna, on Crete, at the beginning of his reign: Anastasius Bandy, *The Greek Christian Inscriptions of Crete* (1970) X: 50–51, no. 23. The practice persisted from much earlier imperial eras.

[64] Hypotheses of Archibald W. Dunn, "Heraclius 'Reconstruction of Cities' and Their Sixth-Century Balkan Antecedents," in *Acta XIII Congressus Internationalis Archaeologiae Christianae*, Pars 2 (Studi di Antichità Cristiana pubblicata a cura del Pontificio Istituto di Archeologia Cristiana, 54; Vjesnik za arheologiju i historiju dalmatinsku, Sup. Vol. 87–89; Split: Arheoloski Muzej, 1998) 795–804.

[65] Christoph von Schönborn, *Sophrone de Jérusalem* (Paris, 1972) 83–84.

[66] *Synodicon Vetus* c. 129, ed. John Duffy and John Parker (Washington: Dumbarton Oaks, 1979) 108.

place to attempt to conciliate Christian dissidents. George of Pisidia and Sophronios both praised Heraclius' restoration of the Cross.[67]

Heraclius utilized this time to try to consolidate his empire by reasserting imperial authority in lost provinces and in attempting to find ways to end religious dissidence. In retrospect these efforts failed. But he risked much personal and imperial prestige in trying to find compromises and in intervening. He expended many patient efforts. The religious challenges were multivariate. Memories of his efforts may well not be entirely accurate, colored as they are by sectarian outlooks and distorted by the passage of time and elimination of his own and his partisans' versions of his actions and objectives.

One can only speculate what impression his visit to the Holy Land and to many religious sites may have made on Heraclius. He had campaigned in the vicinity of Antioch back in 613, but had apparently never journeyed south of it. He now encountered new geography, new personalities, new communities, and new attitudes. How these travels and religious experiences altered his outlook is uncertain. He was now mature in age, in his mid-fifties. Precisely what effect the vistas of Jerusalem made on Heraclius is unknown. And unplanned, he was gaining some impressions about the countryside and people of Syria about whom he soon would have to make major military decisions. We have no idea whether he was very conscious of any Arabs while visiting or returning from Jerusalem.

It was extraordinary for a sovereign to have visited Jerusalem and Galilee and to have seen Nineveh (or its edge), however unappreciated, and Carthage as well. Heraclius had acquired a richer perspective on his contemporary world than any emperor since Theodosius I. His experiences probably developed in him deeper religious feelings and greater geographical, political and military perspectives. But did that diversity of experience improve his judgmental skills or affect them in any way at all?

A major question is whether Heraclius possessed or developed, while at Jerusalem or soon thereafter, any vision of the future. It is unclear whether he really expected that he could simply restore the *status quo ante* with respect to institutions, fiscality, and political loyalties. He was not a philosopher, but a man of action. He faced many day-to-day problems. He could not face nor was he intellectually inclined to afford, given contemporary political, fiscal, and ecclesiastical pressures, the luxury of engaging in abstract thought. No grand intellectual synthesis would emerge from the totality of his diverse

---

[67] George of Pisidia, *In restitutionem S. Crucis*, lines 25–31 (226 Pertusi). Sophronios, *In venerandum Crucem*, lines 53–56, 85–90, 17–20, 73–76. Mary Whitby, "A New Image for a New Age: George of Pisidia on the Emperor Heraclius" (n. 1) 197–225.

experiences. There is no evidence whether he even attempted to sit back, reflect, and try to make sense of his life at this juncture. Certainly he sought to do more than restore the *status quo ante* with respect to religion. There he was seeking to reach a definitive solution that no one had previously achieved.

Heraclius was essentially restoring, for the moment at least, previous institutions and practices, while also trying to slash military expenses by demobilizing and cutting the payroll and subsidies. He was not, at the start of the 630s, attempting some major overhaul of provincial and military institutions. He recognized that there were problems in the provinces. So he did not choose, as he could have done, to return to Constantinople and simply enjoy accolades for his triumph over Persia. Instead he chose to involve himself in difficult and unrewarding tasks of trying to solve difficult problems. He spent his time in areas where the population was not primarily Greek-speaking. He probably began to gain some feel for the region, a better sense of it than he or his predecessors would have possessed, especially if they confined their residence to Constantinople and its vicinity.

Bishop Elias from Persia met Heraclius at Jerusalem and accompanied him back to Constantina, in northern Syria. It is possible that Heraclius passed through Damascus on his return from Jerusalem.[68] Christian and Muslim traditions about Heraclius' visit to Damascus are problematical, and may simply seek to associate him with that locality. Although an extremely valuable province with respect to agriculture and tax revenues, and although it was wracked with religious dissensions and had suffered at the hands of its recent Persian occupiers, Heraclius did not turn south from Jerusalem, via land or sea, to visit Egypt. In fact no one ever reflects on Heraclius' neglect of Egypt when he visited the Holy Land. No one expected him to visit Egypt. It was simply expected that he would return northward after visiting Jerusalem. Egypt remained an important part of his empire yet one that he had probably never seen (we do not know his exact sailing routes to and from Africa, but it is improbable that he ever visited Egypt). This was an important gap. His neglect of his subjects and conditions in Egypt was a serious omission, but no contemporary made any known comment on that failure. He did not use the occasion of the restoration of Byzantine rule in Egypt to make a personal visit of inspection and of celebration of the restoration of Byzantine authority. He might have used such an occasion to improve relations with his subjects there,

---

[68] Kaegi, *BEIC* 75–78; Flusin, *Saint Anastase le Perse* II: 320.

and to understand the problems of its inhabitants, of its agriculture, of its ecclesiastics, and of its internal and external security. He did not.

It is probable that Byzantine military forces strenuously attempted to secure areas adjacent to and through which Heraclius would pass during his visit to and from Jerusalem. Echoes of that visit to Palestine probably appear in some Arab traditions about the earliest *maghāzī* (Muslim raids in the era of the Prophet Muḥammad)[69] in areas east of the Jordan River and east of the Dead Sea. Byzantine forces were seeking to extend control and order to make certain that Heraclius' pilgrimage was an undisturbed and peaceful one. At the same time, residents east of the Dead Sea had not experienced significant direct Byzantine or Roman rule for a long time. There was a vacuum and the question was who would fill it, the Byzantines or someone else. Heraclius did not personally visit that strategic if forbidding area, which very soon would be the scene of important combat.

This was the zenith of Heraclius' power. It seemed that almost everything was awaiting transformation and he, Emperor Heraclius, had the power to transform the world as he saw fit, in conformity with religious truth. For one brief moment everything seemed to be moving within his grasp, with respect to religion, to political and military power, to foreign relations, and to domestic policy. The giddiness of several months of glory quickly passed, as a rapid sequence of events eliminated some opportunities. There was no total reversal, but any possibility of total mastery quickly disappeared. The fruits of victory were elusive.

The Persian situation soon deteriorated. Shahrbarāz had Ardashīr assassinated on 27 April 630, but he in turn was slain on 9 June 630.[70] That event ripped away the fragile underpinnings of Heraclius' arrangements with Persia, even though Persia remained very weak. More troubles followed. Probably Heraclius used these troubles as an excuse to station or maintain some Byzantine troops in Persia to keep an eye on the situation and to be ready to try to intervene there if the right opportunity offered itself. Yet there were limits to what Byzantium could do. Heraclius was in a strong position, but the situation was extremely volatile and unstable. It was potentially very dangerous for Byzantium. The wrong outcome, given recent memories and experiences, might even have threatened to revive the specter of an evil Persian threat to the empire's existence. We can only make inferences about the Byzantine presence and role in those volatile times and circumstances.

A daughter of Khusrau II, Boran II, became Persian sovereign, and requested the Nestorian Catholicos Ishoyahb II to carry a message to

[69] M. Hinds in *EI*² V: 1161–1164, s.v. "al-Maghāzī."
[70] Flusin, *Saint Anastase le Perse* II: 306–307, 320.

Heraclius, asking for a renewal of the truce between Byzantium and Persia. Probably Ishoyahb met Heraclius at Aleppo (Berrhoea) in the summer of 630.[71] They reviewed and settled remaining issues about the border, which nominally reverted to that delineated in the reigns of the deceased Khusrau II and Maurice. There Heraclius and Ishoyahb entered into doctrinal discussions. Heraclius asked him about his beliefs and he explained his own views on theology. Heraclius asked him to celebrate mass in his presence and asked that the two take communion. He repeated his request, asking that other prelates be allowed to take it, but Ishoyahb first insisted on the removal of the name of Cyril of Alexandria from the diptychs. Then he gave his profession of faith in writing, which Heraclius distributed to others.[72] This accord was fashioned to conform to the Monotheletic one of Patriarch Sergios of Constantinople, the associate of Heraclius. This was really an improvisation.[73] Ishoyahb gave Heraclius communion at his request. At Hierapolis Heraclius reportedly already had heard of the assassination of the Persian King Kawadh-Siroy (September 628?).[74]

Heraclius stayed a while in Mesopotamia, in particular at Edessa and Constantina, in late 630–631 to oversee the arrangements of the borders with Persia. Among the attendant responsibilities would have been making sure that all Persian troops and unwanted civilians evacuated Byzantine territory, reception and processing of Byzantines who were or had been either prisoners, hostages, or refugees and displaced persons in Persia, who wished to return to Byzantine territory. The resettlement and determination of actual borders were important. Another aspect of the process probably was determination of arrangements for resumption of trade and peaceful communications between the two empires.

Heraclius began to engage in public efforts to solve the long intractable problems of Christology that had racked the church. He may have turned his mind to these issues earlier, but in northern Syria earlier mental preoccupations now resulted in public actions. He had probably consulted extensively with his friend Sergios, the Patriarch of Constantinople, before leaving the capital, but there are no details.[75] The exact itinerary of Heraclius

[71] Flusin, *Saint Anastase le Perse* II: 321.

[72] *Histoire Nestorienne/Chronicle of Si'irt, PO* 13: 557–559. *Lettre christologique du patriarche Syro-oriental Iso'yahb II de Gdala (628–646)*, ed. Louis R.M. Sako (Rome, 1983) 45–49 and esp. 59–60.

[73] Flusin, *Saint Anastase le Perse* II: 326. Background: Friedhelm Winkelmann, "Die Quellen zur Erforschung des monoenergetisch-monotheletischen Streites," *Klio* 69 (1987) 515–559.

[74] Speck, *Das geteilte Dossier* 160–161, 378.

[75] Winkelmann, "Die Quellen zur Erforschung des monoenergetisch-monotheletischen Streites," *Klio* 69 (1987) 515–559.

in 630 is uncertain. He returned through Hierapolis (Mabbug, Mambij), which he had previously visited coming from the north to Jerusalem. At Hierapolis, he negotiated, reportedly for twelve days, with the Monophysite Patriarch of Antioch, Athanasios, and twelve Monophysite bishops, for a formula on union, to which Athanasios agreed, in the spring of 631. Heraclius demanded a written statement. He praised their faith and asked for them to give him communion and then accept a written statement of his confessing one will and one energy in Christ "according to Cyril," which they refused, angering him.[76] According to one tradition Archbishop Athanasios seemed to accept Chalcedon, but only with a sly stratagem, which allegedly resulted in the creation of Monoenergism as a theological doctrine to explain the mysteries of Christology.[77] Heraclius' award of the Great Church of Edessa to Chalcedonians provoked a major rift with Monophysites. George of Pisidia predictably praises Heraclius' efforts to reeducate religious dissidents at Hierapolis.[78] Meanwhile (July 631), Athanasios had died. Again, Heraclius' efforts to impose unity were frustrated.[79]

Armenian affairs also required attention from an emperor who was of Armenian descent. Somehow Heraclius soon prevailed on the Armenian Catholicos Ezr to accept a compromise formula of one activity or one energy of the God–man. Supposedly Ezr received as a reward one-third of the komopolis of Kolb and the revenues from its salt mines.[80] Heraclius had a general encyclical issued to the church espousing his views. A synod at Theodosiopolis (Armenian Karin, modern Erzurum) in 631–633 confirmed that policy. Heraclius was actually present.[81] The authenticity of the canons of the synod of Theodosiopolis is very doubtful.[82] Heraclius

---

[76] Michael the Syrian, *Chronique* 11.2, 11.4 (405–408, 412 Chabot). Also: Theoph. *Chron.* A.M. 6021 (329–330 De Boor; 460–461 Mango-Scott).

[77] Theoph. *Chron.* A.M. 6021 (329–330 De Boor; 460–461 Mango-Scott). Frend, *Rise of the Monophysite Movement* 346–347.

[78] George of Pisidia, Κατὰ δυσσέβους Σευέρου 'Αντιοχείας, in *Carmi* 1.706, p. 304 (Tartaglia). Benzinger in *RE* II.2: 2843–2844, s.v. "Bambyke"; Thomas Leisten, "Bambyke," *Der Neue Pauly* 2 (1997) 429–430. Beihammer, *Nachrichten* nos 41, 42, pp. 61, 62; W.E. Kaegi, "A Misunderstood Place-name in a Poem of George of Pisidia," *BF* 26 (2000) 229–230.

[79] Penetrating analysis by L. MacCoull, "George of Pisidia, *Against Severus*: In Praise of Heraclius," in *The Future of the Middle Ages and the Renaissance. Problems, Trends, and Opportunities for Research*, ed. R. Dahood (Arizona Studies in the Middle Ages and the Renaissance, 2; Turnhout: Brepols, 1998) 69–79.

[80] Yovhannes Drasxanakertc'i, *History of Armenia* 18.6–14, trans. K.H. Maksoudian (Atlanta: Scholars Press, 1987) 98–99. *De rebus Armeniae*, p. 310 Garitte. See Sebeos, *Hist.* c. 41 (91–92 Thomson) with J. Howard-Johnston, Historical Commentary, 228.

[81] Michael the Syrian, *Chron.* 11.2 (II: 405 Chabot trans.). Frend, *The Rise of the Monophysite Movement* 345. On broader trends in the relationships of emperors and patriarchs: Gilbert Dagron, *Empereur et prêtre. Etude sur le 'césaropapisme' byzantin* (Paris: Gallimard, 1996) esp. 35–168.

[82] Michel le Grand, *Chronique*, trans. Langlois (1868) 226; Stephen Asolik of Taron = *Des Stephanos von Taron. Armenische Geschichte*, ed. trans. Heinrich Gelzer, A. Burkhardt (Leipzig, 1907) 62–63. Jean-Pierre Mahé, "Confession religieuse et identité nationale dans l'église arménienne du VIIe au

apparently threatened to establish a rival hierarchy if Ezr refused to accept imperial theological preferences. Therefore Ezr, having been deprived of Sasanian protection, yielded, but there was no pure and simple adhesion to the dogma of the Council of Chalcedon.[83]

It was at that time that Mzezh Gnuni, Byzantine commander in Armenia, exerted pressure on Catholicos Ezr to accept Chalcedon, which he did. He communicated with Heraclius. Having accepted these terms, he was given responsibility for supervising the distribution of the troops and for assigning military stores.[84] Friction broke out between the Persian *aspet* Varaztirots and his son Rostom versus Mzhezh Gnuni. Heraclius cultivated good relations with the *aspet*, received him in northern Syria, upper Mesopotamia, gave him a fine palace, cushions of silver coins, and other treasures. But Varaztirots became involved in a plot of Heraclius' bastard son Athalaric against Heraclius. Mzhezh Gnuni arrested some of Dawid (Dawit, David) Saharuni's soldiers and planned to attack him. Mzhezh Gnuni was slain and Heraclius appointed Dawid as *aspet* for three years.[85] Those events stretched over the course of more than five years after the adhesion of Ezr to Heraclius' religious formulae. Not every Armenian accepted and agreed with Ezr's submission.

Heraclius returned to Constantinople, where he was received with joy. He brought four elephants with him.[86] Heraclius cannot have returned to Constantinople before the middle of 631.[87] He then celebrated a triumph, distributed largesse to the public, and ordered an annual subsidy to be given to the church clergy to reimburse it for his earlier seizures of ecclesiastical property.[88]

The remains of St. Anastasios the Persian were transferred, after their pious theft from a monastery in Persia, with great publicity and emotion, from Persia to Palestine at that time (631). Heraclius' authorities were not officially involved in the transfer of the remains, but Arab allies tacitly cooperated in moving the relics of the saint to their final resting-place in Caesarea Maritima on 2 November 631.[89] The event was another aftermath of the Byzantine–Persian war.

XI siècle," in N. Garsoïan, Jean-Pierre Mahé, *Des Parthes au Califat. Quatre leçons sur la formation de l'identité arménienne* (Travaux et Mémoires du Centre de recherche d'histoire et civilisation de Byzance, Collège de France, Monographies, 10; Paris: De Boccard, 1997) 62 n. 11, 63. On the broader background of Armenian ecclesiastical relations with Byzantium: N. Garsoïan, *L'Eglise arménienne et le grand schisme d'Orient* (*CSCO* Subsidia, 100; Leuven, 1999) 386–387.

[83] Garsoïan, *L'Eglise arménienne* 386–390.
[84] Sebeos, *History* 131–132, ch. 41 (91–92 Thomson); *Storia* c. 39 (101 Gugerotti).
[85] Sebeos, *History* 132, ch. 41 (92 Thomson); *Storia* c. 39 (102 Gugerotti).
[86] Suidas, *Lexikon*, ed. A. Adler, II: 582. Speck, *Das geteilte Dossier* 378–379.
[87] Mango, comment. on Nikephoros, *Short History* c. 19, p. 186.
[88] Nikephoros, *Short History* c. 19 (66–69 Mango). Suidas, *Lexikon*, ed. A. Adler, II: 582.
[89] Flusin, *Saint Anastase le Perse* II: 329–352.

The challenge of Christology was not easily solved, despite Heraclius' pressures. In 631 Heraclius appointed Kyros, Bishop of Phasis, to be Patriarch of Alexandria. He had met him in 625/626 when he was campaigning in Anatolia and found him to be someone with whom he could work. Kyros arrived in Egypt in autumn of 631. That appointment enraged the Monophysites/Copts and their Patriarch Benjamin, who fled into exile. During the summer of 633 Kyros managed to hold a synod at Alexandria, where two bishops signed a Tome of Union that acknowledged one single energy/activity in Christ (3 June 633).[90] Dissent spread and prevailed in Egypt. Heraclius' support for Kyros was to no avail.

The outcome was fingerpointing, recriminations, and purges of alleged collaborators with the Persians, especially Jews. Heraclius ordered the forcible baptism of Jews in Africa by the prefect of Africa on 31 May 632.[91] The scope and intent of this decree is controversial,[92] though it involved local Jews and Samaritans as well as foreign ones. Heraclius may have arrived at that decision while at Jerusalem in 630. Although an extremely harsh and unrealistic and ineffective measure, it was consistent with Heraclius' other strenuous efforts to achieve religious uniformity among the subjects within his empire. But other factors may have been present. The large influx of foreigners, including refugees from Persia, probably spread alien ideas, which may have exacerbated already hostile sentiments against Jews. At the beginning of Arab raiding, some Byzantines may have, however

---

[90] Frend, *Rise of the Monophysite Movement* 349–350; *PLRE* III: 377–378, s.v. "Cyrus 17."

[91] Dagron and Déroche, "Juifs et Chrétiens au VIIe siècle," 31–32; R. Devreesse, "La fin inédite d'une lettre de saint Maxime: un baptême forcé de Juifs et de Samaritains à Carthage en 632," *Revue des sciences religieuses* 17 (1937) 25–35; Joshua Starr, "St. Maximos and the Forced Baptism at Carthage," *Byzantinisch-neugriechische Jahrbücher* 16 (1940) 192–196; Olster, *Roman Defeat* 85–86, 123, 162. Jews in seventh-century Byzantium: Averil Cameron, "Byzantines and Jews: Some Recent Work on Early Byzantium," *BMGS* 20 (1996) 248–274. Authenticity of the *Doctrina Jacobi*: R. Hoyland, *Seeing Islam as Others Saw It* (Princeton: Darwin Press, 1997) 55–61. On the life of Maximos: Jean-Claude Larchet, *La divinisation de l'homme selon Saint Maxime le Confesseur* (Paris: Cerf, 1996) 8–18.

[92] Günter Stemberger, "Zwangstaufen von Juden im 4. Bis 7. Jahrhundert. Mythos oder Wirklichkeit?," in *Judentum – Ausblicke und Einsichten. Festgabe für Kurt Schubert zum siebzigsten Geburtstag*, ed. Clemens Thoma, Günter Stemberger, Johann Maier (Judentum und Umwelt, 43; Frankfurt, New York: Peter Lang, 1993) 99–100 on Justinian's *Novel* 37 that prohibited the Jewish cult in Africa; see on Heraclius 106–111 esp. 107–111. Outside Carthage, we have no certain proof for compulsory baptism under Heraclius. Learned and ingenious but unconvincing revisionist interpretations about Heraclius' forcible conversion of Jews, by Paul Speck, *Beiträge zum Thema Byzantinische Feindseligkeit gegen die Juden* (Varia VI; Ποικίλα Βυζαντινά 15; Bonn: Habelt, 1997) 441–467; cf. skeptical review by A. Külzer, *BZ* 91 (1998) 583–586; also Külzer, *Disputationes graecae contra Judaeos* (Stuttgart, Leipzig: Teubner, 1999) 142–147. Speck argues that references to Samaritans as well as Jews in sources on compulsory conversion in Africa indicate the spuriousness of the African materials and instead point to a later and Christian Palestinian provenance for stories about Heraclius' decree for compulsory baptism of Jews. But Samaritans are often paired with Jews in legislation against Jews, irrespective of whether there are likely to be any Samaritans in a given region: Cod. Theod. 16.8.16 (404, Rome), 16.8.28 (426, Ravenna). But see Beihammer, *Nachrichten* no. 48, pp. 67–69. I am grateful for the advice of W. Van Bekkum.

falsely, linked Jews and the Arab menace.[93] According to the Merovingian historian Fredegarius, Heraclius sought to have the Frankish King Dagobert order the baptism of his Jews within his kingdom, which Dagobert hastened to do. Although Fredegarius dates this to 629, it probably took place slightly later.[94] These policies fit into an apocalyptic age with its associated mentalities and expectations. The Qiliri text may refer to the mood of Jews after Heraclius' reoccupation of Jerusalem and before the Muslim conquest.[95] According to the *Doctrina Jacobi nuper Baptizati*, Heraclius ordered that Jews everywhere be baptized.[96] Ecclesiastical constituencies were not enthusiastic about this forceful imperial policy.[97] The only explicit references to the application of this order within the Byzantine Empire locate such policies in Africa. The much later historian Michael the Syrian erroneously dates the decree to 634.[98] It is unclear whether this law was enforced elsewhere in the empire with the vigor that the exarch George used in Africa.[99] It is significant that this action of Heraclius increased instability, uncertainty, unhappiness, and anger in Africa as well as Palestine just contemporary with the start of the Muslim invasions. Many Jews fled from Byzantine control, reportedly some fled from Edessa to areas under Arab control or to Persia or elsewhere.[100] News spread speedily in that interconnected Mediterranean coastal world. But hostility to Jews was the mood elsewhere in the Mediterranean: the epitaph of the contemporary Pope Honorius (625–638) exults that, "In your time the perfidy of the Jewish people was conquered and thus you brought unity to the pious shepherding of the Master." Although vague, it underscores the breadth and depth of contemporary hostility to Jews without explicitly mentioning forcible baptisms. A contemporary poem of the Patriarch Sophronios of Jerusalem likewise asserts "Let the vituperation of the unlawful Jews turn upon their heads."[101]

[93] Carl Laga, "Judaism and Jews in Maximus Confessor's Works. Theoretical Controversy and Practical Attitudes," *Byzsl* 51 (1990) 177–188; also Külzer, *Disputationes graecae contra Judaeos* 144.

[94] Fredegarius, *Chronicle* 65 (54Wallace-Hadrill); Dagron and Déroche, "Juifs et chrétiens," 32. This story may well deserve skepticism.

[95] E. Fleischer, "Solving the Qiliri Riddle," *Tarbiz* 54.3 (1984–5) 383–427; Fleischer, "New Light on Qiliri," *Tarbiz* 50 (1980–1) 282–302.

[96] *Doctrina Jacobi nuper baptizati* 1.2 (70–71 Dagron).

[97] Dagron and Déroche, "Juifs et chrétiens" 35–38, make excellent observations.

[98] Michael the Syrian, *Chronique* 11.4 (II: 414 Chabot).

[99] Averil Cameron, "Byzantines and Jews: Some Recent Work on Early Byzantium," *BMGS* 20 (1996) 248–274. Dagron and Déroche, "Juifs et chrétiens" 17–248.

[100] To Persia: Michael the Syrian, *Chronique* 9.4 (II: 414 Chabot). To Arabs: Sebeos, *Hist.* ch. 42 [134] (95 Thomson).

[101] Jean Durliat, "L'épitaphe du pape Honorius," in *Aetos: Studies in Honour of Cyril Mango*, ed. Ihor Sevcenko, Irmgard Hutter (Stuttgart, Leipzig: Teubner, 1998) 72. ψόγος ἐκνόμων Ἑβραίων: Sophronios, εἰς τὸν τίμιον σταυρόν 85–86 (ed. M. Gigante, *Anacreontica* (Rome: Gismondi, 1957) 117).

According to one tradition, Heraclius went in public procession with the Patriarch Sergios to a domed tetrastyle built by Constantine I, to initiate the display of a casket of gold and the accompanying letter of Theodore the shipmaster, who miraculously managed to return it to his creditor, the Jew Abraham, to whom he had sworn an oath in front of the icon later called "Antiphonetes." The exact date is uncertain. Abraham sought baptism for himself and his household and was ordained a priest, and his two sons as deacons, inside the oratory of the tetrastyle.[102] The incident underscores the contemporary anti-Jewish sentiments, Heraclius' public support for Christian triumph over and conversion of Jews, as well as the growing prestige of icons.

New troubles already beset parts of the east in 632. St. Maximos the Confessor speaks of barbarian ravages, which are surely Arab raiding, as a scourge in that year:

What more unfortunate circumstances could be here than these that hold the inhabited world in their grip? . . . What could be more lamentable and more terrible to those upon whom they fell? To see how a people, coming from the desert and barbaric, run through land that is not theirs, as if it were their own; how they, who seem only to have simple human features, lay waste our sweet and organized country with their wild untamed beasts.[103]

That is two years before the normal date for the outbreak of Muslim raiding in 634, after the battles of Dāthin (near Gaza) and Ajnādayn. Whether those raiders mentioned by Maximos in 632 were Muslim is uncertain, but it was a sign that the Heraclian restoration was very fragile and incomplete indeed. The news was troubling. Some, like Maximos, related it to apocalyptic or eschatological signs.

The Byzantine central government did not have time to reestablish itself after the Persian withdrawal. To the extent it made any effort, it botched its chances. Local governmental decisions, at that time, made in order to save money by terminating monetary payments to friendly Arabs and also to attempt to tighten controls on Arabs' trading and smuggling and evasion of "borders" probably increased tensions, resentments, and violence, and disrespect for imperial authority in some areas on the margins of settled regions in Palestine and Syria.[104]

How much Heraclius understood and sought to remedy this situation is uncertain. Other than restoring the fragments of the Cross, he encouraged

---

[102] Paul Magdalino, "Constantinopolitana," in *Aetos: Studies in Honour of Cyril Mango*, 220–227.
[103] Translation adapted from Carl Laga, "Judaism and Jews in Maximus Confessor's Works. Theoretical Controversy and Practical Attitudes," *Byzsl* 51 (1990) 186.
[104] Theophanes, *Chron.* A.M. 6123 (335–336 De Boor). Nikephoros, *Short History* 20 (68–69 Mango).

and donated to the rebuilding of Christian buildings and communities in the Holy Land.[105] We do not know how he began to appreciate the significance of Arab raiding on the edges of Palestine, whether by Muslims or non-Muslims. But the situation was very troubling. We learn from Leontios of Neapolis[106] that it was necessary to ransom prisoners from Arabs in the Negev and adjacent regions, which were overrun by Midianites (probably trans-Jordanian Arabs, or Arabs from east of the Dead Sea). So parts of that region were out of effective governmental control before the great invasions of 634. Insecurity was rampant. That news may have spread widely and have caused Maximos to deplore Arab depredations already in 632.

Could matters return to the *status quo ante*? Probably not, for there had been too much demographic disruption, with Christians from Persia settling in Byzantine territory and bringing new ways and valuable but new information. The war had widened horizons in diverse and unanticipated ways. Some Persian refugees remained inside Byzantine territory and Byzantines appear to have retained some kind of leverage inside extreme western parts of the Persian Empire. Heraclius apparently either never withdrew all Byzantine troops from Persia, or, in the increasingly volatile struggle for the succession after the death of Kawadh-Siroy, and especially through the medium of supporting Shahrbarāz's grasp for power, injected small but potent numbers (exact figures are impossible to know) of Byzantine troops and commanders in the extreme northwest territories that nominally were under the jurisdiction of the Sasanian Empire. That may help to explain why, at the moment of the Muslim conquest of Iraq, some Byzantine commanders and forces are mentioned roughly from Hīt on the middle Euphrates to Takrīt on the Tigris. Fredegarius, or his oriental source, stated that for almost three years Heraclius subjugated Persia after invading it.[107] These forces may well have included more friendly Arabs than soldiers of Greek or even of Armenian extraction. These measures were preventive, covering sensitive Byzantine territories, and offering excellent strategic advantages and some potential for gathering intelligence about and possibly even trying to intervene in the Sasanian Empire. Heraclius simply exploited Sasanian weakness.

Through his ties with the family of Iesdem, who had managed finances in Persia, Heraclius now had a potential new handle on Persia with respect

[105] Robert Wilken, *The Land Called Holy* (New Haven: Yale University Press, 1992).
[106] Leontios, *Life of John the Almoner*: E. Lappa-Zizicas, "Un épitomé inédit de Saint Jean l'Aumônier," *AB* 88 (1970) 276; also Kaegi, "Egypt on the Eve of the Muslim Conquest," in *The Cambridge History of Egypt*, ed. Carl Petry (Cambridge: Cambridge University Press, 1998) I: 56–57; V. Déroche, *Etudes sur Leonce de Néapolis* (1995) 117–119.
[107] Fredegarius, *Chronicle* 64 (53 Wallace-Hadrill); cf. Kaegi, *BEIC* 151–157.

to finances and the broader information, and with respect to the local important Christian community. Probably hopes soared for something dramatic, a breakthrough in the conversion of Persians to Christianity, and even to Orthodox Christianity (in communion with Constantinople). This may seem unrealistic but those were heady days, when many undreamed-of eventualities now seemed possible, in the wake of the unprecedented Byzantine triumph and the abject humiliation of the Persian ruling family. The exquisitely crafted "David Plates" and perhaps even the prototype of the Joshua Roll (now in the Vatican Library) may date to this period of Heraclius' life.[108] Yet whether there is any Heraclian imperial message or ideology in the "David Plates" is controversial. Mary Whitby argues that George of Pisidia wrote his *Hexaemeron* at this time.[109] This was an era of great expectations.

Georgian traditions assert that Heraclius vigorously encouraged ecclesiastical unity in Georgia. He "dispatched priests to Tp'ilisi and Mc'xet'a and Ujarma so that all Christians would be united in [his Imperial] Church, and all the magi and fire-worshippers who would not receive baptism were exterminated."[110]

But George of Pisidia lightly referred to another problem that had not entirely disappeared from Byzantium: the envy that Heraclius had encountered many times earlier in his life and career. The wishes of the poet that

---

[108] David Plates: Susan Spain Alexander, "Heraclius, Byzantine Imperial Ideology, and the David Plates," *Speculum* 52 (1977) 217–237; also, M. Mango, "Imperial Art in the Seventh Century," in *New Constantines: The Rhythm of Imperial Renewal*, ed. Paul Magdalino (Aldershot: Variorum, 1994) 122–131; S. Wander, "The Cyprus Plates: The Story of David and Goliath," *Metropolitan Museum Journal* 8 (1973) 89–104; S. Wander, "The Cyprus Plates and the Chronicle of Fredegar," *DOP* 29 1975) 345–346. J. Trilling, "Myth and Metaphor at the Byzantine Court. A Literary Approach to the David Plates," *Byzantion* 48 (1978) 249–263. A different interpretation: Ruth E. Leader, "The David Plates Revisited: Transforming the Secular in Early Byzantium," *Art Bulletin* 82 (2000) 407–427. On the possible relationship of the Joshua Roll to Heraclius: Cyril Mango, "The Date of Cod. Vat. Regin. Gr. 1 and the 'Macedonian Renaissance'," in *Acta ad Archaeologiam et Artium Historiam pertinentia, Institutum Romanorum Norvegiae* 4 (1969) 126, who speculates for the possible celebration in the Joshua Roll's prototype of Heraclius' triumph over the Persians and his triumphal entry into Jerusalem; cf. A. Cutler, *ODB* 1075–1076, s.v. "Joshua Roll," and esp. facsimile edn. by Otto Mazal, *Die Josua-Rolle* (Vienna, 1983–1984); K. Weitzmann, *The Joshua Roll* (Princeton: Princeton University Press, 1948 and reprints). Contemporary conceptions of David and Heraclius: Claudia Ludwig, "Kaiser Herakleios, Georgios Pisides und die Perserkriege," ed. P. Speck (*Varia* III, Ποικίλα Βυζαντινά, 11; Bonn, 1991) 95–127; C. Rapp, "Comparison, Paradigm and the Case of Moses in Panegyric and Hagiography" 295–296.

[109] Mary Whitby, "The Devil in Disguise: the End of George of Pisidia's Hexaemeron Reconsidered," *Journal of Hellenic Studies* 115(1995) 115–129, esp. 127–129, and Luigi Tartaglia, *Carmi di Giorgio di Pisidia* (Turin: UTET, 1998) 25–30, arguing against David Olster, "The Date of George of Pisidia's Hexaemeron," *DOP* 45 (1991) 159–172, who continues to maintain his opinions. I have not yet seen the new study on and edition of the *Hexaemeron* by F. Gonnelli, *L'Esamerone* (Pisa: Edizioni ETS, 1998). Also Claudia Ludwig, "Kaiser Herakleios, Georgios Pisides und die Perserkriege," 104–127.

[110] Sumbat Davitis-dze, *Life and Time of the Georgian Bagratids*, trans. S. Rapp, forthcoming.

Heraclius be preserved from envy[111] ("tearing friends and dividing relationships, knotting up brothers and brothers, and raising fraternal hypocrisy") indicate that there continued to be some kind, or more than one kind, of internal resentment against Heraclius even at the summit of his triumphs, that is, immediately after the restoration of the fragments of the Cross to Jerusalem in 630. We do not know the particulars, but the subsequent abortive *coup* attempt and friction about the imperial succession, and the exiling of certain Armenian commanders, are symptomatic of the problem, which may have extended beyond these figures. George of Pisidia vaguely alludes to the fragility of internal conditions.

Reduction of imperial expenses on the army was a problem that existed in other environments as well. A wagon driver who had served with the Persians in Mesopotamia at the Persian capital had already encountered problems in receiving payment for his services. The Persian authorities sneeringly told him that they had no more need for his services. Only with the intervention of St. Anastasios the Persian did he receive his compensation. Then he left and made his way to Constantinople, making himself a part of the vast displacement of peoples in the wake of those wars. He found a new life in Constantinople.[112] His complaints probably had echoes among Byzantine soldiers as well. Demobilization was not a problem unique to Byzantium. It was a time of exaltation and a time everywhere for governmental leaders to reduce high public expenditures on armies and related activities. It is impossible to ascertain how much Heraclius and his financial advisers reduced the size of his armies and other military expenses after the conclusion of peace with Persia. The problems did not end with the death of Khusrau II. Two more years were necessary for Byzantine armies to remain alert and ready to enforce Persian withdrawal and the reoccupation of former Byzantine territories. Whether he kept Byzantine armies at their peak strength is unlikely, but a skeletal force would have been inadequate for the multiple needs for security. News of the death of Shahrbarāz, in itself, did not require any major mobilization, but probably served to remind Heraclius to retain some troops who would be capable of intervening in unforeseen contingencies and crises.

Probably demobilization and reduction of military expenses accelerated in 631 and 632, after the conclusion of the pilgrimage to Jerusalem

---

[111] George of Pisidia, *Exped. Pers.* 3.444, [quotation =] 3.449–451, 3.457, *Poemi panegirici* 135, 136 Pertusi. Mary Whitby, "Defender of the Cross: George of Pisidia on the Emperor Heraclius and His Deputies," in M. Whitby, *Propaganda of Power* 247–273, emphasizes George's efforts to explain Heraclius' absence from Constantinople to Constantinopolitans in a positive way.

[112] Flusin, *Saint Anastase le Perse, Miracles anciens* I: 123–125.

and Heraclius' return to upper Mesopotamia. Soldiers who served in Mesopotamia did receive payments in silver as well as booty and of course cheers and honors when they returned to Byzantine territory. But the temptation was to cut expenses to the bone. Recovery of lost territories did not instantly restore the old high stream of revenues to Constantinople. Many constituencies were seeking imperial funds for worthy purposes and for recompensing recent losses. It was hard to justify paying large sums for the army when no great enemy was in sight. No budgetary records or muster lists survive.

Heraclius reinforced his policy of consolidating power in the hands of his family and securing the imperial succession. He raised his son Constantine III to the consulship on 1 January 632, which was an indubitable announcement of his decision about his succession.

Other important questions remain obscure. How had Heraclius' own health survived those events? Heraclius was now in his mid-fifties, having been born around 575. How had his experiences on these campaigns changed his outlook? How did his outlook change in light of his difficult experiences with trying to settle ecclesiastical strife about Christology? What did he now wish to accomplish at his full maturity and as he crossed over the threshold of what some Byzantines would have regarded as old age?[113]

Heraclius was a known and fixed quantity and personality by the beginning of the 630s. He was almost sixty years of age, quite old for those days. By the end of his fifties Heraclius had acquired the fullest possible range of experiences and wisdom. He probably was contemplating his eventual death and his prospects for eternal life. He may well have preferred to stay away from Constantinople as much as possible, to allow his subjects to accustom themselves to his eventual succession by his son, Constantine III. He also probably preferred to avoid controversy about himself and his marriage with Martina. He had become accustomed during the campaigning against Persia to absenting himself from Constantinople. During his absence from Constantinople he probably deepened and enriched his non-Constantinopolitan perspectives on the empire and its conditions, which, theoretically, strengthened his ability to appreciate events. Despite his advancing age, he was still in shape to endure the rigors of travel, although probably not the still greater ones of campaigning again in the field, especially in challenging terrain and climate. His face and his eyes on his

---

[113] A.-M. Talbot, "Old Age in Byzantium," *BZ* 77 (1984) 267–278; Judith Herrin and A. Kazhdan in *ODB* 36, s.v. "Age."

Fig. 4. Heraclius' portrait from solidi ca. 629–631, with Heraclius Constantine; Constantinople (obverses, a. *DOCat* 27; b. *DOCat* 26a; c. *DOCat* 26g).

portraits on his coinage seem to depict a man who has undergone many strange experiences. There is an unusual gaze in his visage and eyes. He looks more tired and wiser. His portrait on his gold coinage reflects aging and fatigue (Fig. 4).[114] The beginning of the 630s was a brief moment when there was one single dominant power in the Mediterranean and Near East. Comparable circumstances had not existed since the end of the Parthian state at the end of the second century and beginning of the third. There was a brief window of opportunity. Contemporaries had no way of understanding or predicting how briefly that window was to remain open. No one in the seventh century would have tried to peer back and make comparative judgments about possible historical parallels and perils.

At the end of the five years since victory over Persia, despite reverses and turmoil in Persia, and continuing religious dissent within the church throughout much of his empire, and despite the existence of immediate crises and others on the horizon, Heraclius and most of his contemporaries would not have judged his five-year record to have been one of total failure. It would have appeared to have been a mixed record. No irrevocable slide off any precipice appeared to be in sight.

Heraclius' extensive absences from Constantinople make it difficult to understand precisely his relationship in those years with Patriarch Sergios, but probably it was satisfactory and somehow they maintained adequate communications and a smooth relationship. There was a mutual dependence, which had started at the beginning of his reign, and which had developed and matured over the course of decades.

Heraclius' empire in the early 630s was benefiting but also being shaken by an influx of refugees from recent and contemporary upheavals. Some Persians, and not exclusively Christian ones, had fled Persia during his campaign in Persia and during the subsequent chaos there, to seek either asylum or better opportunities within the borders of the Byzantine Empire, including at Constantinople. Some of these brought valuable skills. Some

[114] *DOCat* 27.

Persian refugees brought detailed knowledge of the financial structures of the Persian Empire. Jews such as the Banū Naḍīr had been expelled from the Arabian peninsula and took refuge on the edges of Byzantine Syria. The empire and its leaders and subjects did not all welcome or appreciate these newcomers, despite their multifaceted talents and knowledge.

Heraclius had potentially strong individuals who could provide him with valuable information about conditions, resources, personalities, and changes within Sasanian Persia: Shahrbarāz and the family of Iesdem (Yazdin). But the rivalries and intense hatred among some of these individuals complicated the quality and nature of the information and advice that he was receiving about Persia. The situation in Persia was already quite unstable and volatile. These rivalries worsened it. Moreover Persia was not the entire Middle East.

The influx of refugees increased religious and cultural turmoil. The mood was less one of exhaustion than of pulsating and palpitating exultation. An out of control dynamism seemed to drive events. Inhabitants of regions who had not been very accustomed to strangers suddenly confronted peoples with differing ways of speaking and dressing, and who possessed different practices and outlooks. This contributed to intellectual ferment, but not everyone welcomed such ferment and change in an era when many simply wished a return to the old *status quo* in society, culture, and religion. Demobilization of Byzantine troops and their transfers, the return of captives and hostages all contributed to spreading some knowledge of other parts of the world, of other ways of doing things, and accelerated processes of change. It is uncertain how much Heraclius understood and appreciated the ferment caused by the influx of refugees, who potentially could contribute much to the empire in many ways. The dispersion and displacement of peoples and cultures in the early 630s created opportunities for cultural interchange, but many did not want or actually feared or opposed that process. But displaced peoples also probably spread communicable diseases for which no immunities or remedies existed. They exacerbated resentments between local communities and sects. They contributed to tensions and fear of change and of the future. The empire was becoming still more polyglot and diverse but not everyone welcomed that growing diversity. Extraordinary Christian talent became more available, as well as talented rejects from non-Christian communities who lost out in the internal struggles of adjacent states.

What could Heraclius have done better than he did in the early 630s? With hindsight, we can criticize many of his strategies and policies. Yet, knowing what he did in the face of those conditions and the light of his recent experiences, his policies were understandable, however faulty. Heraclius did undertake some institutional changes. He apparently reorganized the imperial mints.[115] But not all was innovation. In Palestine, the Byzantine reoccupation witnessed a revival of old institutions and festivals.[116] It was a complex and mixed process, which included both innovation and restoration. Extreme modern skepticism about the testimony of Greek primary sources from the beginning of the 630s concerning events and conditions is unjustifiable.[117]

As powerful as he was and as prestigious as he was at the beginning of the 630s, when he was theoretically at his zenith, Heraclius did not enjoy unlimited power. In particular, his power over his armies and their commanders was limited unless he personally assumed direct command. At the beginning of the 630s he probably assumed that armies and their commanders were at his disposal, but he learned quickly, as indicated by Peter of Numidia's refusal to move to relieve Arab (Muslim?) pressure on Egypt at his command in 632/633, that some commanders and their soldiers might reject or ignore his commands, without necessarily engaging in open rebellion. But already before the decisive Muslim victories, his ability to give effective orders to distant armies was not unlimited.

What Heraclius did not do was make any major redeployment of troops from Asia into the Balkans. Perhaps he was mindful of the fate of Maurice, who had done so in the 590s. His historian Theophylact reminded contemporary readers of the fate of Maurice. Heraclius himself cannot have remained oblivious to those terrible precedents. He did not wish to risk destabilizing his armies by moving potentially recalcitrant troops from Asia, especially any of Armenian origin, who already had shown their dislike of such service in the reign of Maurice, or from Egypt to the Balkans. Perhaps his own lack of personal experience with the Balkans acted as another deterrent or caution. Furthermore, his own embarrassing experience in the "Avar Surprise" may have contributed to his discouragement at undertaking any active policy of military campaigning in the Balkans to reassert Byzantine control over areas devastated by or lost to occupation or even settlement

[115] M. Hendy, "On the Administrative Basis of the Byzantine Coinage, c. 400–c. 900, and the Reforms of Heraclius," *University of Birmingham Historical Journal* 12 (1970) 129–154.

[116] Kaegi, "Some Seventh-Century Sources on Caesarea," *Israel Exploration Journal* 28 (1978) 179–180.

[117] Paul Speck, *Beiträge zum Thema Byzantinische Feindseligkeit gegen die Juden im frühen siebten Jahrhundert* (Bonn: Habelt, 1997) is excessively skeptical about accounts of St. Anastasios the Persian, Strategios on the Persian capture of Jerusalem, and of the *Doctrina Jacobi*. His efforts to impute all of this to later (eighth- and ninth-century) interpolations, and hypotheses about an upsurge of anti-Semitism in Palestine in the eighth and ninth century, are unconvincing for a number of reasons, including lack of corroboration from Arabic and Hebrew sources.

by Avars and Slavs. There is no convincing evidence for the hypothesis of a Heraclian offensive to recover the Balkans between 626 and 634, one that allegedly was led by Heraclius' brother Theodore.[118] It is even unclear how accurate the information was that he was receiving about the Balkans. Recent Byzantine military experience had taken place in the east and many of the lessons learned were not easily transferable, because of differences in terrain and climate and ethnography, to conditions in the Balkans. In any case, the Balkans did not constitute a priority for him at the beginning or end of the 630s, irrespective of the dire conditions there of his present or former imperial subjects.

It was even more unrealistic to contemplate reasserting Byzantine territorial control of strong-points or footholds in southern Spain or elsewhere in the extreme western Mediterranean. Exigencies had compelled Heraclius to allow their abandonment in the first two decades of his reign, but even at the zenith of his prestige at the beginning of the 630s he could not allocate resources and time and thought to their recovery. At the beginning of his reign the empire included most of what long before had been the Carthaginian Empire: not only Carthage, but also Carthago Nova, that is, New Carthage (modern Cartagena), in Spain, with its excellent port and valuable nearby mines of silver and lead. The empire had controlled valuable ports and points for taxing or developing rich maritime trade networks. By the early 630s, those ports and coastlines, with their resources, had slipped out of Byzantine hands. As long as the empire continued to control Septem (modern Ceuta), it was possible to monitor the straits of Gibraltar and even contemplate a return to Spain, or extension of authority along the Atlantic coast of Mauretania Tingitana. But resources were lacking and communications were slow and difficult to maintain with Septem and its environs when he was in Constantinople, let alone when he was in Anatolia or Syria. Yet, more than other emperors, he probably continued to remember and possess some appreciation of the potential of the western Mediterranean, at least from hearsay.

It is equally unclear what kind of military stocktaking took place on the part of Heraclius and his generals in the light of their recent campaigning against the Persians. Probably he perceived no great urgency to revamp his army. He turned to his brother Theodore for help now that his cousin Niketas was dead. Theodore had responsibility, as earlier in upper

---

[118] R.-J. Lilie, "Kaiser Herakleios und die Ansiedlung der Serben," *Südost-forschungen* 44 (1985) 23–26, 42–43. Lilie's criticisms are persuasive. Also, Lilie, "Bisanzio e gli Avari: tentativo di un'analisi," *Rivista di Bizantinistica* 1 (1991) 81–90; F. Curta, *The Making of the Slavs* (Cambridge: Cambridge University Press, 2001).

Mesopotamia and northern Syria, for mopping up dissidents and restoring Byzantine authority east of the Dead Sea, in trans-Jordania.

At the bureaucratic level, important was the emergence of the *sakellarios* as the critical comptroller of the treasury, in the wake of the obscure breakup of the old Pretorian Prefecture. The *sakellarios* also quickly became a critical intermediary between Heraclius and important constituencies among his subjects and within the ruling structure. Thus it was a *sakellarios* who was entrusted with the transmission of key correspondence between Heraclius, while he was in the east, and Patriarch Sergios of Constantinople.

A structural weakness in the early 630s was Heraclius' failure to find institutional ways to delegate military authority to commanders who were not members of his family. He probably relied heavily on family members because he did not believe that he could trust others with so much potential for military unrest. He could never be sure of them, even at the moment of his greatest triumphs.

Strong pressures to reduce governmental expenditures invariably restricted the funds available for military purposes. Hence the desire to downsize the military forces and related subsidies to foreign military forces, whose services appeared to be less essential. The outcome was demobilization, reduction or outright elimination of subsidies to barbarian allies. Many imperial subjects welcomed such measures, but those who lost such funding resented those new policies, which negatively affected themselves and their families and associates.

By 633 it was becoming apparent that Persia would not recover its military power very soon. Tentative progress seemed to be occurring with respect to ecclesiastical controversies, but evidence of opposition continued to be strong in almost every direction. The imperial succession seemed to be assured. The Persians had evacuated Byzantine territory and Byzantine authority had at least nominally been restored. The situation in the Balkans was murky. At a minimum, from his enormous expenditure of time and labor on site, Heraclius had now gained much familiarity with local problems, topography, and important civilian and ecclesiastical personalities in Syria, Upper Mesopotamia, and Armenia. None of his predecessors had managed to achieve a comparable grasp of information. Information was indispensable for Heraclius but could not assure him mastery over the course of events.

As the five years since victory over Khusrau II drew to a close, moods altered somewhat, to include both apprehension and tempered pessimism. "Even if it is diminished a little, we expect that it will rise again . . . " was the reputed reply of the Jew Justos, at Sycamina, on the Palestinian coast, to a question about the contemporary state of "Romania," or the Byzantine Empire.[119] Roman greatness was in the past: "the territory of the Romans extended up to our days from the Atlantic Ocean, that is, from Scotland, Britain, Spain, Francia, Italy, Greece and Thrace as far as Antioch, Syria, Persia and the entire east, Egypt, Africa and the interior of Africa. One sees there still the statues of their emperors, in marble as well as bronze. For everyone was subjugated to the Romans by a divine decree, but now we see Romania humiliated."[120] Again, he explained: "Romania is reduced, torn, and shivered asunder."[121] These sentiments reflected fluctuating feelings, which could always reverse themselves in light of new circumstances. Matters were about to take a decisive turn. Other jitters resulted from an earthquake in Palestine and the sighting of an ominous comet: "an earthquake occurred in Palestine; and there appeared a sign in the heavens called *dokites* in the direction of the south, foreboding the Arab conquest. It remained for thirty days, moving from south to north, and was sword-shaped."[122] The window of opportunity was closing, however imperceptible that reality was to Heraclius and most contemporaries.

[119] *Doctrina Jacobi* 3.8.40 (167 Dagron-Déroche).
[120] *Doctrina Jacobi* 3.10.3–8 (169 Dagron-Déroche).
[121] *Doctrina Jacobi* 3.12.6 (171 Dagron-Déroche). cf. 5.1.6 (183 Dagron-Déroche).
[122] Theophanes, *Chron.* A.M. 6124 (467 Mango-Scott).

CHAPTER 7

Tested again

Heraclius probably never was in control of events, even between 628 and 630, but external and internal ones decisively spun out of his ability to control them between 634 and 636, and never returned to any semblance of normality thereafter. He had reached the age of sixty, a very old age for that era, an age at which one might hope to slow down in order to enjoy the rewards of achievements accomplished earlier in life. That was not to be, for volatile conditions persisted and even intensified while health and internal crises took more and more of his attention and thereby impaired his efficient functioning. Unanticipated alien and domestic challenges and conspiracies tested him, his family, his faith, and his empire.

It is unclear precisely when or where Heraclius first heard of Islam, or more accurately, whether he ever heard of it, or when he first perceived there to be a significantly different Arab menace than he and his immediate predecessors had encountered in the Levant.[1] It is hardly surprising that he had no clear and coherent understanding of and insight into it, given that historians of the twenty-first century still disagree sharply about its formation and incipient nature.[2] Probably the elements of what would later become classic Islam were still in flux and had not become a fixed entity. It is understandable that Heraclius and his advisers could not comprehend an evolving religious phenomenon. But the *Doctrina Jacobi* ("What do you tell me about the prophet who has appeared among the Saracens? And he answered me while crying out loudly that 'He is false, for do prophets

---

[1] Robert Hoyland, *Seeing Islam as Others Saw It* (Princeton: Darwin Press, 1997) 218–219, 525. Best interpretation of some Muslim traditions: S. Leder, "Heraklios erkennt den Propheten," *ZDMG* 151 (2001) 1–42. Older inquiry into admittedly legendary materials: Suleiman Bashear, "The Mission of Dihya al-Kalbi," *JSAI* 14 (1991) 84–114 (reprinted unchanged in *Der Islam* 74 (1997) 64–91), esp. 94–110, who explicitly states that he is not investigating the historical Heraclius.

[2] Donner, *Narratives of Islamic Origins*; Donner, "From Believers to Muslims: Confessional Self-Identity in the Early Islamic Community," in *The Byzantine and Early Islamic Near East. Patterns of Communal Identity*, ed. L.I. Conrad (Princeton: Darwin, forthcoming). It is inappropriate here to undertake any inquiry into the significant modern debates about the origins of the Islamic community, but for a solid account: H.N. Kennedy, *The Prophet and the Age of the Caliphates* (London: Longman, 1986).

come armed with sword and chariot?' ")³ testifies to the speed with which information about the newly emergent prophet among the Arabs crossed from the shores of the eastern Mediterranean to those African ones in the vicinity of Carthage. There is no doubt that Heraclius swiftly heard some, perhaps many reports, but whatever conclusions he and his advisers drew were faulty. No Byzantine manual of statecraft or warfare offered advice on how to handle the appearance of a major prophet amidst the peoples who surrounded the empire. In fact the recent *Strategikon* of Maurikios offered no advice on how to fight Arabs of any kind. Nor could the family of Iesdem (Yazdin) and other Christian or non-Christian Sasanian advisers offer much helpful advice to Heraclius, for Sasanian relations with Arabs had been terrible during the reign of Khusrau II. Contrary to the Muslim historian al-Azdī al-Baṣrī's testimony that Heraclius was still in Palestine when he learned of the impending Arab invasion, his probable location was somewhere else in the east, whether Antioch, Hierapolis, or Edessa. Byzantine forces had already secured at least much of Palestine prior to, during, and to cover Heraclius' departure from Palestine when he personally returned the fragments of the Cross to Jerusalem. No embarrassing incidents were reported during his visit or his return. What initially appeared to be a simple but pesky matter of clearing out beduin who were taking advantage of the chaos of the Persian withdrawal from Palestine and Egypt imperceptibly, then radically, changed its form and scope. In the murky interim between the Sasanian evacuation and Byzantine reoccupation of Edessa in northern Syria, Jews may well have taken advantage of the vacuum by seizing control, as the *History* attributed to Sebeos claims,⁴ and so may have Arabs, whether Muslims or not, in the regions east of the Jordan and Dead Sea.

When Heraclius realized the severity of this Muslim threat is uncertain: 632 or 633 possibly. He or his advisers may have at first regarded them as some special sect of Jews. By early or the middle of 634 he had already heard of major Byzantine reverses. He had already unsuccessfully summoned troops from African Numidia, surely as part of a much wider effort to collect troops to use against what appeared at first simply to be many Arabs. He had already appointed his brother Theodore to combat them. Theodore already had experience clearing Persians and irregulars and deserters out of upper Mesopotamia. His previous experience there certainly acquainted him with Arabs. But Theodore, according to a hostile tradition, showed contempt for Arabs: "What are the sons of Hagar? Dead dogs!"⁵ But these

---

³ *Doctrina Jacobi* 5.16 (209 Dagron-Déroche).   ⁴ Sebeos, *Hist.* ch. 42 [134] (95 Thomson).
⁵ Michael the Syrian, *Chronique* 11.3 (II: 409–410 Chabot), and the quotation: *Chronique* 11.5 (418 Chabot). [Anonymous] *Chronicon ad annum Christi 1234 pertinens* c. 110 (190–191 Chabot).

were different tribes and somewhat different terrain. There is evidence of
beduin depredations, from the perspective of sedentary agricultural and
town populations, in southern Palestine and the Sinai, and within the
Egyptian desert. In the eyes of his Byzantine subjects, peripheral tribes,
and the Byzantine army Theodore represented Heraclius. To resist him was
to resist the emperor, any defeat for him tarnished the prestige of Heraclius.
Heraclius probably gave him discretion in handling the reoccupation, but
reportedly warned him to avoid open battle with the Arabs and to be wary
of ambushes.

Heraclius himself had never seen cities and rural terrain south of
Jerusalem or east of the Dead Sea, where the initial Byzantine fighting
with Muslims occurred. He had plenty of opportunity to hear descriptions from subordinate commanders and officials. The first engagement
with Muslims took place at Mu'ta, in September 629, probably in effect
a very modest clash between Byzantines attempting to reoccupy areas
southeast of the Dead Sea and Muslims moving northwest into areas that
Persian forces or Persian surrogates had evacuated. This resulted from no
strategic decisions of either side. Heraclius had not planned that battle,
which took place in the vicinity of the lightly populated homelands of the
Biblical Amalek, who figured so prominently in imagery of contemporary
Byzantine literature. Because it was a Byzantine victory, it did not induce
any Byzantine self-doubts or drastic reorganization of Byzantine military
forces in Palestine.

According to Sa'īd b. Baṭrīq (Eutychios), Heraclius had already visited
Damascus in 630 on his trip to Jerusalem to return the fragments of the
Cross. While at Damascus Heraclius had demanded the payment of the
missing tribute that the local prefect, Manṣūr b. Sarjūn, had turned over to
the Persians. Manṣūr protested that he had already given it up to the Persians
and their king, Khusrau II. Heraclius compelled him to pay the sum of 1000
"dinars," and only then confirmed him in his position as chief tax collector.
This story may set a precedent, for later Heraclius and his successors would,
according to Muslim traditions, demand payment of tribute equal to what
local leaders had given to other parties as tribute, whether to Persians or
to Muslims.[6] But it is a story that survives in transformed rendering, in
a Christian Arab text with many question marks about its authenticity. It
reflects a larger tradition that indicates mutual distrust between Heraclius
and local authorities on the eve of the Muslim conquest. There would be

---

[6] Eutychios, *Hist.* 271 (107 Breydy; *Gli anni* 323–325; 332–333 Pirone), for Heraclius' stay in Damascus
after visiting Jerusalem; he demanded money from Mansur. Is this a doublet or second demand for
funds?

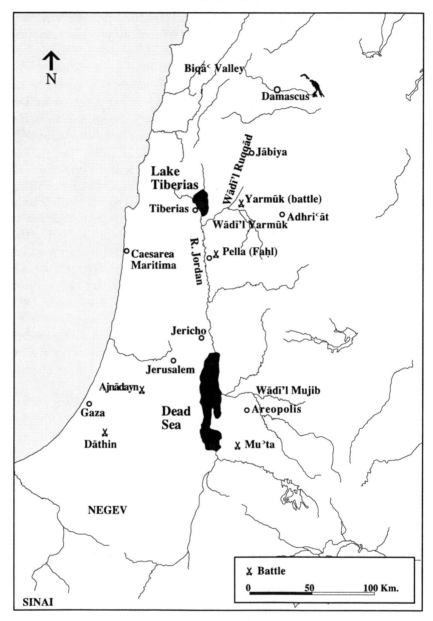

Map 8 Byzantine Palestine and southern Syria, showing sites of principal battles

echoes elsewhere, in Egypt, northern Syria, and Africa, of mistrust and accusations and breakdown of relations because of disputes about revenues owed by local authorities to the imperial government.

The first persistent Muslim raiding, after the initial clash of 629 at Mu'ta, also occurred east of the Dead Sea. Local officials had negotiated terms with Muslims at 'Aqaba, then Areopolis and its fortress (its fuṣṭāt, at present Rabba, in the Moab, in modern Jordan) fell.[7] The immediate sequel included penetration of the Wādī'l 'Araba, initial raids into the Negev,[8] and in the vicinity of Gaza. Gaza lay exposed after local Arabs angrily withdrew their support for the Byzantines in reaction to (1) the insulting refusal of a eunuch to pay them their normal stipends, and (2) governmental efforts to control their illicit commercial transactions.[9] Details of all this probably escaped Heraclius. False rumors claimed that he was leading troops in the vicinity of Areopolis, whose Arabic name is Ma'āb. Perhaps the rumors confused or conflated him with his brother Theodore, or the Byzantines may have deliberately floated such reports. But the generals who fought the Arabs in Transjordania were his appointees.

Word of menacing movements of Arabs had probably reached Heraclius by 633, and possibly before. That is why he unsuccessfully sought to command the shifting of troops from Numidia to Egypt to assist its defense against the Arab threat. Another reason for his request was the absence of any large permanent garrison of effective Byzantine troops in Egypt. In an empire already hard-pressed to find troops to reoccupy and monitor territory that the Persians had evacuated, or to protect what remained of the Byzantine Balkans, it was natural for a former resident of Africa to think of summoning troops from Numidia to assist beleaguered Egypt. The refusal of General Peter, on the advice and admonition of Maximos the Confessor, to move east was a harsh reminder of the limits of Heraclius' power even following his prestigious triumph over the Sasanians.[10] His strategic vision for drawing on resources from diverse parts of his far-flung empire was

---

[7] Wāqidī, *Maghāzī* 760, 990 Marsden-Jones; al-Balādhurī 113; al-Ṭabarī 1.2108; al-Azdī al-Baṣrī, *Ta'rīkh futūḥ al-Shām* 23–24 Lees; Sebeos, *Hist.* 135, ch. 42 (96–97 Thomson, 96 Macler); Beihammer, *Nachrichten* no. 51, pp. 71–72; *contra* commentary by J. Howard-Johnston on Sebeos, *Hist.* 241. On al-Azdī: Suleiman A. Mourad, "On Early Islamic Historiography: Abū Isma'īl al-Azdī and his *Futūḥ al-Shām*," *JAOS* 120 (2000) 577–593.

[8] al-Ṭabarī 1.2108, 2125; al-Balādhurī 108–109 De Goeje.

[9] Theoph. *Chron.* A.M. 6123 (335–336 De Boor; 466 Mango-Scott).

[10] "Relatio factae motionis inter domnum Maximum monachum et socium eius coram principibus in secretario," *Scripta saeculi vii vitam Maximi Confessoris Illustrantia*, ed. Pauline Allen, Bronwen Neil (*CC*, Series Graeca, 39; Turnhout: Brepols, 1999) 12–15. Beihammer, *Nachrichten* no. 48, pp. 68–69. Roman soldiers had been shifted from Africa to Egypt even in the Julio-Claudian period, during the reign of Nero.

unrealizable, even though the continuator of Isidore of Seville's Chronicle and some Muslim traditions state that he summoned troops from all parts of his empire, including islands.[11]

Heraclius passed time in Oriens for several reasons: (1) to investigate conditions firsthand and supervise the restoration of his administration in regions that the Persians had occupied and, in a number of cases, damaged; (2) to participate in negotiations and to exert pressure for the solution of ecclesiastical problems, including theological disputes and quarrels concerning episcopacies, in particular concerning Christology; (3) to settle any grievances of his troops; (4) to stay away from Constantinople while his controversial marriage aroused negative comments; and (5) to visit holy sites. Two additional reasons emerged as Arab raids turned into larger-scale invasion: (1) from a not too distant rear he attempted to assess the changing military situation and devise military responses by raising and dispatching troops, and advising and giving orders to commanders, and (2) he was prepared, if the situation warranted, to engage in diplomatic negotiations with Arab or Muslim leaders and, preferably, learn enough about them to devise ways to capture, kill, or divide them, as had been the custom of the Byzantines and Romans with Arabs, Berbers, and other "barbarians."

Heraclius had gained most of his previous successes through exploiting divisions within the ranks of his opponents, whether Phokas, Khusrau II, or others. He was close enough to the military front that he could rather quickly respond to timely information about divisions within Arab ranks, if he could learn of rivalries or other vulnerabilities. That diplomatic or conspiratorial option would have been less costly in lives and financial resources than battle. Such hopes were not to achieve realization, in part because of the new and blurry phenomenon of Islam. Yet this is part of the explanation for Heraclius' behavior between 634 and late 636, when it became apparent to all that this Arab challenge, whatever it was, involved qualitatively different aspects than earlier ones.

It is difficult to disentangle truth from rumor and propaganda in that critical span of time. Heraclius had acquired some familiarity with terrain that would be crucial between 634 and late 636. He had personally journeyed to Jerusalem; he had seen Tiberias, Damascus, Antioch, and Emesa (Ḥimṣ), and critical portions of the road network of central and northern Syria and their interrelationships with roads and passes in the Tauros and Anti-Tauros

[11] [Ps.-Isidore] *Continuationes Isidorianae Byzantia Arabica et Hispana*, ed. T. Mommsen (*MGH AA* 11) 741, c. 15 (337 Mommsen); *Chron. Hisp.* c. 7 = Pereira/Wolf c. 8; trans. in Hoyland, *Seeing Islam as Others Saw It* 616.

mountain ranges, and the upper Euphrates. He had some feel for the climate and difficulties in moving and supplying troops there. He had observed the strengths and weaknesses of fortifications of some of the major towns, and the potential for improving fortifications and building new watchtowers and defensive positions. He knew many of the commanders and units that were committed to the defense of Syria and upper Mesopotamia, and how some of them had recently performed against the Persians and even during the reoccupation of the Levant in the wake of the Persian evacuation.

Heraclius in the memory of the Arabic sources attempted to arouse popular opposition in Palestine and Damascus to the impending Muslim attack.[12] In earlier struggles he had sought to communicate with the public via bulletins or open letters. Sources also portray him as so curious to learn about the Muslims that he sent spies to investigate them, which is perfectly consistent with earlier Byzantine practices against other non-Roman peoples. His alleged efforts to arouse the public to self-defense in several places in the Levant are consistent with reports in the *Short History* of Nikephoros that on more than one other occasion at Constantinople he convened the public in order to consider controversial issues. That does not, however, prove the truth of Azdī's traditions. What all of the sources agree is that, unlike the campaigns against the Persians, Heraclius did not personally participate in any combats or directly command troops that engaged the Muslims.[13] He spent his time either at Ḥimṣ/Emesa or Edessa or at Antioch, all of which were important communications and supply centers. While at Ḥimṣ or Antioch (or earlier, Hierapolis) he could receive and dispatch communications efficiently, make judgments concerning supplies, and maintain the best possible ties with Constantinople and other critical centers in Anatolia.[14] It is impossible, given extant sources, to identify his exact location within most of those cities, although Hierapolis had served in the 580s, as Antioch many times before, as a critical site for military commanders and even for emperors (Antioch for Julian, Hierapolis for Valens).[15] At Edessa, he lived in a palace that overlooked a spring.[16] Thereby he maintained control of the government despite the fluctuating and rapidly deteriorating military fronts. However bad, the situation could

---

[12] Azdī 23 Lees; al-Ṭabarī (Sayf) 1.2104, cf. 1.2086; Ibn al-Athīr 2.311, 317–318; Kūfī, *Kitāb al-futūḥ* 1.100–101. See on images: Nadia Maria El Cheikh, "Muhammad and Heraclius: A Study in Legitimacy," *Studia Islamica* 89 (1999) 5–21; and her *Byzantium Viewed by the Arabs* (Ph.D. diss. Harvard, 1992) 120–133.

[13] Kaegi, *BEIC* 104–109.

[14] W. Brandes, "Die melkitischen Patriarchen von Antiocheia im 7. Jahrhundert. Anzahl und Chronologie," *Le Muséon* 111 (1998) 37–57.

[15] Hierapolis as site for General Komentiolos in the reign of Maurice: Theophylact, *Hist.* 4.10.9, 4.12.8.

[16] [Anonymous] *Chronicon ad annum Christi 1234 pertinens* c. 102 (185 Chabot).

have been much worse if he had insisted on his personal presence in any of the major combat zones during the campaigns of 634–636. Not only would he have risked his and his family's lives by exposure to combat or capture, but also he would have placed himself in regions where communications with the rest of his empire would have been more time-consuming and difficult. His was a prudent policy if not a glorious one.

There is no evidence whether Heraclius paid any attention to local opinion where he resided when he first heard of the appearance of the prophet Muḥammad, or the impending Muslim invasions. After all, he did not govern by public opinion in the ordinary sense. The Nestorian *Chronicle of Siʿīrt* reports that Heraclius convoked bishops at Antioch to inquire about their opinions on Islam.[17] This may well be a later tradition.

Azdī reports that Heraclius appointed deputies from his armies over the cities of Syria. This is consistent with other reports that Heraclius later appointed a military commander (*stratelates*) Ptolemaios to replace the imprecisely titled *curator* or *epitropos* or governor John Kateas in Osrhoene and Mesopotamia. Local granaries to supply the Byzantine military there had a long history and are not unique creations of Heraclius, although he and his officials may have restored earlier institutions. Appointments such as that of Ptolemaios may or may not be significant emergency measures of an extraordinary sort, improvisations that created special temporary military commands or governorships, not a calculated and carefully planned institutional reform. These temporary measures may well be forerunners of the later "theme" system in Anatolia and elsewhere, but documentary evidence does not exist to ascertain details about titulature or other aspects of their character and functioning.[18] The collapsing military front caused these particular commands to be overrun and disappear.

Any evaluation of Heraclius must confront the issue of how he and his advisers miscalculated the Muslim challenge. Although it is possible that the Prophet Muḥammad did actually attempt to send some courier to Heraclius, to summon him to Islam, such a messenger would not have reached him or received any kind of imperial audience or recognition.[19] In the eyes of some Byzantine sources, Heraclius did have a prudent plan, which his commanders failed to follow and thereby incurred this disastrous sequence of defeats. But he was close enough to the scene of events to share

---

[17] *Histoire Nestorienne/Chronicle of Siʿīrt* 116 (*PO* 13: 626).
[18] Seventh-century institutions: John Haldon, *Warfare, State and Society in the Byzantine World 565–1204* (London: UCL Press, 1999) 71–85, 107–115. But see W. Brandes, *Finanzverwaltung in Krisenzeiten*, Appendix XVI: "Die Provinzen Mesopotamien und Osrhoene im 6. und im beginnenden 7. Jahrhundert – Vorbild für spätere Entwicklungen?" 590–595.
[19] I have not seen the paper that Irfan Shahid is preparing on this topic.

responsibility for the outcome. It was an unprecedented event that he could not have anticipated. Yet local inhabitants of the region had already in the sixth century, in 540, and again in the wake of Persian successes after 610, surrendered their cities, including walled ones, to the Persians in negotiated deals. His religious policies did not earn him the love of his Jewish and dissident Christian populations, but the propensity of locals to cut separate deals with invaders, instead of fighting to the death in popular resistance, had already manifested itself. No one was eager for any repetition of the massacre of the inhabitants and clergy that took place in 614 at Jerusalem at the hands of the Sasanians as a consequence of the townspeople's prolonged resistance. Yet recent experiences with the Sasanians provided imperfect guidelines for action in the 630s and early 640s.

Heraclius probably encouraged his commanders to delay battle in Syria, and later in Egypt, to try to learn more about the Muslims, to seek out their vulnerabilities and probably to try to decapitate their leadership or use diplomacy to lure away key leaders or important clans or tribal group-ings. That may well be another reason for the pauses before battle that Byzantine commanders reportedly practiced. Anecdotes of desultory ne-gotiation during Muslim blockades or sieges of cities, such as Gaza, may not be so implausible. Using such negotiations to probe for the enemy's weaknesses was an old technique that Byzantines used in some instances as part of their efforts to check or defeat the Muslims.

This was not the first time that Heraclius had delegated authority to other military commanders. He trusted and instructed Theodore Trithyrios, the important treasurer (that is, *sakellarios*), as early as 634 concerning how to conduct himself with Arabs. A *sakellarios* had already been the critical transmitter of important missives between Patriarch Sergios and Heraclius during his stay in the east, in 632. Heraclius allegedly warned Theodore Trithyrios to beware of Arab ambushes, and to avoid battle with them. Another source, from Spain, reports that he gave such a warning to his brother Theodore. But official historiography and propaganda that sought to exonerate him and his dynasty for responsibility for military disasters may contaminate and distort these traditions. He is represented as having given wise advice that his deputies imprudently ignored, to their own and to the empire's detriment. But another tradition, in the Spanish source, blames Heraclius himself for having been seduced into erroneous policies by popular adulation.

The state of Heraclius' health in this period is a major unknown. Health concerns may explain his avoidance of combat. Probably he was intermit-tently unable to function efficiently while at other moments he could handle decision-making very capably. This judgment rests on assumptions about the capabilities of individuals suffering from "dropsy" before the terminal period. Less clear is whether he also may have suffered from Post-Traumatic Stress Syndrome due to his protracted exposure to military combat and related strains. Heraclius began to confront this massive Muslim invasion when he was crossing the threshold of sixty years of age. That was an advanced age, indeed a remarkable one, at which to remain in the field, with its rigors. The remaining five years of his life were filled with still more crises and the unraveling of events. He was not likely to change his ways much at that late stage of his life. Although he had outlived many contemporaries in that era of short longevity, he was not senile. He had much wisdom, but the challenges required resourcefulness, flexibility, creativity, and stamina. By that time he possessed immense experience with a diversity of threats and options. He had built up a vast network of personal acquaintances with the military commands and in the civilian bureaucracy. But he needed all the talents that he had, for there were no solutions for these new challenges in old ways of doing things.

The state of the health of Heraclius' oldest son, Heraclius Constantine, is almost as important as that of Heraclius. Heraclius Constantine was ill, although how ill is debatable. He was the son of an epileptic and prematurely deceased mother. His poor health overshadowed political and military calculations in the middle and late 630s. This young man did not accompany his father on campaign in Anatolia in 622, 624, and in 627–628, because it was imperative and desirable to have a trusted member of the immediate imperial family at Constantinople during Heraclius' absence, to keep a secure control and to insure continuity of the dynasty and to remain outside of harm's way. But by the 630s Heraclius Constantine was no longer immature or a minor. It was his father who was vulnerable. Yet Heraclius Constantine is not reported to have campaigned in Asia, even when his uncle Theodore and others proved untrustworthy. The explanation may be his own fragile health. We likewise do not know what communications and consultations took place between Heraclius and Heraclius Constantine concerning Syria, Palestine, upper Mesopotamia, and Egypt, and issues of military strategy, theology, and fiscal issues. Heraclius' fears for the health of Heraclius Constantine may help to explain his controversial concerns for incorporating the progeny of himself and Martina into the imperial succession.

The personal presence of Heraclius in no way would have terrified the Muslims into retiring or fleeing to avoid him by late 634. Such false rumors had not cowed them in the vicinity of Areopolis (Rabba) earlier that year,[20] and they certainly would not have done so later in other parts of Palestine or Syria or upper Mesopotamia. Nevertheless, narrative sources give great attention to Heraclius' activities and lack of activities between 634 and 636. What he was or was not doing was regarded as critical to understanding Byzantine policies and actions. That may well have been a simplistic and false assumption, which exaggerated his role and ability to shape events, but nonetheless that is his image.

Contemporary writings of Sophronios, including his synodal letter of 634,[21] and of Maximos the Confessor provide a little evidence about the initial shocked reactions in the provinces to the news of Muslim successes. Sophronios prayed for Heraclius to have grandchildren and to tread on barbarians, especially the unexpected Saracens. His is an explicit acknowledgment that ecclesiastical leaders, who were quarreling about Christology, had not expected the Muslim torrent. His remarks indicated the overweening desire for the dynasty to have generations of offspring and continuity, which was potentially in jeopardy. There is no evidence that Sophronios or other ecclesiastical leaders, Chalcedonian or anti-Chalcedonian, encouraged the populace to resistance *à l'outrance* against the Arabs. But that evidence is fragmentary and does not exist for many provinces and cities. Likewise there are no reports on how Heraclius and his advisers attempted, for their part, to weigh reports on popular reactions to news of major Muslim victories and advances.

Excessive skepticism about the possibility of reconstructing the main events is unpersuasive.[22] Greek, Syriac, and Muslim sources agree that

[20] Wāqidī *Maghāzī* 760, 990 Marsden-Jones, cf. 1015, 1018.

[21] Sophronios, synodal letter, preserved in the Acts of the Sixth Ecumenical Council of 680/681, in the edition of R. Riedinger, *Concilium Universale Constantinopolitanum Tertium* (*ACO* Vol. II, Pt. 1; Berlin, 1990) 410–495, esp. 492. Mansi, *Sacrorum conciliorum nova et amplissima collectio* 11.462–510, esp. 505–508.

[22] On Yarmūk: Beihammer, *Nachrichten* nos. 97, 100–103, pp. 122–126, 128–133. It is misleading and incorrect to argue that the *History* attributed to Sebeos alone can provide a reasonable picture and reconstruction of events, as J. Howard-Johnston does in his commentary to Sebeos, *History* 233–243. He implausibly argues for the location of the major battle east of the River Jordan or Dead Sea, somewhere in the Kingdom of Jordan. He conflates the battle of Yarmūk and the earlier small combat at Rabba (Ma'āb). He ignores Muslim traditions about military action at Ma'āb (Rabba) in assessing their credibility, while exalting that of Sebeos; in fact they mutually reinforce credibility. He ignores the explicit testimony of St. Anastasios the Sinaite in the late seventh century that there were destructive Byzantine military defeats at Gābitha (Jābiya), Yarmūk, and Dathesmon (Dāthin, near Gaza). The late seventh-century Ps.-Methodios *Apocalypse* also refers to decisive combat at Gābitha (Jābiya). The major and decisive fighting took place around the edge of the Syrian side of the Golan Heights. The *History* attributed to Sebeos is very useful and valuable, but cannot stand alone, because its compiler sometimes confuses and conflates proper names, chronology, and offers only one limited perspective on events.

there was a battle of the Yarmūk, or Jābiya-Yarmūk. References to Jābiya (Gābitha) indicate that the battle took place in what is today Syria, near the confluence of twentieth-century Israeli, Syrian, and Jordanian cease-fire lines, not in what is today the Kingdom of Jordan. It is the explicit testimony of St. Anastasios the Sinaite in the late seventh century that destructive Byzantine military defeats (bloodshed) occurred at Gābitha (Jābiya) Yarmūk, and Dathesmon (Dāthin, near Gaza).[23] Likewise references in some Muslim and Christian sources to the presence of a *sakellarios* (Theodore Trithyrios) as a Byzantine commander in the Gābitha-Yarmūk campaign are not imaginary or a *topos*, for this Byzantine office only appears as an important independent one in the 630s, and by the end of that decade receives sigillographic confirmation. The *sakellarios* is not normally a Byzantine military commander in subsequent centuries. That particular tradition derives from an authentic historical core.[24] It cannot have been made up at some much later date. One of the principal tasks for modern historians is the weighing and comparing of non-Muslim and Muslim sources, in particular with reference to specific Late Antique and Byzantine terminology, in the search to evaluate the authenticity of separated bits of memory from the merely spurious.

The *History* attributed to Sebeos, which is invaluable on Armenian affairs and personalities and stimulating for many other purposes, is hopelessly vague about the chronology and location of the battle and related campaigning, sometimes compressing and conflating events virtually out of recognition. It is even confused and incorrect about the name of Heraclius' brother Theodore (not Theodosios). A combat occurred in Arabia, by which the compiler or his source presumably means the province of Arabia. It is unclear whether he refers to the battle of the Yarmūk, or some other clash, such as Faḥl/Pella, which reportedly took place near the Jordan. The author does not identify the Byzantine commander or commanders, whether of Armenian extraction or not. The *History* attributed to Sebeos states that the Muslims invaded, and immediately and permanently overran areas west of the Jordan River after defeating the Byzantines at this non-specific battle in Arabia. Yet the Patriarch Sophronios states in his Christmas

[23] Anastasios the Sinaite, *Sermo adversus Monotheletas* 3.1.86, in *Sermones duo in constitutionem hominis . . . Opuscula contra Monotheletas*, ed. Karl-Heinz Uthemann (*CC*, Series Graeca, 12. Brepols-Turnhout: Leuven University Press, 1985) 60. Gābitha Ramtha (Syrian Der'a), on the modern Syrian–Jordanian border as site of a major battle: Ps-Methodios, *Apocalypse* 11.1–2 (41–42 Reinink).
[24] Theoph. *Chron.* A.M. 6125–6126 (337–338 De Boor, 468–470 Mango-Scott). Ibn 'Asākir, *TMD* 2.144. "Fragment on the Arab Conquests," trans. in Hoyland, *Seeing Islam as Others Saw It* 117, and "A Record of the Arab Conquest of Syria, AD 637," in *The Seventh Century in the West Syrian Chronicles*, ed. A. Palmer (Liverpool University Press, 1993) p. 3 line 15.

sermon for 634 that "Saracens" had already overrun the Palestinian countryside around Bethlehem.[25] The *History* attributed to Sebeos is a good but incomplete source that requires critical evaluation. Moreover one cannot learn from it where Heraclius was at any point during Byzantine–Muslim military operations in Syria; apparently that was not a concern of its compiler or his source or sources. Because its author envisages the Muslim conquest of Palestine in Biblical terms, the modern reader must exercise critical caution in reading the text, for the Biblical echoes and imagery can mislead the reader. The Muslims' crossing of the Jordan and concentration at Jericho after defeating the Byzantines in "Arabia" may be valid, but it is also possible that the author of the *History* attributed to Sebeos is shaping his narrative to imitate or to interpret events in terms of the Biblical deeds of Joshua. One cannot reliably alter the well-established date for the battle, or at least its final day, by appealing to a passage in a Syriac chronicle that refers only to the clash at Dāthin near Gaza, with which it conflates and compresses the entire Muslim conquest of Persia. If it inaccurately telescopes the entire Muslim conquest of Persia under one date, how can one have any confidence in using it to be the firm benchmark for the *terminus ad quem* for Muslim military operations in Syria? The passage in question is the final one by one source for that chronicle, and may well in the course of transmission have been compressed and epitomized and emended beyond the original intent of the compiler. It cannot serve as the benchmark for dating the decisive campaigning in or east of Palestine, given its deficiencies.[26] The account of Ibn ʿAsākir remains essential for understanding the combat and related maneuvering.[27]

Heraclius did not micromanage from afar the Byzantine forces who maneuvered in August 636 between Jābiya and the gorges of the wādī ʾl Yarmūk. Heraclius, who was not personally present, in early 636 collected a very substantial Byzantine and Christian Arab force to reverse recent Muslim victories in Syria, Transjordania, and Palestine, and drive them out of Syria and Palestine. The site strategically included high ground, water supplies, pasture, and domination of important routes between Damascus and Galilee. It was an important sedentary base and crucial pasture-grounds

---

[25] Sophronios, "Weihnachtspredigt," 506.
[26] Andrew Palmer, "Extract from a Chronicle Composed about AD 640," AG 945–947, in *The Seventh Century in the West Syrian Chronicles* 19; *contra*, J. Howard-Johnston, Sebeos, *Hist.*, Historical Commentary 240–243.
[27] Ibn ʿAsākir, *TMD* 2.141–166. Ibn ʿAsākir's history: *Ibn ʿAsākir and Early Islamic History*, ed. James E. Lindsay (Studies in Late Antiquity and Early Islam, 20; Princeton: Darwin Press, 2002). The contributors believe that it contains historical material of value for the seventh century, as does David Cook, "The Beginnings of Islam in Syria" (Ph.D. diss, University of Chicago, 2002).

of the friendly Christian Arab tribe of Ghassān, and lay within traditional Byzantine boundaries, near the intersection of four Byzantine provinces' boundaries. A major battle previously took place near it in 614, at which the Persian General Shahrbarāz resoundingly defeated the Byzantines, opening the way into Palestine for the Persians. The terrain's strategic significance was apparent to both sides and in theory was familiar to both. On the eve of the battle the Byzantines had not succeeded in developing any effective new tactics or strategy for checking the Muslims. The battle of the Yarmūk or Jābiya lasted more than a month, if one includes the preliminary maneuverings. It began in the vicinity of Jābiya, the traditional base of the Ghassān, with maneuverings, and terminated on 20 August 626. Byzantine forces had come from Emesa under General Vahan, who probably was *magister militum per Orientem*, and Theodore Trithyrios, the *sakellarios* (treasurer). Jabala b. al-Ayham, king of the Ghassān, led the Ghassānid forces.[28] Other Christian Arabs, whom Heraclius had recruited in upper Mesopotamia and elsewhere, participated. There are contradictory traditions concerning whether Theodore, the brother of Heraclius, was present. Although he participated in planning some of the campaign, Theodore probably had been recalled to Constantinople and disgrace before the final stages of the battle. Muslim forces under Abū 'Ubayda b. al-Jarrāḥ withdrew from Emesa and Damascus in the face of the approach from the north of stronger Byzantine armies. They retired to a line between Dayr Ayyūb and Adhri'āt, where they waited for more than a month, in a topographically strong position, to deter any Byzantine move further south. On 23 July 636 the Muslims won an initial clash near al-Jābiya. The Byzantines used the waiting period to familiarize their forces with the Muslims and, unsuccessfully, to encourage desertion and dissension within Muslim ranks. Both sides received reinforcements, but the decisive clash took place when the Muslims were continuing to gain more reinforcements. The Byzantines, together with their Christian Arab allies, probably enjoyed numerical superiority, having troops that totaled up to 15–20,000 men, possibly more.

By feigned retreat, the Muslims lured the Byzantines into attacking Muslims and their camp near Dayr Ayyūb. The Muslims penetrated the

---

[28] A lead seal shows that Jabala held the prestigious Byzantine rank of *patrikios*: Werner Seibt, *Die byzantinischen Bleisiegel in Österreich* (Vienna: Verlag der Akademie, 1978) no. 129, p. 262. Discussion: I. Shahid, "Sigillography in the Service of History: New Light," in *Novum Millennium: Studies on Byzantine History and Culture Dedicated to Paul Speck*, ed. Sarolta Takács, Claudia Sode (Burlington, VT: Ashgate, 2001). The seal probably dates to 630 or the immediately following years. It has implications for the credibility of Arabic traditions about early Islamic history: it shows that some Muslim traditions have a historical foundation independent of Christian texts.

exposed Byzantine left flank, and then exploited gaps that yawned between Byzantine foot and cavalry. Byzantine infantry apparently attempted to lock shields and to engage in intricate and complicated and risky exercises (the so-called "mixed formation") that involved opening the ranks of foot for horsemen to pass through and then relocking shields. Poor Byzantine coordination allowed the Muslims to exploit the gap and to slay many exposed Byzantine infantry. Byzantine forces withdrew into territory that lay between the Wādī 'l Ruqqād and Wādī 'l 'Allān, both west of the Wādī 'l Ḥarīr, to what they believed to be a secure encampment that received protection from the high bluffs of the wādīs.

The capable Muslim commander Khālid b.al-Walīd decisively altered the situation by seizing the critical bridge over the Wādī 'l Ruqqād, which offered the only viable retreat route for the encircled men and animals of the Byzantine army, in a night-time raid. The Byzantines found themselves blocked and could not retreat in formation, or fight their way out, or negotiate reasonable terms. The Byzantines panicked, having learned that they were cut off. The Muslims stormed their camps between the wādīs as well as at the village of Ya'qūṣa, on the edge of the Golan Heights. The Byzantines lost cohesion and most were slaughtered, although a few may have managed to flee down the steep sides of the wādīs. The Muslims took few or no prisoners. Some Christian Arabs allegedly wavered in their loyalty to the Byzantine cause and managed to flee, which aided the Muslims. Some dejected and defeated Byzantine troops, having perceived the hopelessness of their situation, fatalistically awaited their slaughter.

The battle destroyed the only viable Byzantine army in Syria and its commanders, who ceased to exist as a fighting force. A rout ensued. The Muslim victory eliminated the possibility of any Byzantine penetration further south, reconfirmed Muslim control of Palestine and Transjordania, and opened the way for the Muslim conquest of the Biqā' Valley, Damascus and, beyond it, all of Syria. The Muslims consolidated their victory by a rapid and far-stretching and ruthless pursuit of retreating Byzantines, giving them no respite. The battle had great psychological as well as material effects: it broke the will of the Byzantines to give more open battle. Henceforth Byzantines avoided open battle with the Muslims in Syria and upper Mesopotamia, and stopped trying to recover or hold Syria.[29]

However much Heraclius wished to probe for fissures within the Muslim ranks, the Byzantine ranks had their own internal tensions. Eutychios,

---

[29] Details: Kaegi, *BEIC* 112–146, and Kaegi, in *EI*[2] ii, fasc. 183–184 (2001) 290–292, s.v. "Yarmūk." Beihammer, *Nachrichten* nos. 97, 100–102, pp. 122–126, 128–133. It is inappropriate to review the material here.

Theophanes, al-Azdī al-Baṣrī and Ibn 'Asākir all report tensions within the ranks of the Byzantines. Tensions involved soldiers and civilians, or commanders who attempted to requisition supplies and funds, or, according to Theophanes or his source, tensions between General Vahan and Heraclius, in addition to tensions between Heraclius and his brother Theodore.[30] Theodore, who had already failed at the battle of Ajnādayn, was not present at the battle of the Yarmūk. Instead he had been recalled to Constantinople, where he was imprisoned. One speculation is that Heraclius suffered by the time of the battle of the Yarmūk from Post-Traumatic Stress Disorder, PTSD, which affected his performance and which may have increased his suspicion of others, including his brother Theodore. There is no present means to verify this hypothesis. General Vahan reportedly rebelled against Heraclius, and then perished at the hands of the Muslims, and in any case did not return to Byzantine territory. It is possible that the government propaganda machine decided to blame him, Vahan, for the disaster at Yarmūk, by blaming his disobedience for the outcome. Ultimate responsibility for the battle and the campaign lay with Heraclius, who appointed the commanders. News of this succession of defeats, underscored by their taking place in the Holy Land, encouraged unrest and exacerbated the incipient imperial succession crisis, that is, tensions within the Heraclian household between Heraclius and his brothers, between his second wife Martina and supporters of his son Heraclius Constantine by his first marriage, to the late Fabia/Eudokia, and the wild card of the ambitions of his illegitimate son Athalaric. Things started to unravel, stimulated by bad news from the Levant, especially from the holy places, and the losses of lives and tax revenues, and loss of prestige. As unreliable elements appeared even within the ranks of Heraclius' immediate entourage and family, his task of ruling became ever more difficult. It was hard to find capable yet reliable military commanders and deputies, and more difficult to find reliable and untainted advice.

Heraclius, despite health problems, found that he had no remaining excellent military commanders to help reorganize new defenses after the disaster at Yarmūk. He probably ordered the evacuation of Syria and approved the truce made at Chalkis (Arabic, Qinnasrīn) that allowed one year for the evacuation of those inhabitants who wished to flee to Byzantine territory, although not the arrangements, including tribute, to stave off a Muslim occupation of Byzantine Mesopotamia and Osrhoene.[31] Historical traditions

---

[30] *Chronicon ad annum Christi 1234 pertinens* c. 110 (190–191 Chabot).
[31] Chase F. Robinson, *Empire and Elites after the Muslim Conquest* (Cambridge: Cambridge University Press, 2000) 19–31.

ascribe to Heraclius himself the responsibility for ordering the creation of new defenses in Cilicia, and the creation of a wasteland.[32] "He ordered his troops and sent them to pillage and devastate the villages and the cities, as if the country had belonged to the enemy. The Romans [Byzantines] robbed and pillaged everything that they found, they devastated the country more themselves than the Arabs did. They withdrew and abandoned the land to the Arabs who held new sway there." He traversed these regions in 613 and subsequently while fighting the Persians unsuccessfully, and finally, in 629, immediately following his successful negotiations with General Shahrbarāz, and again when he accompanied the fragments of the Cross to Jerusalem and back in 630. He appreciated their strategic significance. The successful military evacuation of Syria proceeded under his authority.

Edessa in particular became the object of much direct imperial attention after Heraclius' victory over Persia, probably more indeed than it had ever previously enjoyed. Heraclius used Edessa as a key base first for the restoration of regional Byzantine military and political control after the Sasanian withdrawal and for his efforts to end ecclesiastical divisions. Edessa in particular had been very diverse religiously: Jacobites, Nestorians, Jews, Armenians, Arabs, as well as some Greeks. Skilled Christian craftsmen migrated to Edessa from central Iraq during the Sasanian occupation, perhaps to escape undesirable economic and social and political conditions or merely to improve their own material circumstances. The *History* attributed to Sebeos reports that Edessa and Amida enjoyed "peace and prosperity"[33] under Sasanian occupation and administration. The later memory of those times was positive. Glimpses of that world and its turbulence peer through the narratives about St. Anastasios the Persian.[34]

It was, then, an era of disturbance and dramatic change. Although the process of restoring Byzantine authority after 628 was not a smooth one, it could even have been a lot worse. Inhabitants suffered a lot and had to make many adjustments. There was insufficient time for memories of this chaos and abuses to fade. Many believed that they had reasons for grudges and scores to settle there. There was no opportunity for stability to prevail. All residents suffered. The sources are not, however, explicit about the sufferings or opinions of Armenians in either Amida or Edessa at that time. Economic dislocations probably took place as well as political

---

[32] Michael the Syrian, *Chron.* 11.7 (II: 424 Chabot). Beihammer, *Nachrichten* nos. 108, pp. 136–138.
[33] Sebeos, *History* III, ch. 33 (63 Thomson); *Storia* c. 31 (85 Gugerotti).
[34] Bernard Flusin, *Saint Anastase le Perse* (Paris, 1992), for important historical commentary.

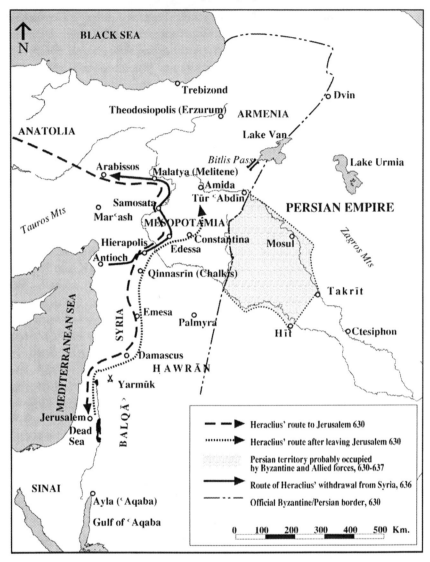

Map 9 Important West Asian localities during the Islamic conquests, AD 634–641

and ecclesiastical ones. Statistics are lacking: we do not know the size of the population (neither gross totals nor demographically segmented portions) or the volume of trade and industry in either city at any time in the seventh century, or the material and human losses incurred in either city during those trying times. It is likely that losses were serious but limited, i.e. not comparable to those that the inhabitants and buildings of Jerusalem suffered in 614 as a result of the Sasanian soldiers' storming of that city.

Al-Ṭabarī, repeating the tradition of Sayf b. 'Umar, plausibly states that after the battle of the Yarmūk (final stage: 20 August 636) Heraclius departed from Syria by way of Edessa and then Samosata, before proceeding to Constantinople.[35] The Syrian tradition preserved by al-Azdī al-Baṣrī, *Ta'rīkh futūḥ al-Shām*, also specifies, without other details, that Heraclius left Antioch for Edessa, where he "dwelled" or "settled" for an indeterminate time, and then made his way towards Constantinople.[36] No more exact chronology is possible, but one infers a date of late 636 or early 637. Heraclius did visit the province of Osrhoene; Edessa was the city that Heraclius needed to hold for a while to permit his Armenian troops to withdraw properly from Syria.[37] Al-Ṭabarī's statement concerning Heraclius' departure from Syria via Edessa and Samosata (and not directly through the Cilician Gates from Antioch) may well be authentic. Heraclius does appear to have been trying to stabilize the military situation southeast of the Tauros Mountains before proceeding to the Anatolian plateau and on to the Asian shores of the Bosphorus; he was not fleeing pell-mell after the defeat of his armies at the Yarmūk.[38] Extreme skeptics[39] might of course question whether Muslim sources really refer to Heraclius himself, or merely in some generic fashion to Byzantine armies, personalizing them under the name of Heraclius, but the best judgment is that Heraclius and his entourage did evacuate Syria by way of Edessa and Samosata. We have no specific information about the numbers of soldiers who accompanied Heraclius or their ethnic composition.

Heraclius ordered the recovery and destruction of Melitene (Malatya) and the implementation of a scorched-earth policy near Antioch and in Cilicia. He tried to build up defenses at the outer edge of Asia Minor. He was not medically or mentally incapacitated soon after the battle of Yarmūk. His anger at the *epitropos* (*curator*) John of Kateas' willingness to arrange a truce with the Muslims and his deposition and replacement by

[35] Al-Ṭabarī 1.2390, 1. 2395–6 (tradent is Sayf b. 'Umar, from Abū Zuhrā. Azdī 212–213 Lees. Ibn al-Athīr 2.384 Tornberg.

[36] Azdī *Ta'rīkh futūḥ al-Shām* 212–213 Lees.

[37] J.B. Segal, *Edessa, the Blessed City* (Oxford: Clarendon Press, 1970).

[38] F. Donner, *The Early Islamic Conquests* (Princeton: Princeton University Press, 1981) 150.

[39] Suleiman Bashear, "The Mission of Diḥya al-Kalbī and the Situation in Syria," *JSAI* 14 (1991) 84–114, is primarily useful for legendary materials, not historical reality. He did not concern himself with problems in the vicinity of Edessa and Amida.

a more forceful military commander is consistent with his vigorous efforts elsewhere to try to harden resistance and even to launch counterattacks.[40]

Heraclius' presumably short stay in Edessa on his retreat from Syria nevertheless put him in a city that he knew well. It was there he had previously (630) negotiated concerning ecclesiastical reunion, and where he had handed over the cathedral to one church faction. He understood and appreciated its strategic significance. He had expended great efforts and human resources in the long struggle for it with the Persians. In late 636, after the decisive destruction of much of his best armies at the hands of the Muslims at the battle of the Yarmūk, Heraclius did not take the shortest route out of Syria. Instead he chose to cover Armenia and his communications with Persia and with other friendly Arab tribes. His was no pell-mell retreat.

Heraclius' withdrawal from Syria via Edessa had consequences. Muslim military forces understandably tracked and covered his withdrawal, to prevent some crafty Byzantine counter-offensive, as improbable as that might seem in retrospect. Scholars have debated whether Muslims invaded upper Mesopotamia from Syria or from Iraq. This controversy reflects analyses of conflicting Muslim historical traditions from those two regions, Syria and Iraq. No original documents or archives survive from that era concerning these problems. Epigraphic and sigillographic sources are likewise lacking or inconclusive. Most extant Arabic and Syriac literary historical or annalistic records date from the ninth century or later. The preponderance of evidence, reinforced by a rereading of the *History* attributed to Sebeos, indicates that Muslims from Syria, in particular those under the command of 'Iyād b. Ghanm al-Fihrī, at the behest of Abū 'Ubayda b. Jarrāḥ, first penetrated to Edessa and Amida/Diyarbekir and imposed terms on the respective leaders and inhabitants. It is inappropriate here to undertake a detailed analysis of Muslim historical traditions, but most scholars of Islamic history concede that whatever the difficulties, there is ultimately a genuine core of historical traditions within Islamic memory. Elucidation of it is not always easy and much requires excision.[41] The principal Edessene source is the lost history or chronicle of Theophilos of Edessa, whose work survives in fragmentary form in several extant histories in Greek (*Chronicle of Theophanes the Confessor*), Arabic (Agapios of Mambij) and Syriac

---

[40] Al-Ṭabarī 1.2349. Balādhurī 164. Michael the Syrian, *Chron.* 11.7 (II: 424 Chabot). Beihammer, *Nachrichten* nos. 104–105, pp. 134–135. On the route from Egypt to Melitene: K. Miller, *Itineraria romana*, Strecke 98, on pp. 680–684. Theoph. *Chron.* A.M. 6128 (340 De Boor). On alleged illness of Heraclius: Nikephoros, *Hist.* 24–25, 27 (72, 77 Mango).

[41] F.M. Donner, *Narratives of Islamic Origins* (Princeton: Darwin Press, 1998).

(*Chronicle* of Michael the Syrian and other shorter chronicles).[42] Heraclius had normally kept Constantinopolitans informed of his military activities against the Sasanians during the 620s, especially victorious ones, through military bulletins or open letters, but there is no reference to any such communications emanating from his stay in the vicinity of Edessa (or Amida/Diyarbekir) in 636/637.

Some facts are simple to understand. Byzantine retention of Mesopotamia first compelled Muslims in Syria and Iraq to divert troops from some other potential target, in particular Anatolia. Secondly, it preserved a forward base that could serve as a springboard for any possible Byzantine counter-offensive to recover territory lost to the Muslims, or for any attempt to make a joint counter-offensive in coordination with remaining Sasanian Persians, given Heraclius' recent good relations with Persians after the end of the long Byzantino–Persian War. Thirdly, it partially protected the Byzantine empire's Armenian territories, which were valuable recruiting grounds for Heraclius' soldiers, and commanders, from Muslim invasion and occupation. It was not clear whether the Muslims would be able to consolidate their hold on Syria. Retention of Mesopotamia provided a good Byzantine listening post and a place from which either an attack or dissension could be spread among the inhabitants of the newly occupied territories. Fourthly, that retention of Mesopotamia could affect recruitment among Arab tribesmen for Heraclius' armies; he had used them extensively in the 620s for his successful comeback against the Persians. By eliminating the Byzantine bulge or threat to Muslim communications, the Muslim conquest of Mesopotamia contributed to the termination of any remaining troublesome Persian resistance, consolidated control of Iraq, and finally was indeed the necessary prelude to any effort to overrun the four Byzantine provinces of Armenia and the local manpower.

Heraclius probably left some Byzantine troops in Persia, specifically in Iraq, in order to maintain Byzantine influence over the Persians, to try to provide a buffer on his own eastern frontier, and to stabilize the internal Persian situation in a manner favorable to Byzantine interests.[43] It may have served as a necessary prop to a friendly but weak Sasanian government

---

[42] L.I. Conrad, "The Conquest of Arwād: a Source-Critical Study in the Historiography of the Early Medieval Near East," in *Byzantine and Early Islamic Near East*, ed. Averil Cameron, L. Conrad, I: 332–341. For a reconstruction of a hypothesized "Syriac Common Source": Hoyland, *Seeing Islam as Others Saw It* 631–671.

[43] Kaegi, *BEIC* 151–157, for evidence for continuing *de facto* Byzantine armed presence in parts of the Sasanian Empire after the overthrow of Khusrau II. Also, Fredegarius, *Chronicle* 64 (53 Wallace-Hadrill), for a statement that Heraclius occupied Persia for three years; this may support that reading of the evidence. Robinson, *Empire and Elites after the Muslim Conquest* 26–27.

that he had installed in power and that was facing potential internal unrest and the risk of chaos.[44] Yet there were real limits to Heraclius' ability to control events and trends. An extended Byzantine presence, however token, also potentially overstrained and overextended Byzantine communications, logistics, manpower, and finance. It could offer little real resistance to the Muslims.

It was natural for the Muslims, having conquered Syria and Iraq, to wish to eradicate that salient or bulge of Byzantine Mesopotamia, which, theoretically at least, threatened the easiest and most convenient communication between Syria and Iraq. Its conquest was a prudent step in the consolidation of an empire. For Byzantium it was an agriculturally fertile and a rich province worth retaining. Yet the Byzantine presence in northern Iraq made it even more desirable for Heraclius to try to hold on to upper Mesopotamia, to the provinces of Osrhoene and Mesopotamia, in order to preserve communications and the ability to reinforce Byzantine garrisons in Iraq. Because some Byzantine troops were stationed in Iraq, there was some temptation and hope, presumably, that perhaps some coordinated action against the Muslims could be arranged and successfully implemented. Of course, that never happened. The basic question is the trustworthiness of the accounts of a Byzantine presence in Persia and a Persian presence in Byzantine territory. There are sufficient numbers of reported Byzantines to conclude that there probably was some overlapping presence. The losers in Persian civil strife probably found employment under the Byzantines. Heraclius probably did wish to draw on Persian advice about administering Syria and defending it from nomads. One would like to know more of the text of agreements between Shahrbarāz and Heraclius at Arabissos, in July 629, which is crucial for understanding the problem.[45] There probably were difficulties in ejecting all Persian troops from northern Mesopotamia. It was necessary for Theodore to besiege them at Edessa, it appears, in late 629 or 630. And it appears that some Persians remained in Syria, for example, in the Biqāʿ Valley at Baʿlabakk, after the other Persians withdrew from

---

[44] The clearest evidence for contemporary Byzantine anxiety about the Sasanian Empire, and the desirability of preserving it from falling into chaos, is Theophylact Simocatta's composition of a speech, written any time between 628 and 640, which he attributed to ambassadors of Chosroes II to Maurice (in 590): Theophylact Simocatta, *Hist.* 4.13.9, 4.13.13. But it helps to illuminate the mood at Heraclius' court that could have stimulated the decision to keep some troops in Persia to try to hold some kind of friendly government together. The internal situation in the Sasanian Empire was extremely fluid at that time. Byzantine hopes were high.

[45] Ibn ʿAbd al-Ḥakam, *Futūḥ Miṣr* 36–37 Torrey. On Arabissos: Friedrich Hild and Marcell Restle, *Kappadokien (Kappadokia, Charsianon, Sebasteia und Lykandos): Tabula Imperii Byzantini* (Vienna, 1981) II: 144–145.

areas they had previously occupied, in conformity with the agreement with Shahrbarāz at Arabissos in July 629.

The recent long war with the Persians left many legacies for the warfare between Byzantines and Muslims. This is especially true for Byzantine Mesopotamia. The existence of Byzantine officials in part of northern Iraq, as well as troops there, made it all the more desirable to try to hold on to Byzantine Mesopotamia in order to preserve communications and the ability to reinforce the others. Their presence made Mesopotamia and northern Syria and their roads and towns all the more vital. They also seriously complicated decision-making on the defense of Byzantine Syria and Mesopotamia. It was much more difficult to decide to evacuate Mesopotamia when there was the recent experience of also occupying part of Iraq. The situation created a natural reluctance to give up all of this, even though that was the rational decision to make in those circumstances. Except for underscoring the provisional and volatile military and civilian and ecclesiastical situation in those areas, the identification of these Byzantine troops in Sasanian Persia and the presence of Persians in Byzantine territory does not, on balance, probably change very much of what we know. But it does provide a fuller and more nuanced historical understanding.

To contemporaries, the recent victory of Heraclius over the Persians, despite the initially great negative odds, may well have strongly affected perceptions and calculations about strategy and military operations after the conquest of Syria. From the Muslims' perspective it was critical to prevent any repeat of successful Byzantine recruiting among Armenians and elsewhere in the Caucasus, which had proved so important to Heraclius in the 620s.[46] For Muslim military interests, in addition to eliminating the Byzantine bulge or threat to communications, the conquest of Mesopotamia was indeed the necessary prelude to any effort to overrun the four Byzantine provinces of Armenia and thereby deny Heraclius access to Armenian recruits. The sparse extant sources do not explain these motives, which simply emerge from any reflection on the actual military situation in the 630s and the immediately preceding military historical events that would have formed the frame of reference for those making military decisions.[47]

---

[46] Hypothesis that (1) the famous Mardaites of the late seventh century may have been stationed earlier in various parts of Armenia IV, including Mardes (Mardin) in upper Mesopotamia, and (2) originated near Theodosiopolis (Erzurum): Hratz Bartikian, Η λύση τοῦ αἰνίγματος τῶν Μαρδαϊτῶν, in *ByzStratos* I: 17–39, makes a strong case.

[47] Muslim conquest of Armenia: Kaegi, *BEIC* 181–204.

The Byzantine situation in Syria became untenable even though they still, after Yarmūk, held major walled towns. The able Muslim commander 'Iyāḍ b. Ghanm had penetrated as far north as Melitene, a key communications point and fortress on the upper Euphrates. Its inhabitants surrendered on terms. Although the compiler may well have erroneously and confusedly compressed a lot of unrelated material under the year 635/636, a reference in that year to the slaying of Simon, doorkeeper of Qedar, brother of Thomas the priest (the compiler would remember the date of his brother's death, unless errors in transmission have garbled the entry), in the Tūr 'Abdīn region at the hands of raiding Arabs may corroborate that deep penetration by 'Iyāḍ b. Ghanm or other Muslims.[48] 'Iyāḍ imperiled Byzantine communications with any troops in Syria and upper Mesopotamia. They needed a rest, not more battle. The empire had territorial depth and could, at a terribly high price, purchase time to try to reorganize and recover.

At Melitene (Malatya) in late 636 Heraclius showed resoluteness. Ibn Isḥāq reports, after the battle of the Yarmūk, according to al-Ṭabarī,

And when the Byzantines were defeated, Abū 'Ubayda sent 'Iyāḍ b. Ghanm in pursuit of them. He followed them, passing through al-A'māq until he reached Malatya. He made a treaty with its inhabitants for the payment of the headtax [*jizya*] and he returned. When Heraclius heard about this he sent to the military forces and their commander and ordered them to Malatya. On Heraclius' order Malatya was burned.[49]

Heraclius' reaction in this instance was consistent with his rejectionist policies elsewhere in Syria and later in Egypt, but the incident also underscores his alertness and readiness to develop an active defense of the edge of Anatolia.

Heraclius was in no position to direct the defense of remaining Byzantine positions in Palestine and Syria. Some of the essential outlines of events emerge dimly, even though contradictory and fragmentary sources admittedly leave many loose ends. Only scraps of information exist about the fall of individual towns, such as the unique and generally plausible account, despite martyrological embellishments, of the "Sixty Martyrs of Gaza."[50] Jerusalem fell, and Gaza's garrison yielded soon thereafter. Heraclius could

---

[48] Andrew Palmer, "Extract from a Chronicle Composed about AD 640," AG 947, in *The Seventh Century in the West Syrian Chronicles* 19.

[49] Al-Ṭabarī (Ibn Isḥāq) 1.2349.

[50] H. Delehaye, "Passio sanctorum sexaginta martyrum," *Analecta Bollandiana* 23 (1904) 289–307; J. Pargoire, 'Les LX Soldats Martyrs de Gaza," *EO* 8 (1905) 40–43.

do nothing for the small garrison that surrendered to the Muslims at Gaza.[51]

Heraclius, reportedly while still at Antioch, presumably in late 636, ordered his commanders to try to hold on to whatever they could, but to avoid open battle with the Muslims.[52] This tradition seems plausible. He sought to take advantage of Byzantine fortifications, preference for fighting behind fortifications, and the need to rebuild shattered confidence. He ordered Melitene recaptured and burned because his troops were unable to hold it.[53] But this was part of Heraclius' efforts to take successful control of remaining Byzantine strongpoints. He did not want any locals or their leaders to negotiate separate terms with the Muslims. His orders to try to hold out from fixed positions may reflect his early experiences in Africa, where locals survived temporary infestations of Berber raiders by taking short-term asylum in walled towns or fortresses. But most Syrian cities soon fell.[54]

Consistent with his advanced age, Heraclius developed a very conservative strategy for preserving territory, manpower, and what limited governmental funds remained. He tried to minimize risk by avoiding more risky battles. Although he had been a risk-taker in military campaigns earlier in his life, he now adopted a more cautious course. In the short run his policy effectively conceded vast territories and towns to the Muslims, unless and until some strategy of reconquest and recovery could be conceived and implemented. It was not to be.

[51] The Latin martyrological account cannot receive completely uncritical acceptance, but its essential details are plausible. The skepticism of R. Hoyland, *Seeing Islam as Others Saw It* 347–351, is unjustifiable. Its reference not merely to names of soldiers but also to their specific military units is important and decisive. For example, the *Scythae Iustiniani* are a genuine Byzantine unit mentioned in sixth-century papyri, and moreover, were stationed while in Egypt sometimes in Sinai, near to southern Palestine: Jean Gascou, "La table budgétaire d'Antaeopolis (*P. Freer 08.45 c-d*)," in *Hommes et richesses dans l'Empire byzantin* (Paris: Editions P. Lethielleux, 1989) I: 281, 290, 301 line 26, 309–310. Also see sixth-century papyrus (*P. Oxy.* XVI 1920.3–5, XVI.2046.10–12, 17–25, 42–43) of Apion family estates, ed. by T.M. Hickey, "A Public 'House' but Closed: Fiscal Participation and Economic Decision Making on the Oxyrhynchite Estate of the Flavii Apiones" 159. Military units were shifted around in the military emergencies of the seventh century, irrespective of their normal postings; this was no normal situation, so older epigraphic attestions of proper names, to which Hoyland appeals, are irrelevant in the emergency. Units were moved from one end of the Empire to the other. The Latin martyrological text about Gaza has a historical core. It uses the correct contemporary term *bandum* for military units, and above all a documented specific *bandum*, which no tenth-century copyist or writer could have discovered or interpolated in the tenth or eleventh century.
[52] Michael the Syrian, *Chronique* II: 424–425 Chabot. *Histoire Nestorienne/Chronicle of Si'irt* 116 (*PO* 13: 626). Agapios, *Kitāb al-Unvān, PO* 8: 471. [Anonymous] *Chronicon ad annum Christi 1234 pertinens* c. 117 (196–197 Chabot). Beihammer, *Nachrichten* no. 108, pp. 136–138.
[53] Ṭabarī (Ibn Isḥāq) 1.2349.
[54] Beihammer, *Nachrichten* nos. 107–120, 122–159, pp. 136–150, 152–185.

It was extremely embittering for Heraclius to see land and people in Syria and upper Mesopotamia again slip out of Byzantine hands, after only recently recovering them, at a high cost in lives, money, and strain. Heraclius himself was somewhat familiar with Anatolia, given his repeated campaigning there since 612/613. But he also witnessed the utility of forti-fying strongpoints in Africa, which could serve as places of temporary refuge for the military and civilians and their livestock. Although aging, he had endured conditions of severe heat in Africa in his early maturity, be-tween roughly twenty-five and thirty-five years of age. He could appreciate some conditions in the east better because of that experience. Yet his earlier African experiences could not really prepare him well to cope with the rise of Islam. The problem was whether this was simply an unusually large infestation of beduin raiders that could be waited out, or was it something more, of a different qualitative sort. Yet he was able to think in terms of an empire that stretched to the ends of Africa. He conceived, whether for drawing on military resources or for exiling undesirables, of his control of Africa in the larger scope of his range of policy options.

Heraclius was too fixed in his ways, at age sixty, especially given the rigid intellectual frameworks of the era, to be able to find flexible, creative solutions to the Muslim invasions. The new challenge was too radical for him and his mental horizons and repertory of experiences and the repertory of writings that he and his advisers could rapidly consult.

There was a related problem. By the late 630s, the aged Heraclius was po-tentially a known quantity to his opponents, who could draw on previous experience to anticipate just how he would react to their specific military moves. There was less mystery to him. They were more of a mystery to him than he was to them. They could understand the potential repertory of his responses to military challenges. They had ways, through conversa-tions with those Arabs who had served with him against the Sasanians, to understand his strengths and weaknesses. That was a significant asset for them.

Despite the horrendous territorial losses that the empire suffered in Syria and upper Mesopotamia, no breakaway Byzantine leaders emerged, as would be the case in the eleventh century in the wake of the Seljuk in-vasions. There was no Byzantine Shahrbarāz, just as there was no Muslim one. No successful mutinies or revolts by frustrated military comman-ders occurred on the edge of Muslim-conquered territories in Syria and upper Mesopotamia. No autonomous princes appeared. That contrasted completely with the centrifugal rebellions and autonomy movements a few decades later in Byzantine North Africa, in Sicily, and in Italy, all of which, significantly, were more remote from Constantinople and from imperial control. Heraclius managed, despite the terrible defeats, to keep tight control of the Byzantine armies and soldiers who evacuated Syria and upper Mesopotamia in the years 636–639. The evidence is circumstantial: the absence of any major rebellions in Anatolia or adjacent areas in the wake of the Muslim victories in Syria. That speaks strongly for his ability, even in the midst of familial quarrels, to dominate the internal security situation. How he managed to do that is uncertain. Somehow he managed to maintain the initiative, somehow he managed to convince contemporaries that he had taken charge and was doing his best to stop the hemorrhaging. He assumed responsibility for overseeing the withdrawal and regrouping of Byzantine forces. He still knew how to maintain or reassert some controls on his best troops.

Sources, probably deriving from those transmitted by Theophilos of Edessa, report that Heraclius became furious at a special agreement that John Kateas, the *epitropos* of Osrhoene, made with the Muslim conqueror of upper Mesopotamia, 'Iyāḍ b. Ghanm, at Chalkis. This *patrikios* had agreed to pay a heavy tribute to the Muslims to persuade them from invading his two provinces of Osrhoene and Mesopotamia. Heraclius removed him and replaced with a general, Ptolemaios.[55] But the Muslims under 'Iyāḍ b. Ghanm then invaded Mesopotamia. In these circumstances, the inhabitants of Edessa were forced to beg for terms for themselves and for Ptolemaios, who was then sent back to what remained of Byzantine territory, after the Muslims occupied Edessa and the surrounding province. The specificity of the terminology of Theophanes' source (e.g. Osrhoene and Mesopotamia, and *epitropos*) argues for the authenticity of this account even though some parts of Theophanes derive from a later period.

Heraclius had not simply thrown up his hands and evacuated. He tried to continue to maintain control and to avoid allowing local commanders to cut their own deals with the Muslims, which would have, in effect, undercut the supreme authority of the central imperial government. By taking this action Heraclius made an important point, even though the outcome was a swift Muslim invasion by 'Iyāḍ b. Ghanm, whose troops quickly overran

---

[55] Theoph. *Chron.* A.M. 6128 (340 De Boor, 472 Mango). Michael the Syrian, *Chronique* 11.7 (II: 426 Chabot). Agapios, *Kitāb al-Unvān, PO* 8: 476, who adds that Heraclius exiled Paul, which is an error for John Kateas, to Africa. Beihammer, *Nachrichten* nos. 121, 160–171, pp. 151–152, 185–200, persuasively argues for a separation of information about a 637 negotiation at Chalkis between Abū 'Ubayda and an unidentified Byzantine *patrikios* for a truce, from that of 638 between 'Iyāḍ b. Ghanm and John Kateas. Arguments that John Kateas may simply be a governor whose function has been lost in the Greek rendering of an unknown Syriac term: Brandes, *Finanzverwaltung in Krisenzeiten* 590–595.

the provinces. Heraclius needed the local revenues and certainly did not wish those revenues to flow to and to strengthen his enemies, the Muslims. This occurred in 638/639. The Muslims, for their part, offered no face-saving solutions to Heraclius. It quickly became apparent that the Muslims would not become even nominal *foederati* or allies of the empire. It later became inconceivable to consider such an outcome, but to some Byzantine contemporaries, there might have been some momentary hope for that. But it was not to be.

We have no actual records of Heraclius' reaction to the loss of the Holy Places to the Muslims.[56] This was a great reversal of fortune. The religious significance may have cut several ways. First, there was the aspect of some kind of evidence of divine wrath, but divine anger for what reason? It is clear that some contemporaries were very aware that a prophet had arisen among the Muslims, but just how much these events, and the fall of Jerusalem and other holy places was seen as an immediate sign of triumph of another religion, instead of primarily as a much larger infestation of savage beduin than normal, is unclear. At least some valuable relics, such as the fragments of the Cross, had been saved and dispatched to Constantinople.

Heraclius did not call for any Crusade against the Muslims, nor did Patriarch Sophronios of Jerusalem, as is evident from his Christmas (634) sermon.[57] There is no initial evidence, that is, in the context of the early and middle 630s, of any Byzantine consciousness of the Muslim invasions as the expression of a new religion. It would be incorrect to read back later experiences and perspectives into those years when seeking to evaluate Heraclius. He skillfully had striven to maintain close relations with his subjects through open letters and military bulletins during his campaigning against the Persians. Muslim traditions suggest that he did endeavor to communicate with his subjects during the Muslim conquests, but no reliable records exist of those communications or how he or his advisers sought to portray or explain imperial strategy, tactics, military experiences, or the successes of the empire's opponents. Records of such communications could have disappeared from the historical records for many reasons, but any conclusions about his handling of public relations are sheer speculations.

---

[56] Muslim and hostile Christian traditions that Heraclius regarded the Muslims as a flail of God or the will of God (Agapios, *Kitāb al-Unvān, PO* 8: 471, 473) deserve skepticism.

[57] Sophronios, "Weihnachtspredigt," ed. H. Usener, *Rheinisches Museum für Philologie*, N.F. 41 (1886) 506–515. Rejection of the conception of Byzantine holy war or crusading: G. Dennis, "Defenders of the Christian People: Holy War in Byzantium," in *The Crusades from the Perspective of Byzantium and the Muslim World*, ed. Angeliki E. Laiou, Roy Parviz Mottahedeh (Washington: Dumbarton Oaks, 2001) 31–39; Haldon, *Warfare, State and Society* 27–33.

Heraclius might have tried to remain at Antioch or some other town south of the Tauros Mountains, to try to devise some new defenses against the Muslims. But no such city, including Antioch, was an optimal place to reside. To the extent that the empire's problems were primarily in Syria, or upper Mesopotamia, that might have been the case. But the Muslims also threatened Egypt. Antioch or other northern Syrian cities, or those in upper Mesopotamia, lacked good communications with Egypt. Land communications with Egypt had been interrupted by the Muslim advances for some time, probably almost from the beginning of the Muslim invasion of Palestine in 634. Although the permanent invasion of Egypt did not begin until late 639, the threat had arisen earlier, and there were other ecclesiastical and fiscal problems to arrange with Kyros and other officials and commanders in Egypt. Constantinople was a better place from which to arrange that, if at all possible anyway, than was Antioch. Muslim successes against Egypt understandably caused Heraclius to grieve.[58]

Another problem probably affected Heraclius' decision to evacuate Syria and his timing. Heraclius left Syria via Samosata or Edessa, where he had presumably found himself in territory and an environment highly volatile and of problematic loyalty due to the extensive presence of Monophysites there,[59] While probably not openly disloyal, Heraclius and his advisers may have viewed the local peoples as more ready to switch sides or become neutral or passive. This was not a propitious place for him to stay after the stunning defeat of his armies and allies at Yarmūk. But in the meantime he identified places for resistance against the Muslims. His earlier travels and campaigns in these areas probably helped him to choose strongpoints and areas to turn into scorched-earth zones of devastation.

The cascading defeats of the Byzantines probably worsened Heraclius' health. Such news depressed him, caused him to grieve. And the news from the fronts with the Muslims simply became worse; it never improved during his lifetime.

We do not know whether Heraclius and his advisers attempted to comprehend the reasons for their defeats, or how they rapidly sought to devise new methods to resist the Muslims. That process occurred, but we cannot trace it closely. There surely would have been many special review sessions where Heraclius and his commanders and advisers tried to argue through, thrash out, and explain what had happened and how to find formulae for avoiding more defeats and for transforming the still deteriorating military

---

[58] John of Nikiu, *Chron.* 116 (184 Charles).
[59] Al-Ṭabarī 1.2390–2391. Azdī 212–213 Lees. Ibn al-Athīr 2.384 Tornberg.

situation. Some blame fell on his brother Theodore.[60] Fatigue from protracted war with the Sasanians is a common explanation for Byzantine or Heraclius' inability to resist the Muslim advance in the 630s. Although exhaustion of finances and will power may well have been causes, contemporary sources (and even later Muslim ones) do not ascribe the outcome to them. If anything, the public representations of Heraclius emphasize his generosity, and his renewal and reconstruction of physical damages. These are unsurprising *topoi*. But exhaustion, however real, is not an element of the contemporary public culture. The zealous public expenditures for reconstruction and for beautification in fact competed with and reduced available resources for financing military resistance to the Muslims. They probably contributed to weakening military resistance although they encouraged popular appreciation of the imperial government and its concern for their local well-being.

Heraclius' forces had continued to occupy part of Sasanian territory after the triumph over Khusrau II, probably as far into the Sasanian Empire as Hit on the Euphrates and Takrīt on the Tigris.[61] The *de facto* Byzantine occupation or stationing of some troops in northwestern Sasanian territory, as some Muslim sources and Fredegarius attest, is at odds with one modern claim that Heraclius in 628–630 accepted borders short of the former Byzantine ones with the Sasanians. There had been no formal redrawing of the borders, but this presence of small numbers of Byzantine troops, together with allied Arabs, allowed the Byzantines the opportunity to monitor the situation in Persia, with some potential to intervene. Such action also protected Byzantine interests in Armenia. Muslim accounts of their conquest of Iraq refer to the presence of Byzantine troops and commanders among the opposing forces. The enfeebled internal Sasanian political situation helps to explain that situation. The lines of communication with the Sasanian leadership were potentially open, in ways that had been inconceivable in early decades and centuries of their relations, but Heraclius was unable to devise any satisfactory mutual collaboration against the Muslims. The Muslim conquest of upper Mesopotamia in 639 cut off Byzantine and Sasanian communications, except by extremely circuitous and hazardous routes that were closed in inclement times of the year. So the hopes for the conversion of Christians in Iraq to Orthodoxy, for collaboration, began to fade quickly in the 630s, especially by the late 630s. Yet wisps of those hopes remained. A member of the powerful Sasanian Christian family of Iesdem (Yazdin) participated

[60] Michael the Syrian, *Chronique* 11.5 (II: 418 Chabot).   [61] Kaegi, *BEIC* 153–157.

in an important court ceremony in early 639, almost two years after the battle of Qādisiyya had already shattered the Sasanian Empire in regions close to Byzantium. But those wisps remained. How much advice the family of Iesdem gave to Heraclius and his advisers about how to handle the Muslims is unknown and in any case it did not solve the crisis. Monetary confusion and chaos engulfed areas of the Sasanian empire adjacent to Byzantium.[62]

Heraclius' earlier experiences in Africa probably stimulated him to take a greater interest than some of his predecessors in diplomacy with Spain and with Merovingian Franks. In itself this does not explain the Frankish king Dagobert's order for the conversion of Jews. But Heraclius was probably mindful of the strategic and commercial significance of Spain and Gaul, given his ten years in Africa.

There were stark contrasts between images of Roman and Biblical triumphalism[63] and the realities of terror, flight, devastation, financial ruin, famine, and death. An earlier earthquake and earlier sightings of an ill-omened comet intensified fears.[64]

In the first twenty-five years of his reign Heraclius unwittingly tilted the empire towards becoming more Middle Eastern through his continued presence in western Asia, during and after his campaigns against the Sasanians. External pressures, not his own volition, were the cause. It was impractical, in those years of such great stress, to take time to visit or reside in Latin-speaking provinces or to dwell on their problems and circumstances. The empire that he had wrested from Phokas was not an innately Near Eastern one, for its dimensions stretched to the Atlantic. But by the end of his reign the western and central Mediterranean elements, however important, had become more tenuous and exposed and were slipping away, leaving a torso that was more Middle Eastern, although never completely so, given its Romano-Hellenic heritages. And it was losing key parts of its Middle Eastern territories and populations and urban and rural culture as well, as the Muslims overran Syria, Palestine, upper Mesopotamia, and began to invade Egypt.

Yet in the final decade of his life and reign no living holy man or saint stands out as special counselor to Heraclius. There was no new Theodore of Sykeon, in so far as tradition has preserved any names. Heraclius sought to

---

[62] Stuart D. Sears, "A Monetary History of Iraq and Iran, ca. 500 to 750" (unpub. Ph.D. diss., University of Chicago, 1997) 366–376, provides the most thorough investigation of fiscal and economic conditions within the Sasanian Empire.

[63] Triumphalism: David Olster, *Roman Defeat, Christian Response and the Literary Construction of the Jew* (Philadelphia: University of Pennsylvania Press, 1994) 35–45, 63–64.

[64] Theophanes, *Chron.* A.M. 6124 (467 Mango-Scott).

identify himself, his reign, and his success with holy men earlier in his life. If anything, dreams allegedly were an influence on Heraclius, but that may well result from selective preservation of memory. His critics later stressed that certain contemporary holy men delivered hostile predictions about him and his family.

Another limitation on Heraclius' power was internal unrest in Armenia and its outcome. This shook up the imperial family, the court, and Heraclius' relationships with Armenian commanders. The unsuccessful plot in 637 to slay Heraclius and replace him with Heraclius' illegitimate son Athalaric involved Heraclius' nephew the *magister officiorum* Theodore, the son of Heraclius' brother Theodore, various unidentified local magnates in Constantinople, and a powerful Armenian general, David Saharuni, whom Heraclius had arrested in 637. A palace *curator* exposed the plot before its conspirators could act. But David, who had been arrested and bound, escaped, killed his captor the *aspet* Mzhezh Gnuni, and ultimately was able to have himself accepted as *ishan* (prince) of Armenia. Heraclius was unable to get rid of him. The Armenian *aspet* Varaztirots', whose friendship Heraclius had cultivated, was aware of, but did not directly participate in, the conspiracy. His conduct was sufficiently suspicious that Heraclius exiled him to Africa:

"In return for your acting thus towards me, and not wishing to lay your hand on my life and that of my sons, I shall not set my hand on you or your sons. But go and stay where I shall command you, and I shall have mercy upon you." Although his supporters often cried out: "Let him die," yet he [Heraclius] did not wish to heed them. But he ordered him and his wife and children to be taken to an island and the city of constraint which they call "Exile."[65]

As in Italy and the Balkans, at times Heraclius had to acquiesce. This was a remarkable case of such acquiescence. His victories over the Sasanians had not enabled him to gain absolute control of Armenia. Heraclius could not afford and may well have been physically unable or sufficiently wealthy to campaign in Armenia personally to suppress David Saharuni, who enjoyed the support of many prominent Armenian commanders.

The background to the conspiracy is hard to understand, but some elements stand out. Heraclius' power remained very fragile in his final years, especially his ability to control regions beyond the perimeters of Constantinople and environs. Heraclius' brother Theodore had, according to Nikephoros' source, harshly criticized Heraclius' marriage to Martina

---

[65] Sebeos, *Hist.* 133, ch. 41, 143, ch. 44 (93, 107 Thomson); *PMBZ* V: 84, no. 8567, s.v. "Varaztiroc'." The precise locale in Africa is unidentified.

("His sin is continually before him").[66] Heraclius ordered his son Heraclius Constantine to dishonor him publicly and imprison him. Angry reaction to parental disgrace probably caused Theodore's son, the *magister officiorum* Theodore, to participate in the abortive plot in favor of Athalaric.[67] Heraclius already resorted to using public dishonor in the cases of Priskos, Theodore senior, and would soon again, in the case of Kyros, the Alexandrian Patriarch and Augustalis. Presumably Theodore's father Theodore was no longer a possible candidate. In any case Athalaric and Theodore the *magister* were mutilated, that is, their noses and hands were cut off. There ensued the exile of Athalaric to nearby Prinkipo Island and Theodore to the island of Gaudomelete (Malta). Theodore suffered still more mutilation on Heraclius' order: one leg was cut off. Their plot threatened Heraclius Constantine and Heraclius as well as Martina, that is, all members of the core of the imperial household. But any possible solidarity between Martina and Heraclius Constantine was fleeting.[68] Nikephoros has drawn on some source hostile to the Heraclian dynasty, possibly a source hostile to Monotheletism or a source that emerged after the fall of the Heraclian dynasty, possibly even the mysterious late seventh-century Trajan, who is mentioned as a chronicler by Photios. There probably had been considerable internal political troubles within Heraclius' empire before he had set out to eject the Persians.[69]

News of the conspiracy, even though it failed, can only have increased dismay and disillusionment among the empire's subjects at this moment of great external threat. It increased doubts and increased finger-pointing, fear, controversy, and uncertainty. It did not boost morale and solidarity in opposition to the Muslims. The conspirators became an object lesson of the fate of plotters, but all of this was a major distraction to Heraclius, who was probably trying to dream up ways to split the Muslims and to utilize such divisions to cause their invasion to disintegrate. The conspiracy took place at a terrible time, just when the empire's leaders were trying to devise responses to the Muslims and to solve the difficult ecclesiastical dissensions. It shocked and grieved Heraclius. It indicated that he could not rely even on members of his family. Heraclius was at the Hiereia palace near Constantinople at the time of the conspiracy, according to Nikephoros, and

---

[66] Nikephoros, *Short Hist.* p. 69 Mango trans.   [67] *PLRE* III: 1284–1285, s.v. "Theodorus 171."
[68] Comments on possible rivalry within the family: P. Speck, *Das geteilte Dossier* 416–418.
[69] George of Pisidia, *Exped. Pers.* 3.444, 449–51, 457 (135, 136 Pertusi). See the analysis of Claudia Ludwig, "Kaiser Herakleios, Georgios Pisides und die Perserkriege," in *Varia* III, Ποικίλα Βυζαντινά, 11 (1991) 87–88. There are no extant details, except for difficulties in Italy. Constantinopolitans' nervousness about Heraclius' absence from Constantinople: Mary Whitby, "Defender of the Cross: George of Pisidia on the Emperor Heraclius and His Deputies," in Whitby, *The Propaganda of Power* 250–253.

Fig. 5. Heraclius' portrait, with Heraclius Constantine to his left and Heraklonas to
Heraclius' right, from a solidus ca. 635–636; Constantinople (obverse, *DOCat* 33b).

Sebeos adds the details that Heraclius ordered the arrest of the conspirators
the next morning.[70]

The conspirators probably tried to use the embarrassing Byzantine defeats as another incentive or opportunity to incite and take advantage of
unhappiness and disillusionment with Heraclius. News of the conspiracy,
even though a failure, can only have encouraged the Muslims and even
other remaining discontents, for not all of them had been identified and
eliminated, in peripheral regions, such as Italy. The plot increased mistrust
at a critical time. It poisoned the atmosphere at Constantinople, at the
court, and in many regional centers. It exacerbated the existing volatility of
many variables. The aging process had already taken its toll on Heraclius,
to judge from his portrait on imperial coinage from the early 630s, possibly
632–635 (?). By 636/7 he looked more aged (Fig. 5).[71]

The failure of the conspiracy made Heraclius even more dependent
on the shrinking number of reliable individuals whose ranks included
Philagrios. Philagrios evidently was in no way implicated with the conspirators, for otherwise he would not have survived as powerful *sakellarios*
at the end of Heraclius's reign. His position was too powerful to concede
to anyone of doubtful loyalty. An unidentified *curator* reported the conspiracy. Viraztirots' was partially implicated, but was exiled with his family.
Armenian military leaders as well as prominent men of Constantinople
were implicated and ruined.

The conspiracy probably increased Heraclius' suspicions of others. It
forced him to keep some of the best troops at Constantinople as a safe-
guard against more plots, as well as to investigate, interrogate, and remove
other potentially fine soldiers but who were of doubtful loyalty, if not proven
disloyalty in the light of this and other events. It might well have exacerbated any Post-Traumatic Stress Disorder that afflicted him. It complicated
the devising of the defense of Anatolia and Egypt, and made it even more

[70] Sebeos, *History* 133, ch. 41 (92–93 Thomson); *Hist.* c. 29 (93 Macler). Nikephoros, *Short History* 24
(72–73 Mango).
[71] *DOCat* 33b (632–635(?), 36b dated tentatively to 636/637(?).

unlikely to contemplate Heraclius, or his son Heraclius Constantine, assuming direct personal command at or near the front against the Muslims. He continued to surround himself with Armenian guards and officers, but turned to ones that he believed were loyal. It was necessary for Heraclius and Heraclius Constantine to remain at or near Constantinople. They could not afford to leave and run the risk of other plots at the capital. It was too risky, therefore, in addition, for reasons of internal security. The public reaction to all of this at Constantinople is unclear. No records exist of any special ceremonies of public thanksgiving, however stylized and contrived, for the safety and welfare of the emperor and his family after the failure of this conspiracy. It was impossible to hide the news of the conspiracy, which diverse sources, relying on different traditions, transmit. Probably some reacted, looking through the lens of respective ecclesiastical points of view, seeking to interpret this as a vindication of their own Christologies.

What Heraclius did not do was threaten, as he once had during the war against the Persians, to move to Carthage. His own health and perhaps his alleged fear of water both made that impractical. Moreover, the external situation in the east was even riskier than in the previous war against the Persians, so flight could have proved fatal for Anatolia and possibly even Constantinople.

Heraclius' extended presence in the east exacerbated Byzantine challenges in Italy and Africa. In such circumstances, in the absence of close supervision, it is even more understandable that there were problems for soldiers in Italy receiving timely stipends. Other aspects of Byzantine administration in Italy, Sicily, and Africa probably suffered from neglect and drift, resulting in autonomous or centrifugal tendencies. However much Heraclius was interested in those western regions, he was not in a position to give them, with their own extensive problems and challenges, the attention that they deserved. This tempted others who were aware of the military crisis in the east to exploit circumstances.

The deteriorating situation in the Balkans worsened.[72] Slavs settled in the Peloponnese in the second and third decades of the seventh century. Economic conditions there exacerbated the shortage of imperial revenues due to actual and impending territorial losses in Syria, Palestine, and Egypt.[73] Insecurity intensified, as papal correspondence of Honorius I concerning

---

[72] Paul Lemerle, *Les plus anciens recueils des miracles de Saint Démétrius* II: 139–140.

[73] Anna Avramea, *Le Peloponnèse du IVe au VIIIe siècle: changements et persistances* (Paris, 1997) 71, 158–159. T.E. Gregory, *Isthmia*, V: *The Hexamilion and the Fortress* (Princeton, 1993) 145. J. Karayannopoulos, "Zur Frage der Slavenansiedlung im griechischen Raum," in *Byzanz und seine Nachbarn*, ed. Armin Hohlweg (Südosteuropa-Jahrbuch, 26; Munich: Südosteuropa-Gesellschaft, 1996) 177–218.

Epirus Nova indicates in 625 that travel had become too risky for Hypatios, the metropolitan of Nikopolis, to attempt to journey to Rome.[74] Eastern challenges made it impossible for Heraclius to contemplate relief for beleaguered subjects in the Balkans. As always, the unhappy memories of Phokas' rebellion and earlier mutinies there at the end of the previous century contributed to a disinclination to intervene in any massive way.

[74] Ep. Honorius VIII, *PL* 80: 478.

CHAPTER 8

Losing control

Everything coalesced to compel Heraclius to remain in the vicinity of Constantinople after the debacle of the Yarmūk: his health, danger of conspiracies, and the need to be at the communications center of the empire to filter and coordinate news from Egypt as well as other far-flung, and more proximate but vulnerable fronts. After returning to Constantinople, he participated in public ceremonies and engaged with the public. He needed to reinforce his image, and that of his potential successor, Heraclius Constantine. There was not much to celebrate as a triumph, for the news was pessimistic on all external frontiers of the empire. At Constantinople, some semblance of old practices persisted to keep up the spirits of the public and the imperial family itself. Liturgical feasts continued. The Hippodrome remained the location of games, as in previous eras. Customary activities did not halt for the external crises.

Heraclius and his advisers sought to project an image of imperturbability, foresight, harmony, mastery, and orderly process, partly out of respect for tradition, but also to make a contrast with recent experiences of internal chaos and disturbances and external calamities far from Constantinople and its environs. Accidental preservation or calculation may explain the survival of several records of ceremonies at Constantinople from the final years of Heraclius' reign and life. They provide invaluable glimpses into the public memories of the waning moments of Heraclius' reign. For example:

...on 4 July, eleventh indiction [AD 638], the Imperator (*Autokrator*) and great emperor [Heraclius] wishing to announce the promotion of his son from the rank of Caesar to the dignity of emperor acted in the following manner. The Patriarch and all of the senators were summoned. The Patriarch approached the emperor, with Constantine his [Heraklonas'] brother being present. Prayer took place in the [chapel] of the holy Stephen of Daphne. His *kamelaukion* [a kind of cap or head covering] was removed from his head and the imperial crown was placed on his head. There was prayer for the *despotes* David as the *kamelaukion* was placed on his head as he ascended to the rank of Caesar. That having been done, the most glorious Patricians were summoned according to custom, and they entered the Augusteum and received the great emperor and his sons, with the Caesar being present. All ex-consuls and those with ranks as high as *illustres* departed and stood on the steps of the forecourt. The gates of the armory were opened and all of the standards (*signa*) and *scholae* and demes [factions] entered. The Patriarch exited with them [the emperor and his sons]. And with everyone acclaiming them, the emperor and his sons departed for the Great Church. Everything took place according to form in the Great Church.[1]

This ceremony celebrated a great and joyous and solemn occasion, but it masked and smoothed over genuine tensions and rivalries between the descendants of Heraclius' first and second marriages. Pageantry was a fundamental component of the event. Orderly continuity, legitimate succession, and religious sanctification of the process were essential. Heraclius himself had probably been crowned in the same chapel of St. Stephen in the palace complex on 5 October 610. The ritual endeavored to underscore a well-thought-out and sanctified familial and imperial succession. Heraclius had made his son Heraclius (Heraklonas) emperor on 4 January 638, then consul in 639, probably on 1 January. He reportedly proclaimed his sons David and Martinos Caesars, the former on 4 January 638, but the latter may have only been named *nobilissimus*, and his daughters Augustina and Martina Augustas.[2] His efforts solidified nothing, merely arousing more controversy and resentment. They were occasions for a little more ceremonial and pageantry at Constantinople in an otherwise doleful era. These formal acts raise another question: did Heraclius try to intervene to handle sensitive issues of potential rivalry between his heirs, and their wives? In the long term, no such effort succeeded, but we simply have no reliable information of any possible efforts of his to heal strife within his own family.

Heraclius' coinage likewise proclaimed familial unity and provision for a smooth transition in any imperial succession, showing an elderly long-bearded Heraclius standing taller but nevertheless between his sons Heraclius Constantine and Heraklonas (Fig. 6).[3] The official picture is a forced show of harmony despite the underlying rivalries and tensions that Heraclius was unable to dispel or control. There is a gap between external appearances and internal realities.

[1] Constantine VII Porphyrogenitus, *De cerim.*, ed. J. Reiske (*CSHB*; Bonn, 1829) 627–628.
[2] Constantine VII, *De cerim.* 629–630 Reiske.
[3] Grierson, *DOCat* 41a, 41c, 42a, 42b dated to 638/639?, 43b, 43g both dated to 639(?)–641; Hahn, *Moneta Imperii Byzantini* III: nos. 48, 49.

Fig. 6. Heraclius' portrait with Heraclius Constantine and Heraklonas, each with crown, from solidi; Constantinople (obverses, a. *DO Cat* 42a, ca. 641; b. *DO Cat* 43b, ca. 639–641).

Another solemn event occurred almost a half year later:

On the first of the month of January, 12th indiction [639], the emperor made a procession to the Great Church. The *despotes* Constantine departed with him, wearing a tunic, and the *despotes* Heraclius and [his, the emperor's] son wore the toga *praetextata*, and was supported on the arm of his own brother. The Patricians Niketas and John and the Patrician attached to Iesdem [Yazdin] and the Patrician Dometios and the *magister* Eustathios wore togas, while the other officials wore pure silk tunics, and some of the ex-consuls wore the consular *loros* [sash]. Having entered the Great Church they lit candles and everything went according to form and was valid.[4]

Here again a splendid ceremony displayed minute attention to dress and to the show of harmony within the imperial family. The presence of a Sasanian or former Sasanian dignitary (Yazdin had been Treasurer or Comptroller of the Sasanian Empire) underscores the vain hopes that still burned for exploiting the fruits of Heraclius' earlier victories over Khusrau II for the sake of the church and empire, even as the Muslims were triumphing over both empires.

The strongest demonstration of familial and imperial solidarity, despite the rivalries between the descendants of Fabia/Eudokia and Heraclius' second wife Martina, appear in the following document for an event just three days after the previously recorded one:

On the fourth of the same month [January 639], there being a horse race, the emperor received the usual persons in the Augusteum, and he ordered them to come to him in the Hippodrome. He received all of the officials, and having entered the Augusteum, they found the emperor and the Augusta standing. In front of them stood Augustina and Anastasia, their daughters and Augustae. The Patricians were present and on the right stood the other children of the emperor, and on the left were the *cubicularii* [chamberlains] and they cried out, saying: "Good fortune to the government, good fortune to the government, good fortune

4 Constantine VII, *De cerim.* 628–629 Reiske.

to the government. Heraclius Augustus, conquer! Anastasia Martina, conquer! Constantine Augustus, conquer! Heraclius Augustus, conquer! Augustina Augusta, conquer! David Caesar, conquer! Martina most noble, conquer!" Then the emperor left for the Hippodrome.[5]

This document gives impressions of the sounds and cadences of the Heraclian era. Scraps of Latin (*tu vincas*, conquer!) in the Greek text reinforce the echoes of the empire's Roman heritage. The document is reminiscent of much more ancient Roman protocols and public culture, and public spectacles. Heraclius and his family made a point of showing themselves to their subjects in ways that matched public expectations even as illness and age was taking its toll on Heraclius himself.

A final Heraclian document records Heraclius' actions when his old friend and associate the Patriarch Sergios died:

On the thirteenth of December, a Sunday, 12th indiction [638], Sergios the Patriarch of Constantinople was buried. At the services the emperor received the officials according to custom and sent them to the burial service. The senators, after going to the Great Church, changed out of white tunics and put on colored ones, and followed the procession to the Church of the Holy Apostles. The clergy were asked if there was a protocol for other patriarchs. This is the same one, they said. They observed the similar ritual for the burial of Bishops Kyriakos and Thomas. For these were performed on Sunday. After the service, those officials who wished to remain remained until the deposit of the corpse, but the rest went home.[6]

Ritual offered regular process, sanctification, and some assurance that all was proceeding in a correct way, despite the volatility, horrors, and reverses on the empire's far-flung borders, financial hemorrhaging, and despite any whispers or doubts about the imperial marriage, imperial ecclesiastical policies, the health and harmony of members of the imperial family, and any murmurs about any approach of apocalyptic events. This was Byzantium. These documents provide some understanding of how ritual offered some solace and even helped calm the population in those turbulent and momentous times. It was a legitimate means for drawing collective participation in support of the preservation of themselves and their empire. It represented steadiness in the midst of chaos and may well have contributed to Byzantine survival in the face of great perils.

The death of Sergios on 9 December 638, with burial on the 13th, led Heraclius to choose Pyrrhos to replace him, who remained Patriarch from 20 December 638 until 29 September 641, that is, beyond Heraclius' own

[5] Constantine VII, *De cerim.* 629–630 Reiske.   [6] Constantine VII, *De cerim.* 630–631 Reiske.

death on 11 February 641.[7] He also approved the issuance of the *Ekthesis*, in September/October 638, which proclaimed Monotheletism as the Christological doctrine of the empire.[8] It condemned discussion of one or two energies, on penalty of suspension from sacred offices for clergy and from sacraments for monks and laity.[9] There were various motives for the publication of the *Ekthesis*. Heraclius hoped to settle remaining issues before his death, including the thorny problem of the imperial succession, theological disputes, and the Patriarchate. He probably also wished to show that he and his government could still do something. He may have timed its issuance for the centenary of Severos of Antioch's death in 638.[10] There was a political price to pay, but the temptation was to stay busy and produce something for the public in a moment of otherwise distressing news. The issuance of the *Ekthesis* did not settle matters, it only inflamed them. Heraclius continued to tighten his ties with the Patriarchate, when he needed more ecclesiastical support. In a period in which doubts were growing about the loyalty of parts of his family and the army, he reinforced, understandably, his ties with the established church. But this was a fragile and troubled alliance. George of Pisidia could still hopefully address and praise Heraclius at that late date as "shining eye of the inhabited world, its tower, its foundation, feeder of souls,"[11] however little his words corresponded to the realities of power.

Heraclius had already probably heard of a letter from Pope Honorius I to Patriarch Sergios, probably written in 634, in which Honorius praised Patriarch Sergios and accepted the doctrine of one will in Jesus Christ, and warned Sophronios the monk and then Patriarch of Jerusalem, to cease disputing that doctrine with Kyros, Patriarch of Alexandria.[12] Heraclius' own role and opinions on relations with contemporary Popes such as Honorius I and Severinus are absent from anecdotal accounts. Formal correspondence,

---

[7] Jan Louis Van Dieten, *Geschichte der Patriarchen von Sergios I. bis Johannes VI. (610–715)* (Amsterdam: Hakkert, 1972) 57–63. For a broader evaluation of Sergios, pp. 51–56.

[8] Van Dieten, *Geschichte der Patriarchen* 49–51.

[9] Text: Mansi, *Sacrorum conciliorum nova et amplissima collectio* 10.999C-D. Best: R. Riedinger, "Aus den Akten der Lateran-Synode von 649," *BZ* 69 (1976) 17–29.

[10] Intriguing thesis of L. MacCoull, "George of Pisidia, *Against Severus*: In Praise of Heraclius," in *The Future of the Middle Ages and the Renaissance. Problems, Trends, and Opportunities for Research*, ed. R. Dahood (Arizona Studies in the Middle Ages and the Renaissance, 2; Turnhout: Brepols, 1998) 78.

[11] George of Pisidia, *Contra Severum*, lines 691–692 = *Carmi* p. 304 Tartaglia; trans. adapted from L. MacCoull, "George of Pisidia, *Against Severus*: In Praise of Heraclius" 77.

[12] Jaffé, *Regesta Pontificum Romanorum* 2018. Mansi, *Sacrorum conciliorum nova et amplissima collectio* 11.539; *PL* 80: 472–473; cf. Jaffé, *Regesta* 2024, Mansi 11.579. *PL* 80: 474. Elena Zocca, "Onorio e Martino: due papi di fronte al monotelismo," in *Martino I Papa (649–653) e il suo tempo. Atti del XXVIII Convegno storico internazionale, Todi, 13–16 ottobre 1991* (Spoleto: Centro Italiano di Studi sull'Alto Medioevo, 1992) 103–147, esp. 110–123.

which necessarily originated at Rome, reached his chancery, but no evidence that he bore any special hostility towards bishops of Rome as a group or individually. His years in Africa probably caused him to appreciate the potentially strong influence that popes could exert in many of his imperial provinces.

Heraclius apparently (it is hard to believe that the appointment could have taken place in the face of strong imperial opposition) concurred, at least passively, in the elevation of Sophronios to be Patriarch of Jerusalem. He probably did not appreciate how inveterate an opponent of Monotheletism Sophronios would soon prove to be. Sophronios apparently returned the remains of John Moschos to Palestine some time in 634.[13] Arkadios, the Archbishop of Cyprus, apparently held an initially moderate position on Christological matters, although he was a good friend of Kyros, the Patriarch of Alexandria. The worsening military situation in the east increased the significance of each of those episcopal sees, including that of Cyprus, which sat astride increasingly critical communications between Constantinople, Egypt, and the Levantine ports. Heraclius' opinion of and relations with Arkadios, Archbishop of Cyprus, are unknown.[14] Sophronios wrote a letter to Arkadios, some time between late 634 and mid-636, or possibly as late as 637.[15] In it he rejected Monoenergism and any effort to compromise theological differences through *oikonomia*. The letter contains no references to Heraclius or to Muslims. Stimulated by demands from Sophronios for a hearing, Arkadios then convoked a meeting of bishops in Cyprus, in 634 or a little later, which included Kyros, concerning Maximos the Confessor's theological concerns about the energies and will in Christ.[16] Maximos declined to come.

After much had been said, some of the bishops were saying that "we should accept Maximos' doctrine," while others said, "No, it is pernicious"; and they decided to put this doctrine down in writing and send it to the victorious emperor Heraclius. When they had done this they sent it by the hands of Georgios, the archdeacon of

---

[13] E. Follieri, "Dove e quando morì Giovanni Mosca?," *Rivista di Studi bizantini e Neoellenici*, n.s. 25 (1988) esp. 20–39. The criticisms of Follieri's chronology by Andrew Louth, "Did John Moschus Really Die in Constantinople?" *Journal of Theological Studies*, n.s. 49 (1998) 149–154, are acute but not conclusive, because he does not take into account the relevance of materials such as those in the *Doctrina Jacobi nuper Baptizati*, for example.

[14] But see the imperial letter cited in S. Brock, "An Early Syriac Life of Maximus the Confessor," c. 8–14, *AB* 91 (1973) 315–317.

[15] M. Albert, C. von Schönborn, eds., *Lettre de Sophrone de Jérusalem à Arcadius de Chypre, PO* 39/2 (1978)170–176.

[16] Brock, "An Early Syriac Life of Maximus the Confessor," c. 8–14, 315–317; also, Jean-Pierre Sodini, "Les inscriptions de l'Aqueduc de Kythrea à Salamine de Chypre," in *Eupsychia. Mélanges offerts à Hélène Ahrweiler* (Paris, 1998) 630.

the holy Arkadios, bishop of Cyprus, and of Leon, the deacon of the holy Kyros of Alexandria, and of Elias, the notary of Sophronios.[17]

Sophronios reportedly had reservations about sending the text to Heraclius, but the letter was sent, to await the imperial decision.

When the above-mentioned men reached the imperial city they entered before the victorious emperor Heraclius, and the letter concerning the doctrine of Sophronios and the rascal Maximos was read out in their presence, whereupon they perceived that it was alien to the entire Christian teaching. The emperor at once made a document called an "Edict," and sent it to the four [Patriarchal] sees. In it he rejected this despicable doctrine and ordered it to be brought to naught as being pernicious, and he laid down in the definition he made that everyone who confessed [this doctrine], or believed on such lines, should be ejected from his position.[18]

Such fear reportedly existed after the imperial edict (*Ekthesis*) arrived that, from the point of view of Monophysites, "there was peace until the death of the victorious emperor Heraclius,"[19] for Maximos the Confessor remained in his cell because of fear of the emperor and anathemas by the Patriarchs. Such was the account of a Monophysite raconteur, with a distinct agenda, who attributed great power to Heraclius in the outcome of the controversy during the emperor's lifetime.[20]

Heraclius never wavered in his support of the *Ekthesis*. He tried to convince Pope Severinus, as was the case with Pope Honorius I, to accept the *Ekthesis* and its doctrines.[21] St. Maximos the Confessor falsely tried to invoke Heraclius as having changed his mind about the *Ekthesis* at the end of his life. This is not an unusual tactic, to try to convince others that a great man, or in this case, the founder of an imperial dynasty, and more important, the reigning one, had been incorrectly portrayed as having been a supporter of a controversial policy or measure, that in fact he had changed his mind or had doubts about it. Heraclius will be invoked to justify other matters as well: his will concerning the imperial succession to himself, and also probably concerning the establishment of a new census for a new tax base for the empire. Heraclius' name continued to be invoked in support of and in opposition to various policies, which is additional testimony to the power of his name and reputation in the years that immediately followed his death.

[17] Brock, "An Early Syriac Life of Maximus the Confessor," c. 12 (316 Brock).
[18] Brock, "An Early Syriac Life of Maximus the Confessor," c. 15 (317 Brock).
[19] Brock, "An Early Syriac Life of Maximus the Confessor," c. 16–17 (317 Brock).
[20] Skepticism about the authenticity of the information in the Syriac life of Maximos Jean-Claude Larchet, *La divinisation de l'homme selon Saint Maxime le Confesseur* (Paris: Cerf, 1996) 8–12.
[21] A. Alexakis, "Before the Lateran Council of 649: The Last Days of Herakleios the Emperor and Monotheletism," *Annuarium Historiae Conciliorum* 27/28 (1995/6) 93–101.

Heraclius clung ever closer to Pyrrhos and sympathetic ecclesiastical figures, as the number of his reliable secular civil and military supporters shrank. Probably concerns for his health, his family, and his succession motivated him to turn even more to the church for support and steadfast guidance and assurance.

Public rituals could not forestall fiscal pressures late in the 630s. The streams of the empire's fiscal revenues failed to stabilize or recover after the Byzantine withdrawal from Syria. The fragments of information indicate that in the final years of Heraclius' life his government desperately needed to find funds. It was having much difficulty in paying its essential expenses, such as for the military in that time of desperate military exigencies. Solutions had not yet been found, even though the outlines of newer realities and the scope of governmental control of territories were changing. There was no stabilization or any moment of respite. Resort to various desperate expedients necessarily created surprise, resentments, and even resistance. Those who were believed to be responsible for such expedients were objects of dislike and controversy.

Events continued to outpace solutions. The lucrative tax revenues of Egypt were endangered when they were most needed, for the Muslims began to threaten Egypt itself. It became difficult to discover any remaining reliable sources of revenues. The search for cash to pay the mounting military costs intensified. That search did not spare Italy, not even the rising wealth of the Papacy, with which Heraclius' relations had been mixed. By 640 the *cartularius* Maurice and an exarch Isaac the patrician appropriated much papal treasure at Rome to turn over to soldiers who had not received punctually all of their stipends from Heraclius. A portion of the funds and plate were forwarded to Heraclius:[22]

... it was Maurice who was driven by malice against God's church and entered into a plot with some perverse men: they incited the Roman army saying, "What use is it that so much money has been stored away in the Lateran Episcopium by Pope Honorius while the army gets no support from it? – sometimes that man even buried away the stipends the lord emperor periodically sent you." On hearing this they were all incensed against God's church; in a state of excitement all the armed men who chanced to be in Rome, from youths to old men, came to the Lateran Episcopium. They could not get in by armed force as they met resistance from those who were with the holy lord Severinus. Seeing that they could achieve nothing, Maurice maliciously made the army take up occupation there inside the Lateran Episcopium, where they stayed for three days. After the three days Maurice came in with the judges who were his accomplices in the plot. They sealed up the entire

---

[22] *Liber Pontificalis/Book of Pontiffs*, trans. Raymond Davis (Liverpool University Press, 1989) 65–66.

Vestry of the church and the sacred equipment of the Episcopium, which various Christian emperors, Patricians and consuls had bequeathed to St. Peter for the redemption of their souls, for distribution of alms to the poor at particular times, and for the redemption of captives. Afterwards Maurice sent a letter to Isaac the Patrician at Ravenna about the action that had been taken, how he had used the army to seal up the entire Vestry of the Episcopium, and that they could plunder all its wealth without any trouble. When Isaac had realized how true this was, he came to Rome and sent all the dignitaries of the church into exile, each to a different city, so that there would be none of the clergy likely to resist. Some days later Isaac entered the Lateran Episcopium, and was there for eight days until they had plundered all the wealth. Then he sent a portion of the wealth to Heraclius at the imperial city. After this the holy Severinus was ordained; and Isaac returned to Ravenna.[23]

These actions in Italy were probably not the result of explicit orders from Heraclius, but they fitted into a broader pattern of seizures of ecclesiastical plate to meet the critical needs of the government and army. Back in 622 Heraclius had seized plate and copper at Constantinople, and now the search for plate intensified again. Whatever revenues had been appropriated in Persia had been spent. Now it was necessary to turn to the churches to find enough hoarded wealth to finance the pressing military needs. Rome was not the only place in which that occurred. It took place in Egypt and would soon also take place in the central Mediterranean, in Sicily and Africa, as well as in Italy.

A close reading of Leontios of Neapolis' *Life of John the Almsgiver* reveals strong apprehensions at the end of Heraclius' life,[24] probably because of recent actual experiences, that the imperial government was moving to confiscate or make forced loans of ecclesiastical precious metals, given the desperate fiscal situation. The invocation of Niketas in the *vita* may be indirect testimony to Heraclius' responsibility or initiative in ordering such seizures, because living or dead, his memory or precedent was not invoked, only that of Niketas, in apparently ecclesiastical efforts to forestall more such measures. It may well indicate fear in 641 or immediately thereafter that the imperial government would attempt such measures, so the hagiographer invoked venerable precedents for abstention from depredations on the part of an eminent deceased member of the imperial family, Niketas. This was an era in which religious relics continued to become ever more important

---

[23] *Liber Pontificalis/Book of Pontiffs* 65–66 Davis (I: 328–329 Duchesne).
[24] The date of Leontios of Neapolis' *vita* of John is approximately 641–642: V. Déroche, *Etudes sur Léonce de Néapolis* (Uppsala, 1995) 16. Kaegi, "Egypt on the Eve of the Muslim Conquest," in *Cambridge History of Egypt*, ed. C. Petry (Cambridge: Cambridge University Press, 1998) I: 34–61, esp. 58. On the value of church plate: M. Mango, *Silver from Early Byzantium* (Baltimore: Walters Art Gallery, 1986) 3–15.

in the eyes of the public. The earlier correspondence of Pope Gregory I with Epirus Nova underscores the role of relics and their importance in the flight of refugees from that troubled province, ca. 603/604.[25] A symptom of the importance of relics in that era was an act of Heraclius ca. 628. Heraclius had sent the reputed and highly valued chair of St. Mark, which he had brought from Alexandria presumably to save it from the Sasanian invaders, among other gifts with an embassy to the Patriarch of Grado:[26]

the Patriarch of Grado sent his emissary (*apocrisarius*) . . . to inquire[27] about the fact that the baptismal [parish] churches had been plundered, and that the Lombards had sought to withdraw the bishops [under their territorial control] from his oversight, and that they had held back for themselves the Patriarch's[28] money. Finally, the emperor sent back more gold and silver than [the Lombards] had put to waste, and moreover, he sent . . .[29]

This text may refer not only to Lombard spoliation of baptismal churches, but possibly also to Heraclian authorities' having expropriated church plate during recent extreme emergencies, to help to pay urgent imperial expenses. The text allows the inference. The *Historia* uses the passive voice to express the first hardship at issue (the despoiling), and only then come the Lombards in the active voice. One need not exclude Lombard hands as the denuders, but with knowledge of the broader historical context, one easily sees the chronicler's point and delicacy in not naming Lombards until their business is at issue. The gift of the chair would seem to be a singular substitution of reparations for the spoiled furnishing of the parish churches, a reversal of the taking that possibly was perpetrated by surrogates of Heraclius. The text again attests to the respect in which subjects held Heraclius and, later, his memory, and to the importance of emperors' honoring provincial localities and their churches.

This is a case of restoring precious metals to a prominent church contemporary with Heraclius' victory over Sasanian Persia. It reflects Heraclius' wish to maintain and strengthen relations with a prominent see in Italy.

---

[25] *Registrum epistolarum Gregorii I. papae*, ed. P. Ewald (*MGH* Epist. II) let. no. XIV.7 425–426, XIV.8, 427, XIV.13.432–433.

[26] At vero supra memoratus patriarcha Primogenius apocrisiarium suum dirigens in regiam urbem ad virum piissimum Iustinianum augustum, huius rei indagandae causa, qualiter ipse baptismales ecclesiae denudatae fuissent, quod et Longobardi suos episcopos a diocesi eius subtrahere voluissent et ipsum thesaurum apud se ipsi retinuissent. Tunc demum ipse piissimus imperator aurum et argentum plus rimisit quam perdiderant, et insuper sedem beatissimi Marci euvangeliste dirigens, quam ab Alexandria Heraclius augustus in regiam urbem adduxerat. Dölger, *Regesten* no. 185. *Chron. patr. Grad.* c. 7; SS rer. Lang. 395. See also Dandolo, *Chronicon* 6.6.2 in L.A. Muratori, *Rerum Italicarum scriptores* (Milan, 1728) XII: 114A.

[27] Euphemism for "to complain."   [28] Ipsi, dative of reference.

[29] I thank my colleague Michael Allen for advice.

One wonders about the fate of relics and communal identity in some other provinces and regions at approximately the same time. Earlier in the century Heraclius' cousin Niketas in Alexandria reportedly tried to prevent this kind of wrongful appropriation of church treasures.

In far-away Africa, in 636 or 637, near Constantine, there was additional confirmation of the continuing strength, if not increase, of the cult of saints: the interment of relics of several saints, according to a lead seal that bore the name of Emperor Heraclius.[30]

The frantic search for cash, in addition to military measures – not only the fighting, but also the priority given to military needs – almost certainly negatively affected areas of the economy that did not directly experience warfare. Probably maritime commerce was squeezed for more imperial revenue, and therefore contracted.

The fiscal crisis worsened by 640–641. The rage of Heraclius and his advisers against any unauthorized local arrangements to pay extensive tribute to the Muslims is understandable. They made the task of the *sakellarios* Philagrios and his employees all the more difficult. Multiple pressures and crises were reinforcing one another. Given his concern for keeping his empire intact, Heraclius attempted to rebuke or replace local officials who decided to pay off the Muslims. He likewise supported his fiscal officials' efforts to find new revenues and to maintain those that already existed. The *sakellarios* Philagrios probably was a close adviser concerning the likely fiscal implications of any substantial payments of tribute to the Muslims. Larger Byzantine military units did not dissolve entirely.

The *sakellarios* or treasurer Philagrios as well as Patriarch Pyrrhos were two important leaders whose power waxed stronger in the waning moments of the reign of Heraclius.[31] Heraclius could not escape the economic and fiscal consequences. Heraclius' administration had been in the process of reforming some bureaus, including finance. Thus the office of treasurer or *sakellarios* was emerging into prominence in the middle of the 630s, and certainly this could only happen with the concurrence of Heraclius, but whether he conceived of this administrative reform is unclear. There was a desperate shortage of cash, which already had been evident in the 610s and early 620s. The Muslim conquests and imposition of assessments of tribute quickly aggravated those arrears and in turn made decision-making and the implementation of decisions much more difficult yet more urgent.

After the death of Theodore Trithyrios, the *sakellarios*, at the battle of the Yarmūk, where his presence was occasioned probably by the need to

---

[30] Yvette Duval, *Loca Sanctorum Africae*, no. 112 (I: 234–235, and discussion 236–239).
[31] Brandes, *Finanzverwaltung* 385–431.

have a paymaster present to motivate and calm the troops, Heraclius appointed Philagrios to the rank of *sakellarios*, and he ordered him, perhaps as late as 640 or the initial days of 641, to make a new census (*apographe*) for the entire empire, which was to be surveyed (κηνσευθῆναι).[32] This was a bold step, for no such general census had been taken for a long time. This indicates again that Heraclius remained in active control of the government until his death. How far Philagrios managed to accomplish this imperial instruction is uncertain. After the death of Heraclius it may have been expedient to remind subjects that it was Heraclius himself who had ordered the reassessment.[33] A Georgian tradition of Sumbat Davit'is-dze offers possible corroborative information by reporting a census in K'art'li between 642 and 650 that was taken to Byzantium.[34]

One might have supposed in that dire emergency that Philagrios and his subordinates became unpopular with some elements of the population, for squeezing the population to find cash for the army and government, even though other elements, such as some soldiers and those who were trying to maintain the loyalty of the soldiers and recruit even more of them, may well have been grateful to them. Yet the contemporary John of Nikiu states that Philagrios was popular ("he was greatly beloved") in Constantinople.[35] Contemporary ecclesiastics knew or believed that Philagrios and Heraclius had somehow continued to make gifts to churches, while somehow Patriarch Pyrrhos was believed, immediately after the death of Heraclius, to have halted imperial gifts to churches and to have laid indeterminate but significant charges on them.[36] The popularity of Philagrios for giving gifts to churches probably indicates that late in Heraclius' reign, when Heraclius himself was racked with disease, Philagrios was acting with or was perceived by others as acting with independent discretion. Somehow he was managing to find funds to enrich churches and had thus far staved off the need to despoil or impose forced loans on churches. Some among elites and among the public probably had ambivalent attitudes about Philagrios, for they may not have liked treasury officials, but realized that they could not do without them and their extraordinary measures. The relative power of Philagrios expanded in the final moments of Heraclius' life, but it is impossible to quantify this precisely. It is likewise impossible to know what Philagrios

---

[32] Σύνοψις Χρονική, ed. Constantine Sathas, Μεσαιωνικὴ Βιβλιοθήκη, 7 (1894) 110. On Philagrios, *PLRE* III: 1018, s.v. "Philagrius 3" (identical probably with *PLRE* III: 1019, "Philagrius 6"). Brandes, *Finanzverwaltung* 414–415, esp. n. 234, argues for the historicity of the census.

[33] Theophanes, *Chron.* A.M. 6131 (474 Mango). On Theophilos of Edessa and Syriac transmitters: Cyril Mango, *The Chronicle of Theophanes* (Oxford, 1997) lxxxii–lxxxiv.

[34] Sumbat Davit'is-dze, *Life and Time of the Georgian Bagratids*, trans. Stephen H. Rapp (forthcoming).

[35] John of Nikiu, *Chronicle* 119.24 (191 Charles).   [36] John of Nikiu, *Chronicle* 119.21 (191 Charles).

really wanted. He eventually favored Heraclius Constantine and the troops of Valentinos Arshakuni, instead of Martina and Thracian troops. Presumably he had concern for the fiscal soundness of the empire and probably he diligently sought to promote and aggrandize his bureaucratic office, that of the treasury of the *sakellarios*. He was a critical holder of that office in the early emergence of it. He was a consummate insider, but one who not simply took orders, but was willing to take some initiative and risks, and had some sense of timing at least with respect to internal strife. Otherwise his personality and ambitions remain obscure. On balance, it was fortunate that the empire had an official with his skills at that critical moment. His appointment is an indication that Heraclius still had the ability to select competent bureaucrats late in his own life.

Philagrios while in exile at Septem (Ceuta) after the death of Heraclius may well have gained some ideas about the potential for raising new revenues by increasing taxes on maritime commerce, especially the kinds of commerce that existed in the western Mediterranean. This may help to explain the complaints in Italy, Sicily, and Africa for the raising not only of taxes on the church and on landowners, but also on maritime commerce, and navigation. But there is no explicit documentary evidence on this. No relevant sigillographic evidence has been uncovered in Spain or western North Africa (that is, Mauretania).

The impression emerges that in his final years, after the evacuation of Syria in late 636, Heraclius succeeded only with difficulty in maintaining control of some regions and spheres. Centrifugal tendencies of many kinds asserted themselves and made the task of organizing resistance to the Muslims, to the Lombards in Italy, and to Avaro-Slavic penetration and settlement in the Balkans, even more challenging and at times intractable.

It is far from clear that Heraclius would have been able to solve matters if he had lived a little longer. Because his medical condition worsened over some time, there was an opportunity to anticipate some problems. His death was not sudden and did not suddenly plunge the empire into unexpected crises, as bad as the crises turned out to be. He himself had time to think about and to try to arrange matters before his decease.

One may speculate. Could Heraclius and his advisers have salvaged the Byzantine hold on Syria and upper Mesopotamia after the battle of the Yarmūk? It would have required dramatic leadership and adequate funds to stiffen resistance by remaining Byzantine troops and to recruit and train adequate numbers of additional Byzantine troops to resist the Muslims. Yarmūk vastly increased the feeling that momentum was on the side of the Muslims. At that moment the Byzantines still controlled the most populous and most fertile regions of Syria. The shock was probably too great, the reserves of men and funds were too inadequate, there was too much defeatism, and there was dissatisfaction and unrest among the Byzantine leadership, including the rivalries growing about the succession within the ranks of the imperial family. There was little time to repair the walls of towns, to prepare inhabitants of walled towns to withstand sieges and blockades. The will to resist to the death was not there. There is no evidence of any readiness to conceive of any kind of crusade or religious zeal to defend the faith, or that the faith of the Christians of Syria was at stake at that moment.

But Heraclius, whether at Antioch or Edessa or Samosata, was not in a position to raise still more troops, including traditionally friendly Arab ones. He had raised those he could before the Yarmūk campaign to expel the Muslims. The volatile situation appeared to have shifted. Perhaps someone younger and more vigorous might have done something else. But that would have involved more battle and the concomitant risk. The troops and the money and the right officers just were not there. Something had snapped.

Heraclius had several ways to gain information about the Muslims after he evacuated Syria. Fleeing Christian Arabs, including leaders such as the Ghassānid ruler Jabala b. al-Ayham, brought information that Heraclius and his subordinates could assess. Heraclius encouraged the flight of Christian Arabs to Byzantine territory. Their reports would have received special attention. Other refugees and Christian clergy, including those who helped to negotiate the redemption of hostages and prisoners and civilian captives, may also have brought valuable intelligence. There were some merchants and mariners. There likely continued to be a trickle of refugees who left areas under Muslim control by boat for Cyprus, where their reports would have speedily been passed to Constantinople. Such contacts did exist. But no irrevocable cleavages among the Muslims were apparent. One can only speculate how Heraclius might have exploited internal Muslim strife at the death of Caliph 'Umar or in 656, but that occurred after his own death. No easy cracks appeared in Muslim unity during Heraclius' lifetime. There was no Muslim Shahrbarāz, and perhaps tellingly, the Muslims reportedly executed, on 'Umar's command, a son of Shahrbarāz after the battle of the Yarmūk. It is uncertain how accurate was the information that Heraclius was receiving.

Instead, all was not lost. But the effort was set to limit losses. Probably recent Byzantine experiences with the Sasanian invasion of the Byzantine Levant had created the critical precedents that loomed in the mind of Heraclius and his advisers.

There may well have been another element that helps to explain the conduct of Heraclius. Most of his earlier military victories had not been major, decisive, victories. He had won, in civil as well as in external wars, by small margins, usually accentuated by exploiting vulnerable internal frictions and fissures of his foes to widen minor triumphs into larger successes. Some of these victories, although victories, were less military than political triumphs. After Yarmūk and the earlier reverses in Syria and Palestine, it became clear that it would not be easy through some similar small marginal successes to reverse the victorious momentum of the Muslims and then lure or neutralize their leadership by bribing or deceiving them into rivalries, desertions, switching of sides or by kidnapping or decapitating their leadership. Instead, a major total and comprehensive effort would have been necessary. And it would have been necessary to develop a new and effective strategy, which had not yet happened. This could not be done merely through rhetoric or public relations. The task seemed beyond the means and the will of contemporaries, even though others may well find it hard to understand why someone or some group could not have accomplished it. But it needed to be done quickly, for the situation was sliding fast. Those possibilities and opportunities slipped away. When hopes for transforming small psychological successes into major victories and strategic reversals of the comprehensive situation failed to become reality, there was a magnification of defeat on the Byzantine side. Military defeat turned into larger-scale disaster for the Byzantine side. The process of momentum then worked against the Byzantines, instead of against their foes. There was no point in Heraclius trying to stay in northern Syria or Mesopotamia to try to find a way to split and undermine the Muslims without first smashing them in battle. The contacts and opportunities were not there. One was not going to win victory without a major second battle, yet that was unthinkable in the material and psychological situation of the Byzantines after Yarmūk. There would be future divisions among the Muslims, but not at that critical moment in the late 630s. There was no unexploited pool of Arabs or other tribes (non-Arab ones) who could be recruited or used to play off against the Muslim invaders. Options were limited, and shrinking.

Muslim sources anachronistically attribute almost everything to a personalized depiction of Heraclius having been and having remained in control of decision-making. The fact was, Heraclius' writ did not run very far away from areas where he was not personally present, whether at the capital or in the provinces, by the late 630s. Although he may have done so, there are no reports in the Greek sources of Heraclius' personally mustering, reviewing, or addressing his troops in his final five years of life. He surely saw and communicated with some during the withdrawal from Syria, but there is simply no reference to how he interacted with his troops after the defeat at Yarmūk. Because of his health he may have limited his exposure to them, but there is simply no reliable information.[37] The conspiracy of Athalaric shows that troops might be swayed to conspiracies, but sufficient troops remained loyal to stamp out any whiffs of plots. Except for the conspiracy of Athalaric and associates at Constantinople, and the unrest and alleged mutiny of Vahan and his troops at the battle of the Yarmūk, there is no known instance of a revolt of soldiers in the east in the immediate aftermath of the Yarmūk defeat. That silence indicates that Heraclius managed to maintain control of the critical field armies.

This time, the lesson having been learned in 614 when the Persians overran the Holy Land, the key religious relics in the Holy Land, especially at Jerusalem, including fragments of the Cross, were spirited away to Constantinople, so that they did not fall embarrassingly into the hands of the Muslims. This may or may not have occurred at the express command of Heraclius, but the removal of those objects at least spared Heraclius and his government still more embarrassment and humiliation that would also have shamed him for failing to support Christianity against its foes. The church under Patriarch Pyrrhos became, in his last years, one of his strongest and most reliable supports. But that pillar was also fragile.

Heraclius was unable to control the competing interests and mutual hatreds of his chosen appointees as his own power ebbed. Older tensions between imperial financial and ecclesiastical bureaucracies intensified. The looming Muslim threat did not cause these disputes to fade away in the name of imperial unity and Christian survival. Strained finances and the imperial succession struggle gave more ascendancy to the treasurer or *sakellarios*. Heraclius' powerful treasurer Philagrios and Kyros, his own choice for Patriarch of Alexandria, were enemies.[38] Some of this antagonism may have been personal, but there probably were also jurisdictional roots to their enmities. Similar tensions between church and secular officials had surfaced in earlier decades of Heraclius' reign, and involved Catholic as well as Monothelete and Monophysite clergy; spheres of influence rather than confessional differences lay at their core. As treasurer, Philagrios was desperately seeking to maximize imperial revenues, even seeking new inventive ways to create streams of revenue. Kyros, for his part, understandably sought to preserve the extensive financial resources and prerogatives of his church and the inhabitants of Egypt. Heraclius was unable to persuade

---

[37] Suda [Suidas], *Lexikon* II: 582, ed. Adler, s.v. "Herakleios."
[38] John of Nikiu, *Chron.* 120. 66 (199 Charles).

these rivals to compose their differences, which became one of several critical negative factors that undermined imperial rule and imperial defense of Egypt, and jeopardized the imperial government itself and public morale.

After the Muslims shattered Byzantine armies at the Yarmūk in August 636 and overran Palestine, including the nodal city of Gaza in 637, Egypt became very vulnerable, even though it had thus far suffered no major Muslim invasion. Beduin incursions, whether Muslim or not, may have emerged when some raiders sought to take advantage of the power vacuum when the Sasanians withdrew and only limited Byzantine military forces were available. The fact that in 633 Heraclius unsuccessfully ordered General Peter of Numidia to deploy his troops in the east to come to the defense of Egypt indicates that Egypt was in serious jeopardy long before Muslims decisively invaded it in late 639.[39] It is conceivable that the pre-eminent Muslim commander in southern Palestine, 'Amr b. al-'Āṣ, did threaten Egypt sufficiently that Patriarch Kyros agreed to pay considerable tribute to forestall any Muslim invasion and raiding, just as John Katcas, the *epitropos* of Osrhoene, had done in the north to prevent a Muslim raid on that region.[40] But John of Nikiu does not confirm it.[41] An early Muslim tradition passed on by the tradent Ḥārith ibn Yazīd al-Ḥaḍrāmī (d. ca. 700 CE), reports via Ibn Lahī'a, according to the historian Ibn 'Abd al-Ḥakam, that Abū Bakr made peace arrangements with Kyros for Egypt before the conquests of Syria.[42] He gives no particulars. But any significant disbursements of funds from Egypt by Kyros to Muslims had negative effects on the imperial treasury under the control of the *sakellarios* Philagrios. Philagrios was no military commander, but his influence was growing in the final months of Heraclius' life. He was well situated to criticize and maneuver against Kyros in support of the treasury's interests and possibly also because of personal antipathy for Kyros. Such internal hostilities exacerbated decision-making at the end of Heraclius' reign.

[39] "Relatio factae motionis inter domnum Maximum monachum et socium eius coram principibus in secretario," *Scripta saeculi vii vitam Maximi Confessoris Illustrantia*, ed. Pauline Allen, Bronwen Neil (*CC*, Series Graeca, 39; Turnhout: Brepols, 1999) 12–15.

[40] Theoph. *Chron.* A.M. 6128 (340 De Boor, 472 Mango-Scott).

[41] Alexander Beihammer, *Quellenkritische Untersuchungen zu den ägyptischen Kapitulationsverträgen der Jahre 640–646* (Vienna, 2000) 21–29, rejects the possibility that Kyros bought off 'Amr before 639. See also Beihammer, *Nachrichten* nos. 50, 183, pp. 69–70, 210–227. But after Yarmūk and the fall of Gaza to 'Amr, the Muslim threat loomed large and may well have intimidated Kyros. The text of John of Nikiu is incomplete here, so his silence is inconclusive. For a different perspective and arguments for the authenticity of earlier negotiations between Kyros and the Muslims, see "The Conquest of Egypt," in Robert G. Hoyland, *Seeing Islam as Others Saw It* 574–590.

[42] Ibn 'Abd al-Ḥakam, *Futūḥ Miṣr* 53.

We do not know how Heraclius discussed and thrashed out policies for the defense of Egypt.[43] Just as John the Almoner had once, during the Persian invasion of Egypt, attempted to reach him to plead directly for imperial approval for peace negotiations with the Persians to spare Alexandrians from suffering, so one of his successors, Kyros, also sought to persuade Heraclius to consent to the terms that Kyros had negotiated with 'Amr b. al-'Āṣ, the Muslim commander who had invaded Egypt from southern Palestine via the Sinai coastal route in late 639. The earlier experience and the repetitiousness of the pleading may well have negatively impressed Heraclius. The desperate effort to find revenues pressed on everything. It intertwined with ecclesiastical and military policy-making. Yet Heraclius had never visited Egypt. His cousin Niketas had probably told him much about it. Gregoria, the wife of his son Heraclius Constantine, came from the Barka region of Cyrenaica and may well have transmitted some impressions, whether direct or third-party ones, about Egypt. It is uncertain how much Gregoria lobbied for the interests of Africa or Africans at court in the last years of Heraclius. Her perspectives and interests would not have been the same as those of Martina. She would have had some solicitude for relatives and friends in Cyrenaica and may well have advocated, accordingly, more understanding for and more participation in a vigorous defense of Byzantine Egypt.

Given recent unhappy experiences with local negotiations by on-the-spot commanders in Osrhoene and Mesopotamia, which had not been approved by Heraclius and which resulted in crushingly expensive agreements to pay tribute in return for holding off raiding and invasions, Heraclius had tightened procedures. That is why in Egypt Patriarch Kyros had to forward his tentative pact with 'Amr b. al-'Āṣ to Heraclius for formal approval, which he rejected. Heraclius had conceived, almost certainly, of the strategy of reinforcing Egyptian resistance with Byzantine troops from further west, from the Barka region of Cyrenaica, even though those troops in Numidia under General Peter refused to help. Heraclius had some forewarning of problems in Egypt to defend it against the Muslims. The Muslim threat to Egypt was not a total surprise. It was impractical for Heraclius to micromanage the defense of Egypt. Ibn 'Abd al-Ḥakam identifies the backbone of resistance in Egypt with Heraclius.[44] Ibn 'Abd al-Ḥakam's source, or tradent, is Ibn Lahī'a.[45] He, like John of Nikiu, Nikephoros, Theophanes,

---

[43] W.E. Kaegi, "Egypt on the Eve of the Muslim Conquest". Important observations: Jean-Michel Carrié, "Pouvoir civil et autorité militaire dans les provinces d'Egypte," *L'Antiquité Tardive* 6 (1998) 118–121. Detailed critique of Arabic sources: Beihammer, *Quellenkritische Untersuchungen.*

[44] Ibn 'Abd al-Ḥakam, *Futūḥ Miṣr* 76 Torrey.

[45] Raif Georges Khoury, *'Abd Allah Ibn Lahia (97–174/750–790): Juge et grand maître de l'école égyptienne* (Wiesbaden: Harrassowitz, 1986).

and Michael the Syrian (and like al-Azdī, who describes Heraclius as one who tried to stimulate hard resistance in Syria), characterizes Heraclius as one who rejects expensive tribute-paying arrangements with the Muslims, one who angrily criticizes separatist truces or treaties, as one who urges strong military resistance, whether in upper Mesopotamia or in Egypt.[46] The traditions concur in attributing to him scathing rebuke and contempt and criticism for the policies of Patriarch Kyros.[47] Agapios of Mambij plausibly reports that some Egytians denounced Kyros' negotiations and arrangements with the Muslims to Heraclius, who understandably reacted angrily.[48] Heraclius created important precedents for his successors by insisting that any arrangements or accommodations with Muslims receive prior imperial approval. His ad hoc improvisations with extraordinary military appointments in endangered towns and regions are part of the larger background for the lengthy incremental process of defensive military institutions that would ultimately become what modern scholars call the Byzantine "theme system."

The sources indicate that an imperial concern was loss of tax revenue as well as any strictly military or political considerations. But it was primarily the local Augustales and duces of Egypt, notably from Alexandria and filled with mutual hostilities and rivalries, who led the resistance to the Muslims in 639–642, for only John of Barka was a commander who came from outside Egypt. For better or worse, Heraclius and his family selected and appointed military commanders for the defense of Syria and Mesopotamia against the Muslims. Heraclius' abortive order for Peter to move from Numidia to aid in the defense of Egypt fitted into the Syrian and Mesopotamian pattern. But although the Byzantine commanders who defended Egypt acted in the name of Heraclius, they came from prominent local Egyptian constituencies and were not appointees that Heraclius selected from his most experienced and most successful field commanders from, say, his campaigns against the Sasanians or from fighting the Muslims in Syria, Palestine, and Mesopotamia. John of Nikiu reports Heraclius' reaction to Muslim successes in Egypt, in 640: "And Heraclius was grieved by the death of John the chief of the local levies, and of John the general who had been

[46] For the conquest of Egypt: Jorgen Baek Simonson, *Studies in the Genesis and Early Development of the Caliphal Taxation System* (Copenhagen: Akademisk Forlag, 1988) 135–140. Kaegi, "Egypt on the Eve of the Muslim Conquest". I thank Dr. John Meloy for letting me see an advance copy of his unpublished paper "The Initial Muslim Settlement of Alexandria."

[47] P. Speck, *Das geteilte Dossier* 401, 411, believes that the thrust of the source of Nikephoros is criticism of Heraclius, ultimately placing the blame on him for the loss of Egypt and Mesopotamia, because he was too obdurate to permit paying tribute to the Muslims.

[48] Agapios, *Kitāb al-Unvān*, PO 8: 472. See also, [Anonymous] *Chronicon ad annum Christi 1234 pertinens* c. 118 (197 Chabot).

slain by the Moslem, as well as by the defeat of the Romans that were in the province of Egypt."[49] Theodore, who probably was Augustalis of Egypt,[50] led Byzantine forces in the Fayyum against the Muslims in 640, and retrieved the body of John, and sent it to Heraclius: "And Theodore sought with great diligence for the body of John, who had been drowned in the river. And with much lamentation he had the body drawn forth in a net, and placed in a bier and sent to the governors, who also (in turn) sent it to Heraclius."[51] Probably it was sent to Heraclius in order for him to give the body of a distinguished opponent of the Muslims an honorable burial ceremony with full dignity, to show, however vicariously, the priority and recognition that Heraclius and the imperial government gave to the defense of Egypt, that it was not forgotten, nor were those who resisted firmly to suffer oblivion; there was the possibility of reward. But such acts did not stimulate any stouter local resistance to the Muslims.

This may be excessive personalization. Heraclius appreciated the value of Egypt to his government and to his empire. He may well have thought of it in terms of the prism of his experiences in seizing power from Phokas back in 608–610. He could not afford to let Egypt disappear into the hands of his foes, with attendant losses of revenue to himself the equal gain to his foe, without some effort. He may well have realized that its loss even exposed his beloved Africa to conquest and ruin. Yet it was difficult to devise and coordinate anything workable for Egypt from faraway Constantinople. Yet his capital and his people and governmental revenues had managed, with difficulty, to survive from 619 to 629 without aid from Egypt. The loss of Egypt potentially raised issues about the viability of defenses in North Africa itself, which was another valuable source of revenues and a region with multiple ties with the reigning dynasty. Heraclius' relationships with Egyptian elites, such as members of the Apion family or comparable ones, are unknown.[52] Sources such as Agapios probably conflate Heraclius with Heraclius Constantine and with Heraclonas and even Constans II, concerning events in Egypt.[53]

---

[49] John of Nikiu, *Chron.* 116.1–2 (184 Charles). The second John (*PLRE* III, s.v. "Ioannes 246") is probably, contra *PLRE*, John Barkaines, of Barka, in Cyrenaica, whom Nikephoros mentions: *PLRE* III, s.v. "Ioannes 249". See Carrié, "Pouvoir civil et autorité militaire" 118–120.

[50] Carrié, "Pouvoir civil et autorité militaire" 119.   [51] John of Nikiu, *Chron.* 111.15 (180 Charles).

[52] Whether Heraclius could draw on members of the Apion family in the 630s is uncertain. Some pillars of that family had disappeared by now. B. Palme, "Die Doma Gloriosa des Flavius Strategius Paneuphemos," *Chiron* 27 (1997) 96–125, esp. 96–105, investigates Fl. Strategius of the Apion family, whom we lose sight of after 616. See Todd M. Hickey, "A Public 'House' but Closed: Fiscal Participation and Economic Decision Making on the Oxyrhynchite Estate of the Flavii Apiones," concerning the Apion family's landholdings and practices in the sixth century.

[53] For example, Agapios, *PO* 8: 474.

In any case, it was impractical for Heraclius or any other member of the imperial family to make a personal visit to Egypt as he had to Syria, where his presence had not saved the situation. At his age, and in his probable state of health, and given internal tensions within the court and within ruling circles, any trip to Egypt would have been extremely risky and unlikely to succeed, whether to direct military campaigning or to arouse popular support for resistance to the Muslims. In theory there would have been time to raise consciousness and drill elements of the Egyptian population to resist the Muslims, whose menace had already appeared in southern Palestine and northern Arabia. But there is no evidence of any concerted effort to do so. It is improbable that he possessed especially effective ideas for resisting in Egypt, given his personal lack of familiarity with terrain, waterways, and roads, climate and local leaders.

The stages and the location for the devising of policies for the defense of Egypt are unknown. Heraclius did have a fairly good idea about the state of readiness of the Byzantine armies withdrawn from Syria and Mesopotamia. But they were needed *in situ* for the defense of Armenia and the Anatolian plateau, and ultimately, Constantinople. Very few of them could be spared, even for such a rich province as Egypt. Some crack troops from Thrace or the embryonic Thrakesion military unit were sent by ship to Egypt. That was a risky policy but it had to be tried. There is no report of any concerted effort by Heraclius to arm and train the Egyptian population for self-defense against the Muslims. Whether specific formulae were created and missives accordingly sent to Egypt about fortifying and repairing the walls of Egyptian towns, and canals, is unknown.

What is known is that Byzantine authorities were expected to keep Heraclius informed of the local situation. Highly relevant to any discussion of Heraclius and Egypt is the role of Cyprus, and Heraclius' relations with ecclesiastics on Cyprus. Archbishop Arkadios was a friend of Kyros, Patriarch of Alexandria. Cyprus was a key nodal point of Byzantine communications and supplies, and transport of troops, between Constantinople and Egypt. Heraclius' understanding of the situation on Cyprus is unclear. Some aqueducts were repaired there during his reign, and probably with his financial assistance, according to inscriptions.[54]

Heraclius likely considered the defense of Egypt in the light of his experiences in 608–610, during the rebellion against Phokas, and again during the Persian invasion of 619 and the Byzantine reoccupation. He cannot

---

[54] But the date of these repairs is controversial, according to J.-P. Sodini, "Les inscriptions de l'Aqueduc de Kythrea à Salamine de Chypre," in *Eupsychia. Mélanges offerts à Hélène Ahrweiler* (Paris, 1998) 630.

have been oblivious to religious controversy in Egypt, including disputes about the Patriarchate of Alexandria and Christology.

Nikephoros reports that "some years" prior to the death of Patriarch Sergios (638), Heraclius had

recalled to Byzantium Kyros, the bishop of Alexandria, and held him under severe accusation of having surrendered to the Saracens the affairs of all of Egypt. He pursued these charges at the time in front of a large gathering of citizens. But ⟨Kyros⟩ defended himself by saying that he was in no way guilty of these matters, and that if his plan had gone forward and he had raised taxes for the Saracens by means of trade profit, the latter would have remained in peace and the imperial dues would not have been in arrears. And he accused others of having committed the misdeeds in question and alleged that he himself had made charges against them to no avail. But ⟨Heraclius⟩ called Kyros a pagan for having advised that the emperor's daughter should be betrothed to Ambros, phylarch of the Saracens, a pagan, an enemy of God and an opponent of the Christians. Waxing incensed with him and threatening him with death, ⟨Heraclius⟩ handed him over to the prefect of the City for punishment.[55]

Heraclius' convening of a public hearing and public denunciation of Kyros is consistent with other reports, from Muslim traditions, especially al-Azdī al-Baṣrī, that he convoked the public in various places in the Levant to seek to raise their resistance to the Muslims, and consistent with his earlier speech at Hierapolis to persuade its populace to revert to Orthodox Christianity from Monophysitism. It is also consistent with his summoning and public interrogation, excoriation, and judgment on Priskos in 612, in Constantinople. Until virtually the end of his life, Heraclius sought to keep in touch with the public and to shape and direct their sentiments. Although there were some cowards and laggards among Byzantine commanders in Egypt, other generals perished in combat against the Muslims, demonstrating their sacrifices and the fact that not everyone there gave up or fought lethargically.

Ibn 'Abd al-Ḥakam reports:

...the Muqawqis [Kyros] who was the foremost among the Byzantines until he wrote to the king of the Byzantines, informing him what he did. And 'Amr accepted that and he agreed and allowed them to leave. And he wrote a document about it. And Muqawqis wrote to the king of the Byzantines informing him about the reason for the affair in all detail. The king of the Byzantines wrote to him, denouncing his opinion as shameful, called him impotent, and replied to him about his actions. He said in his document: "Indeed 12,000 Arabs reached you while there are innumerable Copts beyond counting in Egypt and the Copts loathe killing and

[55] Nikephoros, *Short History* c. 26 (75–77 Mango). Beihammer, *Nachrichten* nos. 201–202, pp. 240–243.

like to contribute *jizya* [head tax] to the Arabs and they prefer them to us. You have in Egypt Byzantines of Alexandria who together with auxiliary troops number more than 100,000 and the strength of the Arabs...."[56]

This was a tradition of Yaḥyā b. Ayyūb and Khālid b. Ḥumayd.[57]

Heraclius reportedly ordered Kyros to fight the Muslims, to "triumph or die."[58] "And the king of the Byzantines wrote a letter/document similarly to the community of the Byzantines."[59] Kyros accordingly went to 'Amr and reported that Heraclius had denounced him and rejected what they had agreed upon and ordered him to fight until he was victorious or died.[60]

Layth b. Sa'd from Yazīd b. Abī Ḥabīb reported that

Muqawqis [Kyros] reached an agreement with 'Amr that those among the Byzantines who wished to leave might depart, those who wished might stay on the terms of the agreement. When the king of the Byzantines heard of it he was angry with him [Muqawqis] and severely criticized him and rejected it and sent armies and they besieged Alexandria.'[61]

Ibn 'Abd al-Ḥakam remarked of Heraclius, "God broke the strength of the Byzantines with his death."[62] This narrative corroborates the traditions of Nikephoros and John of Nikiu that Heraclius disapproved of Kyros' decisions about terms in his negotiations with the invading Muslims concerning Egypt.

Although his career caused him to pass through many regions and towns with important historical associations, Heraclius probably had only minimal consciousness of their historical significance. His troubled final years were not ones in which he had the leisure to investigate, even if he had so desired.

Problems of the imperial succession occupied Heraclius after his return to Constantinople, reportedly over a special bridge to hide the waters of the Bosphoros from him.[63] After evacuating Syria Heraclius initially had not returned to Constantinople itself, but had been residing on the Asian side of the straits at his beloved palace of the Hiereia:

At this time Heraclius returned home and resided in the palace called Hiereia; for he was afraid of embarking on the sea and remained unmoved by the noblemen and citizens who repeatedly begged him to enter the City. On feast days he would dispatch only his sons who, after attending holy liturgy in the church, immediately returned to him. And likewise, when they watched the hippodrome games, they

---

[56] Ibn 'Abd al-Ḥakam, *Futūḥ Miṣr* 71 Torrey.   [57] Ibn 'Abd al-Ḥakam, *Futūḥ Miṣr* 70 Torrey.
[58] Ibn 'Abd al-Ḥakam, *Futūḥ Miṣr* 71 Torrey.   [59] Ibn 'Abd al-Ḥakam, *Futūḥ Miṣr* 71 Torrey.
[60] Ibn 'Abd al-Ḥakam, *Futūḥ Miṣr* 71–72 Torrey.   [61] Ibn 'Abd al-Ḥakam, *Futūḥ Miṣr* 72 Torrey.
[62] Ibn 'Abd al-Ḥakam, *Futūḥ Miṣr* 76 Torrey.
[63] P. Speck, *Das geteilte Dossier* 406–407, is rightfully skeptical of this story.

went back to their father. . . . After a considerable lapse of time the noblemen of the court caused the prefect to collect a great many ships and tie them one next to the other so as to bridge the straits called Stenon, and to make on either side a hedge of branches and foliage so that ⟨the emperor⟩, as he went by, would not even catch sight of the sea. Indeed, this work went ahead speedily, and the emperor crossed the sea on horseback, as if it were dry land, to the shore of the bay of Phidaleia (as it is called). Avoiding the coastal area, he reached Byzantium . . . [64]

This unique story may be simply that: a story. It may reflect some neurological disorder, or a misreading by Heraclius of some astrological or other occult messages or prophecies. More likely, it may be an exaggerated elaboration of Heraclius' decision to remain in isolation during the crisis of the Muslim invasion, but on the Asian side of the straits, where he could, unencumbered and discreetly and more speedily, consult with his military about the critical situation in Anatolia. Already, during the winter of 621–622, Heraclius may have retreated to the palace of Hiereia when he was studying and reflecting before his offensive against the Persians.[65] He may have liked the palace so much that he simply preferred it, as in that earlier challenging time of his life, to the bustle and pressures of Constantinople, while he was trying to sort out what to do. The Hiereia Palace had many fond memories for Heraclius. He spent his first summer there after seizing control of the empire, in 611. It was there then that his first daughter, Epiphania, was born. He resided there when he received the blessings of St. Theodore of Sykeon, and again, on his return from his overthrow of Khusrau II in Persia. That palace, on the Asian side of the straits, had many favorable associations for him. He beautified its grounds by filling in its cisterns and constructing gardens and parks. Two centuries later the Byzantine court still retained memories of his beautification of the Hiereia palace grounds.[66] The story of his reluctance to return to Constantinople may simply be an echo of a malevolent spin on an old and ailing man's preferences for comfortable, familiar, snug, and secure quarters where he could reflect and convalesce most efficiently.[67] Whatever the truth, his prolonged stay at Hiereia gave rise to ugly and disquieting rumors that indicated a widening gap between himself, the Constantinopolitan elite, and the people.

[64] Nikephoros, *Short History* 24–25 (72–75 Mango). See Suda [Suidas], s.v. "Herakleios," *Lexikon*, ed. Adler, II: 582.

[65] Speculations about Hiereia by A. Stratos, Βυζάντιον I: 326, II: 654–655 = *Byzantium in the Seventh Century* II: 135–136.

[66] Theophanes Continuatus, *Vita Basilii* c. 92, ed. I. Bekker (Bonn, 1838) 338.

[67] Janin, *Constantinople byzantine* (Paris: Institut français d'études Byzantines, 1964) 148–150, and map XIII.

There is no convincing evidence whether or not Heraclius turned more passionately to astrological predictions and calculations in the final years of his life, under the strain of so many Byzantine reversals and Muslim triumphs.

The ever deteriorating situation in the east and in Egypt made it impractical for Heraclius to contemplate any serious military action in the Balkans, to bring relief or restoration of Byzantine rule to its inhabitants and its shrinking ecclesiastical hierarchy. His contemporary, Isidore of Seville, records in his chronicle that under Heraclius the Slavs "took Greece [Graecia]" from the Byzantines, although he provides no details for this tantalizing generic statement.[68] Isidore may vaguely refer to the overrunning of the Greek mainland while the Persians were occupying those other eastern provinces not in any precise year, but in the middle of the second decade of the seventh century, approximately, and the phrasing indicates that this was no temporary act. Heraclius welcomed the opportunity to accept diplomatic detente with Kuvrat (Koubratos), the nephew of Organas and lord of the Onogundurs, who successfully rebelled against the Khan of the Avars and drove their army out of his territory. Any weakening of the Avars potentially aided Byzantium. Kuvrat sent an embassy to Heraclius. They concluded a treaty which both observed for the duration of their lives. Heraclius, in the typical manner of Byzantine emperors dealing with barbarian leaders, sent him gifts and honored him with the rank of Patrician. This act did not involve the recovery of the Balkans for Byzantium, however. The precise identity and affiliations of Kuvrat are unclear and very controversial. But Heraclius could not find comparable other barbarian leaders to play off against the Muslims in Asia and against their threat to Byzantine control of Egypt.

In his final span of life, Heraclius had difficulties urinating, which was extremely painful, as the historian Nikephoros, or his source, explained: "it grew to such an extent that when he was about to urinate, he would place a board against his abdomen: (otherwise) his private parts turned round and discharged the urine in his face."[69] Critics saw this as evidence of divine wrath against him for his illicit marriage with Martina, "on account of which he suffered the ultimate punishment," so judged Nikephoros. Scholars debate the character of this disease: dropsy, prostate problems, or another

---

[68] Isidore of Seville, *Chron. MGH* AA 11: 479: on the sixteenth year of the reign of Heraclius, "cuius initio Sclavi Graeciam Romanis tulerunt, Persi Syriam et Aegyptum plurimasque provincias." On this, see P. Charanis, "Graecia in Isidore of Seville," *BZ* 64 (1971) 22–25; A. Avramea, *Le Peloponnèse du IVe au VIIIe siècle: changements et persistances* (Paris, 1997) 71–72.

[69] Nikephoros, *Short History* c. 27 (77 Mango).

opinion, epispadias.[70] Of course, there well may have been a polemical motive for the source, who is hostile to Heraclius, to describe him in this fashion, and the report therefore may need discounting. It may simply be a malevolent story that Heraclius' critics spread to embarrass and humiliate him.

A multitude of troubles beset Heraclius, from every side, at the end of his reign. There was no respite, and no one on whom to lean, given the vulnerability of his eldest son, Heraclius Constantine, let alone that of his wife Martina and her children. Yet there is no evidence that he spent those years in grief, retreat, or withdrawal, for there was too much to confront. He remained busy with public affairs until the end of his life. He did have time to contemplate the end of his life, for he left detailed instructions about the succession and about his final wishes for his funeral ceremony and burial.

There is no evidence that Heraclius returned to Anatolia to supervise personally the organization of local structures of defense against the Muslims. He passed through Anatolia on his return from Syria, during which time he certainly had the opportunity to observe conditions and opportunities to create defenses. He may have conversed with local leaders about options and their own counsel. But the sources are silent. In the final year of his life he suffered another disappointment: the empire's last foothold in the Holy Land, and a vital port and administrative center, Caesarea Maritima, fell to the Muslims.[71]

Heraclius had the time to think carefully about details of his own funeral and burial. Therefore he may well have also endeavored, however unrealistically, to try to leave the most positive picture of his reign preserved for public and historical memory, through the panegyrists and other writers and other forms of public art and monuments. However, there is no explicit proof that he encouraged or directed any systematic effort to purge or cleanse the record in his favor. He was trying to think ahead and he did have time to try to anticipate. His decease was not sudden or an unanticipated event.

Nikephoros described Heraclius' death, on 11 February 641:

He set forth a testament whereby his sons Constantine and Heraclius were to be emperors of equal rank and his wife Martina was to be honored by them as

---

[70] J. Lascaratos et al., "The First Case of Epispadias: An Unknown Disease of the Byzantine Emperor Heraclius (610–641 A.D.)," *British Journal of Urology* 76 (1995) 380–383. This identification is not conclusive. It is unusual for someone to have survived so long with such an excruciatingly painful and trying disease, if that indeed was his illness. His tomb was white marble, whether Proconnesian or Docimian: P. Grierson, "The Tombs and Obits of the Byzantine Emperors," *DOP* 16 (1962) 48.

[71] Balādhurī 212–213; Muḥammad ibn ʿAlī ʿAẓīmī, *Taʾrīkh Ḥalab*, ed. Ibrāhīm Zarūr (Damascus, 1984) 167.

mother and empress. So he died of this ⟨disease⟩ at the age of sixty-six after a reign of thirty years, four months, and six days. He was buried in the church of the all-praised Apostles and for three days, as he had ordained while he was still alive, the tomb containing his body remained uncovered and attended by ministering eunuchs.[72]

The Latin Spanish chronicler reports, "Eraclius morbo intercutis aquae mortalem mundum deseruit."[73] According to the "Anonymous Guidi" Chronicle, and the Chronicle of Si'irt or *Nestorian Chronicle*, Heraclius died weighed down with sorrow, in the words of the Nestorian Chronicler, "plunged in despair and overcome by affliction because of the events."[74] It is very likely that Heraclius was depressed and saddened by the turn of military and internal political and dynastic developments in the last years of his life. There is no reason to reject this tradition, despite the hostility of its transmitters to Heraclius. There is no way to ascertain whether any aging process had in itself impaired his mental functioning or other abilities to perform his imperial duties. There are no meaningful data on the aging process in the early seventh century.

Already Heraclius' historian Theophylact Simocatta had described in the 630s the provisions that two legitimate emperors, Tiberius II and Maurice, had taken to provide for their successions, including the writing of wills.[75] Tiberius, like Heraclius now, according to Theophylact, had also been described as having been worn down by disease.[76] Such remarks would have resonated meaningfully in the entourage of the disease-racked Heraclius in his final years. While Heraclius was terminally ill, he had provided money to Patriarch Pyrrhos "on behalf of Empress Martina so she would not be lacking in funds if she were driven out of the palace by her stepson, Emperor Constantine."[77] The exact size of these funds is unknown, although later Philagrios persuaded the reluctant Patriarch to hand the funds over to him. Philagrios ultimately provided his adjutant Valentinos with 2,016,000 solidi, to procure military support against Martina and her sons, but not all of that need have come from the sum that Pyrrhos surrendered to Philagrios.[78] Heraclius' final moments and words with members of his family remain unrecorded.

---

[72] Nikephoros, *Short History* c. 27 (77, 191 Mango).

[73] *Cont. Isidorianae* 18, *MGH AA* 11: 338. Another interpretation of the date (January 641) of his decease: cf. P. Grierson, "Tombs and Obits," *DOP* 16 (1962) 48.

[74] *Chronicum Edessenum*, in *Chronica Minora*, ed. I. Guidi (*CSCO*, SS, 1903–1905) p. 31. Quotation: *Histoire Nestorienne* 116 (*PO* 13: 627).

[75] Theophylact, *Hist.*1.1.5–20, 7.11.7 (19–21, 227–228 Whitby).

[76] Theophylact, *Hist.* 1.1.7–9 (20 Whitby). [77] Nikephoros, *Short History* c.29, p. 79 Mango trans.

[78] *PMBZ* V: 69–74, no. 8545, s.v. "Ualentinos."

The *History* attributed to Sebeos carefully adds another dimension to the last will of Heraclius:

He made his son Constantine swear to exercise [mercy] on all the transgressors whom he had ordered to be exiled, and to restore them to each one's place. He also made them swear regarding the *aspet* [Varaztirots, whom Heraclius had sent into exile after the failed conspiracy of Athalaric] that he would bring him and his wife and children back, and establish him in his former rank. "If he should wish to go to his own country, I have [so] sworn to him. Let not my oath be false. Release him, and let him go in peace."[79]

Like others, including Leontios of Neapolis who invoked the name of Niketas to save church plate and property from subsequent imperial spoliation, or to justify a census for the empire, the author seeks to insists on respect for Heraclius' last words and testament to implement and perpetuate specific policies relevant to Armenian families. Heraclius' name was invoked for all kinds of reasons soon after his death.

We do not know what judgment Heraclius placed on his own accomplishments and failures at the end of his life, what regrets he may have had for taking certain decisions and courses of action. Probably he became aware of his limits, that he could not do everything. Yet given the poor state of health of his eldest son, and familial complications and recent conspiracies, he could not contemplate abdication, however frustrated he may have been. Only he himself had the awareness of terrain and communications and military leadership in the east, especially on either side of the Tauros Mountains, as well as any feel for the potential resources of other sections of his empire, especially in the west, and how to marshal them in this great emergency. His final years were so busy that he may not have had so much time for stocktaking, any summing up, and reminiscences. Although his poet George of Pisidia had composed a poem *On the Vain Life*,[80] it is unclear whether Heraclius himself had made or even attempted to make comparable reflections. The events of 638–639, with the elevation of Heraclius Constantine and Heraklonas, are probably indicative of Heraclius' own stocktaking and recognition that his own life was finite. One cannot determine precisely when, or even whether, he ever realized that he had peaked and that many of his efforts were ending in failure, but if there was such a moment, 638–639 was probably it. He had little free time to take solace.

---

[79] Sebeos, *Hist.* ch. 42. [137–138] (99 Thomson); *PMBZ* V: 84, no. 8567, s.v. "Varaztiroc."

[80] Possibly dated to 629/630: Mary Whitby, "Defender of the Cross" 271; Mary Whitby, "Devil in Disguise," *Journal of Hellenic Studies* 115 (1995) 116, 128; George of Pisidia, *Carmi* 30, text: 428–444 Tartaglia; *PG* 92: 1581–1600.

Theophylact, Heraclius' historian, pointed out that Maurice had wrongfully failed to show respect for the miracles of St. Euphemia and had stripped her sepulchral tomb of silver, perhaps trying gently to warn Heraclius not to repeat such depredations even as his subordinates were doing so in the provinces and elsewhere.[81] In Rome, Pope Honorius I (625–638) lavished much silver on St. Peter's, St. Andrew's, and on the basilica to St. Pancras. So some churches did have vast sums of silver to expend on the beautification of churches and chapels, even in dire times.[82] The trend towards belief in miracles continued to intensify. Likewise, Theophylact noted the recent continuation of troubled predictions about the future of the empire.[83] He mentioned cases from several decades earlier but the very recording of them here added to their fame and encouraged their proliferation and continuation. Prophecies and portents, such as comets, abounded, and unsettled some. Heraclius had to deal with that socio-psychological reality. A Syriac report of a saint's prediction of ill fate for those espousing Monothelete policies in the 630s, although preserved in a later source, is consistent with such references and provides a little insight into contemporary popular mentalities in the final years of Heraclius' life.[84]

In his last years Heraclius probably reflected on the premature death of so many whom he had known: his first wife, so many of his children, his able cousin Niketas, so many generals, and his aides, and even Patriarch Sergios of Constantinople and their opponent, Patriarch Sophronios of Jerusalem, who died in 638.[85] The circle of close counselors had changed radically over the course of the years. But however much he trusted and confided in them, Patriarch Pyrrhos, Empress Martina, and treasurer Philagrios were unable to provide Heraclius with military advice for coping with the invading Muslims on the edge of Anatolia and in Egypt. His counselors were a narrow group, of circumscribed capacities with respect to urgent measures of internal and external security.

One of the most important yet understandably obscure questions is how Heraclius attempted to prepare Heraclius Constantine and Martina to assume direction of imperial policy-making.[86] Heraclius had accumulated unparalleled experience from his lifetime service in far-flung corners of the

[81] Theophylact, *Hist.* 8.14.1–9.
[82] *Liber Pontificalis/The Book of Pontiffs* 64–65 Davis, ed. L. Duchesne, lxxii Honorius, pp. 323–324.
[83] Theophylact, *Hist.* 8.13.14–15.
[84] Michael the Syrian, *Chronique* 11.5, 11.7 (II: 418, 422–423 Chabot).
[85] Mortality of emperors and their children: Walter Scheidel, "Emperors, Aristocrats, and the Grim Reaper: Towards a Demographic Profile of the Roman Elite," *Classical Quarterly,* n.s. 49 (1999) 254–281.
[86] Dionisia Misiu, Η διαθηκη τοῦ Ηρακλειου Αʹ και η κριση τοῦ 641 (diss., Thessalonica, 1984).

empire, a record that would never be equaled in the future by any of his successors. Passing on that accumulated wisdom was a potential invaluable legacy. There is no evidence that Heraclius ever wrote down any memorandum of advice for his immediate or future successors. Oral advice in the corridors of the palaces is even more elusive to uncover. It is quite possible that he conferred extensively with Gregoria, his daughter-in-law, and left her detailed advice. It is unclear what insights and advice he passed on to any of them concerning imperial defenses in the east, the critical situation in Egypt, the Balkans, or theology. Presumably he urged them to follow the leadership of Philagrios in troubled fiscal matters and Patriarch Pyrrhos with respect to ecclesiastical issues. Unresolved, however, was how to reconcile competing fiscal needs to tap ecclesiastical wealth and ecclesiastical leaders' understandable resolve to preserve it untouched by bureaucratic predators. With respect to military crises, it is likewise uncertain how he counseled his successors to handle sensitive issues of military personalities and their rivalries and ambitions, as well as the pressures coming from their units and men. It is unclear whether he advised these successors about the wisdom or urgency of campaigning in person. Likewise obscure is his advice on how to handle public opinion, whether in Constantinople or in the broader stretches of the empire.

Soon after Heraclius' death, in particular, following the brief reign of his son Heraclius Constantine, who reigned only about a hundred days, the Alexandrian or Egyptian public mocked both Heraclius and Heraclius Constantine. So after his death he swiftly had become an object of criticism and derision. According to John of Nikiu, the marriage of Martina with Heraclius and the offspring of that marriage received harsh criticism and ominous predictions in Egypt after the death of Heraclius: "And people mocked at Heraclius and his son Constantine,"[87] "they rejected the will of the elder Heraclius [Emperor Heraclius]."[88] Probably those sentiments were also present before Heraclius' decease, but there is no explicit corroboration from sources that purport to reflect provincial opinion. The controversy concerning Heraclius' uncanonical marriage with Martina and the poor state of health of Heraclius Constantine were both divisive elements that undermined morale among imperial subjects at the end of Heraclius' life and at the moment of maximum peril from the Muslims. Yet one cannot quantify the negative effects. There is no explicit testimony that the scandal affected the morale of Byzantine troops and commanders during the first six or seven years of early Islamic conquests – that is, the final years of the life of Heraclius.

---

[87] John of Nikiu, *Chron.* 116.9 (186 Charles).   [88] John of Nikiu, *Chron.* 120.2 (192 Charles).

The regime's apportionment of blame for its reverses had begun long ago. The first object of this had been the fallen Phokas, to whom were ascribed many territorial losses both in Europe and in Asia, against the Avars and Slavs, and at the hands of the Persians. Later the conspiracies of Vahan, of Theodore's son Theodore and his allies, the disobedience and unsatisfactory conduct of his own brother Theodore, and the disloyalty of hostile ecclesiastics, were all part of the rogues' gallery of those responsible for imperial defeats and humiliations. Heraclius had personally criticized Patriarch Kyros of Alexandria in front of a convened assembly at Constantinople. Heraclius himself had started the process of aggressively blaming others for the failure to defend rich provinces against the Muslim conquests. Ironically he failed to blame his imperial predecessor Maurice for grievously harming the Ghassānid shield that had protected imperial borders surprisingly well.[89] He had personally taken charge of and participated in publicizing such scapegoating. He had even begun it with the public shaming and interrogation of Phokas before his execution. He frequently resorted to the public shaming of others, and his publicists circulated such reports widely during and after his lifetime. It was inconceivable for the emperor to assume personal responsibility for these military defeats and Heraclius did not. He had to offer some explanation for what had happened and what was happening, one that deflected blame from himself. Yet the panegyrists had a problem. They had praised him for his triumphs over civil strife and over the tyrant Phokas, and over the Persians, using stratagems and strategic skills. Why could these methods not work against the Arab invaders? The problem was too sensitive for an easy reply except to impute the blame, in some fashion, to others, and not to himself. The circumstances were so dire that it was understandable that he and his subordinates lashed out against insubordination and sought to identify and blame traitors and punish them. The insubordinate included ecclesiastics, irrespective of Christological position, whether a Kyros, a Sophronios, or a Maximos the Confessor.

An extreme situation demanded extreme measures. This does not justify but helps to explain the resort to harsh imprisonments and mutilations of the accused. There was no time or inclination for tolerance. These punishments occurred at the same time as the arrival of bodies of eminent men who had fallen in combat against the Muslims. It was no time for half-measures, it was a time for extreme ones. In doing this Heraclius set precedents for the conduct of his successors in similar circumstances, who

[89] Shahid, *Byzantium and the Arabs in the Sixth Century* gives the best description.

also needed to deflect blame and to defend their dynasty. Heraclius' criticism of Kyros implicitly imperilled the reputation of Patriarch Pyrrhos of Constantinople, who had been one of Kyros' strong supporters and allies.

Heraclius lashed out not only at those who rejected Monotheletism, but even at prominent Monotheletes, such as Kyros, in his efforts to deflect blame for the costly military disasters in the east and in Egypt. Implicit in Heraclius' reported criticism of Kyros is criticism of his failure to rouse the Egyptian population to defend itself and its province against the Muslims. Yet one papyrus preserves possible evidence of clerical efforts in rural Egypt to encourage popular prayer for the Byzantine defenders of Egypt against the Muslims: "For our benefit, in order to wage war together against them, and for them to subdue all that belongs to the enemy host. We pray on behalf of the citizens living in faith among them. For our city and all cities, and our land and the villages and our common faith."[90] Clergy may have offered similar prayers elsewhere in Egypt and elsewhere in the east, with or without governmental advice or pressure, but without avail.[91] Things were flying apart. The interactive Mediterranean world with its ports quickly reverberated with news of Byzantine defeats. News may have trickled only slowly into the interior, away from the coasts, but inhabitants of the ports and littoral quickly learned of the basic pace and course of events. Heraclius probably was aware that they were in receipt of reports and rumors. He began to understand that he could not keep everything under control, yet he could find no one to fill his shoes. The empire had faced the horrors and perplexities of two-front wars many times, and they had often overstrained his predecessors, but the situation at the beginning of the 640s was even worse. It was a multi-front conflict, including several dimensions of internal stress. There were no textbook solutions at hand. It was not that he had ignored some of these, but it was beyond him to solve all of them even though he personally attempted to intervene and impose or apply pressure to bring about solutions. That was insufficient.

One does not know how the public reacted to the memory of recent panegyrics in favor of the military wisdom of the emperor, now that, after just a few years, vast military disasters were engulfing the empire, which

---

[90] Penelope J. Photiades, "A Semi-Greek Semi-Coptic parchment," *Klio* 41 (1963) 234–235. The language of the Greek text resembles the nearly contemporary letter of Pope Martin I to Heraclius' grandson Constans II, Mansi, *Sacrorum conciliorum nova et amplissima collectio* 10: 796E, and interestingly, Heraclius' role-model, Constantine I, in the words of Eusebius, *Vita Constantini* 1.46, see trans. and commentary, Averil Cameron and Stuart G. Hall, *Life of Constantine* (Oxford, Oxford University Press, 1999) 88, 222.

[91] This prayer offers some support for Azdī's source, who claims that in Syria Heraclius did stir up the populace to resist the Muslims: Azdī, *Ta'rīkh futūḥ al-shām* 22–23 Lees; Kūfī, *Kitāb al-futūḥ* 1.100–101.

was imploding. It was a swift reversal of fortunes. So the old praises and clichés about his victories and achievements may well have rung hollow in popular memories, as did such epithets as "savior/deliverer of the universe [*Kosmorustes*],"[92] and intensified the necessarily muted yet multifaceted criticism of him and his dynasty.

Byzantine emperors always sought to preserve respect and honor for their reputations. Heraclius was no exception. The violent character of his initial seizure of power and the military reverses made it imperative for him to pay careful attention to his standing with his subjects. Already during his campaigning against the Sasanians in the Caucasus he had the townspeople of Tiflis slaughtered for mocking him during a siege. In the immediate aftermath of the battle of the Yarmūk his official ("*patrikios*") strongly protested and demanded restitution for an inadvertent defacing of his eye on a temporary pillar erected to mark the border between Byzantium and the Muslims, following the evacuation of much of Syria.[93] The incident underscores the sensitivity and extreme insistence on avoidance of injury to the reputation and image of Heraclius, probably made even stronger by the major military defeats. It was a rearguard action, indeed part of an ignominious retreat, but a reminder that Heraclius' officials were still strenuously fighting to insist on honor for his image. Heraclius did not personally intervene in this incident, which illustrates the policy that his subordinates followed.

Contemporary writing, from the reign or within a decade or two of the reign of Heraclius, offers some additional appreciation of the awe in which subjects held emperors such as Heraclius, and reference to some acts of respect and obedience, including kissing imperial seals and prostrating themselves. The symbolic significance of the imperial crown is also noteworthy. Leontios, Bishop of Neapolis, explained how subjects regarded the emperor: "he who receives an order from the emperor does not offer homage to clay or paper or lead while kissing the seal, but addresses him with προσκύνησις [prostration] and respect, just as we also, the children of Christ, when we adore the symbol of the Cross, we do not render homage to the nature of the wood, but we consider it as the seal, the ring and the symbol of Christ . . . "[94] "In the same way when a good emperor makes with his own hands a shimmering and precious crown, all of the loyal subjects of the emperor kiss and honor the crown, not because they honor the gold and the pearls, but because they honor the head of that emperor and his expert

---

[92] George of Pisidia, *In Bonum patricium* 7 (*Poemi panegirici* 163 Pertusi).
[93] Eutychios, *Hist.* 141–142 Arabic text (120–121 Breydy trans.).
[94] Vincent Déroche, "Léontios, Apologie contre les juifs," *TM* 12 (1994) 67.

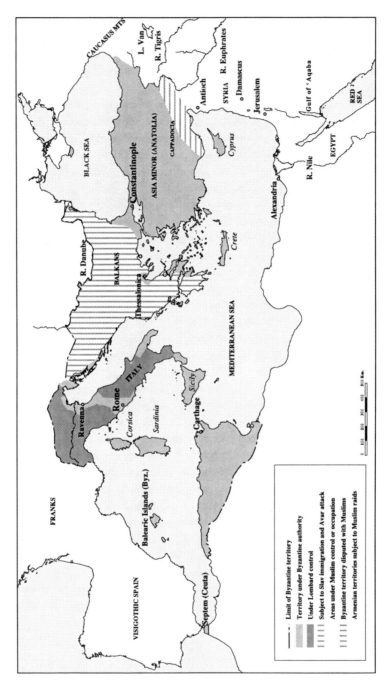

Map 10 The shape of the Byzantine Empire soon after the death of Heraclius, ca. 645

Legend:
- – · – Limit of Byzantine territory
- Territory under Byzantine authority
- Under Lombard control
- Subject to Slav immigration and Avar attack
- Areas under Muslim control or occupation
- Byzantine territory disputed with Muslims
- Armenian territories subject to Muslim raids

CAUCASUS MTS
L. Van
R. Tigris
R. Euphrates
SYRIA
Antioch
Damascus
Jerusalem
Gulf of ʿAqaba
RED SEA
EGYPT
R. Nile
Alexandria
Cyprus
BLACK SEA
Constantinople
ASIA MINOR (ANATOLIA)
CAPPADOCIA
Crete
MEDITERRANEAN SEA
R. Danube
BALKANS
Thessalonica
ITALY
Rome
Ravenna
Corsica
Sardinia
Sicily
Carthage
FRANKS
Balearic Islands (Byz.)
VISIGOTHIC SPAIN
Septem (Ceuta)

0 100 200 300 400 500 Km.

hands who made the crown."[95] Leontios does not specify the emperor, but he was writing contemporary with Heraclius and his immediate successors.

In 634 Heraclius had become aware of a number of great disappointments and failures, both with respect to personal relations and with respect to policy, but nothing had changed irrevocably. By the end of the next quinquennium, or by the eve of his decease, let alone the start of 641, the situation of the empire and his family had become more perilous. Even at that time, nothing was irrevocably lost, in theory, but the dimensions of defeat and disaster were ever more evident. The situation had been radically transformed for the worse since 634, despite his unceasing efforts to halt and reverse the slide. His inability to reverse matters was surely bitter for one who had not resigned himself to passivity or to be a mere spectator to events.

[95] Déroche, "Léontios, Apologie contre les Juifs," *TM* 12 (1994) 69.

CHAPTER 9

Conclusions

The name of Flavius Heraclius, Byzantine emperor 610–641, is associated with many events. For most Christians, he is most clearly associated with victory over the Persians in 628, and his personal restoration of what he believed to be the fragments of the True Cross to Jerusalem, which he entered on 21 March 630 via the Golden Gate (which is now sealed). Yet he is also the emperor in whose reign the Slavs and Avars overran the Byzantine Balkans, and more important, Muslims began and accomplished many conquests that permanently changed the nature of the Middle East. So there was a dramatic reversal, tragedy as well as triumph, a mixed and contradictory picture.

Heraclius faced thirteen major crises during the course of his life (ca. 575–641): (1) seizure of power from the unpopular Emperor Phokas in 610, and consolidation and legitimization of his own authority after seizing power; (2) death of his first wife Fabia/Eudokia in 612; (3) failure of initial efforts in 610–612 to end war with the Persians, who had taken advantage of Phokas' illegitimacy to invade and overrun territory; (4) Persian (that is, Zoroastrian) capture of Jerusalem in 614, massacre of its inhabitants, removal of fragments of the Cross to Persia, which embarrassed the government and the church, and Persians' overrunning Egypt in 619, with resulting loss of huge tax revenues and food supplies; (5) fiscal crisis, which peaked between 619 and 622; (6) Balkans overrun by Avars and Slavs, especially in the middle of second decade of the century and following, that is, between 610–615 and 626; (7) zenith of military threats in August 626, in the form of a Perso-Avar joint blockade, siege, and short assault on the empire's capital, Constantinople; (8) Heraclius' risk of everything while rushing off to invade Persian territory in 622, 624–628; (9) theological divisions within the church over the nature of Christ, and proclamation of the doctrine of One Will (Monotheletism); (10) the Muslim conquest of the Holy Land, Jerusalem, Syria, Mesopotamia between 633 and 639, beginnings of the Muslim invasion of Egypt in 639–641, again embarrassing his government and creating enormous challenges and loss of prestige, wealth, resources; (11) efforts to cope with the renewed fiscal crisis; (12) his controversial second marriage to his niece Martina and the related succession crisis, with strife between his children by his first marriage and those from his second marriage; and, (13) his health, terminating with his death in January or February 641.

Heraclius and his panegyrists compared Heraclius with David, with Moses, and with Constantine I.[1] They celebrated his many virtues, including his mental and physical versatility, his mildness and clemency, and sought to keep him, while absent from Constantinople on campaign or other missions, reassuringly in the minds of Constantinopolitans.[2] It remains, however, unclear whether he really liked and felt comfortable in Constantinople. In his final years, considerations of security required his presence at or near the capital, in order to quash any potential unrest, but, not unlike the early 620s, he preferred the palace of the Hiereia, which lay across the straits, to Constantinople and its political perils and gossip. Those were the palace grounds that he embellished with gardens and parks, leaving an enduring legacy for palace aficionados of subsequent centuries.

An evaluation of Heraclius as a military commander involves several considerations. His earliest victories were in civil war, between 608 and 610, in which he and his father Heraclius and his cousin Niketas triumphed not simply through land and naval combat but through winning over critical elements of the forces and leadership from the ranks of their opponents, or at least neutralizing them, by causing them to withdraw actively from participation in the fighting, perhaps to betray their own usurping Emperor Phokas. Heraclius profited from subversion within, from shared intelligence, espionage, of which he was a master. He knew how to consolidate power for himself and purge his opponents systematically after initially seizing control of the leadership. The initial political skills that he demonstrated he could use in warfare remained a distinctive part of his art of command throughout many of his subsequent campaigns.[3]

---

[1] Claudia Rapp, "Comparison, Paradigm and the Case of Moses in Panegyric and Hagiography," in *The Propaganda of Power: The Role of Panegyric in Late Antiquity*, ed. Mary Whitby (Leiden: Brill, 1998) 295–296.

[2] Mary Whitby, "Defender of the Cross: George of Pisidia on the Emperor Heraclius and His Deputies," in Whitby, *The Propaganda of Power* esp. 250–270.

[3] Excellent review of scholarship on Late Roman military practices and conditions: J.-M. Carrié, S. Janniard, "L'armée romaine tardive dans quelques travaux récents. 1e partie. L'institution militaire et les modes de combat," *L'Antiquité Tardive* 8 (2000) 321–341.

Evaluation of Heraclius' struggles with the Persians leads to mixed conclusions. Heraclius did ponder Persian military techniques and vulnerabilities in battle and he devised ways, according to textbook prescriptions, to defeat them. He demonstrated at the battle of Nineveh that he knew how to choose terrain for battle that maximized his potential for victory. He delayed and used multiple and protracted official diplomatic and covert informal contacts to identify weak spots to exploit politically and militarily. He resorted to bold initiatives that unsettled his opponents and forced them to react to his moves. He created a new operational dynamic in the years 622, 624, 625, 626, and above all in 627–628. He never conceived of warfare against the Persians in terms of the four phases into which we have subdivided it for modern historical analysis. He did not simply react to his Persian opponents. His bold risk-taking worked. Unlike Julian, the previous Roman emperor who invaded but met disaster in the heart of the Persian Empire in AD 363, Heraclius returned in triumph. Julian probably had hoped to exploit decisive military victory over the Persians to gain sufficient prestige and clout to be able to bend his diverse subjects to his pagan religious policies. But Heraclius' case is instructive. Decisive victory in Persia may well have encouraged him to seize the opportunity of his momentary prestige to resolve religious problems of his own era. But that joyous victory, achieved so tenuously with the assistance of diverse Sasanian opponents of Khusrau II, was insufficient to break the gridlock.

Heraclius' victories display some of the same qualities and skills that enabled him to overthrow Phokas. His final victory over the Persians was not one of simple triumph on the battlefield, but one also of espionage, subversion, luring a key Persian general, Shahrbarāz, to withdraw his support from the Persian King Chosroes or Khusrau II. And he profited from spreading false information, disinformation. Heraclius took a lot of calculated risks. That covert diplomacy and subversion was a critical element that permitted Heraclius to take his greatest calculated risk: invasion of the heartland of Persia's empire, Mesopotamia, a feat no one had accomplished since the Roman Empire had become Christian. It was dangerous because he was cut off from Byzantium temporarily and there were risks from Persian armies and from the heat and disease. So his ultimate victory over Persia, even though it involved a victory in battle not far from the site of Alexander the Great's triumph over the Achaemenid Persian King Darius at Gaugamela (Arbela) in 332 BC, of which he probably was unaware, was not simply a military one. It is easy to make retrospective analyses. The collapse of Byzantine resistance in Syria, Palestine, and Mesopotamia in Heraclius' third decade of rule was extremely serious, and the great Muslim victories over the

Sasanians indicated that something unique was happening, but everything was not played out. Muslim control was still fragile. It was unclear whether the Muslims would successfully establish tight and lasting and effective administrative control over the areas that they had so quickly overrun. There was still hope for the resolution of ecclesiastical fissures. The situation in Italy and Africa was no worse than before. The Byzantine imprint on Armenia was deeper than ever, even though many problems persisted. The Balkans, it is true, were mostly lost to the Byzantines. Everything had been very tenuous in 610, much as it still was in 641. Experience had been gained, but how well lessons had been learned remained to be seen. The empire was in worse shape than it had been when Heraclius seized power in the autumn of 610, but not much worse. It was for his successors to try to cope, just as he had. Yet almost all of the basic external and internal problems that he had inherited in 610 remained in 641. What he was managing to do, however hard, was to root his family as an imperial dynasty. It was a painful process, but it was taking place. By his tenacity he founded a long-lived dynasty. He managed to seize and to hold on to power, even though it had demanded unceasing struggle and vigilance, and even at the end of his life, the internal situation was tenuous. He and his family were in a stronger position at the end of his life than he had experienced for the first half of his life. He had accomplished a lot, despite the terrible fluctuations in his fortunes.

One internal threat to security had drastically diminished due to imperial policy, whether active or passive. No longer were restive Byzantine armies in the Balkans a threat to the throne. Whether by neglect or purges or destruction at the hands of Avars and Slavs in repeated campaigns, Byzantine troops in the Balkans ceased to be a major source of military unrest.[4] Even during lengthy imperial absences in the east on campaign against Persians or Muslims, or while reorganizing ecclesiastical matters, there are no reports of mutinies or revolts. No local Balkan commander took advantage of what would have been good opportunities. This silence probably reflects Heraclius' policies.

Heraclius at the end of his life established a policy and line of aggressively deflecting responsibility for the Byzantine defeats at the hands of the Muslims on to either his religious critics or on to others, even his own associates and appointees, such as Bishop Kyros and John Kateas, the *epitropos* in Osrhoene and Mesopotamia, and Theodore Trithyrios and Heraclius' own

---

[4] Kaegi, *Byzantine Military Unrest* 89–119, for instances of unrest in the Balkans in the sixth and early seventh centuries. Also, M. Whitby, *Emperor Maurice and His Historian* (Oxford, 1986) 151–168.

brother Theodore. All of these received blame for disobeying instructions. Heraclius laid down the foundations of this approach, which his successors would follow and elaborate in their struggles with their own critics. He did not passively wait for criticisms to fall upon himself; he actively sought out scapegoats and cast opprobrium on them. He did not stay on the political defensive, but instead he took the offensive against his critics. It was a risky strategy, but he probably believed that he could not afford to admit error on his own part, and he probably genuinely was angry at and frustrated with botched defenses that did not fully take advantage of the full human and material resources of the empire. That did not mollify all of his critics. It may well have complicated efforts to find and build up capable military commanders, because they did not wish to become sacrificial victims themselves. His stance probably discouraged flexible military initiatives. But he did stabilize a deteriorating military situation and prevented complete dissolution of military units.

Heraclius demonstrated extraordinary skill as a commander, strategist, and tactician who excelled at discerning, calculating, and exploiting volatile and reversible situations. He possessed rare timing skills that he occasionally used to great advantage. This was not an unerring skill, however, for he showed it only occasionally. He understood, at times, how to use the right talent, resolve, and pressure at the critical moment, to succeed, militarily and politically, with modest resources, in tough strife. He could appreciate tenuous, wavering military and politico-military situations, in which the ultimate outcome was not predetermined. Such situations present fascinating challenges, without firm rules. That is why he probably was so frustrated and angry at the end of the 630s, when he perceived that the situations in northern Syria and Egypt were not totally hopeless, but redeemable with proper moves and resolves and timing, which his subordinates evidently were failing to execute. He was unable to impart the skills for exploiting terrain that he showed in December 627 at Nineveh to other Byzantine commanders at the moment of the early Islamic conquests in Syria, Mesopotamia, and Egypt. Their failure to know and adapt to terrain greatly contributed to the decisive Byzantine defeat at the Yarmūk.

Heraclius exploited internal divisions and treachery among his foes in the case of Phokas (Priskos), Komentiolos, brother of Phokas (Justinos, commander of the Armenians), Priskos (summoning him to Constantinople, where he was condemned and publicly shamed), and Shahrbarāz and Kawadh-Siroy (who both betrayed Khusrau II). Heraclius probably hoped to find some vulnerable point among Muslim ranks. That may be a partial explanation for truces and pauses and even for Heraclius' order to try to hold on to existing positions without engaging in open combat. This is a hypothesis, not a securely documented fact. He was probably seeking to learn more about his new opponents, and then hoped to find ways to divide, undermine, and destroy them. That is consistent with his earlier practices. Although he did not wish his subordinates to negotiate on their own with Muslims, Heraclius probably did encourage some diplomatic contacts with the Muslims, in order to feel them out and find ways to divide and conquer them, just as he had successfully done with the Sasanians. Besides Byzantine weaknesses, that is probably a hidden reason – never, of course, admitted by chroniclers or rhetoricians – for some of his actions. He was playing for time, even though Byzantine withdrawal in the east was a military necessity and a prudent course. But the right opportunity did not present itself this time, not in his lifetime. Heraclius vainly sought a lever, or some powerful stratagem, to use against the Muslims. It was this kind of warfare, fight–talk, talk–fight, in which he excelled. He was not in optimal health to have exploited such an opportunity if one had briefly occurred. Nor did he have an adequate striking force to exploit such vulnerabilities, if they had appeared in the late 630s. He had no grasp of embryonic Islam. The Muslims probably were aware of his predilections. Some reports of Byzantine efforts to kidnap or assassinate Muslim commanders in the course of parleys during the early Islamic conquests may have some basis in fact, for such activities were typically Byzantine and especially typical of Heraclius. But probably by the end of his life he realized that such hopes were mere phantoms.

Heraclius devoted much time and effort to religious issues. Success and failure in religious dimensions are the most important elements of his reputation. He attempted to solve difficult religious issues and policies by cultivating personal relations with many important ecclesiastics within his empire. Whenever possible, he made generous donations to important churches. He supported efforts to proselytize remaining pockets of unbelievers in peripheral regions on the empire's borders, such as in the Caucasus. His efforts to shape and promote a Monothelete compromise solution for Christological problems failed decisively. Historical tradition associates his memory less with Monotheletism and the zealous promotion of Christianity than with the emergence of Islam. Heraclius faced a new religion that was in the process of formation. That made it especially difficult for him to try to cope with the challenge of Muslims. That religion was probably not fixed in form, but was in flux. It is no wonder that he and his advisers did not know how to understand, react to it, and formulate policies to contain or destroy it. His effort to unify fractious Christians proved to be his greatest failure and many will doubt whether anyone could have succeeded in the task that frustrated him. He inherited but exacerbated an extremely divided church and laity. The embittered internal religious situation that he left at his death encumbered his successors for decades. Inadvertently his ecclesiastical policies created opportunities for Islam, even though religious divisions in themselves did not cause the Islamic conquests.

Heraclius had to cope with ecclesiastics whose priorities were not military. However critical the military situation was against the Persians or Muslims, ecclesiastics and monks often had their minds on other priorities. If one looks at *The Spiritual Meadow* of John Moschos (d. 619),[5] which he dedicated to Sophronios, the later Patriarch of Jerusalem and opponent of Monotheletism, one finds stories of God saving monks and other ascetics from Mauretanians (Moors)[6] and Saracens or Arabs, but even though the work was completed around 619, in a dire era, there is no indication in the work of the exigencies of the empire or any need for ecclesiastics to work for the empire's salvation. If anything, the anecdotes offered hope for individuals for divine aid to escape injury from Saracens. Of course that was different from the empire and government and polity receiving such miraculous aid. All ecclesiastical skills and resources were not harnessed for concentrating on opposing barbarians. Some anecdotes seemed to report that God would somehow provide for the just. All attention was not focused on external affairs, even though the invaders might disrupt the very lives of the ascetics and other ecclesiastics. Heraclius cultivated holy men and sacred images for their support, but never put all of his trust in them.

Retrospective judgments are easy to make. Heraclius could have done more to conciliate Arabs and non-Arab subjects in territories that he was seeking to reoccupy and revive after his triumphal return from the Sasanian Empire. He could have ordered his brother Theodore and other subordinates to act more sensitively and responsibly when trying to fill the vacuum and authority and power after the Sasanian withdrawal from the Levant. He inherited the legacy of the poor Arab policies of Emperor Maurice and even of Khusrau II, both of whom had abused their respective Arab allies,

---

[5] John Moschos, *The Spiritual Meadow*, trans. John Wortley (Kalamazoo, MI: Cistercian Publications, 1992).

[6] John Moschos, *Spiritual Meadow* 20 (14 Wortley). In c. 21, a bird seizes, carries away a Saracen who slew an anchorite, and then dropped him to the ground dead, where he was turned to carrion (15 Wortley). In c. 99, a Saracen who attempted to slay a monastery elder was swallowed up by the earth in answer to the prayer of the elder (80 Wortley); c. 133, a monk in vicinity of Clysma/Suez, paralyzed a Saracen for two days when he threatened him with bodily force (109 Wortley); c. 155, three Saracens became possessed of demons and slew each other, permitting their prisoner to escape and become a monk (129 Wortley), in the region of Wadi Betasimon. See Daniel J. Sahas, "Saracens and Arabs in the Leimon of John Moschos," *Vyzantiaka* 17 (1997) 123–138.

leaving bitter memories in the ranks of their descendants. Yet on the eve of and during the initial Muslim invasions, Heraclius was able to recruit and enjoy the loyalty of important Christian Arab tribal entities. More sensitive and realistic policies of (1) subsidizing friendly Arabs, and (2) tolerating the smuggling and trading that Arabs developed on the periphery of Palestine and Syria during the obscure period of ostensible Sasanian control and occupation might have dampened or discouraged any violent response or removed grievances that could turn into rebellion or collaboration with other exogenous invaders.

Yet the negotiating and covert skills and strategic and tactical knowledge that enabled Heraclius to defeat the Persians were not the appropriate ones for defeating his next set of challengers: those Arabs who were already or in the process of becoming Muslims. He was much more cautious in reacting to them. There were no textbook solutions for fighting them, except to use other Arabs against them. And now there was some sort of an evolving new religion, Islam, which made it much more difficult to subvert them, and some of their leaders were likely aware of earlier Byzantine attempts to kidnap Arab leaders during parleys. The winning combination was no longer present. The responsibilities did not completely lie at the feet of Heraclius. It was Emperor Maurice who had dismantled and ruined the previous imperial policy of using a federated or allied Arab shield to protect the eastern and southeastern frontiers of the empire.[7] There was irony in Heraclius' panegyrists evoking the memory of Emperor Maurice in nostalgic and praiseworthy terms, even though the heritage that he unwittingly left to Heraclius was a very harmful one. Heraclius himself never developed a deep familiarity with Arabs during his extensive campaigning against the Persians, for most of his campaigning fell outside the normal range of most friendly and even hostile Arab settlement and pastoral zones. In the final ledger of Heraclius' life, internal strife inflicted the greatest damage on his empire and endangered his dynasty. Ironically, it had been internal strife on which he thrived and which he himself used to raise himself to power and to overcome the Persians, which would in the form of a bitter struggle to succeed him contribute to overwhelming his own empire, in large part because of his own marital and inheritance decisions. That struggle would greatly ease and accelerate Muslim victories in his last years and in the years that immediately followed his death in 641. At the end of his life Heraclius could not rely upon familial solidarity, given his troubles with his brother and nephew Theodore, let alone with his quarrelsome sons by two different

---

[7] Irfan Shahid, *Byzantium and the Arabs in the Sixth Century* I: 464–478, 529–563, 609.

marriages. Essentially, internal strife not dissimilar to the situation in which he seized power in 608–10 reemerged very late in his reign to undermine his final years and his efforts to provide for a smooth transition to his successors. Internal strife contributed to the evisceration of much that he had provisionally achieved. His erstwhile rival sovereign Khusrau II, who had almost fallen irrevocable victim of a conspiratorial military rebellion by Bahram in 590, ultimately succumbed to a complex military conspiracy with exogenous as well as internal dimensions in 628 that Heraclius partially precipitated or manipulated but in any case exploited. Heraclius himself fared better than Khusrau II in the face of conspiracies, but only to a limited degree. At the end of his life he could no longer master that strife, which burst forth at his death. Already it was evident in his final years and seriously complicated his efforts to create an effective resistance to the Muslims in the east and Egypt, let alone to the Slavs and Avars in the Balkans. As expert as he was in exploiting others' internal fissures, he failed to seal the fissures within his own family and regime. They endangered Byzantium as much as the formidable external threats did. Internal threats were multidimensional. The almost pathetic and falsely proclaimed harmony between his two sons Heraclius Constantine and Heraklonas and their constituencies is a prominent feature of the public culture of his final years, but the steadfast repetition of the theme of unity merely highlights how tenuous arrangements were.

From his proclamation in Africa as consul alongside his father to his final issues of gold coinages and public ceremonies, Heraclius and his advisers continually strove to establish and confirm the legitimacy and continuity of his authority, given the realities of its tenuousness. He could never stop trying to root the legitimacy of his power as firmly as possible in the face of embarrassing reminders of its fragility.

If we turn to look at the military side of Heraclius' victories over the Persians – how he defeated them – we have some good fortune. A Byzantine military manual written ca. 600, the so-called *Strategikon* of Maurikios, which includes Book 11 on how to fight other peoples, among them, the Persians, does describe contemporary conditions. Here we learn of the Persian preference to fight from or in rough terrain, and to avoid level and open fields, where Byzantine and Roman superiority in fighting in fixed formation at close quarters would likely be decisive. We learn of the Persians' preference for fighting in triple formation and of their vulnerability to flanking attacks. As one studies the extant contemporary accounts of Heraclius' conduct in battle, we see that he followed the advice of such a manual. The question then arises, why could not he have done this back in

612 and have avoided seventeen or eighteen years of ruinous warfare? If we study Heraclius' conduct in 622 and 627 we see him following a formula in fighting the Persians: lure them by simulated or feigned flight into pursuing you, have a carefully prepared counterattack, lure them onto a plain, counterattack and, using flanking attacks, crush them. We can, furthermore, read other sections of the *Strategikon*; we can locate probable actual tactical formations chosen and described in the narrative accounts. That is not usually possible in other periods of Byzantine military history. But the use of such tactics was part of a bold offensive strategy that unnerved his opponents and relied on excellent intelligence and excellent diplomatic alliances with other peoples, especially in the Caucasus. Those are qualities of a great commander, one who possesses some tactical and strategic genius.

But other political and diplomatic and institutional conditions were not propitious for that simple formula to work in Heraclius' favor for many years. It required more than formulae to win. Heraclius exploited multidimensional approaches and tools – timing, espionage, subversion, disinformation, and treachery, and skillful public relations and use of religion, exploitation of internal fissures within the ranks of his enemies – to defeat the Persians. Persian and Arab sources transmit traditions about that struggle as one of craft, cunning, and deception.

Heraclius was at the height of his powers mentally when he triumphed. However, even he could not adequately adjust to the sudden acceleration in the rate of historical change that occurred in the final decade of his life. He probably only began to comprehend the magnitude of his internal and external problems in the final five years of his life, during which the dangers merely continued to grow in intensity and multiply in number. Radically new variables made it difficult to think in terms of older and more familiar frames of reference. The old handbooks fitted a different group of circumstances. Historical precedents were of limited value. A man who had demonstrated a masterful sense of timing found that new contingencies were overwhelming him and his contemporaries materially and conceptually. Old techniques ceased to bring success. He had not done enough. His worsening and very painful medical condition complicated any efforts of his to devise solutions. Everything was going wrong at the end of his life. Troubles were cascading.

Longer term, more subtle processes continued. Like his contemporaries throughout his empire, Heraclius embraced and furthered the spread of saints' relics and their cults. Heraclius' reign saw the continuing conversion of the disappearing number of classical monuments and statues, either in the form of destruction by meltdown and stripping, or preservation by transformation into Christian uses. Two of the latter examples are the conversion in Rome of the Pantheon into a church, and similarly the conversion of the Roman senate building in the Roman forum into a church of St. Adriano, the first late in the first decade of the seventh century, just before Heraclius began to reign, and the second with Heraclius' permission around the year 630. The shortage of metal encouraged the scrapping of older classical monuments and works of art and sculpture, such as the Ox in the Forum of the Ox, in Constantinople. A broader process of conversion of classical remains to Christian purposes was occurring in literature and in other forms of culture, including in the visual arts. Although he participated in it, Heraclius did not initiate or cause that process, and he probably could not have halted it if he had wished. It had started long before his reign and continued far beyond it. He had too many other higher concerns to worry about it during his problem-plagued reign. The last traces of the imperial post system vanished with his reign. Similarly, he was apparently the last Byzantine emperor who founded or renamed cities for himself on a large scale, after the fashion of earlier Roman emperors.[8]

There was a great concern, underscored and probably exaggerated by the nature of the religious sources that survive, for the wealth of churches and cult sites. That wealth existed and was measured in terms of ornamentation in silver, other precious metals, and precious stones. Heraclius accepted and encouraged the prevailing admiration of the wealth of churches expressed in precious metals, although he and his subordinates found it necessary to tap that wealth to help to pay for military emergencies. Accidental finds of silver plate from Heraclius' reign, such as the David Plates, provide some glimpse of the private, public, and ecclesiastical wealth and craftsmanship that still existed in his age. Subsequent Byzantine eras have not left comparable lavishly crafted silver objects.

Financial matters reached a snapping point by Heraclius' death. Somehow fiscal officials had scrambled to manage to keep things going. Somehow churches continued to receive imperial largesse and privileges, but the paucity of governmental funds was about to compel resort to seizure of ecclesiastical treasures once more. His was the end of an era. For some churches on the periphery, compulsory expropriations had already begun. In some peripheral regions, like Italy, troops did not receive their pay regularly. Things had to change.

---

[8] Thomas S. Brown, Antony Bryer, David Winfield, "Cities of Heraclius," *BMGS* 4 (1978) 15–38.

Heraclius alternated between borrowing from churches and lavishing wealth on them. He similarly alternated between generosity and penuriousness in handling public funds for buildings and public works. At the termination of his victorious war with the Persians, he found himself in control of a seemingly vast surplus of financial resources, so he released substantial funds in many localities for reconstruction, repair, and new construction. He could not afford such expenditures during the long period of warfare with the Persians and Avars. But the Muslim invasions abruptly cut off his imperial generosity with public funds in the early and middle 630s. So his was a fluctuating policy that followed the course of imperial military fortunes. Although ridden with contradictions, it reflected fiscal and military realities. Heraclius was unable to escape from such constraints.

Heraclius exacerbated the financial exhaustion of the empire by liberal spending on reconstruction of secular and religious structures, thereby fulfilling deferred expenditures that were expected of an emperor as part of his generosity. He committed great sums for public works and for churches in various parts of the empire. Military expenditures that soared to meet the Muslim threat left Heraclius' treasury even emptier, much emptier. Contemporary authors, unlike modern commentators, do not display awareness of and probably did not dare to speak of any "exhaustion" of the empire whether from protracted warfare or from excessive financial commitments to construction and reconstruction. Instead they speak of Heraclius' restoration or revival of empire and structures within it. He had spent the war spoils and more by the middle of the 630s. Whether tax collections had ever been restored to normal after reoccupying the east (from the Persians) is doubtful – some anecdotal information (Eutychios) suggests that there was still haggling on the part of local authorities in the east about money owed to Constantinople from the time of their occupation by the Persians. He may have had little choice, for contemporary memory recalled the violent end of his predecessor Emperor Maurice, whose stinginess attracted opprobrium.

There are other qualifying observations. Significantly, unlike against the Persians, Heraclius did not appear in battle against the Muslims, nor even show himself near them. Court-inspired historians and chroniclers are careful to exonerate him and to claim that he warned his commanders about the dangers of Arabs ambushing Byzantines, that it was his commanders who failed to follow his all-wise counsel and that is what caused their terrible defeats. His decision to remain far to the north in Syria had its positive elements: he avoided personal exposure to risky combat, he covered his vital lines of communications. He remained in a position that gave him options. His pivotal location in northern Syria put him astride key communications with Constantinople and with Persia. And his very presence in northern Syria threatened or at least could influence the actions of the fragile political leadership in the Sasanian Empire, for the Sasanian decision-makers could not be certain what he might do if he strongly objected to some of their policies. He apparently ended up advocating that his commanders follow a defensive strategy of holding to seemingly secure fixed positions against the Muslims. That policy failed decisively in the short term.

It is hard to envisage the Muslim conquests without Heraclius, or Byzantine defenses without his having inspired their beginnings. He set the precedent for leading vigorous yet realistic resistance against the Muslims, and some Monophysite sectarians, such as Jacobites, as well as Muslims, associated his memory and name with Byzantine military resistance to the early Islamic conquests. He personalized Byzantine resistance for posterity, however deficient his actual policies and leadership were. He did help to play for time, avoid unnecessary risks to what remained of his armies (by avoiding another major battle where all of them might be lost), and he did help to create a strategic withdrawal and regrouping. He or his commanders and his immediate successors and advisers did learn something from Byzantine mistakes. They did succeed in devising some tactical, operational, and strategic responses to Muslim techniques of avoiding assaults on Byzantine walled towns, overrunning the countryside, and establishing new military bases and settlements of their own. That process began in his lifetime, even though no winning formulae had yet been found. That will, in addition to topography, did help the Byzantines to fashion an ultimately successful defense of Anatolia, and with it, their empire. Heraclius, in sum, helped to make Byzantium survive another 800 years while its old competitor Persia crumbled to the Muslim invaders. Although no great institutional reformer, he stamped his forceful yet ambiguous and torn personality on historical memories.

Heraclius' greatest institutional achievement was not so much military as a permanent transformation of fiscal institutions, the details of which remain obscure. Most notably he encouraged the emergence of the office of treasurer, or *sakellarios*, from the ruins of the once powerful institution of the pretorian prefecture.

As a Latin Spanish chronicler put it in the following century, using some unidentified eastern source: "he subdued the rebellious Persians and restored the imperial lands through his fighting. Seduced, as they say, by the praises of his people, he heaped the honor of victory not on God but on himself, [but] grimly foreseeing no small rebuke [for himself] by means of a vision, he was frequently in terror."[9]

What should we make of Heraclius' reported astrological investigations?[10] Did they deceive him? Or are they merely another story or legend, or possibly a malevolent tale to depict him engaged in wrongful acts that somehow led to implicit divine retribution, part of a series of legends of Heraclius the immoderate and the proud, whose improper actions led him down a road to ruin?

Particularly difficult to evaluate is the expanded role of Armenians within the Byzantine army during the course of Heraclius' reign, and in particular, at the end of it. The wars with the Persians and the Muslim invasions, the loss of the Balkans with its formerly formidable recruits, and the reticence of hitherto reliable African troops to fight for Heraclius had, almost by default, catapulted Armenians into a highly valued category. He probably never trusted troops from the Balkans, given the history of their restiveness and former support of Phokas. That process had been intensifying in the 630s. Heraclius again had thought that he knew how to manage them, but as his health deteriorated and the struggle for the succession intensified, their role became more crucial, and for some, more threatening. Heraclius had not solved that problem at his death, and in fact it would overcome his wife, his children by his second marriage, and severely threaten his grandson, Constans II, when he became emperor and for a number of years of his reign. Heraclius probably had not anticipated that in his other efforts to overcome and confound internal political and military threats to his regime and family. Still more ironies would surround his efforts to turn to Armenians as a reliable cohort, even though he was to punish a number of them, including with exile, before his own death.[11] The upshot was that his reign, especially the final fifteen years, experienced a significant strengthening of the role of Armenians within the armies and as holders of important commands.

Heraclius confronted the distressing news of the premature death of his first wife, Fabia/Eudokia, and the ill health of their son and his first heir and successor, Heraclius Constantine. His marriage to his niece Martina remains one of the major puzzles of his life. It and its offspring complicated

[9] Trans. from Hoyland, *Seeing Islam as Others Saw It* 614–615. Latin text: *Cont. Isidorianae, Cont. Hisp., MGH AA* 11: 337: ". . . Persas rebellantes edomuit, imperiales patrias belligerando reformavit, seductus a laudibus populi non deo, sed sibi, ut ferunt, honorem victorie exaggerando, increpationem per visum non modicam graviter presagando crebrem expavit."

[10] François Nau, "Appendice. Héraclius astrologue et astronome," at end of his edn. of "La didascalie de Jacob, première assemblée," *PO* 8 (1912) 742–744. Also, Fredegarius 4.65 (52–54 Wallace-Hadrill).

[11] Sebeos, *History* 133, 143, ch. 41, 44 (93, 107 Thomson); *Hist.* c. 39, 42 (102, 110 Gugerotti).

his final years and raises other puzzling questions: just how aware was he of the criticism of that marriage and, if so, how did he react and what were his options?

Other enigmas persist. It is unclear whether Heraclius ever had regrets for his Jewish policies, in particular the compulsory baptisms in Africa, although some believe that he did have contrition for some purges after his visit to Galilee in early 630. But again, this is obscure. It is likewise unclear whether he changed policy at the end of his reign – certainly there is no source for that – and how the Muslim conquests affected, if at all, his policies and his attitudes towards Jews. Although he engaged in an aggressive effort to deflect the blame for external reverses onto scapegoats, he did not, apparently, try to blame the Jews for his reverses at the hands of the Muslims or Slavs and Avars, even though very recently contemporaries had blamed Jews for collaborating with the Persians in the capture, massacre, torture, and captivity of Christians at Jerusalem and in the Holy Land.

Heraclius died at a moment of intensifying apocalypticism within the Near East and Mediterranean. Sources such as the *Doctrina Jacobi* from his own reign anticipate the end. The following decades would witness the circulation of still more apocalyptic texts, such as the *Apocalypse* of Pseudo-Methodios as well as the expectations of final days or the end of time in the body of broader sources such as the *History* attributed to Sebeos.[12] But we cannot ascertain to what degree he ever shared in such apocalyptic beliefs.

Heraclius cannot have regarded his entire life and career as a total failure at the moment of his death. His empire still stretched from the straits of Gibraltar to the edge of the Caucasus, although his armies had now evacuated Syria. After all, Byzantine armies were still resisting in Egypt and upper Mesopotamia, and extreme northern Syria had not been irrevocably written off, as we know from final Byzantine probes into them. He believed that he had purged the army of unreliable elements. That was to prove to be a false hope, but the situation looked better than it had in 610 or 612, when Komentiolos, the brother of Phokas, and Priskos were still able to control significant forces within the armies. So however dire, the military situation at the beginning of 641 still looked better than it had in the ten years between 619 and 629. The empire still controlled much more land and many more subjects than it had in 619–629. Things were looking perilous and were teetering, but no one could then have been certain that Syria and Palestine were lost, or that Egypt and Libya would soon fall. Although Muslims had

---

[12] See interpretations of apocalypticism in Sebeos according to Dr. Tim Greenwood, "A History of Armenia in the Seventh and Eighth Centuries." F. Donner and David Cook believe that it is a vital element in many of the earliest Muslim communities.

penetrated as far as Melitene, on the far side of the Tauros Mountains, they did not probe into the Anatolian plateau until a year or two after his death and they did not begin the devastating "winterings" in Anatolia until the year 662–663.[13] He had not had to witness that. Counterfactual speculations are dangerous. There is no evidence that if he had lived longer, even with better health, he would have been able to devise an effective way to check the Muslims, let alone roll back their recent conquests. There is no evidence that he was on the verge of finding some great successful formulae to meet or overcome their challenge.

It is not easy to ascertain how much Heraclius changed over his lifetime. He continued to accumulate wisdom about his empire and its diverse localities throughout his life. His breadth of experience stretched from western regions of the empire to the eastern frontiers and beyond, and was without parallel since emperors of the Constantinian and Theodosian dynasties, especially Constantine I, for whom he had much admiration and with whom he and his panegyrists chose to compare himself, as well as Constantius II, and Julian, and Theodosius I. There were many layers to Heraclius' Byzantine Empire. There were echoes of Carthage as well as those of Rome, the Assyrians, Medes and Persians, and Alexander the Great. How conscious Heraclius was of those or any of them other than Rome is uncertain. He did not have the leisure at any point in his long reign to think much about such matters in isolation. At his accession the empire controlled or virtually controlled every major maritime and commercial opening to the Mediterranean – the straits of Gibraltar, the Bosphorus, and the northern end of the Red Sea – but at his death this last one was being overrun by the Muslims. Heraclius' vast experience proved of limited value in meeting the new challenges of the 630s and early 640s.

It is unclear whether Heraclius continued to grow intellectually. Potentially his diverse experiences gave him the possibility to develop an integrated appreciation of his changing yet multifaceted empire. Like Theodosius I, he had come to Constantinople from the west, bringing with him very different perspectives. Yet unlike Theodosius, his paternal family came from much further east, with experiences from the virtual edge of the Caucasus. Throughout his life he reinforced his heritage with more layers of travels and encounters. How much of his unique heritage and insights he imparted to his heirs is impossible to ascertain. There were to be no more Byzantine emperors who gained comparable experience and perspectives

---

[13] Three sources give the date: AH 42 (= 662–663 CE): Ibn Sa'd, *Kitāb al-Ṭabaqāt al-kabīr*, ed. E. Sachau, K.V. Zettersteen (Leiden: Brill, 1905) 5.166; Ibn 'Asākir, *TMD* 37.114; Muḥammad ibn 'Alī 'Aẓīmī, *Ta'rīkh Ḥalab*, ed. Ibrāhim Za'rūr (Damascus, 1984) 177. I thank Paul Cobb for help.

from service in the west. With the important exception of members, especially female, of the imperial family, he does not appear to have surrounded
himself with advisers or commanders from the west.

A unique and extraordinarily rich and complex mix of experiences and
influences formed Heraclius. Their complexity probably left some unresolved contradictions in his personality, but also complicated the task of
internal and external opponents who sought to understand and confound
him. It contributed to his mystique. One could not simply interpret him
as a new David, new Moses, or new Constantine, nor was he simply an
African or Armenian, or simply an echo of earlier Roman emperors. There
were loose ends.

Heraclius held complex if incompletely formed views. He did not consider his empire to be a Near Eastern state. It was a Roman one, however
vague that was in his mind. However, his empire was in the process of transformation into a more Near Eastern one irrespective of his wishes during
his reign. He had a social consciousness, for he wished to have a reputation
for justice and righteousness and as a leader who remedied the sufferings
of the weak. But social and economic redistributions were not policies that
he pursued.

Late in his life Heraclius grew more cautious and conservative. Perhaps
this was a natural process for someone of his age, but risks from internal
threats as well as consciousness of limited resources probably reinforced
that proclivity. It probably was wise for him to avoid taking great military
risks at the end of his life. He had, moreover, no trustworthy captain to
whom he could turn over military responsibilities, especially as the imperial succession crisis intensified. His former trustworthy associates died,
disappeared, disqualified themselves by questionable actions, leaving him
increasingly isolated and dependent on those who lacked the requisite military and diplomatic skills to reverse trends. It is impossible to ascertain
how much any aging process had affected him in his final years, given
the lack of specific data. There is no evidence that his intellectual faculties were failing.[14] Heraclius may have suffered by the time of the battle
of the Yarmūk from Post-Traumatic Stress Disorder, PTSD, which could
have affected his performance and which may have increased his suspicion
of others, including his brother Theodore. But there is no reliable test to
ascertain whether that was the case.[15]

---

[14] Mortality among Roman emperors and within the imperial family, including that of Heraclius:
Walter Scheidel, "Emperors, Aristocrats and the Grim Reaper: Towards a Demographic Profile of
the Roman Elite," *Classical Quarterly* 49 (1999) 254–281.

[15] Lawrence Tritle suggested that Post-Traumatic Stress Disorder may explain Heraclius' irregular
conduct and psychological reactions in the middle and late 630s, in the Conference on "Perspectives
on War and War Experience, Ancient and Modern," 14 October 2000, Loyola University of Chicago.

Because no record of Heraclius' daily calendar survives, unlike for some sovereigns and statesmen of later periods, one cannot judge how much, if at all, his daily routine changed over the course of his lifetime. There is no evidence whether he had special avocations or pleasures in his final years. There are some limited observations to make. In his final six or seven years, he showed himself to wage war cautiously, perhaps reflecting a lifetime of lessons learned, but he had demonstrated caution in his 622 campaign as well. He probably changed too little to confound his new Arab foes. He retained enough sense about military politics to know how to snuff out and severely punish conspiracies; his old experiences kept him ahead, even in advanced years, of ambitious younger plotters.

Heraclius remained sensitive to public criticism and tried to manipulate public opinion and his reputation. Whether he succeeded in becoming more adept at that in older age than in his young maturity is uncertain. In historical traditions, he remained in control of public affairs until his death and did not relinquish decision-making to others, such as a regency or council, especially since he resided at Constantinople in his last years.

We can never know what was inside Heraclius' head. Such psychological insights are impossible to uncover, given the nature and limitations of our sources. Sources personalize details about him. A few inferences may be possible from anecdotes, but they are risky to draw. Intimate details of his relationships with his children are unavailable. Likewise we cannot know how tender he was with members of his immediate family. There is every outward indication that his family meant a great deal to him, that he tried to be considerate to all of them, but intimate details are lacking. We do not know his dietary preferences or his favorite pastimes, except for his reported liking for fighting lions, probably as a young man, and this may be no more than a *topos*. There is no evidence about his likes and dislikes during his lifetime of travels, that is, which of the lands that he visited did he like the most, and did he bring back and cherish any mementos, other than some renowned relics? Throughout most of his life he demonstrated that he was not shy, even though at the end he probably and understandably avoided many public appearances.

Heraclius' regnal formulae or official titulature varied somewhat during his long reign. It could be "Reign of our most divine and most pious *despotes*/ruler greatest benefactor Fl. Heraclius eternal Augustus and Autokrator..." or "Reign of our most pious *despotes* Fl. Heraclius eternal Augustus and Autokrat or..." or "reign of most pious and lover of mankind [*philanthropos*] *despotes* Fl. Heraclius eternal Augustus" or "Reign of the our most divine and serene and God-crowned *despotes* Fl. Heraclius eternal Augustus and Autokrator and greatest benefactor . . . "[16] His first consular year was 611/612.[17] Contemporary Armenian inscriptions from the 630s, the dating of which by Byzantine regnal years testified to spreading Byzantine prestige, echo Greek usage by commemorating him on churches as "King Heraclius protected by God" (Bagavan, 632), "Heraclius pious king" (Alaman, 638), and "victorious king Heraclius" (Mren, 640).[18]

Various historical and literary sources may exaggerate Heraclius' centrality to seventh-century events and developments. However, there are cases in which his name and influence are surprisingly absent. The *Miracles of St. Demetrios*, for example, which concern Thessalonica and its vicinity, are silent about Heraclius despite references to Constantinople and to events that unmistakably took place between 615 and 620.[19] Everything did not revolve around him in every locality of the empire. Local memories do not always preserve a prominent place for him.

Institutional history is no longer a central topic of historical inquiry and theory. It ceases, therefore, to be important whether Heraclius was a great institutional reformer, even though it now may appear that he was not. He was a conservator rather than a gambler. Yet he made some improvisations. He had no master plan for defending or reorganizing the empire, although his experiences in exploiting his various earlier opponents helped him to appreciate issues of internal strife and his regime's vulnerability to it, and accordingly to start the process of tightening controls over local officials and commanders, even though that process would take many decades, if not a century or more. He was no superman, although he tried very hard, within the limits of human abilities and his thought world.

Heraclius seized power at a time of imperial overstretch. He could not have anticipated that the pace of change was suddenly accelerating after many years of almost glacially slow rates of change. Such an intensification of the rate of change would have tested anyone. Although unable to master those processes, he succeeded in avoiding total destruction in their wake.

Heraclius after Heraclius is another story. Advocates for a host of causes and policies invoked his name and alleged final wishes to support their agenda soon after his decease. To posterity, his life and reign served as a

---

[16] K.A. Worp, "Regnal Formulas of the Emperor Heraclius," *JJP* 23 (1993) 217–232.

[17] Bernhard Palme, "Das erste Konsulat des Kaiser Heraclius," *JJP* 26 (1996) 117–126. See Constantin Zuckerman, "La formule de datation du *SB* VI 8986 et son témoignage sur la succession d'Héraclius," *JJP* 25 (1995) 187–202.

[18] I gratefully acknowledge Tim Greenwood's translations, from chapter 5, "Armenian Epigraphy of the Seventh and Eight Centuries," in his dissertation on Sebeos, "A History of Armenia in the Seventh and Eighth Centuries," pp. 287–288.

[19] Paul Lemerle, *Les plus anciens recueils des miracles de Saint Démétrius* II: 110.

benchmark. His grandson dug up his crown, and in similar fashion others exhumed and reused parts of his heritage, sometimes with respect and sometimes not. He left his stamp on the grounds of his favorite imperial palace, the Hiereia. Memories of that lasted at least a couple of centuries. Heraclius loomed as a tragic figure in Arabic poetry, as a verse of the pre-Islamic poet al-A'shā referred to the "Heraclius at the day of Sātīdamā" (*yawm Sātīdamā*), even though the literary representation and later historical commentaries on the verse distorted the actual historical context, chronology, and significance of that specific battle.[20] The tenth-century Emperor Constantine VII Porphyrogenitus referred back to him as "Heraclius the Libyan," after whose reign the empire was "reduced in the east and the west and its limits cut down."[21] For Constantine VII, Heraclius was also the Byzantine emperor with whom the early sovereigns of the Croats and Serbs initiated diplomatic relations and dependencies, thereby establishing useful precedents for Byzantine international policy in the tenth century.[22] Heraclius, through the agency of his general at Belgrade, reportedly settled Serbs from Macedonia in Zakhlumia, Terbounia, and Kanalite lands. For Muslims and for his Christian opponents, he served as an example of overweening pride and ignorance, a lesson in arrogance for the future, even if those memories diverged from historical realities. Posterity attributed many critical decisions and precedents to Heraclius, sometimes for self-serving reasons that were meaningful only in later ages. These attributions may have artificially lengthened his shadow over subsequent eras. Heraclius and his contemporaries showed great interest in not only religious relics. But contemporaries inside and outside the empire also coveted physical relics of Heraclius himself that had great prestige immediately following his decease. His grandson Emperor Constans II in 660 bestowed a belt of Heraclius on Juansher, son of Varaz-Grigor, prince of Albania, "he girt about him the royal belt of his valiant grandfather Heraclius and his grandmother Niketas (Nikita) . . ."[23] Despite significant military defeats late in his life, Heraclius and objects that were associated with him still enjoyed great prestige in the immediately following decades inside and outside the empire.

[20] Rudolf Geyer, *Gedichte von Abu Bashir Maimun ibn Qais al-'A'sha* (London, 1928) poem 36, line 10, p. 160, cf. gloss on p. 158; locality and context: Yāqūt, *Jacut's Geographisches Wörterbuch*, ed. Ferdinand Wüstenfeld. (Leipzig, 1924) 2.6–8, 552. Observations: Werner Caskel, "Ein Sonderbarer Anonymus des ersten Jahrhunderts d.H.," *Oriens* 16 (1963) 89–98, esp. 91.

[21] Constantine VII, *De thematibus*, Pr., ed. A. Pertusi (Rome, 1952) 60.

[22] Constantine VII, *De administrando imperio* c. 31, 32, ed., trans. G. Moravcsik, R. Jenkins (Washington: Dumbarton Oaks, 1967) 146–150, 152–154.

[23] Moses Dasxuranci, *History of the Caucasian Albanians* 2.22 (119 Dowsett). Niketas was not Constans II's grandmother's name, which really was Fabia/Eudokia, although his uncle was Niketas and there were other prominent Niketas' at court and intermarried with the imperial family.

Nothing can demonstrate the desperate character of financial conditions at the end of Heraclius' reign more than the shocking fate of his own crown. He and it could not remain in his white marble tomb in the traditional burial church for emperors, the Church of the Holy Apostles at Constantinople.[24] Reportedly, Constans II was told that his crown had been buried with Heraclius. Constans II had it dug up and removed from the grave; its value was seventy pounds of gold.[25] His action can be interpreted several ways: (1) to save it from theft by those who resented his succession, or simply by graverobbers; (2) to demonstrate that he controlled it, instead of his rivals – that he, Constans, was the legitimate emperor; (3) because Constans and his empire lacked the financial resources to create a comparable new crown for the emperor – it was then nonsensical to allow it to remain buried and unused. In any case, Heraclius' crown was not allowed to rest undisturbed with Heraclius himself in the grave. The only surviving contemporary European crowns are those of the Visigothic King Reccesvinth (653–672)and his wife, which they donated to the church in Spain just a decade or two after the death of Heraclius, and that of the Visigothic King Reccared (586–601) They now rest respectively in the Madrid Archaeological Museum and in the Louvre, but, however fascinating, they are likely to be far more modest than that of Emperor Heraclius, and so give little idea of what his crown might have looked like. For that one must examine numismatic representations of Heraclius. Emperor Leo IV more than a century later reportedly coveted Heraclius' crown, which had been deposited in the treasury of St. Sophia. When he placed it on his head, the boils that broke out on his head caused him to die of fever. Such was the story that Empress Irene's agents or other iconodule constituencies circulated and that found its way into later traditions.[26] So the heritage of Heraclius remained a strange and seemingly potent one long after his decease.

Later Byzantines invoked Heraclius' name for many reasons. Even though he engaged in some *de facto* truces or provisional arrangements with Muslims, by the Latin conquest of Constantinople in 1204 some Byzantines believed an equestrian statue of Justinian I at Constantinople was really Heraclius "and he was holding out his hand toward heathendom, and there were letters written on the statue which said that he swore that the

---

[24] Heraclius' tomb was white marble, whether Proconnesian or Docimian: P. Grierson, "Tombs and Obits of the Byzantine Emperors," *DOP* 16 (1962) 48.

[25] Nikephoros, *Short History* 30 (81 Mango).

[26] Georgios Kedrenos, *Hist.*, ed. I. Bekker (Bonn, 1839) 2.20; W. Treadgold, "An Indirectly Preserved Source for the Reign of Leo IV," *JÖB* 34 (1984) 69–76.

Saracens should never have truce from him."[27] Twisted memories invoked Heraclius as an inveterate foe of Islam, having made him into a kind of falsified yet usable past. But his superlative military distinctions continued to reverberate. Early in the thirteenth century Michael Choniates praised Heraclius in a letter to Emperor Theodore I Laskaris: "For I believe no emperors who have reigned in the City are equal to you, except for the great Basil the Bulgar-slayer in modern times, and the noble Heraclius in more ancient times. For these alone until the end prevailed against the enemy and remained undefeated while subjugating the greatest nations."[28]

Heraclius' reign was lengthy. Some of his subjects may well have tired of him and the repeated tests they or their families had suffered during his reign. It is not surprising that his immediate successors struck coins invoking, without further explanation, the concept of *ananeōsis*, "Renewal," for he left an empire that needed that process.[29]

No Byzantine emperor experienced such a great spread between success and failure in the same reign.[30] Heraclius never gave up completely. He was no quitter;[31] he could not afford to be one. He acted responsibly until the end, no matter what his physical pain. He took responsibility for trying to salvage matters. In the end, somehow the Heracles legend embedded in Heraclius' own name seems more appropriate than any Davidic[32] one to characterize his life and work, and the crises that he confronted that formed the major story and stuff of his life.

The skeptic may ask whether Heraclius made a difference. Yes, perhaps because he had, through his extensive campaigning in Anatolia, especially at Caesarea, become familiar with the key role of mountain passes as choke points, he was able to stabilize the front after the disastrous early great victories of the Muslims in Syria and Mesopotamia. Even his wary stationing of troops in 628–629 along the Tauros passes in order to block any possible penetration by Shahrbarāz's forces reinforced his and his commanders' already considerable appreciation of the strategic importance of those

---

[27] Robert de Clari, *The Conquest of Constantinople*, trans. Edgar Holmes McNeal (Columbia Records of Civilization; New York: Columbia, 1936) 107. Original: *La conquête de Constantinople* c. 86, ed. Philippe Lauer (Les Classiques français du Moyen Age; Paris: Champion, 1924) 86.

[28] *Michael Akominatou tou Choniatou ta sozomena* Ep. 179.4, ed. Sp. Lampros (Athens, 1880) II: 354.

[29] P. Grierson, *DOCat* II.2: 391–392, 394, *DOCat.* nos. Heraclonas 5a, 5b (6); Constans II nos. 59–69, 90–95.

[30] Judicious comment of P. Lemerle, "Quelques remarques sur le règne d'Héraclius," *Studi medievali* 1 (1960) pondering whether Heraclius dominated his age or was dominated by it.

[31] N.H. Baynes remarked, "It was the glory of Heraclius that he did not despair of the Roman state," in "The Military Operations of the Emperor Heraclius," *The United Services Magazine*, n.s. 45 (1913) 533.

[32] P. Speck, *Das geteilte Dossier* 337f; Claudia Ludwig, "Kaiser Herakleios" 101f.

gateways to the Anatolian plateau. Likewise he energetically removed local officials who were negotiating local deals with the Arab Muslims; that is, paying them off to avoid Arab military action. He emphatically did not give up. He started the process of creating a new land census for what remained of his entire empire, even though there would understandably be many complaints about the new tax liabilities. From these points one might cautiously conclude that one leader could affect the course of events even though he was unable to halt or reverse them entirely. He displayed independent leadership and decision-making that did not simply reflect or yield to long-term processes, even though it would be otiose to attempt to understand him outside his contemporary historical context.

The life and reign of Heraclius raise issues concerning just how much one can expect an individual, even one of exceptional talents and effort, to accomplish in the face of adverse circumstances and trends. Heraclius managed to do a lot, yet he could not prevent his Late Roman world and empire from imploding. But within his lifetime many events occurred that were not merely parts of larger trends. Could he have checked or altered them? A related issue is whether at certain turning-points, if one concedes that such may ever exist, an individual can have decisive influence. It was the Muslims rather than Heraclius who permanently transformed a fluid and volatile situation. All of these remarks are speculative. Phokas on the verge of his own execution allegedly asked Heraclius, "Will you be able to do better?" One modern commentator remarked, "In spite of the transient victories of the 620s, Heraclius failed the test; the year 602, adopted by Jones, is an appropriate terminus for the Roman empire in the east."[33]

Heraclius' true aims and will became, like his policies, the subject of controversy immediately following his death, as they had been during his lifetime. Controversy in different forms has plagued his reputation and significance even in the twentieth century, and very likely will in the twenty-first.

Heraclius' own poet George of Pisidia prophetically reflected on the instability of life, and his words are in some way applicable to Heraclius himself and his entourage even though the poet would never have dared to make such an association:

Suddenly fades the splendor that surrounds and all the unstable vanity of human glory stretches out and again constricts, like an evil lowly serpent with its contortions it seems to stretch and then constricts, in order that we may learn the nature and offspring of the arrogant like vipers.

---

[33] M. Whitby, "The Successors of Justinian," in *Cambridge Ancient History* XIV (2000) 111.

The whole course of life and the soft lump of everything human passes like a ball inflated with air: in appearance the ball rises toward the height of the heavens, but it is sufficient that accidentally some trifle makes it fall in the middle – a straw, a crumb, a drop – because its empty lightness is pressured by the violent impact.[34]

---

[34] George of Pisidia, Εἰς τὸν μάταιον βίον, "On the Vain Life" 10.215–225 (*Carmi* 442 Tartaglia).

Chronological table

Ca. 575	Birth of Heraclius
586/7–589	Father Heraclius serves in combat on eastern frontier and near Nisibis
ca. 600	Heraclius the Elder appointed exarch in Africa
602	Phokas overthrows and executes Emperor Maurice and his family
603	Persians under Khusrau II start war against Byzantines, ostensibly to avenge Maurice
608	Heraclius and his father launch rebellion against Phokas in Africa, proclaim themselves *consules*
609–610	Niketas, cousin of Heraclius, overruns Egypt
610	Heraclius departs from Africa for Constantinople with expeditionary force
18 April 610	Sergios appointed Patriarch of Constantinople
3 October 610	Heraclius lands at Hebdomon fort near Constantinople, resistance crumbles
5 October 610	Phokas and his officials are seized and executed
5 October 610	Heraclius is crowned by Patriarch Sergios, marries Eudokia, who is raised to rank of Augusta
late 610	Rebellion of Komentiolos, brother of Phokas, terminates with his murder
610–620	Phase I warfare with Persia: defeat and stabilization
610–611	Persians decisively penetrate Byzantine defenses in northern Syria
7 July 611	Daughter Epiphania is born, crowned 4 October 612
3 May 612	Oldest son, Heraclius II Constantine, born
6 August 612	Death of Heraclius' wife Eudokia, of epilepsy
5 December 612	Heraclius dismisses Priskos as Count of Excubitors because of his failure to trap Persians at Caesarea
22 January 613	Coronation of Heraclius Constantine

spring 613	Heraclius unsuccessfully campaigns to save Antioch in Syria; Persian victories split the empire into parts; fall of Emesa and Damascus
17 or 20 May 614	Persians storm Jerusalem
615	Failed diplomatic contacts with Persians, including meeting with Shāhīn
615	Hexagram coin struck with inscription *Deus adiuta Romanis*
619	Persians complete occupation of Egypt by capturing Alexandria
617, 619	Failure of rebellions in Italy
winter 621/622	Heraclius withdraws to Hiereia Palace
early 622	Heraclius borrows church plate for military emergency
622/623	Heraclius marries his niece Martina
622	Phase II warfare with Persia: testing techniques of offensive warfare
5 April 622	Heraclius leaves Constantinople to campaign in Asia Minor where by late autumn he wins morale-building victories against Persians
5 June 623	Avar Khan attempts to seize Heraclius during negotiations
624–628	Phase III warfare with Persia: shift to large-scale offensive expeditionary warfare
25 March 624	Heraclius departs from Constantinople for Armenia
624	Heraclius passes through Theodosiopolis, Ayrarat, destroys Dvin, Takht-i-Suleiman
end of 624	Heraclius defeats Shahrbarāz near Arcesh, encamps north of Lake Van
1 March 625	Heraclius commences rapid withdrawal from east via Nymphios River, Amida, Samosata, to Cilician Gates, with Shahrbarāz in hot pursuit
29 June–1 August 626	Avar-Persian siege and blockade of Constantinople
late 626, early 627	Shahrbarāz and Khusrau II develop mutual mistrust and dislike, Heraclius begins covert contact with Shahrbarāz
mid-September 627	Phase IV warfare: Heraclius, having contacted Kök Turks, sets out from Tiflis to invade Mesopotamia
1 December 627	Heraclius reaches Zāb River

12 December 627	Battle of Nineveh. Heraclian victory, Persian disintegration
22 January 628	Khusrau II evacuates Dastagard Palace
January–early February 628	Heraclius probes Nahrawān Canal region, turns north
23/24 February 628	Khusrau II is overthrown and executed (29 February)
24 March–3 April 628	Heraclius receives Persian delegation for peace from King Siroy
21 March 629	Heraclius at Constantinople designated "Faithful in Christ *Basileus*"
July 629	Phase IV ends: Heraclius and Shahrbarāz reach understanding at Arabissos
14 September 629	Holy Sponge arrives in Constantinople, through efforts of Patrikios Niketas, son of Shahrbarāz, is exaltated with the Cross
28 October 629	Holy Lance arrives in Constantinople, is venerated
21 March 630	Heraclius accompanies fragment of the Cross to Jerusalem from Hierapolis for its reinstallation
31 March 630	Word reaches Constantinople of Heraclius' reinstallation of the Cross in Jerusalem
summer 630	Heraclius meets Nestorian Catholicos Ishoyahb III at Berrhoia/Aleppo
630/631	Heraclius' appointee Kyros assumes Patriarchate at Alexandria, Egypt
spring 631	Heraclius negotiates with Monophysite Patriarch Athanasios of Antioch at Hierapolis, Syria
631 or 632/633	Heraclius supports negotiations with Armenian ecclesiastics at Theodosiopolis, some clerics agree to accept Chalcedon
632	Forcible baptism of Jews in Africa, although its universal application uncertain
632–633	Troubles among Arab tribes causes Heraclius to try to shift troops from Africa to defend Egypt, but their general Peter resists
634	Muslim raiding intensifies in southern Palestine and east of the Dead Sea
20 August 636	Byzantine defeat at Jābiya-Yarmūk
late 636	Heraclius evacuates Syria, tries to regroup troops, stiffen Anatolian defenses

637	Unsuccessful palace plot against Heraclius; purges
4 July 638	Heraclius raises his son Heraklonas from Caesar to Augustus
September/October 638	Proclamation of Monothelete doctrine in the *Ekthesis*
9 December 638	Patriarch Sergios dies
20 December 638	Pyrrhos selected as Patriarch of Constantinople
late 639	Muslims begin to invade Egypt
640	Heraclius summons and criticizes Patriarch Kyros for failure to defend Egypt against Muslims
?640 or initial days of 641	Heraclius orders *sakellarios* Philagrios to initiate new census
11 February 641	Death of Heraclius
20 April 641	Death of Heraclius Constantine
September 641	Constans II raised to Augustus; Martina and her sons Heraklonas and David are deposed and mutilated soon thereafter
28 November 641	Byzantine treaty surrenders Egypt to Muslims

Select bibliography

PRIMARY SOURCES: GREEK

ANONYMOUS WORKS

Chronicon Paschale, ed. L. Dindorf. *CSHB*. 2 vols. Bonn, 1832. English trans.: Michael and Mary Whitby. Translated Texts for Historians, 7. Liverpool: Liverpool University Press, 1989.

Concilium Universale Constantinopolitanum Tertium, ed. Rudolf Riedinger. *ACO*, ser. 2, Vol. II, Pts. 1–3. Berlin: W. De Gruyter, 1990–1995.

Doctrina Jacobi nuper Baptizati in G. Dagron and V. Déroche, "Juifs et chrétiens dans l'Orient du VII siècle," *Travaux et Mémoires* 11 (1991) 17–248.

The Miracles of St. Artemios, ed., trans. V.S. Chrisafulli and John W. Nesbitt. Leiden: Brill, 1997.

La narratio de rebus Armeniae, ed., comment. Gérard Garitte. *CSCO*, Subsidia, 4. Louvain, 1952.

Παραστάσεις Σύντομοι Χρονικαί = *Constantinople in the Eighth Century*, ed., trans. Averil Cameron, Judith Herrin, et al. Leiden: Brill, 1984.

Patria Constantinopoleos, in *Scriptores Originum Constantinopolitarum*, ed. Th. Preger. Vol. 2. Leipzig: Teubner, 1907.

[Pseudo-Methodios]. *Die Apokalypse des Pseudo-Methodius. Die ältesten griechischen und lateinischen Übersetzungen*, ed. W.J. Aerts and G.A.A. Kortekaas. *CSCO*, Subsidia, 97–98, Vols. 569–570. Leuven: Peeters, 1998. (See also 'Other Non-Arabic Eastern Sources' below.)

Synaxarium ecclesiae Constantinopolitanae, ed. H. Delehaye. Brussels: Société des Bollandistes, 1902, repr. 1964.

Three Byzantine Military Treatises, ed., trans. G.T. Dennis. Washington: Dumbarton Oaks, 1985.

SEALS, PAPYRI, INSCRIPTIONS

Byzantine Lead Seals, ed. G. Zacos and A. Veglery. Basel, 1972–1985.

Die byzantinischen Bleisiegel in Österreich, ed. Werner Seibt. Vienna: Verlag der Akademie, 1978.

Catalogue of Byzantine Seals at Dumbarton Oaks and in the Fogg Museum of Art, ed. John Nesbitt and Nicholas Oikonomides. 4 vols. Washington: Dumbarton Oaks, 1991–2001.

Greek Papyri of the Byzantine Period, ed. Georgina Fantoni. Griechische Texte, X, *Corpus Papyrorum Raineri*, XIV. Vienna: Verlag Brüder Hollinek, 1989.

The Greek Christian Inscriptions of Crete X, ed. Anastasius Bandy. Athens: Christian Archaeological Society, 1970.

Inscriptions grecques et latines de la Syrie, ed. Louise Jalabert and René Mouterde. Bibliothèque archéologique et historique, 12, 32, 46, 51, 61, 66, 78, 89, 104. Paris: Geuthner, 1929–.

OTHER WORKS

Agathias. *Historia*, ed. R. Keydell. *CFHB*. Berlin: De Gruyter, 1967.

Anastasios the Sinaite. *Anastasii Sinaitae Opera. Sermones duo in constitutionem hominis secundem imaginem Dei necnon Opuscula adversus Monotheletas*, ed. Karl-Heinz Uthemann. *CC*, Series Graeca, 12. Turnhout: Leuven University Press, 1985.

—*In Hexaemeron. PG* 89: 851–1078.

—"Le texte grec des récits du moine Anastase sur les saints pères du Sinaï," ed. F. Nau. *Oriens Christianus* 2 (1902) 58–89.

Constantine VII Porphyrogenitos. *De administrando imperio*, ed., trans. G. Moravcsik, R. Jenkins. 2nd edn. Washington: Dumbarton Oaks, 1967.

—*De cerimoniis aulae byzantinae*, ed. J.J. Reiske. *CSHB*. 2 vols. Bonn, 1829.

—*Three Treatises on Imperial Military Expeditions*, ed., trans. John Haldon. Vienna, 1990.

Constantine Manasses. *Breviarium chronicum*, ed. Odysseus Lampsides. *CFHB* 36. Athens: Academy, 1996.

Eusebios. *Vita Constantini*, ed. F. Winkelmann. *GCS*. Berlin: Akademie Verlag, 1991. *Life of Constantine*, trans., comment. Averil Cameron, S.G. Hall. Oxford: Clarendon Press, 1999.

Evagrios Scholastikos. *Ecclesiastical History*, ed. J. Bidez and L. Parmentier. London, 1898.

Gelasios. *Kirchengeschichte*, ed. G. Loeschcke, M. Heinemann. *GCS*. Leipzig: Hinrich'sche Buchhandlung, 1918.

George of Pisidia. *Carmi di Giorgio di Pisidia*, ed. Luigi Tartaglia. Turin: Classici Unione Tipografico-Editrice Torinese, 1998.

—*Poemi, Panegirici epici*, ed., trans. Agostino Pertusi. Ettal: Buch-Kunstverlag-Ettal, 1959.

—*Hexaemeron = L'Esamerone*, ed., Italian trans., comment. F. Gonnelli. Pisa: Edizioni ETS, 1998.

Georgios Kedrenos. *Historiarum compendium*, ed. I. Bekker. *CSHB*. 2 vols. Bonn, 1838–1839.

Georgios Monachos. *Chronicon*, ed. C. de Boor. 2 vols. Leipzig: Teubner, 1904.

[Georgios, monk.] *Vie de Théodore de Sykéôn*, ed. A.J. Festugière. Subsidia Hagiographica, 48. 2 vols. Brussels: Société des Bollandistes, 1970.

John of Antioch. *Chronicle = Fragmenta Historicorum Graecorum*, IV: 535–622; V: 27–39.

John Malalas. *The Chronicle of John Malalas*, trans. Elizabeth Jeffreys, Michael Jeffreys, Roger Scott. Byzantina Australiensia, 4. Melbourne: Australian Association for Byzantine Studies, and Sydney: University of Sydney, 1986.

John Moschos, *The Spiritual Meadow*, trans. John Wortley. Kalamazoo, MI: Cistercian Publications, 1992.

John Zonaras. *Epitome historiarum*, ed. L. Dindorf. 6 vols. Leipzig, 1868–1875.

Lemerle, Paul. *Les plus anciens recueils des miracles de St. Démétrius et la pénétration des Slaves dans les Balkans.* 2 vols. Paris, 1979, 1981.

Leontios of Neapolis. *Vie de Syméon le Fou et Vie de Jean de Chypre*, ed., comment. A.J. Festugière, Lennart Rydén. Institut français d'archéologie de Beyrouth, Bibliothèque archéologique et historique, 95. Paris: Geuthner, 1974.

Mansi, Joannes Dominicus. *Sacrorum conciliorum nova et amplissima collectio.* Repr. Graz: Akademische Drück- und Verlagsanstalt, 1960.

Maurikios. Greek edn., German trans.: *Das Strategikon des Maurikios*, ed. G.T. Dennis, trans. E. Gamillscheg. *CFHB*. Vienna: Akademie, 1981. *Maurice's Strategikon: Handbook of Byzantine Military Strategy*. English trans. George T. Dennis. Philadelphia: University of Pennsylvania Press, 1984.

Maximos the Confessor. *Opera. PG*: 90–91.

—"Relatio factae motionis inter domnum Maximum monachum et socium eius coram principibus in secretario," *Scripta saeculi vii vitam Maximi Confessoris Illustrantia*, ed. Pauline Allen, Bronwen Neil. *CC*, Series Graeca, 39. Turnhout: Brepols, 1999. Pp. 12–51.

Menander Protector. *The History of Menander the Guardsman*, ed., trans. R.C. Blockley. ARCA, 17. Liverpool: Francis Cairns, 1985.

"Nicephori Sceuophylacis Encomium in S. Theodorum Siceotam," ed. C. Kirch, *AB* 20 (1901) 252–272.

Nikephoros. *Short History*, ed., trans. Cyril Mango. Washington: Dumbarton Oaks, 1990.

Pantaleon. "Un discours inédit du moine Pantaléon sur l'élévation de la Croix *BHG* 427 p.," ed. F. Halkin, *OCP* 52 (1986) 257–270.

Prokopios of Caesarea. *Opera omnia*, ed. J. Haury, G. Wirth. 4 vols. Leipzig: Teubner, 1905–1913; repr., 1962–1964.

Sargis d'Aberga. *Controverse Judéo-Chrétienne*, ed., trans. Sylvain Grébaut, F. Nau. *PO* 3: 551–643; 8: 711–780; 13: 5–109.

Sergia. "Narratio Sergiae de translatione Sanctae Olympiadis," *AB* 16 (1897) 44–51.

Sokrates Scholastikos. *Historia ecclesiastica*, ed. G.C. Hansen, *GCS*. Berlin: Akademie Verlag, 1995.

Sophronios. *Sermones. PG* 87.3: 3201–3364.

—"Weihnachtspredigt des Sophronios," ed. H. Usener, *Rheinisches Museum für Philologie*, N.F. 41 (1886) 500–516.

Theodore Skutariotes. Σύνοψις Χρονική, ed. Constantine Sathas. Μεσαιωνική Βιβλιοθήκη, 7. Venice, 1894.

Theodore Synkellos. *Analecta Avarica*, ed. L. Sternbach. Dissertationum philologicarum Academiae Litterarum Cracoviensis, 30. Cracow, 1900. Pp. 297–365. cf. Sternbach, below. French trans.: Ferenc Makk, *Traduction et commentaire de l'homélie écrite probablement par Théodore le Syncelle sur le siège de Constantinople en 626* (Acta Universitatis de Attila Joszef Nominatae, Acta Antiqua et Archaeologica, 19; Opuscula Byzantina, 3; Szeged, 1975).

Theophanes. *Chronicle of Theophanes Confessor*, trans., comment. Cyril Mango, Roger Scott, with aid of Geoffrey Greatrex. Oxford: Clarendon Press, 1997.

—*Chronographia*, ed. C. de Boor. 2 vols. Leipzig, 1883.

Theophanes Continuatus, *Chron. Vita Basilii*, ed. I. Bekker. *CSHB*. Bonn, 1838.

Theophylact Simocatta. *Historiae*, ed. C. de Boor. Leipzig: Teubner, 1887; repr., 1972. English trans.: *The History of Theophylact Simocatta*, trans. Michael Whitby and Mary Whitby. Oxford: Clarendon Press, 1986.

PRIMARY SOURCES: LATIN

ANONYMOUS WORKS

Auctarii Havniensis Extrema = *Continuatio Havniensis Prosperi*, ed. T. Mommsen. *MGH* ΛΛ 9. Berlin: Weidmann, 1892, repr. 1961. Pp. 337–339.

Corpus Juris Civilis, ed. T. Mommsen, P. Krueger, R. Schoell, W. Kroll. 3 vols. Berlin: Weidmann, 1928.

Epistolae merowingici et karolini aevi, I. *MGH, Epistolae*, III. Berlin: Weidmann, 1892.

Liber Pontificalis, ed. Louis Duchesne. Repr. Paris, 1957. *Liber Pontificalis/Book of Pontiffs*, trans. Raymond Davis. Liverpool: Liverpool University Press, 1989.

OTHER WORKS

Fredegarius. *Chronicle*, ed. Bruno Krusch. *MGH* Scriptores Rerum Merovingicarum, 2. Hannover, 1888, repr. 1984. English trans.: *The Fourth Book of the Chronicle of Fredegar with its Continuations*, trans. J.M. Wallace-Hadrill. London: Thos. Nelson & Sons, 1960.

Hrabanus Maurus, *Homiliae*, *PL* 110: 1–468.

Isidore of Seville. *Historia Gothorum Wandalorum Sueborum*, ed. T. Mommsen. *MGH* AA 11, Chronica Minora II (repr. Berlin: Weidmann, 1961) 241–333.

[Ps.-Isidore].*Continuationes Isidorianae Byzantia Arabica et Hispana*, ed. T. Mommsen. *MGH* AA 11, Chronica Minora II (repr. Berlin: Weidmann, 1961) 334–369.

PRIMARY SOURCES: ARABIC

Agapios. *Kitāb al-Unvān*, ed. A.A. Vasiliev. *PO* 5.4 (1910) 557–692; 7.4 (1911) 457–591; 8.3 (1912) 399–547.

Al-Aʿshā. *Gedichte von Abû Bashîr Maimûn ibn Qais al-ʾAʿshâ*, ed. Rudolf Geyer. E.J.W. Gibb Memorial Series. London: Luzac, 1928.

Azdī = al-Baṣrī. Muḥammad b. ʿAbdullāh Abū Ismaʿīl al-Azdī. *Taʾrīkh futūḥ al-Shām*, ed. William Nassau Lees. Bibliotheca Indica. Calcutta, 1857. Al-Baṣrī. *"The Fotooh al-Shám: "being an Account of the Moslim Conquests in Syria...,"* ed. William Nassau Lees. Bibliotheca Indica, 16. Calcutta 1853–1854. Also Arabic edn. by ʿAbd al-Munʿim ʿAbdullāh ʿĀmir. Cairo: Muʿassasa Sijill al-ʿArab, 1970.

Balādhurī, Aḥmad b. Yaḥyā. *Futūḥ al-Buldān*, ed. Michael Jan de Goeje. Leiden: Brill, 1866; repr. Leiden.

—*The Origins of the Islamic State*, trans. Philip K. Hitti, F.C. Murgotten. New York: Columbia University Press, 1916, 1924.

Chronicle of Siʿīrt = Histoire Nestorienne. Chronique de Séert, ed. A. Scher, R. Griveau. *PO* 4 (1908) 215–312; 5 (1910) 221–334; 7 (1911) 99–201; 13 (1919) 437–636.

Al-Diyārbakrī, Ḥusayn ibn Muḥammad. *Taʾrīkh al-khamīs fī aḥwāl anfasi nafīs.* 2 vols. in 1. 1866, repr. Beirut, 1970.

Eutychios. *Das Annalenwerk des Eutychios von Alexandrien*, ed., trans. Michael Breydy. *CSCO*, 471–472. Scriptores Arabici, 44–45. Louvain: E. Peeters, 1985. (= Eutychios, *Hist.*) Italian trans.: *Gli anni*, introd., trans. Bartolomeo Pirone. Cairo: Franciscan Centre, 1987.

Ibn ʿAbd al-Ḥakam. *Futūḥ miṣr wa akhbāruhā*, ed. Charles Torrey. New Haven: Yale, 1922.

Ibn ʿAsākir, ʿAlī b. al-Ḥasan. *Taʾrīkh Madīnat Dimashq*, ed. Ruḥīya al-Naḥḥas, Riyāḍ. Dār al-Fikr, ʿAbd al-Ḥamīd Murād, Muḥammad Muṭī al-Ḥafiz. Damascus: Dār al-Fikr, 1984.

Ibn ʿAsākir, ʿAlī b. al-Ḥasan. *Taʾrīkh Madīnat Dimashq*, I, ed. Ṣalāḥ al-Dīn al-Munajjid. Damascus: al-Majmaʿ al-ʾIlmi al-ʿArabī, 1951.

Ibn ʿAsākir, *TMD* = Ibn ʿAsākir, ʿAlī b. al-Ḥasan. *Taʾrīkh Madīnat Dimashq*, ed. ʿUmar ibn Gharāma ʿAmrawī. 80 vols. Beirut: Dār al-Fikr, 1995–1998.

Histoire Nestorienne = Chronicle of Siʿīrt

Kūfī = Ibn Aʿtham al-Kūfī, Abū Muḥammad Aḥmad. *Kitāb al-futūḥ*, ed. Muḥammad ʿAlī al-ʿAbbasī, and Sayyid ʿAbd al-Wahhāb Bukhārī. 8 vols. Hyderabad: Dāʾirat al-Maʿārif al-ʿUthmāniyya, 1968–1975.

Ibn al-Athīr, ʿIzz al-Dīn. *al-Kāmil fī-l Taʾrīkh*, ed. C.J. Tornberg. 13 vols. Repr. Beirut: Dār Ṣādir, 1965.

Ibn Hishām, ʿAbd al-Malik. *Sīra al-nabawīyya*, ed. Heinrich Ferdinand Wüstenfeld. *Sīra Rasūl Allāh = Das Leben Muhammads....* 2 vols. Göttingen: Dieterischen Buchhandlung, 1858–1860.

Ibn Saʿd, Muḥammad. *Kitāb al-Ṭabaqāt al-kabīr*, ed. Eduard Sachau, et al. 9 vols. Leiden: Brill, 1905–1940.

al-Mas'ūdī, Abū'l Ḥasan 'Alī b. al-Ḥusayn. *Livre de l'avertissement et de la revision,* trans. B. Carra de Vaux. 2 vols. Paris: Imprimerie nationale, 1897.

—*Murūj al-dhahab = Les Prairies d'or,* ed. B. de Meynard, Pavet de Courteille. 9 vols. Paris: Imprimerie Impériale, 1861–1917; repr. Paris: Société asiatique, 1962.

Muḥammad ibn 'Alī 'Aẓīmī, *Ta'rīkh Ḥalab,* ed. Ibrāhīm Za'rūr. Damascus, 1984.

Strategios. *Expugnationis Hierosolymae A.D. 614 Recensiones Arabicae,* ed. Gérard Garitte. *CSCO,* Scriptores Arabici, 26–29. Louvain, 1973–1974. (See also Strategios, *La prise de Jérusalem* . . . in Other Non-Arabic Eastern Sources.)

Ṭabarī = al-Ṭabarī, Abū Ja'far Muḥammad b. Jarīr. *Ta'rīkh al-rusul wa al mulūk = Annales,* ed. M.J. de Goeje et al. 15 vols. Leiden: Brill, 1879–1901.

Ṭabarī/Nöldeke = Theodor Nöldeke, *Geschichte der Perser und Araber zur Zeit der Sasaniden aus der arabischen Chronik des Tabari.* Leiden: Brill, 1879.

al-Ṭabarī, *The History of al-Ṭabarī,* V: *The Sasanids, the Byzantines, the Lakhmids and Yemen,* trans. C. E. Bosworth. Albany: State University of New York Press, 1999.

al-Wāqidī, Muḥammad b. 'Umar. *Kitāb al-maghazī,* ed. Marsden Jones. 3 vols. Oxford: Oxford University Press, 1966.

Yāqūt. *Jacut's Geographisches Wörterbuch,* ed. Ferdinand Wüstenfeld. 6 vols. Leipzig: DMG, 1924.

PRIMARY SOURCES: OTHER NON-ARABIC EASTERN SOURCES

ANONYMOUS WORKS

Chronicon ad annum Christi 1234 pertinens, ed., trans. J.B. Chabot. *CSCO,* SS 14. Louvain, 1937.

OTHER WORKS

Ananias of Shirak. *The Geography of Ananias of Shirak, Asxarhacouyc, The Long and Short Recensions,* ed., trans. R.H. Hewsen. Beihefte zum Tübinger Atlas des Vorderen Orients, Reihe B, Geisteswissenschaften, 77. Wiesbaden: Reichart, 1992.

Le Calendrier Palestino-Géorgien du Sinaiticus 34 (Xe siècle), ed., trans. Gérard Garitte. Subsidia Hagiographica, 30. Brussels: Société des Bollandistes, 1958.

Chronica Minora, ed. Ignatius Guidi. *CSCO,* SS, ser. 3, 4, Pts. 1–3. Paris, Leipzig, 1903–1905.

Firdawsi. *Le livre des rois par Abou'lkasim Firdousi,* trans. Jules Mohl. 7 vols. Paris: Imprimerie Nationale, 1878.

Ishoyahb III, Patriarch. *Liber epistularum,* ed., trans. R. Duval. *CSCO,* SS, 12. Ser. 2, vol. 54. Louvain, 1904–1905, 1955.

John, Bishop of Nikiu. *Chronicle*, trans. R.M. Charles. Oxford: Oxford University Press, 1916; repr. Amsterdam, APA-Philo Press, n.d.

Michael the Syrian. *Chronique*, ed., trans. J.-B. Chabot. 4 vols. Paris: E. Leroux, 1899–1910.

Moses Dasxuranci. *History of the Caucasian Albanians*, trans. Charles Dowsett. London Oriental Series, 8. London: Oxford University Press, 1961.

Pseudo-Methodios. *Die syrische Apokalypse des Pseudo-Methodius*, ed., trans. G. Reinink, *CSCO*, 541, SS, 221. Leuven: Peeters, 1993. (See also Greek sources, above.)

Sebeos. *The Armenian History Attributed to Sebeos*, trans., annot. R.W. Thomson, hist. comment. James Howard-Johnston. Translated Texts for Historians, 31. Liverpool: Liverpool University Press, 1999. French edn.: *Histoire d'Héraclius*, trans. F. Macler. Paris, 1904. Italian edn.: *Storia*, trans. Claudio Gugerotti. Verona: Casa Editrice Mazziana, 1990.

The Seventh Century in the West-Syrian Chronicles, ed., trans. Andrew Palmer. Translated Texts for Historians, 15. Liverpool: Liverpool University Press, 1993.

Strategios. *La prise de Jérusalem par les Perses en 614*, ed., trans., Gérard Garitte. *CSCO*, 202–203, Scriptores Iberici, 11–12. Louvain, 1960. (See also Strategios, *Expugnationis Hierosolymae . . .* in Arabic Sources.)

Thomas Artsruni. *History of the House of the Artsrunik'*, ed., trans. R.W. Thomson, Detroit: Wayne State University Press, 1985.

Yovhannes Drasxanakertc'i. *History of Armenia*, trans. K. H. Maksoudian. Atlanta: Scholars Press, 1987.

SECONDARY SOURCES

Alexakis, A. "Before the Lateran Council of 649: The Last Days of Herakleios the Emperor and Monotheletism," *Annuarium Historiae Conciliorum* 27/28 (1995/1996) 93–101.

Bartikian, Chr. (Hratz) M. τό Βυζάντιον εἰς τας 'Αρμενικας πηγάς. Byzantina Keimena kai Meletai, 18. Thessaloniki: Center for Byzantine Studies, 1981.

Bashear, Suleiman. "The Mission of Diḥya al-Kalbī," *JSAI* 14 (1991) 84–114, repr. in *Der Islam* 74 (1997) 64–91.

Baynes, N.H. "The Date of the Avar Surprise," *BZ* 21 (1912) 110–128, 677.

—"The First Campaign of Heraclius against Persia," *EHR* 19 (1904) 694–702.

—"The Military Operations of Emperor Heraclius," *United Service Magazine*, n.s., 46 (1913) 526–533, 659–666; 47 (1913) 30–38, 195–201, 318–324, 401–412, 532–541, 665–679.

—"The Successors of Justinian," in *Cambridge Medieval History* (Cambridge, 1913; repr. 1926) II: 263–301.

Beihammer, Alexander D. *Nachrichten zum byzantinischen Urkundenwesen in arabischen Quellen.* Ποικίλα Βυζαντινά, 17. Bonn: Habelt, 2000.

— *Quellenkritische Untersuchungen zu den ägyptischen Kapitulationsverträgen der Jahre 640–646*, Sitzungsberichte, Österreichische Akademie der Wissenschaften, Philosoph.-Hist. Kl., 671. Vienna, 2000.

Bombaci, A. "Qui était Jebu Xak'an?," *Turcica* 2 (1970) 7–24.

Brandes, Wolfram. *Finanzverwaltung in Krisenzeiten. Untersuchungen zur byzantinischen Verwaltungsgeschichte zwischen dem ausgehenden 6. und dem beginnenden 9. Jahrhundert.* Frankfurt, forthcoming.

—"Die melkitischen Patriarchen von Antiocheia im 7. Jahrhundert. Anzahl und Chronologie," *Le Muséon* 111 (1998) 37–57.

—*Die Städte Kleinasiens im 7. und 8. Jahrhundert.* Berliner Byzantinische Arbeiten, 56. Berlin: Akademie-Verlag, 1989.

Braunlin, Michael, and John Nesbitt. "Selections from a Private Collection of Byzantine Bullae," *Byzantion* 68 (1998) 157–182.

—"Thirteen Seals and an Unpublished Revolt Coin," *Byzantion* 69 (1999) 187–205.

Breydy, Michel. *Etudes sur Sa'īd ibn Baṭrīq et ses sources. CSCO,* 450. *Subsidia,* 69. Louvain: E. Peeters, 1983.

—"Mamila ou Maqella? La prise de Jérusalem et ses conséquences (614 A.D.) selon la recension alexandrine des *Annales* d'Eutychès," *Oriens Christianus* 65 (1981) 62–86.

Brock, Sebastian. "An Early Syriac Life of Maximus the Confessor," *AB* 91 (1973) 299–346.

—"Syriac Sources for Seventh-Century History," *BMGS* 2 (1976) 17–36.

—"Syriac Views of Emergent Islam," in *Studies on the First Century of Islamic Society.* Papers on Islamic History, 5, ed. G.H.A. Juynboll (Carbondale: Southern Illinois University Press, 1982) 9–22.

Brown, Thomas S. *Gentlemen and Officers: Imperial Administration and Aristocratic Power in Byzantine Italy, A.D. 554–800.* London: British School at Rome, 1984.

Brown, Thomas S., Anthony Bryer and David Winfield. "Cities of Heraclius," *BMGS* 4 (1978) 15–38.

Butler, Alfred. *The Arab Conquest of Egypt.* Revised by P.M. Fraser. Oxford: Oxford University Press, 1978.

Cameron, Alan. *Circus Factions: Blues and Greens at Rome and Byzantium.* Oxford: Clarendon Press, 1976.

Cameron, Averil. "Agathias on the Sassanians," *DOP* 23–24 (1969–1970) 67–183.

—"Byzantines and Jews: Some Recent Work on Early Byzantium," *BMGS* 20 (1996) 248–274.

—"The Theotokos in Sixth-Century Byzantium," *Journal of Theological Studies,* N.S., 29 (1978) 79–108.

—"The Virgin's Robe: An Episode in the History of Early Seventh-Century Constantinople," *Byzantion* 49 (1979) 42–56.

—ed. *The Byzantine and Early Islamic Near East,* III: *States, Resources and Armies.* Studies in Late Antiquity and Early Islam, 1. Princeton: Darwin Press, 1995.

—ed. *Cambridge Ancient History,* XIV. Cambridge: Cambridge University Press, 2000.

Cameron, Averil, and Lawrence Conrad, eds. *The Byzantine and Early Islamic Near East,* I: *Problems in Literary Source Material.* Studies in Late Antiquity and Early Islam, 1.1. Princeton: Darwin Press, 1992.

Carrié, Jean-Michel. "Pouvoir civil et autorité militaire dans les provinces d'Egypte," *L'Antiquité Tardive* 6 (1998) 105–121.

Carrié, J.-M. and S. Janniard. "L'armée romaine tardive dans quelques travaux récents. 1e partie, L'Institution militaire et les modes de combat," *L'Antiquité Tardive 8* (2000) 321–341.

Cernik, Josef. "Technische Studien-Expedition durch die Gebiete des Euphrat und Tigris," *Petermanns Geographische Mitteilungen* No. 45, *Ergänzungsband* (1876).

Chichurov, I.S. "O kavkazkom pochode imperatora Irakliya," *Vostochnaya Evropa v drevnosti i srednevekov'e. Sbornik statei* (Moscow: Institut istorii SSSR. Akademiya Nauk SSSR, 1978) 261–266.

Christensen, Arthur. *L'Iran sous les Sassanides.* 2nd edn., Copenhagen, 1944; repr. Osnabrück: O. Zeller, 1971.

Clark, Elizabeth. "Sergia's Narration," in *Jerome, Chrysostom, and Friends. Essays and Translations* (Studies in Women and Religion, 2; New York, Toronto: The Edwin Mellen Press, 1979) 145–157.

Clover, Frank M. and R.S. Humphreys, eds. *Tradition and Innovation in Late Antiquity.* Madison: University of Wisconsin Press, 1989.

Conrad, Lawrence I. "Al-Azdī's History of the Arab Conquests in Bilād al-Shām: Some Historiographical Observations," in *1985 Bilād al-Shām Proceedings* (Amman: University of Jordan and Yarmouk University, 1987) I: 28–62.

—"Theophanes and the Arabic Historical Tradition," *BF* 15 (1990) 1–44.

Cosentino, Salvatore. "L'iscrizione ravennate dell'Esarco Isacio e le guerre di Rotari," *Atti e Memorie della Deputazione di Storia Patria per le Antiche Province Modenesi,* ser. 11, 15 (1993) 23–43.

—*Prosopografia dell'Italia bizantina.* 2 vols. Bologna: Editrice lo scarabeo, 1996, 2000.

Curta, Florin. *The Making of the Slavs.* Cambridge: Cambridge University Press, 2001.

Dabrowa, E., ed. *The Roman and Byzantine Army in the East.* Cracow: Uniwersytet Jagiellonski Instytut Historii, 1994.

Dagron, Gilbert, and Vincent Déroche, "Juifs et chrétiens dans l'Orient du VIIe siècle," *TM* 11 (1991) 17–46.

Delehaye, Hippolyte. "Passio sanctorum sexaginta martyrum," *AB* 23 (1904) 289–307.

Déroche, Vincent. "L'Apologie contre les Juifs' de Léontios de Néapolis," *TM* 12 (1994) 45–104.

—*Etudes sur Léontios de Néapolis.* Acta Universitatis Upsaliensis, Studia Byzantina Upsaliensia, 3. Uppsala: Alqvist and Wiksell, 1995.

—"La polémique anti-judaïque au VIe et au VIIe siècle. Un mémento inédit, *Les kephalaia,*" *TM* 11 (1991) 275–311.

—"L'authenticité de l'Apologie contre les Juifs' de Léontios de Néapolis," *BCH* 110 (1986) 655–669.

Dillemann, Louis. *Haute mésopotamie orientale et pays adjacents. Contribution à la géographie historique de la région, du V^{e}s. avant l'ère chrétienne au VIe de cette* *ère*. Institut français d'archéologie de Beyrouth, Bibliothèque archéologique et historique, 72. Paris: P. Geuthner, 1962.

Dölger, F. *Regesten der Kaiserurkunden des oströmischen Reiches von 565–1025*. Munich, Berlin: Verlag R. Oldenburg, 1924–1965. Facs. 1–5.

Donner, Fred. *The Early Islamic Conquests*. Princeton: Princeton University Press, 1981.

—"From Believers to Muslims: Confessional Self-Identity in the Early Islamic Community," in *The Byzantine and Early Islamic Near East. Patterns of Communal Identity*, ed. L.I. Conrad. Princeton: Darwin Press, forthcoming.

—*Narratives of Islamic Origins: The Beginnings of Islamic Historical Writing*. Studies in Late Antiquity and Early Islam, 14. Princeton: Darwin Press, 1998.

Duval, Yvette, ed. *Loca Sanctorum Africae*. 2 vols. Collection de l'Ecole française de Rome, 58; Rome: Ecole française de Rome, 1982.

El Cheikh-Saliba, Nadia. "Byzantium Viewed by the Arabs." Unpub. Ph.D. diss. in History, Harvard University, 1992.

—"Muhammad and Heraclius: A Study in Legitimacy," *Studia Islamica* 89 (1999) 5–21.

Evangelides, Tryphon. Ἡράκλειος ὁ Αὐτοκράτωρ τοῦ Βυζαντίου (575–641 μ.χ.) [*Herakleios ho autokrator tou Byzantinou (575–641 m. Chr.) kai he kata ton Z' m. Chr. aion katastasis tou Byzantiakou kratous*] Odessa: Ekdotes P. Zervates-Perakes, 1903.

Fine, John V.A. *The Early Medieval Balkans: A Critical Survey from the Sixth to the Late Twelfth Century*. Ann Arbor: University of Michigan Press, 1983.

Flusin, Bernard. *Saint Anastase le Perse et l'histoire de la Palestine au début du VIIe siècle*. 2 vols. Paris: Editions du CNRS, 1992.

Foss, Clive. "The Persians in Asia Minor and the End of Antiquity," *EHR* 90 (1975) 721–747.

Frend, W.H.C. *The Rise of the Monophysite Movement*. Cambridge: Cambridge University Press, 1972.

Frendo, D. "The Early Exploits and Final Overthrow of Khusrau II (591–628): Panegyric and Vilification in the Last Byzantine–Iranian Conflict," *Bulletin of the Asia Institute*, n.s. 9 (1995) 209–214.

Frendo, Joseph D.C. "History and Panegyric in the Age of Heraclius: The Literary Background to the Composition of the *Histories* of Theophylact Simocatta," *DOP* 42 (1988) 143–156.

Frolow, A. *La relique de la Vraie Croix*. Archives de l'Orient Chrétien, 7. Paris: Institut français d'études byzantines, 1961.

—"La Vraie Croix et les expéditions d'Héraclius en Perse," *REB* 11 (1953) 88–105.

Fulford, M.G. "Carthage: Overseas Trade and the Political Economy c. AD 400–700," *Reading Medieval Studies* 6 (1980) 68–80.

Garsoïan. Nina. *Armenia between Byzantium and the Sasanians*. London: Variorum, 1985.

—*L'Eglise arménienne et le grand schisme d'Orient*. *CSCO*, Subsidia 100, vol. 574. Leuven: Peeters, 1999.

Garsoïan, Nina, and Jean-Pierre Mahé. *Des Parthes au Califat. Quatre leçons sur la formation de l'identité arménienne*. Travaux et Mémoires du Centre de recherche d'histoire et civilisation de Byzance, Collège de France, Monographies, 10. Paris: De Boccard, 1997.

Goffart, Walter. "The Fredegar Problem Reconsidered," *Speculum* 38 (1963) 206–241.

Golden, Peter B. *An Introduction to the History of the Turkic Peoples. Ethnogenesis and State Formation in Medieval and Early Modern Eurasia and the Middle East.* Wiesbaden: Harrassowitz, 1992.

—*Khazar Studies.* Bibliotheca Orientalis Hungarica, 25/1. Budapest: Akadémiai Kiadó, 1980.

Goossens, Godefroy. *Hiérapolis de Syrie. Essai de monographie historique.* Leuven: Bibliothèque de l'Université, 1943.

Goubert, Paul. *Byzance avant l'Islam.* 2 vols. in 3. Paris: Geuthner, 1951–1965.

Graf, Georg. *Geschichte der christlichen arabischen Literatur.* 5 vols. Studi e Testi, 118, 133, 146, 147, 172. Vatican City: Biblioteca Apostolica Vaticana, 1944–1953.

Gray, Patrick T.R. "Theological Discourse in the Seventh Century: The Heritage from the Sixth Century," *BF* 26 (2000) 219–228.

Greenwood, Tim. "A History of Armenia in the Seventh and Eighth Centuries." D.Phil. diss., Oxford University, 2000.

Grierson, Philip. *Catalogue of the Byzantine Coins in the Dumbarton Oaks Collection and in the Whittemore Collection*, Vol. 2, Pts. 1–2. Washington: Dumbarton Oaks, 1968.

—"The Consular Coinage of 'Heraclius' and the Revolt against Phocas of 608–10," *NC* ser. 6, 10 (1950) 71–93.

—"The Isaurian Coins of Heraclius," *NC* ser. 6, 11 (1951) 56–67.

—"Tombs and Obits of the Byzantine Emperors," *DOP* 16 (1962) 3–63.

Guillou, André. "La prise de Gaza par les Arabes au VIIᵉ siècle," *BCH* 81 (1957) 396–404.

—*Régionalisme et indépendance dans l'empire byzantin au VIIᵉ siècle.* Rome, 1969.

Gyselen, Rika. *La géographie administrative de l'empire sassanide: les témoignages sigillographiques.* Res Orientales, 1. Paris: Groupe pour l'étude de la civilisation du Moyen-Orient; Leuven: Peeters, 1989.

Hahn, Wolfgang. *Moneta Imperii Byzantini.* 3 vols. Vienna: Österreichische Akademie der Wissenschaften, Denkschriften, Philosophische-Historische Klasse, Österreichische Akademie der Wissenschaften, 109, Vol. 148. 1973–1981.

Haldon, John. *Byzantine Praetorians: An Administrative, Institutional, Social Survey of the Opsikion and the Tagmata, c.500–900.* Ποικίλα Βυζαντινά, 3. Bonn: R. Habelt, 1984.

—*Byzantium in the Seventh Century.* 2nd. edn.; Cambridge: Cambridge University Press, 1997.

—"Military Service, Military Lands, and the Status of Soldiers: Current Problems and Interpretations," *DOP* 47 (1993) 1–67.

—"Recruitment and Conscription in the Byzantine Army c.550–950," *Sitzungsberichte,* Österreichische Akademie der Wissenschaften, Philosophisch-Historische Klasse, 357. Vienna: Verlag der Akademie, 1979.

—*Warfare, State and Society in the Byzantine World.* London: UCL Press, 1999.

Haldon, John, and Hugh Kennedy. "The Arab-Byzantine Frontier in the Eighth and Ninth Centuries: Military Organisation and Society in the Borderlands," *ZRVI* 19 (1980) 79–116.

Hendy, Michael. *Studies in the Byzantine Monetary Economy, c.300–1450*. Cambridge: Cambridge University Press, 1985.

Hickey, Todd. "Observations on the Sasanian Invasion and Occupation of Egypt" (1992 University of Chicago Department of History seminar paper, now under revision for publication).

—"A Public 'House' but Closed: Fiscal Participation and Economic Decision Making on the Oxyrhynchite Estate of the Flavii Apiones." Ph.D. diss. in History, University of Chicago, 2001.

Hommes et richesses dans l'Empire byzantin I. Paris: Editions P. Lethielleux, 1989.

Howard-Johnston, James. "Heraclius' Persian Campaigns and the Revival of the East Roman Empire, 622–630," *War in History* 6 (1999) 1–44.

—"The Official History of Heraclius' Persian Campaigns," in *The Roman and Byzantine Army in the East*, ed. E. Dabrowa (Cracow, 1994) 57–87.

Hoyland, Robert. "Sebeos, the Jews and the Rise of Islam," in *Studies in Muslim-Jewish Relations*, ed. R. Nettler (1996) II: 89–102.

—*Seeing Islam as Others Saw It*. Studies in Late Antiquity and Early Islam, 13. Princeton: Darwin Press, 1997.

Jones, A.H.M. *The Later Roman Empire*. Oxford: Blackwell, 1964.

Kaegi, Walter. *Army, Society and Religion in Byzantium*. London: Variorum, 1982.

—"The Battle of Nineveh," *AABSC* 19 (Princeton University, 1993) 3–4.

—*Byzantine Military Unrest, 471–843: An Interpretation*. Amsterdam, Las Palmas: Hakkert, 1981.

—*Byzantium and the Early Islamic Conquests*. Rev. edn., Cambridge: Cambridge University Press, 1995.

—"Challenges to Late Roman and Byzantine Military Operations in Iraq (4th–9th Centuries)," *Klio* 73 (1991) 586–594.

—"Egypt on the Eve of the Muslim Conquest," in *Cambridge History of Egypt*, ed. C. Petry (Cambridge: Cambridge University Press, 1998) 34–61.

—*Some Thoughts on Byzantine Military Strategy*. Ball State University Hellenic Studies Lecture. Brookline, MA: Hellenic College Press, 1983.

Kawar, I. *see* Shahid.

Kennedy, H.N. ed. *Al-Ṭabarī: The Historian and His Work*. Princeton: Darwin, 2002.

—*The Prophet and the Age of the Caliphates*. London: Longman, 1986.

Kolbaba, Tia. "Fighting for Christianity. Holy War in the Byzantine Empire," *Byzantion* 68 (1998) 194–221.

Konidaris, Johannes. "Die Novellen des Kaisers Herakleios," in *Fontes Minores* (Forschungen zur byzantinischen Rechtsgeschichte, 8) V: 33–106.

Kountoura-Galake, Eleonora, ed. οι σκότεινοι αἰῶνες τοῦ Βυζαντίου (705-905 αι.). Athens: Ethniko Idryma Ereunon, Institouton Vyzantinon Spoudon, 2001.

Kouymijian, D. "Ethnic Origins and the 'Armenian' Policy of Emperor Heraclius," *REArm* n.s. 17 (1983) 635–642.

Kremmydas, Vasiles, Chrysa Maltezou, and Nikolaos Panayiotakis, eds. Ἀφιέρωμα στόν Νίκο Σβορῶνο. 2 vols. Rethymno: University of Crete, 1986.

Kulakovskii, Julian. *Istoriya Vizantii.* 3 vols. Kiev, 1913–1915; repr. London: Variorum, 1973.

Külzer, Andreas. *Disputationes Graecae contra Iudaeos. Untersuchungen zur byzantinischen antijüdischen Dialogliteratur und ihrem Judenbild.* Stuttgart, Leipzig: Teubner, 1999.

Larchet, Jean-Claude. *La divinisation de l'homme selon Saint Maxime le Confesseur.* Paris: Cerf. 1996.

Lascaratos, J., E. Poulakou-Rembelakou, A. Rembelakos and S. Marketos. "The First Case of Epispadias: an Unknown Disease of the Byzantine Emperor Heraclius (610–641 A.D.)," *British Journal of Urology* 76 (1995) 380–383.

Lemerle, Paul. "Note sur les données historiques de l'Autobiographie d'Anania de Shirak," *REArm*, n.s., 1 (1964) 195–201.

—"Quelques remarques sur le règne d'Héraclius," *Studi medievali*, 3a ser., 1 (1960) 347–361.

Lilie, Ralph-Johannes. *Die byzantinische Reaktion auf die Ausbreitung der Araber.* Miscellanea Byzantina Monacensia, 22. Munich, 1976.

—"Kaiser Herakleios und die Ansiedlung der Serben," *Südost-forschungen* 44 (1985) 17–43.

—"Die zweihundertjährige Reform. Zu den Anfängen der Themenorganisation im 7. und 8. Jahrhundert," *Byzsl* 45 (1984) 27–39, 190–201.

Ludwig, Claudia. "Kaiser Herakleios, Georgios Pisides und die Perserkriege," in *Varia* III, Ποικίλα Βυζαντινά, 11, ed. P. Speck (Bonn, 1991) 73–128.

MacCoull, L.S.B. "George of Pisidia: *Against Severus*: In Praise of Heraclius," in *The Future of the Middle Ages and the Renaissance: Problems, Trends and Opportunities for Research*, ed. Roger Dahood (Arizona Studies in the Middle Ages and the Renaissance 2; Turnhout, 1998) 69–79.

Magdalino, Paul, ed. *New Constantines: The Rhythm of Imperial Renewal.* Aldershot: Variorum, 1994.

Manandian, H.A. "Maršrut'i persidskich pochodov imperatora Irakliya," *VV* 3 (1950) 133–153.

Mango, Cyril. "Deux études sur Byzance et la Perse Sassanide," *TM* 9 (1985) 91–118.

—"The Temple Mount, AD 614–638," in *Bayt Al-Maqdis. 'Abd al-Malik's Jerusalem*, ed. Julian Raby and Jeremy Johns (Oxford: Oxford University Press, 1992) 1–16.

Mango, Cyril, and G. Dagron, eds. *Constantinople and Its Hinterland.* Aldershot, UK; Brookfield, VT: Variorum, 1995.

Mango, Cyril, and Marlia Mundell Mango. "Inscriptions de la Mésopotamie du Nord," *TM* 11 (1991) 465–471.

Martino I Papa (649–653) e il suo tempo. Atti del XXVIII Convegno storico internazionale, Todi, 13–16 ottobre 1991. Spoleto: Centro Italiano di Studi sull'Alto Medioevo, 1992.

Maspero, Jean. *Organisation militaire de l'Egypte byzantine.* Paris, 1912.

Mayerson, Philip. "The First Muslim Attacks on Southern Palestine," *TAPA* 95 (1964) 155–199.

McCormick, Michael. "Bateaux de vie, bateaux de mort. Maladie, commerce, transports annonaires et le passage économique du bas-empire au moyen âge," in *Settimane di Studio del centro italiano di studi sull'alto medioevo* 45 (Spoleto, 1998) 35–118.

—*Eternal Victory. Triumphal Rulership in Late Antiquity, Byzantium, and the Early Medieval West*. Cambridge: Cambridge University Press, 1986.

—*The Origins of the European Economy: Communications and Commerce, A.D. 300–900*. Cambridge: Cambridge University Press, 2001.

McCotter, Stephan E.J. "The Strategy and Tactics of Siege Warfare in the Early Byzantine Period: from Constantine to Heraclius." Ph.D. diss., Queen's University, Belfast, 1996.

Misiu, Dionysia. Η διαθήκη τοῦ Ηρακλείου Α΄ και η κρίση τοῦ 641. Συμβολή στο πρόβλημα τῆς διαδόχης στό Βυζάντιο. Thessaloniki, 1985.

Morrisson, Cécile. "Du consul à l'empereur: les sceaux d'Héraclius," in *Novum Millennium: Studies on Byzantine History and Culture Dedicated to Paul Speck*, ed. Sarolta Takács and Claudia Sode (Burlington, VT: Ashgate, 2001) 257–265.

Mourad, Suleiman A. "On Early Islamic Historiography: Abū Ismaʿīl al-Azdī and His *Futūḥ al-shām*," *JAOS* 120 (2000) 577–593.

Nöldeke, Theodor. "Zur Geschichte der Araber im 1. Jahrhundert d. H. aus syrischen Quellen," *ZDMG* 29 (1875) 76–85.

Noth, Albrecht, in collaboration with Lawrence I. Conrad, trans. Michael Bonner. *The Early Arabic Historical Tradition: A Source-Critical Study*. Studies in Late Antiquity and Early Islam, 4. Princeton: Darwin Press, 1994.

Oates, David. *Studies in the Ancient History of Northern ʿIrāq*. London: British Academy, 1968.

Oikonomides, Nicholas. "A Chronological Note on the First Persian Campaign of Heraclius (622)," *BMGS* 1 (1975) 1–10.

—"Correspondence Between Heraclius and Kavadh-Siroe in the Paschal Chronicle," *Byzantion* 51 (1971) 269–281.

—*Les listes de préséance byzantines des IXᵉ et Xᵉ siècles*. Paris, 1972.

—"Middle-Byzantine Provincial Recruits: Salary and Recruits," in *Gonimos. Neoplatonic and Byzantine Studies Presented to Leendert G. Westerink at 75*, ed. John Duffy and John Peradutto (Buffalo, NY: Arethusa, 1988) 121–136.

Olster, David M. "The Dynastic Iconography of Heraclius' Early Coinage," *JÖB* 32/2 (1982) 399–408.

—*The Politics of Usurpation in the Seventh Century: Rhetoric and Revolution in Byzantium*. Amsterdam, Las Palmas: Hakkert, 1993.

—*Roman Defeat, Christian Response, and the Literary Construction of the Jew*. Philadelphia: University of Pennsylvania Press, 1994.

Palme, Bernard. "Die doma gloriosa des Flavius Strategius Paneuphemos," *Chiron* 27 (1997) 95–125.

—"Das erste Konsulat des Kaiser Heraclius," *JJP* 26 (1996) 117–126.

Pargoire, J. "Les LX soldats martyrs de Gaza," *EO* 8 (1905) 40–43.

Pernice, Angelo. *Imperatore Eraclio, saggio di storia bizantina.* Florence: Galletti e Cocci, 1905.

Pertusi, Agostino. "L'iscrizione torcellana dei tempi d'Eraclio," *Bollettino dell'Istituto di storia della società e dello stato veneziano* 4 (1962) 9–38.

Photiades, Penelope J. "A Semi-Greek Semi-Coptic Parchment," *Klio* 41 (1963) 234–235.

Pringle, Denys. *The Defence of Byzantine Africa from Justinian to the Arab Conquest. An Account of the Military History of the African Provinces in the Sixth and Seventh Centuries.* Oxford: *BAR* International Series 99, 1981.

Pryor, John. *Geography, Technology, and War.* Cambridge: Cambridge University Press, 1988.

Reynolds, Paul. *Trade in the Western Mediterranean, AD 400–700: The Ceramic Evidence.* Oxford: *BAR* International Series 604, 1995.

Robinson, Chase F. *Empire and Elites after the Muslim Conquest.* Cambridge: Cambridge University Press, 2000.

Rotter, Ekkehart. *Abendland und Sarazenen. Das Okzidentale Araberbild und seine Entstehung im Frühmittelalter.* Studien zur Sprache, Geschichte und Kultur des islamischen Orients, N.F., 11. Berlin, New York: Walter de Gruyter, 1986.

Sahas, Daniel J. "Saracens and Arabs in the Leimon of John Moschos," *Vyzantiaka* 17 (1997) 123–138.

Sarre, F. and E. Herzfeld. *Archäologische Reise im Euphrat- und Tigris Gebiet.* 4 vols. Berlin: D. Reimer, 1911–1920.

Schick, Robert. *The Christian Communities of Palestine from Byzantine to Islamic Rule: A Historical and Archaeological Study.* Studies in Late Antiquity and Early Islam, 2. Princeton: Darwin Press, 1995, publ. in 1996.

Schönborn, Christoph von. *Sophrone de Jérusalem. Vie monastique et confession dogmatique.* Théologie historique, 20. Paris: Editions Beauchesne, 1972.

Semple, E.C. *The Geography of the Mediterranean Region. Its Relation to Ancient History.* London: Constable, 1932.

Sevcenko, Ihor, and Irmgard Hutter, eds. *Aetos: Studies in Honour of Cyril Mango.* Stuttgart, Leipzig: Teubner, 1998.

Shahid, Irfan. *Byzantium and the Arabs in the Fifth Century.* Washington: Dumbarton Oaks, 1989.

—*Byzantium and the Arabs in the Fourth Century.* Washington: Dumbarton Oaks, 1984.

—*Byzantium and the Arabs in the Sixth Century.* Washington: Dumbarton Oaks, vol. I (Parts 1–2) 1995; vol. II (Part 1) 2002.

—*Byzantium and the Semitic Orient Before the Rise of Islam.* London: Variorum, 1988.

—"The Iranian Factor in Byzantium During the Reign of Heraclius," *DOP* 26 (1972) 293–320.

—"Sigillography in the Service of History: New Light," in *Novum Millennium: Studies on Byzantine History and Culture Dedicated to Paul Speck,* ed. Sarolta Takács and Claudia Sode (Burlington, VT: Ashgate, 2001) 369–377.

Sharf, A. "Byzantine Jewry in the Seventh Century," *BZ* 48 (1955) 103–115.

Sherwood, Polycarp. *Date-List of the Works of Maximus the Confessor.* Studia Anselmiana, 30. Rome, 1952.

Sodini, J.-P. "Les inscriptions de l'aqueduc de Kythrea à Salamine de Chypre," in *Eupsychia: Mélanges offerts à Hélène Ahrweiler* (Byzantina Sorbonensia, 16; Paris: Publications de la Sorbonne, 1998) 619–633.

Speck, Paul. "Epiphania et Martine sur les monnaies d'Héraclius," *RN* 152 (1997) 457–465.

—*Beiträge von Paul Speck.* Varia VII, Ποικίλα Βυζαντινά, 18. Bonn: R. Habelt, 2000.

—*Beiträge zum Thema Byzantinische Feindseligkeit gegen die Juden im frühen siebten Jahrhundert.* Varia VI, Ποικίλα Βυζαντινά, 15. Bonn: R. Habelt, 1997.

—*Das geteilte Dossier. Beobachtungen zu den Nachrichten über die Regierung des Kaisers Herakleios und die seiner Söhne bei Theophanes und Nikephoros.* Ποικίλα Βυζαντινά, 9. Bonn: R. Habelt, 1988.

—"War Bronze ein knappes Metall? Die Legende von dem Stier auf dem Bus in den 'Parastaseis' 42," Ελληνικά 39 (1988) 3–17.

—*Zufälliges zum Bellum Avaricum des Georgios Pisides.* Munich, 1980.

Starr, Joshua. "Byzantine Jewry on the Eve of the Arab Conquest," *Journal of the Palestine Oriental Society* 15 (1935) 280–293.

Stein, Sir Aurel. "Notes on Alexander's Crossing of the Tigris and the Battle of Arbela," *Geographical Journal* 100 (1942) 155–164.

Stein, Ernest. "Heraclius," in *Menschen die Geschichte machten,* ed. Peter Rohden and G. Ostrogorsky (Vienna: L.W. Seidel & Sohn, 1931) I: 257–264.

—*Histoire du Bas-Empire.* 2 vols. Paris: Desclée de Brouwer, 1949–1959.

—*Studien zur Geschichte des byzantinischen Reiches vornehmlich unter den Kaisern Justinus II. und Tiberius Constantinus.* Stuttgart: J.M. Metzler, 1919.

Stemberger, Günter. "Zwangstaufen von Juden im 4. bis 7. Jahrhundert. Mythos oder Wirklichkeit?," in *Judentum – Ausblicke und Einsichten. Festgabe für Kurt Schubert zum siebzigsten Geburtstag,* ed. Clemens Thoma, Günter Stemberger, Johann Maier. Judentum und Umwelt, 43. Frankfurt, New York: Peter Lang, 1993.

Sternbach, Leo. *Analecta Avarica. Rozprawy, Polska Akademii Umiejetnosci, Wydzial Filologiczny,* ser. 2, vol. 15 (Cracow, 1900) 297–365.

Stratos, Andreas. "La première campagne de l'Empereur Héraclius contre les Perses," *JÖB* 28 (1979) 63–74.

—Τό Βυζάντιον στόν Ζ´ αἰῶνα. 6 vols. Athens: Estia, 1965–1978. English trans.: *Byzantium in the Seventh Century,* trans. Marc Ogilvie-Grant and Harry Hionides. 5 vols. Amsterdam: Hakkert, 1968–1980.

Stratos, Zia, ed. Βυζάντιον.᾽Αφιέρωμα στόν ᾽Ανδρέα Στράτο. *Byzance. Hommage à Andreas Stratos. Byzantium. Tribute to Andreas Stratos.* 2 vols. Athens, 1986.

Thierry, Nicole. "Héraclius et la vraie croix en Arménie," in *From Byzantium to Iran ... In Honour of Nina Garsoian,* ed. J.-P. Mahé and R.W. Thomson (Occasional Papers and Proceedings, 8; Columbia University Program in Armenian Studies, Publication No. 5; Atlanta: Scholars Press, 1997) 165–179.

Thomson, R.W. *Rewriting Caucasian History: The Medieval Armenian Adaptation of the Georgian Chronicles.* Oxford: Clarendon Press, 1996.

Toumanoff, Cyril. "Caucasia and Byzantium," *Traditio* 27 (1971) 111–158.

—"The Heraclids and the Arsacids," *REArm* n.s. 19 (1985) 431–434.

—*Studies in Christian Caucasian History.* Washington: Georgetown University Press, 1963.

Trombley, Frank. "War and Society in Rural Syria c. 502–613 A.D.: Observations on the Epigraphy," *BMGS* 21 (1997) 154–209.

Turtledove, Harry. "The Immediate Successors of Justinian: A Study of the Persian Problem . . . ." Ph.D. diss., UCLA, 1977.

Vallejo Girves, Margarita. *Bizancio y la Espana Tardoantigua (SS. V-VIII): Un Capitulo de Historia Mediterranea.* Memorias del Seminario de Historia Antigua, 4; Alcala de Henares: Universidad de Alcala de Henares, 1993.

Van Dieten, Jan Louis. *Geschichte der Patriarchen von Sergios I. bis Johannes VI. (610–715).* Amsterdam: Hakkert, 1972.

Wander, Steven H. "The Cyprus Plates: The Story of David and Goliath," *Metropolitan Museum Journal* 8 (1973) 89–104.

Wenger, Antoine. *L'Assomption de la T.S. Vièrge dans la tradition byzantine du VIe au Xe siècle. Etudes et documents.* Archives de l'Orient Chrétien, 5. Paris: Institut français d'Etudes Byzantines, 1955.

Wheeler, Brannon. "Imagining the Sasanian Capture of Jerusalem," *OCP* 57 (1991) 69–85.

Whitby, Mary. "The Devil in Disguise: The End of George of Pisidia's *Hexaemeron* Reconsidered," *Journal of Hellenic Studies* 105 (1995) 115–129.

—ed. *The Propaganda of Power: The Role of Panegyric in Late Antiquity.* Leiden: Brill, 1998.

Whitby, Michael. *The Emperor Maurice and His Historian.* Oxford: Clarendon Press, 1988.

—"The Persian King at War," in *The Roman and Byzantine Army in the East*, ed. E. Dabrowa (Cracow, 1994) 227–263.

—"The Successors of Justinian," in *Cambridge Ancient History* XIV (2000) 86–111.

Whittow, M. *The Making of Byzantium.* Berkeley: University of California Press, 1996.

Wiita, John Earl. "The Ethnika in Byzantine Military Treatises." Ph.D. diss., University of Minnesota, 1977.

Winkelmann, Friedhelm. "Ägypten und Byzanz vor der arabischen Eroberung," *Byzsl* 40 (1979) 161–182.

—ed. *Byzanz im 7. Jahrhundert. Untersuchungen zur Herausbildung des Feudalismus.* Berliner Byzantinische Arbeiten, 48. Berlin: Akademie-Verlag, 1978.

—"Die Quellen zur Erforschung des monoenergetisch-monotheletischen Streites," *Klio* 69 (1987) 515–569.

—*Quellenstudien zur herrschenden Klasse von Byzanz im 8. und 9. Jahrhundert.* Berlin: Akademie-Verlag, 1987.

Winkelmann, F., R.-J. Lilie, C. Ludwig, et al. *Prosopographie der mittelbyzantinischen Zeit. Erste Abteilung (641–867).* Berlin, New York: De Gruyter, 1998–.

Worp, K. A. "Regnal Formulas of the Emperor Heraclius," *JJP* 23 (1993) 217–232.

Yannopoulos, Panayotis. *L'Hexagramme. Un monnayage byzantin en argent du VII*ᵉ*siècle.* Publications d'Histoire de l'Art et d'Archéologie de l'Université Catholique de Louvain, XI; Numismatica Lovaniensia, 3. Louvain-la-Neuve: Institut Supérieur d'Archéologie et d'Histoire de l'Art, Séminaire de Numismatique Marcel Hoc, 1978.

Zuckerman, Constantin. "Epitaphe d'un soldat africain d'Héraclius servant dans une unité indigène découverte à Constantinople," *L'Antiquité Tardive* 6 (1998) 377–382.

—"La formule de datation du *SB* VI 8986 et son témoignage sur la succession d'Héraclius," *JJP* 25 (1995) 187–202.

—"Heraclius in 625," *REB* 60 (2002) 189–197.

—"The Khazars and Byzantium," in *Proceedings of the International Colloquium on the Khazars* (2002).

—"La petite Augusta et le turc: Epiphania-Eudocie sur les monnaies d'Héraclius," *RN* 150 (1995) 113–126.

—"The Reign of Constantine V in the Miracles of St. Theodore the Recruit (*BHG* 1764): Appendix. Heraclius' First Campaign in Miracles # 2 and # 3," *REB* 46 (1988) 191–210.

Index

Printed in the United States
135424LV00001B/124/A